MW01034368

"Beverly Roberts Gaventa offers an enduring gift to those of us who cherish Paul's epistle to the Romans. By revealing the 'Christ event' as Paul's bedrock for Romans, she unearths a theological framework with myriad implications. This illuminating book is a vital resource for all who seek to teach or preach on Paul's conceptions of the Holy Spirit, the cosmos, time, the human family, and much more."

—Donyelle C. McCray, Associate Professor of Homiletics,
Yale Divinity School

"Beverly Gaventa's commentary on Romans is a special event. It evidences, as it carefully works through Paul's text, her trademark accuracy and lucidity. And it engages the secondary literature with a masterful touch; only the most influential and helpful insights are noted and engaged. The result is a commentary that combines to an unusual degree clarity, economy, and profundity. These features of her commentary alone warrant our gratitude. What marks her reading as special for me, however, is the role played by powerful theological claims. Following in the footsteps of her mentor, Lou Martyn, the result is—although here, and finally here, for Romans—a gripping challenge from a divine word that reveals itself within history. And so the word that first challenged the Roman Christians as they listened to Paul's letter being presented by Phoebe—and also had some of its more difficult paragraphs explained—reaches out again through Gaventa's presentation to challenge its readers today, who listen to Paul by way of this signally important, modern letter-bearer and her explanations."

—Douglas A. Campbell, Professor of New Testament,
Duke Divinity School

"This commentary on Romans is more than a resource; it is a reading born of a sustained relationship. Beverly Gaventa's lifetime of engagement with Paul's letter results in something other than a record of possible interpretations. This is an encounter: an encounter with Romans, and also, by way of Gaventa's patient and deep historical and theological interpretation, an encounter with what Paul calls 'the power of God' that, through Romans, encounters us in the gospel of Jesus Christ."

—Jonathan Linebaugh, Professor of New Testament,
Beeson Divinity School, Samford University

ROMANS

Beverly Roberts Gaventa

Romans

A Commentary

WESTMINSTER
JOHN KNOX PRESS
LOUISVILLE · KENTUCKY

Book design by Jennifer K. Cox

Library of Congress Cataloging-in-Publication Data is on file
at the Library of Congress, Washington, D.C.

ISBN: 9780664221003

Most Westminster John Knox Press books are available at special quantity discounts when purchased in bulk by corporations, organizations, and special-interest groups. For more information, please e-mail SpecialSales@wjkbooks.com.

*With gratitude for Phoebe of Cenchreae
and all her sisters*

CONTENTS

PREFACE

Writing a commentary on Paul's letter to the Romans is a bit like trying to capture the Atlantic Ocean with a liter bottle. Anyone who spends much time with the letter knows that each verse opens a host of questions, that every word generates a multitude of interpretations. As I have come to the end of preparing this commentary, I have thought often and sympathetically of Paul Valéry's statement that a poem is never finished but is simply abandoned. There can be no such thing as a finished commentary on Romans, yet the time has come to send this one on its way into a much larger conversation.

Among the pleasures of drawing a line across work on this book is the opportunity to record my great debts to others. My interest in Paul began decades ago in a course taught by J. Louis Martyn, whose preoccupation with Paul was infectious. It was Lou who introduced me to Paul Minear's *The Obedience of Faith*, which helped me to understand Romans as a real letter rather than a treatise. At the same time, Lou also introduced me to Karl Barth's commentary on Romans and to the compelling essays of Ernst Käsemann. The conversation with Paul persisted under the mentorship of W. D. Davies, my doctoral advisor, whose counsel that "you must go your own way"—maintain your independence of thought—has proven invaluable.

Over the course of preparing this commentary, I benefited from conversations with many people, including John Barclay, Greg Barnhill, Dorothea Bertschmann, Lisa Bowens, Matt Calhoun, Douglas Campbell, Greg Carey, Charles Cousar†, Jamie Davies, Martinus de Boer, Thomas Dixon, Kait Dugan, Susan Eastman, Deirdre Fulton, Richard Hays, Erin Heim, Wesley Hill, Ann Jervis, Donald Juel†, Justin King, Jacqueline Lapsley, Raquel Lettsome, Bruce Longenecker, J. Louis Martyn†, Bruce McCormack, Paul Meyer†, Alicia Meyers, Lidija Novakovic, Matt Novenson, Scott Ryan, Ross Wagner, Francis Watson, Natalie Webb, and Brittany Wilson. In addition, Alexandra Brown, Jonathan Linebaugh, Carey Newman, Mikeal Parsons, and Philip Ziegler each read portions of the commentary as I found my way to a draft, and the work is stronger for their wise input. John Duncan's meticulous assistance in the final stages of preparing the manuscript has been invaluable.

John Carroll has been a gracious and wise editor in his role on the NTL editorial board. His comments, questions, and suggestions about drafts of my work have been unfailingly thorough, constructive, and encouraging. Julie Mullins and Dan Braden have unstintingly fielded a long list of editorial questions.

Work on this project began when I was still teaching at Princeton Theological Seminary and continued at Baylor University, and I am indebted to the libraries at both institutions. In addition, David Schmersal at the Stitt Library of Austin Presbyterian Theological Seminary has been generous with assistance, especially when pandemic closures made library access difficult.

My family—Bill, Matt, Sarah, and Charlie—have largely maintained a safe distance from my research and writing, but they have encouraged, distracted, and loved me in season and out. No words suffice for my gratitude to them.

Publishing this volume means adding my name to a long list of interpreters of Romans. At the beginning of that list stands Phoebe of Cenchreae, whose contribution we can only infer. I offer this volume in gratitude for her and for the host of other women whose contributions to understanding the letters of Paul have been lost, discounted, or neglected.

ABBREVIATIONS

Abbreviations of the titles of ancient sources are those employed by *The SBL Handbook of Style*, 2nd ed. (Atlanta: SBL Press, 2014). Full titles for ancient sources also appear in the Index of Ancient Sources.

AB	Anchor Bible
ABD	*Anchor Bible Dictionary*
ABR	*Australian Biblical Review*
AcBib	Academia Biblica
AnBib	Analecta Biblica
ANTC	Abingdon New Testament Commentaries
ASV	American Standard Version
BBR	*Bulletin for Biblical Research*
BDAG	Bauer, W., F. W. Danker, W. F. Arndt, and F. W. Gingrich. *Greek-English Lexicon of the New Testament and Other Early Christian Literature.* 3rd ed. Chicago, 2000
BDF	Blass, F., A. Debrunner, and R. W. Funk. *A Greek Grammar of the New Testament and Other Early Christian Literature.* Chicago, 1961
BECNT	Baker Exegetical Commentary on the New Testament
BETL	Bibliotheca Ephemeridum Theologicarum Lovaniensium
Bib	*Biblica*
BibInt	*Biblical Interpretation*
BibInt	Biblical Interpretation Series
Bijdr	*Bijdragen: Tijdschrift voor filosofie en theologie*
BLG	Biblical Languages: Greek
BTB	*Biblical Theology Bulletin*
BZNW	Beihefte zur Zeitschrift für die neutestamentliche Wissenschaft
CBQ	*Catholic Biblical Quarterly*
CEB	Common English Bible

CEV	Contemporary English Version
cf.	*confer,* compare
ch(s).	chapter(s)
ClIre	*Classics Ireland*
ClQ	*Classical Quarterly*
CNTC	Calvin's New Testament Commentaries
Colloq	*Colloquium*
ConBNT	Coniectanea Neotestamentica
COP	Colloquium Oecumenicum Paulinum
CPJ	*Corpus Papyrorum Judaicarum.* Edited by Victor A. Tcherikover. 3 vols. Cambridge: Harvard University Press, 1957–1964
CSCT	Columbia Studies in the Classical Tradition
CSEL	Corpus Scriptorum Ecclesiasticorum Latinorum
CTJ	*Calvin Theological Journal*
CurBS	*Currents in Research: Biblical Studies*
CurTM	*Currents in Theology and Mission*
DSS	Dead Sea Scrolls
EC	*Early Christianity*
ed(s).	editor(s)
EDEJ	*Eerdmans Dictionary of Early Judaism*
e.g.	for example
EJL	Early Judaism and Its Literature
EKKNT	Evangelische-katholischer Kommentar zum Neuen Testament
ESEC	Emory Studies in Early Christianity
ESV	English Standard Version
ETL	*Ephemerides Theologicae Lovanienses*
ETR	*Études théologiques et religieuses*
ExAud	*Ex Auditu*
ExpTim	*Expository Times*
FC	Fathers of the Church
FNT	*Filologia Neotestamentaria*
GNT	Good News Translation
HBT	*Horizons in Biblical Theology*
HDR	Harvard Dissertations in Religion
HeyJ	*Heythrop Journal*
HNT	Handbuch zum Neuen Testament
HNTC	Harper's New Testament Commentaries
HThKNT	Herders Theologischer Kommentar zum Neuen Testament
HTR	*Harvard Theological Review*

HTS	Harvard Theological Studies
IBC	Interpretation: A Bible Commentary for Teaching and Preaching
ICC	International Critical Commentary
i.e.	that is
Int	*Interpretation*
Int J Osteoarchaeol	*International Journal of Osteoarchaeology*
JBL	*Journal of Biblical Literature*
JETS	*Journal of the Evangelical Theological Society*
JFSR	*Journal of Feminist Studies in Religion*
JGRChJ	*Journal of Greco-Roman Christianity and Judaism*
JQR	*Jewish Quarterly Review*
JRA	*Journal of Roman Archaeology*
JRE	*Journal of Religious Ethics*
JSNT	*Journal for the Study of the New Testament*
JSNTSup	Journal for the Study of the New Testament Supplement Series
JSPL	*Journal for the Study of Paul and His Letters*
JTI	*Journal of Theological Interpretation*
JTS	*Journal of Theological Studies*
KEK	Kritisch-exegetischer Kommentar über das Neue Testament (Meyer-Kommentar)
KJV	King James Version
KTAH	Key Themes in Ancient History
LCL	Loeb Classical Library
lit.	literally
LNTS	The Library of New Testament Studies
LSJ	Liddell, H. G., R. Scott, H. S. Jones et al. *A Greek-English Lexicon.* 9th ed. with revised supplement. Oxford, 1996
LSTS	The Library of Second Temple Studies
LXX	Septuagint
MM	Moulton, J. H., and G. Milligan. *The Vocabulary of the Greek Testament.* London, 1930. Repr., Peabody, MA, 1997
MNTC	Moffatt New Testament Commentary
Moffatt	*The New Testament: A New Translation*, James Moffatt
NA[28]	Nestle-Aland, *Novum Testamentum Graece.* Edited by the Institute for New Testament Textual Criticism, Münster, under the leadership of Holger Strutwolf. 28th ed. Stuttgart, 2012
NAB	New American Bible

NAC	New American Commentary
NASB	New American Standard Bible
NEB	New English Bible
Neot	*Neotestamentica*
NET	New English Translation
NIB	New Interpreter's Bible
NICNT	New International Commentary on the New Testament
NIDB	*New Interpreter's Dictionary of the Bible*
NIGTC	New International Greek Testament Commentary
NIV	New International Version
NJB	New Jerusalem Bible
NKJV	New King James Version
NovT	*Novum Testamentum*
NovTSup	Supplements to Novum Testamentum
NPNF[1]	*Nicene and Post-Nicene Fathers*, Series 1
NRSV	New Revised Standard Version
NRSVue	New Revised Standard Version Updated Edition
NSBT	New Studies in Biblical Theology
NT	New Testament
NTL	New Testament Library
NTS	*New Testament Studies*
OBT	Overtures to Biblical Theology
OECS	Oxford Early Christian Studies
p(p).	pages(s)
PapyCol	Papyrologica Coloniensia
PBM	Paternoster Biblical and Theological Monographs
PEQ	*Palestinian Exploration Quarterly*
PG	Patrologia Graeca. Edited by J.-P. Migne. 162 vols. Paris, 1857–1886
Phil	*Philologus*
PRSt	*Perspectives in Religious Studies*
PSBSup	Princeton Seminary Bulletin Supplements
RB	*Revue biblique*
RBS	Resources for Biblical Study
RStB	*Ricerche storico bibliche*
RSV	Revised Standard Version
SBLDS	Society of Biblical Literature Dissertation Series
SBLTT	Society of Biblical Literature Texts and Translations
SBT	Studies in Biblical Theology
SemeiaSt	Semeia Studies
SJT	*Scottish Journal of Theology*

SNTSMS	Society for New Testament Studies Monograph Series
SNTW	Studies of the New Testament and Its World
SP	Sacra Pagina
SRTh	Studies in Reformed Theology
ST	*Studia Theologica*
StPatr	Studia Patristica
s.v.	*sub verbo*
SymS	Symposium Series
TBT	Theologische Bibliothek Töpelmann
TDNT	*Theological Dictionary of the New Testament.* Edited by G. Kittel and G. Friedrich. Translated by G. W. Bromiley. 10 vols. Grand Rapids, 1964–1976
Them	*Themelios*
THKNT	Theologischer Handkommentar zum Neuen Testament
TLZ	*Theologische Literaturzeitung*
TS	*Theological Studies*
TU	Texte und Undersuchungen
TynBul	*Tyndale Bulletin*
TZ	*Theologische Zeitschrift*
USQR	*Union Seminary Quarterly Review*
v(v).	verse(s)
VC	*Vigiliae Christianae*
VeEc	*Verbum et Ecclesia*
vol(s).	volume(s)
WBC	Word Biblical Commentary
WBTh	Wiener Beiträge zum Theologie
WGRW	Writings from the Greco-Roman World
WMANT	Wissenschaftliche Monographien zum Alten und Neuen Testament
WUNT	Wissenschaftliche Untersuchungen zum Neuen Testament
WW	*Word and World*
ZNW	*Zeitschrift für die neutestamentliche Wissenschaft und die Kunde der älteren Kirche*

BIBLIOGRAPHY

I. Commentaries on Romans Cited

References to commentaries are by author and page number(s).

Ambrosiaster. 2017. *Ambrosiaster's Commentary on the Pauline Epistles: Romans*. Translated with notes by Theodore S. de Bruyn. WGRW. Atlanta: SBL Press.

Aquinas, Thomas. 2012. *Commentary on the Letter of Saint Paul to the Romans*. Edited by John Mortensen and Enrique Alarcón. Translated by F. R. Larcher, OP. Vol. 37 of the Latin/English edition of the Works of Saint Thomas Aquinas. Lander, WY: Aquinas Institute for the Study of Sacred Doctrine.

Augustine. 1982. *Augustine on Romans: Propositions from the Epistle to the Romans; Unfinished Commentary on the Epistle to the Romans*. Edited and translated by Paula Fredricksen Landes. SBLTT 23. Chico, CA: Scholars Press.

Barrett, C. K. 1957. *The Epistle to the Romans*. HNTC. New York: Harper & Row.

Barth, Karl. 1933. *The Epistle to the Romans*. 6th ed. Translated by Edwyn C. Hoskyns. London: Oxford University Press.

Burns, J. Patout, Jr. 2012. *Romans Interpreted by Early Christian Commentators*. Edited by Robert Louis Wilken. The Church's Bible. Grand Rapids: Eerdmans.

Byrne, Brendan, SJ. *Romans*. 1996. SP 6. Collegeville, MN: Liturgical Press.

Calvin, John. 1995. *The Epistles of Paul the Apostle to the Romans and to the Thessalonians*. Translated by Ross MacKenzie. CNTC. Grand Rapids: Eerdmans.

Cranfield, C. E. B. 1975. *Introduction and Commentary on Romans I–VIII*. Vol. 1 of *A Critical and Exegetical Commentary on the Epistle to the Romans*. ICC. Edinburgh: T&T Clark.

———. 1979. *Introduction and Commentary on Romans IX–XVI*. Vol. 2 of *A Critical and Exegetical Commentary on the Epistle to the Romans*. ICC. Edinburgh: T&T Clark.

Dodd, C. H. 1932. *The Epistle of Paul to the Romans*. MNTC. London: Hodder & Stoughton.

Dunn, James D. G. 1988. *Romans*. WBC 38A–B. 2 vols. Dallas: Word.

Edwards, James R. 2011. *Romans*. Understanding the Bible Commentary Series. Grand Rapids: Baker Books.

Erasmus, Desiderius. 1994. *Annotations on Romans*. Edited by Robert D. Sider. Translated and annotated by John B. Payne, Albert Rabil Jr., Robert D. Sider, and Warren S. Smith Jr. Vol. 56 of *Collected Works of Erasmus*: *New Testament Scholarship*. Toronto: University of Toronto Press.

Fitzmyer, Joseph A. 1993. *Romans*. AB 33. New York: Doubleday.

Godet, Frédéric Louis. 1886–1887. *Commentary on St. Paul's Epistle to the Romans*. 2 vols. Edinburgh: T&T Clark.

Haacker, Klaus. 1999. *Die Brief des Paulus an die Römer*. THKNT 6. Leipzig: Evangelische Verlagsanstalt.

Hodge, Charles. 1838. *Commentary on the Epistle to the Romans*. 2nd ed. London: Religious Tract Society.

Hultgren, Arland J. 2011. *Paul's Letter to the Romans: A Commentary*. Grand Rapids: Eerdmans.

Jewett, Robert. 2007. *Romans*. Hermeneia. Minneapolis: Fortress.

Johnson, Luke Timothy. 1997. *Reading Romans: A Literary and Theological Commentary*. New York: Crossroad.

Käsemann, Ernst. 1980. *Commentary on Romans*. 4th ed. Edited and translated by Geoffrey W. Bromiley. Grand Rapids: Eerdmans.

Keck, Leander E. 2005. *Romans*. ANTC. Nashville: Abingdon.

Kuss, Otto. 1957–1978. *Der Römerbrief*. 3 vols. Regensburg: Pustet.

Lietzmann, Hans. 1933. *An die Römer*. 4th ed. HNT 8. Tübingen: Mohr Siebeck.

Lohse, Eduard. 2003. *Der Brief an die Römer*. KEK. Göttingen: Vandenhoeck & Ruprecht.

Longenecker, Richard N. 2016. *The Epistle to the Romans: A Commentary on the Greek Text*. NIGTC. Grand Rapids: Eerdmans.

Luther, Martin. 1972. *Lectures on Romans*. Vol. 25 of *Luther's Works*. Edited by Hilton O. Oswold. Translated by Walter G. Tillmanns and Jacob A. O. Preus. St. Louis: Concordia.

Matera, Frank J. 2010. *Romans*. Paideia. Grand Rapids: Baker Academic.

Michel, Otto. 1966. *Der Brief an die Römer*. 4th ed. KEK. Göttingen: Vandenhoeck & Ruprecht.

Moo, Douglas. 2018. *The Epistle to the Romans*. 2nd ed. NICNT. Grand Rapids: Eerdmans.

Morris, Leon. 1988. *The Epistle to the Romans*. Grand Rapids: Eerdmans.

Mounce, Robert H. 1995. *Romans*. NAC 27. Nashville: Broadman & Holman.

Nygren, Anders. 1949. *Commentary on Romans*. Translated by Carl C. Rasmussen. Philadelphia: Muhlenberg.

Origen. 2001. *Commentary on the Epistle to the Romans, Books 1–5.* Translated by Thomas P. Scheck. FC 103. Washington, DC: Catholic University of America Press.

Osborne, Grant R. 2004. *Romans.* Downers Grove, IL: InterVarsity Press.

Pelagius. 1993. *Pelagius's Commentary on St. Paul's Epistle to the Romans.* Translated with introduction and notes by Theodore De Bruyn. OECS. Oxford: Oxford University Press.

Sanday, William, and Arthur C. Headlam. 1902. *A Critical and Exegetical Commentary on the Epistle to the Romans.* 5th ed. ICC. Edinburgh: T&T Clark.

Schlatter, Adolf. 1995. *Romans: The Righteousness of God.* Translated by Siegfried S. Schatzmann. Peabody, MA: Hendrickson.

Schlier, Heinrich. 1977. *Der Römerbrief: Kommentar.* HThKNT 6. Freiburg: Herder.

Schreiner, Thomas R. 2018. *Romans.* 2nd ed. BECNT. Grand Rapids: Baker Academic.

Stuart, Moses. 1865. *A Commentary on the Epistle to the Romans.* Edited and revised by R. D. C. Robbins. Boston: Gould & Lincoln.

Stuhlmacher, Peter. 1994. *Paul's Letter to the Romans: A Commentary.* Translated by Scott J. Hafemann. Louisville: Westminster John Knox.

Talbert, Charles H. 2002. *Romans.* Macon, GA: Smith &Helwys.

Wilckens, Ulrich. 1978–1982. *Der Brief an die Römer.* 3 vols. EKKNT 6.1–3. Zürich: Neukirchen-Vluyn.

Witherington, Ben, III, and Darlene Hyatt. 2004. *Paul's Letter to the Romans: A Socio-Rhetorical Commentary.* Grand Rapids: Eerdmans.

Wolter, Michael. 2014–2019. *Der Brief an die Römer.* 2 vols. EKKNT 6.1–2. Neukirchen-Vluyn: Neukirchener.

Wright, N. T. 2002. "The Letter to the Romans: Introduction, Commentary, and Reflections." *NIB* 10:393–770.

II. Other Literature

References to literature apart from commentaries are by author and year of publication.

Achtemeier, Paul J. 1990. "Romans 3:1–8: Structure and Argument." Pages 77–87 in *Christ and His Communities: Essays in Honor of Reginald H. Fuller.* Edited by Arland J. Hultgren and Barbara Hall. Cincinnati: Forward Movement Publications.

Adams, Edward. 1997. "Abraham's Faith and Gentile Disobedience: Textual Links between Romans 1 and 4." *JSNT* 65:47–66.

———. 2000. *Constructing the World: A Study in Paul's Cosmological Language.* SNTW. Edinburgh: T&T Clark.

————. 2013. *The Earliest Christian Meeting Places: Almost Exclusively Houses?* LNTS 450. London: Bloomsbury.

Adams, Samuel V. 2015. *The Reality of God and Historical Method: Apocalyptic Theology in Conversation with N.T. Wright.* Downers Grove, IL: InterVarsity Press.

Agamben, Giorgio. 2011. *The Kingdom and the Glory: For a Theological Genealogy of Economy and Government.* Translated by Lorenzo Chiesa. Stanford, CA: Stanford University Press.

Alexander, Loveday C. A. 2005. "Narrative Maps: Reflections on the Toponomy of Acts." Pages 97–131 in *Acts in Its Ancient Literary Context: A Classicist Looks at the Acts of the Apostles.* JSNTSup 289. London: T&T Clark.

Andrews, William, ed. 1986. *Sisters of the Spirit: Three Black Women's Autobiographies of the Nineteenth Century.* Bloomington: Indiana University Press.

Arzt, Peter. 1994. "The 'Epistolary Introductory Thanksgiving' in the Papyri and in Paul." *NovT* 36:29–46.

Auden, W. H. 1976. *Collected Poems.* Edited by Edward Mendelson. New York: Vintage Books.

Aune, David E. 1991. "Romans as a *LOGOS PROTREPTIKOS.*" Pages 278–96 in *The Romans Debate.* Rev. and exp. ed. Edited by Karl Paul Donfried. Peabody, MA: Hendrickson.

Badenas, Robert. 1985. *Christ the End of the Law: Romans 10.4 in Pauline Perspective.* JSNTSup 10. Sheffield: JSOT.

Bailey, Daniel P. 2000. "Jesus as the Mercy Seat: The Semantics and Theology of Paul's Use of *Hilastērion* in Romans 3:25." *TynBul* 51:155–58.

Bammel, Caroline P. Hammond. 1996. "Patristic Exegesis of Romans 5:7." *JTS* 47:532–42.

Barclay, John M. G. 1988. *Obeying the Truth: Paul's Ethics in Galatians.* Minneapolis: Fortress.

————. 1996a. "'Do We Undermine the Law?' A Study of Romans 14.1–15.6." Pages 287–308 in *Paul and the Mosaic Law.* Edited by James D. G. Dunn. Grand Rapids: Eerdmans.

————. 1996b. *Jews in the Mediterranean Diaspora: From Alexander to Trajan (323 BCE–117 CE).* Edinburgh: T&T Clark.

————. 1998. "Paul and Philo on Circumcision: Romans 2:25–29 in Social and Cultural Context." *NTS* 44:536–56.

————. 2010a. "'I Will Have Mercy on Whom I Have Mercy': The Golden Calf and Divine Mercy in Romans 9–11 and Second Temple Judaism." *EC* 1:82–106.

————. 2010b. "Unnerving Grace: Approaching Romans 9–11 from the Wisdom of Solomon." Pages 91–109 in *Between Gospel and Election: Explorations in the Interpretation of Romans 9–11.* Edited by J. Ross Wagner, Florian Wilk, and Frank Schleritt. WUNT 1/257. Tübingen: Mohr Siebeck.

———. 2011. *Pauline Churches and Diaspora Jews*. Grand Rapids: Eerdmans.

———. 2013a. "Faith and Self-Detachment from Cultural Norms: A Study in Romans 14–15." *ZNW* 104:192–208.

———. 2013b. "Under Grace: The Christ-Gift and the Construction of a Christian *Habitus*." Pages 59–76 in *Apocalyptic Paul: Cosmos and Anthropos in Romans 5–8*. Edited by Beverly Roberts Gaventa. Waco, TX: Baylor University Press.

———. 2015. *Paul and the Gift*. Grand Rapids: Eerdmans.

———. 2023. "Rich Poverty: 2 Corinthians 8.1–15 and the Social Meaning of Poverty and Wealth." *NTS* 69:243–57.

Barnikol, Ernst. 1961. "Der nichtpaulinische Ursprung der absoluten Obrigkeitsbejahung von Römer 13,1–7." Pages 65–133 in *Studien zum Neuen Testament und zur Patristik, E. Klostermann Festschrift*. TU 77. Berlin: Akademie-Verlag.

Barr, James. 1988a. "'Abba, Father' and the Familiarity of Jesus' Speech." *Theology* 91:173–79.

———. 1988b. "'Abbā' Isn't 'Daddy.'" *JTS* 39:28–47.

Barram, Michael D. 2003. "Romans 12:9–21." *Int* 57:423–26.

Barreto, Eric D. 2010. *Ethnic Negotiations: The Function of Race and Ethnicity in Acts 16*. WUNT 2/294. Tübingen: Mohr Siebeck.

Barrett, C. K. 1995. *New Testament Background: Selected Documents*. Rev. and exp. ed. San Francisco: HarperCollins.

Barth, Karl. 1954. "The Christian Community in the Midst of Political Change." Pages 51–124 in *Against the Stream: Shorter Post-War Writings, 1946–52*. Edited by Ronald Gregor Smith. New York: Philosophical Library.

———. 1956. *Christ and Adam: Man and Humanity in Romans 5*. Translated by T. A. Smail. Edinburgh: Oliver & Bond.

———. 1957. *The Doctrine of God, Part One*. Vol. 2, Parts 1 and 2 of *Church Dogmatics*. Edinburgh: T&T Clark.

Barth, Markus. 1955. "Speaking of Sin: Some Interpretative Notes on Romans 1.18–3.20." *SJT* 8:288–96.

———. 1969. "The Faith of the Messiah." *HeyJ* 10:363–70.

Bassler, Jouette M. 1982. *Divine Impartiality: Paul and a Theological Axiom*. SBLDS 59. Chico, CA: Scholars Press.

———. 1991. *God and Mammon: Asking for Money in the New Testament*. Nashville: Abingdon.

Bauckham, Richard. 1997. *The Theology of the Book of Revelation*. New Testament Theology. Cambridge: Cambridge University Press.

———. 2002. *Gospel Women: Studies of the Named Women in the Gospels*. Grand Rapids: Eerdmans.

Baxter, A. G., and J. A. Ziesler. 1985. "Paul and Arboriculture: Romans 11.17–24." *JSNT* 24:25–32.

Beker, J. Christiaan. 1980. *Paul the Apostle: The Triumph of God in Life and Thought*. Philadelphia: Fortress.

Bell, Richard H. 1994. *Provoked to Jealousy: The Origin and Purpose of the Jealousy Motif in Romans 9–11*. WUNT 2/63. Tübingen: Mohr.

———. 1998. *No One Seeks for God: An Exegetical and Theological Study of Romans 1.18–3.20*. WUNT 1/106. Tübingen: Mohr Siebeck.

———. 2002a. "Rom 5.18–19 and Universal Salvation." *NTS* 48:417–32.

———. 2002b. "Sacrifice and Christology in Paul." *JTS* 53:1–27.

———. 2005. *The Irrevocable Call of God: An Inquiry into Paul's Theology of Israel*. WUNT 1/184. Tübingen: Mohr Siebeck.

Belleville, Linda. 2005. "Ἰουνιαν . . . ἐπίσημοι ἐν τοῖς ἀποστόλοις: A Reexamination of Romans 16.7 in Light of Primary Source Materials." *NTS* 51:231–49.

Berding, Kenneth. 2006. "Romans 12.4–8: One Sentence or Two?" *NTS* 52:433–39.

Berry, Joanne. 2007. *The Complete Pompeii*. London: Thames & Hudson.

Bertschmann, Dorothea H. 2014. *Bowing Before Christ—Nodding to the State? Reading Paul Politically with Oliver O'Donovan and John Howard Yoder*. LNTS 502. London: Bloomsbury T&T Clark.

———. 2019. "'Revenge Is Mine, I Will Pay Back'—Has Mercy Not the Last Word, After All? Reading Romans 12:19 as Part of an Implicit Discourse of Justice and Mercy." Pages 273–300 in *Biblical Studies: Tensions between Justice and Mercy, Love and Law*. Edited by Markus Zender and Peter Wick. Gorgias Biblical Studies 70. Piscataway, NJ: Gorgias.

Betz, Hans Dieter. 1992. "Apostle." *ABD* 1:309–11.

Bird, Michael F. 2007. *The Saving Righteousness of God: Studies on Paul, Justification, and the New Perspective*. Waynesboro, GA: Paternoster.

Bird, Michael F., and Preston M. Sprinkle, eds. 2009. *Faith of Jesus Christ: Exegetical, Biblical, and Theological Studies*. Peabody, MA: Hendrickson.

Black, David Alan. 1989. "The Pauline Love Command: Structure, Style, and Ethics in Romans 12:9–21." *FNT* 2:3–22.

Black, Matthew. 1972. "The Christological Use of the Old Testament in the New Testament." *NTS* 18:1–14.

Blackwell, Ben C. 2010. "Immortal Glory and the Problem of Death in Romans 3.23." *JSNT* 32:285–308.

———. 2011. *Christosis: Pauline Soteriology in Light of Deification in Irenaeus and Cyril of Alexandria*. WUNT 2/314. Tübingen: Mohr Siebeck.

Blowers, Paul M. 2013. "The Groaning and Longing of Creation: Variant Patterns of Patristic Interpretation of Romans 8:19–23." Pages 45–54 in *Papers Presented at the Sixteenth International Conference on Patristic Studies Held in Oxford 2011*. StPatr 63. Edited by Markus Vinzent. Leuven: Peeters.

Bockmuehl, Markus. 1990. *Revelation and Mystery in Ancient Judaism and Pauline Christianity.* Grand Rapids: Eerdmans.

Bonhoeffer, Dietrich. 2001. *Discipleship.* Vol. 4 of Dietrich Bonhoeffer Works. Edited by Geffrey B. Kelley and John D. Godsey. Translated by Barbara Green and Reinhard Krauss. Minneapolis: Fortress.

Boring, M. Eugene. 1986. "The Language of Universal Salvation in Paul." *JBL* 105:269–92.

Bornkamm, Günther. 1969. "The Praise of God." Pages 105–11 in *Early Christian Experience.* Translated by Paul L. Hammer. New York: Harper & Row.

Boswell, John. 1980. *Christianity, Social Tolerance, and Homosexuality: Gay People in Western Europe from the Beginning of the Christian Era to the Fourteenth Century.* Chicago: University of Chicago Press.

Bowens, Lisa M. 2020. *African American Readings of Paul: Reception, Resistance, and Transformation.* Grand Rapids: Eerdmans.

Braaten, Laurie J. 2006. "All Creation Groans: Romans 8:22 in Light of the Biblical Sources." *HBT* 28:131–59.

Bradley, Keith. 2011. "Resisting Slavery at Rome." Pages 362–84 in *The Ancient Mediterranean World,* vol. 1 of *The Cambridge World History of Slavery.* Edited by Keith Bradley and Paul Cartledge. Cambridge: Cambridge University Press.

Brand, Miryam T. 2013. *Evil Within and Without: The Source of Sin and Its Nature as Portrayed in Second Temple Literature.* Journal of Ancient Judaism Supplements 9. Göttingen: Vandenhoeck & Ruprecht.

Brauch, Manfred T. 1977. "Perspectives on 'God's Righteousness' in Recent German Discussion." Pages 523–42 in *Paul and Palestinian Judaism: A Comparison of Patterns of Religion,* by E. P. Sanders. Philadelphia: Fortress.

Breytenbach, Ciliers. 1989. *Versöhnung: Eine Studie zur paulinischen Soteriologie.* WMANT 60. Neukirchen-Vluyn: Neukirchener.

———. 1993. "Versöhnung, Stellvertretung, and Sühne: Semantische und traditionsgeschichtliche Bemerkungen am Beispiel des paulinischen Briefe." *NTS* 39:59–79.

———. 2010a. "Salvation of the Reconciled." Pages 171–86 in *Grace, Reconciliation, and Concord: The Death of Christ in Graeco-Roman Metaphors.* NovTSup 135. Leiden: Brill.

———. 2010b. "The 'For Us' Phrases in Pauline Soteriology: Considering Their Background and Use." Pages 59–81 in *Grace, Reconciliation, and Concord: The Death of Christ in Graeco-Roman Metaphors.* NovTSup 135. Leiden: Brill.

Brookins, Timothy A. 2013. "The (In)frequency of the Name 'Erastus' in Antiquity: A Literary, Papyrological, and Epigraphical Catalog." *NTS* 59: 496–516.

Brooten, Bernadette J. 1977. "'Junia . . . Outstanding among the Apostles' (Romans 16:7)." Pages 141–44 in *Women Priests: A Catholic Commentary on the Vatican Declaration*. Edited by Leonard Swidler and Arlene Swidler. New York: Paulist.

———. 1992. "Paul's Views on the Nature of Women and Female Homoeroticism." Pages 58–83 in *Homosexuality and Religion and Philosophy*. Edited with introductions by Wayne R. Dynes and Stephen Donaldson. New York: Garland.

———. 1996. *Love between Women: Early Christian Responses to Female Homoeroticism*. Chicago: University of Chicago Press.

Brown, Alexandra. 1995. *The Cross and Human Transformation: Paul's Apocalyptic Word in 1 Corinthians*. Minneapolis: Fortress.

———. 2018. "*Kairos* Gathered: Time, Tempo, and Typology in 1 Corinthians." *Int* 72:43–55.

Brown, Derek. 2010. "'The God of Peace Will Shortly Crush Satan under Your Feet': Paul's Eschatological Reminder in Romans 16:20a." *Neot* 44:1–14.

Brown, Raymond E. 1968. *The Semitic Background of the Term "Mystery" in the New Testament*. Philadelphia: Fortress.

———. 1993. *The Death of the Messiah: From Gethsemane to the Grave*. 2 vols. New York: Doubleday.

Buell, Denise Kimber. 2008. "'Be Not One Who Stretches Out Hands to Receive but Shuts Them When It Comes to Giving': Envisioning Christian Charity When Both Donors and Recipients Are Poor." Pages 37–47 in *Wealth and Poverty in Early Church and Society*. Edited by Susan R. Holman. Holy Cross Studies in Patristic Theology and History. Grand Rapids: Baker Academic.

Bultmann, Rudolf. 1947. "Glossen im Römerbrief." *TLZ* 72:197–202.

———. 1951–1955. *Theology of the New Testament*. Translated by Kendrick Grobel. 2 vols. New York: Scribner's Sons.

Burer, Michael H. 2015. "'ΕΠΙΣΗΜΟΙ ᾿ΕΝ ΤΟΙΣ ᾿ΑΠΟΣΤΟΛΟΙΣ in Rom 16:7 as 'Well Known to the Apostles': Further Defense and New Evidence." *JETS* 58:731–55.

Burer, Michael H., and Daniel B. Wallace. 2001. "Was Junia Really an Apostle? A Reexamination of Rom 16.7." *NTS* 47:76–91.

Byrne, Brendan, SJ. 1979. *"Sons of God"—"Seed of Abraham": A Study of the Idea of the Sonship of God of All Christians in Paul against the Jewish Background*. AnBib 83. Rome: Biblical Institute Press.

———. 1988. "'The Type of the One to Come' (Rom 5:14): Fate and Responsibility in Romans 5:12–21." *ABR* 36:19–30.

Byron, John. 2003. *Slavery Metaphors in Early Judaism and Pauline Christianity: A Traditio-Historical and Exegetical Examination*. WUNT 2/162. Tübingen: Mohr Siebeck.

————. 2008. *Recent Research on Paul and Slavery.* Recent Research in Biblical Studies 3. Sheffield: Sheffield Phoenix Press.

Byrskog, Samuel. 1997. "Epistolography, Rhetoric, and Letter Prescript: Romans 1.1–7 as a Test Case." *JSNT* 65:27–46.

————. 2008. "Christology and Identity in an Intertextual Perspective: The Glory of Adam in the Narrative Substructure of Paul's Letter to the Romans." Pages 1–18 in *Identity Formation in the New Testament.* Edited by Bengt Holmberg and Mikael Winninge. WUNT 1/227. Tübingen: Mohr Siebeck.

Cadbury, Henry J. 1931. "Erastus of Corinth." *JBL* 50:42–58.

Cadwallader, Alan H. 2015. "Paul Speaks Like a Girl: When Phoebe Reads Romans." Pages 69–94 in *Sexuality, Ideology, and the Bible: Antipodean Engagements.* Edited by Robert J. Myles and Caroline Blyth. Sheffield: Sheffield Phoenix Press.

————. 2018. "Tertius in the Margins: A Critical Appraisal of the Secretary Hypothesis." *NTS* 64:378–96.

Calhoun, Robert Matthew. 2011. *Paul's Definitions of the Gospel in Romans 1.* WUNT 2/316. Tübingen: Mohr Siebeck.

————. 2019. "The Gospel(-Amulet) as God's Power for Salvation." *EC* 10: 21–55.

Calvin, John. 1960. *Institutes of the Christian Religion.* Edited by John T. McNeill. Translated by Ford Lewis Battles. Philadelphia: Westminster.

Campbell, Douglas A. 1992. *The Rhetoric of Righteousness in Romans 3.21–26.* JSNTSup 65. Sheffield: Sheffield Academic.

————. 1994. "Romans 1:17—A *Crux Interpretum* for the Πίστις Χριστοῦ Debate." *JBL* 113:265–85.

————. 2009a. *The Deliverance of God: An Apocalyptic Rereading of Justification in Paul.* Grand Rapids: Eerdmans.

————. 2009b. "The Faithfulness of Jesus Christ in Romans 3:22." Pages 57–72 in *The Faith of Jesus Christ: Exegetical, Biblical, and Theological Studies.* Edited by Michael F. Bird and Preston M. Sprinkle. Peabody, MA: Hendrickson.

————. 2014. *Framing Paul: An Epistolary Biography.* Grand Rapids: Eerdmans.

Capes, David B. 2007. "Pauline Exegesis and the Incarnate Christ." Pages 135–53 in *Israel's God and Rebecca's Children: Christology and Community in Early Judaism and Christianity; Essays in Honor of Larry W. Hurtado and Alan F. Segal.* Edited by David B. Capes, April D. DeConick, Helen K. Bond, and Troy A. Miller. Waco, TX: Baylor University Press.

Carey, Greg. 2009. *Sinners: Jesus and His Earliest Followers.* Waco, TX: Baylor University Press.

Carraway, George. 2013. *Christ Is God over All: Romans 9:5 in the Context of Romans 9–11.* LNTS 489. New York: Bloomsbury.

Carter, T. L. 2004. "The Irony of Romans 13." *NovT* 46:209–28.

Cassidy, Ron. 2010. "The Politicization of Paul: Romans 13:1–7 in Recent Discussion." *ExpTim* 121:383–89.

Charlesworth, James H., ed. 1983–85. *The Old Testament Pseudepigrapha.* 2 vols. Peabody, MA: Hendrickson.

Christoffersson, Olle. 1990. *The Earnest Expectation of the Creature: The Flood-Tradition as Matrix of Romans 8:18–27.* ConBNT 23. Stockholm: Almqvist & Wiksell.

Chrysostom, John. 1997. *Homilies on the Acts of the Apostles and the Epistle to the Romans.* Translated by J. B. Morris and W. H. Simcox. Revised by George B. Stevens. NPNF[1] 11:331–564. Edinburgh: T&T Clark.

Clements, Ronald E. 1980. "'A Remnant Chosen by Grace' (Romans 11:5): The Old Testament Background and Origin of the Remnant Concept." Pages 106–21 in *Pauline Studies: Essays Presented to Professor F. F. Bruce on His Seventieth Birthday.* Edited by Donald A. Hagner and Murray J. Harris. Exeter: Paternoster.

Coleman, Thomas M. 1997. "Binding Obligations in Romans 13:7: A Semantic Field and Social Context." *TynBul* 48:307–27.

Collins, J. N. 1990. *Diakonia: Re-interpreting the Ancient Sources.* Oxford: Oxford University Press.

Collins, Raymond F. 2002. "The Case of a Wandering Doxology: Rom 16, 25–27." Pages 293–303 in *New Testament Textual Criticism and Exegesis: Festschrift J. Delobel.* Edited by Adelbert Denaux. BETL 161. Leuven: Peeters.

Cooper, Adam G. 2012. "Degrading the Body, Suppressing the Truth: Aquinas on Romans 1:18–25." Pages 113–26 in *Reading Romans with St. Thomas Aquinas.* Edited by Matthew Levering and Michael Dauphinais. Washington, DC: Catholic University of America Press.

Cousar, Charles B. 1990. *A Theology of the Cross: The Death of Jesus in the Pauline Letters.* OBT. Minneapolis: Augsburg Fortress.

———. 1995. "Continuity and Discontinuity: Reflections on Romans 5–8 (in Conversation with Frank Thielman)." Pages 196–210 in *Romans.* Vol. 3 of *Pauline Theology.* Edited by David M. Hay and E. Elizabeth Johnson. Minneapolis: Fortress.

Cranfield, C. E. B. 1962. "ΜΕΤΡΟΝ ΠΙΣΤΕΩΣ in Romans XII.3." *NTS* 8: 345–51.

Croasmun, Matthew. 2017. *The Emergence of Sin: The Cosmic Tyrant in Romans.* Oxford: Oxford University Press.

Cullmann, Oscar. 1950. *Christ and Time: The Primitive Christian Concept of Time and History.* Philadelphia: Westminster.

Dahl, Nils. 1977. "The Future of Israel." Pages 137–58 in *Studies in Paul: Theology for the Early Christian Mission.* Minneapolis: Augsburg.

————. 1982. "Romans 3:9: Text and Meaning." Pages 184–204 in *Paul and Paulinism: Essays in Honour of C. K. Barrett*. Edited by Morna D. Hooker and Stephen G. Wilson. London: SPCK.

Danker, F. W. 1972. "Under Contract: A Form-Critical Study of Linguistic Adaptation in Romans." Pages 91–114 in *Festschrift to Honor F. Wilbur Gingrich: Lexicographer, Scholar, Teacher, and Committed Christian Layman*. Edited by Eugene Howard Barth and Ronald Edwin Cocroft. Leiden: Brill.

Das, A. Andrew. 2007. *Solving the Romans Debate*. Minneapolis: Fortress.

Daube, David. 1964. "Appended Note: Participle and Imperative in 1 Peter." Pages 467–88 in *The First Epistle of St. Peter*, by Edward Gordon Selwyn. London: Macmillan.

Davies, J. P. 2021. "Why Paul Doesn't Mention the 'Age to Come.'" *SJT* 74: 199–208.

————. 2022. *The Apocalyptic Paul: Retrospect and Prospect*. Cascade Library of Pauline Studies. Eugene, OR: Cascade Books.

Davies, W. D. 1980. *Paul and Rabbinic Judaism: Some Rabbinic Elements in Pauline Theology*. 4th ed. Philadelphia: Fortress.

Dawbarn, Elizabeth. 1794. *A Dialogue between Clara Neville and Louisa Mills on Loyalty &c.: Recommended to the Attention of Every Female in Great Britain*. Wiesbech, UK: John White.

De Boer, Martinus C. 1988. *The Defeat of Death: Apocalyptic Eschatology in 1 Corinthians 15 and Romans 5*. JSNTSup 22. Sheffield: Sheffield Academic Press.

————. 2011. *Galatians: A Commentary*. NTL. Louisville: Westminster John Knox.

————. 2013. "Paul's Mythologizing Program in Romans 5–8." Pages 1–20 in *Apocalyptic Paul: Cosmos and Anthropos in Romans 5–8*. Edited by Beverly Roberts Gaventa. Waco, TX: Baylor University Press.

————. 2020. *Paul: Theologian of God's Apocalypse: Essays on Paul and Apocalyptic*. Eugene, OR: Cascade.

————. 2022. "The Expectation of Cosmic Redemption in Paul." *RStB* 34: 153–71.

De Bruyn, Theodore. 2011. "Ambrosiaster's Interpretations of Romans 1:26–27." *VC* 65:463–83.

Deichgräber, Reinhard. 1967. *Gotteshymnus und Christus-hymnus in der frühen Christenheit*. Göttingen: Vandenhoeck & Ruprecht.

De Roo, Jacqueline C. R. 2007. *"Works of the Law" at Qumran and in Paul*. Sheffield: Sheffield Phoenix.

Dickson, J. P. 2005. "Gospel as News: εὐαγελλ- from Aristophanes to the Apostle Paul." *NTS* 51:212–30.

Dodd, C. H. 1961. *The Parables of the Kingdom*. New York: Scribner's Sons.

Dodson, Joseph R. 2008. *The "Powers" of Personification: Rhetorical Purpose in the "Book of Wisdom" and the Letter to the Romans.* BZNW 161. Berlin: de Gruyter.

Donaldson, Terence L. 1995. "The Law That Hangs (Matthew 22:40): Rabbinic Formulation and Matthean Social World." *CBQ* 57:689–709.

———. 2006. "Apostle." *NIDB* 1:205–7.

———. 2007. *Judaism and the Gentiles: Jewish Patterns of Universalism (to 135 CE).* Waco, TX: Baylor University Press.

Donfried, Karl, ed. 1991. *The Romans Debate.* Rev. and exp. ed. Peabody, MA: Hendrickson.

Downs, David J. 2008. *The Offering of the Gentiles: Paul's Collection for Jerusalem in Its Chronological, Cultural, and Cultic Contexts.* Grand Rapids: Eerdmans.

———. 2009. "Was God Paul's Patron? The Economy of Patronage in Pauline Theology." Pages 129–56 in *Engaging Economics: New Testament Scenarios and Early Christian Reception.* Edited by Bruce Longenecker and Kelly Liebengood. Grand Rapids: Eerdmans.

———. 2013. "Justification, Good Works, and Creation in Clement of Rome's Appropriation of Romans 5–6." *NTS* 59:415–32.

———. 2016. *Alms: Charity, Reward, and Atonement in Early Christianity.* Waco, TX: Baylor University Press.

Duff, Nancy J. 1989. "The Significance of Pauline Apocalyptic for Theological Ethics." Pages 279–96 in *Apocalyptic and the New Testament: Essays in Honor of J. Louis Martyn.* Edited by Joel Marcus and Marion L. Soards. JSNTSup 24. Sheffield: Sheffield Academic.

Duncan, John. 2015. "The Hope of Creation: The Significance of ἐφ' ἐλπίδι (Rom 8.20c) in Context." *NTS* 61:411–27.

Dunn, James D. G. 1997. "Once More, ΠΙΣΤΙΣ ΧΡΙΣΤΟΥ." Pages 61–81 in *Looking Back, Pressing On.* Vol. 4 of *Pauline Theology.* Edited by E. Elizabeth Johnson and David M. Hay. Atlanta: Society of Biblical Literature.

———. 2004. "Did Paul Have a Covenant Theology? Reflections on Romans 9:4 and 11:27." Pages 3–19 in *Celebrating Romans: Template for Pauline Theology; Essays in Honor of Robert Jewett.* Edited by Sheila E. McGinn. Grand Rapids: Eerdmans.

———. 2006. *The Theology of Paul the Apostle.* Grand Rapids: Eerdmans.

———. 2007. *The New Perspective on Paul.* Rev. ed. Grand Rapids: Eerdmans.

Dunnill, John. 1998. "Saved by Whose Faith?—The Function of πίστις χριστοῦ in Pauline Theology." *Colloq* 30:3–25.

Dunson, Ben C. 2011. "Faith in Romans: The Salvation of the Individual or Life in Community?" *JSNT* 34:19–46.

Du Toit, A. B. 2010. "Some More Translation Headaches in Romans." *VeEc* 31.1, art. 385, pp. 1–5. https://doi.org/10.4102/ve.v31i1.385.

Earnshaw, John D. 1994. "Reconsidering Paul's Marriage Analogy in Romans 7.1–4." *NTS* 40:68–88.

Eastman, Susan Grove. 2002. "Whose Apocalypse? The Identity of the Sons in Romans 8:19." *JBL* 121:263–77.

———. 2008. "Imitating Christ Imitating Us: Paul's Educational Project in Philippians." Pages 427–51 in *The Word Leaps the Gap: Essays on Scripture and Theology in Honor of Richard B. Hays*. Edited by J. Ross Wagner, C. Kavin Rowe, and A. Katherine Grieb. Grand Rapids: Eerdmans.

———. 2010. "Israel and the Mercy of God: A Re-reading of Galatians 6.16 and Romans 9–11." *NTS* 56:367–95.

———. 2013. "Double Participation and the Responsible Self in Romans 5–8." Pages 93–110 in *Apocalyptic Paul: Cosmos and Anthropos in Romans 5–8*. Edited by Beverly Roberts Gaventa. Waco, TX: Baylor University Press.

———. 2014. "Oneself in Another: Participation and the Spirit in Romans 8." Pages 102–24 in *"In Christ" in Paul: Explorations of Paul's Theology of Union and Participation*. Edited by Michael J. Thate, Kevin J. Vanhoozer, and Constantine R. Campbell. WUNT 2/384. Tübingen: Mohr Siebeck.

———. 2017. *Paul and the Person: Reframing Paul's Anthropology*. Grand Rapids: Eerdmans.

Edmondson, Jonathan. 2011. "Slavery and the Roman Family." Pages 337–61 in *The Ancient Mediterranean World*. Vol. 1 of *The Cambridge World History of Slavery*. Edited by Keith Bradley and Paul Cartledge. Cambridge: Cambridge University Press.

Ehrman, Bart. 1996. *The Orthodox Corruption of Scripture: The Effect of Early Christological Controversies on the Text of the New Testament*. Oxford: Oxford University Press.

Eisenbaum, Pamela. 2009. *Paul Was Not a Christian: The Original Message of a Misunderstood Apostle*. New York: HarperOne.

Eliot, George. 1959. *Adam Bede*. New York: Harper & Brothers, 1859. Repr., London: Penguin Classics.

Elliott, J. K. 1981. "The Language and Style of the Concluding Doxology to the Epistle to the Romans." *ZNW* 72:124–30.

Elliott, Mark W. 2009. "Πίστις Χριστοῦ in the Church Fathers and Beyond." Pages 277–308 in *The Faith of Jesus Christ: Exegetical, Biblical, and Theological Studies*. Edited by Michael F. Bird and Preston M. Sprinkle. Peabody, MA: Hendrickson.

Elliott, Neil. 1990. *The Rhetoric of Romans: Argumentative Constraint and Strategy and Paul's Dialogue with Judaism*. JSNTSup 45. Sheffield: Sheffield Academic.

———. 1997. "Romans 13:1–7 in the Context of Imperial Propaganda." Pages 184–204 in *Paul and the Empire: Religion and Power in Roman Imperial Society*. Edited by Richard Horsley. Harrisburg, PA: Trinity.

————. 2008. *The Arrogance of Nations: Reading Romans in the Shadow of Empire*. Minneapolis: Fortress.

Engberg-Pedersen, Troels. 2000. *Paul and the Stoics*. Louisville: Westminster John Knox.

————. 2006. "Paul's Stoicizing Politics in Romans 12–13: The Role of 13:1–10 in the Argument." *JSNT* 29:163–72.

Epp, Eldon Jay. 2005. *Junia: The First Woman Apostle*. Minneapolis: Augsburg Fortress.

Erickson, Richard J. 1999. "The Damned and the Justified in Romans 5.12–21: An Analysis of Semantic Structure." Pages 282–307 in *Discourse Analysis and the NT: Approaches and Results*. Edited by Stanley E. Porter and Jeffrey T. Reed. JSNTSup 170. Sheffield: Sheffield Academic.

Eschner, Christina. 2010. *Gestorben und hingegeben "für" die Sünder*. 2 vols. WMANT 122/1–2. Neukirchen-Vluyn: Neukirchener.

Esler, Philip F. 2003a. "Ancient Oleiculture and Ethnic Differentiation: The Meaning of the Olive-Tree Image in Romans 11." *JSNT* 26:103–24.

————. 2003b. *Conflict and Identity in Romans: The Social Setting of Paul's Letter*. Minneapolis: Fortress.

————. 2003c. "Social Identity, the Virtues, and the Good Life: A New Approach to Romans 12:1–15:13." *BTB* 33:51–63.

————. 2004. "Paul and Stoicism: Romans 12 as a Test Case." *NTS* 50:106–24.

Estes, Joel D. 2016. "Calling on the Name of the Lord: The Meaning and Significance of ἐπικαλέω in Romans 10:13." *Them* 41:20–36.

Fee, Gordon. 1994. *God's Empowering Presence: The Holy Spirit in the Letters of Paul*. Peabody, MA: Hendrickson.

Feldman, Louis H. 1993. *Jew and Gentile in the Ancient World: Attitudes and Interactions from Alexander to Justinian*. Princeton: Princeton University Press.

Feldmeier, Reinhard, and Hermann Spieckermann. 2011. *God of the Living: A Biblical Theology*. Translated by Mark E. Biddle. Waco, TX: Baylor University Press.

Finlan, Stephen. 2004. *The Background and Content of Paul's Cultic Atonement Metaphors*. AcBib 19. Atlanta: Society of Biblical Literature.

Fitch, W. O. 1947. "Note on Romans 3:8b, ὧν τὸ κρίμα ἔνδικόν ἐστι." *ExpTim* 59:26.

Fitzgerald, John T. 1988. *Cracks in an Earthen Vessel: An Examination of the Catalogues of Hardships in the Corinthian Correspondence*. SBLDS 99. Atlanta: Society of Biblical Literature.

————. 1992. "Virtue/Vice Lists." *ABD* 6:857–59.

Fox, Arminta. 2017. "Decentering Paul, Contextualizing Crimes: Reading in Light of the Imprisoned." *JFSR* 33.2:37–54.

Fredriksen, Paula. 2017. *Paul: The Pagans' Apostle.* New Haven: Yale University Press.

Fretheim, Terence E. 1994. "The Book of Genesis: Introduction, Commentary, and Reflections." *NIB* 1:319–674.

Friar, Kimon. 1973. *Modern Greek Poetry.* New York: Simon & Schuster.

Friesen, Steven. 2007. "Government, NT." *NIDB* 2:641.

———. 2010. "The Wrong Erastus: Ideology, Archaeology, and Exegesis." Pages 231–56 in *Corinth in Context: Comparative Studies on Religion and Society.* Edited by Steven J. Friesen, Dan Schowalter, and James Walters. NovTSup 134. Leiden: Brill.

Furnish, Victor Paul. 1984. *II Corinthians: A New Translation and Commentary.* AB 32A. New York: Doubleday.

———. 2005. "Uncommon Love and the Common Good." Pages 58–87 in *In Search of the Common Good.* Edited by Dennis P. McCann and Patrick D. Miller. New York: T&T Clark.

———. 2009a. *The Moral Teaching of Paul: Selected Issues.* 3rd ed. Nashville: Abingdon.

———. 2009b. *Theology and Ethics in Paul.* Nashville: Abingdon, 1968. Repr., NTL. Louisville: Westminster John Knox.

Gäckle, Volker. 2005. *Die Starken und die Schwachen in Korinth und in Rom: Zu Heerkunft und Funktion der Antithese in 1 Kor 8,1–11,1 und in Röm 14,1–15,13.* WUNT 2/200. Tübingen: Mohr Siebeck.

Gager, John G. 1983. *The Origins of Anti-Semitism: Attitudes toward Judaism in Pagan and Christian Antiquity.* New York: Oxford University Press.

Gagnon, Robert A. J. 1993. "Heart of Wax and a Teaching That Stamps: ΤΥΠΟΣ ΔΙΔΑΧΗΣ (Rom. 6:17b) Once More." *JBL* 112:667–87.

Gamble, Harry Y. 1995. *Books and Readers in the Early Church: A History of Early Christian Texts.* New Haven: Yale University Press.

Gardner, Gregg E. 2015. *The Origins of Organized Charity in Rabbinic Judaism.* Cambridge: Cambridge University Press.

Garnsey, Peter. 1999. *Food and Society in Classical Antiquity.* KTAH. Cambridge: Cambridge University Press.

Garroway, Joshua D. 2012a. "The Circumcision of Christ: Romans 15:7–13." *JSNT* 34:303–22.

———. 2012b. *Paul's Gentile-Jews: Neither Jew nor Gentile, but Both.* New York: Palgrave Macmillan.

Gathercole, Simon J. 2002a. "A Conversion of Augustine: From Natural Law to Restored Nature in Romans 2.13–16." Pages 147–72 in *Engaging Augustine: Self-Context and Theology in the Interpretation of Romans.* Edited by Daniel Patte and Eugene TeSelle. Romans through History and Cultures. Harrisburg, PA: Trinity.

———. 2002b. "A Law unto Themselves: The Gentiles in Romans 2.14–15 Revisited." *JSNT* 85:27–49.

———. 2002c. *Where Is Boasting? Early Jewish Soteriology and Paul's Response in Romans 1–5.* Grand Rapids: Eerdmans.

———. 2015. *Defending Substitution: An Essay on Atonement in Paul.* Grand Rapids: Baker Academic.

———. 2017. "Locating Christ and Israel in Romans 9–11." Pages 115–39 in *God and Israel: Providence and Purpose in Romans 9–11.* Edited by Todd D. Still. Waco, TX: Baylor University Press.

Gaventa, Beverly Roberts. 2003. *Acts.* ANTC. Nashville: Abingdon.

———. 2004a. "The Cosmic Power of Sin in Paul's Letter to the Romans: Toward a Widescreen Edition." *Int* 58:229–40.

———. 2004b. "Initiatives Divine and Human in the Lukan Story World." Pages 79–89 in *The Holy Spirit and Christian Origins: Essays in Honor of James D. G. Dunn.* Edited by Graham N. Stanton, Bruce W. Longenecker, and Stephen C. Barton. Grand Rapids: Eerdmans.

———. 2005. "God Handed Them Over: Reading Romans 1:18–32 Apocalyptically." *ABR* 53:42–53.

———. 2007a. "Interpreting the Death of Jesus Apocalyptically." Pages 125–45 in *Jesus and Paul Reconnected: Fresh Pathways into an Old Debate.* Edited by Todd D. Still. Grand Rapids: Eerdmans.

———. 2007b. *Our Mother Saint Paul.* Louisville: Westminster John Knox.

———. 2008a. "'For the Glory of God': Theology and Experience in Paul's Letter to the Romans." Pages 53–65 in *Between Experience and Interpretation: Engaging the Writings of the New Testament.* Edited by Mary F. Foskett and O. Wesley Allen Jr. Nashville: Abingdon.

———. 2008b. "From Toxic Speech to the Redemption of Doxology in Paul's Letter to the Romans." Pages 392–408 in *The Word Leaps the Gap: Essays on Scripture and Theology in Honor of Richard B. Hays.* Edited by J. Ross Wagner, C. Kavin Rowe, and A. Katherine Grieb. Grand Rapids: Eerdmans.

———. 2009. "'To Preach the Gospel': Romans 1,15 and the Purposes of Romans." Pages 179–95 in *The Letter to the Romans.* Edited by Udo Schnelle. BETL 226. Leuven: Peeters.

———. 2010. "On the Calling-Into-Being of Israel: Romans 9:6–29." Pages 255–69 in *Between Gospel and Election: Explorations in the Interpretation of Romans 9–11.* Edited by Florian Wilk and J. Ross Wagner with the assistance of Frank Schleritt. WUNT 1/257. Tübingen: Mohr Siebeck.

———. 2011a. "Neither Height nor Depth: Discerning the Cosmology of Romans." *SJT* 64:265–78.

———. 2011b. "The Paradox of Power: Reading for the Subject in Romans 14:1–15:6." *JTI* 5:1–12.

———. 2011c. "Paul and the Roman Believers." Pages 93–107 in *The Blackwell Companion to Paul*. Edited by Stephen Westerholm. Oxford: Blackwell.

———, ed. 2013a. *Apocalyptic Paul: Cosmos and Anthropos in Romans 5–8*. Waco, TX: Baylor University Press.

———. 2013b. "The Rhetoric of Violence and the God of Peace in Paul's Letter to the Romans." Pages 61–75 in *Paul, John, and Apocalyptic Eschatology: Studies in Honor of Martinus C. de Boer*. Edited by Jan Krans, Bert Jan Lietaert Peerbolte, Peter-Ben Smit, and Arie Zwiep. NovTSup 152. Leiden: Brill.

———. 2013c. "The Shape of the 'I': The Psalter, the Gospel, and the Speaker in Romans 7." Pages 77–91 in *Apocalyptic Paul: Cosmos and Anthropos in Romans 5–8*. Edited by Beverly Roberts Gaventa. Waco, TX: Baylor University Press.

———. 2014a. "The Character of God's Faithfulness: A Response to N. T. Wright." *JSPL* 4:71–79.

———. 2014b. "The 'Glory of God' in Paul's Letter to the Romans." Pages 29–40 in *Interpretation and the Claims of the Text: Resourcing New Testament Theology; Essays in Honor of Charles H. Talbert*. Edited by Jason A. Whitlark, Bruce W. Longenecker, Lidija Novakovic, and Mikeal C. Parsons. Waco, TX: Baylor University Press.

———. 2014c. "The Singularity of the Gospel Revisited." Pages 187–99 in *Galatians and Christian Theology: Justification, the Gospel, and Ethics in Paul's Letters*. Edited by Mark W. Elliott, Scott J. Hafemann, N. T. Wright, and John Frederick. Grand Rapids: Baker Academic.

———. 2015. "Freedom in Apocalyptic Perspective: A Reflection on Paul's Letter to the Romans." Pages 195–208 in *Quests for Freedom: Biblical, Historical, Contemporary*. Edited by Mikeal Welker. Neukirchen-Vluyn: Neukirchener.

———. 2016a. "Questions about *Nomos*, Answers about *Christos*: Romans 10:4 in Context." Pages 121–34 in *Torah Ethics and Early Christian Identity*. Edited by Susan J. Wendel and David M. Miller. Grand Rapids: Eerdmans.

———. 2016b. "Thinking from Christ to Israel: Romans 9–11 in Apocalyptic Context." Pages 239–55 in *Paul and the Apocalyptic Imagination*. Edited by Ben C. Blackwell, John K. Goodrich, and Jason Maston. Minneapolis: Fortress.

———. 2017a. "Reading Romans 13 with Simone Weil: Toward a More Generous Hermeneutic." *JBL* 136:7–22.

———. 2017b. "The Revelation of Human Captivity: An Exegesis of Romans 1,18–32." Pages 43–59 in *God's Power for Salvation: Romans 1,1–5,11*. Edited by Cilliers Breytenbach. COP 23. Leuven: Peeters.

———. 2022a. "The Finality of the Gospel: Barth's *Römerbrief* on Romans 9–11." Pages 104–19 in *The Finality of the Gospel: Karl Barth and the Tasks of Eschatology.* Edited by Kaitlyn Dugan and Philip G. Ziegler. SRTh43. Leiden: Brill.

———. 2022b. "Places of Power in Paul's Letter to the Romans." *Int* 76: 293–302.

———. 2022c. "Power and Kenosis in Paul's Letter to the Romans." Pages 24–40 in *Kenosis: The Self-Emptying of Christ in Scripture and Theology.* Edited by Paul T. Nimmo and Keith L. Johnson. Grand Rapids: Eerdmans.

———. 2022d. "Reading Romans on the Brink: The Continuing Challenge of Barth's *Römerbrief.*" Pages 9–24 in *Karl Barth's Epistle to the Romans: Retrospect and Prospect.* Edited by Christophe Chalamet, Andreas Dettwiler, and Sarah Stewart-Kroeker. TBT 196. Berlin: de Gruyter.

———. 2022e. "Where Is the 'God of Israel' in Paul's Reading of the Gospel?" Pages 30–47 in *Gospel Reading and Reception in Early Christian Literature.* Edited by Madison N. Pierce, Andrew J. Byers, and Simon Gathercole. Cambridge: Cambridge University Press.

———. 2023. "'That Grace Should Come into Its Own': Romans 12:1–8 in and with Karl Barth's *Römerbrief.*" Pages 251–63 in *The New Perspective on Grace: Paul and the Gospel after "Paul and the Gift."* Edited by Edward Adams, Dorothea H. Bertschmann, Stephen J. Chester, Jonathan A. Linebaugh, and Todd D. Still. Grand Rapids: Eerdmans.

Gibson, Jeffrey B. 2004. "Paul's 'Dying Formula': Prolegomena to an Understanding of Its Import and Significance." Pages 20–41 in *Celebrating Romans: Template for Pauline Theology.* Edited by Sheila E. McGinn. Grand Rapids: Eerdmans.

Gieniusz, Adrzej. 1993. "Rom 7,1–6: Lack of Imagination? Function of the Passage in the Argumentation of Rom 6,1–7,6." *Bib* 74:389–400.

Given, Mark D. 1999. "Restoring the Inheritance of Israel in Romans 11:1." *JBL* 118:89–96.

———. 2001. *Paul's True Rhetoric: Ambiguity, Cunning, and Deception in Greece and Rome.* ESEC 7. Harrisburg, PA: Trinity.

Glancy, Jennifer. 1991. "Israel vs. Israel in Romans 11:25–32." *USQR* 45: 191–203.

Gloer, W. H. 1984. "Homologies and Hymns in the New Testament: Form, Content, and Criteria for Identification." *PRSt* 11:115–32.

Goodrich, John K. 2012. "'Standard of Faith' or 'Measure of a Trusteeship'? A Study in Romans 12:3." *CBQ* 74:753–72.

———. 2013. "From Slaves of Sin to Slaves of God: Reconsidering the Origin of Paul's Slavery Metaphor in Romans 6." *BBR* 23:509–30.

———. 2016. "Until the Fullness of the Gentiles Comes In: A Critical Review of Recent Scholarship on the Salvation of 'All Israel' (Romans 11:26)." *JSPL* 6:5–32.

Gordon, Benjamin D. 2016. "On the Sanctity of Mixtures and Branches: Two Halakic Sayings in Romans 11:16–34." *JBL* 135:355–68.

Grant, Robert M. 1970. *Theophilus of Antioch: Ad Autoclycum*. Oxford: Clarendon.

Grieb, A. Katherine. 2002. *The Story of Romans: A Narrative Defense of God's Righteousness*. Louisville: Westminster John Knox.

Gruen, Erich S. 2002. *Diaspora: Jews amidst Greeks and Romans*. Cambridge, MA: Harvard University Press.

Guerra, Anthony J. 1995. *Romans and the Apologetic Tradition: The Purpose, Genre, and Audience of Paul's Letter*. SNTSMS 81. Cambridge: Cambridge University Press.

Gundry Volf, Judith M. 1990. *Paul and Perseverance: Staying In and Falling Away*. Louisville: Westminster John Knox.

Günther, Sven. 2016. "Taxation in the Greco-Roman World: The Roman Principate." *Oxford Handbook. Topics in Classical Studies* (online). https://academic.oup.com/edited-volume/43505/chapter/364128738.

Gupta, Nijay K. 2016. "What 'Mercies of God'? *Oiktirmos* in Romans 12:1 against Its Septuagintal Background." *BBR* 22:81–96.

———. 2020. "Reconstructing Junia's Imprisonment: Examining a Neglected Pauline Comment in Romans 16:7." *PRSt* 47:385–97.

Hachlili, Rachel, and Ann Killebrew. 1983. "Jewish Funerary Customs during the Second Temple Period, in the Light of the Excavations at the Jericho Necropolis." *PEQ* 115:109–39.

Haines-Eitzen, Kim. 2011. *The Gendered Palimpsest: Women, Writing, and Representation in Early Christianity*. Oxford: Oxford University Press.

Hanson, A. T. 1981. "Vessels of Wrath or Instruments of Wrath? Romans 9:22–23." *JTS* 32:433–43.

Harink, Douglas. 2020. *Resurrecting Justice: Reading Romans for the Life of the World*. Downers Grove, IL: IVP Academic.

Harrill, J. Albert. 2006. *Slaves in the New Testament: Literary, Social, and Moral Dimensions*. Minneapolis: Fortress.

Harris, William. 1989. *Ancient Literacy*. Cambridge, MA: Harvard University Press.

Harrison, James. 2020. "Paul's 'Indebtedness' to the Barbarian in Latin West Perspective." Pages 143–78 in *Reading Romans with Roman Eyes: Studies on the Social Perspective of Paul*. Paul in Critical Contexts. Lanham, MD: Lexington/Fortress Academic.

Harrisville, Roy A., III. 1994. "ΠΙΣΤΙΣ ΧΡΙΣΤΟΥ: Witness of the Fathers." *NovT* 36:233–41.

Hartwig, Charlotte, and Gerd Theissen. 2004. "Die korinthische Gemeinde als Nebenadressat des Römerbriefs. Eigentextreferenzen des Paulus und kommunikativer Kontext des Längsten Paulusbriefes." *NovT* 46.3:229–52.

Hassold, William J. 2000. "'Avoid Them': Another Look at Romans 16:17–20." *CurTM* 27.3:196–208.

Hay, David M. 1973. *Glory at the Right Hand: Psalm 110 in Early Christianity.* SBLMS 18. Nashville: Abingdon.

Hayes, Christine. 2015. *What's Divine about Divine Law? Early Perspectives.* Princeton: Princeton University Press.

Hays, Richard B. 1980. "Psalm 143 and the Logic of Romans 3." *JBL* 99: 107–15.

———. 1985. "'Have We Found Abraham to Be Our Forefather according to the Flesh?' A Reconsideration of Rom 4:1." *NovT* 27:76–98.

———. 1986. "Relations Natural and Unnatural: A Response to John Boswell's Exegesis of Romans 1." *JRE* 14:192–96.

———. 1989. *Echoes of Scripture in the Letters of Paul.* New Haven: Yale University Press.

———. 1993. "Christ Prays the Psalms: Paul's Use of an Early Christian Exegetical Convention." Pages 122–36 in *The Future of Christology: Essays in Honor of Leander E. Keck.* Edited by A. J. Malherbe and W. A. Meeks. Minneapolis: Fortress.

———. 1996. *The Moral Vision of the New Testament: Community, Cross, New Creation; A Contemporary Introduction to New Testament Ethics.* San Francisco: HarperCollins.

———. 1997. "PISTIS and Pauline Christology: What Is at Stake?" Pages 35–60 in *Looking Back, Pressing On.* Vol. 4 of *Pauline Theology.* Edited by E. Elizabeth Johnson and D. M. Hays. Atlanta: Scholars Press.

———. 2002. *The Faith of Jesus Christ: The Narrative Substructure of Galatians 3:1–4:11.* 2nd ed. Grand Rapids: Eerdmans.

———. 2005. "Apocalyptic Hermeneutics: Habakkuk Proclaims 'The Righteous One.'" Pages 119–42 in *The Conversion of the Imagination: Paul as Interpreter of Israel's Scripture.* Grand Rapids: Eerdmans.

———. 2006. "Made New by One Man's Obedience: Romans 5:12–19." Pages 96–102 in *Proclaiming the Scandal of the Cross: Contemporary Images of the Atonement.* Edited by Mark D. Baker. Grand Rapids: Baker Academic.

Head, Peter M. 2009. "Named Letter-Carriers among the Oxyrhynchus Papyri." *JSNT* 31:279–99.

Heim, Erin M. 2017. *Adoption in Galatians and Romans: Contemporary Metaphor Theories and the Pauline Huiothesia Metaphors.* BibInt 153. Leiden: Brill.

Hill, Wesley. 2015. *Paul and the Trinity: Persons, Relations, and the Pauline Letters.* Grand Rapids: Eerdmans.

Hodge Johnson, Caroline. 2007. *If Sons, Then Heirs: A Study of Kinship and Ethnicity in the Letters of Paul.* Oxford: Oxford University Press.

———. 2012. "'A Light to the Nations': The Role of Israel in Romans 9–11." Pages 169–86 in *Reading Paul's Letter to the Romans*. Edited by Jerry L. Sumney. RBS 73. Atlanta: Society of Biblical Literature.

Hodgson, Robert. 1983. "Paul the Apostle and First Century Tribulation Lists." *ZNW* 74:59–80.

Hofius, Otfried. 1990. "'All Israel Will Be Saved': Divine Salvation and Israel's Deliverance in Romans 9–11." Pages 19–39 in *The Church and Israel: Romans 9–11; The 1989 Frederick Neumann Symposium on the Theological Interpretation of Scripture*. PSBSup 1. Princeton: Princeton Theological Seminary.

———. 2001. "The Adam-Christ Antithesis and the Law: Reflections on Romans 5:12–21." Pages 165–205 in *Paul and the Mosaic Law*. Edited by James D. G. Dunn. Grand Rapids: Eerdmans.

Holladay, Carl. 2016. *Acts: A Commentary*. NTL. Louisville: Westminster John Knox.

Holmes, Christopher T. 2013. "Utterly Incapacitated: The Neglected Meaning of ΠΑΡΕΣΙΣ in Romans 3:25." *NovT* 55:349–66.

Holmstrand, Jonas. 1997. *Markers and Meaning in Paul: An Analysis of 1 Thessalonians, Philippians, and Galatians*. ConBNT 28. Stockholm: Almqvist & Wiksell.

Hooker, Morna. 1960. "Adam in Romans 1." *NTS* 6:297–306.

———. 1989. "Pistis Christou." *NTS* 35:321–42.

———. 2016. "Another Look at πίστις Χριστοῦ." *SJT* 69:46–62.

Horrell, David. 2015. *Solidarity and Difference: A Contemporary Reading of Paul's Ethics*. 2nd ed. New York: Bloomsbury.

Horrell, David G., Cherryl Hunt, and Christopher Southgate. 2010. *Greening Paul: Rereading the Apostle in a Time of Ecological Crisis*. Waco, TX: Baylor University Press.

Horsley, R. A, ed. 2004. *Hidden Transcripts and the Arts of Resistance: Applying the Work of James C. Scott to Jesus and Paul*. SemeiaSt 48. Atlanta: Society of Biblical Literature.

Howard, George. 1970. "Romans 3:21–31 and the Inclusion of the Gentiles." *HTR* 63:223–33.

Hubbard, Moyer V. 2016. "Enemy Love in Paul: Probing the Engberg-Pedersen and Thorsteinsson Thesis." *JSPL* 6:115–35.

Hugo, Victor. 1972. *Les Misérables*. New York: Amsco.

Hultgren, Arland J. 1980. "The *Pistis Christou* Formulation in Paul." *NovT* 22:248–63.

Hunn, Debbie. 2009. "Debating the Faithfulness of Jesus Christ in Twentieth-Century Scholarship." Pages 15–31 in *The Faith of Jesus Christ: Exegetical, Biblical, and Theological Studies*. Edited by Michael F. Bird and Preston M. Sprinkle. Peabody, MA: Hendrickson.

Ilan, Tal. 1996. *Jewish Women in Greco-Roman Palestine*. Peabody, MA: Hendrickson.

———. 2010. "Names." *EDEJ*, 990–91.

Irons, Charles Lee. 2015. *The Righteousness of God: A Lexical Examination of the Covenant-Faithfulness Interpretation*. WUNT 2/386. Tübingen: Mohr Siebeck.

Jervell, Jacob. 1991. "The Letter to Jerusalem." Pages 53–64 in *The Romans Debate*. Rev. and exp. ed. Edited by Karl Paul Donfried. Peabody, MA: Hendrickson.

Jervis, L. Ann. 1991. *The Purpose of Romans: A Comparative Letter Structure Investigation*. JSNTSup 55. Sheffield: JSOT Press.

———. 2007. *At the Heart of the Gospel: Suffering in the Earliest Christian Message*. Grand Rapids: Eerdmans.

———. 2017. "Promise and Purpose in Romans 9:1–13: Toward Understanding Paul's View of Time." Pages 1–26 in *God and Israel: Providence and Purpose in Romans 9–11*. Edited by Todd D. Still. Waco, TX: Baylor University Press.

Jewett, Robert. 1985. "The Redaction and Use of an Early Christian Confession in Romans 1:3–4." Pages 99–122 in *The Living Text: Essays in Honor of Ernest W. Saunders*. Edited by Dennis E. Groh and Robert Jewett. Lanham, MD: University Press of America.

Jipp, Joshua W. 2009. "Rereading the Story of Abraham, Isaac, and 'Us' in Romans 4." *JSNT* 32:217–42.

———. 2015. *Christ Is King: Paul's Royal Ideology*. Minneapolis: Fortress.

Jodoin, Danielle. 2010. "Rm 12,1–2: Une intrigue discursive; De l'offrande des embers à l'offrande des corps." *ETR* 85:499–512.

Johnson, E. Elizabeth. 1989. *The Function of Apocalyptic and Wisdom Traditions in Romans 9–11*. SBLDS 109. Atlanta: Scholars Press.

———. 1995. "Romans 9–11: The Faithfulness and Impartiality of God." Pages 211–39 in *Romans*. Vol. 3 of *Pauline Theology*. Edited by David M. Hay and E. Elizabeth Johnson. Minneapolis: Fortress.

Johnson, S. Lewis, Jr. 1974. "Romans 5:12—An Exercise in Exegesis and Theology." Pages 298–315 in *New Dimensions in New Testament Study*. Edited by Richard N. Longenecker and Merrill C. Tenney. Grand Rapids: Zondervan.

Johnston, J. William. 2011. "Which 'All' Sinned? Rom 3:23–24 Reconsidered." *NovT* 53:153–64.

Judge, E. A. 1984. "Cultural Conformity and Innovation in Paul: Some Clues from Contemporary Documents." *TynBul* 35:2–24.

Juel, Donald H. 1994. *A Master of Surprise: Mark Interpreted*. Minneapolis: Fortress.

Kallas, James. 1965. "Romans XIII.1–7: An Interpolation." *NTS* 11:365–74.

Kanjuparambil, Philip. 1983. "Imperatival Participles in Rom 12:9–21." *JBL* 102:285–88.

Karris, Robert J. 1991. "Romans 14:1–15:13 and the Occasion of Romans." Pages 65–84 in *The Romans Debate*. Rev. and exp. ed. Edited by Karl Paul Donfried. Peabody, MA: Hendrickson.

Käsemann, Ernst. 1960. "Zum Verständis von Römer 3, 24–26." Pages 96–100 in *Exegetische Versuche und Besinnungen: Erster Band*. Göttingen: Vandenhoeck & Ruprecht.

———. 1969a. "Principles of the Interpretation of Romans 13." Pages 196–216 in *New Testament Questions of Today*. Translated by Margaret Kohl. Philadelphia: Fortress.

———. 1969b. "'The Righteousness of God' in Paul." Pages 168–82 in *New Testament Questions of Today*. Translated by Margaret Kohl. Philadelphia: Fortress.

———. 1969c. "Worship in Everyday Life." Pages 188–95 in *New Testament Questions of Today*. Translated by Margaret Kohl. Philadelphia: Fortress.

———. 1971a. "On Paul's Anthropology." Pages 1–31 in *Perspectives on Paul*. Translated by Margaret Kohl. Philadelphia: Fortress.

———. 1971b. "The Saving Significance of Jesus' Death in Paul." Pages 32–59 in *Perspectives on Paul*. Translated by Margaret Kohl. Philadelphia: Fortress.

Keck, Leander E. 1965. "The Poor among the Saints in the New Testament." *ZNW* 56:100–129.

———. 1966. "The Poor among the Saints in Jewish Christianity and at Qumran." *ZNW* 57:54–78.

———. 1977. "The Function of Rom 3:10–18: Observations and Suggestions." Pages 141–57 in *God's Christ and His People: Studies in Honour of Nils Alstrup Dahl*. Edited by Jacob Jervell and Wayne A. Meeks. Oslo: Universitetsforlaget.

———. 1990. "Christology, Soteriology, and the Praise of God (Romans 15:7–13)." Pages 85–97 in *The Conversation Continues: Studies in Paul and John in Honor of J. Louis Martyn*. Edited by Robert T. Fortna and Beverly R. Gaventa. Nashville: Abingdon.

———. 1995. "What Makes Romans Tick?" Pages 3–29 in *Romans*. Vol. 3 of *Pauline Theology*. Edited by David M. Hay and E. Elizabeth Johnson. Minneapolis: Fortress.

Keesmat, Sylvia C. 1999. *Paul and His Story: (Re)Interpreting the Exodus Tradition*. JSNTSup 181. Sheffield: Sheffield Academic.

Kennedy, H. A. A. 1917. "Two Exegetical Notes on St. Paul." *ExpTim* 28: 322–23.

Khobnya, Svetlana. 2013. "'The Root' in Paul's Olive Tree Metaphor (Romans 11:16–24)." *TynBul* 64:257–73.

Kim, Chan-Hie. 1972. *Form and Function of the Familiar Greek Letter of Recommendation.* SBLDS 4. Missoula, MT: Society of Biblical Literature.

Kim, Jung Hoon. 2004. *The Significance of Clothing Imagery in the Pauline Corpus.* JSNTSup 268. London: T&T Clark.

Kim, Seyoon. 2011. "Paul's Common Paraenesis (1 Thess. 4–5; Phil. 2–4; and Rom. 12–13): The Correspondence between Romans 1:18–32 and 12:1–2, and the Unity of Romans 12–13." *TynBul* 62:109–39.

King, Anthony. 1999. "Diet in the Roman World: A Regional Inter-Site Comparison of the Mammal Bones." *JRA* 12:168–201.

King, Justin. 2017. "Rhetorical Chain-Link Construction and the Relationship between Romans 7.1–6 and 7.7–8.39: Additional Evidence for Assessing the Argument of Romans 7–8 and the Identity of the Infamous 'I.'" *JSNT* 39:258–78.

―――. 2018. *Speech-in-Character, Diatribe, and Romans 3:1–9: Who's Speaking When and Why It Matters.* BibInt. Leiden: Brill.

Kirby, John T. 1987. "The Syntax of Romans 5.12: A Rhetorical Approach." *NTS* 33:283–86.

Kissi, Seth. 2017. "Ministry and Market Spirituality in Ghana: Some Tendencies and Lessons from Romans 12:1–8." *Trinity Journal of Church and Theology* 19.1:64–83.

Kiuchi, Nobuyoshi. 2006. "Living Like the Azazel-Goat in Romans 12:1b." *TynBul* 57:251–61.

Klauck, Hans-Josef. 2006. *Ancient Letters and the New Testament: A Guide to Context and Exegesis.* Translated by Daniel P. Bailey. Waco, TX: Baylor University Press.

Klein, Günther. 1991. "Paul's Purpose in Writing the Epistle to the Romans." Pages 29–43 in *The Romans Debate.* Rev. and exp. ed. Edited by Karl P. Donfried. Peabody, MA: Hendrickson.

Kloppenborg, John S. 2017. "Gaius the Roman Guest." *NTS* 63:534–49.

―――. 2019. *Christ's Associations: Connecting and Belonging in the Ancient City.* New Haven: Yale University Press.

Koperski, Veronica. 2009. "Women in Romans: Text in Context." Pages 441–51 in *The Letter to the Romans.* Edited by Udo Schnelle. BETL 226. Leuven: Peeters.

Kotansky, Roy. 1994. *Greek Magical Amulets: The Inscribed Gold, Silver, Copper, and Bronze Lamellae, Part I; Published Texts of Known Provenance.* PapyCol 22. Opladen: Westdeutscher.

Kraftchick, Steve. 1987. "Paul's Use of Creation Themes: A Test of Romans 1–8." *ExAud* 3:72–87.

Kraus, Wolfgang. 1991. *Der Tod Jesu als Heiligtumsweihe: Eine Untersuchung zum Umfeld der Sühnevorstellung in Römer 3,25–26a.* WMANT 66. Neukirchen-Vluyn: Neukirchener.

Krauter, Stefan. 2009. *Studien zu Röm 13,1–7: Paulus und der politische Diskurs der neronischen Zeit.* WUNT 1/243. Tübingen: Mohr Siebeck.

Kugler, Robert A. 1996. *From Patriarch to Priest: The Levi-Priestly Tradition from Aramaic Levi to Testament of Levi.* EJL 9. Atlanta: Scholars Press.

Kujanpää, Katja. 2019. *The Rhetorical Functions of Scriptural Quotations in Romans: Paul's Argumentation by Quotations.* NovTSup 172. Leiden: Brill.

Lampe, Peter. 2003. *From Paul to Valentinus: Christians at Rome in the First Two Centuries.* Translated by Michael Steinhauser. Edited by Marshall D. Johnson. Minneapolis: Fortress.

———. 2015. "Concepts of Freedom in Antiquity: Pagan Philosophical Traditions in the Greco-Roman World." Pages 117–32 in *Quests for Freedom: Biblical, Historical, Contemporary.* Edited by Michael Welker. Neukirchen-Vluyn: Neukirchener.

Lategan, Bernard. 1992. "Reading Romans 13 in a South African Context." Pages 115–33 in *The Reader and Beyond: Theory and Practice in South African Reception Studies.* Pretoria: Human Sciences Research Council.

———. 2012. "Romans 13:1–7: A Review of Post-1989 Readings." *Scriptura* [Stellenbosch] 110:259–72.

Lee, Chul Woo. 2005. "Understanding the Law in Rom. 7:1–6: An Enthymemic Analysis." *Scriptura* [Stellenbosch] 88:126–38.

Leithart, Peter J. 2008. "Adam, Moses, and Jesus: A Reading of Romans 5:12–14." *CTJ* 43:257–73.

Lettsome, Raquel S. 2021. "Mary's Slave Song: The Tensions and Turnarounds of Faithfully Reading *Doulē* in the Magnificat." *Int* 75:6–18.

Levenson, Jon D. 2003. "Did God Forgive Adam? An Exercise in Comparative Midrash." Pages 148–70 in *Jews and Christians: People of God.* Edited by Carl E. Braaten and Robert W. Jenson. Grand Rapids: Eerdmans.

Lin, Yii–Jan. 2020. "Junia: An Apostle before Paul." *JBL* 139:191–209.

Lincicum, David. 2010. *Paul and the Early Jewish Encounter with Deuteronomy.* WUNT 2/284. Tübingen: Mohr Siebeck.

Linebaugh, Jonathan A. 2010. "Debating Diagonal Δικαιοσύνη: The Epistle of Enoch and Paul in Theological Conversation." *EC* 1:107–28.

———. 2013a. "The Christo-Centrism of Faith in Christ: Martin Luther's Reading of Galatians 2.16, 19–20." *NTS* 59:535–44.

———. 2013b. *God, Grace, and Righteousness in Wisdom of Solomon and Paul's Letter to the Romans: Texts in Conversation.* NovTSup 152. Leiden: Brill.

———. 2022. *The Word of the Cross: Reading Paul.* Grand Rapids: Eerdmans.

Long, A. A. 2002. *Epictetus: A Stoic and Socratic Guide to Life.* Oxford: Clarendon.

Longenecker, Bruce W. 1991. *Eschatology and the Covenant: A Comparison of 4 Ezra and Romans 1–11.* JSNTSup 57. Sheffield: JSOT Press.

————. 2005. *Rhetoric at the Boundaries: The Art and Theology of New Testament Chain-Link Transitions.* Waco, TX: Baylor University Press.

————. 2010. *Remember the Poor: Paul, Poverty, and the Greco-Roman World.* Grand Rapids: Eerdmans.

Macaskill, Grant. 2013. *Union with Christ in the New Testament.* Oxford: Oxford University Press.

Madden, John. 1996. "Slavery in the Roman Empire: Numbers and Origins." *ClIre* 3:109–28.

Malherbe, Abraham J. 1980. "MH ΓΕΝΟΙΤΟ in the Diatribe and Paul." *HTR* 73:231–40.

Manson, T. W. 1991. "St. Paul's Letter to the Romans—and Others." Pages 3–15 in *The Romans Debate.* Rev. and exp. ed. Edited by Karl P. Donfried. Peabody, MA: Hendrickson.

Marcus, Joel. 1988. "'Let God Arise and End the Reign of Sin!' A Contribution to the Study of Pauline Parenesis." *Bib* 69:386–95.

————. 1989. "The Circumcision and the Uncircumcision in Rome." *NTS* 35:67–81.

————. 1999. *Mark 1–8: A New Translation with Introduction and Commentary.* AB 27. New York: Doubleday.

Marshall, Jill E. 2017. "The Recovery of Paul's Female Colleagues in Nineteenth-Century Feminist Biblical Interpretation." *JFSR* 33.2:21–26.

Martens, John W. 2014. "Burning Questions in Romans 12:20: What Is the Meaning and Purpose of 'Coals of Fire'?" *CBQ* 76:291–305.

Martin, Dale. 1995a. *The Corinthian Body.* New Haven: Yale University Press.

————. 1995b. "Heterosexism and the Interpretation of Romans 1:18–32." *BibInt* 3:339–49.

Martínez, Florentino García. 1996. *The Dead Sea Scrolls Translated: The Qumran Texts in English.* 2nd ed. Grand Rapids: Eerdmans.

Martínez, Florentino García, and Tigchelaar, Eibert J. C. 1997. *The Dead Sea Scrolls Study Edition.* 2 vols. Leiden: Brill.

Martyn, J. Louis. 1997a. *Galatians: A New Translation and Commentary.* AB 33A. New York: Doubleday.

————. 1997b. *Theological Issues in the Letters of Paul.* Nashville: Abingdon.

————. 2003. "*Nomos* Plus Genitive Noun in Paul: The History of God's Law." Pages 575–87 in *Earliest Christianity and Classical Culture: Comparative Studies in Honor of Abraham J. Malherbe.* Edited by John Fitzgerald, Thomas H. Olbricht, and L. Michael White. Leiden: Brill.

————. 2008. "Epilogue: An Essay in Pauline Meta-Ethics." Pages 173–83 in *Divine and Human Agency in Paul and His Cultural Environment.* Edited by John M. G. Barclay and Simon Gathercole. LNTS 335. London: T&T Clark.

Marxsen, Willi. 1955. "Der ἕτερος νόμος Rom. 13,8." *TZ* 11:230–37.

Matlock, R. Barry. 2000. "Detheologizing the ΠΙΣΤΙΣ ΧΡΙΣΤΟΥ Debate: Cautionary Remarks from a Lexical Semantic Perspective." *NovT* 42:1–23.

―――. 2002. "'Even the Demons Believe': Paul and the πίστις Χριστοῦ." *CBQ* 64:300–318.

―――. 2007. "The Rhetoric of πίστις in Paul: Galatians 2.16, 3.22, Romans 3.22, and Philippians 3.9." *JSNT* 30:173–203.

―――. 2009. "Saving Faith: The Rhetoric and Semantics of πίστις in Paul." Pages 73–89 in *The Faith of Jesus Christ: Exegetical, Biblical, and Theological Studies*. Edited by Michael F. Bird and Preston M. Sprinkle. Peabody, MA: Hendrickson.

McCruden, Kevin B. 2005. "Judgment and Life for the Lord: Occasion and Theology of Romans 14,1–15,13." *Bib* 86:229–44.

McFarland, Ian A. 2010. *In Adam's Fall: A Meditation on the Christian Doctrine of Original Sin*. Malden, MA: Wiley-Blackwell.

McFarland, Orrey. 2012. "Whose Abraham, Which Promise? Genesis 15.6 in Philo's *De Virtutibus* and Romans 4." *JSNT* 35:107–29.

McGinnis, Claire Mathews. 2012. "The Hardening of Pharaoh's Heart in Christian and Jewish Interpretation." *JTI* 6:43–64.

Meeks, Wayne A. 2002. "On Trusting an Unpredictable God: A Hermeneutical Meditation on Romans 9–11." Pages 210–29 in *In Search of Early Christians: Selected Essays*. Edited by Allen R. Hilton and H. Gregory Snyder. New Haven: Yale University Press.

Meggitt, Justin J. 1996. "The Social Status of Erastus (Rom. 16:23)." *NovT* 38: 218–23.

Merkle, Ben L. 2000. "Romans 11 and the Future of Ethnic Israel." *JETS* 43: 709–21.

Metzger, Bruce M. 1971. *A Textual Commentary on the Greek New Testament*. London: United Bible Societies.

―――. 1973. "The Punctuation of Rom. 9:5." Pages 95–112 in *Christ and Spirit in the New Testament: In Honour of C. F. D. Moule*. Edited by Barnabas Lindars and Stephen S. Smalley. Cambridge: Cambridge University Press.

Meyer, Paul W. 1980. "Romans 10:4 and the End of the Law." Pages 59–78 in *The Divine Helmsman: Studies on God's Control of Human Events, Presented to Lou H. Silberman*. Edited by James L. Crenshaw and Samuel Sandmel. New York: Ktav.

―――. 1997. "Pauline Theology: A Proposal for a Pause in Its Pursuit." Pages 140–61 in *Looking Back, Pressing On*. Vol. 4 of *Pauline Theology*. Edited by E. Elizabeth Johnson and David M. Hay. SymS. Atlanta: Scholars Press.

―――. 2004a. "The Holy Spirit in the Pauline Letters: A Contextual Exploration." Pages 117–32 in *The Word in This World: Essays in New Testament*

Exegesis and Theology, by Paul W. Meyer. Edited by John T. Carroll. NTL. Louisville: Westminster John Knox.

———. 2004b. "Romans: A Commentary." Pages 151–218 in *The Word in This World: Essays in New Testament Exegesis and Theology*, by Paul W. Meyer. Edited by John T. Carroll. NTL. Louisville: Westminster John Knox.

———. 2004c. "Romans 10:4 and the 'End' of the Law." Pages 78–94 in *The Word in This World: Essays in New Testament Exegesis and Theology*, by Paul W. Meyer. Edited by John T. Carroll. NTL. Louisville: Westminster John Knox.

———. 2004d. "The Worm at the Core of the Apple: Exegetical Reflections on Romans 7." Pages 57–77 in *The Word in This World: Essays in New Testament Exegesis and Theology*, by Paul W. Meyer. Edited by John T. Carroll. NTL. Louisville: Westminster John Knox.

Miller, James C. 2001. "The Romans Debate 1991–2001." *CurBS* 9:306–49.

Miller, James E. 1995. "The Practices of Romans 1:26: Homosexual or Heterosexual?" *NovT* 37:1–11.

Miller, Patrick D. 2009. *The Ten Commandments*. IBC. Louisville: Westminster John Knox.

Minear, Paul S. 1959. "Gratitude and Mission in the Epistle to the Romans." Pages 42–48 in *Basileia: Walter Freytag zum 60. Geburtstag*. Edited by Jan Hermelink and Hans Jochen Margull. Stuttgart: Evangelische Missionsverlag.

———. 1971. *The Obedience of Faith: The Purposes of Paul in the Epistle to the Romans*. SBT 2/19. Naperville, IL: Allenson.

Mitchell, Margaret. 1992. *Paul and the Rhetoric of Reconciliation: An Exegetical Investigation of the Language and Composition of 1 Corinthians*. Louisville: Westminster John Knox.

———. 2010. "The Continuing Problem of Particularity and Universality within the *corpus Paulinum*: Chrysostom on Romans 16:3." *ST* 64:121–37.

Miyata, Mitsuo. 2009. *Authority and Obedience: Romans 13:1–7 in Modern Japan*. Translated by Gregory Vanderbilt. New York: Lang.

Moltmann, Jürgen. 1990. *The Way of Jesus Christ: Christology in Messianic Dimensions*. London: SCM.

Montanari, Franco. 2015. *The Brill Dictionary of Ancient Greek*. Edited by Madeleine Goh and Chad Schroeder. Leiden: Brill.

Montgomery, Helen Barrett. 1924. *The New Testament in Modern English*. Nashville: Holman.

Moo, Jonathan. 2008. "Romans 8.19–22 and Isaiah's Cosmic Covenant." *NTS* 54:74–89.

Morgan, Teresa. 2017. *Roman Faith and Christian Faith: Pistis and Fides in the Early Roman Empire and Early Churches*. Oxford: Oxford University Press.

———. 2020. *Being 'in Christ' in the Letters of Paul: Saved through Christ and in His Hands*. WUNT 1/449. Tübingen: Mohr Siebeck.

Moule, C. F. D. 1968. *An Idiom-Book of New Testament Greek.* 2nd ed. Cambridge: Cambridge University Press.

Moulton, James Hope. 1908. *A Grammar of New Testament Greek.* 3rd ed. 4 vols. Edinburgh: T&T Clark.

Mueller, Janel, and Joshua Scodel. 2009. *Elizabeth I: Translations, 1592–1598.* Chicago: University of Chicago Press.

Munck, Johannes. 1967. *Christ and Israel: An Interpretation of Romans 9–11.* Philadelphia: Fortress.

Myers, Alicia D. 2017. *Blessed among Women? Mothers and Motherhood in the New Testament.* New York: Oxford University Press.

Myers, Benjamin. 2009. "From Faithfulness to Faith in the Theology of Karl Barth." Pages 291–308 in *The Faith of Jesus Christ: Exegetical, Biblical, and Theological Studies.* Edited by Michael F. Bird and Preston M. Sprinkle. Peabody, MA: Hendrickson.

———. 2013. "A Tale of Two Gardens: Augustine's Narrative Interpretation of Romans 5." Pages 39–58 in *Apocalyptic Paul: Cosmos and Anthropos in Romans 5–8.* Edited by Beverly Gaventa. Waco, TX: Baylor University Press.

Novenson, Matthew V. 2012. *Christ among the Messiahs: Christ Language in Paul and Messiah Language in Ancient Judaism.* Oxford: Oxford University Press.

———. 2022. "The Classical Rhetorical Idiom 'God Is Witness' in Its Pauline Usage." Pages 126–44 in *Paul Then and Now.* Grand Rapids: Eerdmans.

Nussbaum, Martha C. 1994. *The Therapy of Desire: Theory and Practice in Hellenistic Ethics.* Princeton: Princeton University Press.

Obama, Barack H. 2020. *A Promised Land.* New York: Crown Publishers.

Ochsenmeier, Erwin. 2013. "Romans 12,17–13,7 and the Justice of God: Two Neglected Features of Paul's Argument." *ETL* 89:361–82.

Oegema, Gerbern S. 1998. *Für Israel und die Völker: Studien zum alttestamentlich-jüdischen Hintergrund der paulinischen Theologie.* NovTSup 95. Leiden: Brill.

Parmentier, Martin. 1990. "Greek Church Fathers on Romans 9: Part II." *Bijdr* 51:2–20.

Paton, W. R., and E. L. Hicks. 1891. *The Inscriptions of Cos.* Oxford: Clarendon.

Patterson, Orlando. 1982. *Slavery and Social Death: A Comparative Study.* Cambridge, MA: Harvard University Press.

Paulsen, Henning. 1974. *Überlieferung und Auslegung in Römer 8.* WMANT 43. Neukirchen-Vluyn: Neukirchener.

Paulus, Heinrich Eberhard Gottlob. 1831. *Des Apostels Paulus Lehr-Briefe an die Galater und Römer-Christen: Wortgetreu übersetzt mit erläuternden Zwischensätzen, einem Überblick des Lehrinhalts und Bemerkungen über schwerere Stellen.* Heidelberg: Winter.

Payne, John B. 1990. "Erasmus on Romans 9:6–24." Pages 119–35 in *The Bible in the Sixteenth Century*. Edited by David Steinmetz. Durham, NC: Duke University Press.

Peterman, G. W. 1994. "Romans 15.26: Make a Contribution or Establish Fellowship?" *NTS* 40:457–63.

Piper, John. 1993. *The Justification of God: An Exegetical and Theological Study of Romans 9:1–23*. 2nd ed. Grand Rapids: Baker.

Porter, Stanley E. 1989. *Verbal Aspect in the Greek of the New Testament, with Reference to Tense and Mood*. Studies in Biblical Greek. New York: Lang.

———. 1991. "The Argument of Romans 5: Can a Rhetorical Question Make a Difference?" *JBL* 110:655–77.

———. 1999. *Idioms of the Greek New Testament*. 2nd ed. BLG 2. Sheffield: Sheffield Academic.

Porter, Stanley E., and Hughson T. Ong. 2013. "'Standard of Faith' or 'Measure of a Trusteeship'? A Study in Romans 12.3—A Response." *JGRChJ* 9: 97–103.

Porter, Stanley E., and Andrew W. Pitts. 2009. "Πίστις with a Preposition and Genitive Modifier: Lexical, Semantic, and Syntactic Considerations in the πίστις Χριστοῦ Discussion." Pages 33–53 in *The Faith of Jesus Christ: Exegetical, Biblical, and Theological Studies*. Edited by Michael F. Bird and Preston M. Sprinkle. Peabody, MA: Hendrickson.

Powery, Emerson B. 2004. "The Groans of 'Brother Saul': An Exploratory Reading of Romans 8 for 'Survival.'" *WW* 24:315–22.

Quarles, Charles L. 2003. "From Faith to Faith: A Fresh Examination of the Prepositional Series in Romans 1:17." *NovT* 45:1–21.

Rance, Philip. 2008. "'Win but Do Not Overwin': The History of a Proverb from the *Sententiae Menandri*, and a Classical Allusion in St. Paul's *Epistle to the Romans*." *Phil* 152:191–204.

Rathbone, Dominic. 2008. "The Customs Law of Asia: Nero's Reforms of *Vectigalia* and the Inscription of the *Lex Portorii Asiae*." Pages 251–78 in *The Customs Law of Asia*. Edited by M. Cottier, M. H. Crawford, C. V. Crowther, J.-L. Ferrary, B. M. Levick, O. Salomies, and M. Wörrle. Oxford: Oxford University Press.

Reasoner, Mark. 1999. *The Strong and the Weak: Romans 14.1–15.13 in Context*. SNTSMS 103. Cambridge: Cambridge University Press.

Rehmann, Luzia Sutter. 2000. "The Doorway into Freedom: The Case of the 'Suspected Wife' in Romans 7.1–6." *JSNT* 79:91–104.

Reumann, John. 1973. *Creation and New Creation: The Past, Present, and Future of God's Creative Activity*. Minneapolis: Augsburg.

Richards, E. Randolph. 2004. *Paul and First-Century Letter Writing: Secretaries, Composition, and Collection*. Downers Grove, IL: InterVarsity Press.

Richardson, Neil. 1999. *Paul's Language about God.* JSNTSup 99. Sheffield: Sheffield Academic.

Rickert, GailAnn. 1989. 'ΕΚΩΝ *and* 'ΑΚΩΝ *in Early Greek Thought.* American Classical Studies 20. Atlanta: Scholars Press.

Rife, Joseph L. 2010. "Religion and Society at Roman Kenchreai." Pages 391–432 in *Corinth in Context: Comparative Studies on Religion and Society.* Edited by Steven J. Friesen, Daniel N. Schowalter, and James C. Walters. NovTSup 134. Leiden: Brill.

Robinson, Laura. 2021. "Hidden Transcripts? The Supposedly Self-Censoring Paul and Rome as Surveillance State in Modern Pauline Scholarship." *NTS* 67:55–72.

Rosenblum, Jordan D. 2010. "'Why Do You Refuse to Eat Pork?' Jews, Food, and Identity in Roman Palestine." *JQR* 100:96–110.

Roth, Jonathan P. 1999. *The Logistics of the Roman Army at War (264 B.C.– A.D. 235).* CSCT 23. Leiden: Brill.

Rowe, C. Kavin. 2000. "Romans 10:13: What Is the Name of the Lord?" *HBT* 22:135–73.

Russell, Jeffrey Burton. 1977. *The Devil: Perceptions of Evil from Antiquity to Primitive Christianity.* Ithaca, NY: Cornell University Press.

Ryan, Scott. 2020. *Divine Conflict and the Divine Warrior: Listening to Romans and Other Jewish Voices.* WUNT 2/507. Tübingen: Mohr Siebeck.

Sabou, Sorin. 2005. *Between Horror and Hope: Paul's Metaphorical Language of "Death" in Romans 6:1–11.* PBM. Milton Keynes: Paternoster.

Sancken, Joni. 2012. "Elizabeth Dawbarn." Pages 153–55 in *Handbook of Women Biblical Interpreters.* Edited by Marion Ann Taylor. Grand Rapids: Baker Academic.

Sanders, E. P. 1983. *Paul, the Law, and the Jewish People.* Philadelphia: Fortress.

———. 1992. *Judaism: Practice and Belief. 63 BCE–66 CE.* London: SCM.

Sandnes, Karl Olav. 2002. *Belly and Body in the Pauline Epistles.* SNTSMS 120. Cambridge: Cambridge University Press.

Scheidel, Walter. 2011. "The Roman Slave Supply." Pages 287–310 in *The Ancient Mediterranean World.* Vol. 1 of *The Cambridge World History of Slavery.* Edited by Keith Bradley and Paul Cartledge. Cambridge: Cambridge University Press.

Schelkle, K. H. 1952. "Staat und Kirche in der patristischen Auslegung von Rm 13:1–7." *ZNW* 44:223–36.

———. 1956. *Paulus: Lehrer der Väter: Die altkirchliche Auslegung von Römer 1–11.* Düsseldorf: Patmos.

Schellenberg, Ryan S. 2018. "Subsistence, Swapping, and Paul's Rhetoric of Generosity." *JBL* 137:215–34.

Schliesser, Benjamin. 2007. *Abraham's Faith in Romans 4: Paul's Concept of Faith in Light of the History of Reception of Genesis 15:6*. WUNT 2/224. Tübingen: Mohr Siebeck.

———. 2012. "'Abraham Did Not "Doubt" in Unbelief' (Rom. 4:20): Faith, Doubt, and Dispute in Paul's Letter to the Romans." *JTS* 63:492–522.

———. 2015. "'Exegetical Amnesia' and ΠΙΣΤΙΣ ΧΡΙΣΤΟΥ: The 'Faith *of* Christ' in Nineteenth-Century Scholarship." *JTS* 66:61–89.

Schnelle, Udo, ed. 2009. *The Letter to the Romans*. BETL 226. Leuven: Peeters.

Schreiber, Stefan. 2012. "Law and Love in Romans 13.8–10." Pages 100–119 in *The Torah in the Ethics of Paul*. Edited by Martin Meiser. LNTS 473. London: T&T Clark.

Schroeder, Joy A., and Marion Ann Taylor. 2022. *Voices Long Silenced: Women Biblical Interpreters through the Centuries*. Louisville: Westminster John Knox.

Schubert, Paul. 1939. *Form and Function of the Pauline Thanksgivings*. BZNW 20. Berlin: Töpelmann.

Scott, James C. 1990. *Domination and the Arts of Resistance: Hidden Transcripts*. New Haven: Yale University Press.

Scott, Matthew. 2014. *The Hermeneutics of Christological Psalmody in Paul: An Intertextual Enquiry*. SNTSMS 158. Cambridge: Cambridge University Press.

Seifrid, Mark A. 2000. *Christ Our Righteousness: Paul's Theology of Justification*. NSBT 9. Leicester: Apollos.

———. 2001. "Righteousness Language in the Hebrew Scriptures and Early Judaism." Pages 415–42 in *The Complexities of Second Temple Judaism*. Vol. 1 of *Justification and Variegated Nomism*. Edited by D. A. Carson, Peter T. O'Brien, and Mark A. Seifrid. Tübingen: Mohr Siebeck.

———. 2009. "The Faith of Christ." Pages 129–46 in *The Faith of Jesus Christ: Exegetical, Biblical, and Theological Studies*. Edited by Michael F. Bird and Preston M. Sprinkle. Peabody, MA: Hendrickson.

Siegert, Folker. 1985. *Argumentation bei Paulus gezeigt an Röm 9–11*. WUNT 1/34. Tübingen: Mohr Siebeck.

Smit, Peter-Ben. 2007. "A Symposium in Rom. 14:17? A Note on Paul's Terminology." *NovT* 49:40–53.

Smyth, Herbert Weir. 1956. *Greek Grammar*. Revised by Gordon M. Messing. Cambridge, MA: Harvard University Press.

Southall, David J. 2008. *Rediscovering Righteousness in Romans: Personified dikaiosynē within Metaphoric and Narratorial Settings*. WUNT 2/240. Tübingen: Mohr Siebeck.

Southern, Pat. 2006. *The Roman Army: A Social and Institutional History*. Santa Barbara, CA: ABC-CLIO.

Spitaler, Peter. 2006. "Analogical Reasoning in Romans 7:2–4: A Woman and the Believers in Rome." *JBL* 125:715–47.

———. 2007. "Διακρίνεσθαι in Mt. 21:21, Mk. 11:23, Acts 10:20, Rom. 4:20, 14:23; Jas. 1:6, and Jude 22—The 'Semantic Shift' That Went Unnoticed by Patristic Authors." *NovT* 49:1–39.

———. 2009. "Household Disputes in Rome (Romans 14:1–15:13)." *RB* 116: 44–69.

Sprinkle, Preston M. 2008. *Law and Life: The Interpretation of Leviticus 18:5 in Early Judaism and in Paul.* WUNT 2/241. Tübingen: Mohr Siebeck.

———. 2009. "Πίστις Χριστοῦ as an Eschatological Event." Pages 147–63 in *The Faith of Jesus Christ: Exegetical, Biblical, and Theological Studies.* Edited by Michael F. Bird and Preston M. Sprinkle. Peabody, MA: Hendrickson.

Stanley, Christopher D. 1992. *Paul and the Language of Scripture: Citation Technique in the Pauline Epistles and Contemporary Literature.* SNTSMS 69. Cambridge: Cambridge University Press.

Staples, Jason A. 2011. "What Do the Gentiles Have to Do with 'All Israel'? A Fresh Look at Romans 11:25–27." *JBL* 130:371–90.

Starr, Raymond J. 1987. "The Circulation of Literary Texts in the Roman World." *ClQ* 37.1:213–23.

Stendahl, Krister. 1976. *Paul among Jews and Gentiles.* Philadelphia: Fortress.

Stowers, Stanley K. 1981. *The Diatribe and Paul's Letter to the Romans.* SBLDS 57. Chico, CA: Scholars Press.

———. 1989. "Ἐκ πίστεως and διὰ τῆς πίστεως in Romans 3:30." *JBL* 108: 665–74.

———. 1994. *A Rereading of Romans: Justice, Jews, and Gentiles.* New Haven: Yale University Press.

———. 1995. "Romans 7.7–25 as a Speech-in-Character (προσωποποιία)." Pages 180–202 in *Paul in His Hellenistic Context.* Edited by Troels Engberg-Pedersen. Minneapolis: Fortress.

Strawbridge, Jennifer. 2017. "Early Christian Epigraphy, Evil, and the Apotropaic Function of Romans 8.31." *VC* 71:315–29.

Stringfellow, William. 1978. *Conscience and Obedience: The Politics of Romans 13 and Revelation 13 in Light of the Second Coming.* Waco: Word Books.

Stuhlmacher, Peter. 1986. *Reconciliation, Law, and Righteousness: Essays in Biblical Theology.* Philadelphia: Fortress.

Sullivan, Francis A. 2011. "The Development of Doctrine about Infants Who Die Unbaptized." *TS* 72:3–14.

Talbert, Charles. 1969. "Tradition and Redaction in Romans XII.9–21." *NTS* 16: 83–93.

Tannehill, Robert C. 1967. *Dying and Rising with Christ: A Study in Pauline Theology.* BZNW 32. Berlin: Töpelmann.

———. 2007. "Participation in Christ: A Central Theme in Pauline Soteriology." Pages 223–37 in *The Shape of the Gospel: New Testament Essays.* Eugene, OR: Cascade.

Taylor, Marion Ann, ed. 2012. *Handbook of Women Biblical Interpreters.* Grand Rapids: Baker Academic.

Thomas, Samuel I. 2009. *The "Mysteries" of Qumran: Mystery, Secrecy, and Esotericism in the Dead Sea Scrolls.* EJL 25. Leiden: Brill.

Thompson, Michael. 1991. *Clothed with Christ: The Example and Teaching of Jesus in Romans 12.1–15.13.* JSNTSup 59. Sheffield: Sheffield Academic.

Thonemann, Peter. 2020. *An Ancient Dream Manual: Artemidorus' "The Interpretation of Dreams."* Oxford: Oxford University Press.

Thorsteinsson, Runar M. 2002. "Paul's Missionary Duty towards Gentiles in Rome: A Note on the Punctuation and Syntax of Rom 1.13–15." *NTS* 48: 531–47.

———. 2006. "Paul and Roman Stoicism: Romans 12 and Contemporary Stoic Ethics." *JSNT* 29:139–61.

Ticciati, Susannah. 2012. "The Nondivisive Difference of Election: A Reading of Romans 9–11." *JTI* 6:257–78.

Tilling, Chris. 2015. *Paul's Divine Christology.* Grand Rapids: Eerdmans.

Timmes, Pamela. 2004. "'She Will Be Called an Adulteress . . .': Marriage and Adultery Analogies in Romans 7:1–4." Pages 190–203 in *Celebrating Romans: Template for Pauline Theology; Essays in Honor of Robert Jewett.* Edited by Sheila E. McGinn. Grand Rapids: Eerdmans.

Tobin, Thomas H., SJ. 1995. "What Shall We Say That Abraham Found? The Controversy behind Romans 4." *HTR* 88:437–52.

———. 2004. *Paul's Rhetoric in Its Contexts: The Argument of Romans.* Peabody, MA: Hendrickson.

Toney, Carl N. 2008. *Paul's Inclusive Ethic: Resolving Community Conflicts and Promoting Mission in Romans 14–15.* WUNT 2/252. Tübingen: Mohr Siebeck.

Travis, Stephen. 1992. "Wrath of God [NT]." *ABD* 6:997.

Treggiari, Susan. 1991. *Roman Marriage: Iusti Coniuges from the Time of Cicero to the Time of Ulpian.* Oxford: Clarendon.

Turner, Nigel. 1976. *Style.* Vol. 4 of *A Grammar of New Testament Greek.* Edited by James Hope Moulton. Edinburgh: T&T Clark.

Tyra, Steven W. 2014. "When Considering Creation, Simply Follow the Rule (of Faith): Patristic Exegesis of Romans 8:19–22 and the Theological Interpretation of Scripture." *JTI* 8:251–73.

———. 2019. "'Christ Has Come to Gather Together All the Creatures': What a Sixteenth-Century Debate Teaches about the Theological Interpretation of Scripture." *JTI* 13:53–75.

Ubelaker, D. H., and J. L. Rife. 2011. "Skeletal Analysis and Mortuary Practice in an Early Roman Chamber Tomb at Kenchreai, Greece." *Int J Osteoarchaeol* 21:1–18.

Urbanik, Jakub. 2016. "Husband and Wife." Pages 473–86 in *The Oxford Handbook of Roman Law and Society*. Edited by Paul J. du Plessis, Clifford Ando, and Kaius Tuori. Oxford: Oxford University Press.

Van der Horst, Pieter W. 2000. "'Only Then Will All Israel Be Saved': A Short Note on the Meaning of καὶ οὕτως in Romans 11:26." *JBL* 119:521–39.

Vásquez, Víctor Manuel Morales. 2012. *Contours of a Biblical Reception Theory: Studies in the* Rezeptionsgeschichte *of Romans 13.1–7*. Göttingen: Vandenhoeck & Ruprecht.

Wagner, J. Ross. 1997. "The Christ, Servant of Jew and Gentile: A Fresh Approach to Romans 15:8–9." *JBL* 116:473–85.

———. 2002. *Heralds of the Good News: Isaiah and Paul "in Concert" in the Letter to the Romans*. NovTSup 101. Leiden: Brill.

———. 2011. "Paul and Scripture." Pages 154–71 in *The Blackwell Companion to Paul*. Edited by Stephen Westerholm. Malden, MA: Wiley-Blackwell.

———. 2017. "'Enemies' yet 'Beloved' Still: Election and the Love of God in Romans 9–11." Pages 95–113 in *God and Israel: Providence and Purpose in Romans 9–11*. Edited by Todd D. Still. Waco, TX: Baylor University Press.

Walbank, Mary E. Hoskins. 2005. "Unquiet Graves: Burial Practices of the Roman Corinthians." Pages 249–80 in *Urban Religion in Roman Corinth: Interdisciplinary Approaches*. Edited by Daniel H. Schowalter and Steven J. Friesen. HTS 53. Cambridge, MA: Harvard University Press.

Walker, William O. 2001. *Interpolations in the Pauline Letters*. London: Sheffield Academic.

Wallace, Daniel. 1996. *Greek Grammar beyond the Basics: An Exegetical Syntax of the New Testament*. Grand Rapids: Zondervan.

Wallis, Ian G. 1995. *The Faith of Jesus Christ in Early Christian Traditions*. SNTSMS 84. Cambridge: Cambridge University Press.

Wan, Sze-Kar. 2000. "Collection for the Saints as Anticolonial Act: Implications of Paul's Ethnic Reconstruction." Pages 191–215 in *Paul and Politics: Ekklesia, Israel, Imperium, Interpretation*. Edited by Richard A. Horsley. Harrisburg, PA: Trinity.

Watson, Francis. 1997. *Text and Truth: Redefining Biblical Theology*. Grand Rapids: Eerdmans.

———. 2000. *Agape, Eros, Gender: Towards a Pauline Sexual Ethic*. Cambridge: Cambridge University Press.

———. 2004. *Paul and the Hermeneutics of Faith*. London: T&T Clark.

———. 2006. "The Triune Divine Identity: Reflections on Pauline God-Language in Disagreement with J. D. G. Dunn." *JSNT* 80:99–124.

———. 2007. *Paul, Judaism, and the Gentiles: Beyond the New Perspective*. Rev. and exp. ed. Grand Rapids: Eerdmans.

———. 2009. "By Faith (of Christ): An Exegetical Dilemma and Its Scriptural Solution." Pages 147–63 in *The Faith of Jesus Christ: Exegetical, Biblical, and Theological Studies*. Edited by Michael F. Bird and Preston M. Sprinkle. Peabody, MA: Hendrickson.

———. 2013. "Is Paul a Covenantal Theologian?" Pages 102–18 in *The Unrelenting God: God's Action in Scripture; Essays in Honor of Beverly Roberts Gaventa*. Edited by David J. Downs and Matthew L. Skinner. Grand Rapids: Eerdmans.

———. 2016. *Paul and the Hermeneutics of Faith*. 2nd ed. London: Bloomsbury T&T Clark.

Wedderburn, A. J. M. 1980. "Adam in Paul's Letter to the Romans." Pages 413–30 in *Studia Biblica 1978, 3: Papers on Paul and Other New Testament Authors*. Edited by E. A. Livingstone. JSNTSup 3. Sheffield: JSOT Press.

———. 2004. "Pauline Pneumatology and Pauline Theology." Pages 144–56 in *The Holy Spirit and Christian Origins: Essays in Honor of James D. G. Dunn*. Edited by Graham N. Stanton, Bruce W. Longenecker, and Stephen C. Barton. Grand Rapids: Eerdmans.

Weil, Simone. 2006. *The Iliad or the Poem of Force: A Critical Edition*. 3rd ed. Translated by James P. Holoka. New York: Peter Lang.

Weima, Jeffrey A. D. 2016. *Paul the Ancient Letter Writer: An Introduction to Epistolary Analysis*. Grand Rapids: Baker Academic.

Welborn, Larry L. 2015. "The Polis and the Poor." Pages 189–243 in *The First Urban Churches 1: Methodological Foundations*. Edited by James R. Harrison and Larry L. Welborn. Atlanta: SBL Press.

Westerholm, Stephen. 1988. *Israel's Law and the Church's Faith: Paul and His Recent Interpreters*. Grand Rapids: Eerdmans.

———. 2004. *Perspectives Old and New on Paul: The "Lutheran" Paul and His Critics*. Grand Rapids: Eerdmans.

Wiefel, Wolfgang. 1991. "The Jewish Community in Ancient Rome and the Origins of Roman Christianity." Pages 85–101 in *The Romans Debate*. Rev. and exp. ed. Edited by Karl Paul Donfried. Peabody, MA: Hendrickson.

Williams, Margaret. 2004. "Being a Jew in Rome: Sabbath Fasting as an Expression of Romano-Jewish Identity." Pages 8–18 in *Negotiating Diaspora: Jewish Strategies in the Roman Empire*. Edited by John M. G. Barclay. LSTS 45. London: T&T Clark.

Williams, Sam. 1975. *Jesus' Death as Saving Event*. HDR 2. Missoula, MT: Scholars Press.

———. 1987. "Again *Pistis Christou.*" *CBQ* 49:431–47.

Wilson, Brittany E. 2015. *Unmanly Men: Refigurations of Masculinity in Luke-Acts.* Oxford: Oxford University Press.

Wilson, Walter T. 1991. *Love without Pretense: Romans 12.9–21 and Hellenistic-Jewish Wisdom Literature.* WUNT 2/46. Tübingen: Mohr Siebeck.

Winkler, John W. 1989. "Leucippe and Clitophon." Pages 170–284 in *Collected Ancient Greek Novels.* Edited by B. P. Reardon. Berkeley: University of California Press.

———. 1990. *The Constraints of Desire: The Anthropology of Sex and Gender in Ancient Greece.* New York: Routledge.

Wolter, Michael. 1978. *Rechtfertigung und Zukünftiges Heil: Untersuchungen au Röm 5, 1–11.* BZNW 43. Berlin: de Gruyter.

———. 2005. "Apokalyptik als Redeform im Neuen Testament." *NTS* 51: 171–91.

———. 2015. *Paul: An Outline of His Theology.* Translated by Robert L. Brawley. Waco, TX: Baylor University Press.

———. 2017. "'It Is Not as Though the Word of God Has Failed': God's Faithfulness and God's Free Sovereignty in Romans 9:6–29." Pages 27–47 in *God and Israel: Providence and Purpose in Romans 9–11.* Edited by Todd D. Still. Waco, TX: Baylor University Press.

Wright, Benjamin G., III. 1998. "*'Ebed/Doulos*: Terms and Social Status in the Meeting of Hebrew Biblical and Hellenistic Roman Culture." *Semeia* 83–84:83–111.

Wright, N. T. 1991. *The Climax of the Covenant: Christ and the Law in Pauline Theology.* Edinburgh: T&T Clark.

———. 2001. "The Law in Romans 2." Pages 131–50 in *Paul and the Mosaic Law.* Edited by James D. G. Dunn. Grand Rapids: Eerdmans.

———. 2013. *Paul and the Faithfulness of God.* 2 vols. Minneapolis: Fortress.

———. 2018. *Paul: A Biography.* New York: HarperOne.

Yinger, Kent L. 1998. "Romans 12:14–21 and Nonretaliation in Second Temple Judaism: Addressing Persecution within the Community." *CBQ* 60:74–96.

Ziegler, Philip G. 2018. *Militant Grace: The Apocalyptic Turn and the Future of Christian Theology.* Grand Rapids: Baker Academic.

Ziesler, John. 1972. *The Meaning of Righteousness in Paul: A Linguistic and Theological Enquiry.* SNTSMS 20. Cambridge: Cambridge University Press.

Zoccali, Christopher. 2008. "'And So All Israel Will Be Saved': Competing Interpretations of Romans 11.26 in Pauline Scholarship." *JSNT* 30:289–318.

Zsifkovits, Valentin. 1964. *Der Staatsgedanke nach Paulus in Römer 13,1–7 mit Besonderer Berücksichtigung der Umwelt und der Patristischen Auslegung.* WBTh 7. Vienna: Herder.

INTRODUCTION

A Word of Orientation

Before readers turn to the commentary proper, they deserve to know the commitments that have guided this book and a few decisions that have shaped its writing. From my earliest study of the letter, I have been fascinated by the way Romans works, both at the macro level (How does each major portion of the letter contribute to the whole?) and at the micro level (How does this statement—even this word—follow from the one preceding it?). Along with most New Testament scholars, I am interested in what Paul hoped the letter might accomplish among its addressees in Rome. More recently, that question has shifted a bit, as I have pondered how Roman auditors might have heard the letter when read by Phoebe of Cenchreae.

The questions I bring are not only literary and historical in orientation, however. They are also theological. The two are not separable, given that Paul and Phoebe and the Roman auditors are involved in talk about God and God's doings in the world, which makes the letter inherently theological. Attention to the content of Romans necessarily involves attention to those claims. In addition, the letter remains theological for those today who hear in it Paul's witness to the "now time" of the gospel.[1] For him, these statements about God are quite literally matters of life and death, as becomes clear in chapter 6 in particular.

In keeping with these governing questions, my strategy has been to work through each passage on my own, drafting first with the Greek NT and the lexicons as resources before turning to the secondary literature. This is by no means a claim to objectivity, but simply a report on my priorities.

I have kept references to the vast secondary literature to a minimum. My goal is less to engage with the scholarly literature or report on scholarly debates (which in any case can only be a snapshot and inadequate even at that) than to offer a coherent account of Paul's letter, insofar as that is possible and within my capabilities. With unstinted admiration and gratitude for those such as

---

1. That is not to say that a systematic theology can be read off the pages of Romans, or that Paul is doing what would be recognized as systematic theology. Theology can and does take numerous forms.

Cranfield, Moo, Jewett, and Wolter who have written reference commentaries, my own is not intended as such. The notes I do include indicate places of indebtedness, occasionally to those whose conclusions differ enough from my own that they press me to clarify my reading of the letter. When I refer to important debates, I typically do so with only one or two representative references, so that readers who wish to can find an entry point into discussions. Yet nothing here purports to be an account of even recent scholarship on Romans, not to mention the long history of interpretation.[2]

Occasionally I also cite early interpreters, particularly the commentary of Ambrosiaster and the homilies of Chrysostom. For myself, reading these works offers a corrective to the temptation to engage with only the most recent spate of commentaries and counters a tendency to think our more distant predecessors have nothing to teach us. Attending to these commentaries, we quickly realize, for example, that Rom 13 posed concerns for even the earliest interpreters. When I cite their works, it is not because I think their views inherently superior by virtue of their date, but simply because I think they provide fascinating glimpses into the early appropriation of Romans. These early interpreters also offer some gems that need to be shared, as in Origen's observation that in 7:1–6 "Paul seems to be moving between unmarked rooms through hidden passages."

Readers will see that my translation and the accompanying notes attempt to give a sense of the Greek while occasionally incorporating more contemporary idioms. At 2:1, for example, I have used "you there!" instead of "whoever you are," as I think it better captures the jarring nature of the comment. And at 7:24, "I am utterly miserable" is more natural in contemporary English than "Wretched man/person that I am." My goal has been not to aggravate what John Winkler calls the "watchful schoolmaster" (1989, 171), while producing a translation that is not overly stilted. Having translated Romans again and again, I resonate with Kimon Friar's lament that "all translations of any kind are basically absurd" (1973, 651).

An orientation to some stylistic decisions may also be useful. First, I use the uppercase for "Sin" and "Death" at those places where I contend Paul is referring to powers instead of to acts of sin or to dying. The excursus on Sin and Death as powers explains that decision, as well as the decision not to use the uppercase for grace and righteousness. Second, when discussing Paul's treatment of personal pronouns, generally "I" or "we," I employ quotation marks to distinguish Paul's self-reference from my own or from contemporary readers of the letter. The hope is that this distinction will both draw attention to the roles those pronouns play in the text and remind contemporary readers that we stand

---

2. In keeping with this approach, the bibliography largely includes only publications I cite in the commentary.

at considerable distance from Phoebe's auditors. However important the letter is for many of us, it was not originally written to us.

In addition, when referring to Paul, those around him, and the auditors in Rome, I have sometimes used the word "Christian." This choice has become controversial because the term is anachronistic and, more specifically, because it implies that Christianity is somehow separate from Judaism. While I readily grant that Paul does not imagine the creation of a religion independent of Jewish traditions and practices, or the creation of a new religion at all (even the category religion is problematic), I find it important to have some term for those people—both Jews and gentiles—Paul himself identifies as "in Christ" or "called by Jesus Christ." The word "Christian" does appear in the NT (Acts 11:26; 26:28; 1 Pet 4:16), and I find it preferable to some cumbersome alternatives. "Christ-followers" is better fitted for the discipleship language in the Gospels than for Paul's letters, and "Christ-believers" reinforces the notion that this is a movement restricted to ideas.

Finally, it will be clear that I read this letter with a hermeneutic of generosity: put directly, I attempt to read as I would wish to be read (Gaventa 2017a, 20–21). Having taught the letters of Paul in numerous settings throughout my career, I understand that many people approach Paul with distrust or disdain, even those who otherwise read Scripture generously. I also know that Paul's letters have provided fodder for a range of abusive readings, hateful readings, and willful misreadings. And there are, to be sure, elements in the letter that disturb me, particularly Paul's use of same-sex relations as evidence of humanity's refusal to recognize God as God. Yet I choose to give Paul the benefit of the doubt, in part because I fear the consequences if readers in general abandon generosity, and in part because I have long found in Paul a prime example of "a mass of strange delights," to use George Herbert's phrase for Scripture in general. To be quite honest, I do not think I could have labored so long to teach and understand a text in which I did not take delight.

The Distinctiveness of Romans

Romans is the longest of Paul's letters (at least of letters known to us) and arguably also the most influential. Its influence can be mapped through its best-known interpreters, as is often done, invoking such figures as Chrysostom, Augustine, Luther, Calvin, and Wesley. That line of influence needs to be corrected and expanded by our knowledge, limited though it may be, of the importance of Romans in the lives of Christians whose names are unfamiliar or even unknown. Already within the first five or six centuries of the church's life, 1:16 was being used as an amulet invoking divine power (Calhoun 2019), and 8:31 was carved into the door lintels of Christian homes (Strawbridge 2017). Frustrated by male hierarchies as they pursued their vocations, African American women such as Zilpha Elaw and Julia Foote invoked the precedent of Phoebe over a century before recent disputes about her roles (Bowens 2020, 86–87, 169–70; Schroeder and Taylor 2022, 154–55, 160). The influence of this letter persists in disputes regarding same-sex relations and the role of civil government, but it also persists as words of comfort in funeral liturgies, to say nothing of countless well-worn Bibles.

Romans is distinctive in other respects as well, most obviously in the fact that it is the only letter in which Paul addresses gatherings in a city he has never seen. He is not the one who "planted" the gospel in Rome, as he puts it in 1 Cor 3:6–8, where that reminder funds a claim about Paul's authority at Corinth. Elsewhere he can appeal to his addressees' experience with him (1 Thess 2), to his instruction (1 Thess 4:2; 1 Cor 11:23; 15:1), to their relationship (Gal 4:14–16). Paul recognizes the faith of his Roman addressees in 1:8 (however much he also corrects and expands it later), but he is not their "father" (1 Thess 2:11; 1 Cor 4:14–15) or "mother" (1 Thess 2:7; Gal 4:19) as he is with other groups to whom he writes. Although he has individual contacts at Rome, some of whom he regards as quite close to him (16:4, 7), he does not have an ongoing relationship to which he can appeal as he does in even the highly conflictual situation with the Galatians. He must proceed with caution.

That difference in the letter-writing context may account for some important departures from Paul's earlier letters. Romans is distinctive for its extensive engagement with Israel's Scriptures, its use of diatribal style, and what I will refer to as the rhetorical feint. These features of the letter may be related to Paul's status as an outsider who needs to proceed carefully and who does so by employing recognized bases for his appeals that will be shared by the auditors. He cannot draw on his relationship to them or on his apostolic authority.

The Gospel as Intrusion

In common with Paul's other letters, this one is occasional. It was written to address a particular set of people in a particular place, even if Paul was also concerned about other locations as well (notably Jerusalem and Spain). But behind and prior to that writerly occasion there is another, an occasion unlike any other: the occasion of Jesus Christ. The opening lines of the letter make that fact clear. Paul's commission is on behalf of God's good news, which Paul identifies with the life and death and resurrection of Jesus Christ as actions of God's saving power (1:1–4, 16–17). This occasional character of Paul's letters is obvious, but it is easily forgotten, and that forgetting has serious consequences.

Characterizing this occasion, however, proves challenging. Karl Barth frequently called on the word *Krisis*, a term that is apt, though compromised by its association with existentialism (32, 36, 41, and often elsewhere). J. Louis Martyn referred to the occasion of Jesus Christ as God's invasion of the world, a term that rightly captures the unilateral action of God and the resistance of the world to God, even if its violent overtones are disturbing (e.g., 1997a, 22, 105; 1997b, 82, 151, 154–56, 170, 258). "Intrusion" may be a suitable alternative, with its connotation of an unexpected event that has its origin elsewhere, enters uninvited, unmakes the world as it is, and produces results that are urgently needed, although they are not entirely welcome. The importance lies less in finding the right term than in keeping that dynamic character in mind: something—Jesus Christ—has happened, and it has left nothing untouched. That happening is behind and under everything else Paul writes.

This is perhaps the most obvious and the most frequently neglected feature of the letter, something that is understandable given that we operate two millennia forward from Paul. When Paul writes about the apocalyptic revelation of God's wrath (1:18), it is from the vantage point of this decisive event. When he claims that Israel stumbled (9:32), it is also from the vantage point of this event. When he observes that the reign of God is not about food and drink (14:17), it is also from the vantage point of this event.

The fact of this event makes it difficult to write about "the theology" of Romans, if by that we mean something that is fixed and solid, as in a doctrine of the church, for example. This is what drives Paul Meyer to observe that Paul's letters offer a "ringside seat" for observing what happens as the event of Jesus Christ "*forces* the revision and recasting of all the traditional language, concepts, convictions and categories, including the reading of scripture" (1997, 159; ital. orig.).

That "revision and recasting" has important implications for the extended controversy regarding Paul and apocalyptic or Paul and apocalypticism (on which see J. Davies 2022). The quarrel over whether Paul fits within certain preexisting features of apocalyptic thinking presupposes that those are fixed and can be observed and analyzed. More to the point, the quarrel misses the way *Paul's* understanding of God's action in Jesus Christ revises and recasts his notion of apocalypse.

This fact also complicates the recent scholarly discussion of the Judaism of Paul (as in, e.g., Eisenbaum 2009; Fredriksen 2017). Insisting that Paul remained a Jew is and should be utterly noncontroversial. At the same time, it is crucial to understand that this particular Jew has experienced an event and that event has left nothing untouched. It has not made him something other than a Jew, but it has produced a new way of thinking, assessing, and evaluating (2 Cor 5:16). For example, Paul does not necessarily read Scripture as his fellow Jews do; he does not necessarily perceive the law as his fellow Jews do. That is not because he has long harbored criticism of his people and their practices, but because he has been grasped by Jesus Christ (to use his language in Phil 3:12).

The Circumstances of the Letter

Assessing the Sources

The first and most important source for understanding the circumstances that produced Romans is obviously the letter itself, but in what form? We have no access to the letter (or any other biblical text) in its earliest form and are reliant on numerous ancient manuscripts, the earliest of which, the second-century $\mathfrak{P}^{46}$, is partial. The letter is fully attested, however, in several early uncial manuscripts, including Alexandrinus, Sinaiticus, and Vaticanus. In preparing the commentary, I have reviewed the evidence gathered in the most recent edition of the Nestle-Aland *Novum Testamentum Graece* (NA^{28}), although I report in the notes only on those text-critical problems that are of particular interest or affect the letter's interpretation.

By far the most significant question regarding the text of Romans concerns the status of ch. 16. In 1962 T. W. Manson (1991, 13–14) proposed that the letter Paul sent to Rome initially consisted of what we know as chs. 1–15. At the same time, Paul sent a copy of that letter to Ephesus, attaching to it the greetings of ch. 16. That proposal would solve certain interpretive problems, most notably the apparent discrepancy between Paul's greetings to a number of people at Rome and the fact that he has never been to Rome. Although the proposal gained some adherents at the time, recent commentators have largely rejected it, and for good reason. To begin with, Paul's knowledge of individuals at Rome can be accounted for in other ways (see the commentary at ch. 16 for discussion). More significantly, although the doxology of 16:25–27 does appear in several locations in the manuscript tradition, including the end of ch. 14 and the end of ch. 15 (and I will comment on those at the appropriate places in the commentary), there is no textual evidence for a version of Romans without ch. 16. Given this evidence in the manuscript tradition (or the lack thereof), I will assume that ch. 16 is part of the letter Paul sent to Rome.

In addition to Romans itself, I draw freely on the six other letters whose authorship is undisputed (1 Thessalonians, 1 Corinthians, 2 Corinthians, Galatians, Philippians, Philemon), but I do not draw on the remaining letters (2 Thessalonians, Ephesians, Colossians, 1 Timothy, 2 Timothy, Titus) as primary evidence. Occasionally in the commentary proper I may cite a passage as evidence that reinforces Paul's usage of a term, just as I would look to usage in other contemporaneous texts, but I do not turn to the disputed letters for evidence of Paul's life or convictions.

The remaining source to be considered is Luke's account of Paul's endeavors in the Acts of the Apostles. Because that work, written at least some decades after Romans, primarily gives evidence of Luke's own commitments, it can only be used for historical reconstruction with great caution. I draw on Acts largely when it confirms evidence drawn from the letters. This decision will be important in discussing the date of composition below.

Location

When Paul writes this letter, he is in or at least near Corinth. That location is certain if Erastus is to be identified with the so-called Erastus Stone, although there is considerable doubt about that identification (on which see the commentary on 16:23). Quite apart from Erastus, the identification of Phoebe with Cenchreae, the port city of Corinth, puts Paul in or near Corinth, since he is sending the letter to Rome with her. Reinforcing that location is the reference in 15:26 to the fact that Macedonia and Achaia have contributed to fellowship with Jerusalem. Since in 2 Cor 8:1–7 Paul employs the generosity of Macedonia by way of nudging a response from the Corinthians, the completion of the offering in Achaia correlates well with Corinth as the likely location of Paul as he writes.

Paul does not write alone. Phoebe, Timothy, Lucius, Jason, and Sosipater are with him, along with Gaius, Erastus, and Quartus (16:21–23). These individuals, along with others in Corinth, may well have played a role in shaping the letter. Given the length and complexity of this letter, Paul would have written it over a period of time. Presumably he would have discussed its contents with those around him, probably even read sections or full drafts. This process is especially important regarding Phoebe. Before he entrusts it to Phoebe for delivery, reading, and circulation (see further on 16:1–2), Paul will have made sure that she understood what he wanted from the letter.

Date of Composition

Paul's discussion of the collection for Jerusalem also helps to place the letter relative to his other letters. He mentions it for the first time in 1 Cor 16:1–4, where he gives instructions about setting aside money and sending it by trusted figures to Jerusalem.[3] By the time he writes 2 Cor 8, contributions from Macedonia have been completed, and he takes those as leverage for urging completion by the Corinthians. Paul has the fund and anticipates delivering it in Jerusalem when he writes Romans (15:25–28). This slender thread places the composition of Romans after the Corinthian correspondence (so Campbell 2014, 37–39).

Paul's remarks about Prisca and Aquila also provide bits of useful information. In 1 Cor 16:19, Paul sends their greetings to the Corinthians, which means both that they are in Ephesus with Paul at the time (1 Cor 16:8) and they are already known to the Corinthians, presumably because they have been in

---

3. Gal 2 reports that Paul agreed with Jerusalem leaders to "remember the poor," but that commitment is not necessarily a reference to the collection as such (B. Longenecker 2010, 184–89).

Corinth itself. By the time Paul writes to Rome, however, he includes them among those to be greeted, along with the Christian group that meets in their residence (Rom 16:3–5a).

The narrative of Paul's work in Acts confirms this sequence and ties it to a datable event. Luke introduces Prisca and Aquila in Corinth with the comment that they had been driven from Rome by Claudius (18:1–2). Later, again according to Luke, they go with Paul to Ephesus (18:18–19). Admittedly, Paul himself makes no reference to Claudius's expulsion, but neither is there any strong reason to doubt it, especially as the movements of Prisca and Aquila align well with details in the letters, and Luke does not seem to have any animus toward Claudius, who appears only in this reference and in 11:28.[4]

The Claudius expulsion can be placed with modest confidence in 49 CE, although that dating is based largely on the much later word of Orosius that the event occurred in the ninth year of Claudius's reign (*Adversus Paganos* 7.6.15–16). A second potential anchor for the timeline of Prisca and Aquila comes with Luke's report that Paul appeared before the proconsul Gallio, since Gallio's proconsulship in Achaia can be dated to around 51 CE (again, with modest confidence; Barrett 1995, 51–52; Holladay 2016, 354). If Paul is in Corinth at that time, having been joined by Prisca and Aquila (as both Luke and Paul suggest), then they must have left Rome before 51.

Claudius's death in 54 CE means Prisca and Aquila could have returned to Rome at that point, although they could well have returned earlier, given the improbability of monitoring the city's borders. Paul's letter then would have been written after their return, presumably after they had had some time to reestablish themselves.[5]

These minimal details yield a composition date in the period of 55–58 CE, which is when most scholars place the letter (see the convenient list in Wolter

---

4. That is not to endorse Luke's notion that "all Jews" were forced from Rome or to attribute to Claudius any particular reason for this action (Barclay 1996a, 303–6; Gruen 2002, 36–41). It is enough to note that the expulsion could have included Prisca and Aquila.

5. This statement is not intended to support the theory of conflict between Jewish and gentile believers at Rome following the return of Jews from expulsion. According to that theory, the expulsion transformed Roman Christianity into an overwhelmingly gentile population. When it lapsed following the death of Claudius, returning Jewish believers found their leadership questioned or even rejected (Wiefel 1991, 92–101). The theory relies on a statement in Suetonius that Claudius took his action because the Jews "constantly made disturbance at the instigation of Chrestus" (*Claudius* 25.4; LCL). This "Chrestus" is a mistaken reference to "Christ," as the theory runs, and the expulsion came about because of disputes about Christian preaching. Problems abound with the thesis, however. Not only is the name "Chrestus" well attested in the period (Gruen 2002, 39), but Suetonius knew about Christians and would not likely have confused the name (Barclay 1996a, 304, citing *Nero* 16.2) Further, it is by no means clear that those Jews who were expelled returned to Rome, that they returned at a single time, or that their return would have prompted a rift of the sort this theory presupposes.

1:30), even those who rely much more freely on the chronology of Acts than I have done here.

Addressees at Rome

From the greetings in Rom 16, we may infer that Paul's letter addresses several distinct gatherings in Rome rather than a single Roman assembly. At the outset of the list, he greets Prisca and Aquila and the "assembly at their place" (16:2). Each of the succeeding admonitions to "greet" individuals could reflect a separate gathering. Phoebe will take the letter to each one, introducing, reading, and discussing the letter, accompanied perhaps by Romans who are assisting her as Paul requests (see the commentary on 16:3–5).

Within the greetings, Paul identifies Andronicus, Junia, and Herodion as his "kin," by which he means they are fellow Jews (as in 9:3). If Luke's account is correct, Aquila is also a Jew, and Prisca would likely be a Jew as well (Acts 18:2). The remaining individuals named may be gentiles. Identifying both Jews and gentiles in the greetings is significant, even if we do not know how representative the list is of Roman Christianity or what size the groups may be. Nor do we know whether there are Jewish gatherings separate from gentile gatherings, or how the gatherings may have evolved. Based solely on 16:3–16, then, Paul's Roman addressees include both Jews and gentiles.

This preliminary conclusion—that Paul's addressees include both Jews and gentiles—finds some confirmation in the body of the letter. To be sure, at the outset of the letter Paul identifies his own *apostleship* as addressed to gentiles (1:5–6, 13–14), but that statement does not mean the *letter* to Rome addresses only gentiles. The most unambiguous evidence about gentile presence comes in 11:13–24, where Paul admonishes gentiles in harsh terms about the dangers of boasting over that portion of Israel God has, at present, cut off from its root. The words "Now I am talking to you gentiles" intrude into Paul's discourse in a dramatic manner and demonstrate the presence of gentiles in these Roman gatherings (at least as Paul understands them). At the same time, this sharp turn to gentile auditors also undermines the notion that Paul addresses only gentiles, since, if the entirety of the letter addresses gentiles and only gentiles, then the shift at 11:13 becomes superfluous.

The preponderance of the gentiles in these Roman gatherings probably came from among the *sebomenoi,* worshipers of God attracted to Jewish customs and practices who did not become proselytes. Evidence for such attraction is considerable, including writers as diverse as Josephus (*Ag. Ap.* 2.282), Tacitus (*History* 5.5.1), and Juvenal (*Sat.* 14.96–106).[6] Extended exposure of

---

6. Tobin provides an instructive overview of the evidence and possible reasons for gentile attraction to Jewish practices (2004, 23–27).

these gentiles to Jewish life would explain how Paul can draw so confidently on Scripture in this letter. These auditors know that Abraham is "our" father, would be attentive to words from Isaiah, and would notice Paul's peculiar comments about the law, understanding its importance in the life of the synagogue. To conclude, however, that the auditors are exclusively gentile goes too far, given the names in 16:3, 7, 11, as well as the observation above about the shift at 11:13.

The Purposes of the Letter

There is widespread agreement that Romans is an occasional letter, but articulating the purpose(s) of the letter proves challenging, precisely because Paul writes carefully as he addresses gatherings largely unknown to him. He can recall for the Thessalonians the instructions he gave when they were together (1 Thess 4:1–2), and he can remind the Corinthians that he preached only "Jesus Christ and him crucified" (1 Cor 2:2), but no such reminder is possible with the Romans, at least not a reminder based on their relationship with him (see Rom 15:15). Given the length and complexity of the letter, it seems wise to think in terms of purposes rather than a single purpose. In addition, proposals should account both for the specific details offered up in the letter frame (1:1–12; 16:1–23[27]) and for the subject matter of the letter body (1:13–15:33).[7]

Spain

The letter frame identifies three locations (Rome, Jerusalem, and Spain), each of which likely plays a role in Paul's goals. At the far end of Paul's intended travels lies Spain, where he plans to take the gospel in a new phase of his work. As he writes in 15:19, he has completed the gospel "from Jerusalem and around as far as Illyricum," and he intends now to go to Spain by way of Rome (15:24, 28). In addition to a commitment to extend preaching into territory quite unknown to him, such an undertaking would involve significant challenges and resources (on which, see Jewett 74–75). Paul does comment that he hopes the Romans will send him on his way (15:28), which could be a hint about the need for specific material support. Less convincing is the notion that the fruit Paul hopes for in Rome is a contribution for the Spanish mission (1:13, although see 15:28) or the claim that Phoebe's role in Rome centers on preparations for Spain (16:1–2; Jewett 89–91). If Paul is in fact hoping that the Romans will approve and support his work in Spain, then the repeated concern of the letter

7. Donfried's collection provides a snapshot of proposals available late in the twentieth century, and see the subsequent surveys by Das (2007, 26–52) and J. C. Miller (2001).

for all humans would serve that goal (e.g., 1:6, 16; 3:22; 5:18; 11:32). In general, however, tying the letter's purpose tightly to the Spanish mission is highly speculative, based as it is on two slender comments in 15:24, 28.

Jerusalem

The final lines of the letter body give more extensive and direct attention to Paul's upcoming journey to Jerusalem on behalf of the collection. He introduces the Jerusalem trip at the end of announcing his intent to visit Rome on his way to Spain. "But now," he writes, "I am going to Jerusalem," a journey that will take him some 700 nautical miles out of the way. He first explains why he needs to go to Jerusalem, introducing the collection as an act of fellowship by Macedonia and Achaia on behalf of the Jerusalem poor (15:25–29). Then he asks for prayer in strident language, acknowledging two problems: he is under threat from the "disobedient," which prompts him to ask the Romans to pray for his deliverance (15:31a), and he anticipates that the collection may be rejected in Jerusalem (15:31b). Both the importance of the collection for Paul and his anxiety are palpable in these lines. Placement of this appeal at the end of the letter body may also underscore its importance: this is the last thing the Romans will hear prior to the greetings.

These features prompt the hypothesis that the letter rehearses what Paul wishes to say in Jerusalem, and he sends it to Rome by way of soliciting their support (Jervell 1991, 56, 64). The notion that he composes and sends to Rome what he will say in Jerusalem seems far-fetched, but the genuine concern of 15:30–33 is undeniable. Perhaps Paul does fear that he will never reach Rome, that the trip to Jerusalem will produce complete rejection. In that case, he may hope that the letter to Rome serves as his interpretation of the unity of Jew and gentile. If things go badly, Paul wants this witness to the gospel to make its way to Rome. The churches of Macedonia and Achaia will already have responded to this message and acted on it with their contributions. In Paul's view, the Romans also need the letter's witness, perhaps precisely because their own unity is in doubt.

Such an understanding of the purpose fits well with a good bit of the letter, especially chs. 9–11 and the repeated language that draws Jew and gentile together. But it does less to account for the content of chs. 5–8 (although perhaps among the threats Paul itemizes in 8:38–39 is the threat he perceives at Rome). For that we need to turn to Rome itself.

Rome

Most recent theories regarding the purpose of Romans focus on some perceived need or concern at Rome, which is immediately appealing given that Paul's other letters address their audiences directly.[8] Looking first to the opening of the letter, for the obvious reason that the letter opening may set the agenda, several details are at least curious. To begin with, Paul does not address the Romans as an *ekklēsia*, by contrast with his other letters (1 Cor 1:2; 2 Cor 1:1; Gal 1:2; 1 Thess 1:1). The significance of that silence can be overstated, as with the notion that Paul withholds the word because there has been no apostolic foundation at Rome (Klein 1991, 39–43), but the silence is worth noticing nonetheless. Only when he solicits greetings for the gathering (*ekklēsia*) at the home of Prisca and Aquila does Paul use the term (16:5).

A second curiosity is the brevity of the thanksgiving. Paul gives thanks that their faith is known throughout the world (1:8), but he writes nothing further by way of appreciation. In Philippians Paul gives thanks for their partnership and expresses confidence in their perseverance (1:3–6), and in 1 Thessalonians he expands on their reception of the gospel (1:2–10). Even in 1 Corinthians, he expresses gratitude for the spiritual gifts they have received (1:4–8), although he will later challenge their handling of those gifts. In this situation, where he knows only some of the auditors and has not yet visited, he would seem to have ample reason to expand rather than to contract the thanksgiving, precisely so that he could secure their attention (see further on 1:8).

Perhaps most important, Paul announces that he intends to "proclaim the gospel to you in Rome" (1:15). Outside of Romans, Paul employs the verb *euangelizesthai* only to refer to initial declarations of the good news, as in 1 Cor 1:17; 9:16; 15:1–2; Gal 4:13; 1 Thess 2:9. He does not use it of subsequent instruction or encouragement or exhortation. That is consistent with the word's use elsewhere outside the NT (for evidence, see below on 1:14b–15 and especially the texts gathered by Dickson 2005). More to the point, late in the letter Paul again uses *euangelizesthai* when he describes his own labor as limited to preaching where Christ is not already named (15:20; and see 10:15).

This way of writing about the act of bringing the good news—announcing it to people who have not yet heard it—may indicate that Paul suspects there is some deficit among the auditors at Rome. Although he comments on their faith (1:8) and later will characterize the letter as a reminder (15:15), he nonetheless appears to regard Rome as in need of hearing the good news. That is why he can characterize his reminder as an act of boldness (15:15).

---

8. Proposals range widely and include the notion that with this letter Paul anticipates the work of the Jewish Teachers (Campbell 2009a, 495–518), that he addresses misapprehensions the Romans have formed about Paul himself by virtue of news from the Galatian congregations (Tobin 2004, 98–103), that he undertakes to bring Roman Jews into his own gentile church (Watson 2007, 163–91), that he wants to unite Jews and gentiles as preparation for the western mission (N. T. Wright 2018, 324), and that he writes to show gentile believers (only) how it is that they are now right before God (Johnson Hodge 2012, 170).

What is it that the auditors need to hear for the first time (as Paul understands the situation)? They know already that Jesus is the Christ, the Messiah of God. That initial identification is not in doubt, nor presumably the character of his death and resurrection. Paul begins from those elements of the kerygma (1:3–4). They also know that the arrival of God's Christ initiates the inclusion of gentiles among God's people, although some of them may have misconstrued the significance of that inclusion (as in 11:13–24). There may also be differences over implications of the Christ event for the continuance of the Mosaic law (as in 14:1–12).

What Paul announces as news in Romans is not simply the arrival of Jesus as God's Christ, but what that arrival reveals about the situation of humanity—Jew and gentile alike—and what that arrival reveals about the whole of creation. In 1:16 Paul announces, he *identifies*, the gospel as God's power to bring about salvation. Beginning in 1:17 he explains why that power is necessary, first establishing the captivity of both Jews and gentiles to Sin (3:9), tracing that captivity finally to Adam and the world-encompassing powers of Sin and Death (5:12–21). Christ's death and resurrection mean nothing less than the defeat of these powers (6:12–21) and the hope of the liberation of all creation (8:18–25), although the powers persist in their resistance to God's love brought about in Christ Jesus (8:31–39).

Much is left aside in this brief synopsis (and left to the commentary that follows), but it may suffice by way of proposing that Paul offers this good news at Rome in the hope of expanding his auditors' understanding of the gospel.[9] The gospel is not, as some of his auditors may have thought, only a matter of bringing about the inclusion of the gentiles or of fulfilling the promises to Israel, however urgent those goals are. It is nothing less than the reclamation of a cosmos in thrall to Sin and Death.

An Overview of the Letter

1:1–12. The conventions of letter opening introduce Paul as the letter writer and certain Romans who are beloved and called of God, but the focus is on neither of those parties.[10] Immediately Paul's introduction of himself gives way to a terse introduction of the gospel of Jesus Christ, who belongs to the human line of David and whose resurrection discloses publicly that he is God's Son. Paul gives thanks for the faith of his addressees and explains his long-held desire to visit them.

---

9. This understanding of the letter's purpose aligns well with proposals that Romans belongs in the rhetorical classification of protreptic, given its desire to gain Roman adherents for Paul's interpretation of the gospel (Aune 1991; Guerra 1995).

10. The table of contents provides the letter structure. Here I am sketching the contents to provide an overview of the letter's discourse.

1:13–4:25. The body of the letter begins with the disclosure formula "Now I do not want you to be uninformed" in 1:13 (as in 2 Cor 1:8; Phil 1:12; see below on 1:13). This first major section of the letter initially announces that the gospel *is* God's saving power. It apocalyptically reveals both God's righteousness and God's wrath. Taking up divine wrath first, Paul contends that both Jews and gentiles, however different their history, are under the power of Sin (3:9). They violated the Creator-creature relationship by withholding worship from God (1:18–32; 3:10–18). They have different histories with God in that gentiles have not been gifted with the law (2:14) or with Scripture (3:2) as Jews have, and yet the action of God in Jesus Christ reveals that they have arrived at the same place: both are "under Sin" (3:9). In the "now time," God has put Christ forward to liberate both Jews and gentiles, acting through the faith-generating faithfulness of Christ (3:21–26). The story of Abraham, here retold without reference to his legendary obedience, serves as a prototype of God's initiative, God's inclusion of gentiles, and especially God's creative power in the birth of the promised child, but now in the resurrection of Jesus Christ from the dead (4:17, 24–25). Unlike the ominous "they" of 1:21, and by distinction from the withering indictment of human impiety in 3:10–18, Abraham did glorify God (4:21), anticipating the glory of Jew and gentile together in 15:6, 7–13.

5:1–8:39. With the declaration in 5:1 that "we have been rectified," and the ensuing summary of the present situation of peace, hope, and love, Paul seems to be rounding off his earlier introduction and exposition of God's rectifying action (1:16–17; 3:21–26). What follows is no conclusion, however, but a radical recasting of the rectifying act into universalizing and even cosmic terms. While ethnic language has preoccupied chs. 1–4, it disappears entirely in chs. 5–8, where there is no reference to Jew or gentile, to David or Abraham or Israel. The Christ event is nothing less than Adamic in its extent. Adam's disobedience unleashed Sin and Death on the whole world, such that they became its powerful rulers; Christ's obedience instituted a new rule, that of God's righteousness, once again for the whole world (5:12–21). Those who are baptized into Christ belong to his death to Sin; they belong to new life, liberated from the grasp of Sin and Death (6:1–7:6). Confronting the disturbing remarks he has made about the law, in 7:7–25 Paul contends that Sin's power is such that it has taken captive even God's good law, making obedience to that law impossible. With God's action in Jesus Christ, however, Sin is condemned, and the Spirit of Christ is at work to bring life, adoption, and even inheritance (8:1–17). That new life does not remove humans from the present. To the contrary, life in the "now time" brings about identification with the longing of all creation for God's final redemption (8:18–30) and confidence that God's love will triumph even over persistent anti-God powers (8:31–39).

9:1–11:36. The promise that no created thing "will be powerful enough to separate us from God's love in Christ Jesus our Lord" ushers in the lament of 9:1–5: Where is Israel in this God-generated intrusion that is the gospel? Paul addresses the question of Israel's relationship to God in a dense, difficult passage, replete with Scripture and also with possibilities for misunderstanding. He establishes at the outset that the only Israel that exists is God's creation, brought about and sustained unilaterally by God (9:6–13). By extension, Israel's future also depends entirely on God (9:14–29). In the present time, the "now time" of the gospel, however, God has tripped Israel, raising the possibility that God has actually turned away from God's own people (10:1–21). Paul invites gentile auditors to conclude that God is finished with Israel, only to turn in ch. 11 to show how the present division between the "remnant" and the "rest" is itself God-generated, intended to bring about the salvation of gentiles and the saving jealousy of the "rest" of Israel. The apocalyptic mystery is that "all Israel," that is, the whole of the Israel God created, will be saved (11:1–27). God's word, God's promises, are reliable (9:6; 11:28–32). The universalizing claims of 5:12–21 are here reinforced. A doxology that limns God's ways and God's inscrutability cautions against overconfidence in human speculation and concludes the section (11:33–36).

12:1–15:13. Having invited the auditors to join in the "Amen!" of 11:36, Paul turns specifically to the "now time" of the Roman communities. He invokes their gratitude for God's mercies to urge their own bodily sacrifice, which is their life in Christ (12:1–8). He then sketches that life in a series of statements with parallels both in his other letters and in other ethical traditions. Concern for life within the boundary of faith combines with concern for those outside (12:9–21). In a particularly difficult passage, Paul urges recognition that what we would call civil authorities were put in place by God and only by God (implicitly cautioning against the overestimation of their importance) and urging the payment of taxes and other obligations (13:1–7). Two brief passages in the second half of ch. 13 reveal Paul's notion that real obligation is the obligation to love, which fulfills the law. For Paul, however, that love is not an end in itself, but one that knows what time it is, wrapped up as it is in the Lord Jesus Christ (13:8–14). Chapter 14, for which Paul seems to have been preparing throughout this section, addresses conflicts at Rome, arguing both for the integrity of both sides in the discussion *and* for the obligation to act for the good of all. The goal is not uniformity of judgment but harmony in doxology, as the *telos* is the glorification of God (15:1–6). Paul reiterates that point in 15:7–13, which calls on Scripture once again to interpret the event of Jesus Christ as having its goal not simply in the uniting of Jew and gentile, but in their shared and joyous glorification of God's eschatological triumph.

15:14–16:23[27]. The closing of the letter both reflects on the letter in relationship to Paul's vocation and anticipates the next stage in that work (15:14–33). Eager as he may be for his work in Rome, Paul nonetheless prioritizes Jerusalem, where the very doxology he has just celebrated may encounter a severe challenge. Chapter 16 commends Phoebe, who will deliver the letter (vv. 1–2), requests greetings to be shared among various gatherings in Rome (vv. 3–16), promises once more the triumph of God (vv. 17–20), and concludes with greetings from Paul's companions at Rome (vv. 21–23). The additional doxology in vv. 25–27 is likely a later addition.

The Place of Scripture

No overview of Romans is complete without attention to the place of Scripture. Israel's Scriptures thoroughly saturate Paul's letter to the Romans, as is obvious even from the most superficial reading. A single fact tells the tale: over half the scriptural citations in all of Paul's letters are to be found in Romans (Wagner 2011, 155–57). More impressive than sheer quantity, however, is the range of ways in which Paul calls on Scripture. There are general references to Scripture, such as the opening identification of the promised gospel coming through "his prophets in holy Scriptures" (1:2) and the later assertion that God's righteousness is "confirmed by the law and the prophets" (3:21). There are citations of single lines, as in the citation of Hab 2:4 in Rom 1:17 and that of Exod 9:16 in Rom 9:17. Most of ch. 4 is a reworked account of the scriptural story of Abraham, drawing especially on Gen 15 and 17, and Rom 9:6b–18 crafts a story of God and Israel from a variety of texts. Several lengthy catenae serve important functions, as when 3:10–18 encapsulates and reinforces the conclusion of 3:9 that all are "under Sin" with a series of quotations drawn largely from psalms, and when 9:25–29 calls on Hosea and Isaiah to give voice to Paul's understanding of the contemporary situation of Israel. In ch. 10, the stunning midrash on Deut 30:12–14 reads Christ in the place where the law has stood. There are even claims for Scripture's pertinence in the present time, such as the brief note that the words "[faith] was regarded for him as righteousness" (Gen 15:6) were written not only about Abraham but also about "us" (Rom 4:22–24). A more capacious statement appears toward the end of the letter, when Paul claims that "whatever was written previously" was written "for our instruction" (15:4).

This rich diversity in the way Scripture plays through Romans has produced a lively and complex research agenda in recent decades (set in motion by Hays 1989). I will draw on numerous studies in the commentary, while of necessity giving little attention to some of the more specialized debates, such as whether Paul worked from memory or had access to written manuscripts. While such matters are important, my approach as a commentator is to pay attention to what Paul does with Scripture, being open to the possibility that his auditors knew those same lines and *also* to the possibility that they did not. If Phoebe's gentile auditors at Rome did come from the synagogue, they would have been familiar with Scripture, although that does not mean they followed every scriptural resonance in the letter, especially not at first hearing.[11]

For example, the treatment of Abraham in Rom 4 would be intelligible to anyone even slightly familiar with the narratives of Genesis. Hearers need not have deep acquaintance with the psalms in order to make sense of the catena in 3:10–18, although they may not have associated particular lines with particular psalms or the context of lines within those psalms. Some other passages may have been lost on Paul's auditors or at least have required explanation by Phoebe and others. When Paul turns Elijah's prayer *for* Israel into a prayer *against* Israel in 11:2, he may well have left some auditors behind, to take only a single example. My assumption is that those addressed at Rome were generally familiar with Scripture in its Greek form (for which I will use the customary if inadequate word *Septuagint* [LXX]), but not that they could follow every small change Paul introduced.

As for Paul's own reading of Scripture, the comment in 15:4 is revealing: "For whatever was written previously, it was written for our instruction." This statement not only provides Paul's guidance for the Roman gatherings in their own reading but may also suggest how Paul himself reads Scripture. He assumes that it was written for "our instruction," that is, for those who live in the "now time" (and see 1 Cor 9:9–10). In the context of his apostolic vocation, he reads from the present backward. On the face of it, of course, that is obvious; no one can stand inside the past and read forward. But the intrusion of God in Jesus Christ shapes Paul's reading such that he can hear a witness to Christ even in Deuteronomy's witness to the law (Rom 10:5–8) and can find gentiles among the beloved unloved of Hos 2:25 (Rom 9:25). The gospel has intruded even into Paul's reading of Scripture.

Literary and Rhetorical Features

Romans is also replete with literary features and strategies of persuasion. For example, Paul makes use of alliteration (as in the series of alpha-privatives in 1:31), *synkrisis* or comparison (as in the contrast between Adam and Christ in 5:12–21), and a fortiori arguments (i.e., arguments from the lesser to the greater, again in 5:12–21; 11:12).[12] His use of diatribal style in Romans has received

11. In an oral culture, they may well have understood more than contemporary hearers would on first hearing.
12. A particular strength of Jewett's commentary is his extensive discussion of literary features of the text.

widespread scholarly attention.[13] This feature of the letter is especially important, since without recognition of it interpreters have recklessly assumed, for example, that the direct address in 2:1 singled out actual individuals or groups (all Jews) for attack (as in the "typical Jew" of Sanday and Headlam 54; and see Nygren 115–18). Read as diatribal, however, statements of this sort become part of a larger pattern of persuasion, typical of that employed by teachers in a variety of settings.

Such features of the letter display Paul at work, leading his auditors to see things, or at least attempting to do so. In addition to these acknowledged literary features of the text, at several points Romans leads its audience to draw conclusions that prove to be erroneous, engaging in what I have called a practice of rhetorical feint (Gaventa 2008b, 392). In 3:10–18, for example, the catena draws on numerous psalms that critique the unrighteous *before* turning to extol the good standing of the righteous speaker, so that Paul invites the audience to expect a celebration of those who do keep the law, who do honor God. Instead, with 3:19 he shuts the door on any such conclusion, insisting that the law closes every human mouth (see on 3:10–20 for explication). Similarly, in ch. 10, Paul prompts the audience to conclude that God has rejected Israel, only to turn in 11:1 and insist that God has not forsaken Israel, God's own people.

Paul's treatment of the law provides the most developed example of this practice. Throughout the first six chapters of the letter, Paul both affirms the law of Moses (e.g., 3:21, 31) and makes highly provocative claims about the law (e.g., 4:13, 15). This pattern escalates in chs. 5–7, where the law "slips in" (v. 13), where Paul joins it to Sin as a ruler over humanity (6:14–15), and where it lords over people (7:1). This pattern drives to the question of 7:7: "Is the law Sin?" The answer he *seems* to be driving toward is "Yes, the law itself is sin," inviting that judgment. Instead, he answers emphatically, "Of course not." The law is holy, right, and good (7:12), *but* Sin has nevertheless made use of it.

A final feature, of which Paul himself is likely unaware, is the way the letter enacts the dynamic character of the gospel itself, prompting the audience to experience the gospel as it is heard. Having depicted the work of Sin and Death in ch. 5, using language associated with kingship, slavery, and violence (see the excursus on the powers of Sin and Death), Paul characterizes that as the time of slavery to Sin and urges instead obedient slavery to God (righteousness; 6:16, 19–23). Although the two enslavements carry contrasting outcomes (death and life), Paul allows the language of slavery to stand unchallenged— at that point. Later, however, having discussed God's sending of the Son to defeat Sin and having introduced the work of the Spirit, Paul writes, "You did not receive a spirit of slavery to fear again. Instead, you received a spirit of adoption" (8:15). By contrast with the fear, the utter terror, associated with

13. Stowers 1981; for a helpful review of recent research, see J. King 2018, 103–28.

slavery, Paul interprets slavery to God's righteousness as a slavery without fear. More important, it is a "spirit of adoption." What began as slavery to Sin and Death became slavery to the righteousness of God, which then became adoption into the family.

A second example of the dynamic character of the gospel, both depicted and performed within the letter and perhaps even within the Roman gatherings, has to do with the corruption and redemption of human speech. An important feature of 1:18–32 is that humans withhold praise from God, both in their distorted worship of things that are not God and in withholding of glorification and thanksgiving (1:21). The catena in 3:10–18 reinforces that statement, generalizing it with the charge that no one fears God (3:18) and that human speech is vile and bitter (3:13–14), and prompting the conclusion that the law has shut up every mouth (3:19). In the account of the Spirit's work in ch. 8, however, adoption means that "we" cry out to God as father (8:15). And in 15:6 Paul prays that those previously closed mouths will pray together in unison, glorifying God. Reinforcing this notion of speech that is corrupted and redeemed, at key moments in the letter Phoebe will pronounce the word "Amen!"—calling on the auditors at Rome, along with her, to perform her praise for God's action in Jesus Christ (9:5; 11:36; 15:33). By doing so, they do not simply assent to Paul's words. They become with him and with Phoebe a chorus of praise.

COMMENTARY ON THE
LETTER TO THE ROMANS

Romans 1:1–12
Opening the Letter

The letter opens with a prescript (1:1–7) and a thanksgiving (1:8–12), both standard features of ancient letters. Paul expands the customary identification of the sender with a concise summation of the gospel that orients the whole of the letter. The thanksgiving, while short on details regarding the Roman addressees, introduces Paul's long-standing desire to be in Rome.

1:1–7 The Prescript

Introductions of the apostle Paul abound. Artists introduce him visually, whether alone in contemplation (as in Rembrandt's paintings of Paul in prison or at a desk) or addressing a crowd (as in Raphael's rendering of Paul preaching in Athens). Systematicians and ethicists introduce his teachings and their implications. Biblical scholars introduce him through reconstructions of his life and work. Different lenses are brought to bear, but always the focus remains on Paul, and understandably so. Yet when Paul introduces himself, as he does in the opening lines of Romans, writing to Christians in a city he had never visited, he points away from himself and toward God's action in Jesus Christ.[1] That single redirection says much about Paul, about his letters, and about this letter.

All of Paul's letters expand on the standard conventions of Greek letter prescripts, but Rom 1:1–7—a single sentence in Greek—constitutes the most elaborate prescript found in any NT letter. Rather than beginning with the mere necessities of prescript ("X to Y, many greetings," as in, e.g., Acts 15:23;

---

1. The term "Christian" is admittedly anachronistic, yet it is preferable to cumbersome alternatives (see introduction). In addition, I sometimes use the word "church" for the Greek term *ekklēsia*, on the assumption that readers understand that Paul refers to gatherings or assemblies rather than to buildings or to the structured organizations of later centuries. In no way does this practice endorse the view that Paul himself is no longer Jewish or that Christianity is, in Paul's time, a phenomenon separate from Judaism.

23:26), Paul regularly extends the prescript to identify himself and his addressees in terms of the gospel. Even 1 Thessalonians, with its bare naming of Paul,
Silvanus, and Timothy, addresses "the church of the Thessalonians which is in
God the Father and the Lord Jesus Christ" (1:1). But nowhere else does Paul's
prescript extend to encompass a summary of the gospel. Such a significant
departure from his own typical pattern may well have perplexed the auditors at
Rome (so Byrskog 1997, 37–38) and presumably also provoked them to close
attention. The expansion could reflect the fact that Paul has not been to Rome
and does not have extensive acquaintance with Christians in this city, although
the greetings to specific individuals in ch. 16 suggest that Paul knows more
about the situation in Rome than might be anticipated (see the introduction).
The proclamation of the gospel contained within this extended prescript forcefully reminds all these gatherings in Rome that the gospel has to do with God's
action, not their own; further, any point of commonality between the apostle
and the Romans, or among the Romans themselves, is generated by the gospel.

Not only does the prescript include a pithy summation of the gospel, but
the prescript itself is notable for redundancies of expression that intensify its
claims.[2] In v. 1 Paul identifies himself in three distinct ways. He also uses
intensification when he claims that God's promise of the gospel comes through
his prophets and in *holy* Scriptures. Further, he describes Jesus as coming from
David's line, then adds that he is such *physically.* The resurrected Jesus Christ
is associated with a/the spirit *of holiness.* As becomes clear to anyone who
wrestles with the Greek, the work of some of these expressions is more allusive
than explanatory. Shared assumptions are announced, but they are announced
in a way that anticipates their projection onto a far larger canvas.

> 1:1 Paul, slave of Christ Jesus,[a] called to be an apostle, set apart for the
> gospel of God— 2 the gospel God promised earlier through his prophets
> in holy Scriptures,[b] 3 the gospel about his Son who came from David's
> lineage, considered physically, 4 who was also publicly identified as Son
> of God in power, considered in terms of the spirit of God's own holiness,
> at his resurrection from the dead, Jesus Christ our Lord, 5 through whom
> we received grace and apostleship to bring about among all the gentiles
> the obedience that comes from faith for the sake of his name, 6 among
> whom you also are called to belong to Jesus Christ— 7 to all of God's
> beloved who are in Rome,[c] who are called to be holy people. May you
> have grace and peace from God our Father and the Lord Jesus Christ.

a. Some important manuscripts ($\mathfrak{P}^{26}$ ℵ A G K L P Ψ) reverse the order, reading *Iēsou
Christou* (as in $\mathfrak{P}^{10}$ and B). The variant may reflect harmonization to the word order
found in vv. 4, 6, 7, and 8.

2. Rhetoricians would label this *interpretatio* or *synomyny* (Ps.-Cicero, *Rhet. Her.* 4.28.38).

b. Editions of the Greek NT as well as translators disagree over whether a comma should follow *hagiais* at the end of v. 2. With the comma (as above), v. 2 modifies "the gospel of God," and *peri tou autou* ("about his [Son]") refers back to "the gospel of God" (the end of v. 1). Without the comma, *peri tou autou* specifies that the promise found in Scriptures concerns God's Son (so Hays 1993, 129). Although the latter reading is grammatically possible, Paul does not elsewhere speak of Scripture or Scriptures "about" Jesus Christ. (For additional arguments, see Cranfield 1:57.)

c. A few manuscripts omit the words "in Rome." Evidence for this reading is slender, but the omission is noteworthy because it reflects an understanding of Romans as a letter intended for the whole church rather than addressed to specific communities of believers. See the similar omission of "in Ephesus" in Eph 1:1.

[1:1] Paul introduces himself with three phrases, each of which has parallels or near parallels in his other letters, but nowhere else do all three phrases appear together as they do here. This abundance of self-description could imply that Paul anticipates some resistance to his authority on the part of Roman Christians, but the letter offers little else to warrant that interpretation. Taken together, these three phrases state Paul's credentials (Byrskog 1997, 37), and yet they are a peculiar form of credentialing. Paul has not earned or achieved these designations; instead, they have been imposed from the outside.[3] In addition, all three phrases of v. 1 point away from Paul himself and toward the one who commissioned him. Instead of reinforcing Paul's own authority, then, this verse asserts forcefully that Paul is known by reference to the gospel.

First, Paul identifies himself as a "slave of Christ Jesus" (see Phil 1:1; Gal 1:10; see also 1 Cor 7:22; 2 Cor 4:5).[4] English translations often adopt the word "servant" as a way of avoiding the understandable objections to the connotations of slavery (as in NIV, RSV, NRSVue, and NJB), but that translation misleadingly implies that Paul volunteers for this role, that he labors for Christ Jesus as a result of his own decision or his own will.[5] The involuntary character of this role is implied by the usage of the term *doulos* elsewhere (e.g., Aristotle, *Pol.* 1253b–1254a; Lev 26:13; Josephus, *J.W.* 5.443; Philo, *Creation* 85) and is confirmed by Paul's other comments about his vocation as an apostle (Gal 1:11–17; Phil 3:2–11).

Because Scripture refers to Samuel, David, and other central figures in Israel's history as the "slaves of the Lord" (e.g., Josh 24:29 [24:30 LXX]; Judg 2:8;

3. A glance at the opening paragraphs of Josephus's *Life* is instructive. Josephus goes into considerable detail about his priestly and royal lineage, his father's outstanding character, and his own educational accomplishments (*Life* 1–10). Josephus is writing a *bios*, of course, and Paul is not. Yet both are involved in self-presentation.

4. The practice of referring to human beings as God's slaves occurs not only in Paul's letters but widely in NT literature; see, for example, Luke 1:38; Acts 16:17; Eph 6:6; Col 4:12; 2 Tim 2:24; Titus 1:1; Jas 1:1; 1 Pet 2:16; 2 Pet 1:1.

5. See Lettsome 2021, especially pp. 11–13, for a suggestive proposal about Mary's "slave song" in Luke 1:38, 48.

1 Sam 3:9; Ps 89:3 [88:4 LXX]), Paul's reference is sometimes regarded as a straightforward application to himself of an established honorific term, and for that reason the context of Paul's self-reference has been sought in ongoing discussions about Jews as God's slaves.[6] Yet slavery was ubiquitous in the Roman Empire; by some estimates as much as 20 percent of the population was enslaved.[7] Such a statistic makes it difficult to imagine that Paul would use the language of slavery, or that his audience would hear it, without connecting it to the inescapable evidence of human slavery all around them. Paul's self-identification as "slave" may convey some notion of status because of the exalted status of Jesus Christ (just as some slaves of elite figures acquired certain forms of status; Harrill 2006, 86–87, 103–13; Bradley 378–79), but that status nonetheless also connotes being under the control of another person rather than voluntary submission.

Indeed, as Phoebe read the letter in the assorted Christian gatherings around Rome, a number of slaves may well have found themselves elevated by hearing the term. At least we might ask how they would have responded, even if nothing by way of source material helps us with this question. For the auditors, Paul's self-identification as *doulos* may function as a *captatio benevolentiae* in that Paul's self-acknowledged status as Christ's slave brings him closer to the audience.

Taking seriously the compulsory character of slavery undermines the argument that Paul identifies himself this way because of his humility (as found in Pelagius 59). Similarly, it is not at all clear that this is, at least in Paul's usage, an assertion of his leadership or authority. Paul begins by admitting that he is not his own. That admission is consistent with later parts of the letter, particularly ch. 6, which contrasts slavery to the power of Sin with slavery to God's righteousness. Paul does not appear to have thought of himself or anyone else (individual or corporate) as free from constraint, as self-determined.[8] All are enslaved to some power.[9]

Standing at the opening of the letter, Paul's self-depiction as "slave of *Christ Jesus*" simultaneously connects and disconnects his slavery from that of Joshua or David, figures identified by tradition as the slaves of *God*. By naming himself as the property of Christ Jesus, Paul connects himself intimately with the new event of the gospel. Nevertheless, the lines that follow make it clear that to be the slave of Christ Jesus is also to be the slave of God; the two cannot be separated. Perhaps the order here—Christ Jesus instead of Jesus Christ, the order

6. For a helpful discussion of the various proposals, including proposals that Paul is influenced by the Roman institution of slavery, see Byron 2003, 1–16; 2008.

7. Madden (1996, 109–28) estimates that the percentage of the population enslaved empire-wide in the first century CE was 20 percent, rising in Italy to 30 percent.

8. See further on 6:12–23 and on 8:15–17, where slavery language gives way to language about being part of God's household (Gaventa 2015, 203–5).

9. Bob Dylan captures Paul's assumption with his song "Gotta Serve Somebody." For the lyrics, see https://bobdylan.com/songs/gotta-serve-somebody.

more customary for Paul (e.g., Rom 1:4; 1 Cor 1:2; 2 Cor 1:2; Gal 1:1)—draws attention to the claim that God's anointed, God's messiah, has come in the person of Jesus. That term, messiah, plays various roles in Jewish texts, and what Paul intends by it can best be understood when he unpacks it, first in vv. 3–4 and then throughout the letter.[10]

Second, Paul is "called to be an apostle." Contemporary readers may find themselves drawn immediately to the word "apostle" because of its accrued connotations of office or leadership, but it is important not to overlook the statement that apostleship arises from a calling from outside oneself (*klētos*). Paul uses the language not simply for his own calling or for special ministerial roles but for all those who are called into the gospel (e.g., Rom 1:6–7; 8:28; 1 Cor 1:2, 26, 28). Here and elsewhere, Paul forthrightly asserts that he is an apostle, often linking that apostleship directly to Jesus Christ or to God (1 Cor 9:1; 2 Cor 1:1; Gal 1:1; 1 Thess 2:7). An ordinary word for a messenger or agent of another person, "apostle" later becomes a special term for one charged with the urgent task of presenting and re-presenting the gospel.[11] Unlike Luke, who limits the ranks of the apostles to those who were witnesses of the life, death, and resurrection of Jesus (Acts 1:21–22; although cf. 14:4, 14), Paul's letters assume that the group is not closed or fixed in number (1 Cor 9:5; 12:28–29; 15:7; Gal 1:17; Phil 2:25); neither is it limited to males (note the apostle Junia in 16:7).

Third, Paul describes himself as "set apart for the gospel of God." In Gal 1:15 Paul claims he was "set apart" before his birth for the work of declaring the gospel among the gentiles. Luke employs the verb similarly of the Holy Spirit's designation of Paul and Barnabas as those to be "set apart for the work to which I have called them" (Acts 13:2; cf. 19:9). Here Paul describes his "set-apartness" with the bare phrase "for the gospel of God," the emphasis falling on the gospel itself rather than on the special task assigned to one set apart. Like the word "apostle," "gospel" (*euangelion*) also is an ordinary term for "good news," and the exact nature of that good news Paul will introduce in the lines that follow and then unfold in the letter as a whole. The only specification is that the gospel comes from God. The genitive is one of authorship; this is not simply an announcement of good news about God or even a disclosure of news from God but God's own action that is being revealed in the present. Paul seldom describes the gospel with this phrase, "gospel of God" (although see Rom 15:16; 2 Cor 11:7; 1 Thess 2:2, 8, 9),[12] but the emphasis on God's

---

10. Novenson ably traces both the pitfalls in earlier notions of a single "messianic idea" and the range of work "messiah" does across Jewish literature (2012, 34–63).

11. For an introduction to the term and its usage, see Betz 1992; Donaldson 2006.

12. The parallels are not exact, however, since elsewhere the phrase employs the article, which does not appear here.

authorship is consistent with the emphasis on God's role in the lines that follow and throughout the whole of the letter.

[2] As Paul expands on the phrase "gospel of God," the focus of the prescript shifts to the gospel itself, so that the identification of the letter writer falls out of sight. God promised the gospel "earlier through his prophets in holy Scriptures." The reference to the prophets is distinctive, as Paul nowhere else identifies the prophets collectively as the speakers or writers of Scripture.[13] Pelagius attempted to distinguish the two, as if the wording were "through his prophets *and* in holy Scriptures" (59), but the Greek does not support that distinction. That they are "his" prophets also stands out, underscoring God's direction of events, especially as Paul nowhere else refers to the prophets as "his" (i.e., God's).[14] Nor does Paul use the expression "holy Scriptures" elsewhere, customarily referring simply to "Scripture" (as in Rom 4:3; 1 Cor 15:3–4; Gal 3:8, 22). The adjective "holy" may serve to reinforce the promise as coming from God; it is not the prophets or even Scripture itself that makes promises about God's gospel, but the God who is served by both.

The more difficult question is what Paul intends when he says that God's promise of the gospel may be found in Scripture. As is the case also in 1 Cor 15:3–4, nothing here ties the promise to a particular text or section of Scripture. Instead, the force of the statement is to connect God's promise to agents (the prophets) and sources (Scripture) that are recognized as reliable. This unusually full reference to Scripture and prophetic agency anticipates the content of the letter to follow, since Paul draws on Scripture more extensively and explicitly in Romans than in any other of his letters. This early description of the gospel as previously promised in Scripture underscores the relationship between what God has already done and what God is even now revealing, but that is not to say that the gospel is "in complete continuity with God's earlier revelation to Israel" (Dunn 1:10). Certainly some of Paul's claims about Scripture would not have appeared to his fellow Jews to stand "in complete continuity," such as his claim that the "not my people" of Hos 2:25 referred to gentiles (Rom 9:25). Paul declares that the gospel was promised in advance, not that it was already explicated or understood or accomplished (similarly Calvin 15).

[3–4] "About his Son" resumes the phrase "for the gospel of God" at the end of v. 1 and identifies that gospel, authored and promised by God, with "his Son." The remainder of vv. 3–4 unpacks what it means to say that the gospel is about that Son, explicitly named at the end of v. 4 as "Jesus Christ our Lord." Paul may here employ an early creedal formula, although the extent, origin,

---

13. Romans 3:21 refers to "the law and the prophets," but that expression denotes sections of Scripture rather than its human agents (as also in Matt 5:17; Luke 16:16; Acts 13:15; 24:14). Note also Rom 16:26.

14. In Rom 11:3, however, Paul does cite 1 Kgs 19:10: "Lord, they have killed *your* prophets."

and function of the formula are by no means certain.[15] A number of expressions in these verses are not found elsewhere in Paul's undisputed letters: the identification of Jesus as David's offspring, the verb *horizein* ("publicly identified"), and the phrase *pneuma hagiōsynēs* ("spirit of God's own holiness"). Another unusual feature is the absence of reference to the death of Jesus, since Paul typically refers to Jesus's death when he summarizes the gospel (e.g., Rom 4:25; 1 Thess 4:14; 1 Cor 15:3–4). In addition, the parallel expressions are thought to reflect the careful composition characteristic of liturgical texts:

who came (*tou genomenou*)	considered physically (*kata sarka*)
who was publicly identified (*tou horisthentos*)	considered in terms of the spirit of God's own holiness (*kata pneuma hagiōsynēs*)

Paul may well be employing shared Christian language here, but the case for a pre-Pauline creedal formulation is not as strong as is often assumed. If Paul does not elsewhere connect Jesus with the Davidic line, he does identify him as a physical descendant of Israel (Rom 9:5; and see Gal 4:4). Paul does not elsewhere use the verb *horizein*, but he uses the closely related *proorizein* in Rom 8:29–30 (and see 1 Cor 2:7). And notice that there are unusual expressions also in v. 2 ("*his* prophets" and "in *holy* Scriptures"). That a word or phrase is distinctive (even that there are several such unusual expressions in the same passage) does not require the conclusion that it originates elsewhere.

Closer examination also reveals some flaws in the identification of "parallel" expressions. Both phrases open with the combination of genitive article plus participle ("who came"; "who was publicly identified"), but the second has "Son of God" as its object ("who was publicly identified as Son of God"), while the first has no noun complement. To be sure, there are parallel *kata* phrases, but they are not parallel in meaning (as discussion below will clarify). Instead of drawing on and perhaps modifying an earlier creedal formulation, Paul appears to be crafting a definition of the gospel, incorporating some expressions he anticipates will be familiar to the Roman congregations, and anticipating explication of the summary in vv. 16–17 and much more elaborately in the body of the letter to follow (Calhoun 2011, 85–142).

The summary opens with the assertion that God's Son "came from David's lineage, considered physically." As noted earlier, this is an unusual statement in the context of Paul's letters. David's name appears only two other times in the Pauline corpus (Rom 4:6; 11:9), and in both instances David appears as a speaker of Scripture rather than a progenitor. Specifics of Jesus's biography are likewise rare

---

15. On the formula, see Schlier 23–25, Dunn 1:5–6, Jewett 97–98, 103–4. The latter discussion summarizes the more extended review of the debate in Jewett 1985.

(Rom 9:5; Gal 4:4). Associating Jesus with the Davidic line is not at all unusual in other NT writings (e.g., Matt 1:6; Luke 1:27; John 7:42; 2 Tim 2:8; Rev 22:16), however, where it reflects a strand of Jewish expectation that God would send Israel a savior from the line of King David (as in Isa 11:1, 10; Jer 23:5–6; 33:14–18; Ezek 34:23–24; 37:24–28; Pss. Sol. 17.21; 4QFlor 1.10–13; 4QpGen[a]49).

The parallel phrases concerning "flesh" ("physically" in my translation) and "spirit" prompt some interpreters to play these two phrases off against each another, understanding them as referring to the humanity and divinity of Jesus respectively (e.g., Calvin 15–16; Hodge 7). Occasionally, the further suggestion is made that the words "according to the flesh" carry a negative connotation (so Dunn 1:13). Yet Paul never elsewhere distinguishes between a human Jesus who lived and worked in Galilee and Judea and a divine Jesus who rose from the dead. Further, the suggestion that the two phrases have contrasting connotations assumes that *kata sarka* and *kata pneuma* function analogously to their use in Rom 8:4–5, where Paul contrasts living in a way that conforms to the flesh (i.e., merely human standards) with living in a way that conforms to the spirit (cf. Gal 5:16–21). But Romans 1 does not refer to human action or thought that is "fleshly" or "spiritual." Instead, the two phrases underscore and intensify what has already been said. That Jesus is from David's lineage already establishes that he is a biological descendant of David. The phrase *kata sarka* ("physically") intensifies the connection between Christ Jesus and the royal line of David, the line historically associated with God's eschatological intervention on Israel's behalf.

Verse 4 makes a second claim about Christ Jesus, one that extends the traditional promise about the royal offspring of David in a cosmic direction. Almost every word in this verse challenges interpreters, either because of inherent ambiguity (e.g., does "in power" modify the verb "identified" or the title "Son of God"?) or because of their distinctiveness in Paul's letters. Although some observations about individual expressions are necessary, the force of this statement only emerges by taking the whole of it into account, culminating as it does with the resurrection. Because of the emphasis on Jesus's descent from David in v. 3, it is understandable that interpreters have regarded the two statements as contrasting two ways of conveying Jesus's status (Augustine 59; Luther 5) or as indicating a change in Jesus's status. Verse 4 is then read as implying that the resurrection made Jesus into something "he was not before," or that he "took on a role which was not previously his" (Dunn 1:14). Yet a change of status ill fits with Paul's language elsewhere; as already noted, the letters do not distinguish between Jesus as a historical figure and Jesus following the resurrection. His discussion of the resurrection always has to do with the intrusion of God's power as a harbinger of God's final triumph (as in 1 Cor 15), not with some change in Jesus's status or role.[16] The reference to the exaltation of Jesus ("at

16. One possible exception appears in Phil 2:9–11, but that language is of exaltation rather than of resurrection.

God's right hand") in Rom 8:34 may provide a helpful clue to the interpretation of v. 4; that is, 1:4 also implies Jesus's triumphant accession to the right hand of God, awaiting the completion of God's cosmic triumph.

To summarize, vv. 3b and 4 are not in conflict with one another. Neither are they separable stages in Jesus's existence. Verse 4 interprets what the kingship of Jesus looks like, which is later developed in the "reign" of grace in 5:21 and in the reference to the kingdom of God in 14:17.

The verse's claim about the cosmic consequences of Jesus's resurrection opens with the phrase *tou horisthentos huiou theou,* "publicly identified as Son of God." Since Paul does not use *horizein* elsewhere, discerning the particular nuance of the verb becomes a challenge (although see the related *prohorizein* in 8:30). Luke uses it twice of Jesus, both times in kerygmatic speeches and both times closely connected with the resurrection (Acts 10:42; 17:31). There, as here, the implication seems to be that the resurrection demonstrates something about Jesus rather than that the resurrection brings about a change in Jesus. Consistent with that understanding, Chrysostom explains that the verb means "being shown, being manifested, being judged, being confessed" (*Hom. Rom.* 1.4; *NPNF*[1] 11.340).

One further indication that *tou horisthentos* implies no change of status or ontology (much less an early form of adoptionism) is that the title "Son of God" is already conveyed in the introduction (so Cranfield 1:58). By introducing this entire summary of the gospel with the phrase "about his Son" and concluding it with "Jesus Christ our Lord," Paul suggests that the formula has to do with what human beings are able to acknowledge about the gospel, rather than with stages in the development of Jesus Christ.

The public identification of Jesus Christ as God's Son is said to be *en dynamei,* "in power." It is grammatically possible that "in power" modifies the verb *horisthentos* (i.e., "identified powerfully" or "designated powerfully"), but the context requires that the phrase "in power" modifies "Son of God" rather than "identified." The question is not about the nature of the identifying act (whether or not it is powerful), but the identification of Jesus Christ's own power. What is asserted here is that Jesus is "Son of God in power." Language of power and discourses involving power figure importantly in Romans, where the question of who is really in charge of the cosmos is either in plain sight or just beneath the surface. In a few lines, Paul will identify the gospel with God's own power (1:16; and see 1:20; 9:17; 15:13, 19), a statement that sets the agenda for the entire letter. That Jesus Christ partakes of divine power proves crucial, since there are other powers that threaten to undermine humanity, seeking to separate humanity from its rightful Lord (8:38–39; Gaventa 2022c).

The two phrases that follow intensify the identification of Jesus as God's Son in power. My translation ("considered in terms of the spirit of God's own holiness") aims at the general sense of the terse literal expression "according to a spirit of holiness." The phrase *pneuma hagiōsynēs* has been found in only two other places. In T. Levi 18.11 the phrase appears among the blessings that characterize humanity when redeemed from oppression. In an amulet from the second or third century CE, it refers to the divine glory or divine presence (Kotansky 1994, 126–54).

Without the term *pneuma* ("spirit"), the noun *hagiōsynēs* ("holiness") refers to God's own holiness in Pss 30:4 (29:5 LXX); 96:6 (95:6 LXX); 97:12 (96:12 LXX); and 144:5; otherwise it appears only in 2 Macc 3:12 in reference to the holiness of the temple. Given the frequency of language in the prescript that intensifies Paul's claims, "spirit of holiness" likely serves to emphasize the sacred character of this powerful Son of God. In that sense, it loosely parallels the emphatic function of the earlier *kata sarka* phrase in v. 3: just as Jesus Christ is genuinely from David's family line, he is also genuinely God's powerful Son.

In order to grasp the import of the phrase regarding holiness, it must be taken together with the one that follows: "at his resurrection from the dead." This holy, powerful Son of God is publicly identified as such from God's act in the resurrection. The expression *ex anastaseōs nekrōn* ("at the resurrection of the dead" [pl.]) occurs nowhere else in Paul. In 1 Cor 15, however, Paul several times employs the phrase "resurrection of the dead" (*anastaseōs nekrōn*) without the addition of the preposition (1 Cor 15:12, 13, 21, 42). Consistent with his usage there (and see Acts 26:23), Paul appears to have in mind not only the fact of Jesus's own resurrection, but Jesus's resurrection as the inauguration of the general resurrection that signals God's final triumph over all God's enemies (see Rom 8:38–39; 1 Cor 15:27–28). The Greek leaves unclear whether the preposition *ek* designates the time of the resurrection (i.e., since the time when it happened) or whether it designates the resurrection as the cause of Jesus's powerful and public identification (i.e., because it happened). Since time and cause are inextricable, however, I prefer "at" as a way of signaling the pivotal character of that occasion,

The summary culminates with the words "Jesus Christ our Lord," which stand in apposition to "his Son" at the beginning of v. 3. Together those two designations enclose the identifying expansions in vv. 3–4. That Jesus Christ is "our Lord" is axiomatic in Paul (Rom 4:24; 5:1, 11, 21; 7:25; 15:6; 16:20; and often elsewhere), yet its frequency does not suggest that it is mere formula, here or elsewhere. The affirmation that Jesus Christ descended from David as the fulfillment of promises and that Jesus Christ is God's powerful Son, sign of God's victory over Death itself, does not remove Jesus from human life; on the contrary, the affirmation acknowledges him as Lord of human life (as in Phil 2:5–11).

Taken as a whole, vv. 3b–4 constitute a terse and allusive summary of the gospel. Some of the phrases would be familiar to Roman Christians, who know of David and the work of the spirit and the resurrection. They could not, however, anticipate how Paul would develop these terms in the letter that follows.

[5–6] Although Paul now turns (or, perhaps more accurately, returns) to what he and others have received, Jesus Christ remains the actor in v. 5. Both "through whom," which links v. 5 with what precedes, and "we received" point away from human initiative and toward Christ. Since the opening words of v. 1 identify Paul alone as the writer of the letter (by contrast to Paul's other letters; e.g., 1 Cor 1:1; 2 Cor 1:1; Gal 1:2; Phil 1:1; 1 Thess 1:2; Phlm 1), it is striking that he shifts briefly to first-person plural, perhaps anticipating the plural "all" introduced and repeated in vv. 5, 7, and 8.

What "we received" is "grace and apostleship" (v. 5). "Grace" (*charis*) encompasses all that Paul has written since he introduced the expression "the gospel of God" in v. 1; all that God has done both in the past and particularly in the Son constitutes grace. Similarly, in 6:14–15 Paul will speak of people being "under grace," a shorthand way of referring to the grasp of the gospel, humanity as delivered from the tyranny of Sin and Death (see further below on v. 7). The extent to which this gift is made independent of human deserving is not yet clear, as it will become later in the letter.

"Apostleship" likewise reaches back to v. 1, explicitly recalling Paul's self-identification as "called to be an apostle." Interpreters regularly suggest that the words "grace" and "apostleship" comprise a hendiadys in v. 5, so that they constitute a single concept, "the grace of apostleship," instead of standing as coordinated nouns (e.g., Cranfield 1:65–66; Fitzmyer 237; although see Schlier 28). My translation distinguishes them, because apostleship is not the only manifestation of grace to which Paul has referred in these verses. Nevertheless, these are not distinct events for Paul; he cannot reflect first on the arrival of the gospel and then on his own vocation (see Gal 1:11–17; Phil 3:2–11). The calling to faith and the calling to apostleship are inseparable, just as the measuring out of faith and the distribution of gifts are inseparable (Rom 12:3, 6).

"Grace and apostleship," then, encapsulates vv. 1–4, but the phrase is more than recollection and celebration. It points ahead to the activity described in the remainder of the verse: "the obedience that comes from faith," "among all the gentiles," and "for the sake of his name." "The obedience that comes from faith" (*hypakoē pisteōs*) is a striking phrase, one that might be rendered "the obedience that springs from faith" or "the obedience which is faith" (Dunn 1:17–18; Fitzmyer 237; Moo 448–51). In Paul's letters *hypakoē* has less to do with conforming behavior to a specific command or set of commands or even a standard than it does with living in a way that is coherent with one's allegiance or location. The several instances of obedience language in Romans 6 bring this point to expression, as obedience is assumed to be coordinated with lordship, whether the lordship is that of Sin or that of God in the gospel (6:15–23). "The obedience that comes from faith," then, is behavior that reflects the realm of faith—not in an abstract sense of believing as opposed to doing, but faith, reliance, and trust in the gospel of Jesus Christ, from which conduct springs.

Paul's apostleship, therefore, involves cultivating this integrity of life in the realm of the gospel "among all the gentiles." Literally what Paul writes is "among all the nations," but the translation "gentiles" reflects the fact that this is a conventional Jewish designation for non-Jews (as in, e.g., Matt 6:32; Mark 10:42; Acts 11:1, 18). Paul's use of this "insider" term raises interesting questions about how it is heard by the Roman audiences that undoubtedly contain gentiles—indeed, likely a majority of gentiles (see the introduction and on 16:3–16). A number of these gentiles may be former "Godfearers" who are presumably familiar with this "outsider" label.[17] Galatians 1–2 explicitly identifies Paul's vocation with taking the gospel to the gentiles (see also Rom 15:16), however much that specification may collide with stories in Acts in which Paul repeatedly preaches in synagogues (e.g., 13:13–16; 14:1; 17:1–2, 17). The "all" deserves notice, since it returns in vv. 7 and 8, as well as often in the chapters that follow (e.g., Rom 2:1, 9, 10; 3:4, 9, 12, 19, 20, 22, 23). Paul is writing to a specific group of people who have been overtaken by the gospel of Jesus Christ, but the gospel is not for them alone.

"For the sake of his name" points to the doxological goal of apostleship. Not only is apostleship received as a gift from Jesus Christ ("through whom we received"), but it also returns to him. Paul's letters seldom refer to the "name" of anyone apart from God or Jesus (2:24; 9:17; 10:13; 15:9), a fact that is unsurprising in a context where the "name" somehow embodies the person, where Jesus's name itself conveys miraculous healing (as in Acts 3:6, 16) and is invoked at baptism (as in Matt 28:19; Acts 2:38; 10:48). Labor "for the sake [or on behalf] of his name," then, is not simply a matter of enhancing Jesus's honor or reputation but acknowledges the transcendent power of God (compare Phil 2:9–11). This is no trivial point in Romans, where withholding praise from God is a prime symptom of humanity's enslavement to Sin and Death and where the culmination of God's triumph is associated with praise of the name (15:9; see Gaventa 2008a).

Grammatically, v. 6 continues the identification of the letter writer, since "among whom you also are called" specifies the gentiles of v. 5, who are themselves recipients of the gospel for which Paul was set apart (v. 1). The transition to the letter recipients takes place only at the beginning of v. 7. Those who contend that the audience of the letter consists only of gentiles emphasize this phrase, but that notion overinterprets Paul's wording. The stress here falls on the end of the verse, with its emphatic "you also" identified as "called to belong to Jesus Christ." Paul understands that all Christians are such because

---

17. Despite controversy about whether the term "Godfearer" was employed in the first century, there seems little doubt that some gentiles in Rome frequented synagogues and identified themselves with Jewish life. On the attractiveness of Judaism in the city of Rome, see Barclay 1996b, 282–319.

of a summons from outside themselves; they do not so much "decide" as they are "decided upon" (see, e.g., 8:30; 1 Cor 1:9; 1 Thess 2:12).

[7] With v. 7 Paul turns at last to address the audience, which consists of "all of God's beloved who are in Rome." A glance at other prescripts reveals several distinctive features of this way of addressing the Romans. Paul does not refer to this audience with the word "assembly" or "church" (*ekklēsia*), as regularly in other greetings except in Phil 1:1; instead, he opens the prescript with "all" (*pasin*), which is not used in this way in other prescripts.[18] Although Paul frequently addresses his audiences as "beloved" or "my beloved" (e.g., Rom 12:19; 1 Cor 4:14; 2 Cor 7:1), only here does he identify an audience as "God's beloved." Concluding the identification of the Romans is the phrase "called to be holy people," reinforcing the call language of vv. 1 and 6 and once again the divine action of calling these holy people into being. The Romans do not become holy out of their own resources any more than Paul becomes an apostle by his own initiative.

Although brief by comparison with the preceding elements of the prescript, the distinctiveness of this identification of the addressees prompts some observations. The relative fullness of the identification may simply reflect the fact that Paul is unknown to these Christians and wishes to acknowledge, from the very beginning, his awareness of what God has done in their midst. Yet the absence of the word *ekklēsia*, coupled with the presence of *pas,* may hint at another feature of Christianity at Rome, namely, the existence of several gatherings instead of a single congregation (note the reference in 16:5 to the church in Prisca and Aquila's residence). Further, those gatherings may be divided in more than a geographical sense, so that the repetition of "all" serves rhetorically to draw them together.

The words that bring the prescript to a close, "grace and peace," appear in all of Paul's letters, replacing the term "greetings" (*chairein*), which was ubiquitous in ancient Greek letters (as in Acts 15:23; 23:26; Jas 1:1). Each word recurs importantly in the letter. Paul has already referred to the reception of grace, and grace emerges significantly in ch. 3, when Paul will explain how God's free action in the death of Jesus brings about the liberation of humanity. In chs. 5–6 Paul treats it as a metonym for God's action in Jesus (as in 5:20; 6:1, 14–15). Peace with God serves in 5:1 to signal humanity's release from hostile powers and restoration to the rightful lordship of God (and see 2:10; 8:6; 14:17, 19; 15:13). So important is peace that Paul names God "the God of peace" in the letter's closing lines (16:20). The grace and peace extended here to the congregations at Rome originate not with Paul but with God and Jesus Christ.

These opening verses play a highly conventional role in ancient letters. To say that the prescript merely identifies Paul as letter writer and some residents of

---

18. The word *pas* ("all") does appear in 1 Cor 1:2 and in 2 Cor 1:1, but the usage differs, since in those cases the word links believers in Corinth with those outside Corinth and does not refer to the Corinthians themselves.

the city of Rome as his audience would be a considerable distortion, however, since the prescript in Romans repeatedly points in the direction of God's initiative as the one who calls, who promises, and who sends. In other words, Paul is not locating his authority as apostle within himself but within the gospel. In the center of this prescript he includes a summary of the gospel, at least elements of which are familiar to the Roman auditors. Already in these lines the cosmic scope of the gospel comes into view: it is discerned in God's promise long ago, it extends to all the nations, and it concerns power, even to the extent of power that raises the dead.

1:8–12 The Thanksgiving

The letter opened with the ancient convention of the prescript, although in a protracted form, and convention continues with the thanksgiving. Most of Paul's letters include a thanksgiving, with the exceptions of 2 Corinthians, which employs the form of blessing instead, and Galatians, which notoriously omits the thanksgiving altogether. Curiously, the thanksgiving in Romans contains little detail about the addressees, as Paul moves quickly from a single statement about them (v. 8) to an extended statement of his long-standing desire to be with them (vv. 9–12; cf. 1 Cor 1:3–8 and Phil 1:3–11). What comes to expression here is Paul's concern for the well-being of the Romans in the gospel and his sense of responsibility before God for that well-being, rather than a recollection of the gifts or accomplishments of the audience.

Verse 8 clearly marks the opening of the thanksgiving, but identifying its conclusion is challenging because the statements that follow connect tightly with one another. Many analyses understand the thanksgiving to consist of vv. 8–15, with vv. 16–17 set apart as the introduction of the letter's theme (e.g., Käsemann 16–17; Jervis 1991, 89–90; Moo 31). Separating vv. 16–17 out as a distinct unit is highly problematic, however, since Paul's other letters do not begin with a thesis statement. More important, it is difficult to imagine that three statements connected only by the repeated word *gar* ("for" or "because") constitute an independent unit (see especially Holmstrand 1997, 14). Other analyses of Romans identify the thanksgiving and theme as a single unit that runs through v. 17, marking v. 18 as the beginning of the letter body (e.g., Stuhlmacher 14; Byrne 47–48). Yet the statement about God's wrath in v. 18 follows directly on the end of v. 17, resulting in parallel announcements of the revelation of God's righteousness and God's wrath; more to the point, it is hard to justify excluding vv. 16–17 from the body of the letter, and the content of v. 18 is scarcely satisfying as an introduction to the argument of the letter.

Rather than identify the unit as either vv. 8–15 or 8–17, I have marked its conclusion as v. 12 and identified v. 13 as opening the body of the letter. The body begins with a disclosure formula ("Now I do not want you to be uninformed . . .") similar to those appearing in 2 Cor 1:8 and Phil 1:12 (see further below on 1:13 as the introduction to the body of the letter). As in other thanksgivings, Paul here hints at concerns he will address in the letter that follows (Schubert 1939, 24, 27). Those concerns include the faith of the Roman Christians, its implications for the whole world, and the strengthening required of all of them in anticipation of God's final triumph. When the body of the letter opens in vv. 13–17, Paul will return to these concerns more explicitly.

1:8 To begin with,[a] I thank my God through Jesus Christ concerning all of you, because your faith is announced in the whole world. 9 God is my witness—God whom I worship in my spirit, in the gospel of his Son—how I remember you constantly. 10 Always[b] in my prayers I plead that, if possible, now finally I might succeed, by God's will, in coming to you, 11 because I long to see you, so that I can share with you a spiritual gift for your strengthening. 12 What I mean is this: so that I can be comforted along with you through our mutual faith, both yours and mine.

a. Lit., *prōton men* is "first, on the one hand," suggesting that a series of points will be enumerated, but in this case no series follows. Instead, the usage in v. 8 is classical, meaning "from the very outset" or "of first importance" (BDF §232). Paul employs the same expression in Rom 3:2 and in 1 Cor 11:18.

b. *Pantote* ("always") may modify either "I plead," as in the translation above, or "I remember." The decision is insignificant, since Paul's pleading and calling to mind are one and the same action: he remembers them as he prays to be able to be with them. I have connected "always" to "I plead" simply because there is already an adverb of time in v. 9 modifying "I remember."

[1:8] Following the transitional phrase "to begin with" (*prōton men*), the opening words of the thanksgiving repeat exactly the thanksgivings of 1 Corinthians, Philippians, and Philemon: "I thank my God."[19] More than habit is at work here. The personal pronoun "my" reaffirms Paul's earlier claims of being bound to God (see on 1:1); it also introduces a series of such references: "my God," "my witness," "my spirit," "my prayers." This personal language stands alongside numerous second-person plurals: "all of you," "your faith," "remember you," "coming to you," "long to see you," "share with you," "your strengthening," "with you," "yours" (of faith).[20] Rhetorically Paul is beginning to draw the Roman auditors alongside himself as shared recipients of the gospel's power (1:16–17).

Paul thanks God "through Jesus Christ" (*dia*), using a phrase that compactly calls up the whole of God's actions in the death and resurrection of Jesus. This

19. 1 Thessalonians 1:2 is cast in the first-person plural: "We thank God . . ." Some roughly contemporaneous letters similarly begin with thanks to the gods; see 2 Macc 1:10–2:18; the First Letter of Apion (BGU II 423); P Lond. I 42; UPZ I 60,5–8; BGU XIV 2418, 2–10; SB VI 9017 Nr. 23,2; see Arzt 1994; Klauck 2006, 9–14, 267–70.

20. Jewett (117–18) notes the "carefully developed" "interplay" of personal pronouns in these lines.

is not only a mediatorial role (contra Dunn 1:28; Hultgren 63). Instead, God is thanked through the entire event of Jesus Christ. Similarly, Paul will later write: "in the same way grace might rule as king through righteousness . . . through Jesus Christ our Lord" (5:21). Jesus Christ is not simply an instrument of the workings of "grace" or "righteousness"; his death and resurrection becomes the event as a result of which grace and righteousness triumph over the powers of Sin and Death.[21]

The remainder of the verse tersely states the cause of Paul's thanksgiving. First, he gives thanks "concerning all of you." A phrase identical to this one opens the thanksgiving of 1 Thessalonians, and Phil 1:4 differs only in its preposition (*hyper* instead of *peri*). The presence of "all" here anticipates a significant thread in the letter. Paul has already written of "all the gentiles" (v. 5) and "all of God's beloved who are in Rome" (v. 7), and he will frequently in the letter refer to "all" people or "everyone" (as in, e.g., 2:9–10; 3:4, 9, 12, 19–23; 5:12, 18; 10:11–13; 11:32). Given the fragmentation of Roman Christians into multiple small gatherings separated not only by the realities of urban life but also perhaps by convictions and practices (see the introduction; 14:1–15:6), this repetition brings together rhetorically what is not together in fact.

Paul goes on to specify that their "faith is announced in the whole world." "Faith" (*pistis*) stands unqualified, leaving it unclear whether Paul refers simply to the fact of their faith or to some particular qualities or characteristics of their faith. The absence of such remarks indicates that Paul refers simply to the beginning of faith (as in "when we began to believe," 13:11) rather than to its quality, especially since other thanksgivings do remark on particular aspects of the community's faith (1 Cor 1:4–8; Phil 1:3–6; 1 Thess 1:2–5). (Verse 15 will underscore this possibility.)

The "entire world" (*en holō tō kosmō*) knows of faith at Rome. Here some hyperbole is involved, not unlike that of the evangelists who report that "all" of Jerusalem and Judea went out to be baptized by John the Baptist (Matt 3:5; Mark 1:5). In an earlier letter, Paul reports that "all" believers in the geographic regions of Macedonia and Achaia know about developments in Thessalonica (1 Thess 1:7), but here nothing less than the whole world is watching. In 1 Corinthians, the "world" sometimes carries negative connotations, characterized by corrupt epistemology and immorality (e.g., 1:20–21; 5:1), and it is to be avoided by believers (7:31; E. Adams 2000). In Romans, however, the "world" is the whole of humanity (as in 3:6, 19; 5:12–13; 11:12, 15).

More can be said, however. Paul might have referred to the whole of humanity with the term *oikoumenē*, which Luke uses in similar contexts. Caesar's census requires the participation of the whole *oikoumenē* (Luke 2:1; and

---

21. A similarly expanded notion of the phrase "through Jesus Christ" seems to be at work in Rom 7:25; Phil 1:1; 2 Cor 5:18 ("through Christ"); see also Rom 2:16; [16:27]; Gal 1:1; Phil 1:11.

see also, e.g., 4:5; 21:26; Acts 11:28). Josephus similarly identifies Cyrus as God's appointed king over the *oikoumenē* (*Ant.* 11.3) and the Romans as "lords of the *oikoumenē*" (*Ag. Ap.* 2.41; see also *Ant.* 19.193; *J.W.* 4.656). When Paul refers to the whole human population, however, he emphasizes not its existence under particular human rulers but its creation by God. At the outset of the letter body, he will contend that human beings knew of God from "the creation of the cosmos [*kosmos*]" (1:19–20). Abraham and his heirs receive the promise of inheriting the *kosmos* from the God who "calls into being that which does not exist" (4:13, 17; Gaventa 2011a, 266–69).

This claim about the widespread awareness of faith at Rome flatters the audience, to be sure, but this is more than an instance of *captatio benevolentiae*. Later in the letter Paul will contend that the faith of the gentiles plays a role in God's salvation of Israel (11:11–12); further, 15:22–24 and 30–32 seek the support of Roman Christians for Paul's reception in Jerusalem and his eventual work in Spain. What happens in Rome is important not primarily because of the power and status of this capital city, but because these communities may be a catalyst for Paul's work elsewhere, notably in Jerusalem and in Spain. The use of the verb *katangellō* ("announce") elsewhere reinforces this point, since in Paul's letters the gospel itself is the object of announcement (as in 1 Cor 2:1; 9:14; 11:26; Phil 1:17–18).

Formally, the thanksgiving continues through v. 12, but nothing more is said about the Romans themselves, as vv. 9–12 will turn to Paul's desire to be in Rome. The brevity of comment about Christians at Rome stands out in contrast with other letters. The Thessalonians, for example, Paul praises for their "work of faith and labor of love and endurance of hope" and for their mimetic reception of the gospel (1 Thess 1:3, 6), as well as for the way in which their own faith served as proclamation (1 Thess 1:7–10). Even the Corinthians, who later receive sharp reprimands, he initially praises for their spiritual gifts (1 Cor 1:4–8). The fact that Paul has not yet been to Rome does not altogether account for this relative brevity, since the greetings of 16:3–16 suggest at least some awareness of the constituency and the leadership of Roman congregations. To the contrary, if Paul's knowledge of Roman Christians is limited, it would seem all the more important to draw attention to their strengths by way of inaugurating the relationship and securing a sympathetic hearing for the letter that follows. Paul works to gain their favorable attention in other ways (the interweaving of personal pronouns noted above and the effusive claims of vv. 9–12 about his desire to be with them). The brevity of reference to Roman Christianity, alongside the absence of the term *ekklēsia* (see above on v. 7), may indicate that Paul has concerns he must introduce with some delicacy.

[9–10] As the subject shifts to Paul's ardent desire to be in Rome, the language intensifies. The reiteration of this longing in 15:22–24, where Paul announces his plan to go first to Jerusalem and then to Rome before traveling to Spain, prompts the suspicion that he has some genuine concern about the situation at Rome. First, he solemnly calls upon God as witness to the statement that is to follow (Novenson 2022). By contrast with some other NT texts in which the notion of witnessing plays an important role (e.g., Acts 1:8; John 1:7, 19; Rev 1:5), Paul seldom uses the word *martys* ("witness"), and when he does it most often involves the witness of God regarding Paul's apostolic activity. Philippians 1:8, as here, concerns Paul's desire to be in Philippi (similarly 2 Cor 1:23). First Thessalonians 2:5 and 10 invoke God's corroboration of the integrity of the work Paul and his colleagues carried out in Thessalonica.[22]

Paul amplifies his claim about God's witness with an unusual addition characterizing God as the one "I worship [*latreuō*] in my spirit, in the gospel of his Son." The verb *latreuō* conveys something more specific than the rather vague translation "serve" found in NRSVue, NIV, NASB, and elsewhere. In a range of texts it specifically refers to liturgical service.[23] In addition, in 15:16 Paul describes himself as a priestly servant (*leitourgos*) of Christ Jesus. Such language scarcely restricts Paul's role; on the contrary, it interprets his apostolic labor as a kind of worship.

Yet worship is not simply an apostolic function; it pertains to all human beings. The question of who or what is worshiped returns powerfully later in this chapter, where Paul castigates humanity for its service of things that are created instead of serving the Creator (again *latreuō,* 1:25). And in 12:1 he urges the reasonable service (*latreia*) of God (see also 9:4; 15:27). In those instances, as with the self-reference here, worship has to do with the reverence for God that expresses itself in right conduct, and with right conduct that reflects genuine reverence for God (see further on 1:18–32 and 12:1–2).

Two brief prepositional phrases further identify this worship. It is both "in my spirit" and "in the gospel of his Son." Elsewhere Paul speaks of those "[who] are the circumcision, *who serve God in spirit* and have confidence in Christ Jesus" (Phil 3:3), but the addition of "my" is distinctive to Rom 1:9. The fact that Paul has just in the preceding lines offered thanks to "my God" and called on God as "my witness," and that he will next refer to "my prayers" and "my faith," at least raises the possibility that "my" here largely serves to underscore the importance of the utterance.

Paul's service is also "in the gospel of his Son," a qualifying phrase that recalls once again the opening words of the letter and their relentless focus on Paul's obligation to the gospel (and see vv. 14–15 below). Because the phrase does not introduce anything new by way of content, its presence is largely for

---

22. Only in 2 Cor 13:1 is there a "witness" other than God, and that occurs in a citation from Deut 19:15.

23. E.g., Exod 3:12; Deut 10:12; Matt 4:10; Luke 2:37; Heb 9:9; Rev 7:15; Philo, *Migration* 132; Plutarch, *Mor.* 405C.

emphasis. It reveals just how seriously Paul takes the assertion he is about to make regarding his prayers to be in Rome. The significance of prayer for Paul's work he reiterates at the end of the letter, when he asks the Romans to "contend along with" him in prayer for his rescue and the reception of the collection in Jerusalem ("my ministry/service," 15:30–31).

With the remainder of vv. 9–10, Paul reaches the assertions he has been anticipating by his invocation of God: he constantly remembers the Romans in prayer. Specifically, he always prays that he may finally succeed in reaching them. The language of unceasing memory and prayer recalls Phil 1:3–4 and 1 Thess 1:2–3. What follows in v. 10 is a bit awkward syntactically, since it combines two idioms, *ei pōs* ("if possible" or "perhaps") with *ēdē pote* ("now finally" or "now at length"). The additional stipulation that Paul's travel plans rest on the will of God clarifies the reason for uncertainty: Paul is not in charge of his own apostolic agenda. Elsewhere he stipulates that Satan interfered with his travel plans (1 Thess 2:18), or that he reconsidered them because of difficulties (2 Cor 2:1), but here God's will alone is cited. Since Paul returns in chapter 15 to his desire to be in Rome and there outlines his plans in more detail, it is easy to imagine that he has been criticized for not having already traveled to this capital of the *kosmos*. Nonetheless, even with the relative ease of travel in the Roman Empire, a journey of this sort was not undertaken lightly, and it is somewhat difficult to understand why Roman Christians would think Paul obligated to make them a travel priority. (Indeed, it may be that some of them did not imagine themselves in need of instruction from Paul or anyone else.) This emphasis on his desire to be in Rome may not so much sound an apologetic note as underscore Rome's importance for the next stage of Paul's labor.

[11–12] The thanksgiving concludes with an explanation of Paul's hope for his time in Rome, first stated in terms of what he hopes to bestow (v. 11), and then in terms of what he hopes he and the Roman Christians might share with one another (v. 12). Because v. 12 begins with *touto de estin* ("what I mean is this"), it can be read as a correction of v. 11, even a sort of embarrassed reformulation, which Paul hastily offers for fear of being perceived as overbearing or presumptuous (so, e.g., Dunn 1:35). That interpretation does not consider the probability that Paul's letter, dictated to Tertius (16:22), was almost certainly corrected and copied at least once (Richards 2004, 25, 31, 43, 55–56, 82–84) before it was handed over to Phoebe, the bearer and reader of the letter. Had Paul seriously regarded v. 11 as a kind of misstep, he would have recast it, particularly given the importance he attaches to the letter and the delicacy of his situation. He does not have the sort of relationship with Roman congregations that allows for mid-course correction.

If v. 11 is not a diplomatic mistake corrected by v. 12, then how do these two statements stand in relation to each another? Verse 11 opens by repeating Paul's desire to see the Romans, then offering as his reason that he wants to share a "spiritual gift" for their strengthening. Elsewhere in the letters such gifts (*charismata*) are depicted as being bestowed by God (e.g., Rom 6:23; 11:29; 12:6; 1 Cor 1:7); sharing here is scarcely a unilateral act in which Paul of his own will grants the Romans something they do not have. Instead, his sharing with them in a "spiritual gift" that is divinely granted contributes to their strengthening. Verse 12 amplifies this point, making it clear that in this way all of them, both Paul and the Romans, are comforted, but here the emphasis falls on what they have in common. The difficulty Paul faces is not anxiety about maintaining his own authority (contra Käsemann 19); the difficulty is that circumstances make it impossible for him to indicate further what his relationship is to these groups of believers.

The spiritual gift Paul anticipates is not specified, but the goal of that gift is named: it is their strengthening, their establishment. Isolated from its context, such strengthening would be a reference to internal life, either that of the individuals or that of the community. That connotation is not to be excluded, but it needs to be contextualized in light of the cosmic horizon of this letter. The verb *stērizō* ("strengthen") appears in a variety of early Christian texts concerned with the standing of believers in the face of eschatological conflict. As early as 1 Thess 3:2, Timothy's assignment in Thessalonica is to "strengthen" (*stērizō*) Christians against the likelihood of tribulation and the activity of the "tempter" (*ho peirazōn*, 3:5) in anticipation of the *parousia* (3:11–13). Second Thessalonians 3:3 similarly invokes the role of "the Lord" in strengthening (*stērizein*) believers and guarding them against "the evil one." The eschatological context for "strengthening" is explicit in Jas 5:8 and Rev 3:2. This eschatological concern recurs importantly in Rom 1:16 with Paul's claim about not being "ashamed" over the gospel, later in 8:31–39 with reassurance about God's protective role in the face of the powers that wish to separate humanity from its rightful Lord, and finally in 16:20 with the concluding declaration that God will crush Satan.

The language of 1:8–12, with its emphasis on God as witness, God's will, human faith, and the gospel, signals what lies ahead in this letter. Although not a systematic theology or dogmatics, Romans is nonetheless an explication of God's action in the gospel on behalf of the world. The energy with which Paul declares his desire to be in Rome further suggests that he regards this enlarged understanding of the gospel to be an urgent need at Rome where (as we shall see) the gospel has been reduced to gentile inclusion, even gentile inclusion at the expense of Jews.

Romans 1:13–4:25
God Acts to Reveal and Redeem

In the first section of the letter, Paul announces the gospel he will preach in Rome. The declaration in 1:16 identifies the gospel itself with God's saving power, before unpacking it as the apocalyptic revelation of God's righteousness (1:17) and God's wrath (1:18). The remainder of this section explores these claims about God's activity. Paul first shows how, from the vantage point of the "now time" in Jesus Christ, the predicament of both Jew and gentile comes into view: all are under the power of Sin (1:18–3:20). He then returns to his opening statement, this time explicating God's rectifying actions in the death of Jesus Christ (3:21–31). The all-encompassing character of both righteousness and wrath produces a distinctive vantage point on God's dealings with Abraham, whose encounter with God becomes a prototype for God's dealings with all, Jew and gentile alike (4:1–25).

1:13–17 To Proclaim God's Salvific Power

The body of the letter begins, marked by an introductory disclosure formula and familial language: "Now I do not want you to be uninformed, brothers and sisters." Paul's desire to travel to Rome takes on an explicit purpose having to do with his obligation to announce the gospel of God's saving power for all people. The extent of the gospel's reach (to Jew and gentile alike) here emerges as evidence of the power of the gospel itself. God's own righteousness is eschatologically revealed in the astonishing grasp of the gospel on a humanity that is differentiated but not divided.

1:13 Now I do not want you to be uninformed, brothers and sisters,[a] because many times I planned to come to you—and I was prevented until now—so that I might have some fruit also among you just as I have had among the rest of the gentiles, 14 Greeks as well as barbarians, wise as well as foolish.[b] I am under obligation 15 (thus my desire)[c] to proclaim the gospel to you in Rome.[d] 16 Because I am not ashamed of the gospel,[e] which is God's own power now bringing about salvation for everyone who believes, Jew first[f] as well as Greek. 17 Because God's righteousness is now being revealed apocalyptically in the gospel from faith to faith, as it stands written, "The righteous one[g] will live by faith."[h]

a. The Greek reads *adelphoi*, lit., "brothers." The translation "brothers and sisters" reflects the fact that Paul addresses both women and men in this letter, as is unambiguous in the individual greetings of ch. 16. Other ancient texts similarly refer to "brothers" in situations that include both men and women (BDAG, s.v. *adelphos*).

b. Most editions and translations place a full stop at the end of v. 13, but the translation above understands the series of pairs (Greeks and barbarians, wise and foolish) as explicating the phrase "the rest of the gentiles" in v. 13 (Thorsteinsson 2002; Gaventa 2009). Elsewhere Paul speaks of the necessity that drives his proclamation of the gospel (1 Cor 9:16), of the indebtedness of gentile believers to Jewish believers (Rom 15:27), and of the obligation to love (13:8). The notion that his apostolic labor is under obligation to gentiles (or Jews) does not occur elsewhere, however. Paul's obligation is to his vocation from God, as is clear especially in 1 Cor 9:16. Placing a full stop after *anoētos* instead of after *ethnesin* does create an asyndeton (*opheleitēs eimi* carries no conjunctive *gar* nor *de*), but an asyndeton also occurs with the customary placing of a full stop at the end of v. 13.

c. *Houtōs* ("thus") introduces the phrase *to kat' eme prothymon* ("my desire") as a consequence of Paul's obligation to preach the gospel.

d. The words "in Rome" are omitted by G, as earlier in 1:7. This is not an inherently important variant, but it does give evidence of an early attempt to read the letter as an address to the entire church instead of the church in one location.

e. Some manuscripts (D[2] K L P Ψ) add the words "of Christ" here, presumably influenced by Paul's usage elsewhere (Rom 15:19; 2 Cor 2:12; 9:13; Gal 1:7) and by earlier references to the gospel of God (1:1) and the gospel of his Son (1:9). *To euangelion* without the addition of "of Christ," however, is well attested (𝔓[26] ℵ A B C D* G). Most telling, it is easy to understand why a scribe would have supplied the words "of Christ" and difficult to imagine a reason for their omission.

f. *Prōton* ("first") is omitted by B G sa and Marcion, witnessing to the early impulse to erase this claim.

g. C inserts *mou* ("my") after "the righteous one," making the text conform to important LXX manuscripts.

h. The Greek word order creates a much-discussed ambiguity. Is this "The one who is righteous by faith will live" (so RSV, NET, CEV) or "The righteous one will live by faith" (so KJV, NIV, NRSVue)? Although neither option can be ruled out, had Paul been determined to invoke "the one who is righteous by faith," he could easily have done so by inserting an article before *ek pisteōs* or by altering the word order (Fitzmyer 265).

[1:13–14a] The opening words formally announce the transition away from the thanksgiving and into a new section of the letter (also see above on 1:8–12). To be sure, Paul reiterates his desire to visit Rome, but a similar overlap between thanksgiving and body opening appears in 2 Corinthians (affliction in 1:4, 6, 8) and in Philippians (imprisonment in 1:7, 13–14). In addition, the body of each of those letters also begins with a disclosure formula followed by "brothers and sisters" (note also 1 Cor 1:10):

Rom 1:13   Now I do not want you to be uninformed, brothers and sisters . . .
2 Cor 1:8   For we do not want you to be uninformed, brothers and isters . . .
Phil 1:12   Now I wish you to know, brothers and sisters . . .

The address of fellow believers as *adelphoi* ("brothers and sisters") is ubiquitous in Paul's letters (e.g., Rom 7:1; 12:1; 15:14; 1 Cor 12:1; 2 Cor 8:1; 13:11; Gal 3:15; 5:11; Phil 1:12; 3:1, 13; 1 Thess 1:4; see also Acts 1:16; 2:29; 3:17; 22:1; Jas 1:2, 16; 2 Pet 1:10). The use of this and other terminology drawn from the family ("mother" in Rom 16:13; "father" in 1 Cor 4:15) serves to bind together into a new family believers who may not have natural ties of kinship or ethnicity.

As often in Paul's letters, the disclosure formula calls attention to the importance of the statements that follow (e.g., Rom 11:25; 1 Thess 4:13; 1 Cor 10:1; 12:1; 2 Cor 1:8). What Paul highlights seems at first only a repetition of the preceding lines—he has wanted to come to Rome—but here new information enters the picture. Paul has actually made plans to come to them and has previously been prevented; at the close of the letter he will reinforce this point again by saying that he tried "many times" (*ta polla*; 15:22).

What motivates his plan is that he might have "fruit" among them as among the remainder of the gentiles. When ch. 15 returns to Paul's upcoming travel, "fruit" again appears, referring figuratively to the results of the fund Paul has been gathering for the poor in Jerusalem (15:28; and see Phil 4:17), and prompting speculation that the word here refers to assistance Paul hopes to receive from believers at Rome for his upcoming work in Spain (Jewett 80–91, 130). While that possibility cannot be ruled out as part of the "fruit" of Paul's labor, the word elsewhere appears in Paul's letters as the result that organically follows from some activity; for instance, Rom 6:21 asks about the "fruit" that the Romans previously had from their activity as Sin's slaves, and Gal 5:22 refers to the "fruit" of the Spirit (see also Phil 1:11). What makes the word "fruit" somewhat more ambiguous in v. 13 is that the text does not specify from what plant, so to speak, this produce comes. Probably Paul refers in a general way to the outcome of his own apostolic labor (as in Phil 1:22).

The scope of that labor comes to expression in the phrases that follow: "among you as among the rest of the gentiles, Greek as well as barbarian, wise as well as foolish" (vv. 13b–14). This is the second time Paul has located his audience among the gentiles of Rome (vv. 5–6). Although the language does not require the conclusion that the audience is composed entirely of gentiles, it is possible that many, if not most, Roman Christians are themselves gentiles. What is particularly intriguing about the use of the term is that Paul straightforwardly applies this distinctly *Jewish* term for *non-Jews* in a letter addressed to those same non-Jews. An analogous situation might be found in writing a letter to "you foreigners" or "you outsiders" (as noted above regarding v. 5).

One possibility is that this peculiarity emerges because Paul knows that the gentile believers in Rome come from the ranks of the *sebomenoi*; these people would be familiar with the synagogue and, at least to some extent, with its practices and traditions. (On the audience, see also the introduction and below on 16:3–23.)

The phrases "Greeks as well as barbarians" and "wise as well as foolish" unpack the term "gentiles" in ways that underscore the astonishing extent of the gospel's reach. The opposition of Greek and barbarian is standard in Greek and Latin texts of the educated elite, dividing the world between those who participate in Greco-Roman culture and those who do not (e.g., Plato, *Menex.* 242c–e; Dionysius of Halicarnassus, *Ant. Rom.* 1.89.1–4; Livy, *Ab urbe cond.* 31.29.12–15; Cicero, *Quint. fratr.* 1.27–28; Harrison 2020, 143–59). The word "barbarian" itself (*barbaroi*) derives from the sound Greeks heard when others spoke (Fitzmyer 250). The opposition of "wise and foolish" recasts the same division, since to Greeks "barbarians" would sound and seem to be foolish.

[14b–15] In the preceding sentences, Paul has reported on his constant prayer to be in Rome, his hope for mutual encouragement (vv. 11–12), and his goal of having some "fruit" from his work in Rome. With the end of v. 14, his goal becomes explicit: he is obligated to proclaim the gospel in Rome. His use of the verb *euangelizesthai* elsewhere concerns preaching to those who have not been grasped by the gospel, as when 1 Cor 15:1–2 recalls the terms on which Paul initially preached the gospel in Corinth or when Gal 4:13 recalls his former preaching even in a state of illness or incapacity (see also Rom 15:20; 1 Cor 1:17; 9:16; 1 Thess 2:9).[1] This is scarcely surprising, given that Paul's work was precisely the declaring of the gospel among those it had not reached, "planting" rather than "watering," as 1 Cor 3 puts it (and see Rom 15:20), but it is striking that the verb *euangelizesthai* never appears in contexts having to do with the ongoing nurture of believers. Given that pattern, the fact that Paul opens the letter with a forceful declaration that he is obliged to preach the gospel in Rome hints that he is not convinced the gospel has made its way into that city in full. At the close of the letter, Paul may assert his confidence about the Romans (15:14) and his resolution against preaching on the foundation of another (15:20), but those diplomatic comments come after he has already, in the body of the letter, begun the task of declaring the gospel in Rome.

Paul frames this task of proclamation as both obligation and desire. His letters consistently present his own apostolic labor as the result of God's disruption of a life set along another path (Gal 1:11–17; Phil 3:2–11). He was

---

1. This pattern is consistent with the use of the *euangel–* word group elsewhere, as argued by Dickson (e.g., Pausanias, *Descr.* 4.19.5; Plutarch, *Pomp.* 41.3; 66.3; Chariton, *Chaer.* 8.2.5; Aristophanes, *Eq.* 643–647; Philo, *Joseph* 245; Josephus, *J.W.* 4.618, 656).

"overtaken" by the gospel; already in Rom 1:1 he declares himself the slave of Jesus Christ. The parenthetical phrase here, "thus my desire," hints that God's intrusion has now become Paul's own will as well.

For the second time Paul specifies that the "you" he addresses reside in Rome (see v. 7). None of his other letters repeat the place name in the opening lines, and the repetition here may reflect the sense of importance Paul attaches to this particular set of communities. The itinerary sketched out in ch. 15 makes clear that Rome is pivotal for Paul's plans.

[16] Paul's eager obligation to preach the gospel in Rome now ushers in a paramount claim about that gospel, one anticipating the substance of the letter that follows and routinely identified as the letter's thesis. Already vv. 2–4 have firmly connected the "gospel of God" with God's promises and with the fleshly, Davidic birth and powerful resurrection of Jesus Christ. The letter does not so much argue these points as assume them. At this juncture, God's gospel is restated in terms of its salvific power and its determined grasp for the whole of humankind.

To contemporary readers, the move from eagerness and obligation in the preceding lines to the statement "I am not ashamed" sounds a jarring note. It is hard to resist the pull of a Freudian interpretation in which Paul is denying his own sense of shame or embarrassment (Matera 34), and there is something of that view at work in proposals that Paul actually does have in mind his own sense of inadequacy for the task of preaching in the empire's capital or that he here acknowledges the genuine absurdity of taking the gospel into a world consumed with its own power (Jewett 136–37).

Stylistically, "I am not ashamed" is an instance of *litotes*, which Paul will use again in 10:16, "not all have obediently heard" (see also, e.g., 13:10; 1 Cor 1:26; 10:5). More than rhetoric is at stake here, however. Paul's assertion belongs in the sphere of apocalyptic eschatology, as is the case with much of these two verses. The gospel tradition warns those who are ashamed of Jesus in the present that he will be ashamed of them in the impending judgment (Mark 8:38; par. Luke 9:26; cf. Matt 10:33). Other early Christian writings echo that warning, including 2 Tim 1:8, 12; Heb 11:16; 1 Pet 2:6 (citing Isa 28:16); 1 John 2:28; Herm. Sim. 8.6.4 (72.4); 9.21.3 (98.3); Ign. *Smyrn.* 10.2. Whether or not Paul knew that element of the Jesus tradition (so Dunn 1:38–39), his letters elsewhere demonstrate that being ashamed of the gospel or its opposite, having a reason for pride, has an eschatological location. He writes to the Thessalonians of his expectation that they will be his "hope and joy and crown of pride" at the Lord's arrival (*parousia*; 1 Thess 2:19). The eschatological hope Paul introduces in Rom 5:2 and 5 is the ground of pride and not of shame, and in 15:17 Paul writes of having pride "in Christ Jesus" because of his apostolic labor on behalf of the gentiles. The fact that 1:15 is present tense does not undermine its eschatological overtones: Paul's confidence is born of the gospel, which itself announces God's own final triumph.

In the immediate context, Paul asserts that he is not ashamed of the gospel, which he defines with a simple copula as "God's own power now bringing about salvation." Here there is no account, however brief, of the events of Jesus (see 1:3–4); instead, the gospel *is* God's very power for salvation. It is not enough to understand power in this context as a feature of God's character or one of God's attributes in the sense that God *has* power; instead, God's power is inseparable from what it does, which is to bring about salvation. The elusive little phrase of 1:4 ("Son of God in power") has already introduced power as it is associated with Jesus Christ's resurrection (and see 1 Cor 6:14; 2 Cor 13:4; Phil 3:10).

Paul does not explain the term "salvation," but the letter quickly unfolds what it means, first by depicting its absence and then in positive terms. In 1:18–3:20 Paul displays the grasp of Sin over all of humankind (see the conclusion of 3:9), and 5:12–14 recalls the reign of Death by virtue of Sin's power. The primary depiction of salvation in Romans is the release of humanity from these powers into the liberating power of God's own gracious rule (5:15–21). Chapter 8 extends the notion of salvation, so that all creation stretches forward in anticipation of its liberation from enslavement (8:18–30), a liberation so profound as to be new life (6:1–11). In the discourse of Romans, salvation takes place on a canvas that is cosmic and apocalyptic.

What Paul declares with this initial statement, however, is that the gospel is God's salvific power "for everyone who believes" (see also 3:22; 4:11; 10:4, 11). The conventional translation of *pisteuein* as "believe" needs to be expanded, since the English verb constrains belief to the intellectual acceptance of certain facts that are elsewhere under dispute, while Paul's usage carries the sense of trust or reliance or confidence along with that of intellectual assent. When he later discusses Abraham, it is not simply because Abraham somehow managed to accept God's promise intellectually, but because Abraham lived on the basis of confidence in that promise.

Another important issue is how this clause functions in the sentence. Often it is read as setting a limitation on the realm of salvation, specifying that faith is the "necessary, indispensable condition for salvation" (Fitzmyer 256). That seems an exaggerated conclusion to draw from the larger context of the sentence, which focuses on God's action far more than on a human requirement. Additionally, the word "everyone" and the phrase "Jew first as well as Greek" both extend the reach of salvation, rather than zeroing in on faith as a requirement. Even if faith is viewed as the "necessary, indispensable condition," the role of God in calling humanity to faith (note the language of call in v. 6), in bestowing the gift of faith, makes it wrongheaded to interpret v. 16 as a kind of test posed for humanity prior to its salvation.

The "everyone" (*panti*) reinforces the "all" (*pas*) that runs throughout these opening chapters, but here "everyone" is further explicated as for "Jew first as well as Greek" (see 2:9, 10; 3:9; 10:12). The use of "Greek" may come as a bit of a surprise, since Paul has already referred to all gentiles, not to Greeks alone, but there is no Greek word that refers to an individual gentile, since *ethnos* refers to a nation and its plural means "nations." Full cognizance must be taken of the insistence that the gospel's power is for the "Jew first," particularly in light of the church's many attempts to muffle that priority, attempts that extend back at least to the teachings of Marcion, perhaps even to some gentile Christians at Rome (11:13–24). Nor is it acceptable to gloss over this priority as if it were merely chronological (i.e., the gospel historically was first taught among Jews and only later among gentiles), since that point was so obvious in the first century that it hardly required articulation.

The priority of Jews is unambiguous in this statement. A certain irony emerges around this priority as the letter develops (so Byrne 57), since even the priority of Jews does not prevent them from joining with gentiles in their enslavement to Sin and Death (3:9). By the conclusion of Rom 11, priority attaches to the gentiles in themselves becoming the vehicle through which God works to bring about faith among Jews (11:11–12, 15, 30–32). If the Roman audiences of Paul's letters do contain a large number of gentiles who come from the circle around the synagogue, the *sebomenoi*, they may be accustomed to hearing that God's promises are for Jews alone, with provision for gentiles who become proselytes but not for everyone, not for gentiles as gentiles. Instead, they hear that Jewish priority does not mean God is for Jews alone; indeed, salvation is also for gentiles, even as gentiles.

[17a] Yet another *gar* ("because" or "for") connects v. 17 back to v. 16. The gospel of God's powerful salvation is presently revealing something to which Paul refers as the *dikaiosynē theou*, the righteousness of God.

Excursus: The Righteousness of God

Here Paul introduces the phrase *dikaiosynē theou*, to which he returns, with slight variations, in 3:5, 21, 22, 25, 26; 10:3; 2 Cor 5:21; Phil 3:9.[2] Translation poses the first challenge, even though translation decisions always reflect interpretive inclinations. Paul employs both the noun *dikaiosynē* and the related verb *dikaioō*. (Other related words are used less frequently: the adjective *dikaios,* the nouns *dikaiōma* and *dikaiōsis,* and the adverb *dikaiōs*.) Ideally, those relationships should be visible in translation, as when "baptism" and "baptize" render *baptisma* and *baptizō*, but English has no standard verb to accompany the noun "righteousness" (assuming at present the customary translation

2. Irons 2015 reviews the multitudinous interpretations of the "righteousness of God" from Origen through Wright (9–59). In addition, see Brauch 1977; Seifrid 2001; Bird 2007; Ziesler 1972, 1–14.

of *dikaiosynē* as "righteousness"). The problem comes into clear view in Rom 3:26, where Paul plays on these related terms:

> NRSVue: It was to demonstrate at the present time his own *righteousness* [*dikaiosynē*], so that he is *righteous* [*dikaios*] and he *justifies* [*dikaioō*] the one who has the faith of Jesus.
>
> NIV: He did it to demonstrate his *righteousness* [*dikaiosynē*] at the present time, so as to *be just* [*dikaios*] and the one who *justifies* [*dikaioō*] those who believe in Jesus.

Attempts to solve this problem result in such ungainly pairings as "righteousness" with "to righteous" or "to rightwise." "Rectification" and "rectify" (Martyn 1997a, 249–50) convey the relationship, although "rectification of God" becomes a bit cumbersome.

Another strategy is to employ the vocabulary of justice, as in "the justice of God" (Calhoun 2011, 158–60; Harink 2020, 1–4). While I share the urgent concern for contemporary justice, and justice language does capture one important strand of historical usage, the problem with justice language is that it can be and routinely is construed not simply as the demand for just behavior (fairness, equity) but as the demand for retribution.[3]

Lacking better options, in this translation I employ "righteousness" for the noun *dikaiosynē* and "rectify" for the verb *dikaioō*, in the hope that this pairing will signal their relatedness, albeit in a limited fashion.

Behind and beyond the problem of translation, understanding the phrase "God's righteousness" requires attention to its linguistic heritage, that is, how the phrase would be understood by Paul and his contemporaries. Particularly given the role engagement with Scripture plays in this letter, a primary avenue of investigation is through Israel's Scriptures. Although the precise phrase *dikaiosynē theou* does not appear in the LXX, much is said about God's righteousness. Sometimes God's righteousness is inflected in terms of rewarding good and punishing wrong, as in Ps 72:

> O God, grant your judgment to the king
> and your righteousness to the king's son,
> to judge your people with righteousness
> and your poor with justice.
> Let the mountains return peace to your people. (71:1–3 LXX; see also Ps 96:13 [95:13 LXX])

Elsewhere, however, God's righteousness is associated with God's actions rescuing Israel from its enemies, as in the Song of Moses:

> You led your people with righteousness,
> this people, whom you redeemed.

---

3. In *Les Misérables*, what separates Javert from Monsieur Madeline (Valjean) pertains exactly to this problem in understanding justice. In their confrontation over Fantine, both appeal to justice, Javert to the justice of the law, Madeline to the justice of conscience (Hugo 1972, 154–55).

> You called them through your strength
> into your holy dwelling. (Exod 15:13 LXX)

This association between God's righteousness and salvation figures importantly in the Psalter and Isaiah, two books that loom large in Romans. Psalm 31 opens with a cry:

> In you, LORD, I hoped.
> May I not be put to shame forever.
> In your righteousness deliver me
> and rescue me. (30:2 LXX)

Similarly, Ps 35 cries out for God to awaken and come to the speaker's defense:

> Judge me according to your righteousness, LORD my God,
> and do not let them rejoice over me. (34:24 LXX)

Psalm 40 praises God for deliverance in terms of divine righteousness:

> I told your righteousness in the great congregation.
> Behold, my lips I did not forbid, Lord, as you know.
> Your righteousness I did not hide in my heart.
> Your truth and your salvation I spoke.
> I did not hide your mercy and your truth from the great assembly.
> (39:10–11 LXX)

Isaiah 51 similarly associates God's saving strength with God's righteousness:

> My righteousness is soon at hand, and the light of my salvation will come near.
> . . . .
> My salvation will be forever,
> and my righteousness will not fail.
> . . . .
> My righteousness will be forever
> and my salvation for generations of generations. (51:5–6, 8 LXX)

Particularly important is Isa 59:17, which identifies righteousness as God's own armor:

> He wrapped himself in righteousness as a breastplate
> and put a helmet of salvation on his head. (LXX)

In this sense, God's righteousness reflects God's faithfulness to Israel, although the terms "covenant" and "righteousness" rarely appear together (Seifrid 2001, 423). Some of Paul's auditors, particularly Jews and those gentiles who had been attracted to the synagogue, likely would immediately hear a reference to God's righteousness in these terms—as God's commitment to justice, to the deliverance of Israel, to Israel itself.

This linguistic practice is only part of the story, however, since for the larger Greco-Roman world the *dik-* word group connotes justice. Central to Plato's *Republic* is the character of justice, both for the individual and for the state. Aristotle explored justice among the virtues in his *Eudemian Ethics*. In *Res gestae* (34), the emperor Augustus boasts of the Senate's recognition of his virtues, including his justice. (What Augustus counts as justice, to be sure, others experienced as violence and oppression, which is one reason for avoiding justice language in translation, as noted above.) Musonius Rufus, arguing the necessity for rulers to study philosophy, laments the general confusion about what constitutes justice (*Fragment* 8.18–29). Phoebe's Roman auditors may well have heard Paul's reference to God's "righteousness" in this vein, as an assertion of God's practice of justice. What Phoebe's audience heard in the phrase at this first announcement will have been shaped by their own experience, but that does not yet tell us how Paul employs the expression and, more importantly, where he will go with it.

A third question, and one that has generated immense interpretive dispute, is that of grammar: How does the genitive "of God" relate to the noun "righteousness"? One construal is that God is the origin or author of this righteousness (i.e., genitive of source or origin; Smyth 1956, §1298, 1410). In this case, God's righteousness is the righteousness God gives to human beings. Another construal is that Paul makes reference to God's own righteousness, often referred to as the subjective genitive, but perhaps better as that of possession or belonging (Smyth 1956, §1297). Since the work of the genitive case is always to limit the meaning of the substantive (in this case "righteousness"), only the context can determine the appropriate nuance.[4]

These observations about prior usage and syntactical possibilities may tell us what *Phoebe's listeners* hear, but they do not necessarily tell us what *Paul* is doing with the phrase. Three features of the text, often overlooked, call for attention. First, "God's righteousness" is the grammatical subject of v. 17, paralleling the phrase "God's own power" in v. 16 and anticipating "God's wrath" in v. 18. That sequence of three descriptors attached to God suggests that these are indeed statements about God (i.e., favoring the subjective genitive interpretation). In addition, the three are also best understood as remarks about divine activity (rather than divine attributes, as least to the extent that the term "attributes" favors being rather than acting).

Second, Paul claims that "God's righteousness" is "being apocalyptically revealed" in the gospel, that is, in the event of Jesus Christ (which is how Paul has defined the gospel in vv. 3–4). Later, and at several points in the letter, he invokes the present time: "but now" (e.g., 3:21; 6:22; 7:6), the "now time" (3:26; 8:18; 11:5). Whatever people may have previously associated with God's righteousness, that understanding is currently being changed. And if it is being "apocalyptically revealed," then it is not already known; it is not accessible simply by reading Israel's Scriptures or by consulting philosophical discussions. The righteousness of God "is what happens in Jesus" (Linebaugh 2022, 9).

Third, while "God's righteousness" is commonly understood as the thesis of the letter, that thesis is a beginning point, not an ending point. This is not Paul's only comment about God's righteousness. In 3:21–26 he will return to it. There he will connect it again with God's action in Jesus's death, employing language that is, by turns, cultic, forensic, and liberative. Later he will elaborate on that right-making event, connecting

---

4. Bird 2007 helpfully reviews the debate, especially in its recent permutations.

it with God's defeat of Sin and Death (5:12–21). Later still he will claim that Israel does not presently know God's righteousness, that Israel has not "submitted" to it, closely identifying God's righteousness with Christ himself (10:1–12).

This brings to the surface a flaw in Käsemann's otherwise profound discussion of the righteousness of God in Paul, in that he attempts to draw a straight line from prior Jewish usage to Paul's understanding (see Käsemann 1969b, 172–73). But that is to misconstrue the world-remaking impact of the gospel that Käsemann otherwise limns with such insight (so Linebaugh 2022, 5–8; similarly S. Adams 2015, 106–40) when he writes that the righteousness of God is "for Paul God's sovereignty over the world revealing itself eschatologically in Jesus. . . . It is the rightful power with which God makes his cause to triumph in the world which has fallen away from him and which yet, as creation, is his inviolable possession" (1969a, 180).

Understanding the place of God's righteousness in the letters of Paul is rightly informed by prior usage, but prior usage does not predict Paul's usage, nor does prior usage constrain Paul. That statement holds true at the most obvious level of linguistics: language changes over time. (That is a major reason why the KJV is no longer a viable translation of the Bible for most readers.) It is also true theologically: the gospel is an action of God, an event, even a cataclysm (as in the personal cataclysm on evidence in Phil 3:7–11). As such, it intrudes, it changes, it unmakes in order to make again (see the introduction).

Advocates of Christian supersessionism might look for a toehold in this discussion, somehow imagining that Paul is now rejecting what the prophets have said about God's righteousness or that Paul is undermining Israel's Scriptures. The letter itself constitutes an important argument against such conclusions, for Israel's Scriptures play a major role here, but they are read through the gospel, from the "now time," even as they provide Paul with language for that "now time."

God's righteousness is being revealed apocalyptically. The addition of the adverb "apocalyptically" intends both to convey something closer to the Greek verb *apokalyptein* and to preclude the notion that this is merely an unveiling in the sense of the public display of a new work of art. In that case, a cover is removed from a work that stands inert, ready to be seen whenever the cover is put aside. For Paul, however, God's power and God's righteousness are *happening* in the present time. They intrude in the world in God's sending of Jesus Christ, in God's defeat of Sin and Death in the death and resurrection of Jesus, such that they disrupt the world as it is. To be sure, that disruption does make known (it unveils) the captivity of humanity under Sin (1:18–3:21); in that limited sense, unveiling is not wrong, but it does not capture the fullness of the apocalypse.

Paul characterizes this action by God as "from faith to faith," a simple combination of words that generates several interpretive possibilities, ranging from individual growth in faith (Fitzmyer 263) to emphatic endorsement (i.e., it is used for emphasis, Käsemann 31) to movement from divine faithfulness, either that of God (Barth 41–42) or that of Jesus (Campbell 1994, 281). Study of the construction "from [*ek*] A to [*eis*] A" across a range of Greek literature shows that such series elsewhere convey "range, duration, repetition, source and destination, previous state and new state or progression" (Quarles 2003, 13). That observation does little to eliminate interpretive possibilities, however, since Paul leaves the noun "faith" unspecified (Whose faith? What kind of faith? When does this movement take place?). That omission may be deliberate (so Calhoun 2011, 169–71), provoking the auditors themselves to consider several possible understandings.

The context provides some helpful clues. Paul has just declared his own obligation to proclaim the gospel and has identified that gospel as God's saving power for "everyone who believes," Jew and Greek. The assertion that God's righteousness is apocalyptically revealed "from faith to faith" ties together Paul's proclamation and its reception (Calhoun 2011, 186, informed by Augustine). It may also concern the gospel's spread among the gentiles and the invasion of the gospel's saving power among all people, Jew as well as gentile. In either case, "from faith to faith" reflects the gospel's grasp for all, wise and foolish, Greek and barbarian, Jew and gentile. It finds a geographic counterpart in Paul's later remark about the extent of the mission from Jerusalem to Illyricum (15:19).

[17b] Verse 17 concludes by introducing a version of Hab 2:4—"The righteous one will live by faith"—with the phrase, "As it stands written." This is the first of numerous such formulae in Romans (2:24; 3:4, 10; 4:17; 8:36; 9:13, 33; 10:15; 11:8, 26; 15:3, 9, 21). Paul interprets the phrase himself in 15:4 when he claims that Scripture was written for "our" instruction. But if Scripture is for instruction, what lesson is to be learned? In the case of Hab 2:4, the answer is far from obvious.

To begin with, Paul's wording of Hab 2:4 differs from that of the LXX, which in turn is found in several forms, the most important of which are "*my* righteous one will live by faith/faithfulness" or "the righteous one will live by *my* faith/faithfulness." Paul's version, both here and in Gal 3:11, does not contain the word *mou* ("my"). In addition, all these versions of the line differ from the Hebrew, which reads "but the righteous one will live by his faith/ faithfulness." Since Paul uses this same line in Gal 3:11, with exactly the same wording, presumably either he has such a text (or remembers it that way) or he has deliberately suppressed the *mou* (so Calhoun 2011, 188). In any case, without language identifying the righteous one or the faith/faithfulness at issue, the line become highly ambiguous.

Given that Paul quotes the same passage in Gal 3:11, it is tempting to look to that context for light on this one. In that passage, Paul invokes language from Deuteronomy to show that reliance on law observance leads to being cursed. He then contrasts the law in the form of Lev 18:5 with faith: "The righteous one will live by faith." That is, in Galatians Hab 2:4 speaks over against Lev 18:5, making Hab 2:4 a voice for faith/faithfulness over against the Teachers and their understanding of the law. Reference to the law (i.e., *nomos*) has not occurred to this point in Romans, however, and it will not do so until 2:12. That difference in context means that Gal 3:11 need not be read into this passage. Paul may well be pursuing different goals with the same text.

Instead of assuming that the use of Gal 3:11 is being replayed here, it is more helpful to attend to the words themselves in the context in Romans. Each term signals crucial aspects of the gospel event and, as is often noted, Hab 2:4 is the only line in the LXX in which the three key words (righteous, faith, live) appear. The term *dikaios* ("righteous," an adjective used here as a substantive) plays a central role in Paul's exposition of the human situation from the viewpoint of God's wrath as well as God's righteousness. In Rom 2:13 he claims that it is law-doers, not only law-hearers, who are *dikaios* before God, a statement that paves the way (among many others) for the conclusion in 3:10 that no one is *dikaios*, not even one, and that law observance cannot rectify humans (3:20). It is only in God's action through the death of Jesus Christ that humans are delivered from Sin, an action that demonstrates that God alone is *dikaios* (3:26). Chapter 5 elaborates on the consequences of Jesus's death, which established many as *dikaios*.[5]

This usage in Romans makes it difficult to accept proposals that the righteous one in 1:17 is actually a reference to Jesus Christ (Hays 2005). Vigorous arguments in that direction have been based on usage elsewhere. There is little doubt that 1 Enoch refers to the "righteous one" as a messianic figure (38.2; 53.6). Acts applies that title to Jesus in 3:14; 7:52; and 22:14; similarly 1 Pet 3:18 and perhaps Heb 10:38 (in another citation of Hab 2:4). Yet Paul does not elsewhere use that expression of Jesus, and it would be odd to do so in this leading place in the letter without following through on that quasi-title later on.

Pistis ("faith" or "faithfulness") Paul has already placed at the center of his own apostolic work (Rom 1:5), named as a well-known feature of the auditors (v. 8) and as something he shares with them (v. 12). Later he will speak of God's own *pistis* (3:3) as well as of *pistis* as something generated by Jesus himself (3:26; see the excursus on *pistis christou* below) and of Abraham's *pistis* as a prototype for those caught up in the Christ event (4:16, 19, 20). *Pistis* becomes a shorthand expression not only for belief but also for reliance on and living out of the actions of God in Jesus Christ.

The third word (*zēsetai*, "will live") carries considerable weight as well, even if it has not yet been introduced in the letter (although note the reference to Christ's resurrection in v. 4). Those who are baptized into Christ Jesus no longer live in the power of Sin (6:2); they are dead to it and are living in Christ

---

5. The perplexing comment of 5:7, that someone might choose to die for a human who is *dikaios*, does at least theoretically allow for the possibility of a human being righteous on her own, apart from the "now time" of Jesus Christ, but that use of *dikaios* seems to be something of an outlier, contrasting as it does a righteous person with a good one.

Jesus instead (6:11). They live by the power of the Spirit (8:11, 13). They do not belong to themselves but to the Lord who is himself lord of both the dead and the living (14:8–9).

Returning to Paul's citation of Hab 2:4 in the light of these admittedly partial sketches of three important terms, 1:17b emerges as a declaration, a promise, conveying Paul's utter conviction that those whom God makes righteous ("the righteous one[s]") will live (both now and into the future) out of the faith in Jesus Christ that has been given them by Christ himself. God's power for salvation, the apocalypse of God's righteousness in Jesus Christ, is nothing less than the triumph of life over both Sin and Death.

Auditors who are familiar with Habakkuk may find Paul's interpretation coherent with the book itself, especially 2:1–4 and its word of assurance that God will not delay. Interestingly, Habakkuk follows that promise with a series of warnings for the wealthy, the arrogant, and the violent, perhaps allowing the auditors also to conclude that they themselves do not belong among such people. Paul will shortly dismantle any sense of complacency.

Although I have ventured proposals concerning classic exegetical questions posed by 1:16–17, I have also noted the indefinite character of Paul's words. Indeed, given the elaborate way in which the letter unfolds, it may be that the audience is being "teased into active thought," to borrow a phrase from C. H. Dodd's classic work on the parables (1961, 16). In that case, we must sit lightly with these conclusions, allowing "Paul's own line of thought to disclose his understanding" (Meyer 2004b, 160). Before he unfolds the character of God's righteous-making activity in 3:21–4:25, Paul must introduce the apocalypse of God's wrath in its universal proportions.

1:18–32 God Handed Them Over

In 1:13–17 Paul has announced God's powerful saving action in the gospel as the arrival of God's righteousness; in 3:21–26 and further in 5:12–21 he will unpack that righteousness for his Roman audience. Before doing so, however, he takes up another aspect of the gospel, which is the apocalyptic revelation of God's wrath in the face of universal human rebellion against God.[6] Initially he writes of God's wrath in terms that superficially appear to pertain only to gentiles (1:18–32), but 2:1–3:9 unmasks and finally destroys any assumption that Jews are somehow exempt from the reach of God's wrath. The catena of Scripture texts in 3:10–18 powerfully reinforces the claim that God has handed over humanity as a whole (1:24, 26, 28), with the result that all are under the power of Sin (3:9). In 5:12–7:25 Paul will elaborate the power of Sin and its partner, Death. Prior to that

---

6. Karl Barth has this passage, among others, in view when he writes that God's revelation is that "of God's opposition to the opposition" exhibited by humanity against God (1957, 362).

elaboration, however, in 3:21–26 Paul returns to God's powerful act of rectification in the death of Jesus Christ, and in 3:26–4:25 he reinterprets Abraham as the recipient of God's promises for both Jew and gentile.

A number of ancient traditions and attitudes are at work in 1:18–32.[7] It reflects some traditional Jewish convictions that idolatry and immorality are integrally related to one another and that both are characteristic of gentiles. Scriptural language appears at numerous points, which prompts some scholars to emphasize the connections between this passage and the early chapters of Genesis in particular.[8] Further, ancient understandings of gender roles and sexual behavior underlie the comments in vv. 26–27. And in vv. 29–31 Paul draws on the literary convention of the vice list. It is important to be aware of these features of 1:18–32, but the thrust of the passage is not explained by any one of them or even by all of them taken together. What Paul begins here (and will continue, especially in 5:12–21) is a universal and cosmic account of the human situation, an explanation of humanity's captivity to the powers of Sin and Death, a captivity that has its origin in human rebellion against God and in God's delivering up of rebellious humanity.[9]

Following the opening statement of v. 18, which declares what is being revealed in the present time (the time of the gospel), the story of humanity's captivity unfolds in three movements. First, vv. 19–20 assert that humanity received God's self-revelation. In the second movement, vv. 21–23, Paul argues that, despite this revelation, humanity did not worship God as God; in effect, humanity rebelled against God's very being as God. And in the last, most extensive, and most relentless movement, vv. 24–32 lay out the result of humanity's rebelliousness: God handed humanity over to the powers of Sin and Death. Throughout this section, the use of the third-person "they" and of well-known Jewish conventions of characterizing gentiles permits Paul's audience to imagine that he is speaking only of gentile culpability. At 2:1, however, he will confront that misunderstanding forcefully: "the human" (*anthrōpos*) is under discussion here, not only the gentile human.[10]

1:18 For God's wrath is being apocalyptically revealed[a] from heaven against all ungodliness and wrong[b] of human beings who suppress the

7. This discussion of 1:18–32 adapts Gaventa 2017b and is used by the kind permission of Peeters Press.

8. Proposals vary, but one recurrent claim is that Paul has Adam in mind as the primal figure who knew of God but declined to worship God properly (see esp. Hooker 1960), yet much in this passage fits poorly with Gen 3, especially the charge of idolatry and the resultant sexual immorality.

9. See the excursus at 5:21 on the powers of Sin and Death. Paul uses neither term here, although see 1:32.

10. Hence Linebaugh's perceptive claim that in 1:18–32 "Paul announces the essential oneness—*coram deo*—of all persons; he announces the human" (2013b, 120).

truth with wrong. 19 Now what can be known about God is plainly set
before them, for God made it plain to them. 20 For what is not visible of
God is rendered clearly visible since the creation of the cosmos, because
it is perceived in the things that are made—namely, his eternal power and
deity—so that human beings are without excuse.

21 Now although they knew God, they did not glorify or give thanks
to God as God, but their thinking became vacuous and their senseless
heart was darkened. 22 Claiming to be wise, they actually became foolish,
23 and they changed the glory of the immortal God for the likeness of an
image of a mortal human—even of birds and of four-footed animals and
of reptiles![c]

24 Therefore God handed them over, because of[d] the desires of their
hearts, to impurity so that their very bodies[e] were dishonored. 25 And they
exchanged the truth about God for a lie, and they venerated and worshiped the created instead of the Creator, who is blessed forever. Amen!

26 Therefore God handed them over to dishonorable passions, for
their females exchanged the natural sexual practice[f] for one that is
unnatural. 27 Similarly the men left aside the natural sexual practice
with the female and burned in their lust for one another, men behaving
shamefully with men and taking upon themselves the reward their error
ought to have.

28 And because they did not suitably acknowledge God, God handed
them over to an unsuitable way of thinking, to do what is not done,
29 being filled up with all wrong, wickedness, greed, vice; being full of
envy, murder, discord, malicious cunning; being gossips, 30 slanderers,
God-haters, violent, haughty, braggarts, inventors of evil, disobedient
to parents, 31 senseless, faithless, heartless, merciless. 32 Those people
recognize the right decree of God, namely, that those who do such things
as these are worthy of death. Yet they not only do them—they approve
those who do them!

a. See above on 1:17 for "apocalyptically revealed."

b. Since *adikia* stands in contrast with the *dikaios* of v. 17, the reference appears
to be larger than either "wickedness" or "injustice" might suggest. The discussion that
follows confirms this more capacious translation.

c. The Greek does not, of course, contain the punctuation added here, which reflects
a judgment that the movement from humans to animals is emphatic, underscoring the
decline even within idolatrous practices.

d. Often translated as "to" or "in" but best understood as instrumental or causal (so
also BDAG, s.v. *en*; MM 210; Kennedy 1917, 322–23).

e. Lit., "their bodies." "Very" has been added for emphasis, to indicate the intensity
involved in Paul's move here from the heart to the body, since *sōma* pertains to the
whole person.

f. This phrase may be rendered literally as "natural use," but both the context and usage elsewhere indicate that the particular connotation at work here is sexual (see BDAG, s.v. *chrēsis*).

[1:18] The Greek word *apokalyptetai* ("is being apocalyptically revealed") opens this discussion while simultaneously recalling the revelation of God's righteousness in the lines just above. The Romans have heard of Paul's vocation, his anticipated visit, his compulsion to preach the gospel among them, and particularly of the gospel as God's saving power for all humankind. Now they are to hear the context in which God's saving action takes place: it is not just that gentiles are at last to be incorporated into the people of Israel or that Jews require forgiveness; instead, the whole of humanity has been handed over (vv. 24, 26, 28) to Sin's captivity as a result of their rebellion against God, and that captivity has produced a range of wrong, both wrong thought and wrong action.

The claim that God's wrath "*is* being revealed apocalyptically" needs to be taken seriously. Changes of Greek tense can be distorted and overworked by interpreters, but the shift from the present tense of *apokalyptetai* ("is being revealed apocalyptically") in 1:17, 18 to the aorist tenses in the account that follows is not a minor one. The arrival of the gospel of God's Son (1:3–4, 16–17) forces Paul, as a slave of Christ who is obligated to the gospel, to perceive what happened to humanity in the past (Watson 1997, 260). Shifts from past to present elsewhere in Romans underscore this observation (e.g., 3:21; 6:19, 21; 8:1; 11:30). The arrival of this new knowledge has important counterparts in 1 Cor 1:18–31, where the gospel reveals the bankruptcy of human knowledge; in 2 Cor 5:16–17, where the Christ event produces a new epistemology; and in Phil 3, where Paul characterizes his own position and achievements as excrement because the gospel has overtaken him. From the vantage point of the "now time," the reality of humanity's captivity becomes visible. The gospel, then, reveals human captivity even as it overthrows it.[11]

Discussion of the revelation of divine wrath frequently turns on the question whether this should be imagined as God's personal anger or whether it is an impersonal response to wrongdoing (Barrett 33; Cranfield 1:109; Byrne 66; Travis 1992, 997). The difficulty extends beyond the perceived distastefulness of imputing to God a negative emotion or of imagining "wrath" as somehow existing independently of God. The Bible necessarily draws on human characteristics in its witness to God, but discussion of those features seldom acknowledges the incommensurability of language about God and language about humanity. God's wrath is not simply a larger version of human anger, a cosmic-sized

11. This seems consistent with Markus Barth's observation that righteousness and wrath are not opposites but that God's righteousness "triumphs even *in*" God's wrath (1955, 294; ital. orig.).

temper tantrum. Speaking about God's wrath is instead a way of conveying God's unwillingness to let creation simply continue in its captivity to Sin.

The clue to that understanding comes when we observe that, in the Pauline corpus, the word "wrath" is virtually always associated with eschatological judgment, as in Rom 2:5, which anticipates the future "day of wrath," and 5:9, which speaks of being saved from "wrath" (similarly 1 Thess 1:10 and 5:9; perhaps also 2:16).[12] Here Paul's usage is generally consistent with the usage in the LXX and other Jewish texts that refer to God's wrath, particularly in eschatological terms.[13] The combination of "God's wrath" with "from heaven" underscores the solemnity of the declaration. Since the heavens belong to God and God is identified with heaven, declaring that the wrath of God is being revealed from heaven makes for a certain redundancy, likely for emphasis (as in Rev 3:12; 21:2, 10).

The object of God's wrath is first stated in the sweeping indictment of v. 18 as "all ungodliness and wrong of human beings who suppress the truth with wrong." From the very outset this claim is striking both rhetorically and conceptually. The repetition of sounds draws the ear, as Paul joins *pasan* with *asebeian* ("all ungodliness") and then *adikian* with *anthrōpōn* ("wrong of human beings"). The return of *pas* ("all" or "every"), which has played an important role already in vv. 5, 7, 8, signals the all-encompassing character of this heavenly wrath.

The attribution to humanity of ungodliness and wrong (that is, both wrongdoing and wrong-headedness) touches on powerful themes in this letter, themes that encompass humanity's sinfulness as well as God's salvific intervention. Later Paul will insist that God makes right the ungodly (*ton asebē*; 4:5) and that Christ died for the ungodly (*asebōn*; 5:6). The wrong, even wrong-headedness, of humanity (*adikia*) as demonstrated in this passage contrasts with the preceding assertion of the righteousness of God, the right-doing, the setting right of what has gone powerfully wrong (*dikaiosynē*). At this early point, the only specification of human "ungodliness" and "wrong" is that humans "suppress the truth with wrong." Although ambiguous in this early line, the lines that follow will make clear that this is not truth in some abstract or philosophical sense; the truth humanity suppresses is truth about God as Creator and the corresponding human role of praise and gratitude.[14] What is also clear is the human initiative in "suppressing" the truth.[15]

12.The one time Paul clearly attributes wrath to human beings is in Rom 12:19, where he urges listeners *not* to give way to anger (*orgē*), because vengeance belongs to God. That instance of proscribed anger seems to confirm my point, that wrath is for Paul both divine and eschatological.

13. See, e.g., Exod 15:7; Num 16:46 [LXX 17:11]; Pss 69:24 [LXX 68:25]; 79:6 [LXX 78:6]); 1 En. 91.7; Sib. Or. 1.165.

14. As Aquinas observes regarding this passage, "Ungodliness is a sin against divine worship" (39; and see Cooper 2012, 118).

15. Readers eager to identify human initiative in Romans may find it disconcerting that this is among Paul's most unambiguous attributions of agency to human beings. For Paul, as for Luke, human "initiative" often expresses itself over against God (see Gaventa 2004b).

Because the lines that follow reflect conventional Jewish polemic about gentiles, especially about idolatry and sexual immorality, it is easy to overlook the word *anthrōpos* here. On closer reflection, however, forced especially by the sharp turn at 2:1, the universal implications of Paul's comments will come to the surface. This text operates on two levels simultaneously. It can be read (and continues to be read) as having to do only with the actions of "those" gentiles. Yet *anthrōpos* includes all humanity, as is especially clear in 2:9: "There will be affliction and anguish on every human life [*anthrōpos*] that produces evil, the Jew first and also the Greek."[16]

[19–20] With vv. 19–20 Paul begins to explicate the origin of humanity's captivity. In the first movement of this story, God makes known what humanity is capable of knowing about him. So important is this point for Paul that he states it in three slightly different ways in these two verses. First, he asserts that what can be known about God is clearly accessible to human beings, then that God actually made it clearly visible, and finally how that visibility takes place.

The charge opens with the assertion that "what can be known" of God is "plainly set before" human beings (v. 19). Literally, "the known of God," *gnōston tou theou*, is usually understood as a partitive genitive, one that expresses only a portion of the whole (as in, e.g., "the slice of cake" or "the member of the chorus"). This does not mean God has some attributes that can be known and others that cannot (as espoused by Origen, *Comm. Rom.* 1:16, 17; Burns 26), but that humanity's knowledge of God is always limited. Whatever is knowable about God is also made known by God rather than through human effort, as v. 19b explains: "God made it plain to them." The repetition of "plainly set before" and "made it plain" (*phaneron* and *ephanerōsen*) continues the elevated language of v. 18.

With v. 20 Paul explains how this disclosure *by* God and *of* God works, shifting the language from knowing to seeing, ironically declaring that "what is not visible" (*aorata*) is in fact clearly visible (*kathoratai*). This visibility is connected with creation, and the phrase "since [or from] the creation of the cosmos" can refer either to the time of creation (i.e., since the time of creation) or to the fact of it (i.e., from observing the created world). Because *apo* ("from") can have a temporal reference (e.g., Rom 5:14; 15:23; 2 Cor 5:16; Phil 1:5), and because the consequences of creation are referred to in the next phrase, the connotation seems to be that God has been revealed in the world ever since the time of its creation. "The things that are made" give evidence of God, although

16. Jewett rightly observes that Paul's reference to "humans" in 1:18 eliminates any "loophole" by which some in the audience might imagine themselves excluded from the accusation (158). That would not prevent auditors of Romans—whether ancient or modern—from concluding that the text refers to people other than themselves. The relentless character of Paul's argument, especially in 3:10–18 and 5:1–21, reveals his assumption that this point will not be readily absorbed on first hearing.

again here Paul states the matter generally and does not specify or elaborate. The point is not to expound upon the beauty of nature, as do some of Paul's contemporaries (see, e.g., Wis 13:5; Cicero, *Tusc.* 1.69–70; Philo, *Rewards* 41–42), but simply to assert that God reveals himself through creation.

The rather vague phrases "what can be known" and "what is not visible" become specific with the language of God's "eternal power and deity." What is known to humanity from the time of creation has to do with God's power and God's very character as God. In isolation, such language seems a bit static, yet power has already entered the letter twice, and in both cases the power of which Paul speaks is anything but a static quality. The opening lines of the letter describe Jesus Christ as "publicly identified as Son of God in power," connecting power directly with the resurrection (1:4). In addition, the body of the letter opens with a declaration that the gospel itself is God's power to bring about salvation (1:13–17). The phrase "eternal power and deity," then, refers not to features inherent in a remote and uninvolved deity but to God's own involvement in and with creation, an involvement already hinted at in "the things that are made."

The claim that God makes himself known through the natural world was not an unusual one among Paul's contemporaries.[17] Yet it would be quite far-fetched to conclude that Paul affirms the capacity of human beings to discern God from nature. The verses that follow will recall the refusal of humanity to acknowledge God, a refusal that in turn degrades the human mind such that it is no longer capable of seeing God where it ought to have been able to see God.

Verses 19–20 turn almost entirely on God's action of creation and revelation, but the end of v. 20 returns to the subject of human beings and the accusation of v. 18: "so they are without excuse." Because Paul does not, either here or later, specify who is included in the "they" of this accusation, his audience remains free to imagine themselves as outside this group of accused persons (Brooten 1996, 230). The next movement in this drama will put specificity to the accusation of impiety and wrongdoing announced in v. 18, but already here Paul anticipates the verdict of v. 32: there is no excuse.

[21–23] The second movement of this drama concerns humanity's rejection of God, a rejection Paul locates firmly in worship that is not merely withheld from God but actively perverted into practices of idolatry. Careful attention to the unfolding of the argument is important: humanity is without excuse because they knew God but they would not glorify or give thanks to God. What went wrong with the human condition did so, in the first instance, because of a refusal

---

17. It appears in both Jewish literature (e.g., Job 12:7–9; Ps 8:4; Sir 42:21–23; 43:1–33; Wis 13:1–9; Philo, *Embassy* 3.97–99; *Rewards* 41–43; *Spec. Laws* 1.33–35; 3.187–89) and Stoic texts (e.g., the reports in Cicero concerning the teaching of Zeno [*Nat. d.* 2.58], Cleanthes [*Nat. d.* 2:13–15], and Chrysippus [*Nat. d.* 2:16]; Epictetus, *Diatr.* 1.6.19).

to recognize the human condition, a refusal to recognize God as God and creature as creature.

The explication of this failure to glorify and give thanks follows closely on the preceding assertion that "they" are without excuse because "they knew God." Removed from its context, this comment might be thought to contradict other passages in which Paul describes believers as not having God (Gal 4:8) or distinguishes them from those who do not know God (1 Thess 4:5). More important, it could be understood to suggest that "they" continue to have an option to "decide" to worship God. But that is precisely what the remainder of the verse denies: "their" capacity to know and to worship is lost by virtue of the rejection of God. Only where God is acknowledged in worship is the knowledge of God retained (so also Schlier 55–56; Bell 1998, 49).

The force of v. 21 emerges in the charges that follow, beginning with the words "they did not glorify or give thanks to God as God." The patterns of behavior Paul specifies later in the passage should not deflect attention from this fundamental charge. The origin of humanity's failure appears here, in the refusal to offer glory and thanks to God, rather than in the details of vv. 26–31.[18] As the argument of the letter nears its end, these activities of glorifying and giving thanks return. The admonitions of chapter 14 begin with the recognition that differing practices all derive from giving thanks to God (14:6). In chapter 15 Paul prays that God will grant the Romans the gift of together "glorifying" God (15:6, 9), signaling that a humanity released from captivity to Sin is at last able to offer God glory.[19]

At this juncture, Paul carefully unpacks this refusal to worship God, a refusal that culminates in God's surrender of humanity to the power of Sin (vv. 24–32). Verse 21b vividly connects the refusal to worship God with the loss of faculties of intelligence and perception. Recalling the language of Ps 94:11 (93:11 LXX; see also 1 Cor 3:20) and Ps 75:6 LXX, Paul claims that human thinking became vain and human hearts grew darkened. Verse 22 continues the depiction of the loss of faculties, this time adding the charge that although "they" were "claiming to be wise, they actually became foolish" (cf. 1 Cor 1:18–31). The text is not explicit on this point, but it appears that the need to acknowledge God is essential to the human being, so that when God is not genuinely worshiped the primary faculties of thinking and perceiving become distorted. This human refusal produced a genuine corruption in human thinking.

The seriousness of this claim is not to be missed. Paul does not know of DNA, but it is as if he had written that the DNA itself had been altered. No hope remains for some other way of perceiving and thinking, once the faculties of the

---

18. So Minear 1959, 46: This withholding of worship is "the deepest, most stubborn root of sin."

19. As Karl Barth observes, "What the creature does in its new creatureliness, which in Jesus Christ has become gratitude, is to glorify God" (1957, 669).

62   Romans 1:18–32

human are altered. This is why speaking of vv. 19–20 as "natural theology" or "natural revelation" misses the point (as in, e.g., Osborne 47; Mounce 77–78; Witherington and Hyatt 66). The fact that "they knew God" led to rebellion or rejection of God, and there is not the slightest hint here that this knowledge can be retrieved apart from the revelation of Jesus Christ. The human cannot simply repent or change her mind.[20]

That incapacity comes to expression in terms of idolatry in the final statement of this second movement (v. 23). By supplanting God's own glory with that of a human being or, even worse, with that of an animal, idolatry is the most concrete expression of human ingratitude, human rebellion against God. Interpreters recognize similarities to the language of Jer 2:11 and Ps 106:20 (105:20 LXX), but those texts refer to the glory of the people themselves rather than to God's glory.[21] Paul thereby underscores the outrageous character of idolatry (so Jewett 160).

That much is to be expected, but the reference to divine glory is itself significant. In the LXX and other Jewish literature, God's glory refers to God's own presence (e.g., Exod 24:16; 40:34; Lev 9:23; Ps 56:6; Ezek 11:23), often in contexts of conflict, where God's presence signals the downfall of God's enemies (e.g., Exod 15:6–7; Isa 2:10; Hab 3; Bar 4:24; 5:6, 7, 9; and see 1QHª 11.33–37; CDᵇ 20.26; Mark 8:38; 13:26; Gaventa 2014b; and see below on 6:4). What humans "changed," therefore, was the powerful, saving presence of God in their midst. Later Paul will affirm that, as a result, all of humanity has been removed from God's glory, that is to say, from the presence of God (3:23).

The attack continues as Paul contrasts not simply "immortal God," on the one hand, with "mortal human," on the other, but God's "glory" with the vaguely described "likeness of an image" of a human being. *Homoiōma* ("likeness") and *eikōn* ("image") are virtually interchangeable, so that employing both of them is not only redundant but emphasizes the gross error of the exchange (Barrett 38). The addition of "birds and four-footed animals and reptiles" only compounds the assault (see, e.g., Deut 4:15–18 and Wis 11:15; 12:24; 15:18).

The introduction of idolatry allows Paul's audience to *imagine* that his target is restricted to gentiles. Here he reflects a common Jewish revulsion at the practice of idolatry, a revulsion widely reflected in the OT and depicted with special vividness in Wis 13:10–14:31 (see also, e.g., Sib. Or. 3.11–45; Philo, *Decalogue* 76–80; *Contempl. Life* 8–9; *Spec. Laws* 1.13–27; Acts 17:22–31). To an audience with a larger number of gentiles (see the introduction on audience) who are now followers of Christ, this critique may have been soothing, as

20. Francis Watson observes regarding this passage that "the effect of the primal revelation was, simply and solely, its own distortion into idolatry" (1997, 261).
21. To be sure, the Hebrew of Ps 106:20 does refer to "God's glory."

they assume that idolatry is a problem of their neighbors or their own past, not yet imagining that they themselves are still included in the criticism.

At the same time that the subject matter indicts gentile idolatry, some phrases here reflect OT texts that associate Israel itself with idolatry. For example, Ps 106:20 (105:20 LXX) describes the golden calf incident as "they exchanged their glory for the image of an ox" (see also Deut 4:15–18; Wedderburn 1980). A subtle irony emerges, as the "gentile problem" is cast in language that also applies to Israel, laying the groundwork for 2:1 and what follows. One difference from the texts cited above, however, is that their critiques of idolatry directly identify gentiles as the culprit. By contrast, the unidentified "they" of Romans 1 simultaneously invites the audience to conclude that "they" points to gentiles and leaves open the possibility that Jews themselves are liable to equally severe charges.

[24–32] With the beginning of the third movement of this story, the subject changes from humanity to God. Since the assertion that humanity is "without excuse" in v. 20, every verb has depicted the action of human beings or the result of that action. With the opening of v. 24, God again is the agent (as at the end of v. 19), and here God's action takes a form that is genuinely terrifying, for Paul declares that "God handed them over."[22] This declaration shifts the terms of the story, for there is now a new character to whom God is handing over an ingrate, worshipless humanity, a character as yet unnamed who will produce in humanity not simply more idolatry but a massive harvest of misconduct that requires the remainder of the chapter to enumerate. And the distinctiveness of this assertion is the more impressive when compared with the often-adduced Wis 13–15, which does not attribute to God a direct role in the handing over of sinners. (The same is true also of other texts customarily cited in connection with Rom 1:18–32: Let. Aris. 132–38; Sib. Or. 3.8–45; T. Naph. 3.3; Josephus, *Ag. Ap.* 2.236–54; Philo, *Spec. Laws* 1.13–31.)

The repetition of the phrase "God handed them over" in v. 26 and again in v. 28 marks it as crucial to the passage, perhaps even to the whole letter. Comparison to Paul's use of repetition near the beginning of earlier letters is instructive. In the opening lines of Galatians, Paul twice pronounces a curse on those who would preach "another gospel" (1:8–9), and 2 Cor 1:3–7 repeats *paraklēsis* ("exhortation") and the related verb *parakaleō* ("exhort"). In both contexts, the repetitions signal a major concern of the letter. Syntactically, Rom 1:24, 26, 28 are closer to 1 Cor 1:27–28 in that there also Paul repeats a verb three times, in each case with God as the subject. Translated rather woodenly:

---

22. This discussion of *paradidōmi* and its implications for understanding Romans 1 draws on research presented in Gaventa 2005; 2007b, 113–23, 194–200.

The foolish things of the world God chose,
the weak things of the world God chose,
the lowborn things of the world and the despised God chose.

As with the examples from Galatians and 2 Corinthians, here Paul announces a key issue of the letter, in this case the authority of God over human ways of knowing and assessing. Such passages strengthen the supposition that the repetition in 1:24, 26, and 28 similarly signals a major concern of the letter.

The three *paredōken* (God handed over) clauses in vv. 24, 26, and 28 introduce three subsections of this final movement in the passage (vv. 24–25, 26–27, and 28–32):

> v. 24: Therefore God handed them over
> > because of the desires of their hearts
> > to impurity
> v. 26: Therefore God handed them over
> > to dishonorable desires
> v. 28: And because . . . God handed them over
> > to an unfit way of thinking

Earlier commentators understood these *paredōken* statements in a permissive or privative sense, according to which God withdraws, permitting humanity to go its own way (Chrysostom, *Hom. Rom.* 3.24; *NPNF*[1] 11.354; Augustine 59; Dodd 29), and more recent commentators have treated them forensically with the understanding that God hands humanity over to judgment (Sanday and Headlam 45; Schlatter 42; Cranfield 1:120–21; Haacker 51–52; Lohse 89; Hultgren 92).

More needs to be said of this handing over, both as it involves God and as it suggests the involvement of a third party. Xenophon writes that Cyrus intimidated the Syrians to surrender (*paradidōmi*) a fort (*Cyr.* 5.4.51); Pausanias recounts Antiope's surrender (*paradidōmi*) of a stronghold to Heracles (*Descr.* 1.2.1).[23] In the LXX, the verb *paradidōmi* regularly refers to the turning over of someone or something to a third party, often in a situation of conflict. For example, in Deut 2:24, Moses recounts God's words: "Look, I have handed over to your hand King Sihon."[24] The prophets routinely use *paradidōmi* when declaring God's intention to hand Israel itself over, as when Jer 21:10 announces that Jerusalem will be handed over to Babylon (and see 22:25; 24:8; 39:28). Ezekiel warns that God will turn over Israel's possessions to "the wicked of the earth" (7:21; see also 11:9; 16:27; 21:36 LXX [21:31]; 23:28; 25:4). Paul

23. See also P. Hib. 92.11, 17; P. Lille 3.59; P. Tebt. 38.6; BDAG s.v.; LSJ s.v.
24. The verb occurs more than twenty times in Deuteronomy, virtually always following this same pattern (e.g., 2:30, 31, 33; 3:2, 3; 7:2, 23, 24; 20:13, 20; 28:7). The usage in Joshua is similar (e.g., 2:14, 24; 6:2, 16; 7:7; 8:18; 10:8, 12).

himself uses the verb similarly in 1 Cor 5:5; 15:24; Rom 4:25; 6:17; 8:32 (see also 1 Cor 11:23; Gal 2:20).

Additionally, in most instances of "handing over," the third party is an identifiable agent rather than an abstraction. Even in prophetic texts warning about the outcome of unfaithful or disobedient behavior, the "handing over" involves another power (e.g., the Chaldeans, the "hands of foreigners," "the will of your enemies," or "the people of the East") rather than an abstraction depicting the consequences of wrongdoing.[25]

This widespread pattern of usage suggests that in Rom 1:24, 26, and 28 also, the handing over takes place in a situation of conflict that involves God, humanity, and a third party. The third party has not yet been identified, but it will be explicitly named as Sin in 3:9: "All are under the power of Sin." Paul does point in the direction of the third party even here, however, since all three instances of the *paredōken* phrase in Rom 1 are followed by *eis* ("to" or "into") and an object identifying the power to which humanity has been delivered up.

The first *paredōken* clause, unlike the second and third, is followed immediately by "because of the desires of their hearts." Although Paul can write of desire (*epithymia*) in a positive sense, as conveying his longing to be with Christ (Phil 1:23) or his longing to be reunited with the Thessalonians (1 Thess 2:17), desire often has the connotation of forbidden desire or desire that is out of control (Rom 13:14; 1 Thess 4:5; Gal 5:16, 24).[26] In this particular context, the "desires of their hearts" stands as an apt summary of vv. 21–23. What humanity has desired is release from the obligation to acknowledge God, resulting in the senseless heart of v. 21. Because of these very desires, God handed them over.

With the remainder of the verse—God handed them over "to impurity so that their very bodies were dishonored"—Paul gives the first indication of the captor to whom humanity has been delivered. The language of "impurity" (*akatharsia* or its cognate, the adjective *akathartos*) seldom appears in Paul's letters (1 Cor 7:14; 2 Cor 6:17; 12:21; Gal 5:19; 1 Thess 2:3; 4:7), but in Romans it appears again in 6:19 as Paul recalls that the audience earlier had "presented your limbs as slaves to impurity." The following verse picks up the same point, this time with the wording "when you were slaves of Sin." "Impurity" in 6:19 metonymically represents Sin itself, and the same conclusion may be appropriate for 1:24. Gospel usage confirms this perception, since

25. Micah 6:16 might be regarded as an exception, but even there the "destruction" and "hissing" to which Israel is to be handed over are obviously references to captivity by the nations. Similarly in Ps 118:18 (117:18 LXX), the "death" to which the speaker is handed over comes about at the hands of human enemies.

26. See also, e.g., 1 Tim 6:9; 1 Pet 1:14; Eph 4:22; and often in Stoic texts such as Epictetus *Diatr.* 2.16.45; 2.18.8–10; 3.9.21; see BDAG, s.v. *epithumia*).

the "unclean" or "impure" spirits that subject human beings to possession are there closely associated with the powers of God's enemy, Satan (e.g., Mark 3:11; Luke 4:33, 36).[27]

The result of this captivity by impurity is the dishonoring of human bodies. In view of the association of impurity and sexual immorality elsewhere in Paul's letters (2 Cor 12:21; Gal 5:19; 1 Thess 4:7), and in the lines that follow, the dishonoring of the body refers to the physical body, that is, inappropriate and shameful sexual conduct. More is included here, however, than sexuality. The *sōma* ("body") is the entire person, the "capacity for communication" (Käsemann 1969c, 191). The whole person is dishonored, which means that dishonoring involves not just the sexual human but the intellectual one, the emotional one, the commercial one, and so on—hence the long list of vices in vv. 28–31. It is this total dishonoring Paul has in mind, as is clear when he returns to the topic of idolatry in v. 25. In addition, this dishonoring is reversed when the rescued humanity is enabled to deliver up the entire body as a sacrifice in 12:1.

Verse 25 returns to the problem announced for the first time in v. 21, the distorted worship of what is created rather than of the Creator. Idolatry is clearly included in this indictment, but it is framed in a way that includes far more than the worship of images. The charge of substituting "the lie" for "the truth" about God pertains to idolatry, but it also pertains to much of the behavior depicted in ch. 2 (e.g., presuming to know God's judgment on others without recognizing one's own liability to judgment, masquerading as an advocate of God's law while violating the law). Similarly, worship of what is created applies quite narrowly to idolatry, yet it also extends to include the acts of boasting of one's relationship to God (2:17), of boasting over the "root" (11:16–17), of thinking more highly of oneself than one ought to think (12:3), and of judging others whose convictions and practices differ from one's own (14:1–23).

Reference to the Creator prompts the blessing at the end of the verse. This conventional blessing of God has parallels in Paul's letters (Rom 9:5; 2 Cor 1:3) and often elsewhere (e.g., Gen 9:26; 1 Sam 25:32; 2 Sam 18:28; 1 Kgs 1:48; 8:15; 2 Chr 2:12; Ps 41:13; Luke 1:68; Eph 1:3; 1 Pet 1:3). Its function here may be construed negatively, as an indication of Paul's revulsion at the very idea of idolatry (so Dunn 1:64), but it may also be construed positively, exemplifying the acknowledgment of God that is the first proper role of the human.

---

27. Ambrosiaster seems to draw the same conclusion when he writes of this passage, "They, in turning away from God, were given up to the devil" (29). And see the perceptive comments on *paradidōmi* here and elsewhere in the NT in K. Barth 1957, 458–506: "[God] makes [humans] so powerless that He gives them over to the authority of a power which is too great for them—the power, in fact, of their enemy—that he may rule them" (484).

The blessing culminates with "Amen," the first of several instances of the word in Romans (9:5; 11:36; 15:33; [16:27]).[28] Importantly, when the Hebrew word "amen" appears in the OT, the context is usually that of corporate worship (see, e.g., 1 Chr 16:36; Neh 5:13; 8:6; Pss 41:13; 72:19; 89:52; 106:48).[29] Similarly, the Dead Sea Scrolls employ the term "amen" in liturgical settings (e.g., 1QS 1.20; 2.10; 2.18; 4Q286 7.ii.1; 7.ii.5; 7.ii.10). Consistent with this pattern, 1 Cor 14:16 assumes that with the "amen" those present in worship assent to what is being said and done (even in the case of outsiders to the Christian community). Culminating the blessing with "amen," then, invites those present at the reading of the letter to join their voices with those of Phoebe and Paul in assent to the claims Paul is making about God (Gaventa 2008a, 59–62; Martyn 1997a, 92). In effect, then, Paul's letter enacts or at least invites worship of God—worship that is newly restored following the death and resurrection of Jesus Christ—even as it charges that humanity's generative problem is the withholding of worship to God.

Verse 26 replays the initial *paredōken* clause of v. 24 (see above for discussion), but now the object of the handing over is "dishonorable passions" (*eis pathē atimias*). With the same phrase, 1 Thess 4:5 warns believers against the sexual immorality of those outside the community, but otherwise Paul does not use the word *pathos*. The closely related expression "sinful desires" (*ta pathēmata tōn hamartiōn*) does appear in Rom 7:5, where these "sinful desires" are said to work through (*energeisthai*) the law to bring about death; "sinful desires," then, are capable of being the subject of action, capable of ensnaring human beings. As with impurity in v. 24, "dishonorable passions" anticipates the explicit introduction of the anti-God powers later in the letter.

The remainder of vv. 26–27 offers specific examples of the working of these sinful passions in the form of homoerotic behavior. Many features of these verses and the concerns that give rise to them warrant attention, but understanding their place in the argument is crucial. Paul has already identified human "ungodliness and wrong" with the refusal to give God thanks and praise, *as a result of which* God surrendered humanity to God's own enemies, here identified as impurity, dishonorable passions, and an unfit mind (in v. 28). The behavior of vv. 26–27, as well as the actions that follow in vv. 28–31, stand as illustrations of the consequences of Sin, not as Sin in and of itself.

The behavior adduced as the first example of the control of the "dishonorable passions" is that of same-sex relations. In the context of an accusation

28. Although Rom 16:25–27 may well have been added at a later time, the presence of the "amen" is consistent with the pattern of the letter. It appears elsewhere in 1 Cor 14:16; 2 Cor 1:20; Gal 1:5; 6:18; Phil 4:20; 1 Thess 3:13.

29. The LXX, however, does not have *amēn* in all of these instances, but only in 1 Chr 16:36; Neh 5:13; 8:6.

about idolatry, the introduction of what Paul regards as sexual immorality is scarcely surprising, since the two are regularly linked in Jewish tradition (e.g., Isa 57:1–13; Jer 8:4–21; Ezek 16:36; 18:15; Hos 2:12–13; Mic 1:7; Wis 14:12; see also Acts 15:20, 29; 21:25). Given the rhetorical force of this passage, pulling hearers in so that they stand alongside Paul and Phoebe in indignation at "their" behavior, the decision to comment specifically on same-sex relations is a shrewd one, as it plays on the widespread revulsion at homoerotic behavior in Paul's social world. Same-sex relations are rarely mentioned in biblical texts, but they are routinely condemned when mentioned (see Lev 18:22; 20:13; and cf. 1 Cor 6:9; 1 Tim 1:10).[30] Paul's comments do not merely replay the strictures of Leviticus, however. They also reflect the Roman world's understanding of gender hierarchy. In non-Jewish texts, sexual relations between people of the same gender were understood to be abnormal, not because of divine disapproval but because masculinity was associated with the act of penetration. "Real" men were those who penetrated; and men who were sexually passive, acted upon rather than acting, were regarded with disdain (e.g., Aristotle, *Eth. nic.* 1148b.15–1149a.20; Artemidorus, *Onir.* 1.78–80; Winkler 1990, 33–41; Martin 1995a, 29–34). In the context of a larger indictment on the charges of refusing to serve God as God, refusing to conform to the order of creation, this ancient understanding of homoeroticism as a violation of the "natural" order serves Paul's argument particularly well.

Paul begins with reference to the behavior of women, a striking decision since most ancient texts that refer to homoeroticism make no reference to women, and the conventional pattern would be to speak about men first, women only secondarily, if at all. Instead of the more usual noun for women, *gynē*, Paul uses *thēlys*, which appears in contexts having to do with created sexual differences (see Gen 1:27 LXX; Gal 3:28). Paul writes that "their females exchanged the natural sexual practice for the one that is unnatural," repeating the change/exchange language earlier in the passage. Sexual behavior is not explicitly mentioned, but *chrēsis* has the connotation of sexual use (BDAG s.v.), and the explicit language of v. 27 leaves no doubt that Paul refers to sexual use here.

Precisely because Paul does not unambiguously say that women engaged in sexual relations with one another, it has been argued that what he has in mind

---

30. Others have posited a link between this passage and Gen 1:27–28 and 2:18–24, arguing that the references to God as Creator in 1:18–32 suggest that he and his audience would recollect the Genesis account (e.g., Hays 1996, 386–87). Of course, interest in God as Creator is in no way confined to Genesis (see, e.g., Job 26:7–13; Pss 8; 19:1–4; 33:6–9; Isa 40:21–28; 42:5; 45:12; Jer 10:10–16; Neh 9:6), making it precarious to assume that Gen 1:27–28 and 2:18–24 are in play here, simply by virtue of creation language. More importantly, those texts demonstrate the divine origin of procreation and marriage; they do not restrict marriage to male-female couples capable of procreation or prescribe heterosexual marriage for everyone (Fretheim 1994, 345–46; Furnish 2009a, 63–66).

here is not same-sex relations at all but impermissible heterosexual behavior.[31] The "likewise" at the beginning of v. 27, however, firmly connects the two statements with one another. In addition, since v. 27 clearly refers to homoerotic sexual relations, it is highly likely that v. 26 does also. Paul's indirectness in v. 26 may derive from a certain discomfort with any discussion of female sexual behavior.

The phrase *para physin*, here translated "unnatural" (i.e., contrary to nature), has evoked considerable discussion. Because the preposition *para* can have the connotation of "beyond" as well as "contrary," some have argued that here it should be taken as "beyond" nature, that is, behaviors outside of one's natural proclivity, so that persons of heterosexual orientation would be acting "beyond" their nature if they engaged in homosexual acts (Boswell 1980; cf. Hays 1986). As has been well established, however, the ancient world did not operate with an understanding of heterosexual or homosexual orientation, so that this proposal transposes a distinctly modern concept into an alien framework. In addition, while the preposition *para* can imply "more than" or "beyond" (as in "they worshiped and served the created instead of [*para*] the Creator" [1:25], or "more highly than [*para*] you ought to think" [12:3]), the phrase *para physin* regularly occurs in texts concerning sexual conduct, where it is contrasted with *kata physin* ("in conformity to nature"; see, e.g., Josephus, *Ag. Ap.* 2.273, 275; Philo, *Spec. Laws* 3.39; Plutarch, *Amat.* 751C, E).

What one society construes as natural, however, another may regard as unnatural. For example, Paul regards nature as requiring that men have short hair and women long hair (1 Cor 11:14–15), a conviction that seems quaint to contemporary readers (and see his reference to gentiles who do not have the law "by nature" in Rom 2:14). And especially in the arena of sexual conduct, understandings of what is or is not regarded as natural have a great deal to do with assumptions about the social order. For Roman society, as noted above, the sexual hierarchy reflected the assumption of the superiority of the active penetrator over the passive penetrated. The notion of women engaged in sexual relations with one another, then, was "contrary to nature," since women were regarded as naturally passive, and their sexual relations were thought to reflect that passivity (Brooten 1996, 216).

Verse 26 is relatively indirect in its comments on sex between women, but the condemnation of same-sex relations among men is scarcely to be accused of similar indirectness. Here Paul not only states the matter explicitly ("men with men"), but describes it as burning with strong desire, as shameful behavior, and as deserving of its reward. The striking image of burning desire provides

31. J. E. Miller 1995. This view was evidently debated as early as the fourth century, as Ambrosiaster initially takes v. 26 to refer to "unnatural" acts between men and women and subsequently modifies his view so that it refers to same-sex relations (de Bruyn 2011).

a clue to Paul's concern (and see the similar notion in 1 Cor 7:9). In common with his contemporaries, he regarded desire of any kind as dangerous, sexual desire as especially dangerous, and same-sex relations as evidence of desire out of control.[32] Homoerotic conduct serves Paul's argument especially well, then, because according to assumptions prevalent at the time, it epitomizes the cancerous passions that result from God handing over humankind to its own desires.

When introducing the third and final *paredōken* clause in v. 28, Paul extends the brief introductions of vv. 24 and 26 to the statement "and because they did not suitably acknowledge God." This statement reinforces the earlier charge that humanity has refused to acknowledge God as God, that the underlying problem is one of false worship and ingratitude. The behaviors introduced, whether sexual or otherwise, result from this fundamental refusal to acknowledge God. In this third instance, God hands humanity over to "an unfit way of thinking." "Unsuitable" (*adokimos*) here plays on the phrase "did not suitably acknowledge" (*edokimasan*) that opens the verse. Although this third phrase, "an unsuitable way of thinking," does not appear again in Romans, a closely related expression appears in 8:6–7, referring to the "thinking" (*phronēma*) of the flesh that is death, a way of thinking that sets itself over against God. As in the first two *paredōken* clauses of vv. 24 and 26, this is yet another instance of metonymy; what God hands humanity over to is Sin, here expressed as an "unfit mind," with the result that "they" did things that are not to be done.

With vv. 29–31, Paul enumerates other results of this "handing over" in the form of a list of vices, similar to other such lists found elsewhere in the NT and in other literature of the period.[33] This one is notable in that it is the only such list in the Pauline letters that makes no reference to sexual immorality, presumably because vv. 26–27 have already done so. When read in translation, the list seems to conform to no order whatever, but it does in fact reflect careful construction. Verse 29 consists of two parallel adjectival constructions beginning with "being filled up" or "full of." The first is followed by four nouns (evil, wrong, wickedness, greed), and the second by four nouns (envy, murder, discord, malicious cunning). Verses 30–31 itemize twelve vices, the final four of which (v. 31) are all alpha-privatives, combining the alliteration of the "a" sound with the accusation against humankind (Byrne 32–33). Far from random, the presentation is highly organized and rhetorically dramatic. A number of the items included appear in other such lists, but the opening is particularly appropriate to the letter. It begins with "being filled up with all wrong" (*pasē adikia*), recalling the "all" motif earlier in the chapter; equally important,

32. See, for example, Philo, *Abr.* 133–41; Dio Chrysostom, *Or.* 7.151–52; and Martin 1995b, 343, who comments, "Gluttony was 'too much eating'; homosexuality was 'too much sex.'"
33. For an overview of the genre and numerous examples, see Fitzgerald 1992.

"wrong" underscores both the opening announcement of God's wrath against "all wrong" and the rectification of that wrong announced in 1:16–17.

The summation of v. 32 draws the list to a close: although humans know the ordinance of God that those who do these things deserve death, they not only do them but approve of those who do them. It is hard to understand how approving those who do wrong ranks alongside—or even ahead of—actually doing the wrong. Second Corinthians 8:10, however, may offer a parallel move; there Paul recalls how the Corinthians began not only to act in the matter of the collection but also to will that act. By prioritizing the approval of bad actions, Paul may be anticipating the turn in 2:1 to the accusation about judging others.

The declaration that people who do these things deserve death seems extreme, particularly when the list includes offenses such as gossip and bragging. This hyperbolic claim confirms the observation that Paul is not so much drawing up a bill of particulars, making a case against each and every individual based on observed actions, as he is analyzing the results of human rejection of God. What precisely does it mean to say that they are "worthy of death"? Customarily this assertion is read as "deserve to die," to be deserving of the end of life.[34] When the word "death" reenters the letter in chapter 5, however, it does so as a power by the name of Death that enters the world to take humanity captive. It is not at all unlikely that this notion of captivity to the powers is at work in chapter 1 as well.

The sweeping character of the accusation and the rhetoric in this passage prompts some readers and hearers to react with incredulity. It is simply wrong to say that all (even all gentiles) have committed the actions so confidently recited here. Indeed, in a few short lines, Paul himself will praise some gentiles for their unwitting keeping of the law. After all, even the Areopagus speech of Acts 17, which places on Paul's lips another attack on idolatry, credits those same idolaters with a desire for God, albeit a falsely directed search.

Yet complaining that Paul is guilty of hyperbole misses the nature of the accusation. This is not a legal argument in which Paul presents a bill of particulars and documents the offenses of every single human being. It more closely resembles an observation that "the voting public has no concern for the long-term flourishing of the economy," or that "car buyers pay too little attention to gas mileage." Like such statements, Paul's analysis takes place on a large canvas. Although the audiences gathered in Rome may relish momentarily the thought that the "they" Paul indicts are *other* people, by the time Phoebe reaches 3:9 in her reading of the letter, it is clear that this canvas involves all of humankind. Indeed, the story is even larger than all of humanity, since it involves

---

34. Stephen Sondheim's disturbed and disturbing character Sweeney Todd sings in his towering rage, "They all deserve to die" ("Epiphany"). Todd goes on to include himself and his partner, Mrs. Lovett, in that death sentence, something Paul will do as well later in the letter.

not only God but also the captors of humankind: Sin and Death. The letter shows plainly that the wrath of God stems from human rejection of God, and that humanity is handed over to Sin as a consequence, which in turn produces captivity to the various behaviors depicted.

If some contemporary readers recoil at the ferocity of Paul's argument, others will be profoundly angered by his decision to use same-sex relations as a primary illustration of the workings of Sin. Far too many readers may resemble the small gatherings of believers who listened to Phoebe read this passage for the first time, happily identifying themselves as the unspoken "we" and urging Paul on in his accusation against "them," "those" gentiles who deserve death. They may anticipate that this accusation serves as a prelude to a word of comfort for God's faithful people, both Jews and the gentiles who have joined them. Wisdom of Solomon, after all, moves from its castigation of the gentiles to assuring its audience that Israel will not sin (15:1–6). Phoebe's hearers are about to receive a rude awakening if they imagine that somehow they are exempt from the accusation of this drama.

2:1–29 No Excuses, No Favoritism

Phoebe's auditors may have relished Paul's dramatic presentation of the rebellion and subsequent captivity of humanity, assuming that its stinging accusations are meant for people other than themselves. With 2:1, however, Paul pivots to attack precisely those who fancy that they agree with him, those who presume themselves innocent of his earlier accusations. Here he undermines the notion that there are exceptions to the "handing over" (1:24, 26, 28) by contending that no one escapes divine judgment. The argument is complex, including assertions and insinuations about specific wrongdoings, appeals to divine impartiality, and a radical destabilizing of the categories of Jew and gentile. The extent of this destabilizing becomes clear at the chapter's end, where even the physical, visible, objective difference between "circumcision" and "uncircumcision" is undermined. The result is to seal the exit doors against those who regard themselves as removed from captivity to Sin and Death.

The chapter begins with a direct address attacking the presumption to judgment by a corrupt judge and asserting the comprehensiveness and impartiality of God's judgment (vv. 1–11). A second section (vv. 12–16) then considers how gentiles might become recipients of "glory and honor and peace" in the day of God's judgment. The remainder of the chapter (vv. 17–29) reverses the scenario, considering the possibility that Jews may stand condemned.

This latter possibility, that those who identify themselves as Jews might be condemned, emerges in the third section (vv. 17–24), which returns to the use of direct address. Although vv. 25–29 initially concede the benefit of circumcision, the argument further undermines the categories of circumcision and uncircumcision, prompting the stunning question of 3:1: Does being a Jew carry any benefit whatsoever?

Elements of Greco-Roman diatribal style appear in this chapter, especially the use of direct address to an interlocutor (vv. 1, 3, 17), raising the possibility that Paul's comments here do not address an actual situation at Rome but are intended as a response to hypothetical arguments, a response Paul wants Roman believers to overhear. Yet the concerns expressed here dovetail considerably with other parts of the letter, especially 1:18–32; 3:1–26; 5:12–21; and 14:1–15:6, making it likely that Paul regards the stance of the interlocutor as a genuine possibility at Rome as elsewhere.

2:1 Therefore you have no excuse—you there!ᵃ—every one of you judges. For while you are judging the other person, you judge yourself condemned,ᵇ since you, the judge, are doing the very same things. 2 We know that God's judgment falls in truth on those who do such things. 3 But do you imagine—you there—the judge of those who do such things while doing them yourself,ᶜ that *you*ᵈ will flee God's judgment? 4 Or do you look down on the riches of God's goodness and endurance and patience, not knowing that God's goodness leads *you* to repentance? 5 Because of your hardened and unrepentant heart you treasure for yourself wrath on the day of wrath and the apocalyptic revelationᵉ of the right judgment of God. 6 God will "repay to each according to works." 7 On the one hand, for those who, through persistence in work that is good, seek glory and honor and immortality, there will be life forever. 8 But on the other hand, for those who, out of selfishness, both reject the truth and obey the wrong, there will be wrath and rage. 9 On the one hand, there will be affliction and anguish on every human life that produces evil, the Jew first and also the Greek. 10 On the other hand, there will be glory and honor and peace for everyone who works the good, the Jew first and also the Greek. 11 For there is no favoritism with God.

12 For those outside the law who have sinnedᶠ will also perish outside the law, and those within the law who sin will be judged through the law. 13 For mere hearers of the law are not right before God, but instead doers of the law will be rectified. 14 For whenever gentiles, who do not have the law by nature, keep the obligations of the law, they are law for themselves, even though they do not have the law. 15 People like that show that the work of the law is written in their hearts, their conscience testifying for them and their own inner imaginings accusing or defending them 16 in the day when God judgesᵍ people's private thoughtsʰ in accordance with myⁱ gospel through Christ Jesus.

17 But if *you* call yourself a Jew and you rely on the law and boast in God, 18 and you know God's will and you discern the things that matter

because you are taught by the law, 19 and you are confident that you are a guide to the blind, a light to those in darkness, 20 an instructor for the foolish, a teacher of babes, having the embodiment of knowledge and truth in the law— 21 then, while you are teaching another, do you teach yourself? While preaching against stealing, do you steal? 22 While speaking against adultery, do you commit adultery? While detesting idols, do you commit sacrilege? 23 While you boast in the law, do you dishonor God through transgression of the law? 24 For "the name of God is blasphemed among the gentiles on your account," as it is written.

25 Now circumcision is valuable if you practice the law; but if you are a transgressor of the law, your circumcision has become uncircumcision. 26 Therefore if uncircumcision keeps the right decrees of the law, isn't his uncircumcision counted as circumcision? 27 And the natural uncircumcision who fulfills the law will judge you to be a transgressor of the law even if you do have Scripture and circumcision.ʲ 28 For there is no such thing as an obvious Jew, nor is even circumcision in the flesh something obvious, 29 but the Jew is not visible (i.e., not apparent), and circumcision of the heart is through the spirit rather than the letter. Praise of such a person comes not from human beings but from God.

a. Lit., "O human" or "O man," but "you there" reflects more idiomatically the abrupt move into second-person speech.

b. "Judge yourself condemned" displays the relationship between *krineis* ("you judge") and *katakrineis* ("condemn").

c. The addition of "yourself" brings out the accusation of hypocrisy against the unjust judge.

d. The addition of italics here and below in vv. 4 and 17 reflects the presence of the emphatic pronoun *sy*.

e. Consistent with 1:17–18, this *apokalypsis* is not simply the revealing of information but a disruption of cosmic proportions, as becomes clear in the argument that follows.

f. The aorist "sinned" is a "collective historical aorist" (Cranfield 1:153) that views the situation from the time of judgment; thus, the translation renders it into the English perfect tense (see also 3:23).

g. Some manuscripts (D² K L 33 81 et al.) read the future "will judge" rather than the present "judges." Since the difference consists of a single accent mark and most early manuscripts have no accent, little external evidence informs a decision. It does, however, seem easier to understand why scribes would have altered the present tense to a future tense than the reverse (so also Jewett 193).

h. Lit., "the inner things," but this expression (*ta krypta*) appears elsewhere with reference to thoughts, plans, purposes (BDAG s.v.; e.g., T. Reu. 1.4; 1 Cor 14:25). These are not "hidden" thoughts in the sense that they are deliberately concealed; instead, they are thoughts inaccessible to other human beings.

i. A few manuscripts omit "my," presumably because of concerns about the connotation of Paul claiming the gospel for his own.

j. Lit., "through letter and circumcision." The "letter" (*gramma*) clearly refers to Scripture itself, given the discussion of the characteristics of Jews and especially "the sayings" of God in 3:2.

[2:1] The abrupt introduction of direct address creates the initial impression that this verse marks a change of direction from 1:18–32, but a closer examination of the passage reveals consistency in subject matter.[35] The opening word, *dio* ("therefore"), indicates that what follows draws out conclusions from the previous section, even if the connection is not yet clear. The charge that "you have no excuse" (*anapologētos*) repeats the charge 1:20 introduced against all humanity (again *anapologētous*, "they have no excuse"). Similarly, the repetition of "all" or "every" (*pas*), "doing" (*prassein*), and "truth" (*alētheia*) connects the two passages.

The use of direct address in vv. 1, 3–5, 17–23 is a familiar rhetorical feature in a wide range of texts.[36] In this case, the interlocutor is someone who imagines she stands outside the depiction of 1:18–32 and the concluding judgment that "those who do such things are worthy of death." Further, the interlocutor is familiar with Scripture (2:6 in particular), recognizes the priority of Jews (2:9–10), and, whether Jewish or gentile, self-identifies as a Jew (see below on 2:17).[37] Paul is not directly addressing actual persons at Rome, because the sharpness of the attack is ill-suited for the Roman setting where he himself is unknown and for which he requires careful diplomacy.[38] Nonetheless, as the audience overhears this attack, it will (or it should) find itself implicated; if not, the later treatment of the universal reign of Sin (3:9, 20, 23; 5:12–21) should bring this section to mind, to say nothing of the specific arguments later in the letter about overconfidence in one's own judgment (12:3, 16) and about judgment within the community (14:1–23).

The initial characteristic ascribed to the interlocutor is that of distorted judgment. Four times this single verse uses the verb "judge" (*krinō*) or "judge condemned" (*katakrinō*). The second half of the verse specifies the problem: the judge is doing the "same things" as those whom he is judging. Questions about

35. This startling shift is not the only trick Paul plays on his auditors, although it may be the most obvious. See the introduction and below on 3:19; 5:3; 11:1, 13.

36. E.g., Plato, *Symp.* 172a; Philo, *Mos.* 2.199; Jas 2:20; Plutarch, *Alex.* 69.4; Epictetus, *Diatr.* 2.17.35.

37. Some scholars contend that the interlocutor is initially a gentile and that Paul shifts to a Jewish interlocutor (or someone who identifies as a Jew) at 2:17 (e.g., Stowers 1994, 103–4; Tobin 2004, 115), but the unity of the argument throughout ch. 2 and the attribution of Jewish assumptions to the interlocutor throughout 2:1–16 make that shift unlikely.

38. In 11:13, where Paul does address gentile Christians at Rome, his remarks are direct but less barbed than here in 2:1–5.

the identity of the "judge" prompt the claim that the interlocutor in 2:1–11 cannot be a Jew, on the assumption that Jews did not do *ta auta* ("the same things"); that is, they did not practice idolatry and were sharply critical of same-sex relations (Byrne 86). A little suspicion regarding such generalizations is warranted, however, particularly of the notion that Jews did not engage in same-sex relations; this is obviously a matter on which no direct evidence is available. And indeed, the practice of idolatry was so ubiquitous in the ancient world that it is difficult to imagine that Jews living in Rome or elsewhere entirely escaped being implicated in service of the gods. There are differences between what texts prescribe or depict and what takes place in practice.

Even if we imagine that Jews did not engage in idolatry and same-sex relations, *ta auta* ("the same things") could refer to any and all of the vices listed in 1:29–31. More to the point, the initial, generative problem of humanity is its refusal to recognize God as God (see above on 1:18–32), and that rebellion against God can happily coexist with even the most careful adherence to religious norms. Whatever precise content Paul has in mind for *ta auta*, he claims that those who know about God's judgment (as in 2:2) and who see the faults of others are nonetheless culpable. With this opening verse, then, Paul begins to undermine the assumption that 1:18–32 has to do exclusively with gentiles.

The condemnation the interlocutor ("the judge") executes upon himself while judging others anticipates Paul's discussion of the universal condemnation brought about through Adam's disobedience (5:16, 18). The interlocutor represents only one of many ways in which Sin exerts its power. Later still, Paul will announce that there is no condemnation in Christ Jesus (8:1) and that no one will be able to bring charges against or condemn Christ's own (8:33–34), signaling the gospel's power (as in 1:16) to redeem humanity from its captivity.

[2] Paul moves from accusation ("you have no excuse") to a statement of shared knowledge ("we know") that succinctly recalls the end of chapter 1, this time inviting the audience to his side with "we" (see also, e.g., 3:19; 7:14; 8:22, 26, 28). The phrase "those who do such things" repeats the wording in 1:32, where "they" are said to be worthy of death (or perhaps of the power of Death, which has them in its grasp). The contrast with 2:1 goes well beyond the shift in pronouns, however, since here it is God's judgment that is rightly at work rather than the false and inappropriate human judgment in v. 1. The additional phrase *kata alētheian* ("in truth") finds parallels in Paul's contemporaries who similarly associate truth with divine judgment.[39] The reference to truth does not suggest that there is some standard of truth external to God, but that truth is identified with God; in 1:18, when humans suppress the truth, what they are suppressing *is* knowledge of God.

39. See especially 1QS 4.19–20 because of its association with eschatological judgment, and also 1QS 11.14; CD 20.29–30; see also 4 Ezra 7.34; 2 Bar. 85.9.

[3–4] The concession to shared knowledge about God's reliable judgment vanishes quickly with v. 3, which forcefully recasts the opening question of v. 1. Verse 1 addresses ("you there!—every one of you judges") and then accuses: "For while you are judging the other person, you judge yourself condemned, since you, the judge, are doing the very same things." In v. 3, the address and the accusation are collapsed into a single act: " . . . you there—the judge of those who do such things while doing them yourself." "Every one of you [who] judges" now becomes "the judge of those who do such things while doing them yourself." And the question that follows returns to God's judgment, not in a general apodictic form but as a pointed accusation: Do you imagine that *you* will escape God's judgment? The addition of the emphatic pronoun "you" (*sy*) leaves little to the imagination. The interlocutor, in Paul's view, imagines that it is possible to escape God's judgment even while she is doing "the same things" as those excoriated in 1:18–32.

The introductory "or" (*ē*) in v. 4 indicates that the question restates v. 3: To expect to escape God's justice is the equivalent of looking down on God's generosity, which is intended to produce repentance. The language used here of God, particularly of God's goodness (*chrēstotēs*), is conventional in Jewish literature (e.g., Pss 31:19 [30:20 LXX]; 119:65–68 [118:65–68 LXX]; 145:7–9; Wis 15:1; Jer 33:11 [40:11 LXX]; and see Rom 3:26; 9:22; 11:22).

Precisely because these are conventional expressions about God, the question whether the interlocutor "does not know" about God's goodness carries a certain sharpness: How is it possible that anyone would not know of God's goodness? That is particularly the case when the question is contrasted with the shared "we know" at the opening of v. 2.[40] The accusation of ignorance and condescension to God recalls 1:18–32, where Paul charges that humanity (with a focus particularly on gentile humanity) knew God but did not act on that knowledge, and here it is said that humanity (with a focus particularly on Jewish humanity) does not know God despite God's goodness.

Specifically, the interlocutor does not know that God's goodness is intended to produce repentance (*metanoia*). The language echoes that of Wisdom of Solomon:

> You show mercy to all people, because you are able to do all things,
> and you overlook the sins of human beings to bring about repentance.
> (Wis 11:23)

Similarly Wis 12:10 and 19 affirm that God generously allows sinners to repent (and see elsewhere, e.g., Pr. Man. 12.7, 13; Sir 17:24; Joel 2:13; Isa 46:8). And of

---

40. Admittedly, *agnoeō* often occurs in Paul's letters as part of a disclosure formula (as in Rom 1:13; 11:25; 1 Cor 10:1; 12:1; 2 Cor 1:8; 1 Thess 4:13), but in Rom 2:4 the usage is more than formulaic. Here the participle is subordinate to the finite verb *kataphroneō* ("look down on"), which carries a distinctly negative connotation, as in 1 Cor 11:22.

course language of repentance is familiar from elsewhere in the NT (e.g., Matt 3:8; Luke 24:47; Acts 5:31; 11:18; Heb 6:1; 12:17). Second Peter 3:9 seems especially close to Rom 2:4 and Wis 11:23:

> [God] is patient for your sake, not wanting anyone to perish but wanting all to reach repentance.

In the context of Jewish and early Christian writings, then, Paul's comments about repentance in 2:4 are commonplace.

Yet within the context of Paul's letters the comments are quite unusual, as Paul seldom refers to repentance before God. Outside of this passage, the noun appears only in 2 Cor 7:9, 10 and the related verb "repent" only in 2 Cor 12:21, and in those passages it refers to specific instances of misconduct; it does not refer to repentance in the sense of humanity's need for righteousness. The virtual absence of repentance language in Romans and elsewhere in Paul's letters is easier to understand than its presence here. When Paul depicts the human situation in 1:18–3:26 and especially later in 5:12–21, he depicts it as an all-encompassing subjection to Sin and Death. Because humanity is ruled by such powers, repentance is ineffective (see further on 5:12–21).

That observation in turn raises the question why Paul introduces the language of repentance in 2:4–5, since it does not recur later in the letter in calls for repentance or, more pertinent for this Christian audience, recollections about their repentance. For now, it seems enough for Paul to say that there is both need and opportunity to repent. What unfolds will show that repentance does not suffice to address the universal problem that has been revealed by the gospel.

[5–8] Verses 5–8 move from the actions of corrupt judges to the inevitable consequences of those actions. Assuming for the sake of argument that the answers to the questions of vv. 3–4 are affirmative (the interlocutor does actually imagine escape from God's judgment, does look down on God's goodness, is ignorant of the purpose of God's goodness), Paul draws the conclusion that the heart of such a person is "hardened and unrepentant" (literally, "because of your hardness and unrepentant heart"). The notion of "hardening" or "stubbornness" appears with some frequency in the LXX (e.g., Deut 10:16; Ps 94:8; Prov 17:20; Jer 4:4; Ezek 3:7) and elsewhere in the NT (e.g., Matt 19:8; Acts 7:51; Heb 3:8, 13, 15; 4:7). Paul will later refer to the hardening of Pharoah's heart as God's unilateral act (see Rom 9:18). The alpha privative *ametanoētos* ("unrepentant") occurs only rarely in texts roughly contemporary with Paul (T. Gad 7.5; Onasander, *Strategikos* 8.1.3; Epictetus, *Gnom.* frag. 25.4), and here obviously serves to reinforce the preceding claim about the need for repentance.

Because of this hardened and unrepentant heart, "you" create a treasure. The verb "treasure" appears in biblical literature for storing up what is good (e.g., Tob 4:9; Prov 13:22; Pss. Sol. 9.5; Matt 6:19–20) as well as what is evil (e.g., Prov 1:18; 16:27; Jas 5:3). Paul has already introduced the notion of God's wrath in Rom 1:18, but his comment is now restated more fully as "wrath on the day of wrath and the apocalyptic revelation of the right judgment of God."

Verse 6 draws the conclusion in the language of Ps 62:12 (61:13 LXX) and Prov 24:12: God will "repay to each according to works."[41] It may well be that this is a widely held view,[42] but as Paul develops this principle in the lines that follow, he simultaneously reinforces it and subverts it. He elaborates on ways in which human beings do both good and evil and the consequences of those actions. He also subverts the principle by undermining any notion the interlocutor entertains that Jews are predictably among those who do what is right and gentiles predictably among those who do evil. What exactly Paul has in mind by this "repayment" remains unclear, perhaps because his concern here is less to predict specific outcomes than to expose the problem involved in judging others.

Verses 7–8 elaborate on what it is God will render and to whom, and the explication takes the form of two parallel statements linked by *men . . . de* ("on the one hand," "on the other hand"). First, picking up the reference to "works" in v. 6, Paul describes those who demonstrate "persistence in work that is good." In doing so, they seek "glory and honor and immortality." "Glory and honor" appear paired in a wide variety of texts in Paul's environment, both biblical (Pss 28:1 LXX; 95:7 LXX; Job 37:22; 40:10; Wis 8:10; Dan 2:37) and otherwise (Dio Chrysostom, *Or.* 4.116; *Or.* 44.10; Appian, *Bell. Civ.* 3.18; Plutarch, *Mor.* 486b; Josephus, *Ant.* 12.118; BDAG, s.v. *timē*). "Immortality" does not customarily appear with "glory and honor," but it does appear in 1 Cor 15:50–54 as a characteristic of resurrected life (and see Wis 2:23; 6:18–19; 4 Macc 9:22; 17:12). All three of these desiderata may be heard by the Romans as virtues to which they aspire (so Jewett 204), but for Paul these are gifts to be granted by God rather than human achievements. Romans 1 has already associated "glory" and "immortality" with God,[43] so that humans who seek after these things are seeking God's gifts.[44] What is given them is life unending. Paul does not bother to explain what this life looks like, here or elsewhere (Rom 5:21; 6:22–23; Gal 6:8; see also 2 Cor 5:1), although chapter 6 refers to the radically new life given by virtue of Christ's own resurrection.

41. See also, e.g., Job 34:11; Ezek 33:20; Jer 17:10; Hos 12:2 (12:3 LXX); Sir 16:12; Pss. Sol. 9:5; Matt 16:27; 2 Tim 4:14; Rev 2:23; Josephus, *Ant.* 1.14.

42. Dunn, for example, depicts it as "a broad principle which would gain wide acceptance among people with any degree of moral sensibility" (1:86).

43. Paul does not ascribe "honor" (*timē*) to God, although see 1 Tim 1:17; 6:16.

44. Karl Barth's elegant discussion of divine glory that "overflows" "into co-existence with the creature" seems to have captured the gist of Paul's comments here, although Barth is referring primarily to the relationship between God's own glory and the human glorification of God (1957, 666–77, citation on p. 673).

The parallel statement in v. 8 concerning the "reward" granted to others describes them abundantly. First, they are said to act *ex eritheias*, which I have translated as "out of selfishness," although the precise connotation of the word is disputed (BDAG, s.v. *eritheia*; cf. 2 Cor 12:20; Gal 5:20; Phil 1:17; 2:3). Second, they "reject the truth," again recalling the charge in 1:18, 25 that humanity suppresses the truth about God. As in those earlier cases, truth here is not general or philosophical but theological. And third, they are obedient to wrong, again recalling the human wrong (*adikia*) of 1:18, 29. The "reward" in this case is described as both wrath and rage.[45]

[9–11] At first glance, these verses seem only to repeat, but in reverse order, the claims regarding a final accounting in vv. 7–8. Instead of beginning with those who do the good, Paul now begins with those who produce evil. The following schema clarifies the relationship:

v. 7	Those who seek glory and honor and immortality	life forever
v. 8	Those who reject truth and obey wrong	wrath and rage
v. 9	Affliction and anguish	on every human life that produces evil
v. 10	Glory and honor and peace	for everyone who works good

The consequence earlier expressed as "wrath and rage" now becomes (or perhaps produces) "anguish and affliction." "Life forever" is described with "glory and honor and peace."[46]

Yet this is more than restatement for the sake of emphasis, since each verse concludes with the phrase "the Jew first and also the Greek." A new element is added here, or rather, an earlier element in the letter reappears in an unsettling way (see 1:16). The reward for evil falls on "the Jew first and also the Greek." And the reward for good also falls on "the Jew first and also the Greek."

Verse 11 provides the principle at work in Paul's reasoning: "There is no favoritism with God." Paul's Scriptures taught God's impartiality in the sense that God does not favor the wealthy and powerful over the poor and disenfranchised (as in Deut 10:17; 2 Chr 19:7; Sir 35:14–16). Paul applies this claim now to judgment of Jew and gentile, implying what he will develop below: there is no correlation between those who do what is right and ethnicity (see also Acts 10:34; Bassler 1982, 123–54, 176–78).

45. Elsewhere in Paul's letters *thymos* ("rage") refers to human rage (2 Cor 12:20; Gal 5:20; cf. Eph 4:31; Col 3:8).
46. See below on 5:1, where Paul describes the result of rectification as having "peace with God" (cf. 8:6; 14:17, 19; 15:13), and also 15:33, 16:20, where God is described as the "God of peace."

Generalizations about what first-century Jews thought are perilous and can become pernicious, but at least some of Paul's contemporaries would have been surprised by this application of divine impartiality to ethnicity. To take but a single example, the author of the Wisdom of Solomon, which is often invoked for parallels with Rom 1:18–32, contends that Israel does not sin:

> You, our God, are kind and true,
> patient, and ruling all things in mercy.
> For even if we [i.e., Israel] sin we are yours, knowing your power;
> but we will not sin because we know that you acknowledge us as yours.
> (Wis 15:1–2 NRSVue)

For the author of these lines, the assumption is that Jews know their worth to God and will do what is right.[47] Paul is in the process of destabilizing any such assumption.

[12–13] The firm assertion of God's impartial judgment of both Jew and gentile persists in vv. 12–16, but now Paul introduces the law (*nomos*) as the criterion for judgment. Substituting the specific term "law" for the more general term "works" (v. 6) extends the question of ethnicity, since the law to which Paul refers is Mosaic law.[48] Verse 12 affirms that the two groups of people, those who do not have the law and those who do, are both accountable to God: those outside the law who sin perish without the law, and those within the law are judged based on the law.[49]

Again underscoring Paul's earlier, unsettling implication that those who do good and those who do evil come in *both* sorts of humans, Jew as well as Greek, the argument shifts in v. 13. There are other distinctions to be made, as some who are in the law merely hear the law while others actually keep it (see also, e.g., Matt 7:21; Jas 1:22). These two groups are contrasted with one another in yet another set of parallel statements, presented somewhat literally as follows:

Not the hearers of the law   *dikaios* before God
But the doers of the law   *dikaiōthēsontai*

---

47. As Linebaugh puts it, "From *Wisdom's* perspective, Romans 2.7 describes Israel and Romans 2.8 describes non-Israel" (2013b, 131). See also Josephus, *Ant.* 3.22–23; and the discussion in Barclay 2010a, 88.

48. The context situates this difference between having and not having law alongside the question of circumcision and uncircumcision (in vv. 25–29), indicating that Paul is referring specifically to Mosaic law.

49. For the identification of gentiles as "lawless," see also 1 Cor 9:21; 3 Macc 6:9; Pss. Sol. 17.11; Wis 17:2.

Contrasting those who merely hear the law with those who observe it anticipates the point that becomes explicit in vv. 17–24: there may be Jews who do not in fact keep the law.

This verse also undermines any notion that a person who is *dikaios* ("right") before God has some special moral or spiritual trait or characteristic. In the first place, there would be no way to claim that someone who merely listens to the law is morally or spiritually "right." More to the point, the claims here are relational. Paul parallels being *dikaios* before God (v. 13a) with being made right (*dikaiōthēsontai*; v. 13b), rather than with being a righteous person. Consistent with what Paul will claim in 3:26; 4:5; and 5:1, 9, humanity's "rightness" comes about as a result of God's action.

[14–15] Having touched on the difference between hearing the law and actually doing the law, to which he will return in vv. 17–24, Paul introduces a curious category—that of gentiles who somehow observe the law even though they never received it. Such a possibility has entered the argument indirectly with v. 10, which includes both Jew and Greek among those who do the good, yet v. 12 appeared to equate being outside the law with sinning. For the interlocutor who clings to the identification of gentiles with wrongdoing, this concession about the hypothetical possibility of gentiles who observe the law may prove unsettling. And "hypothetical" is the right modifier here, since no example is given either of individuals who are obedient or of specific laws that are observed. With vv. 17–24 Paul at least introduces some specific instances in which Jews might be found violating their own law; here the language remains at the level of generality.

Paul calls these people "gentiles, who do not have the law by nature." The reference to nature (*physis*) can be understood to modify the phrase that follows, so that they "keep the law by nature" (as in NRSV, NIV, NASB), but both the context and Paul's usage elsewhere favor "gentiles, who do not have the law by nature." Just lines later he refers to uncircumcision as "natural" (*ek physeōs*, 2:27), not simply because the foreskin is present at birth but because he assumes that Jew and gentile are identities produced by nature. Galatians 2:15 similarly refers to Jews being such by nature (again using *physis*). For Paul, the distinction between Jew and gentile is to be taken as natural, just as it is natural to him that women and men have different hairstyles (*physis,* 1 Cor 11:14) and that the sex roles require male assertiveness and female passivity (*physis,* Rom 1:26–27). The law is part of the constitution, as it were, of the Jew.[50]

Despite the fact that gentiles do not have the law as part of their makeup, there are gentiles who keep the law (*ta tou nomou poiōsin*) and thereby are the law among themselves. In light of the condemnation of 1:18–32, identifying

50. Later on, especially in chs. 4 and 9–11, Paul's comments emphasize the role of God in creating Israel and sustaining Israel in every generation, which implies that even being a Jew "by nature" is not so much a *biological* as a *theological* event.

these hypothetical gentiles who do keep the law as gentile Christians is one way to reconcile this affirmation with the condemnation of 1:18–32 (e.g., Cranfield 1:156; N. T. Wright 2001; Gathercole 2002b; Barclay 2015, 467–70).[51] Yet there are significant problems with identifying law-observing gentiles in this passage as Christians. To begin with, Paul does not elsewhere unambiguously say that Christians keep or observe the law (see below on Rom 8:4 and 13:8). Even when Paul implies that Christians somehow "fulfill" the law, he associates that activity with the work of the Spirit, which is curiously absent from 2:12–16. Further, reference to gentile Christians would be a significant and inexplicable change of subject matter in a context where the discourse concerns the revelation of God's wrath. Given his previous, heated struggles in the Galatian churches, it seems highly unlikely that Paul would lift up gentile Christian accomplishment of things of the law.

The tension between this group of gentile law-keepers and the argument in 1:18–32 is more apparent than real. Paul is not describing individuals like the worthy centurion of Luke 7:1–10 or the devout Cornelius of Acts 10.[52] Instead, he is undermining the very categories of Jew and gentile by destabilizing any tendency to equate gentile with sinner (despite the fact that he did precisely that in Gal 2:15). Most important, whatever Paul is conceding gentiles are able to do, they are not exempt from the conclusion of 3:9 that all are "under Sin," much less the argument in 5:12–21 that the rule of Sin and Death are universal.

Verses 14b–15 carry the claim further. Those gentiles who observe the law, even though they did not receive it, are in some sense a law to themselves.[53] What that elusive statement might mean becomes a bit clearer in the explication of v. 15: by their actions, they show that the "work of the law" is written in their hearts (cf. Isa 51:7; Jer 31:33). And the effectiveness of that integration of the law into the person is such that their consciences and their imaginations (their internal life) serve either to accuse or defend them (v. 16). In vv. 25–29 Paul will take the obvious next step to say that such people warrant the name "Jew" more than some who claim to be Jews but do not act in ways consistent with their gifts.

[16] Verse 16 returns to the eschatological setting. It is not human beings who judge these gentiles. To the contrary, God judges them according to the gospel. The phrase "in the day when" does not follow easily on v. 15 and probably refers back to v. 13 instead, with vv. 14–15 serving as explication of the "doers of the

51. Elsewhere Gathercole traces Augustine's changing treatment of this passage (2002a).

52. A more relevant Lukan text might be Acts 15:21, in which James defends the decision at Jerusalem by observing that "Moses" is read in the synagogues every Sabbath, implying that, although gentiles do not have the law, those who have been present in the synagogue will be familiar with its expectations; and see Philo, *Special Laws* 2.62.

53. Aristotle, *Eth. nic.* 1128a.31–32 employs similar language for the person whose behavior reflects internalized norms (cited in Cranfield 1:157).

law" in v. 13. At first glance, the reference to judgment seems only to reinforce and perhaps round off the earlier statements about the day of wrath in v. 5 and the payment to people according to their works in vv. 6–10. Earlier Paul has not used the language of "inaccessible thoughts" (literally, "the hidden things of people," *ta krypta tōn anthrōpōn*), language that will come into play again later in the chapter (v. 29). A literal translation, "hidden things," tends to suggest that all that is involved is some judgment of the inner self, the internal life, which seems odd given the insistence here on doing. The sense of the word here, and later as well, reflects its association with God; that is, there are aspects of human beings known only to God, as in 1 Cor 14:25 (cf. 1 Pet 3:4).

The remainder of the verse is crucial, because it redefines—or at least recontextualizes—the judgment discussed earlier. God judges "in accordance with my gospel through Christ Jesus." Given that the gospel Paul preaches ("my gospel") is the gospel of Jesus Christ (1:3), this assertion is redundant. Paul describes the judgment in both ways to emphasize that judgment is integral to the gospel, just as the apocalypse of God's wrath is integral to the apocalypse of God's righteousness (1:17–18).

As the letter unfolds, so will the further implications of God's saving power come to the foreground, so that in 14:1–12 the prospect of giving an account before God is joined with the promise that God enables his people to "stand" (14:4; cf. Phil 2:15; 1 Thess 3:13; 5:23). In the context of ch. 2, however, Paul is less concerned to offer eschatological reassurance than he is to blur the lines between Jew and gentile on the way to declaring that both Jew and gentile are under Sin's power (3:9).

[17–20] The third section of the chapter (vv. 17–24) turns from gentiles who in some sense observe the law to those Jews (or Jewishly identified gentiles) who do not. Verses 17–20 form a single, sustained protasis (an "if" clause), creating the expectation of an apodosis (a concluding "then" clause), an expectation that is disappointed at the outset of v. 21 (see below).

The earlier direct address of 2:1–11 speaks to anyone who takes on the role of judge, but v. 17 turns explicitly to the emphatic "you" who takes on the name "Jew." It opens with a striking statement: "But if *you* call yourself a Jew . . ." Is the one who takes on the name "Jew" in fact a Jew? Paul elsewhere regularly employs *Ioudaios* for those who are Jews by birth (e.g., 1:16; 1 Cor 1:22–24; and especially Gal 2:13–15), making that seem the most likely implication here as well. Yet the groups gathered to hear Phoebe read this letter contained gentiles who had been associated with synagogues in Rome and who found the proclamation of the gospel attractive because it offered them a way of being Jewish without undergoing the full process of proselytism (see the introduction). Some of these synagogue-identified gentiles may have called themselves *Ioudaios*. There is evidence for applying the name *Ioudaios* to those who are not Jews by birth, as when Plutarch recounts the denigration of a freedman who is called a Jew because he is suspected of Jewish practices (*Cic.* 864c). More pertinent, Epictetus makes reference to people who act as if they are Jews when they are actually Greek (*Diatr.* 2.9.20; and see Dio Cassius, *Hist. rom.* 37.17; TDNT 3:3.70). Whether Jews by birth or by affiliation, Paul addresses those who assume they have the law and who understand themselves accountable to it (unlike the "lawless" in 2:12).

To Jews and those gentiles who call themselves Jews, then, Paul turns in vv. 17–20. Given the favorable depiction in vv. 14–16 of gentiles who observe the law, it is reasonable to expect that he will continue in that vein. And in fact all the descriptions in vv. 17–20 are positive, making the sharp turn taken with the questions of vv. 21–23 even more stunning. Following the initial verb of naming, vv. 17–18 describe the addressee with four verb phrases ("rely," "boast," "know," and "discern") and then vv. 19–20 add a series of attributes modifying a participle ("being convinced," rendered above as "you are convinced").

The first statement, "you rely on the law," has been widely perceived as a critique of Jewish "legalism" or more recently as a critique of ethnic self-aggrandizement on the part of Jews (e.g., Dunn 1:lxiv–lxxii, 110). Such a view would be more persuasive if the text were being read backward, moving from vv. 21–24 to vv. 17–20, on the assumption that the violations of the law introduced by the questions in those verses *result* from relying on the law. Paul does not make that association, however, and the identification of Israel with the law is deeply rooted in Scripture (as in Exod 19:1–8; 20:1–17; Lev 18:5; Deut 4:1–8; Neh 8; and often elsewhere). Indeed, it might be said that what non-Jews regarded as making a person Jewish had to do with the law, particularly circumcision and dietary law (see, e.g., Epictetus, *Diatr.* 1.11.12–13; 1.22.4; Tacitus, *Hist.* 5.4–5; Juvenal, *Sat.* 14.96–106), in addition to devotion to one God.

Similarly, in numerous passages Scripture admonishes "boasting in God," which is synonymous with glorifying or praising God (see the use of *kauchaomai* in 1 Chr 16:35; Pss 5:11 [5:12 LXX]; 32:11 [31:11 LXX]; 149:5; Jer 9:24; Sir 50:20). To be sure, Paul can castigate boasting when it is misplaced, as he often does in the Corinthian correspondence (e.g., 1 Cor 3:21; 4:7; 2 Cor 11:18). Later in Romans he will conclude that human boasting has been excluded (3:27; 4:2), but he will go on to commend boasting in the hope of God's glory (5:2, 3, 11). Nothing in 2:17 itself suggests a problem with "boasting in God"; as with relying on the law, the problem emerges only later with the suggestion that at least some Jews fail to honor God or the law with their behavior.

The assertions of v. 18 make more specific the general descriptions of v. 17. Not only do those who call themselves by the name "Jew" boast in God, but they know "the will," clearly a shorthand for "God's will" (as in 12:2; 15:32; 1 Cor 1:1; 2 Cor 1:1; 8:5; Gal 1:4), which they have learned from the law. That this is not a presumptuous claim on the surface is clear from Paul's own comment in 12:2 that believers are able to discern God's will. Those who discern what is important stand in contrast with the indictment of 1:28 against those who do not see fit to acknowledge God (also *dokimazō*). This discernment is possible because they are taught by the law.

The participle (*pepoithas,* literally, "being convinced") at the outset of v. 19 introduces a chain of epithets regarding Israel's vocation. Israel is to be a guide for the blind and a light in darkness (as in Isa 42:6–7; 49:6; see also Matt 15:14; Luke 2:32; Acts 26:18). Verse 20 recalls Israel's role as a pedagogue, as in Deut 4:10; 11:19; Ps 78:5–6.

Finally, the "you" being addressed is said to have in the law the embodiment of knowledge and truth. This "you" constitutes the polar opposite of the one whose mind is corrupted by refusal to recognize God, the one who suppresses the truth (1:18). These are entirely positive descriptions, unless and until the accusations implied in 2:21–24 are read back into these statements. Second, this statement, like its predecessors, heavily emphasizes the Mosaic law. It should come as no surprise, then, that Paul later addresses the possible inference that the law itself is the problem (an inference he will finally reject in 7:7–25 by concluding that the problem is with Sin's overtaking of the law rather than the law itself), but here he lets the implication stand without further comment.

[21–24] The apodosis anticipated by vv. 17–20 is not forthcoming; in its place stands the chain of questions and statements in vv. 21–24 introduced by "therefore" (*oun*). Verses 21–24 sharply counter the self-understanding of the "you" addressed in vv. 17–20. A gap opens up between these two parts of the section (so Byrne 97), a gap that undermines any assumption that Jews are exempt from Sin's power.

Paul begins with a question about teaching, which appears to follow closely on v. 20's concern with disciplining the foolish and teaching infants. The following three questions—theft by the one who preaches against theft, adultery by the one who proscribes adultery, and robbing idols by the one who proscribes idolatry— are closely associated with the Decalogue (Exod 20:3–17; Deut 5:6–21).

The final question (v. 23) recasts what has preceded in more general terms: the one who boasts in the law may dishonor God by transgressing the law. To make matters even worse, that dishonor extends outside the circle of Jews so that God's name is blasphemed among the gentiles (v. 24). Here Paul, using the language of Isa 52:5, takes his interlocutor back to 1:18–19. If God's name is dishonored, that is the equivalent of failure to give honor to God in the first place. Verse 24, far from being a decoration to the argument, actually demonstrates how people who call themselves Jews are themselves no better than gentiles.

Particularly given the history of Christian interpretation and misinterpretation of Judaism, great care is needed in discussing these questions. They should not be read as a dispassionate analysis of either Jews in particular or of first-century Judaism in general. Just as it is unlikely that Jews avoided all the accusations lodged in 1:18–32, neither is Paul saying that all Jews violated the law they claimed to serve or that Judaism is inherently susceptible to hypocrisy.

He is instead opening up a space for the argument to come in 3:1–20 and again in 5:12–21 about the universal extent of Sin. He does that not by critiquing Judaism as such or Jews as a whole, but by showing that the law does not itself protect Jews from Sin.

[25–29] The final verses further destabilize the categories of Jew and gentile. Earlier in the chapter Paul has spoken in terms of Jew and gentile, of having or not having the law. Now he introduces yet another way of describing these two groups: "circumcision" (*peritomē*) and "uncircumcision" or "foreskin" (*akrobystia*). These labels refer to the Jewish practice of circumcision, which physically marks the male as well as marking out the males whom Jewish women marry (Josephus, *Ant.* 1.192; 20.139, 145–46; Philo, *QG* 3.61; Barclay 1996b, 411–12). In that sense, the concern about circumcision pertains to both men and women.

The language is used symbolically, of course, as elsewhere in early Christian texts (Phil 3:3; Col 2:11; Barn. 9.4; Justin, *Dial.* 24.1–2). But with these symbolic names, Paul now refers to Jew and gentile with terms that are objective, physical, and visible. That is particularly the case with *akrobystia*, which refers to the visible foreskin of the uncircumcised. Paul is taking up the most objective, verifiable way of marking the boundary between Jew and gentile, and it is exactly that boundary he now destabilizes, making the distinction between Jew and gentile even less clear and eventually prompting the question of 3:1: What is the benefit of being a Jew?

Verse 25 takes the first step in that direction. Paul begins with the affirmative claim that circumcision is profitable for the one who "does" the law, recalling the implications of vv. 7, 14–16 and perhaps even vv. 17–20 that there are such people. (Note, however, that 3:10–20 will vacate this category, and 5:12–21 will further interpret all of humanity as captive to Sin.) With v. 25b, however, he states the corollary in startling terms: transgressing the law is not simply "without profit"; instead, transgressing the law means that circumcision has become uncircumcision. A circumcised male who does not keep the law has grown a foreskin. This outrageous assertion takes vv. 12–16 to its logical conclusion.

Having stipulated that circumcision is of benefit when the law is kept, Paul continues with the assertion that where the law is not observed, circumcision has become uncircumcision (literally, "a foreskin"). Verse 26 reinforces this astonishing claim with its opposite: if the uncircumcised person practices the law's requirements, then that person is regarded as if circumcised. Verse 27 presses even further: not only are the visible signs of Jew and gentile now confused with one another, but the foreskinned male who keeps the law will actually be the judge of the circumcised male who does not. [54] And the transgressor is specifically said to have both "Scripture and circumcision." This last

---

54. As Hultgren comments, "The statement that gentiles who keep the law 'will condemn' . . . those who possess the 'written code' . . . and practice circumcision is not to be taken as a doctrinal aspect of the final judgment, but as a hyperbolic figure of speech within a diatribe" (130).

phrase underscores the advantage of circumcision and the law and thereby also increases the volume on the accusation, since the advantage could be thought a protection against transgression.

Verses 28–29 are extremely challenging. The syntax is elliptical, and the introduction of terms conveying openness and hiddenness as well as spirit and letter further challenges the interpreter. An important anchor for interpretation comes with the "for" (*gar*) at the outset of v. 28, which links vv. 28–29 with the preceding verses. This is not a principle of interiority or a reference to Christians as "secret" Jews or "real" Jews. Instead, it continues the argument about circumcision and uncircumcision in vv. 25–27, again undermining this verifiable boundary between Jew and gentile.

First, v. 28 claims that there is no such thing as the "visible" Jew and no such thing as "visible," "in the flesh" circumcision. There is instead the Jew who is "unseen." Rendering *kryptō* with "hidden" or "secret" introduces an element of intentionality unwarranted by the text. The context suggests instead that what qualifies one for the descriptor "Jew" is not publicly verifiable, just as v. 16 indicated that God would judge what is not visible. Paul amplifies this point with a further reference to circumcision as "of the heart" and "in the spirit rather than by the letter." Here he recalls a traditional way of speaking about effective service of God as involving circumcision of the heart (e.g., see Deut 10:16; 30:6; Jer 4:4; 9:25–26; Lev 26:41; Ezek 44:7, 9; Jub. 1.23; 1QpHab 11.13; Odes Sol. 11.1–3; Barclay 1998, 551).

The quest to identify these various statements with specific groups, such as unbelieving Jews and believing Christians, constitutes a winsome attempt to sidestep the argument. When, in Rom 9–11, Paul does take up the question of God's relationship to Israel (past, present, and future), he does not do so in terms of whether Israel has kept the law but in terms of whether and when Israel has been called into faith.[55] Nor does he identify Christians as the "real" Jews; that line of thought will wait for the Epistle of Barnabas. Instead of elevating one group over against another, Paul is undermining what his auditors would have regarded as utterly certain: one either was a Jew or one was not.

This passage (vv. 25–29 but also vv. 6–10 and 16) often plays a role in discussions of Paul's view of eschatological judgment, but again the context needs to be given due consideration.[56] Paul is leading his auditors inexorably to the conclusion of 3:9 that all are under Sin's power and to his declaration of God's redemption from that power in 3:21–26 and, later, 5:12–21. To be sure, he elsewhere anticipates future accountability (e.g., 14:10–12; 1 Thess 3:11–13), but

---

55. See below on 9:30–33, which might be thought to contradict this statement (and see also Gaventa 2016a).

56. "As with parables, so also with diatribe, not everything said, or put forcefully, should be raised to the level of doctrine" (Hultgren 117).

words of reassurance often accompany those announcements about judgment (as in Rom 8:1, 31–39; and 14:4).

Romans 2, especially vv. 17–29, is often read as a critique of Judaism, whether in the traditional guise of supposed "legalism" or the more recent charge of national boasting or ethnic superiority. Yet neither here nor elsewhere in Romans does Paul argue with Judaism per se. His argument has to do with *anthrōpos*, with the human (as in 1:18; see Linebaugh 2013b, 120). The human comes in two groups, as Paul understands it: Jew and gentile (as in 1:16 and elsewhere). These groups are differentiated by their historic relationship with God, by God's action in them; nonetheless, the gospel reveals that these differences do not prevent Sin from capturing Jews along with gentiles. As becomes explicit in 3:1–20, Jews are not exempt from Paul's argument about the apocalyptic revelation of God's wrath or, as he frames it later on, the universal reign of Sin and Death. Yet that is quite another statement than claiming that he is concerned about a Jewish sense of superiority or ethnic/national pride as such. Instead, he is showing that the good gifts of God to Jews have not rendered them immune to the power of Sin. The same point will be made, albeit more vividly, in 7:7–25, where it becomes quite clear that even the one who earnestly desires to observe the law is not able to do so—not because the law is a problem, but because of Sin's engorging power.

As the argument proceeds into Romans 3, it will emerge that although Jews and gentiles are differently situated by virtue of their histories with God, they both fall under the power of Sin. Both Jews and gentiles participate in the *anthrōpos* of 1:18, not because of some inherent flaw in Judaism (whether legalism or national pride) and not because of some particular temptation peculiar to Jews, but because both are human. Together they are alike subjects of territory occupied by Sin and Death (5:12–21).[57]

3:1–20 The Power of Sin Over All

Having introduced the captivity of humanity to Sin and Death (1:18–32) and the distinction between Jew and gentile (2:1–29)—a distinction that permitted some at Rome to imagine themselves as having been exempted from that captivity—Paul now reinforces his argument by means of an imagined conversation (3:1–9) and a catena of quotations from Scripture (vv. 10–18), driving toward the conclusion of vv. 19–20.

The imagined conversation of 3:1–9 again involves Paul's interlocutors. Those Jews who confidently identify themselves as "the circumcision," as well

---

57. Markus Barth's lament is apropos: "If only Paul's interpreters had spoken of their own depravity and not of the total corruption of others, their doctrine of sin might somehow have corresponded to Rom. 1–3" (1955, 294).

as gentiles who understand themselves to be Jews (see above on 2:17), press Paul's claims to logical but quite untenable conclusions (vv. 1, 3, 5, 7–8). Paul's responses (vv. 2, 4, 6, 9) underscore the fidelity of God's dealings with humankind and drive toward the conclusion he has been establishing through a variety of strategies since 1:18: the gospel reveals that all humanity lives under the power of Sin. Of course, the distinction between two "voices" in the conversation should be held lightly, since Paul is the one articulating both positions.

The scriptural catena of vv. 10–18 provides a rhetorically powerful reinforcement for the argument, as it once more invites auditors to imagine themselves outside the "they" of its relentless critique, only to find that no one lives outside that circle. The catena thereby makes the conclusions of vv. 19–20 inescapable: those who are "in the law" share with the gentiles of 1:18–32 their liability to God's judgment, since the law reveals human captivity to Sin without itself rectifying human beings.

3:1 Someone may ask, "What has become of the advantage of the Jew? Or the value of circumcision?" 2 Much in every way. Of first importance,[a] they were entrusted with the sayings of God.

3 What then? If some were untrustworthy, does their faithlessness destroy the faithfulness of God? 4 Of course not! Let God be true,[b] and every human be a liar. As it is written:
So that you might be established as right[c] in your words
and you will triumph[d] in your judging.

5 But if our wrongdoing establishes God's righteousness, what do we say? God is not wrong for bringing about wrath, is he? (I speak in a human fashion.) 6 Of course not! Since how else will God judge[e] the cosmos?

7 But if God's truth actually increased for his glory through my lie, why am I still judged a sinner? 8 Are we saying (as we are accused and as some report that we say) that we should do evil so that good may come? In that case, their condemnation of us is just.[f]

9 What then? Are we defending ourselves?[g] Not at all! For we have already charged that both Jews[h] and Greeks—all—are under the power of Sin,[i] 10 just as it is written:
There is no righteous one—not even one;
11 there is no one who understands;
there is no one who seeks out God.
12 For all turned aside, together they became depraved;
there is no one who does the good, there is not even one.
13 An opened grave is their throat,
with their tongues they deceive,
the venom of asps is under their lips,

14 their mouth is filled with cursing and bitterness,
15 swift are their feet for shedding blood,
16 destruction and wretchedness are in their paths,
17 and the way of peace they did not know.
18 There is no fear of God before their eyes.

19 Now we know that whatever the law speaks to those who are in the law,ʲ it says so that every mouth might be stopped and the whole cosmos might be under God's judgment. 20 Therefore from observance of the lawᵏ no flesh will be rectified before God, since through the law comes recognition of Sin.

a. *Prōton men* is construed here as "of first importance" rather than "first of all." See the note on 1:8, where the same phrase appears.

b. A single manuscript, G, reads *estō*, the present imperative of the verb "to be," rather than the present imperative *ginesthō* from *ginomai*. The variant could result from simple haplography, the first three letters of *ginesthō* having been omitted under influence from the immediately preceding *genoito*, but the variant may also reflect discomfort arising from the implication that God needs to *become* true. For the implications of the imperative, see the comments below on v. 4.

c. Lit., "you might be rectified." In the context here, as well as in Ps 50:6 LXX, however, the point is not that God needs to be rectified or justified, but that God's own righteousness is publicly witnessed.

d. Following Ps 50:6 LXX, a number of manuscripts read the subjunctive *nikēsēs* (including B G L Ψ 365 1175 1505 1739 1881) instead of the future indicative (attested in ℵ A D K 81 2464). The future indicative is reflected in this translation, based on the assumption that the variant arises from harmonization to the LXX.

e. Some manuscripts read the present form, including B² D² K* 365 629, and others the future, including Ψ 1739 1881. The difference between the two readings consists of a single accent mark, and a number of early mss. have no accent (ℵ A B* D* G 33), which means that decisions on this issue need to be held lightly.

f. Lit., "the judgment of them is just." The context seems to make it clear that this is not neutral judgment but judgment with a negative result—hence the translation "condemnation." The *hōn* ("of them") is ambiguous; it could refer to condemnation of the evil things being done, condemnation of the people who make the accusations (i.e., objective genitive), or the condemnation made by the accusers (i.e., subjective genitive; so Fitch 1947). In the mouth of Paul's imagined conversation partner, who utters both vv. 7 and 8, the question of v. 8a is a complaint about the consequences of Paul's argument. Verse 8b, in the interlocutor's mouth, does not judge the accusers but comments that the accusers' judgment is just (again, in the view of the interlocutor).

g. The variants here are several, and they likely arise because of the difficulty of translating *proechometha*. Most modern translations render this verb as if it were in the active voice, resulting in the question, "Do we have any advantage?" (NIV) or "Are we any better off?" (CEB, NRSVue), while some understand it as having the passive meaning "Are we excelled?" or "Are we at a disadvantage?" (Fitzmyer 330–31; Stowers 1994, 173–74). I translate it in the normal middle sense of having something to put forward for oneself, or "Are we defending ourselves?" (for such usage, see Sophocles, *Ant.* 80; Thucydides, *Hist.* 1.140.4; Dionysius of Halicarnassus, *Ant. rom.* 7.32.1; and see Dahl 1982; Dunn 1:146; Bell 1998, 211–12). In any translation, the question serves entirely to set up the following unequivocal declaration of Sin's grasp of human life, both Jewish and gentile life.

h. The word *prōton* is inserted here by A, almost certainly by virtue of the harmonizing influence of 1:16; 2:9–10.

i. Lit., "under Sin." For the translation "under the power of Sin," see the discussion of 3:9 below.

j. Neil Elliott rightly suggests this translation (1990, 144–45), which honors the parallel indicative verbs "it says" (*legei*) and "it speaks" (*lalei*) and the fact that "those who are in the law" follows the first verb. In addition, this translation better conveys the universal implications of this statement: What the law says to Jews who have the divine word (3:2), it says in order to close every human mouth.

k. Although the phrase *ergōn nomou*, translated literally, is "works of law," that rendering readily feeds the perception that Paul is actually contrasting "works" or "working" with "faith" or "believing." The more capacious word "observance" not only avoids that difficulty but reflects the historic insistence on "keeping" or "observing" the law, as in, e.g., Exod 18:20; Deut 31:12; 1QS 5.21–22 (Martyn 1997a, 260–63; Bell 1998, 224–37). Despite energetic arguments that Paul's use of the phrase concerns only certain boundary-making practices of the law (esp. circumcision and food laws) rather than observance of the law in toto, Paul's comments do not lend themselves readily to restriction (contra Dunn 1:153–55, 158–60; Wright 460–61). That is particularly the case in Rom 3, because what the catena in vv. 10–18 attacks includes corrupt attitudes toward God, toxic speech, and deadly action.

[3:1] The opening question, again from an imagined interlocutor, follows directly from Paul's comments about the shared liability of Jew and gentile to judgment (2:1–11), the possibility that Jews might not have conducted themselves in accordance with their gifts (2:17–24), and especially the possibility that circumcision might become uncircumcision and vice versa (2:25–29). If Paul's observations there are applied strictly, then it seems unlikely that he would attribute any advantage whatsoever to being a Jew (Dodd 43; Barclay 1998, 546). Paul's interlocutor is still a Jew or Jewishly identified gentile (as in 2:1, 17) who has followed Paul's argument carefully and drawn the obvious conclusion.

Technically there are two questions here, one regarding being a Jew and the other regarding circumcision. In fact, for Paul and his contemporaries, this was a single question, since Jewish identity was so closely connected with the practice of circumcision (as is clear in the language of 2:25–29). As noted above, despite the fact that only men underwent the rite of circumcision, the symbolic status of circumcision included both men and women. As circumcision defined the Jewish male, circumcision also defined the women who would marry those males.

From the convenient vantage point of the present, it is altogether too easy to fault the question for reflecting a kind of Jewish exceptionalism. More than personal or even corporate identity issues are at stake here, as will become evident especially in chs. 4 and 9–11. To disturb the distinction between Jew and gentile is to raise a question about God, who called Israel into being and made promises to Israel (as in 4:13; 9:4; 11:29). That the question concerns the relationship between God and Israel becomes clear in the verses that follow.

[2] Logic would have compelled a negative response to v. 1: what Paul has just written in 2:25–29 concerning the impartiality of God's judgment and the permeability of the line between Jew and gentile requires the conclusion that there is no advantage to being a Jew. The answer Paul gives is emphatically positive, however, even though only one advantage is identified at present (others will be introduced at 9:1–5). As at 2:1 (and as will happen at 3:19 also), Paul has led the auditors to expect a particular conclusion, only to turn sharply in another direction.

The particular advantage Paul introduces at this point is crucial for the argument. Jews "were entrusted with the sayings of God." Paul does not elsewhere refer to the *logia tou theou*. In the LXX, however, the phrase refers to Balaam's oracles as instances of hearing the words of God (*logia theou*; Num 24:4, 16), and in Ps 106:11 it stands in parallel with "the counsel of the Most High" (*boulē tou hypsitou*). Elsewhere in the NT the phrase or its near equivalent refers in a general way to Scripture as God's gift to Israel (Heb 5:12; 1 Pet 4:11; Acts 7:38); similar references appear in Philo (*Rewards* 1.1; *Contempl. Life* 25.3) and Josephus (*J.W.* 6.311–13). The same connotation is at work here: the whole of Scripture is understood as the most important advantage of the Jews, and Scripture is understood precisely as being *God's*. (The phrasing *tois logois* in v. 4b may have influenced Paul's selection of words in v. 2: *logia tou theou*.)

Of at least equal significance alongside these sayings of God is that "they [Jews] were *entrusted* with them." No mere stylistic device, the passive voice summons up the agency of God and overturns any impulse to read the "advantage" or "value" of Jews as a property that inheres in them or a possession they have earned. Similarly, "entrusted" (*episteuthēsan*) implies that the "advantage" of Jews is not a gift for their own use but a commission that carries with it certain responsibilities. Paul does not specify the nature of the responsibility; given 2:17–24 and 3:3, it may refer to general trustworthiness and integrity with respect to God. Elsewhere Paul refers to his own apostolic labor as being "entrusted" with the gospel (1 Thess 2:4; Gal 2:7; 1 Cor 9:16–17). First Corinthians 9:16–17 is particularly relevant, because there Paul directly connects being "entrusted with a commission" with the obligation to carry it out ("Woe to me if I do not proclaim the gospel!"). Being entrusted with Scripture is a distinctive advantage, and it is also a fearsome responsibility.

Paul adduces a single advantage before the imagined interlocutor interrupts with another question (v. 3). Yet the specific advantage he identifies has everything to do with the case under construction. The advantage of Jews is that they are entrusted with Scripture, but Paul will shortly introduce an extended set of scriptural quotations in order to make his argument about the captivity of all humanity to Sin (v. 9). Ironically, then, this most important *advantage* of Jews serves not as their defender but as their *accuser* (as in v. 19).

It can scarcely be incidental that Paul refers to Jews in the third-person: "*They* were entrusted." The implied distance is overturned later on, at 4:1 and emphatically at 9:1 and 10:1, but it is worth noticing that Paul at this point speaks as an outsider, identifying neither with Jew nor with gentile (see also the third-person in 1:18–32). That does not mean the Jews spoken of here are only those who do not acknowledge Jesus Christ, since the gift of God's sayings is not limited in v. 2, and v. 9 explicitly includes "all." Instead, the third-person reflects the fact that this entire section of the letter (1:18–3:20) presents evidence of God's handing over of humanity, all of humanity, to the powers of Sin and Death *prior to* the arrival of God's Son.

[3] "What then?" marks the return to the question Paul imagines might be asked by Jewish or Jewishly identified auditors. Continuing the language of "entrust" (*pisteuō*) from the preceding verse, the question juxtaposes the untrustworthiness (*apisteuō*) or faithlessness (*apistia*) of "some" with the possibility of nullifying God's own faithfulness (*pistis*). This is the first appearance of the word *pistis* or its cognates since 1:16–17, but it will move to the center in 3:21–31 and especially in ch. 4. The fact that both the English words "trust" and "faith" are required to render the shared Greek stem reflects the range of meanings associated with *pistis* (Morgan 2017, especially 1–35). The word and related terms have something to do with the possibility of relying on another object or person, as in the confidence involved in stepping out onto a bridge, the trust that it will carry one's weight without crumbling. In some instances, then, that reliance or *pistis* will require the language of "faith," even "belief," while in others, terms such as "trust" or "confidence" will better suit the context.

The preposterousness of questioning God's faithfulness is signaled by the *mē* that introduces the question, which indicates that a negative answer is expected: "What then? If some were untrustworthy, does their faithlessness destroy the faithfulness of God?" That both Paul and his conversation partners would regard such a deduction as outrageous may be suggested by formative understandings such as are found in Deut 7:9:

> Know, therefore, that the LORD your God is God, the faithful God who maintains covenant loyalty with those who love him and keep his commandments, to a thousand generations. (NRSVue; see also Deut 32:4; Isa 49:7; 1 Cor 1:9; 10:13; 2 Cor 1:18)

The question of v. 3 is often read, and rightly, as an anticipation of the much-extended discussion of God's dealings with Israel in chs. 9–11. More is at work here than an anticipation of that later argument, however. Paul, or at least his imagined conversation partner, also follows through quite naturally on the concerns raised in ch. 2. Paul has not explicitly accused Jews (whether "some" as in v. 3 or "all" as later in v. 9) of being faithless; 2:17–29 is far more subtle in its reasoning than that (and, indeed, far less direct than much prophetic critique of Israel). Yet the radical undermining of the distinction between Jew and gentile in 2:25–29 might well prompt the question whether God would then abandon Jews, whether God would keep faith with Jews. Hence, the question in v. 3 is deeply implicated in the logic of ch. 2.

[4] As with the response in v. 2 to the initial question, here also the response to the imagined interlocutor is vehement. The expression with which Paul rejects the possibility of God's faithlessness, "Of course not!" (*mē genoito*), further reflects the absurdity of the inquiry.[58]

A solemn response follows this interjection. First Paul asserts, "Let God be true, and every human be a liar," and then he quotes Ps 50:6 LXX. Many passages in Scripture associate God with truth or truthfulness (e.g., Gen 41:32; Exod 34:6; Deut 32:4; Ps 30:6; John 3:33; 17:3; Rev 16:7; 19:9), but understanding the precise claim made here requires attention to the whole of the verse. Paul contrasts the truthfulness of God with humanity's lack of truthfulness: "and every human be a liar." Although the topic is the advantage of Jews, this assertion about the falseness of humanity recalls the opening of this major section and the claim that humanity has suppressed the truth about God (1:18) and exchanged God's truth for a lie (1:25). The conversation partner's question in v. 3 concedes that some Jews may have been untrustworthy, but Paul's answer ratchets up the argument as he reframes the minimal account of "some" Jews who are false in terms of the larger depiction of humanity's falseness toward God (and see also Ps 115:2 LXX).

The connection between v. 3 and 1:18 helps to explain the otherwise puzzling word *ginesthō*. "Let God be true" or even "Let God become true" implies something more than that truth inheres in God as a static quality or a personality trait. Nor does the verb suggest that God is not yet true but is becoming so, a conclusion that would likely elicit from Paul another emphatic *mē genoito*. *Ginesthō* reflects instead God's saving activity, an activity that is already underway, the culmination of which is yet to come. Like God's presently-being-revealed righteousness and wrath (1:17, 18), God's truth is also being established as right (so Käsemann 80).

---

58. This is the first of several points in the letter at which this phrase appears (3:6, 31; 6:2, 15; 7:7, 13; 9:14; 11:1, 11; see also 1 Cor 6:15; Gal 2:17; 3:21; 6:14), a phrase associated particularly with Epictetus (e.g., *Diatr.* 1.29.9–11; 2.8.26–27; 3.1.44; see Malherbe 1980).

The citation of Ps 50:6 LXX confirms this active understanding of the working out of God's truth, which takes place so that God's righteousness might be publicly witnessed through God's words and so that God will triumph in God's own judging. The psalm's reference to God's words (*logois*) recalls the gift of God's speech or Scripture (*ta logia tou theou*) in v. 2, and the reference to judging anticipates God's role as judge in vv. 6–7. The only term that has not already entered the letter is that of triumph (*nikaō*), but its notion of God's victory over the powers of Sin and Death is crucial to understanding Romans (5:12–21; 8:18–39; 16:20; see also 1 Cor 15:23–28). Without such an apocalyptic interpretation of God's truth, the second half of v. 4 dangles, only vaguely connected to the context as a way of reintroducing the language of righteousness.

[5] The conversation now reverts to Paul's imagined conversation partner, who again takes the logic of Paul's argument to an extreme conclusion. Moving away from the terminology of *pistis/apistia* and of *alēthēs/pseustēs*, Paul returns to the language of *dikaios/adikia*. Having contrasted God's faithfulness with the unfaithfulness of humans, and God's truthfulness with the falseness of human beings, Paul now uses a third pair, concluding (from the imagined conversation partner's viewpoint) that human wrong actually demonstrates God's righteousness. From that correct conclusion, yet another question follows for which both parties know the answer must be emphatically negative: Is God then wrong for bringing about wrath? The choice of "wrath" transforms the question from one of justice or fairness per se to one about God, since "wrath" is thoroughly associated with God, particularly in the Pauline corpus (see above on 1:18). Because "wrath" belongs to God, it is absurd to conclude that God is wrong to bring about wrath. The final words of the verse demonstrate this absurdity, as Paul's imagined conversation partner recoils with "I speak in a human fashion."

[6] Paul himself recoils from the possibility with a second "Of course not!" His further answer reinforces the sense that the passage, which at one level concerns the divine gifts of being a Jew, also has to do with all of humankind and perhaps all of creation. To say that God will judge the *cosmos* at least raises this possibility, particularly since 8:18–23 anticipates the redemption of all creation (*ktisis*). God cannot be regarded as unjust to inflict wrath on humanity, since God is both the Creator and the final judge of the entire created order.

In each of three responses to the imagined conversation partner, Paul has significantly transposed the questions. Verse 2 transposes a question about privilege into a statement about God's entrusting of Jews with God's own speech. Verse 4 transposes a question about God's faithfulness into a declaration about the impending triumph of God's righteousness. And v. 6 transposes a question about God's wrath into a question about the judging of the entire cosmos. Given this pattern, it should not be surprising to find that vv. 7–8 produce in v. 9 an even more radical transposition of the questions raised.

[7–8] The conversation partner puts forward two final questions. The first (v. 7) reframes the question of v. 5, again pressing the logic of the disparity between human faithlessness and God's faithfulness. A few alterations are revealing. Instead of the earlier direct contrast between faith and unfaith or truth and falsehood, the question now introduces a third element, that of God's glory (*doxa*). By connecting "my" lie, God's truth, and God's glory, the question recalls 1:23 with its charge that human beings traded their worship of God's glory for that of animals. In addition, this version of the question is cast in terms of the individual "I," thereby making the question sharper and perhaps anticipating the contrasting "all" of v. 9. And the "I" protests, not that God is the bearer of wrath, but specifically that the individual is judged as a "sinner," anticipating the power of Sin that will be identified explicitly in v. 9 (and see 5:8).

Nothing indicates a shift of speaker or perspective between vv. 7 and 8, which resumes the first-person plural of v. 5. (Contrast the "much in every way" of v. 2 and the "of course not" of vv. 4 and 6.) Paul's imagined conversation partners continue here, perhaps introducing the slander of their neighbors against Christians, slander that may have been precipitated by Paul's position as reflected in Galatians (so Tobin 2004, 70–76). Taking the questions of vv. 5 and 7 to their logical conclusion, people could in fact protest that human evildoing actually brings about a good result and, hence, that more evildoing results in more glory for God.

If v. 8 comes from the imagined conversation partner, then the final statement ("Their condemnation of us is just") does not reflect Paul's judgment on his own accusers, a judgment that seems both disproportionate to the slander and out of keeping with the tone of the passage. Instead, with this final statement the interlocutor concedes that those who accuse Christians of advocating a "more evil, more good" policy have a point. They are right to condemn such nonsense; their condemnation of such a viewpoint is just.

[9] In ch. 6 Paul will return to the question whether the gospel actually encourages wrongdoing, placing that question firmly in the context of the conflicting lordships over human life. Here, however, the case that has been unfolding since 1:18 reaches its outcome. Verse 9 is pivotal in this development, since it both explicitly states Paul's understanding about the power of Sin and introduces the scriptural catena that serves as the final argument for that understanding. Literary details confirm this pivotal function for the verse, since the *ti oun* ("What then?") replays the introduction to v. 1, and the *kathōs gegraptai* ("just as it is written") of v. 10 tightly connects v. 9 to what follows.

With "What then? Are we defending ourselves?" Paul interprets the preceding questions as attacks on his understanding of the gospel and quickly moves ("Not at all") to the main point toward which he has been driving: "We have already charged that both Jews and Greeks—all—are under the power of Sin." Whether Paul's audience, ancient or modern, agrees with his analysis, a careful reading of the charge reveals how it suits the argumentative setting, both forward and backward.

To begin with, "We have already charged" need not signal that Paul has already completed his case, as if he were in a court of law and had now concluded the argument for the prosecution. That is to put too much weight on the verb to "charge" or "state the accusation ahead of time" (*proētiasametha*). The verb only loosely connects what follows with the argument that began in 1:18 regarding the apocalyptic disclosure of God's wrath. Here Paul will bring together his earlier comments—his discussion of God's handing over of humanity to the powers of Sin and Death (1:18–32), his critique of those who fail to see their own judging in the light of God's impartial judging of all humanity (2:1–11), and his undermining of the distinction between Jew and gentile (2:12–29)—to make the charge that follows.

The charge concerns "both Jews and Greeks," which is consistent with what has become a refrain in this letter. The gospel is God's salvific power for "Jew first as well as Greek" (1:16). The resulting judgment also falls on "the Jew first and also the Greek" (2:9–10). The absence of the "first" (*prōton*) in 3:9 is noteworthy, as it presumably was to the scribe who inserted the word in one early manuscript (see translation note h on v. 9).

If Paul does not insist on Jewish priority at this juncture, he does add a crucial word: *all*. As at several other important points in Romans (5:18; 11:26, 32), much depends on the connotations of this word. The notion that "all" includes every single individual human being raises the specter of rendering Hitler indistinguishable from Moses (so Stowers 1994, 176, 181). Perhaps "all" might be taken distributively, in the sense that sinning takes place across the ethnic divisions between Jew and Greek (so Engberg-Pedersen 2000, 206–7). The difficulty with such attempts to restrict the word "all" here, as elsewhere in Romans, is that Paul has relentlessly invoked "all" since the opening lines of the letter. Because Paul has declared that the gospel's scope extends to "all" (1:5, 16) and has also repeatedly included "all" in his depiction of human captivity to Sin (1:18, 29; 2:1, 9, 10; 3:4), it is difficult now to suggest that Paul has reined in his rhetoric, rendering "all" as something other than universal. Later on, Paul quite dramatically depicts the universal extent of Sin's sovereignty:

> . . . as Sin entered the world through one person and Death entered through Sin, in the same way Death also entered and extended its reach to all people, so that all sinned. (5:12)

> . . . where Sin increased, grace multiplied even more. So as Sin ruled as king through Death, in the same way grace might rule as king through righteousness for eternal life through Jesus Christ our Lord. (5:20b–21)

To be sure, this passage does not constitute proof of Paul's belief that every single individual in human history is sinful; however, as the next phrase ("are under the power of Sin") reveals, Paul is not itemizing and calculating trespasses but analyzing a condition from which, in fact, no one has escaped. What does it mean to be "under the power of Sin"? Going well beyond affirming the possibility of sinning or the tendency of all people to make mistakes (as in Stowers 1994, 184–85; Engberg-Pedersen 2000, 207), Paul's language points in the direction of a power that controls human life. When he employs the preposition "under" (*hypo*) with an object in the accusative, and often with some form of the verb "to be" (*einai*), Paul signals an existence that is actually controlled by that object, under its power (Martyn 1997a, 370–73). This pattern is most readily seen in Gal 3:24–25:

> The law was our custodian until Christ came, so that we might be rectified by faith, but now that faith has come, we are no longer under a custodian [*hypo paidagōgon*].

In this instance, it seems quite unavoidable that being "under" the custodian has to do with being under that figure's power. Similarly, Gal 4:3 speaks of being "under the elements of the cosmos," then immediately describes that as a time of "enslavement"; that is, these "elements" constitute a power over human lives (see the same construction in Gal 3:10, 22, 23; 4:4, 5, 21; 5:18; Rom 6:14–15; 7:14). Although Paul does not explicitly designate Sin here as a power, the later description of Sin's rule in chs. 5–7 makes the conclusion unavoidable that Sin is, for Paul, to be understood as a genuine power, a power that extends its grasp to include all of human life (Gaventa 2007b, 125–36, 198–200; 2013b).

This charge has been making its way toward explicitness since 1:18, especially since the dramatic repetition of God's handing over of humankind (1:24, 26, 28). Paul's case, however, is far from complete. It comes to fruition only with the highly structured and rhetorically powerful catena of biblical texts that follows.

[10–18] "Just as it is written" signals that a scriptural citation follows, but it also indicates that the citation and v. 9 belong together, each interpreting the other. In this instance, the citation does not take the form of a single, brief quotation (as, e.g., at 1:17 or 3:4) but comprises a lengthy catena of direct and indirect quotations from several psalms and a passage from Isaiah.[59] And unlike

---

59. For further on vv. 10–20, see Gaventa 2008b. Several features of the catena prompt the suggestion that it derives from someone other than Paul or that Paul composed it prior to its use in this letter (see esp. Keck 1977). Reinforcing these suggestions is the fact that comparable indictments of humanity appear in other contemporaneous apocalyptic literature (e.g., 4 Ezra 7.22b–24), and in some cases they are comprised of several scriptural allusions and quotations (*As. Mos.* 5.2–6; CD 5.13–17). The possibility of independent composition cannot be dismissed, but the subject matter of the catena coheres with Paul's argument from 1:18 to 3:9 and also anticipates 3:19–20, which suggests that Paul himself may have compiled it.

the lengthy quotation of Scripture in 15:9–12, which repeatedly reminds hearers of its origins ("as it is written . . . and again it says . . . and again . . . and again Isaiah says"), here a single formula introduces the catena, providing no clue that multiple passages are involved.

The content of the catena is also distinctive. Paul's other lengthy citations of Scripture typically address divine actions or promises, but this catena entirely concerns the attitudes and actions of human beings. Romans 9:25–29 focuses on God's dealings with Israel, as do 10:18–21; 11:18–20; and 11:26–27. Even 15:9–12, which announces the shared praise of Jew and gentile, also announces the arrival of the "shoot of Jesse." God is not the initiating agent in 3:10–18, however. On the contrary, God is referred to simply as the one whom human beings have failed to seek, the one for whom they have no awe or respect.

The solemn declaration that "there is no righteous one—not even one" (v. 10b) sets an incessantly negative tone from the beginning. The first three Greek words (*ouk estin dikaios*) correspond to a phrase in Eccl 7:20 LXX, although the brevity of the phrase makes it perilous to argue for dependence. Rather than a quotation as such, this initial line may have been crafted as an introduction to the catena that follows, every line of which details, sometimes graphically, the absence of rightness in human beings. And the choice of *dikaios* summons up all the language of righteousness since 1:17. As a whole, this initial statement both recasts v. 9 and anticipates vv. 19–20.

"There is no" (*ouk estin*) recurs five more times in the catena, sounding a relentless refrain of the absence of the good:

> There is no one who understands. (v. 11a)
> There is no one who seeks out God. (v. 11b)
> There is no one who does the good, (v. 12c)
> there is not even one. (v. 12d)
> There is no fear of God before their eyes. (v. 18)

Verses 11 and 12 both derive from Ps 14:2–3 (13:2–3 LXX), but the relationship is a complex one (Watson 2016, 52–53). The psalmist asserts:

> The Lord peered out from heaven at humanity's offspring
> in order to see whether anyone understands or seeks out God. (13:2 LXX)

However, the catena at Rom 3:11 renders this as a thoroughly negative statement:

> There is no one who understands;
> there is no one who seeks out God.

Although the psalm still allowed for the possibility that some humans might try to understand or find God, v. 11 does not, by contrast with Acts 17:27. This recasting of the psalm not only makes it more negative but also aligns it more closely with Paul's argument to this point of the letter, since 1:21–23 identifies the beginning of human rebellion with an unwillingness to glorify or offer thanks to God, and 1:31 characterizes humans as "without sense" or "without understanding" (*asynetos*).

Verse 12 reproduces Ps 14:3 (13:3 LXX) almost exactly, with the single difference that Romans adds the definite article ("the") just prior to the phrase "one who does the good." Where the first two lines of the catena (i.e., v. 11, bracketing v. 10b as title or introduction) concerned attitudes toward God, this pair has to do with behavior, turning away and failing to do anything that is good. The statement concerning good (*chrēstotēs*) that is not done by humans recalls Paul's earlier charge against those who look down upon the wealth of God's goodness (*chrēstotēs*; 2:4), as well as the contrast between humanity and God in 3:1–8.

The next four lines of the catena (vv. 13–14) concern parts of the body, all of which are involved with speech: the throat, the tongue, the lips, and the mouth. The first two lines of v. 13 reproduce Ps 5:9b (5:10b LXX), and the third comes from 140:3b (139:4b LXX). Verse 14 only slightly abbreviates Ps 10:7 LXX. Placed together in this new context, these four lines constitute a stinging rebuke of human speech as a matter of nothing less than death (poisonous venom, the grave).[60] As with previous lines, one does not have to search far to find antecedents in 1:18–32, where several of the activities of human beings that come under scathing critique concern speech, especially gossip, slander, and bragging (1:29–30). And in that context also, such actions are associated with death (1:32).

Paul is not alone in his concern about human speech, of course. Biblical literature, especially in the Wisdom tradition, frequently expresses concern about speech practices (e.g., Prov 10:18; 17:4; Sir 20:18, 24; cf. Jas 3:5, 6, 8–10a). Similarly, philosophers and moralists contemporary with Paul taught about right and wrong speech practices (e.g., Epictetus, *Ench.* 33.1–3; Diogenes Laertius, *Lives* 1.105; Plutarch, *Mor.* 502B–C). Importantly, however, these diverse traditions all assume that humans are capable of controlling their speech; they are able to cultivate the virtue of disciplined speech. Paul, however, allows no such exception.

Verses 15–16 also begin with bodily imagery, that of the feet, but these two lines concern the ways in which "the feet," human actions, produce the shedding of blood, destruction, and wretchedness. Paul here excerpts from the longer description in Isa 59:7 LXX:

---

60. Calvin remarks aptly regarding v. 13a, "This is more than if he had said that they were man-eaters . . . since it is the height of enormity that a man's throat should be big enough to swallow and devour men entirely" (67).

Their feet run toward evil,
swift at shedding blood.
And their thoughts are the thoughts of fools;
destruction and wretchedness are in their paths.

Abbreviating and combining the first and second lines of Isaiah and deleting the third gives the catena a more direct focus on action as distinct from thought: "Swift are their feet for shedding blood, destruction and wretchedness are in their paths" (Rom 3:15–16).[61] That choice may have to do with the fact that the catena opens by lamenting the absence of understanding or seeking for God—that is, thought as distinct from action—but here moves to the topic of action.

The final two lines of the catena summarize what has been said up to this point with the dreadful assessment that "the way of peace they did not know" and "there is no fear of God before their eyes" (vv. 17–18). The first part of this charge comes almost exactly from Isa 59:8. The second quotes Ps 36:1b (35:2b LXX). Both claims resonate with large strands of biblical literature, however,[62] and Paul has already identified peace among those things to be granted at the final judgment (Rom 2:10; and see also 5:1; 8:6; 14:17, 19; 15:13; 16:20). The assertion that people do not know the ways of peace anticipates the final line, which characterizes humanity as having no fear of God (3:18). Given the ubiquity with which Scripture identifies fear or awe as the appropriate response to God, this concluding charge powerfully summarizes what Paul has been saying since 1:18.[63]

The original settings of the various texts quoted here may provide some hint to Paul's overall purpose in the catena. In the LXX, all of the psalms included here (Pss 5, 10, 13, 35, 139 LXX) begin with the heading *eis to telos*, the LXX's rendering of "to the leader." That phrase was interpreted eschatologically early in the church's life (as in "to the last hour"),[64] and it would scarcely be out of character for Paul, too, to read these texts eschatologically (15:4).[65]

More important is the fact that these psalms all position themselves alongside the innocent and over against the guilty. Psalm 14 (13 LXX) contrasts "those" foolish people with the righteous, for example, and Ps 10 LXX castigates

61. Curiously, Paul will later call on other Isaianic words about feet when invoking the joyous arrival of the gospel's messengers (10:15, quoting Isa 52:7; and notice 16:20 as well).

62. The desire for and promise of peace are especially prominent in the psalms (e.g., Pss 29:11; 34:14; 72:7; 85:8, 10; 119:165; 120:6). For Luke, peace becomes a hallmark among the promises that accompany the birth of Jesus (Luke 2:29; cf. Acts 10:36; and also John 14:27).

63. E.g., Exod 20:20; Lev 19:14, 32; Deut 6:24; 31:12–13; Ps 61:5; Isa 11:2–3.

64. Bell 1998, 218. Note also Jerome, *Tract. Ps.* 2; Augustine, *Enarrat. Ps.* 5.1; Theodoret, *Comm. Ps.* 4.

65. The fact that roughly a third of the psalms open with *eis to telos* makes it difficult to weigh that phrase too heavily here.

"those" who are wicked with the warning that God will deliver "the orphan and the oppressed" (10:18). That observation also holds for many psalms other than the ones represented in the catena. If Phoebe's auditors have even passing acquaintance with the psalms, they will hear in the catena the refrain of human wickedness that constitutes a major motif of the psalms. They will also expect to hear the catena turn to address those who are innocent. For example, Ps 5 (quoted in Rom 3:13a) urges that God punish the wicked but then concludes:

> But let all who take refuge in you rejoice;
>> let them ever sing for joy.
> Spread your protection over them,
>> so that those who love your name may exult in you.
> For you bless the righteous, O LORD;
>> you cover them with favor as with a shield. (Ps 5:11–12 NRSVue)

Phoebe's auditors would surely have expected to hear her turn to comment on the wise, the righteous, the innocent (as in, e.g., Pss 11, 12, 14, 28, 31), but instead they hear only that there are no such persons.

The catena is far more than a scriptural decoration employed to increase the volume of Paul's argument. As noted above, the connections between the catena and the argument that has preceded it are impressive. Not only are terms and thoughts from the preceding argument repeated, but the movement of the catena recalls that of 1:18–32 in that both passages begin with a discussion of the failure of the human mindset (1:21; 3:11) and culminate in actions that lead to death (1:32; 3:15–16). This move constitutes a rhetorical feint: the text induces its auditors to anticipate a certain conclusion about God's dealings with the faithful; instead, v. 19 will draw another conclusion altogether.

[19] The effect of the catena continues into v. 19. The introductory phrase "Now we know" assumes that Paul and his audience will be in agreement about what follows (as earlier in 2:2): the law speaks to those who live in the realm of the law. "We" are all in agreement about this matter, a point that might be a restatement of 3:2: what the law says it speaks to those to whom it is given (see not only 3:2 but also 7:1 and 9:4).

Whether "law" (*nomos*) here refers to Scripture in general or whether the preceding catena is to be thought of as a commentary on the law (so Watson 2016, 51), an unmistakable relationship exists between the catena and the claim of v. 19; the catena is in some sense among those things the law "says," even though Paul is not quoting from Mosaic Torah. And remarkably, what the law says it utters so that "every mouth might be stopped." The contrast between the law's speech (mentioned not once but twice in v. 19a) and the silencing of human speech is rhetorically elegant, the more so since vv. 13–14 of the catena bring together three psalm texts that have to do with the vileness of human speech. What the law says actually renders humanity unable to speak, thus terminating the disastrous speech of vv. 13–14 as well as the speech against God implied in the charge of idolatry in 1:18–32. Little wonder that Paul regards this as the equivalent of bringing the entire cosmos under God's judgment.

A significant question arises at just this point: How would Phoebe's audiences hear this statement? Is what the law says, in Paul's voicing of the law, something that his contemporaries would expect to hear the law say? Would Jews in Rome, together with those gentiles who identified themselves with Jews and their traditions, have declared that the law speaks *in order to* bring about judgment, especially judgment on all humanity, Jew and gentile alike? The evidence concerning early Jewish understandings of the law is highly complicated and difficult to assess, and the scholarly debates on these questions are more diverse and complex even than the evidence, but it is hard to imagine that Jews and Jewishly identified gentile listeners would have nodded their heads in assent as Phoebe read this assertion. To be sure, the notion that all people are liable to transgress the law appears in Jewish literature roughly contemporaneous with Paul (e.g., 1 En. 80–81; 4 Ezra 3.22–22; 7.19–25; 9.11; Jub. 23.11–31; CD 6.10, 14; 15.7–10). It also has a venerable history in Scripture, in both historical and prophetic literature, as well as in the Psalter, such as the psalm texts taken up in the preceding catena. At the same time, the law of Moses is itself spoken of as a gift that sets Israel apart (Deut 4:8; 33:4), as that which must be cherished and obeyed alongside Israel's God (Deut 27:3; 31:11; Pss 1:2; 40:8). Dire consequences threaten those who disobey the law (e.g., Deut 27:26; 28:61), but those who keep it are promised security, prosperity, and wisdom (e.g., Josh 1:8; Ps 119:1; Sir 15:1). In light of such a wealth of perception, Paul's claim that the law—a paramount gift from God to Israel—*speaks in order to reveal that all humanity is liable to judgment* is a claim that must have seemed peculiar at best.

[20] In Rom 7:12 and 9:4, Paul will again identify the law among those gifts of God to Israel, but at this juncture he does not soften the sting of v. 19. The final step taken in this passage is to move from indicting human sin to insisting that observance of the law does not bring about righteousness, since Paul here identifies the law entirely with the awareness of sin.

Paul draws on Ps 143:2b (142:2b LXX) in v. 20, as he did already in his letter to the Galatians. In both letters he adds the phrase "from observance of the law," introducing an element that connects the psalm's claim about humanity specifically with the law.

Ps 142:2b LXX	because *any living one* [*pas zōn*] will not be rectified before *you*
Gal 2:16	because *from observance of the law* [*ek pisteōs nomou*] *all flesh* [*pasa sarx*] will not be rectified.
Rom 3:20	because *from observance of the law* [*ek pisteōs nomou*] *all flesh* [*pasa sarx*] will not be rectified before *him*.

How exactly the law and Sin are connected Paul does not say at this stage, leaving that question for ch. 7. Here, however, what he accomplishes is the closure of any escape from the dire words of 3:9: *all* are under the power of Sin. Having so graphically depicted the causes and results of the event in which God turned humanity over to the powers of Sin and Death, Paul returns in vv. 21–26 to God's rectifying action in the advent of Jesus Christ.

3:21–26 "But Now . . ."

In the death and resurrection of Jesus Christ, God has disclosed humanity's captivity to Sin's power. There is no exit from God's wrath, not for the gentile sinner, not even for the law-observant Jew. This astonishing reading of the human situation has been revealed apocalyptically (1:18) as part of the gospel itself. That disclosure is far from being the final word, however. With the dramatic "but now" of 3:21, Paul takes up the revelation of God's righteousness, which is to say, the action of God in Jesus Christ, an action that simultaneously reveals the human situation and makes it right through the liberative, holy, and rectifying event of the cross.

This passage is crucial to the letter and has generated endless discussion by exegetes and systematic theologians alike. Yet it cannot be understood in isolation; nor can individual statements or terms within it be taken in isolation. Paul's comments regarding the law in v. 21 will continue in 3:27–31, return at various points in chs. 4–6, and culminate in ch. 7. In addition, the provocative and fluctuating imagery used here regarding Jesus's death can scarcely be understood apart from the more sustained discussion in 5:12–21. One reason for the intense disagreement over the exegesis of this passage is that its interpreters have placed too much weight on individual words within it, without probing their connections to the larger context of Romans.

One of the ongoing debates over this passage during the last half century has concerned the possibility that Paul is making use of early Christian tradition in vv. 24(25)–26. Several features of the passage prompt this proposal: (a) the presence of words or phrases that are otherwise rare in or missing from Paul's vocabulary (including *hilastērion, paresis, protithēmi,* and *haima*); (b) the abrupt transition to a participle at the beginning of v. 24; (c) the awkward intrusion in v. 25 of the typically Pauline phrases "through faith" (rendered here as "through God's own faithfulness") and "as a demonstration of God's righteousness."[66] My discussion treats these lines as Paul's own composition because, while some of the terms that appear here are unusual, they do not

---

66. For the development of this proposal, see Bultmann 1951–1955, 1:46; Käsemann 1960, 96–100. For reviews of the discussion, see S. Williams 1975, 5–19; Kraus 1991, 1–20; Jewett 269–71. Campbell (1992) offers a sustained argument for the identification of pre-Pauline tradition in 3:24(25)–26, summarized on pp. 201–3.

constitute a sufficient "mass" to require appeal to an author other than Paul. In addition, the uncharacteristic expressions can be understood within the context (both narrow and wide) of the letter. Also, the transition at the beginning of v. 24 is less abrupt if the participle is read as modifying the *pantes* of v. 23 (see translation below). And if Paul has supplied the phrase "through faith" in order to brand the quoted material with his own terminology, as it were, it seems very peculiar that he would insert the phrase in a way that renders the quotation more rather than less difficult to understand. Finally, even if Paul is making use of earlier tradition, he has made the language his own and used it to forward the understanding of the gospel announced in 1:17.

3:21 But now, without the law's involvement, God's righteousness has been made plain, although it is confirmed by the law and the prophets, 22 that is, God's righteousness through Jesus Christ-faith[a] for all who believe (for there is no distinction, 23 since all have sinned and are thereby deprived of[b] the glory of God, 24 yet all are rectified freely through God's grace[c]) through the liberation from slavery that comes about in Christ Jesus, 25 whom God put forward publicly as the very cover of the ark of the covenant.[d] God did this through God's own faithfulness,[e] by means of Jesus's bloody death, as a demonstration of God's righteousness because of the incapacity[f] resulting from previous sins 26 and through God's forbearance, as a demonstration of God's righteousness at the present time, so that God might be right and might make right the one who is part of this Jesus-faith.[g]

a. See the excursus on the faith of Christ (pp. 116–19).

b. "Are deprived of" (as in the NAB) construes *hysterountai* as passive rather than middle, as in the more customary translations "lack" or "fall short of." This translation makes for a closer connection to 1:18–32, where humanity is "handed over" and thereby deprived of God's presence. A similar passive translation, "be deprived of," would also make sense in 1 Cor 1:7; 8:8; see also Ps 22:1 LXX; Eccl 9:8.

c. The nominative participle *dikaioumenoi* is construed most naturally as modifying the nominative *pantes* in v. 23 rather than the accusative *pisteuontas* in v. 22. In addition, the participial phrase counterbalances the content of the first part of the statement: just as there is no distinction in the working of Sin, there is also no distinction in the working of God's righteousness. The statement then ends with "freely through God's grace," so that the following *dia* clause ("[righteousness] through the liberation from slavery") stands in parallel to the *dia* clause that precedes in v. 22 ("righteousness through Jesus Christ-faith"), drawing on Campbell (1992, 87–95).

d. *Hilastērion* in the LXX regularly translates the Hebrew *kapporet*, which is often rendered "mercy seat" (e.g., Exod 25:17–21; Lev 16:13–15), but the texts describe it as a cover or top piece for the ark of the covenant, making "seat" misleading. (See further the comment on v. 25a below.)

e. Some manuscripts (including ℵ C* D* F G) omit the definite article here (*dia tēs pisteōs*, rendered "through God's faithfulness" in my translation), and others include it (𝔓⁴⁰ᵛⁱᵈ B C³ D²). It might have been added as a resumptive reference to the *pistis* phrase in v. 22, although note the article with *pistis* in vv. 30–31 (and see Metzger 1971, 508).

f. The extensive discussion of *paresis* (which is a hapax legomenon in both the NT and the LXX) perseverates over the alternative translations "passing over" or "forgiveness," but the most obvious and widely attested meaning of *paresis* is that of paralysis, found not only in medical texts (including works of Hippocrates, Soranus, Galen, and Aretaeus; see the discussion in Holmes, as well as LSJ s.v.) but also in Josephus (*Ant.* 9.240, paralysis of the limbs because of fear; 11.236, Esther's paralysis as a result of fear) and Philo (*Rewards* 143, 145, inability to use the tongue because of disease; *Worse* 168, the "paralysis" of the remaining parts of the soul when the mind is gone). In addition, Chrysostom explains *paresis* in this text as *nekrōsis* ("death") that requires divine healing (*Hom. Rom.* 7.25; *NPNF*¹ 11.378), and Theophylact also understands *paresis* here in this sense of paralysis, which God cures through Jesus Christ (PG 124:388). Similarly, the related verb *pareinai* is used of paralysis or incapacity, as in, e.g., Heb 12:12; Deut 32:36; 2 Sam 4:1; Sir 25:23 (see Holmes, who notes Luke 11:42 as an exception to this usage).

g. The *kai* ("and") is omitted in F G it and Ambrosiaster (thus, God is right by rectifying); a few manuscripts insert *christou* following *Iēsou*; F G and a few others omit the reference to Jesus altogether; and some read the accusative *Iēsoun* instead of the genitive *Iēsou*. These are all minor textual variants, largely serving to show the difficulties perceived in this phrase.

[3:21] "But now" (*nuni de*) alerts the audience that something has happened: God has attacked the dire situation under discussion in the previous chapters, and Paul is now turning to explain that attack. The word choice is warranted, even if attack seems a strident term. Already in 1:16–17 God's power has been invoked, and the conflict language of chs. 5–8 will reinforce this notion of God's powerful intervention. Nonetheless, for Paul, God's attack on the way things are does not participate in conventional equations of power with sheer force or control over others. God's attack takes the form of love (5:1–5), radical giving (8:32), even weakness (15:3).

As often in Romans, "now" (whether *nyn* or the more intensive form used here, *nyni*) conveys a sense of urgency (e.g., 3:26; 5:9, 11; 6:19, 21–22; 7:6, 17; 8:1, 18, 22; 11:5, 30–31; 13:11; 15:23, 25). Paul can anticipate that the gatherings at Rome will respond to this time reference, since one thing that distinguishes those who have been called by Jesus Christ (1:1, 6) is that they know what time it is. All of creation may be in labor, but it is "we" who know what is happening at present (8:22). Salvation is closer now than when "we" first believed (13:11).

Central to the "now" event is "the righteousness of God" (*dikaiosynē theou*), a phrase that returns to Paul's introductory comment about the gospel itself as God's saving power (1:16–17). Paul begins to explain how that power has been acting in the world. Already in 3:5 he has referred to God's righteousness;

unlike human beings, who have proven themselves faithless (3:3), God has proven faithful through righteousness (3:5). God's righteousness is the grammatical subject of the entire passage 3:21–26, leaving aside the parenthesis of vv. 22b–24a. Quite apart from grammatical considerations, the importance of the term may be gauged from the fact that it appears seven times in this short passage: in the noun phrase "God's righteousness" or "his righteousness" (3:21, 22, 25, 26), the verb "rectify" or "make right" (3:24, 26), and the adjective "right" (3:26). This repetition could lend itself to the misperception that Paul is composing a treatise on one of the divine attributes, unless we attend carefully to the time references at the beginning and the end ("but now" and "at the present time") and to the specific reference to the event of Jesus's death. Put differently, if God's own "rightness" is under discussion here, it is because humanity comes to know that "rightness" entirely through the death of Jesus Christ.

The adverb "entirely" may seem extreme, but the shift from v. 20 to v. 21 suggests otherwise. The catena in 3:10–18 relentlessly depicts the situation of humanity under Sin ("all," v. 9) and the multitudinous ways in which human beings have gone wrong, culminating with the indictment regarding "all flesh" (*pasa sarx*) in v. 20. Verse 21 shifts dramatically from the action (or inaction) of humanity to that of God; humanity has been rendered silent, captive to Sin's power, so that only God is able to act. This point is underscored if we attend to Ps 143, which seems to be at work in both 3:20 and 21 (Hays 1980). Although Paul takes up the psalmist's affirmation that no human is rectified before God and affirms God's own saving righteousness, he does not follow the whole of the psalmist's logic. Here there is no claim that humanity cries out to God for deliverance or trusts in God for vindication, and no plea for the destruction of enemies (Ps 143:5–12) because, in Paul's view, there is no one who fears God.

Verse 21 modifies the phrase "God's righteousness" in two ways, both of which are deeply connected to the ongoing argument of the letter and also employ the rhetorical feint observed earlier in the letter (see on 2:1; 3:1). Initially, Paul describes God's righteousness as *chōris nomou*, "without the law's involvement," which builds upon the conclusions drawn in vv. 19–20. The law itself has spoken in order to shut every human mouth, since law observance cannot make a person right before God. Every expected avenue has been closed off, and the conventional notion that the good would be rescued has been thwarted with Paul's remarkable conclusion that there are in fact no such good people whom God might vindicate. The phrase "without the law's involvement," then, both reinforces 3:19–20 and announces that God is free to act apart from the law (Keck 105).[67]

67. Linebaugh rightly observes, "It is easy to miss the contextual absurdity of Paul's claim. Paul is saying that the divine righteousness is revealed apart from the very thing which, in his tradition, was the revelation of the divine righteousness" (2010, 121).

Yet the law is not entirely absent, as is already clear in v. 19, since it is the law that speaks in such a way as to reveal human sin. So Paul again modifies "God's righteousness" by saying that it is confirmed (*martyroumenē*) by "the law and the prophets."[68] Here he draws on the *martys* word group that is associated with witness, especially in the Gospel of John (e.g., 1:7–8; 5:31–33; 19:35) and in Acts (1:8; 2:32; 13:31; 26:16). Paul seldom uses this terminology, and when he does it appears as confirmation of assertions made by others: God confirms Paul's desire to be in Rome (Rom 1:9; 2 Cor 1:23); Paul's conscience is confirmation (2 Cor 1:12); he confirms the affection the Galatians had for him earlier (Gal 4:15). (See also Rom 10:2; 1 Cor 1:6; 15:15; 2 Cor 8:3; 13:1.) If the usage is similar here, what Scripture does is to *confirm* what God has done rather than to *anticipate* it. Which particular writings confirm Paul's argument about God's righteousness he does not specify, although it is by no means incidental that Romans makes more explicit and extensive use of Scripture than any of Paul's other letters.

The relationship between these two statements about the law ("without the law's involvement"; "confirmed by the law and the prophets") is important, and interpreters vary in their assessments of that relationship. Is Paul moving between two distinct connotations of *nomos*—on the one hand, the law as a constraint on human action, and on the other, the books of the Pentateuch (so Fitzmyer 344)? Is the first reference (without the law's involvement) limited to the specific legal requirements that marked the social boundaries of Israel, such as circumcision and food laws, while the second (confirmed by law and prophets) reveals Paul's real conviction that there is continuity "right through the scriptures" (so Dunn 1:165)? Is the second intended to counteract the possibly adverse impact of the first on an audience prepared to reject Paul as a radical critic of Jewish tradition? The fact that all of these possibilities can be argued suggests that once again Paul is employing the sort of rhetorical sleight of hand already seen in the move from 2:25–29 to 3:1–2, where he undermines the distinction between Jew and gentile and then insists on the prerogatives of "the Jew." Having said that God has acted apart from the law, Paul asserts the confirming importance of the law and the prophets. Similarly, at the end of this chapter he will insist that—contrary to appearances—he is upholding the law. By doing this, Paul appears to be gentling the comments he made about the law in Galatians (so Tobin 2004, 153–54), but it is by no means clear that his argument about the law in Romans is ultimately less radical than his argument in Galatians.

[22a] Having announced the arrival of God's righteousness ("but now") apart from the law, Paul begins to reaffirm the identification of that arrival with

---

68. Paul nowhere else uses this phrase to refer to Scripture, but it is found in 2 Macc 15:9; 4 Macc 18:10; Sir, Prologue 1, 24; Matt 7:12; 11:13 ("the prophets and the law"); 22:40; Luke 16:16; Acts 13:15; 24:14; 28:23.

Jesus Christ (as also in 1:3–4, 16, where "the gospel" refers to God's Son). A long series of prepositional clauses running through v. 26 unpacks the nature of God's action (the series being broken by the parenthesis in vv. 22b–24a).

The initial phrase modifying "God's righteousness" is "through Jesus Christ-faith." As the excursus below explains, this phrase refers to faith associated with Jesus Christ. It originates in God's action in Jesus Christ and returns to Jesus Christ in human confidence or trust. Human faith (*pistis*) is not for Paul isolated from this event as a virtue or state to be contrasted with "works" or "unbelief" but is integrally associated with Jesus Christ. This is not to say that faith *as such* only enters human history with the Christ event, since Paul knows of Abraham's trust in God (4:3, 17–20). "Jesus Christ-faith" is not generic human faith in God but specifically faith inaugurated by God in the sending of Jesus Christ. That it comes as a result of God's own action will be clearly enunciated in 10:14–17, where faith is attributed to God's sending of messengers (and see also 12:3).

This Jesus Christ-faith is for all. Because *pas* ("every," "all") has run like a red thread through the letter until this point (1:5, 7, 8, 16, 18, 29; 2:1, 9, 10; 3:2, 4, 9, 12, 19, 20), its appearance here should not be surprising. The qualification "who believe" does not limit God's action or stipulate how one "taps into" God's righteousness so much as it acknowledges that at present only some have been called (as in 1:1, 7) to understand what God has done.

[22b–24a] Paul now explicates "all who believe" with a statement that simultaneously summarizes 1:18–3:20 and anticipates the interpretation of the Christ event that begins here and extends at least through ch. 5. The statement applies particularly to the "all" of v. 22a, the "all who believe" (Johnston 2011). In a sense the statement is superfluous, as Paul has already argued at length for the universal extent of Sin, and he will reinforce that argument in 5:12–21. Reiterating it at precisely this point, where he has just referenced "all who believe," puts them in the spotlight: even those who believe are among the "all who have sinned and are thereby deprived of [or removed from] the glory of God." Paul lets no one escape, as earlier at 2:1. He will insist that the very "we" who are at peace with God were weak, godless sinners, enemies of God (5:1–11).

The initial assertion that "there is no distinction" seems to contradict earlier statements about the priority of Jews (1:16; 2:9, 10) and the advantages of being a Jew (3:1–2), but Paul's argument since 1:18 has moved in the direction of showing that, whatever advantages Jews have, the power of Sin is such that it has enslaved both Jews and gentiles (3:9), and that point is reinforced in 3:19–20: every human being stands under judgment. So Paul restates the point in v. 23. The shift in tenses from the aorist "all have sinned" to the present "[all] are thereby deprived of" reflects the account of Sin's triumph in 1:18–32. "All have sinned" in that all participated in the rejection of the rightful worship and service of God, and as a result all are presently deprived of "the glory of God."

"The glory of God" (*doxa theou*) is often understood as a reference to the glory of created humanity in Adam prior to the fall (Cranfield 1:204; Käsemann 95; Dunn 1:168; Wright 470). Examples from Jewish literature can be adduced in support of the claim that other Jews in Paul's general environment attributed to Adam a glory that was lost in the fall (1QS 4.23; CD 3.20; 3 Bar. 4.16; *LAE* 20.2; 21.6). Yet Paul never refers to the glory of Adam; nor does he speak of the loss of the created glory of humanity. In fact, when he does speak specifically of human glory in 1 Cor 11:7, he assumes that males *continue* to bear the glory of God.

By contrast, in Romans the language of glory is associated primarily with God. One of the main charges lodged against humanity in Rom 1 is that, in its false worship, humanity exchanged God's glory for that of images, withholding the giving of proper glorification to God alone (1:21, 23; see also 3:7). By contrast, Abraham is recalled for giving glory to God (4:20), and Paul's vision in 15:7–13 is of Jew and gentile together glorifying God (15:6, 9). The resurrection is said to have taken place through the glory of God (6:4), God acted in Israel's history for God's own glory (9:23; and see 9:4; 11:36), and Christ's welcome of all is for God's glory (see also 15:7).[69] To be sure, glory is also associated with humanity, but in Romans human glory is always an eschatological glory, as in 2:7, 10, and especially in 8:18, 21, where glory awaits God's children (probably this is also the sense at 5:2; and see 1 Thess 2:12; 1 En. 50.1; 2 Bar. 51.1, 3; 54.16, 21). Humanity's loss in rebellion was the loss of its worshipful relationship to God. When Paul says that humanity is deprived of God's glory, then, he refers to the loss of its proper, worshipful relationship to God, not its inherent or created glory (Gaventa 2014b, 30–31).

The parenthesis ends with what initially appears to be a mild redundancy, in that "all" are said to be rectified both "freely" and "through God's grace," as in the English expression "a free gift." For many of Paul's contemporaries, this would have seemed a peculiar statement, to put it mildly. The widespread expectation was that gifts should be reserved for those who are worthy of them. Paul's claim that God's rectifying act takes place without regard for the appropriateness of the recipient—indeed, in the face of the utter inappropriateness of the recipient—was distinctive in the ancient world (Barclay 2015, especially pp. 72–73, 315–18, 324, 563–66). Later, in 5:20–21, grace takes on verbs; that is, it is revealed not simply as a character trait of God but as God's activity. A similar notion is at work here as well.

[24b] The remainder of v. 24 stands outside the parenthetical summary and resumes Paul's explanation of God's righteousness; it takes place "through

69. Agamben (2011, 197–202) helpfully distinguishes this notion of God's presence, God's "terrifying appearance . . . the Kingdom, Judgment, and the throne," from the aesthetic interpretation of glory in Hans Urs von Balthasar.

the liberation from slavery that comes about in Christ Jesus." The Greek word *apolytrōsis*, often translated "redemption," is rare in Paul's letters.[70] *Apolytrōsis* is also infrequent outside biblical usage, but when it does appear it almost always refers to liberation from captivity or slavery.[71] Given the violent history of Roman conquest and the ubiquity of slavery in the Roman world, the term would be familiar to Paul's audience in connection with the very real situation of being set free; indeed, a number of them are likely to be slaves or freedmen/women themselves (Lampe 2003, 153–83; and see below on 16:3–16). It should not be surprising, then, if he uses such a term for deliverance from the captivity he has already depicted in stunning detail and will later name as slavery to Sin (6:17). This understanding of *apolytrōsis* appears in some of Paul's earliest interpreters. Ambrosiaster, for example, speaks of this redemption as "release from slavery" and continues:

> For he [Christ] surrendered himself to the raging devil, who, however, did not know what was coming. Believing that he could hold Christ captive, the devil received him, seemingly, but because the devil could not bear Christ's power, he let go all whom he held captive at the same time he let Christ go. (68–69)

Similarly, Origen comments that the word *apolytrōsis* "designates something given to enemies in exchange for their captives, whom they then restore to their prior freedom" (*Comm. Rom.* 3.7; Burns 76).[72] Paul identifies this particular redemption as "in Christ Jesus," and v. 25 begins to clarify what this phrase means.

[25a] At this point cultic language displaces the language of redemption from slavery that precedes, as Paul affirms that God put Christ "forward publicly as the very cover of the ark of the covenant." Although the verb *protithēmi* can have the nuance of "plan" or "intend" (as in 1:13 and in the related noun *prothesis* in 8:28 and 9:11), here the emphasis falls not simply on God's purpose but on God's public action (e.g., Exod 29:23; 40:4, 23; Lev 24:8). God puts Jesus forward publicly in the cross, as in Gal 3:1, where the crucifixion of Jesus Christ is said to have been publicly proclaimed.

---

70. See Rom 8:23; 1 Cor 1:30. It is also rare in the remainder of the Bible; see Dan 4:34 LXX; Luke 21:28; Eph 1:7, 14; 4:30; Col 1:14; Heb 9:15; 11:35. The related noun *lytron* ("ransom") and the verb *lytroō* ("to redeem, to liberate") appear frequently (e.g., Exod 6:6; 13:15; 21:8; Lev 19:20; 27:31; Deut 7:8; 1 Kgs 1:29; Ps 24:22; Isa 43:1; 44:24).

71. See, e.g., *Let. Aris.* 12.3; Josephus, *Ant.* 12.27; Philo, *Prelim. Studies* 109; Plutarch, *Pomp.* 24.4; Cos Inscription 29 (Paton and Hicks 1891, 52); Campbell 1992, 119.

72. The fact that such redemptions from slavery or captivity involve the payment of a price need not work against this interpretation. Metaphors ought not be read rigidly; moreover, there is a kind of "price" at work here in that Christ is later said to be "handed over" on behalf of humankind (4:25; 8:32).

God puts Christ forward as *hilastērion*, "the very cover of the ark of the covenant." The fact that Paul uses this word only once should caution against taking it as the key to his understanding of the death of Jesus, and that fact also makes it challenging to understand the precise nuance of the term. The long-standing debate about *hilastērion* comes down to whether it should be understood as a figurative reference to the cover of the ark of the covenant or whether it should be understood more abstractly as a "means of expiation" or "propitiation." The linguistic evidence overwhelmingly favors the rendering "cover of the ark of the covenant." *Hilastērion* in the LXX regularly appears as a translation for *kapporet* (the cover of the ark of the covenant; e.g., Exod 25:18–22; Lev 16:2, 13–15; Num 7:89; and see Heb 9:5). *Kapporet* appears four times in the Dead Sea Scrolls, always with reference to a feature of the temple (4Q364 17.3; 4Q365 8a–b.1; 11Q19 3.9; 11Q19 7.9; similarly in Philo, *Cherubim* 25; *Flight* 100; *Moses* 2.95–96). *Hilastērion* can also be used for gifts offered to the gods, as an offering made to Athena (Dio Chrysostom, *Or.* 11.121), or a tomb built by Hyrcanus (Josephus, *Ant.* 16.182). The word is used metaphorically in 4 Macc 17:22, where the phrase "the *hilastērion* of their death" refers to the death of martyrs; yet this phrase, like Rom 3:25, seems to be the figurative use of a conventional term for a place or a thing rather than an abstract concept (Bailey 2000).

Despite this strong evidence, translating *hilastērion* as a figurative reference to the cover of the ark of the covenant prompts some objections. One such objection is grammatical; in the LXX *hilastērion* virtually always carries the definite article, as it does in Heb 9:5, but there is no definite article in 3:25, leading to the conclusion that the referent is a general act of mercy rather than a specific place (Cranfield 1:214–15). However, *hilastērion* is a predicate accusative, which does not regularly take the article (Smyth 1956, §1614); in addition, *hilastērion* could be understood by Paul as a one-of-a-kind object, which again does not require the article (Wallace 1996, 248).

A second objection to translating *hilastērion* as a figurative reference to the cover of the ark of the covenant is that gentiles among Phoebe's auditors at Rome would not understand the reference (Käsemann 97). This objection loses considerable force, however, if the Roman gentile Christians are understood as *sebomenoi* who are familiar with Scripture—knowledge of which is certainly presumed in the letter.

Third, the identification of Jesus with a "thing," even with "a piece of furniture" (Cranfield 1:215), proves unimaginable to some, yet this objection misunderstands the role of the cover of the ark of the covenant, to say nothing of misconceiving metaphorical language. It appears not to be problematic when the Johannine Jesus compares himself with a vine or with bread (John 6:31–58; 15:1–6), and it should not be problematic in Romans if Paul compares Jesus Christ with the cover of the ark of the covenant.

To the contrary, the identification of Jesus Christ with the *hilastērion* is a powerful one. Among the most obvious features of the ark of the covenant is that human beings constructed it following God's specifications. The instructions in Exod 25:10–22 repeatedly insist, "You shall make" or "You shall put." In Romans, of course, it is explicitly God who puts Jesus forward as the cover. Consistent with the contrast between divine and human action elsewhere in this letter, Paul once again draws attention to God's role in making this *hilastērion* happen.

More to the point, Scripture identifies the *hilastērion* as the place at which God makes himself known. Culminating the building plan in Exod 25 is the declaration "There I will meet with you, and from above the cover, from between the two cherubim that are on the ark of the covenant, I will tell you all that I am commanding you for the Israelites" (Exod 25:22 NRSVue). This point comes to expression even more forcefully in Lev 16, with God's instructions regarding the Day of Atonement ritual. Aaron is warned against coming before the *hilastērion* at any time other than the Day of Atonement, because he will die there, so powerful is God's holy presence in that place (16:2; and see Num 7:89).[73] In the Second Temple there is, of course, no ark of the covenant, and thus no *hilastērion*. As Josephus writes (*J.W.* 5.219), at the very center of the holy of holies there is nothing. Yet an association is made between *hilastērion* and God's glory (as in Philo, *Moses* 2.95–100; *Cherubim* 25). The identification of Christ Jesus with this *hilastērion*, then, also calls up the very holiness of God and God's self-revelation. Jesus is put forward as the holiest place at which God makes himself known to humankind. Given the emphasis in the early chapters of Romans on the glory of God and of humanity's refusal to acknowledge that glory, this reference to Jesus as the center of the holy of holies is significant.

One thing that should be noted here is the easy way in which Paul refers to "his" blood and then "his" righteousness, without carefully sorting out which "his" belongs to which agent. This slight unclarity may suggest that disengaging the two agents is less an issue for Paul than for his interpreters. To be sure, the actor here is God, but the notion that redemption is "in Christ Jesus" already indicates that God is not acting with this agent in the same way as God acted with Moses or Abraham or David. God's self-revealing act is bound up with Jesus.

Construing the relationships among the string of prepositional phrases that follow is a challenge. The *hilastērion* is said to be both "through faith" (*dia tēs pisteōs*) and "by his blood" (*en tō autou haimati*), which can be rendered "through faith in his blood," as in the KJV and the NIV. Nowhere else, however, does Paul or any other NT text refer to belief *in the blood of Jesus*. Paul rarely follows either the noun *pistis* or the verb *pisteuō* with *en*, as in "belief in" or

---

73. While the term *hilastērion* has clear associations with the Day of Atonement, that does not necessarily mean that Paul sees Jesus as a replacement for the temple sacrifice, a move that would be more at home in the book of Hebrews than in Paul.

"believe in."[74] It is also unclear how God's offering of Jesus as the cover of the ark of the covenant is accomplished *through* belief in blood. Instead of linking "through faith" with "by his blood," the two prepositional phrases stand in apposition: God acted through faith, that is, through God's own faithfulness, as in Rom 3:3, *and* God acted by means of Jesus's blood. Coupled with the reference to the holy of holies, the graphic reference to blood suggests a connection to sacrifice, but that connection should not be overstated, especially as 5:9 again uses "blood" metonymically to refer to death.

[25b–26] The remainder of vv. 25 and 26 comprises two lengthy prepositional phrases set in parallel to each other, each of which is governed by the noun *endeixis* ("demonstration"; see also 2 Cor 8:24; Phil 1:28):

> as a demonstration of God's righteousness
>> because of the incapacity resulting from previous sins
>> and through God's forbearance,
> as a demonstration of God's righteousness
>> at the present time,
>> so that God might be right and might make right the one who is part of this Jesus-faith.

God's action in the death of Jesus Christ inaugurates the eschatological event of making right what has gone disastrously wrong. Paul offers two coordinated claims about this righteousness. First, God does it because of the incapacity resulting from previous sins. By retrieving the widespread use of *paresis* as "incapacity" (see translation note f on v. 25), the translation coheres with what Paul has said in 1:18–32 about gentiles and worked out in 2:1–3:20 about all humans: the refusal of humanity to acknowledge God prompted God to surrender humanity to the powers of Sin and Death. That he would now speak of the result of that handing over as incapacity is not far-fetched, especially since he will present that incapacity in an even starker sense in 5:12–21 and in 7:14–25. The plural "sins" may result from the influence of earlier tradition, but the power of Sin is that it is able to bring about sins and transgressions (as in 5:16).

"Through God's forbearance" is the most difficult part of this statement to understand. Paul uses the term *anochē* ("forbearance") only one other time, at 2:4, where it refers not to God's action to defeat Sin and Death or to forgiveness but instead to God's restraint, which is intended to provide an opportunity for repentance—though a repentance that apparently never comes. In some instances, *anochē* can refer to a temporary pause or letup in a situation of conflict (as in 1 Macc 12:25; Josephus, *J.W.* 1.173; Philo, *Embassy* 100; see S. Williams 1975, 27), and that connotation may be at work here. After God handed humanity

---

74. Rom 10:9 refers to the location of trust or belief as "in your heart," and Gal 3:26 to faith or trust "in Christ Jesus."

over to Sin and Death (Rom 1:24, 26, 28), withdrawing from conflict for a time, incapacity comes over humanity as a result of Sin's workings.

The second *endeixis* clause ("as a demonstration") decisively relocates the emphasis to the present time, literally "the now time" (*en tō nyn kairō*), recalling the urgent *nyni de* that marks the beginning of this passage (v. 21; and see 8:18; 11:5; 2 Cor 8:14). Now no longer forbearing with Sin's control, God has acted both to show God's own "rightness" and to make right the one who belongs to Jesus-faith.[75] Notably, Paul does not at this point spell out the consequences of this right-making for humans. When he does so later, the forensic sense of being made right with God ushers in terms that go well beyond the sphere of judgment into language of peace, reconciliation, and new life (as in 5:1–11; 6:1–5; 8:9–11).

The shifting imagery in this passage—from righteousness to liberation from slavery, then to the holy of holies, and again back to righteousness—tempts us to lose track of Paul's overarching claim that in Jesus's death God has both revealed himself and secured the liberation of humankind from its enslavement to Sin and Death. Just as interpreters labor to catch the precise nuance of one image in the text, that image recedes when another arrives immediately in its wake. It is helpful to understand the passage not as Paul's ultimate statement on the atonement, but as a development of the overture of 1:16–17, each element of which will be restated in the chapters that follow. Release from the enslaving captivity of Sin and Death becomes a dominant concern in chs. 5–7. Chapter 8 returns to the revelation of God's own glory. The public demonstration of God's righteousness is reflected in chs. 9–11 as well as in chs. 12–16.

The sheer difficulty posed by the content of this passage should not prevent taking notice of some features that are not present. Notably there is no invitation to obedience, no recollection of repentance, no restatement of the demands of the covenant. The utter focus on God's action in Jesus Christ may prompt concerns about what humanity is to do in response to or even as part of God's righteousness. In addition, it is once again unclear what has become of the profit that attached to being a Jew (3:1–2). These are the issues to which Paul turns briefly in 3:27–31.

Excursus: The Faith of Christ

The translation and commentary above render *dia pisteōs Christou* in Rom 3:22 as "through Jesus Christ-faith" and *ek pisteōs Iēsou* in v. 26 as "part of this Jesus-faith."

---

75. The construction consists of an article referring to a person followed by the preposition *ek*. The closest parallels are the partitive genitives of Rom 16:10, 11, where Paul refers to the people who are *ek tōn Narkissou*; see also Rom 4:16; Acts 6:9; 11:12; Gal 2:12; 3:7, 9; Phil 4:22. The translation "who is part of" is my attempt to reflect that same relationship here.

These translations reflect my position on the infamous *pistis Christou* debate, which is routinely characterized as a decision between the subjective and objective genitives.[76] To illustrate from English usage, the phrase "the persecution of Paul" can refer either to persecution Paul experienced as its object (the objective genitive) or persecution he carried out as its subject (the subjective genitive). Later in Romans Paul writes of the *agape tou theou* being "poured out into our hearts," which could refer either to God's own love for "us," or "our" love for God (5:5; similarly, "God's zeal" versus "zeal for God" in 10:2). Rendered as an objective genitive, the phrase *pistis Christou* refers to faith in which Christ is the object: "faith in Christ." Rendered as a subjective genitive, the phrase instead refers to faith of which Christ is the subject: "the faith/faithfulness of Christ."

As recently as 1975 Cranfield could assume the objective genitive and give only a terse footnote to a single scholar contending for the subjective genitive (203).[77] The scholarly literature on this question has exploded since Cranfield wrote, and the argumentative lines have hardened accordingly.[78] Treatments of the phrase have exploited considerations of several sorts. Grammatical, syntactical, and lexical arguments can be made for either position, but these arguments will not settle the dispute, and most scholars concede that point. Some have attempted to enlist patristic discussions into the debate, because early interpreters of Paul stood much closer to his audience and their understanding of Greek than does the recent scholarly community. Those attempts have also proven of limited usefulness, especially as some examples are themselves ambiguous (Harrisville 1994; Wallis 1995, 175–221; M. Elliott 2009).

It is past time to acknowledge that the entire debate is riddled with problems. Both sides verge on reifying subjective and objective uses of the genitive, almost as if (to be slightly mischievous) Paul were reading the standard Greek grammars rather than the other way around. And both arguments minimize the versatility of Greek (de Roo 2007, 238). More to the point, both these options, at least as they are normally presented, have serious flaws.

Reading *pistis Christou* as an objective genitive ("faith in Christ") presupposes a human agent who is able to make a decision, positive or negative, about Jesus Christ. This assumption comes through when commentators speak about faith as the "means" or "mode" or "vehicle" through which humans appropriate the benefits of the gospel (e.g., Dunn 1:166; Fitzmyer 346; Byrne 127). Yet Paul has argued in the preceding chapters that God acted in Jesus Christ to reclaim a humanity handed over to *incapacity* (see especially 1:21, 28).[79] That incapacity returns in 5:12–6:23 as Paul traces the universal

---

76. This excursus concerns only Rom 3:22, 26, although many of the same issues would arise in the related texts (Gal 2:16, 20; 3:9, 22).

77. The brevity of Cranfield's remarks is even more impressive in view of the fact that his commentary gives substantial attention to the history of interpretation. Yet there was considerable discussion about the phrase in nineteenth-century scholarship, on which see Schliesser 2015.

78. Particularly influential have been the contributions of Hays (1997, 2002) and Dunn (1997), although the literature on this question is vast. See the instructive survey by Hunn 2009.

79. Those concerned with the outworking of Paul's letters in practice will want to consider the problems an objective genitive ("faith in Christ") raises in the case of individuals who have limited or compromised intellectual ability. Those who emphasize human faith as a prerequisite or means

rule of Sin and Death and the resultant enslavement of human beings. Understanding *pistis Christou* as a human decision apart from divine action seriously distorts Paul's argument.[80]

The argument for the subjective genitive also has serious weaknesses.[81] Apart from the passages in which the disputed phrase *pistis Christou* or similar expressions (e.g., *pistis Iēsou* in 3:26) appears, neither the noun *pistis*, the adjective *pistos*, nor the verb *pisteuō* is attributed to Christ by Paul. Appeals to Christ's obedience as the equivalent of Christ's faithfulness also do not persuade, since Rom 5:19 refers to Christ's obedience, but Paul does not use that language elsewhere of Christ. Further, 5:19, by way of emphasizing the contrast between Christ and Adam, plays on the words *parakoē* ("disobedience") and *hypakoē* ("obedience"), which may explain the use of "obedience" for Christ in that context. Paul's only other explicit reference to Christ's obedience comes in Phil 2:8.

In addition, especially in Rom 3, the emphasis falls on what God does by means of Christ Jesus rather than on Christ's own actions. This point is reinforced in later references to Jesus being "handed over" (4:25; 8:32) and dying "on our behalf" as a result of God's love (5:8). Paul pairs this language not with terminology of faithfulness or obedience, but with that of Christ's exaltation to the right hand as mediator (8:34) and his lordship over both death and life (14:9). As the history of interpretation shows, a significant risk of the subjective genitive reading is overstating Jesus's human obedience and understating his exaltation.[82]

The translation "Jesus Christ-faith," while ungainly, attempts to move beyond this problematic stalemate in order to capture several features of the phrase in its context in Rom 3. First, "Jesus Christ-faith" (or "Jesus-faith" in v. 26) has the virtue of wedding *pistis* to the context, in which Paul addresses the "now time" of Jesus Christ. This is not a general treatise about the virtue of faith versus the peril of human activity. The contrast for Paul is between what came before (i.e., the captivity of the whole of humanity to Sin) and what has happened, namely, the apocalypse of God's righteousness in the event of Jesus Christ. As a result, "Jesus Christ-faith" both stems from God's action in Jesus Christ and returns to God in the form of human trust in that action in Jesus Christ. It is both generated by God's action in Jesus Christ and oriented toward Jesus Christ. Human

---

of entry have great difficulty making space for those whose cognitive function may be impaired in some way. That is not to say that Paul himself considered such issues, but they are very much part of Christian reflection on these texts, or they need to be.

80. Meyer 2004b, 197: "Faith cannot mean some prerequisite condition to be fulfilled by human beings before God can act." In an important contribution, Linebaugh shows that Luther's argument for the objective genitive by no means isolates the human act of faith: "The *sola fide* is the confession of the *solus Christus*" (2013a, 544).

81. This conclusion represents a change from my earlier advocacy of the subjective genitive reading (Gaventa 2007b, 109–10, 194).

82. Seifrid notes the dangers here (2009, 145–46), and they are illustrated well in Schliesser's review of the relevant literature; e.g., H. E. G. Paulus treats *pistis Christou* as Christ's "sincerity of conviction" (1831, 164–65; discussed in Schliesser 2007, 262–63; 2015, 66). More recently, Stowers speaks of Jesus's heroic faithfulness (1989, 674).

pistis originates by virtue of God's intervention, as is quite clear when Paul speaks of having been "overtaken" by Christ in Phil 3:12 and of being called (Rom 1:1; Gal 1:15; Phil 3:14) along with other believers who are called into faith (Rom 1:6; 8:30; 1 Cor 1:2, 9; Gal 1:6; 1 Thess 2:12; 5:24).[83] Surrendering to the challenge to provide a grammatical label, I would invoke the genitive of origin (BDF §162; Smyth 1956, §1298).

3:27–31 One God, One Righteousness

The relentless "all" whom Paul has identified as being "under Sin" (3:9; see also 3:19, 23) and redeemed by the death of Jesus prompts once more the question whether Jews have any advantage (3:1–2). Reverting to language of boasting (2:17–24), Paul again draws on diatribal practice in an imagined conversation. In this case, the dialogue ties righteousness to the Shema even as it also separates righteousness (again) from law observance. Paul affirms both that righteousness does not come through law observance and that he is nevertheless upholding the law, a tension he will only address explicitly in ch. 7.

3:27 So, what has become of boasting? It has been excluded altogether. By what law? Is this because of the law of works? No, it is because of the law of faith, 28 since we are convinced that a person is rectified through faith apart from law observance. 29 Otherwise, is God the God of Jews alone? Is God not also God of the gentiles? Yes, of course, God is also God of the gentiles, 30 since "God is one," who rectifies circumcision on the basis of faith and also uncircumcision through the same[a] faith. 31 Does this mean we are doing away with the law through faith? Not at all! We are actually upholding the law.

a. God is said to act *ek pisteōs* ("on the basis of faith") in the case of Jews and *dia tēs pisteōs* ("through faith") in the case of gentiles. The difference between the two prepositions is minimal (at least in this context), although see the comment below. The addition of *tēs* ("the") in the second phrase is anaphoric (Howard 1970, 233).

[3:27] The opening question ("What has become of boasting?") lends itself to various arguments about the character of boasting in the Roman context in general and by Jews in particular. Yet boasting is put aside as soon as it is mentioned (although see 4:2), because the main subject is not boasting but the claim that the singular God rectifies all humanity in the same way, through the faith generated by and oriented toward Jesus Christ.

---

83. Succinctly put by Seifrid (2009, 146): "Our faith is the work of another." As articulated by Morna Hooker, "Faith derives, *not* from the believer, but from the fact that he or she is already in Christ and identified with him" (1989, 341).

Already Paul has referred to boasting once in this letter: "If you call yourself a Jew and you rely on the law and boast in God . . ." (2:17). As he expanded on that statement, it became clear that some Jews (or those gentiles who identify themselves as Jews) may claim a status that they undermine in their behavior. Although calling themselves by the name "Jew" and presenting themselves as law observant and reliant on God, their actions (theft, adultery, violation of shrines, dishonoring God through other transgressions) unmask their boasting as invalid. The discussion in ch. 2 is not narrowly restricted to boundary issues or to national pride but extends into several areas of law observance.

More to the point, the discussion in ch. 2 focused on the division between Jew and gentile (the division between insider and outsider, in the world as viewed from Paul's birth and education), but the discussion was not confined to claims some Jews might make. That point will come into piercing clarity later in the letter, when Paul speaks directly to gentile believers with the imperative, "Do not boast over the branches" of the tree into which you have been grafted (11:18). To the extent that Paul, either in 2:17 or in 3:27, rejects boasting about one's own standing, he returns to the question forcefully later. Any gentile, ancient or modern, who hears 2:17 or 3:27 as an indictment of Jews or Judaism should find herself squirming when 11:18 comes around, which is explicitly addressed to gentiles: "Do not boast over the branches."

Removed from the context, "boasting" could be connected with any and every sort of pride in human achievement. In Rom 5, however, Paul freely encourages boasting. In the peace that follows rectification, Paul encourages boasting "in our hope for the coming of God's glory," that is, in the firm expectation of God's ultimate triumphant glory (see on 5:2). And "we" even boast in the midst of "afflictions," presumably signs of the impending triumph of God (5:3). As elsewhere in the letters, boasting (as well as shame, see on 1:16) is an eschatological event:

> Who is our hope and joy and crown of boasting—is it not you—before our Lord Jesus at his coming? (1 Thess 2:19)

> We are your cause for boasting in the day of our Lord Jesus just as you are ours. (2 Cor 1:14)

However much conflicts over honor were a hallmark of the ancient Mediterranean world in general and the Roman Empire in particular, for Paul the language of honor and shame includes not merely contests among human beings but confidence in God's eschatological triumph.

The statement that boasting has been excluded prompts the follow-up question and answer: "By what law? Is this because of the law of works?" "Law of works" is an unusual expression, and it may be that Paul is simply playing on the more typical "works of the law" (as in 3:20 and in the singular in 2:15;

Keck 115). Elsewhere, however, when Paul uses *nomos* with a noun in the genitive case, he refers to the law as it is controlled by or understood through the genitive noun, as in "the law of Christ" (Gal 6:2), "the law of Moses" (1 Cor 9:9), "the law of God" (Rom 7:22; 8:7) (see Martyn 2003). The same pattern obtains here: Paul is not discussing a general principle or norm but the Mosaic law as it is governed by a notion of observance versus the law as governed by faith.

"Law of faith" is also an unusual expression, found neither in Paul nor elsewhere in the NT or LXX. The introduction of "faith" recalls vv. 21–26 and the contrast drawn there between human observance and God's own faithful, faith-generating intervention. Throughout this passage, then, *pistis* is not simply a human decision or affect, but God's action in Jesus Christ that gives birth to human faith, calling it into being (see 1:1, 7). This is not a general contrast between "doing" and "believing," since "law of faith" and "law of works" are both shorthand expressions, the first connected to God's action in Jesus Christ, the second to the Mosaic law. In other words, these are better thought of as eras—before the "now time" and in the "now time" of Christ. This even further removes the passage from being a critique of Jews or Judaism as such; it is not that Jews observed the law by doing rather than by believing, but that now (3:21) the world has changed. This phrase will be clarified in 8:1–4 with its identification of the liberating power of the law in the hands of the Christ's life-giving Spirit.

To be sure, Paul has already argued that the law closes every mouth and brings judgment on all people, presumably because no one observes the law (3:10–20), but here he establishes the same point differently. He adds that rectification cannot come about through the law because it comes by faith—that is, by the Christ event. This amounts to an intensification of the argument in light of what he has just written in 3:21–26.

[28] The pithy phrases of v. 27 are clarified here with a concise restatement of 3:21–22a. What has just been said negatively regarding boasting is now restated positively about God's rectification. A comparison of key elements in the two sentences is revealing:

v. 27	Boasting	is excluded	not by the law of works	but by the law of faith
v. 28	A person	is rectified	by faith	apart from works of law

The two events (the exclusion of boasting and the event of rectification) come about on the same terms. The agent of the first act, boasting, is presumably the human being, and the agent of the second, consistent with 3:21–26, is God's own intervention. The parallel to Gal 2:16 is especially close: no one is rectified by law observance but by Jesus Christ-faith (and see Gal 3:24).

[29] Between v. 28 and v. 29 stands an unstated premise: if law observance is the means by which God rectifies people, then only Jews and those gentiles who join them in law observance can be rectified. That premise then produces the question in v. 29, in which Paul presses the logic of his imagined interlocutor to its extreme conclusion. If only Jews and those gentiles who identify with them can be rectified, then God is actually God only of Jews. Of course, no one would claim such a thing. Although diverse Jewish groups understandably had different attitudes toward gentiles, and some expressed quite negative attitudes, the notion that God is only God over Jews would have been unthinkable. To be sure, Jewish texts of the period vary in their assessments of the standing of gentiles before God (Donaldson 2007, 469–513), but that very question itself presupposes that God is indeed the God of gentiles. God is understood to be the God of all. By raising this question, Paul does not so much attack a supposedly particularistic, exclusivist form of Judaism as he offers the equivalent of the debater's "nuclear holocaust" strategy: anyone who disagrees with his point about God's rectification is guilty of denying the universal extent of God's own sovereignty.

As has been the case earlier in the letter, Paul refers to "Jews" rather than to "Israel." Given the introduction of a crucial phrase from the Shema in v. 30 ("God is one"), Paul might have written, "Is God the God of Israel alone?" Yet the word "Israel" comes into Romans only in ch. 9 in connection with Paul's peculiar rendition of the history of God's creation of Israel. Neither here, there, nor anywhere else does Paul identify God as "the God of Israel," however (Gaventa 2022e). The closest Paul comes to such an affirmation is this question whether God is God of the Jews *alone*, a proposition he sharply rejects, because God is the God of all, the One who raised Jesus Christ from the dead (see 4:24).

[30] God is God of Jew and gentile alike precisely because "God is one." Paul cites a crucial phrase of the Shema (Deut 6:4), but he then draws a conclusion from it with which at least some of his contemporaries would have disagreed: God treats Jew and gentile in the same way (see, e.g., 4 Ezra 2.1–14; 3.28–36; Wis 11:9–10; 12:20–22; 15:1–2; 16:1–4). Invoking the claim that "God is one," Paul transfers that "oneness," that singularity, to the singularity of God's dealings with Jew and gentile. At first glance, this seems an innocuous move, except that in Deuteronomy the Shema concerns Israel and makes no reference to other nations: "Hear, O Israel, the LORD our God, the LORD is one" (Deut 6:4; see also 10:12–22; Num 15:41). Perhaps more surprising still, Paul separates the Shema from law observance, despite the fact that, in the context of Deuteronomy, the Shema introduces the law and its binding nature (Deut 6:5–9). Similarly, when the Shema appears elsewhere in the NT, it serves to introduce the law's requirements (Mark 12:28–34) or at least the expectation of works (Jas 2:19). Stunningly, Paul both connects the Shema to gentiles and disconnects it from the law.

Paul employs two slightly different expressions for God's treatment of Jews and gentiles: God will rectify "circumcision *on the basis of faith* and also uncircumcision *through the same faith*." "On the basis of faith" reintroduces the phrase at the end of 3:26, *ek pisteōs*. What is said in 3:26 without reference to ethnicity is said here of Jews in particular: God will rectify based on faith, that is, the confidence in Jesus Christ generated by God. When Paul turns to the case of "uncircumcision" (literally, the foreskin), he uses a slightly different phrase, but one that ties the two together: literally, "through the faith," referring back to the faith already introduced. The definite article resumes the initial use of *pistis.* That is, God acts for gentiles through the same faith as God acts for Jews. These are not different activities or processes; if anything, the difference of expression actually emphasizes the unity of the two in Christ. In 15:8–9, as Paul reaches the climactic moment in his argument, he will make a similar move, interpreting Christ's own service as involving both Jew and gentile. There too the statements differ—Christ serves Jews (circumcision) on behalf of God's truth and gentiles (uncircumcision) on behalf of God's glory—but both are united in the same act of Jesus Christ.

God rectifies "the circumcision" and "uncircumcision" in the same way, by faith-granting faithfulness. By reintroducing the terms used earlier, Paul shows that discussion of "righteousness" is not simply a discussion of God's attributes or of God's action confined to a "spiritual" realm; it is a claim about God's action in the midst of the daily world of conflicts and strife, of name-calling and stereotype (Marcus 1989).

[31] Here, paralleling the question of 3:1 regarding the advantage of being a Jew, the question that surfaces is what these statements imply concerning the Mosaic law: Are we doing away with the law? The verb *katargoun* can be rendered rather neutrally as "abolish" or "set aside" (BDAG s.v.), as in releasing something or someone (see Rom 7:2, 6; 1 Cor 13:11).[84] Yet elsewhere in Paul's letters it carries a strong sense of defeating another power, as when he writes in Rom 6:6 that "the body that was governed by Sin would be done away with," or when 1 Cor 15:24 anticipates God's victory, after Christ "has destroyed every ruler and every authority and power" (see also 1 Cor 1:28; 6:13; 15:26).[85] Given the presence of conflict language in Rom 3:21–26 (in *apolytrōsis, anochē*), and what follows in chs. 5–8, we may have here a notion of actually defeating the law through faith. The objection Paul anticipates is that "faith" (i.e., God's own faithful act) has destroyed the law, having treated it as a hostile power. His answer is a sharp negation: the law is not destroyed; on the contrary, it is validated. Exactly how Paul is validating the law remains to be seen, however.

Paul's treatment of the objection bears a striking similarity to the answer at 3:1–2, where he insists that there are prerogatives to being a Jew but then says little by way of explaining what those prerogatives might be. Here also,

84. *Katargoun* appears in the LXX only in Ezra (4:21, 23; 5:5; 6:8) and seldom in the NT outside the letters of Paul (Luke 13:7; Eph 2:15; 2 Thess 2:8; 2 Tim 1:10; Heb 2:14).

85. Jewett (302) cites several passages from T. Sol. as evidence of the meaning "neutralize." Interestingly, two instances of the verb are in conflict settings: T. Sol. 6.5–6, where Deception and Strife are evil angels who are neutralized.

Paul insists that "we" are not destroying the law, but he will first insist that the promise did *not* come to Abraham through the law (4:13) and then that "the law brings about wrath" (4:15). An explication of how Paul "establishes" the law awaits ch. 7.

4:1–12 Abraham as Prototype

The appearance of Abraham's name at 4:1 seems abrupt, since prior to this point the only individuals referred to by name are Jesus and David (in 1:3). And now, without explanation or introduction, Abraham arrives on the scene. Yet this discussion extends the argument Paul has been developing in several important ways. In Rom 1–3, Paul invokes conventional assumptions about the line separating gentiles and Jews while simultaneously undermining that same line. He has written about the "all," about "the human." That discussion culminates with the declaration in 3:29–30 that God is God of "all" and deals with "all" in the same way.

Paul now extends and reinforces that discussion in a peculiar manner—by turning to Abraham, the quintessential "forefather" of Israel. First, Paul locates the wedge he has been driving between law observance, on the one hand, and faith, on the other, all the way back in the life of Abraham. Given the place occupied by Abraham in many Jewish writings of Paul's era, texts that celebrate Abraham for his obedience, this move is quite a bold one. Second, Paul rewrites the title of Abraham: "our forefather" now becomes the "father" of gentiles as well as Jews. Viewed from the vantage point of the Christ event, Abraham thus becomes not the founder of Israel or the archetypical Christian, but a prototype of God's dealings with all of humankind. The narrative in which Abraham figures is that of God and the world, not that of Jew and gentile.

The chapter opens as a comment on Abraham's righteousness by faith, identifying him with the "ungodly" (vv. 2–8). It then shifts to consider the context in which Abraham received God's blessing of righteousness, namely, his own *uncircumcision* (vv. 9–12).

4:1 So, what shall we say that Abraham our forefather learned, thinking in a merely human way?[a] 2 For if Abraham was rectified on the basis of his works, he then has a basis for boasting (thinking in that same merely human way[b]). But so far as God is concerned, that is not the way it happened.[c] 3 For what does Scripture say?

"Abraham believed God and that was regarded as righteousness."

4 Now in the case of a worker (in everyday life[d]), a wage is not regarded as a gift but as an obligation. 5 But in the case of someone who is not a

worker, someone who believes the One who rectifies the ungodly, that person's faith is regarded as righteousness. 6 It is just the same as when David speaks about the blessing of the one to whom God regards righteousness apart from works:

7 "Blessed are those whose lawlessnesses have been taken away and whose sins have been covered over.

8 Blessed is the man whose sin the Lord will regard not at all."

9 So, is this blessing for the circumcision or for the uncircumcision? For we say, in the case of Abraham, faith was regarded as righteousness. 10 So how exactly did that happen? Was it while he was circumcised or while he was uncircumcised? It was not while he was circumcised but while he was uncircumcised. 11 And then he received a sign—circumcision[e]—a seal of righteousness that came about through faith while he still was uncircumcised, so that he might be father of all who believe who are uncircumcised, in order that righteousness might be regarded in their case, 12 and also so that he might be the father of the circumcised, not only for those who are circumcised but also for those who follow in the footsteps of the uncircumcised faith of our father Abraham.

a. This introductory question is difficult to translate, as it follows a question encountered frequently in Romans ("What shall we say then?")[86] with an infinitive that either supplements the "we say" or has "Abraham our forefather" as its subject. Difficulties attend either decision; here I have taken a traditional line of translation, connecting the "finding" or "learning" with Abraham. Yet what is crucial for my translation is not the subject doing the finding but the phrase *kata sarka*. This phrase can be used in a neutral sense to refer to human flesh (e.g., 1:3; 9:3, 5), as is reflected in the adjectival rendering of the NRSVue and NIV (ancestor [or forefather] "according to the flesh"). "Forefather" already conveys Abraham's paternity, however, making this neutral sense redundant. *Kata sarka* can also have the negative sense of a merely human way of perceiving and evaluating (e.g., 8:4, 5, 12, 13; 2 Cor 5:16). In addition, just a few lines above Paul writes that "no flesh" (*sarx*) is rectified before God. Taken adverbially as a modification of Abraham's learning, then, the phrase contrasts with the *pros theon* (lit., "before God") at the end of v. 2 (Schliesser 2007, 327).

b. The parenthetical phrase is added to make explicit the contrary-to-fact character of the protasis, since Abraham was not rectified by his actions.

c. The Greek is elliptical, concluding with the words, literally rendered, "but not with/before/in the presence of God." Customarily, this is taken to refer to boasting in God's presence (as in NRSVue, NIV). By placing this phrase at the outset, the translation

86. As in 7:7; 8:31; 9:14, 30; and see also 3:5, where there is no *oun* ("therefore").

brings out the contrast between *kata sarka* at the end of v. 1 and *pros theon* at the end of v. 2 (see note a on v. 1).

d. The phrase "in everyday life" is added to indicate the shift to this analogy from ordinary labor.

e. Lit., "sign of circumcision," here understood as a genitive of apposition (see Wallace 1996, 95–100) or epexegetical genitive (Moulton 1908, 3:214). See also 4:11; 6:4.

[4:1] Introducing Abraham might well signal to Paul's audience that what follows will concern the priority of Israel, but the arc of Paul's thought extends well beyond Israel's borders. Despite the claim of 3:30 that God deals with all people in the same way, Paul has in 3:2 asserted the multiple advantages of being a Jew, and invoking Abraham as the forefather further underscores that possibility. *Propatōr* is a hapax legomenon in the NT, and elsewhere it can refer not simply to an ancestor but to the founder of a people (BDAG s.v.). Josephus uses it in that way of Abraham, although only once (*J.W.* 5.380). To the extent that *propatōr* suggests a founding figure (a George Washington or Alexander Hamilton, for example), then Paul is introducing a notion about Abraham that he will quickly undermine. Perhaps he is even inviting misunderstanding, since the account that follows makes of Abraham little that resembles a human founder.

[2] Thinking of Abraham's experience with God in a merely human way, "we" would conclude that Abraham has a basis for boasting, that he was rectified because of his actions. Here Paul reflects widespread ancient understandings of Abraham. Genesis itself narrates Abraham's obedient migration from Haran (12:4), his obedient circumcision of the males in his household (17:23–27), and his obedient preparation for the sacrifice of Isaac in response to the divine command (22:1–19). Later interpreters draw attention to Abraham's obedience, as when Sirach praises Abraham for keeping the law and being faithful when tested (44:20–21), and when Jubilees specifies that Abraham kept the feast of Shebuoth (6.19) and urged obedience to all of God's commands (Jub. 20–22). Similarly, early Christian writers praise Abraham for his actions obeying God's commands (Jas 2:21–23; Heb 11:8–12; Acts 7:1–8).

With the terse phrase "but not with God," which I have translated as "so far as God is concerned," Paul introduces a version of Abraham that sets it at an angle from this tradition. It may well have seemed odd to those more attuned to the notion of Abraham's obedience to God. To be sure, Paul has already said in 3:20–21 and in 3:28 that people are not rectified by law observance (literally, "works of the law"), but to restate that point in the case of the forefather Abraham is to provoke, precisely because Abraham was famous for his obedience to God's commands, for his "works."

[3] In support of his claim that Abraham had no boast before God on the basis of his works, Paul cites Gen 15:6 ("Abraham believed God and that was regarded as righteousness") and then returns to it repeatedly in this chapter.

The verse fits Paul's argument well, given that it is the single verse in the LXX in which the three key terms (belief, regard, righteousness) all appear. But of course Paul has already made use of this verse in Galatians, so there is no need to imagine that he went in search of it for his letter to Rome; in addition, the passage was widely influential in contemporaneous Judaism (Schliesser 2007, 152–220). Paul makes this the signal scriptural witness to Abraham, however, leaving behind many other elements in the Abraham story, such as Abraham's obedient move from Haran, his obedient act of circumcising the males of his household, and his obedient preparation to sacrifice Isaac.

Taken on its own, the statement that "Abraham believed God" can appear somewhat abstract, as if the question is simply whether or not Abraham is capable of trust, whether he does or does not perform a particular cognitive act. Already in the letter human faith, or trust, has been identified as generated by God in the gospel of Jesus Christ (1:16; 3:22, 26) and with a trusting response (or the lack thereof) to the "oracles" given by God (3:2–3). Here as well there is a divine act that generates Abraham's belief, although Paul will only later indicate that it is the promise that brings forth Abraham's belief (4:17–18).

[4] Now Paul might commence retelling the story of Abraham, but he does not yet do so. Instead, he turns to the world of everyday labor, playing on slightly different meanings of "work" and how it is "counted" or "regarded." "The worker" (or one who works) now refers not to obedience to God or the law but simply to the ordinary experience of working for a wage (*misthos*). It is obvious that a worker receives a wage because it is due to that person; it is not a gift (*charis*). Yet even this seemingly obvious example carries within it a bit of a sting, since in Gen 15:1 (LXX) God announces that he will give Abraham a *misthos.* The language of "gift" or "grace" reappears in 4:16 regarding the promise freely given to Abraham (see also 3:24), and the term will return in ch. 5 as a metonym for the event of the gospel, the powerful saving apocalypse itself.

[5] With v. 5 the context changes again, shifting from the arena of everyday labor to the much larger context of God's activity. God does not deal in what is "owed" to a worker, since Paul has already shown in stark terms that humanity is under the power of Sin and cannot act appropriately toward God. The translation "believes" shows the verbal connection between this statement and others using the *pistis* word group, but the translation is problematic if it is understood as simply an act of cognition, as in assenting today (or not) to the proposition that the evidence supports climate change. Here the connotation is more that of trust, reliance, acknowledgment. That understanding is supported by the untranslated *epi* ("on" or "on the basis of"); what is expressed is reliance on "the One who rectifies the ungodly."

As a circumlocution for God, "the One who rectifies the ungodly" is particularly important in this context. Already in 1:18, the gentiles have been identified as ungodly, but it is not only they who live outside a proper relationship to God, as the catena in 3:10–18 makes clear. There is no one who seeks after God, Paul insists (3:11). And God is the one who is trusted, the one who rectifies the ungodly (a category that apparently includes all humanity). The point made about Abraham in 4:2 is now generalized. Paul's comments about God's dealings with Abraham are simultaneously about God's dealings with "all," as becomes explicit in vv. 23–25.

[6–8] For the first time in the letter a citation from Scripture is attributed to the author or, as in this case, the speaker, something Paul will do often in chs. 9–11 (e.g., 9:25, 27, 29; 10:19, 21; 11:9; and see 15:12). The reference to David in 4:6–8 may reflect the fact that the psalm itself concerns David's experience of repentance and forgiveness, but Paul also invokes Abraham's own sinfulness. When v. 9 connects "blessing" with Abraham, it then also connects Abraham with the blessing of v. 8 and by implication with sinfulness and forgiveness. Indeed, the general reference to the human (*anthrōpos*) that introduces the quotation reaches beyond both David and Abraham to the blessing of God on humankind in general.

This point may help explain why Paul quotes three lines from Ps 32:1–2 (31:1–2a LXX) rather than simply the third line. Verse 8 (Ps 31:2a) would seem to be all that is needed, since it picks up the language of "counting" or "regarding" (*logizomai*) as well as that of sin. But the first two lines (v. 7; Ps 31:1) reinforce the situation, not only of David but also of Abraham and by implication all people. Given Paul's customary preference for the singular "sin" rather than the plural "sins" and the virtual absence of the language of divine forgiveness from his letters, the inclusion of v. 7 is otherwise unusual.

These verses further reinforce the notion that Abraham is not only godless but also sinful.[87] And he is blessed by God based on what *God* does, with no reference to repentance. Psalm 32 continues with assertions of guilt (31:3–4 LXX) followed by declarations that "I" confessed sin and received forgiveness (vv. 5–7), but that section of the psalm falls by the wayside in Paul's quotation of the psalm. As we will see in Rom 5 (and have observed already in 3:21–26), the problem Paul perceives is too large for what is usually understood by repentance and forgiveness. The human problem requires rescue.

[9–12] Paul now takes up the third and most extensively developed feature of the circumstances in which Abraham received righteousness (i.e., he didn't work, he was godless and sinful)—namely, the fact that he was *uncircumcised*.[88] Not only was his righteousness based on his belief in the God who

---

87. As Orrey McFarland observes, "Abraham does not emerge from ungodliness in any way but is justified precisely as one who *is* ungodly" (2012, 120; ital. orig.).

88. See above on 2:25–29. Circumcision was the primary identifier of Jewish identity (both male and female in that women would typically marry only circumcised men; Barclay 1996b, 411–12). Paul in Romans neither criticizes the practice nor warns away from it (by contrast with Galatians), which suggests that it was not a matter of controversy at Rome or between Paul and Roman congregations.

rectifies the ungodly rather than on any behavior of his own, but Abraham was rectified *before* he was circumcised. The way Paul embroiders this point suggests its importance for him. First, in v. 9a he introduces the question of fact: Was the blessing on the circumcised or on the uncircumcised? In vv. 9b–10b he explicitly introduces Abraham again: Was Abraham's faith considered righteousness while he was circumcised or not? The answer at the conclusion of v. 10 plays on the ordering of events in Genesis: God's rectifying of Abraham in Gen 15:6 precedes the act of circumcision in 17:9–14, 23–27; thus it is an uncircumcised Abraham who is blessed by God.

Paul goes on to say that Abraham received a *sēmeion*, or "sign," which was circumcision, but he dissociates circumcision from obedience and from covenant; indeed, here circumcision does not even set the circumcised apart from the uncircumcised. First, v. 11 specifies that Abraham "received a sign, namely, circumcision." Gone is Genesis 17's account of God's command followed by Abraham's obedient action of circumcising all the males in his household. Circumcision in Rom 4 is a sign linked to God's righteousness, yet in Gen 17:11, 13, 14 (and Acts 7:8), it is a sign of the covenant, a term never used here in Rom 4.[89]

The sign—circumcision—is further linked with God's action through the second appositional phrase, "a seal of righteousness that came about through faith," since Paul has repeatedly demonstrated that righteousness is God's own action. To specify once again that this sign or seal of circumcision came when Abraham was uncircumcised (a seal of the righteousness of faith *while uncircumcised*) seems peculiar in the extreme: How else could it have happened? Paul's insistence on the importance of Abraham's uncircumcised state generates a bit of unintended humor at this point, since one would scarcely circumcise the circumcision.

The reason for this insistence comes into view in the second half of the verse: because Abraham was uncircumcised, he is the father of all uncircumcised believers so that they can be rectified. The priority given to gentiles here is quite astonishing. Paul inverts the expected priority of Israel, a priority that characterizes the opening chapters of the letter (e.g., 1:16). Verse 12 goes on to affirm that Abraham is the father of the circumcised too, but even there Paul qualifies the "circumcised" by specifying that Abraham's paternity of circumcision is not just a paternity of those who are circumcised but of those who also walk in the footsteps of Abraham's faith while he was uncircumcised. Even as Paul includes Jews in this statement, he incorporates a kind of priority for the uncircumcised.

Abraham enters this discussion as "forefather," but he is not a founder, either of obedience or of a people. Viewed from the "now time" of the gospel,

---

89. Covenant assumptions can be present without being named as such, of course; yet it may be more accurate to identify Paul as engaging in scriptural rather than covenantal reflection (so Watson 2013).

the customary depiction of Abraham's obedience morphs into a different portrait, one in which God rectifies ungodly Abraham because of Abraham's trust. Crucially for Paul's depiction, that act takes place before Abraham's circumcision, making him "our" forefather, meaning those who share his confidence in the One who made alive both the promised child Isaac and the crucified Jesus Christ (4:24).

4:13–25 God's Powerful Promise to Abraham

Having introduced Abraham as the ungodly and uncircumcised figure who is rectified by God, in vv. 13–25 Paul turns to the divine promise that elicits Abraham's confidence in God's creative, redemptive power. Verses 13–17a introduce the divine promise as God's unilateral gift to Abraham and "all of us." Abraham's faith comes to the forefront in vv. 17b–22, where his faith is characterized as elicited by God, who has power over both life and death. The closing verses (vv. 23–25) move from Abraham's faith to the present time, leaping over both the birth of Isaac and the entire history of Israel. Here Paul simultaneously recalls the power of God limned in ch. 1 and anticipates the way that same power triumphs over Sin and Death (5:12–21).

4:13 As for the promise to Abraham or to his seed that he would be the heir of the world, that promise did not come through law but through righteousness of faith.[a] 14 For if the heirs were from the law, faith itself would be emptied out and the promise would be destroyed. 15 For the law brings about wrath, but where there is no law there is no transgression. 16 For this reason the promise was from faith, that it might be a gift, in order to confirm the promise to all the seed, not only to the seed that comes from the law but also to the seed from Abraham's faith. Abraham is the father of all of us. 17a As it is written, "I have appointed you as father of many nations."[b]

17b Faced with this statement,[c] Abraham believed God, who makes the dead live and who calls into being that which does not exist. 18 Hoping against hope, Abraham believed he would be the father of many nations, as it was said, "Thus will be your offspring." 19 And although he was not weak in faith,[d] Abraham did take note of his own body, which was already as good as dead (he was about 100 years old), and the death of Sarah's womb. 20 But in view of the promise of God he did not hesitate[e] in faithlessness. Instead, he increased in faith, giving glory to God 21 and being convinced that what had been promised God was also powerful to bring about. 22 For that reason "it [faith] was regarded for him as righteousness."

23 Now this was not written only about Abraham that "it [faith] was regarded for him" 24 but also about us, those who are to be regarded, those

who trust the One who raised Jesus our Lord from the dead, 25 who was handed over for our transgressions and was raised for our righteousness.

a. A more literal translation would draw attention to the structure of this verse, which begins with the negative statement "not through law" and closes with the positive "but through the righteousness that comes from faith," thus highlighting the emphasis on the promise. I have placed that contrast at the end, simply to make the English more comprehensible.

b. Verse 17a belongs both with what precedes and with what follows (see also Cranfield 1:226). Because it amplifies the identification of Abraham as father of "all of us," I have connected it with vv. 12–16. I have placed v. 17b with the following section to set apart these remarks about Abraham's faith, characterized as it is with a string of finite verbs (*katenoēsen, diekrithē, enedynamōthē*) and modifying participles (*asthenēsas, dous, plērophorētheis*) in vv. 19–21.

c. The Greek here is ambiguous; it reads either "in the presence of the God whom he believed" or "in the presence of which [i.e., the divine statement that precedes]." Paul uses the preposition *katenanti* elsewhere only in 2 Cor 2:17 and 12:19, and both of those instances refer to God's presence. That is a very small sample of usage, however, and *katenanti* can also be used of material objects (as in Mark 12:41; 13:3; Campbell 2009a, 741–42). The difference here is slight, since both translations connect Abraham's faith to God's action.

d. The relationship between the circumstantial participle "was not weak" (lit., not being weak) and the main verb "Abraham did take note" is ambiguous. The translation reflects the judgment that Abraham's comment on his own age and that of Sarah might be understood as weakness.

e. This verb is usually rendered "doubt" or "waver," on the assumption that the word *diakrinomai* ("to judge" or "dispute," BDAG s.v.) acquires a particular meaning in early Christian texts. Yet the evidence for a special Christian nuance is tenuous, especially as early interpreters of Romans do not reflect such an understanding of the verb (Spitaler 2007; Schliesser 2012). "Hesitate" reflects the customary usage of *diakrinomai* (as in Acts 10:20) and also does justice to the following phrase, "in faithlessness." See also on Rom 14:23.

[4:13–17a] By the end of v. 12 Paul has referred to Abraham's faith, righteousness, circumcision, and his fatherhood of both uncircumcised and circumcised, but not specifically to the promise. That term arrives with v. 13, where the first claim regarding the promise is negative: "not through the law." This frontloading of the negation of the law in v. 13, together with the repeated claims about the law in vv. 14–16, can scarcely be meaningless. It stands out all the more because of the claim of 3:31 to be establishing or upholding the law—how can Paul be establishing the law while dissociating it from the promise? Paul's comments about the law will continue to be provocative (as in 5:20; 6:14), and only with ch. 7 will he resolve the tension.

Paul identifies the promise in a way that is simultaneously both more capacious and more restricted than in the Genesis account. Here the promise is

summed up with one word: *kosmos*, or "world." Such a promise does not appear
in Genesis, although this wording might be understood as a terse reframing of
the promise that Abraham's children would outnumber the sand and the stars
(as in Sir 44:21; Jub. 19.21–22). Closer to hand, Rom 1:8 says that the faith
of the Romans is known in the whole world (*kosmos*), and presumably that
nuance is at work here. However, given the emphasis in ch. 1 on creation and
in ch. 8 on the created world, there may be something more at work here than
simply inheriting the human population, in the sense of having a large body of
offspring. The *kosmos* for Paul is God's creation (as in 1:20), and he anticipates
the eschatological redemption of creation in 8:19–22 (*ktisis*). In other words, a
cosmic and eschatological overtone is at work here.

Casting the promise to Abraham in such an all-encompassing way passes
over the Genesis promise of a land for Abraham's inheritance (Gen 12:1, 7;
13:14–15; 15:7, 18–21; 17:8; 24:7) and honor for Abraham (12:2–3). Given that
Paul's mission largely lies outside the land of Israel (although he is scarcely
indifferent to the community or communities of Jerusalem, as in Rom 15:25–
33), it is scarcely surprising that he omits reference to inheritance of the land.
The omission of reference to Abraham's honor is worth noting, however,
especially in light of ancient concerns about honor and shame. The account in
vv. 17–23 does bestow a kind of honor on Abraham, but the honor lies in God's
power to do for him what he and Sarah are powerless to bring about on their
own. Even the repeated expressions of the promise of a son and of numerous
offspring (Gen 12:3; 13:16; 15:4–5; 17:4–6; 18:10, 13) are here condensed
and reinterpreted as the inheritance of the *kosmos* (and later the fathering of
nations/gentiles, in Rom 4:17); perhaps more to the point, the promised son is
never named. Paul is more concerned with the originator and guarantor of the
promise than with its content.

Verses 14–17a largely serve to reinforce Paul's introductory comment
regarding the promise in v. 13. First, heirs are not produced by the law, as
that would vacate both faith and the promise (v. 14). This happens because
the law actually produces wrath (v. 15); divine wrath is surely in view here, as
elsewhere in Paul (e.g., Rom 1:18; 3:5; 5:9). Again, these statements are not
fully developed, as Paul waits until later in the letter to do that. Earlier in the
chapter he argues based on chronology (Abraham is rectified by faith before he
is circumcised), but now he alludes to the gospel-generated knowledge that the
law produces not just the awareness of sin (3:20) but sin itself. In ch. 7 Paul will
explain how it is that God's holy law can produce sin, but for now he allows
that provocation to linger uninterpreted.

Verse 16 turns from law and its nonrole in the promise to affirm the promise
and Abraham's faith. It opens with a terse comment (literally, "for this reason,
from faith") resuming the topic of the promise, which is "from faith" that it
might be "according to grace" or "as a gift." Already the language of gift or

grace has been used to refer to the reception of the "grace and apostleship" in 1:5 and to the gift of righteousness in 3:24, and it will become prominent in ch. 5, where we learn that God's grace triumphs over Sin (5:15, 17, 20–21). Here its juxtaposition to *pistis* at least suggests that faith itself is a gift, and possibly that the *pistis* referred to runs in two directions; that is, God's faithful treatment of Abraham generates Abraham's trust.

The remainder of v. 16 restates the claim in vv. 11–12 about righteousness for all of Abraham's children: the promise also is for "all the seed." This time, however, the inclusive character of the "all" is defined in categories of "law" and "faith," not "circumcision" and "uncircumcision." The statement is perplexing, since "not only to the seed that comes from the law" implies that indeed some of Abraham's seed are "through the law," which appears to conflict with the stark claim of v. 13. Yet v. 13 refers to the way in which the promise came to Abraham, and v. 16 offers two ways of defining Abraham's offspring: those who came about through the law and those who came through faith. Confusing as it is, Paul here anticipates his later conclusion in 11:26 that "all Israel will be saved." The citation of Gen 17:5 in v. 17a signals the inclusive character of Abraham's paternity. He is now the "father of many nations," which includes the "all of us" of v. 16b as well as the others hinted at in the phrase "through the law" just prior to that. For the first time we learn what exactly it is that Abraham believed.

[17b–22] Paul makes four affirmations about Abraham's faith (vv. 17b, 18, 19, and 20–21), leading up to the repetition of Gen 15:6 in v. 22, although even here Abraham is no spiritual athlete or hero figure. He is instead one who witnesses God's power over life and death.[90] The initial statement (v. 17b) is perhaps the most astonishing, since the audience might well expect a statement focused tightly on believing the content of the promise or Abraham's conviction that there would be a child. Instead, Paul identifies God as the one "who makes the dead live and who calls into being that which does not exist" (v. 17b); this "name" for God simultaneously reflects God's action with Abraham and Sarah and God's action in the death and resurrection of Jesus Christ. To characterize the conception of Isaac as bringing life to the dead is dramatic, even hyperbolic, although this is precisely the language Paul uses in v. 19: Abraham and Sarah were as good as dead. Putting it that way, of course, connects God's action in the case of Abraham and Sarah to the resurrection of Jesus Christ, which Paul does explicitly in v. 24. And the language of death here and in v. 19 anticipates the discussion in ch. 5 of Death's terrifying power and its defeat.

The second half of the characterization of God in v. 17b recasts this act as an act of creation: God brings into being things that do not exist (as in Isa 41:4;

---

90. "Abraham's righteousness is constituted purely by his trusting acceptance of God's promise to act on his behalf" (Watson 2016, 268).

48:13; 2 Clem. 1.8; Philo, *Spec. Laws* 4.187). Already Rom 1:20 has referred to God's creation of the world, and God's redemption of creation returns in 8:19–22. But for Paul creation is not a theoretical proposition or a scientific argument. Creation is instead witnessed in the creation of Isaac out of nothing and the creation of Israel (ch. 9) and the fact of redemption for all things in ch. 8. The creation of Isaac and God's creation of the universe are mutually interpreting. The cosmic character of Paul's thought is not disconnected from specific history but is actually witnessed in that history.

Verse 18 interprets Abraham's faith in the context of events in Genesis. "Hoping against hope," in the face of all the evidence that he would not father a child (which is to be spelled out further in v. 19), Abraham believed what had been said to him. What Abraham believes is that he will be the "father of many nations." No reference here ties Abraham's fatherhood to the line through Isaac, who never appears in Rom 4. What is important for Paul is not the immediate history of Abraham's biological line but his trust in God and his cosmically proportioned offspring, both gentile and Jew. The repetition of the earlier citation of Gen 17:5 with "many nations" and its reinforcement with the declaration of Gen 15:5 ("Thus will be your offspring") confirm this point: Abraham is the father of "many nations," not of "a son" or of "our people Israel." As far as Rom 4 is concerned, the paternity of Abraham is always of "many."

The third statement regarding Abraham's faith (v. 19) does address the specific circumstances of Abraham and Sarah, although in terms that anticipate the turn to the death and resurrection of Jesus (in v. 24b–25, as already in v. 17b). Even though Abraham was not "weak" (an issue to which Paul returns in 5:6 and again at length in ch. 14), Abraham frankly reflected on the situation from the perspective of his confidence in God's promise. Here Paul gives specificity to the earlier expression "hope against hope" by conjuring up the age of both Abraham and Sarah. Abraham's body had died already, and death is located in Sarah's womb, placed *in* the organ that nurtures life.[91] These graphic expressions enhance the statement of God's power, but they also anticipate the resurrection of Christ from the dead (v. 24) and the grasp of Death for all humankind (5:14).

The final expression of Abraham's faith, and the most elaborate, comes in vv. 20–21, this time couched in reference to the promise. Abraham did not hesitate, remaining in unbelief, but he grew in faith. That faith was evidenced when Abraham was confident that what had been promised God was able also to do and gave glory to God. The element that stands out is the reference to glorifying God. It is unusual in the immediate context, which has focused on Abraham's faith. Yet in the larger context of Romans, glorifying God is anything

---

91. Interestingly, when Chrysostom comments on *paresis* ("incapacity") in 3:25, he explains it as death, using *nekrōsis* (see the translation note on 3:25).

but unusual. Already ch. 1 has identified failure to glorify God as a leading characteristic of humanity's rebellion, and the catena in 3:10–18 reinforces that notion, since the fact that "no one seeks for God" suggests that God is not glorified. As 15:6–13 demonstrates, the giving of glory to God is among the characteristics of the newly created humanity; eventually all of Abraham's children will together glorify God.

The final statement in v. 21 is crucial: what Abraham believes is that God has the power to do what God says. Here Paul echoes his interpretation of the gospel as divine power, announced in 1:4, 16–17, and promised again in the closing lines of Rom 8 (see also 14:4 and 16:20). With ch. 5, Paul will extend his argument regarding the need for this power: just as only divine power can bring life from the dead womb of Sarah, so only divine power can rescue humanity from its captivity to Sin and Death.

Here the story of Abraham's confidence in God's power veers away from what might have been anticipated, as there is no reference to the birth of Isaac (see 9:7–9); nor is there reference to any of the other physical descendants from Abraham and Sarah. Abraham does not go home and father a child (as Elkanah is said to do; see 1 Sam 1:19). He does not receive the "power of procreation" (Heb 11:11). Sarah is not said to "conceive" a child (see Gen 21:3; 29:32; 30:23; Luke 1:24). Instead, v. 22 returns to Gen 15:6, which has been pivotal for the entire discussion: Abraham was regarded as righteous.

[23–25] Any sense that this is a "once upon a time" account evaporates with the opening of v. 23. The Genesis account does not simply pass along information about Abraham; it is about "us." The shift to first-person here is significant. Paul's use of first-person plural in the letter has been limited until now (1:5; 2:2; 3:5, 9, 19, 28, 31; 4:1, 9), but here he moves—and seamlessly—from Abraham's trust in God to "ours." "We" are defined, as Paul is in 1:1, by relationship to God, not by names or descent or achievement. And God is not said to be Abraham's God or Israel's God but "the One who raised Jesus our Lord from the dead." That is God's name (Watson 2006, 104).

Verse 25 further explicates Jesus's own identity, as the one "who was handed over for our transgressions and was raised for our righteousness." Isaiah 53 will have suggested this phrasing, as it does in Rom 8:32, where again Paul will write that Jesus was "handed over" on behalf of "all of us." The connection with the suffering-servant tradition does not exhaust the implications of v. 25, however. Already in 1:24, 26, and 28 Paul has written of the "handing over" of humanity, and in 5:12–21 he will return to that "handing over" in terms of the universal power of Sin and Death. In the crucifixion, Jesus is subjected to those same powers, and his resurrection signals the end of their reign (as in 5:12–21; 8:31–39; 1 Cor 15:24–28, 54–55).

For the Roman congregations, especially if some of them regard themselves as having been grafted into Israel's story, what Paul writes is remarkable. They are all among Abraham's children, but that means the children of God's action (as in Luke 3:8), not the children of Abraham's story.[92] Indeed, there is no story here apart from God's promise. The promise is not just about continuity for Abraham, certainly not about Abraham's honor as the father of a people. Instead, it is nothing less than the power to bring life out of death. In ch. 5 Paul will show how that power extends to the defeat of Death itself.

---

92. On just this point, Luke's Gospel offers a compelling companion text, when John the Baptist warns those who take for granted that they are Abraham's offspring (Luke 3:8; cf. also 13:16; 19:9).

Romans 5:1–8:39
Christ, Cosmos, and Consequences

The peculiar account of God's actions with Abraham in Rom 4 leaps across the centuries from Abraham and Sarah to Jesus's death and resurrection (4:24–25). Paul has interpreted Abraham as the prototype of the rectified ungodly (4:5) and simultaneously tied the miracle of new life for Abraham and Sarah to the resurrection of Jesus Christ (4:17). Later on, in chs. 9–11, Paul will have much more to say about God's dealings with offspring (or more precisely, God's repeated *creation* of offspring for Abraham and Sarah).

Before returning to the question of offspring in chs. 9–11, however, chs. 5–8 address at length the consequences of the death and resurrection of Jesus Christ.[1] Often these chapters are described as addressing "new life in Christ" (e.g., Hultgren 202) or the "consequences of faith in Christ" (e.g., Dunn 1:242; Fitzmyer 393), but such designations do not do justice to the complex subject matter of these chapters.

In an earlier dense and evocative passage, 3:21–26, Paul identified the death of Jesus Christ with righteousness, with redemption from slavery, and with the holy of holies. Now he returns to interpret the consequences of Christ's death in ch. 5 by casting the problem in cosmic terms. The powers of Sin and Death had invaded the entire human cosmos and were defeated only through Jesus Christ and his life-giving work (6:1–7:6). Not even the holy law of God remained exempt from the enslaving grasp of Sin (7:7–25). In ch. 8 Paul turns to the liberating work of the Spirit (introduced in 5:5), which means the "slaves of righteousness" have become nothing less than siblings of Jesus Christ, anticipating God's final triumph and the redemption and vindication of God's whole creation.

If Roman Christians, especially those who are gentiles, imagine that the gospel has to do only or primarily with the engrafting of gentiles into Abraham's

---

1. Some commentators would connect ch. 5 tightly with what immediately precedes in ch. 4 and begin a new section only at 6:1 (e.g., Wilckens 1:286–87; Dunn 1:242–44; Stuhlmacher 14–15, 57; Sanday and Headlam xlviii–xlix; Godet 1:314, 340–41; Kuss 1:198–99; Morris 217). Others begin a new section at 5:12 (Keck 102, 133–34; Talbert 129–31). The connection between the end of ch. 4 and the beginning of ch. 5 is admittedly a close one, but the same should be said also for the connection between chs. 5 and 6. In any case, identifying "sections" of Romans is a heuristic endeavor, and any conclusions from such an analysis need to be held lightly.

biological family (and perhaps even replacing that biological family, as in 11:17–24), this part of the letter serves to recast the gospel as something altogether larger and more encompassing.

5:1–11 Peace by the Death of Jesus Christ

Paul returns to his comments about the crucifixion of Jesus (3:21–26), but here the language of righteousness, which played a prominent role earlier, is joined by that of peacemaking and reconciliation, language that anticipates God's action in the conflict with Sin and Death that comes to expression in 5:12–21. Romans 5:1–11 serves as something of a hinge in the argument, in that it both recalls a number of elements in 1:18–4:25 and anticipates those that follow in 5:12–8:39. The opening phrase, "since we have been rectified by faith," epitomizes 1:18–4:25. "God's wrath," announced in 1:18 (and see also 2:5, 8; 3:5; 4:15), is that from which "we" have been saved (5:9), and the language of salvation appears here for the first time since 1:16. The boasting Paul rejected earlier (2:17, 23; 3:27) is now encouraged, although with an unsettling twist. God's rectification of the ungodly Abraham (4:5; and see 1:18) is replayed here as Jesus's death for the ungodly "we" (5:6–8); Abraham's trust and hope in God's promise (4:17–21) returns in "our" hope in God's glory (5:2). God's "grace" has already appeared (1:5, 7; 3:24; 4:4, 16), and it will return in Paul's depiction of the cosmic reach of the gospel in 5:12–21 (5:15, 17, 20–21; see also 6:14, 15, 17).

The passage does more than summarize, however; it also prepares for the discussion that will follow, especially in 8:18–39. "Hope for the coming of God's glory," introduced in 5:2, anticipates the discussion of hope for the glory of God's children (8:21; and see 8:20, 24). "Affliction" has been referred to in 2:9, but it returns in 8:35 and also is included among the "sufferings" discussed in 8:18. "God's love" poured into human hearts (5:5) will return in 8:39 as the divine love in Christ Jesus that will not permit God's enemies to triumph over God's beloved. Perhaps most important, the brief reference in 5:5 to the gift of the Holy Spirit anticipates extended comments about the work of the Spirit in 8:1–27. And while there is little verbal linkage (although see 8:6), the language of peace and reconciliation prepares Paul's audience for the conflict that will follow in 5:12–21 and that persists in 8:31–39 (and see 15:33; 16:20).

The thick web of connections to what precedes and what follows signals the importance of this passage, and its numerous rhetorical features reinforce that judgment. Throughout 5:1–11, Paul continues the use of first-person plural that he took up in 4:24, attempting to draw the Roman auditors to understand God's actions along with him. The repetition of the phrase "through our Lord Jesus Christ" in vv. 1 and 11 constitutes an inclusio that knits the passage together (and see the similar phrase at 5:21; 6:11, 23; 7:25; and 8:39). In addition, Paul employs another rhetorical feint in v. 3, a "stairstep" argument (climax) in

vv. 3–5, a dramatic aside in vv. 6–8, and argument from the lesser to the greater in vv. 9–10.

5:1 Therefore, since we have been rectified by faith, let us enjoy[a] the peace we have with God through our Lord Jesus Christ, 2 through whom we have entrance[b] to this grace in which we stand. And let us boast[c] in our hope for the coming of God's glory.[d] 3 Not only that, but let us boast also in afflictions, knowing that affliction produces endurance 4 and that endurance produces character and character produces hope. 5 And hope will not put us to shame,[e] because God's love has been poured out into our hearts through the Holy Spirit[f] that has been given to us.

6 For Christ—while we were still weak, still at that very time—Christ died on behalf of the ungodly. 7 (Why, scarcely will someone die on behalf of a righteous person, although perhaps for a good person someone might dare even to die.) 8 God establishes God's own love for us in that while we were still sinners Christ died on our behalf.

9 Therefore, even more *now* since we have been rectified through his blood, we will be saved by him from wrath. 10 For if, when we were enemies, we were reconciled to God through the death of his Son, even more will we be saved by his life. 11 And not only that, but we also boast in God through our Lord Jesus Christ through whom *now* we have received reconciliation.

a. The difference of a single Greek letter stands between the indicative *echomen* ("We have peace") found in some manuscripts (א[1] B[2] F G P Ψ) and the subjunctive *echōmen* ("Let us have peace") found in others (א* A B* C D K L). The manuscript evidence favors the subjunctive reading followed above, even if many translations and commentaries opt for the indicative because they judge that the context requires it (NRSVue; Käsemann 133; Cranfield 1:257; Dunn 1:245; Wilckens 1:288–89). Resolving this particular problem matters less than it may seem, because the exhortation is based entirely on God's work, as is clear in the rest of the passage, and because the exhortation is to "have peace" rather than to "make peace." Moffatt's rendering, "Let us enjoy peace," which is anticipated by Chrysostom (*Hom. Rom.* 9.1; *NPNF*[1] 11.396) and Origen (*Comm. Rom.* 4.8; Burns 104), is adopted here as particularly effective (and see 4 Macc 3:20; John 16:33; Acts 9:31).

b. At this point some manuscripts insert *tē pistei* or *en tē pistei* (both of which are rendered "in the faith"). The evidence is rather evenly divided. Given the phrase *ek pisteōs* in v. 1, neither the presence nor absence of the phrase makes for a substantive change.

c. The form *kauchōmetha* can be translated either "we boast" (indicative) or "let us boast" (subjunctive); the latter translation follows better from the opening exhortation (so also in v. 3).

d. Lit., "our hope for God's glory." The addition of "the coming" reflects the judgment that Paul's concern here is largely with God's own glory in the sense of

God's powerful presence. See the comment on glory at 3:23, and note especially the role of God's glory in 6:4.

e. The form *kataischynei* can be either present or future indicative, but the future better reflects not simply Paul's conviction about the future fulfillment of God's glory but the future tense of vv. 9–10 (although note the present tense in 1:16).

f. The uppercase "Spirit" is used here and elsewhere in instances where an agent is referred to, as distinct from the "spirit" of an individual (as in 1:9) or "spirit" rather than "letter" (as in 2:29).

[5:1–2] The first-person plural continues from 4:24–25, encouraging Paul's hearers to align their viewpoint with his. "We" are those who trust in Jesus (4:25), yet Paul does not identify the "we" further. No definition of a "they" separates the "we" from other human beings; "we" unites the sender of the letter and Phoebe who reads it with the audience in Rome, but without specification. And the repeated use of "all" in 5:12–21 stands as a warning against any presumption that the actions of God are limited in their scope to those who presently constitute the "we" (to say nothing of texts such as 9:14–23; 11:17–18).

By virtue of being rectified *ek pisteōs* ("by faith"), Paul is able to write what follows. Paul does not explain whose *pistis* is meant (whether "our" faith or the faithfulness of God/Jesus Christ), since by this time the audience is expected to understand that *pistis* is God's faithful action on behalf of humankind that generates human trust. Thus, faith is the sort evidenced in the peculiar story of Abraham, faith strengthened by God, not an individual virtue or an intellectual victory of conviction over doubt. The content specified in ch. 4, of course, is Abraham's confidence that God will do as God has said and "our" confidence in the One who raised Jesus from the dead (4:20, 24). (The noun "faith" or "trust" does not appear again until 9:30; the verb "to believe" or "trust" appears once in 6:8.)

With the words "Let us enjoy the peace we have with God," we come to the exhortation that might have been expected following 3:26 but never materialized. And yet it is a peculiar exhortation, which may account for the conflicted manuscript tradition (see translation note a on v. 1). What makes the exhortation peculiar is that nothing follows to indicate what exactly the exhortation means. It is not that "we" can do something to bring peace about; on the contrary, everything that follows indicates that God has already acted to bring about peace. "Let us enjoy peace" captures the sense of this exhortation as an invitation to celebrate God's intervention in Jesus Christ, and that invitation in turn coheres with the numerous doxological elements throughout the letter.

The language of peace may seem surprising, as it has scarcely entered the letter before this point. God is the one who grants peace, whether it is in the greeting of the letter ("grace and peace from God"; 1:7), in the eschatological gifts promised Jew and gentile alike (2:10), or in prayer (15:33). Among Paul's designations for God is "God of peace" (15:33; 16:20; 1 Thess 5:23; Phil 4:9;

see also Heb 13:20). Reference to peace with God is especially apt here, where Paul is about to demonstrate how humanity has been at enmity with God due to its enslavement to Sin and Death.

This particular phrase ("peace with God") is not found elsewhere in Paul's letters, but the LXX does associate peace with divine activity (as in 1 Chr 12:19; Ps 84:9; Isa 26:12; 54:1), as Paul has already done in 2:10. The notion of peace with God is especially urgent for Paul, given his analysis of the human situation. This phrase recalls 3:17, with its citation of Isa 59:8: "They do not know the way of peace." The way of peace that humanity does *not* know now becomes the peace with God that humanity knows and enjoys because of God's actions in Jesus Christ.

If being rectified means that "we" may and should enjoy peace with God, then that peacemaking in turn has to do with the resolution of conflict, since an admonition regarding peace is only appropriate or necessary where two or more parties have previously been in conflict. The question, then, is which parties are involved in the conflict. This opening line permits us to imagine that the conflict is between two parties only, God and human beings, or perhaps that the conflict and therefore its resolution are confined to the human arena. As early as 1:24, 26, and 28, however, we glimpse the existence of another party to the conflict, and in 3:9 the party is named as Sin. In the remainder of this passage and continuing through 8:39, we will find ample confirmation of an all-encompassing conflict between God and those powers that attempt to "separate us from God's love in Christ Jesus" (8:39). The peace with God that Paul celebrates in this opening line of ch. 5 is the result not simply of a reconciliation between God and human beings (whether individuals or corporate groups), but of *the defeat of Sin and Death*. This point is reinforced by the language of reconciliation later in the passage (vv. 10–11). Such discourse may have a particular freight in Rome, where the empire declares itself to be the maker of peace (as in Augustus's *Res gestae*), yet that fact does not reduce or limit this passage to an anti-empire statement.

The phrase "through our Lord Jesus Christ" both begins and ends this passage (v. 11), and it echoes through the entire section 5:1–8:39 (5:21; 6:11, 23; 7:25; 8:39), but it is no mere literary twitch. Until this point the letter has commented relatively little on Jesus Christ; the opening lines of the letter do so, of course, as does 3:21–26. But beginning with 4:23–25 and now especially in ch. 5, the actions of and through Jesus Christ come to the foreground.[2] In ch. 4 Paul has written a peculiar history that leaps directly from Abraham to the cross, and now he explicates that cross, unpacking the highly condensed references to

2. The name Jesus, Christ, Jesus Christ, or Christ Jesus, appears ten times in all of Rom 1–4, but seven times in Rom 5 alone, and that observation does not account for the indirect references such as "someone" (5:7) or "the coming one" (5:14).

Jesus's death in 3:21–26. Having identified God as "the One who raised Jesus our Lord from the dead," Paul now turns to account for that identification and its implications.

Because of Jesus (and specifically because of his death, as vv. 6–11 will explain), "we have entrance to this grace in which we stand" and "boast in our hope for the coming of God's glory" (v. 2). The word "entrance" (*prosagōgē*) does not appear in the LXX and appears elsewhere in the NT only in Eph 2:18; 3:12, where it concerns access to God's presence. Its connotation of physical access or entry point is underscored by the reference to "standing" in grace; the death of Jesus has located "us" in a different place. Paul's other references to standing confirm that this is not for Paul the equivalent of having a conviction or belief (as in statements such as "This is where I stand on that issue"); it is instead the "place" where one lives, the sphere of influence that determines one's existence (Rom 11:20; 14:4; 1 Cor 10:12; 15:1; 2 Cor 1:24), not unlike Paul's expression "in Christ." This is why the designation "believers" is problematic for Paul, as it suggests that what distinguishes the Christian is a matter of the head rather than of the whole person, indeed of the whole of humanity (as in 12:1).

The specific location is identified as the "grace" or "gift" "in which we stand," reinforcing the notion that "we" have been moved from one place and into another. Already, of course, Paul has identified God's action in Jesus Christ as a "grace" (1:5), given specifically in the cross (3:24), and has retold the story of Abraham to emphasize God's gift (4:4, 16). In all these cases, the gift is bestowed without regard for the recipient's worthiness, a fact Paul's contemporaries would have found peculiar (Barclay 2015, 24–51). In the argument that follows, Paul will cast that unworthiness onto a universal canvas in terms of the unworthiness of all Adam's offspring (5:12–21), and "grace" or "gift" will become a metonym for the divine action itself (5:21).

This change of location prompts a further exhortation to boasting "in our hope for the coming of God's glory" (v. 2). Paul earlier made a brief, caustic remark about the possibility that some Jews might boast in God while not keeping the commandments (2:17, 23), and he rejected boasting about law observance (3:27), which makes the endorsement of boasting in 5:2 something of a surprise. But not all boasting has been excluded, as is clear elsewhere in Paul's letters (e.g., 1 Cor 1:31; 2 Cor 5:12; 12:1; Gal 6:14; Phil 2:16; 1 Thess 2:19). Given the ubiquity of boasting in Paul's culture (not unlike that of contemporary North American culture), it would have been unthinkable to reject boasting altogether, but boasting normally pertained to one's own achievements or that of one's family or city (Jewett 49–51).

By contrast, the boasting Paul encourages is based on hope for the arrival of "God's glory." The verses that follow, as well as the later remarks in 8:18–24, demonstrate that hope is an eschatological conviction, not a disposition to optimism or a personal virtue to be cultivated. The hope referred to here is that of the coming triumph of God's glory, God's eschatological presence that accomplishes God's will, rather than a future glorification of human beings. Paul does refer to God's glorification of human beings in 8:17, 21, and 2 Cor 3:18 refers to the conforming of humans to the image of Christ, but the "glory of God" is the powerful presence of God, as is the case in Rom 6:4. Humanity's refusal to acknowledge God's glory (1:21) precipitated their being handed over to Sin and deprived of God's presence (3:23). Boasting on the basis of God's own glory, then, coheres with the numerous doxological expressions in the letter (1:25; 7:25; 9:5; 11:36; 15:33).[3]

[3–5] The move from v. 2 to v. 3 bears watching; as Paul repeats his admonition about boasting, he also recasts it in an unexpected way:

v. 2b   Let us boast in our hope for the coming of God's glory
v. 3a   Let us boast also in afflictions

By separating these two admonitions with the phrase "not only that," Paul prepares the auditors to hear a boast about human achievement or strength or advantage.[4] Instead, the boast is about affliction. Once again Paul has used a rhetorical sleight of hand. In place of what might have been anticipated, even expected—namely, a boast about one's own achievements or triumphs—he admonishes instead boasting in tribulations.[5] Paul's own experience may be reflected here. In his dealings with the Corinthian congregations, Paul had encountered those who would make assessments based on verbal agility or charismatic power (e.g., 1 Cor 4; 2 Cor 10–13). Romans 8:18–25 will address the future glorification of humanity and the redemption of creation, but in 5:3 the boasting lies elsewhere.

In v. 3b "affliction" (*thlipsis*) becomes the subject, both grammatically (the subject of the verb in v. 3b) and substantively. Affliction is said to do certain things that lead to "hope" in v. 5, where hope becomes the subject. Although *thlipsis* can refer to a wide range of hardships (as in, e.g., 1 Cor 7:28; 2 Cor 2:4; Jas 1:27), it often appears in contexts that involve conflict (e.g., 1 Thess 3:7; Gen 42:21; Deut 28:53; Neh 9:27; 1 Macc 5:16; 4 Macc 14:9; Ps 54:4; and

3. Michel suggests that this boast has the character of "shouts of joy in worship" (177–78, cited in Gathercole 2002c, 256).
4. In 8:23, e.g., "not only that" (*ou monon de*) introduces the groaning of the human "we," escalating the argument about the anticipation of all creation; similarly in 2 Cor 7:7, "not only that" announces Paul's elevated rejoicing over Timothy's report on his visit to Corinth; see also Rom 1:32; 9:10; 2 Cor 8:10, 19; 9:12. In Phil 1:29, "not only that" marks the movement from "believing" to "suffering."
5. Boasting about one's hardships was not unique to Paul, to be sure (see Fitzgerald 1988, 47–116), but in 5:3, with Paul having just boasted about God's own glory, one might expect that the consequences for "us" would be glorification rather than affliction.

Josephus, *Ant.* 4.108; 1 Clem. 57.4), and especially in eschatological contexts (e.g., Isa 8:22; 10:3; 37:3; Jer 6:24; Dan 12:1; Matt 24:9, 21, 29; Mark 13:24; Rev 7:14). Given the language of reconciliation and peace in Rom 5:1–11, as well as the conflict between God and the anti-God powers that has already come into view in 1:24, 26, and 28 and will return more explicitly with 5:12–21 and beyond, *thlipsis* acquires the full connotation of eschatological conflict here.[6]

The reference to afflictions becomes more intense by virtue of the rhetorical move that follows as Paul proceeds by "stairsteps":

> Affliction produces endurance
> Endurance produces character
> Character produces hope

This is a common rhetorical device, often referred to as climax (as in, e.g., Wis 6:17–20; Maximus of Tyre, *Diss.* 16.3). Although it is tempting to take up each of these terms to discern precisely what sort of process Paul envisions and how it comes about,[7] such a query sheds little light on the text. This is neither a truism about human nature nor a moralizing claim that promises a good outcome for those who persevere. It is, instead, a rhetorical flourish; it elaborates in order to emphasize both the reality of affliction and the reality of hope. The stairstep then underscores Paul's call for boasting in afflictions and his emphasis on hope.

This stairstep reasoning comes into sharp focus when Paul reaches the end of ch. 8. If affliction produces endurance, and endurance produces character, and character produces hope, it is because of God's determination that "nothing will separate" humanity from its rightful lord. These changes happen not as little lessons in personal growth (à la Nietzsche's famous claim that whatever did not kill him would make him stronger) but because God will not allow the separation. And that hope will not "put us to shame"; that is, eschatologically speaking, confidence in God's glory cannot possibly lead to shame (see on 1:16; and see also Rom 9:33; 10:11; Phil 1:20; Mark 8:38; Luke 9:26; 2 Tim 1:12; 1 Pet 2:6; 1 John 2:28).

Hope arises in precisely the circumstances that could well produce its opposite, both in this passage and in 8:18–25. It is affliction that produces hope, just as in 8:18–25 "the sufferings of the present time" are the context in which hope comes about. Here "our" hope recalls the confidence of Abraham, who trusted God even as he took note of his own failing body and that of Sarah (4:18–19).

---

6. As in English, the term "affliction" suggests something that comes from the outside; it is also more evocative than the bland and trivializing "problems" of the CEB.

7. For similar associations between affliction and endurance, see 2 Cor 1:6; 6:4; for affliction and character, see 2 Cor 8:1–2.

If "our" hope does not face eschatological shame, that is because (*hoti*) of God's love "poured out into our hearts through the Holy Spirit that has been given to us" (v. 5). The subject (grammatically) is God's love; both God's love and the gift of the Holy Spirit are in turn connected to Jesus's death (note the *gar*, "for," in v. 6). The Greek phrase *hē agapē tou theou* ("the love of God") is just as ambiguous as the English, susceptible of being understood either as God's love of "us" or "our" love of God, and neither connotation can be altogether excluded. Paul's argument to this point weighs in favor of reading this as God's own love. He has relentlessly argued that humanity does not fear God (3:18), has sinned, and has been deprived of God's glory (3:23), and it is hard to reconcile that description with an affirmation of human love for God. To the extent that human beings love God "now" (i.e., in the time of the gospel), it is only because of God's own initiating love (as trust or faith comes about through God's initiating act in Jesus Christ). The phrase "God establishes God's own love" in v. 8 also confirms that what Paul has in mind here is love that comes from God and is given to humanity.

The extravagant character of God's love comes through with the verb *ekcheō*, "poured out." The "pouring out" from God is associated most often in the NT with the Holy Spirit (as in Acts 2:17–18 [quoting Joel 3:1–2 LXX], 33; Titus 3:6), but other gifts from God are also said to be "poured out" (e.g., grace in Ps 44:3 LXX; mercy in Sir 18:11; BDAG, s.v. *ekcheō*). Blood is also "poured out" (as in 3:15; Acts 22:20; Matt 26:28), and although the death of Jesus is scarcely said to be "poured out in our hearts," Paul is about to connect God's love specifically with Jesus's death. God's love is no abstraction, not a characteristic of God that can be isolated from what God does. Since Paul's claim about God's love in v. 5 is linked by *gar* immediately to the death of Christ in v. 6, it is clear well before v. 8 that God's love is demonstrated in this death. God's love looks like this death on behalf of the enemy.

Paul's comment that God's love is poured "into our hearts" further intensifies the effusive claim about the "pouring out" of God's love. Paul might have written simply "for us," as he does rather often (e.g., 5:8; 8:31, 32, 34); this particular wording conjures up an intimacy of relationship.[8] Earlier in the letter the heart is the location of resistance to God (1:21, 24; 2:5), but now the heart is the recipient of God's love, a love that proves transformative.

The outpouring of God's love is brought about "through the Holy Spirit that has been given to us." This is the letter's first explicit reference to the Holy Spirit (although see 1:4), whose activity is only hinted at here and comes to the foreground in ch. 8. Like the love of God, the Holy Spirit also is a gift.

---

8. Consistent with his contemporaries, Paul uses "heart" (*kardia*) to refer to the location of human emotion, will, etc. (e.g., Mark 7:21; Acts 7:23; 11:23; 1 Pet 3:4; Epictetus, *Diatr.*1.27.21; Sophocles, *Ant.* 1105; Diogenes Laertius, *Lives* 7.159).

Superfluously, Paul adds that the Spirit is given "to us," but that addition simply reinforces the passive character of the reception of the Spirit. It is not a prize, a reward, or an achievement.

Taking into account the comments on Christ's death in v. 6, this short passage touches on the web of relationships Christians will later call the Trinity. God's love is poured out through the Spirit, which is in turn given by God. This happens adjunctively to the peace "we" have with God "through our Lord Jesus Christ," who died "for us." God's love shows itself in Christ's death. Paul may not delineate this relationship with anything approximating precision, but the concerns and connections that give rise to Trinitarian thought can be glimpsed here.

[6–8] In v. 6 Christ becomes the agent of the action for the first time in the letter. The "we" who was the subject of vv. 1–3a yielded in vv. 3b–5 to "affliction," "hope," and "God's love." God's love returns in v. 8, and the "we" returns as the subject in vv. 9–11. Here, however, in the center of the passage, the subject of the verbs is Christ himself:

v. 6   Christ died on behalf of the ungodly
v. 8b   Christ died on our behalf

Earlier in the letter, Paul referred briefly to Jesus's death (1:4; 3:25; 4:24), but now for the first time he puts the matter directly: Christ died. This emphasis on Christ's death is coupled repeatedly with the claim that Christ's death was "on behalf of" others. What 3:21–26 announces, 5:1–21 explains. Yet what Paul does at this point is not merely to dispense information but to demonstrate the extent of God's achievement, in order both to compel the audience to recognize its own need and to introduce the cosmic horizon of the gospel.

Just as hope arises where it might not be expected, it is also the case that God has brought about reconciliation and righteousness where they were previously impossible. In Greek, v. 6 begins with the name of Christ and ends with his death, but those references bracket a double reference to the timing of Christ's death. The genitive absolute of v. 6 ("while we were still weak") places Christ's death while "we" were still in a condition of helplessness, which Paul then underscores with *kata kairon* ("at that very time"). The emphasis on timing lays the groundwork for the conflict between the enslaving powers of Sin and Death and the power of God's righteousness discussed later in the chapter. It is precisely *while* "we" were unworthy that Christ acted, with no regard to "our" readiness or preparation.

Repeatedly vv. 6, 8, and later 10 identify the "we" in negative terms: we were "weak" and "ungodly" (v. 6), we were "sinners" (v. 8), we were "enemies" (v. 10). Standing at the beginning of this series of descriptors, "weakness" is the least negative and the most puzzling. The Greek adjective *asthenēs* and the related noun *astheneia* can refer to physical illness (Acts 4:9), to "weaker" body parts (1 Cor 12:22), to the "weaker" sex (1 Pet 3:7), to any sort of limitation or incapacity (Rom 6:17; 8:3), and to the weakness of Christ at his crucifixion (2 Cor 13:4). In the context of this letter, where it appears that some Romans are labeling others as "weak in faith" (14:1–2), Paul signals a solidarity among human beings who are all characterized by weakness, in anticipation of his instruction about what genuine power looks like in 15:1–2.[9]

The declaration of "weakness" pales beside the second description of humankind as "the ungodly" (*asebeis*).[10] The full power of this assertion that Christ died for the "ungodly" emerges when this claim is read alongside the many passages in Paul's Scriptures that assume a veritable abyss separating the "ungodly" from the "righteous" (see v. 7). The Psalter opens by pronouncing blessing on the one "who does not walk in the way of the ungodly" (1:1 LXX: *asebēs*).[11] That sharp line between the "ungodly" and the "righteous" comes into early Christian texts as well (1 Tim 1:9; 1 Pet 4:18; 2 Pet 2:4–10; 3:7; Jude 4, 15). Paul has already insinuated that Abraham himself once belonged among the "ungodly" (see above on 4:5). For those Roman auditors who may have imagined themselves exempt from the charges of 1:18–32, this phrase stands as yet another reminder that all are "under Sin" (3:9), that there is no one in the right (3:10).[12]

Verse 8 introduces the third label for human beings; not only "weak" and "ungodly," they are also identified as "sinners." Even in Romans, where concern with Sin is prominent (see the excursus on the powers of Sin and Death, pp. 162–65), Paul seldom uses the word "sinner" (an adjective used substantively; see 3:7; 5:19; 7:13). In Gal 2:15, 17, the term identifies gentiles who are sinners by (Jewish) definition (and thus is similar to the Gospels' identification of "sinners" with the socially marginal; Carey 2009, 17–36). In the context of Romans, however, a "sinner" is not someone who belongs to the "others" but someone who belongs to Sin itself, as becomes clear in 5:12–21 and well into ch. 6. The time reference is significant; Christ died "while we were still sinners," not "after we had repented" or "when we began to live righteously."

Between these identifications of "us" in vv. 6 and 8, v. 7 constitutes an elaborate aside on the improbability of dying for another. Many ambiguities attend this statement, including whether Paul has in mind two different sorts of

9. This concern about weakness may have been especially pronounced among males (B. Wilson 2015, 39–75).

10. Because there is no personal pronoun modifying "ungodly," we might imagine that Paul distinguishes between "us" who were merely "weak" and some unidentified others who were "ungodly." The first-person plurals of v. 8 and v. 10 immediately undercut any such distinction: "we" also are among the "ungodly."

11. Among many other examples, see Gen 18:23, 25; Ps 58:10 (57:11 LXX); Prov 3:33; 10:6–7; Wis 3:10; Hab 1:4.

12. As in the elegant remark of Jeffrey Burton Russell: "The worm is in my rose too" (1977, 22).

people (the "righteous" and the "good") and whether "the good" is a person or an abstraction.[13] Puzzling out these ambiguities matters less when we recognize the rhetorical direction of the statement, which reinforces how outrageous God's act is: while an unspecified "someone" might imagine death on behalf of the admirable, death on behalf of the weak, ungodly sinner lies beyond imagining.

That implicit comparison introduces v. 8, with its interpretation of Christ's death as an embodiment of God's love. God's "own love" (the pronoun is emphatic), already described as being poured out in "our" hearts (v. 5), is demonstrated "in that while we were still sinners Christ died on our behalf." However much Romans depicts a conflict between God and anti-God powers, God's action on behalf of humankind does not come about simply to demonstrate power or to establish control for its own sake; rather, God's action is born out of love. And the connection between the two parts of the verse is important: God's love is demonstrated in Christ's death. God's action of loving and Christ's action of dying are connected, not in that God sends Christ to die (although see 8:3 and Gal 4:4), but it is as if the two are identical (the *hoti* that connects v. 8a with v. 8b is epexegetical; Wallace 1996, 460). Paul does not articulate the relationship between God and Christ as the church later would, yet this statement implies a deep connection.

The statement that "while we were still sinners Christ died on our behalf" marks the fourth time in three verses that Paul has used the expression "die on behalf of":

v. 6   died on behalf of the ungodly
v. 7   die on behalf of a righteous person
        die on behalf of a good person
v. 8   died on behalf of us

Central to Paul's interpretation of Jesus's death is the notion that it was "on behalf of" humankind, as is clear from his use of the phrase elsewhere (see Rom 14:9; 1 Thess 5:9–10; Gal 2:21; 1 Cor 8:11; 15:3; 2 Cor 5:15).[14]

Identifying the significance of the phrase does not yet mean understanding its nuance, however, as "on behalf of" can mean "in place of" (as in substitution) or "for the sake of" (as in some more general sense of benefiting the other). The initial announcement of Jesus's death in 3:21–26 does not resolve this ambiguity, since the imagery shifts, moving from redemption from slavery to cultic language and then to judicial language. Only the context can resolve

13. Dispute about it reaches back into the earliest centuries of commenting on Romans, on which see Bammel 1996. On the question whether the "good" here is an abstraction or a person, see Gathercole 2015, 87–89.

14. On the extensive use of combinations of the verb *apothnēskein* ("die") with the prepositions *hyper, peri, pro,* and *anti* in Greek literature, see Gibson 2004; Eschner 2010.

the ambiguity. The assumption that Paul must mean Christ died instead of ("in place of") is pervasive, fueled by passages such as John 11:50–51. Yet in Rom 6 Paul will connect the death of Jesus with the death of believers to Sin and their new life in Christ (Breytenbach 2010b, 75–78). In Romans, Christ's death does not substitute for human death; to the contrary, Christians are incorporated into the death and new life of Christ. In this setting, then, "for the sake of" is the better understanding of the phrase.

On either interpretation of this expression, this is an event in which God acts through Jesus Christ without human cooperation or initiative.[15] Paul will take up the resulting change later on, even calling it newness of life, but the change comes from God's action, not from human action. God's action happens "while we were still sinners" (and ungodly, weak), not after "we" have repented or when "we" began to live righteously.

[9–11] Verses 6–8 foreground Christ's death on behalf of a humanity that is weak, godless, and sinful, but in vv. 9–11 the consequences of that death "for us" come again to the foreground, as "we" becomes the subject of the verbs once again ("we will be saved," "we were reconciled," "we boast," "we have received reconciliation"). In v. 10 Paul will add to the names "weak," "ungodly," and "sinners" the most negative name of all, "enemies," which in turn anticipates the conflict Paul highlights in ch. 6.

The opening words of v. 9 repeat the opening of 5:1 ("therefore, since we have been rectified") but with the addition of *pollō mallon* ("even more") and *nyn* ("now"), which intensifies the sense of urgency. Earlier, in 3:21, Paul identified "now" as the time of God's rectifying action in Jesus Christ and contrasted the "now" time with the uniform history of human enslavement to Sin. The peculiar story of ch. 4, with its yawning gap between the time of Abraham and the time of the present, reinforces the sense that "now" is the time of God's action.

The "now" time is not the whole of the story, however, and vv. 9–11 point to a future that is even greater than the present. With the "even more" (*pollō mallon*) in v. 9 and again in v. 10, Paul constructs a *qal wahomer* argument—an argument from the lesser to the greater—that reinforces his point (as he will do again in 5:15, 17). The contrast here is conventional, as when Jesus teaches his disciples not to worry about food or clothing, since the God who clothes the grass will surely clothe human beings (Matt 6:30). Paul moves from God's actions for "us" in the death of Jesus to the even more astonishing actions of God expected in the future, anticipating a move he will make again in 8:18–25.

Verse 9 contrasts being rectified "through his blood" with the future action of salvation from wrath (recalling 1:18), also carried out "by him." This contrast seems to separate rectification from salvation, a separation hard to reconcile

---

15. Käsemann comments that *hyper hēmōn* can mean either "on behalf of" or "in place of," but especially it means "without us," apart from any human cooperation or initiative (138).

with 1:16–17, where the two are closely connected. Yet the distinction antici-pates 8:18–25, with its contrast between what has already begun and its escha-tological fulfillment. That coheres with the reintroduction in 5:9 of the term "wrath," the eschatological overtones of which are clear in 2:8.

That rectification is "through his blood" recalls the claim of 3:25 and sum-marizes vividly Paul's repeated statements about Christ's death in vv. 6–8. Here death is no abstraction; it is the very real human blood of Jesus. Especially given the cultic language in 3:21–25, the sense may also be sacrificial. As in that earlier passage, so here: language that is forensic (judicial) and language that is cultic stand side by side .

Verse 10 introduces yet another language arena, when the "wrath" of v. 9 employs the language of reconciled enemies. Earlier "we" were described as weak, godless, and sinners, but now Paul ratchets up the argument a final step, revealing a perspective that will emerge sharply in the second half of this chap-ter: "We were enemies." In the Greek, the term "enemies" is frontloaded, so that it strikes the auditor with force. And it is followed quickly by "we were reconciled." This language emerges from the realm of diplomacy or, more accurately, the failure of diplomacy.[16] Humanity was no neutral observer in the conflict between God and the anti-God powers; instead, humanity existed as a genuine enemy of God. This may well be the most disturbing of the claims made in the wake of Paul's announcement of divine wrath in 1:18. The language of enemies will return in 8:7, where Paul characterizes the mindset of the "flesh" as being God's enemy, and 11:28, where Paul refers to that portion of Israel that remains (in Paul's time) in conflict with God's gospel. There, as here, enemy status is alleviated by and only by the love of God.

The section ends by returning to the initial statement about "our" boasting in God. And again, as in v. 1, boasting is "in God through our Lord Jesus Christ." Jesus is no mere alternative here or an add-on but is the very way in which "we" have received reconciliation. This statement returns to the claim of v. 1 with the language of reconciliation, but it expands it simultaneously. Central to Paul's understanding of Jesus's death is that it reconciles a humanity at odds with God. Chapter 4 places "us" who trust in Jesus Christ in the family of Abraham, whether Jew or gentile. Belonging to that family does not suffice to describe God's act in Jesus, however, as ch. 5 makes clear. Paul dramatically depicts the rescue of humanity from its enmity to God, a rescue brought about by Jesus's unlikely act of dying for those who are utterly undeserving. The insistence on the undeserving character of "us" may well sound off-key for some in Paul's audience. Some Jewish auditors will surely object to the notion that they were ever weak, ungodly sinners at enmity with God. Some gentile auditors may be

16. See, e.g., Dionysius of Halicarnassus, *Ant. rom.*3.9.2; 3.50.4; Josephus, *Ant.* 15.136 (Brey-tenbach 1989, 40–83; 2010a).

no less offended, especially those who have heard the gospel precisely because they had earlier been affiliated with the synagogue. For this reason Paul will press on in vv. 12–21 to show the depth and extent of the rescue required. It involves rescue from terrifying enemies by the names of Sin and Death.

5:12–21 The Triumph over Sin and Death

Weak, godless, sinners, enemies—Paul has slipped some disturbing language into the welcome declaration of peace and the eschatological anticipation of hope and salvation in 5:1–11. And he has done so in first-person plural, placing himself and the Roman Christians alike under the burden of these troubling epithets. Even though he casts the statements in past tense, it is easy to imagine Phoebe's hearers responding with puzzlement, perhaps even irritation, to the notion that "we," the very people "who trust the One who raised Jesus our Lord from the dead" (4:24), were ever to be regarded as weak or godless or sinners, to say nothing of having been enemies of God.

To be sure, Paul has already written in 2:1 that "you" who judge are doing the very same things, and he has declared that all are under the power of Sin (3:9; also 3:23), that there is no one who is right (3:10b), and that no one has been rectified (3:20). He has even identified Abraham among the ungodly (4:5). Despite those statements, Paul does not assume that the audience will have understood themselves as numbered among the indicted. Not only is this repetition rhetorically forceful, but—as the long history of reading Romans demonstrates—readers are capable of assuming that its indictments somehow exclude themselves. Paul closes the door to any such temptation in 5:12–21. By reaching back to the disobedience of Adam, Paul shows how Sin and Death have been at work in the human world from its beginning. They became its rulers. No one has escaped their reign.

But that is not the whole of the story. Paul not only rehearses how human beings came under the control of Sin and Death; he also emphasizes God's defeat of Sin and Death through the triumph of Jesus's death and (in ch. 6) his resurrection. By the time we reach 5:21, the reign of grace, which is to say, the reign of God, has been established. Taken together, then, 5:1–11 and 5:12–21 unpack the terse argument of 3:21–26 about the significance of Jesus's death— indeed, of the Christ event as a whole.

The passage is carefully composed around a series of six comparative statements using *hōsper / hōs . . . houtōs* ("just as . . . so also") that display the dire universal consequences of Adam's disobedience and then the astonishing and equally universal consequences of Christ's obedience (vv. 12, 15, 16, 18, 19, 21). The first in this series of comparisons stands apart, with its piercing depiction of the catastrophic consequences of Adam's sin. The second and third comparisons contrast the consequences of Adam's single human act with the divine gift of God (vv. 15–17); Christ's obedience is *not* like the disobedience of Adam. The last three statements compare positively Adam's action with that of Christ in that both shape all of humanity (vv. 18–21). The final *hōsper . . . houtōs* clause draws out the conclusion: where Sin and Death once ruled, now grace (that is to say, God) rules (v. 21). In addition to this series of comparative statements, again here as in 5:1–11, Paul argues from the lesser to the greater ("even more" in vv. 15 and 17). He also makes use of homoioteleuton in vv. 15–16 as he repeats the *–ma* ending in the words *paraptōma, charisma, dōrēma, krima, katakrima,* and *dikaiōma* (trespass, grace, gift, judgment, condemnation, righteous act).

These rhetorical details become more intriguing when we recognize that Paul's argument would remain intact if he had moved immediately from v. 12 to v. 21 (or perhaps to v. 19; K. Barth 1956, 7). What he needs and wants to demonstrate is that the lordship of Sin and Death over all humanity has now been defeated by the surpassing lordship of Jesus Christ. The reality of v. 12 is defeated by the new reality of v. 21, the reign of grace. And in both cases "all" means *all*, because God's power to redeem humanity exceeds even the combined powers of Sin and Death. If grace does not reign over all without exception, then grace is less powerful than Sin and Death. Verses 12 and 21 together constitute the argument. The remainder of the passage elaborates the case, but it is worth pondering why so much explanation is needed—or appears to Paul to be needed—to get from one place to another.[17]

The intricate structure, the contrasts, and the repetition make this passage rhetorically compelling, and such care signals its importance for the argument: Paul has arrived at the heart of his discussion of Jesus's death and resurrection. "Our" identity is not described by the title "heirs of Abraham" alone, however important that may be (and it is important, as emerged in ch. 4 and will be reinforced in chs. 9–11). "We" are also involved in a conflict between God and the powers of Death and Sin. "We" have been God's enemies, because "we" were captive to those enemies (surrendered by God), but "we" have been rescued (see also Gal 1:4). "We" have been rescued by God's action in Jesus Christ, and this took place before, apart from, and utterly without any action or response. The language of faith or trust is altogether missing in this section, where emphasis on the unilateral divine gift in the event of Jesus Christ is unmistakable. It is only with ch. 6 that Paul touches on the implications of this rescue for understanding where "we" now live, whose "we" are, and what "we" do in the new lordship, although even there he is not finished with his discussion of Sin and Death, which extends into ch. 8 (see the excursus on the powers of Sin and Death, pp. 162–65).

17. In a sermon on this passage, Richard Hays cleverly imagines 5:12–19 as a student paper, the author of which would be referred for remedial writing instruction (2006, 97).

5:12 Because of our reconciliation with God we now understand that[a] as Sin entered the world through one person and Death entered through Sin, in the same way[b] Death also entered and extended its reach to all people, so that[c] all sinned. 13 Of course, even before the law Sin was already present in the world, although it is not recognized[d] without the law. 14 But Death already ruled as king from the time of Adam until Moses, even in the case of those who did not sin just[e] as Adam did, and Adam is a type of the one to come.

15 Saying that Adam is a type does not mean that his trespass is like the gracious gift. Since many people died through the trespass of one person, even more God's grace and the gift through that grace of the one person Jesus Christ multiplied for many people. 16 And neither is the consequence of the one who sinned like the consequence of the gift. For the judgment that followed one act produced condemnation, but the gracious gift that followed many trespasses produced righteousness.[f] 17 Since by the trespass of one person Death ruled as king through that same one, even more will those who receive the abundance of grace and the gift of righteousness rule in the life that comes to them[g] through the one person, Jesus Christ.

18 This means that Adam and Christ *are* alike in this way: as the trespass of one brought all people to condemnation, so the righteous act of one brought all people to rectification, that is, to life.[h] 19 They are alike also in this way: as through the disobedience of one person many were established as sinners, so through the obedience of one person many will be established as rectified. 20 Now the law sneaked in so that it might increase the transgression, since where Sin increased, grace multiplied even more. 21 So as Sin once ruled as king through Death, in the same way grace might rule as king through righteousness for eternal life through Jesus Christ our Lord.

a. *Dia touto* can be translated simply as "for this reason," but a lengthier clause is needed to show the relationship between vv. 1–11 and 12–21.

b. Here the word order is *kai houtōs* rather than *houtōs kai* as in vv. 15, 18, and 19. Because *kai houtōs* elsewhere in Paul is always used consecutively or consequentially ("and in this way," as in 11:26), some scholars argue that v. 12 introduces a protasis, for which the apodosis comes only in v. 18 (e.g., Cranfield 1:272–63; Moo 346–47). But that argument presumes rigid consistency in Paul's prose and overlooks the careful construction of this passage, as well as the fact that there are other variations in the comparative statements that follow:

v. 12	*hōsper*	*kai houtōs*
v. 15	*hōs*	*houtōs kai*
v. 16	*hōs*	[implied]
v. 18	*hōs*	*houtōs kai*

v. 19   *hōsper   houtōs kai*
v. 21   *hōsper   houtōs kai*

In addition, *hōsper* introduces comparisons in both 6:19 and 11:30, neither of which uses *houtōs kai*. Given these factors, my translation renders v. 12 also as a comparison, the first half of which addresses the initial arrival of Sin and Death, and the second half the consequential grasp of Sin and Death for all people.

c. The *eph' hō* of v. 12d is among the most disputed phrases in Romans (see Cranfield 1:274–81; Fitzmyer 413–16). The phrase can be a relative clause that refers to an antecedent earlier in the verse (e.g., "the place on which you are standing is holy," Acts 7:33). Augustine, to take the most influential example of this view, took *eph' hō* to mean that "in Adam" all sinned (relying on the Vulgate's *in quo*; in *C. Jul. op. imp.* 2.63). More recently, Jewett has argued that the antecedent of *eph' hō* is "the world" in v. 12 (376). Both these options identify as antecedents words that stand at considerable remove from the phrase itself, and Augustine's reliance on the Vulgate confuses *epi* ("on") with *en* ("in"). A second and more widely held option is that *eph' hō* functions as a conjunction, where it can mean simply "because" or "so that" (e.g., Phil 3:12; 4:10; 2 Cor 5:4). Interpreters often prefer "because" or "since" rather than "so that" in order to avoid the implication that Adam's sin is passed along genetically, to emphasize personal responsibility, and to avoid the implication that Death itself somehow causes human beings to sin (e.g., Cranfield 1:278–81; Wolter 1:344–45). But "so that" better fits the context (and see Fitzmyer 416–17). Nothing else in this passage faults individuals other than Adam for the arrival of Sin in the world (however much they cooperate with it); indeed, v. 19 explicitly claims that the disobedience of one person made many into sinners. Adam's act opened the door for the enslaving powers of Sin and Death; just as Sin brought Death into the world, Death's pervasive power produced even more sinfulness because Sin and Death are mutually reinforcing powers (see the excursus on the powers of Sin and Death, pp. 162–65).

d. This clause is difficult to translate because the verb *ellogeō* is rare, appearing only one other time in the NT (Phlm 18). Here in the passive voice, Sin is said not to be *ellogeitai* unless the law is present. It is generally understood as a reference to God's activity, as in the NRSVue's "reckoned"; that is, God keeps an account of sin. That interpretation, however, implies that Adam's action is somehow not sin because it happens prior to the arrival of the law, which is clearly in conflict with Paul's argument. A better alternative, reflected here, is to take *ellogeitai* as a reference to the humans to whom the account is presented; Sin is perceived or recognized as such by human beings only in the presence of the law (so Hofius 2001, 194–97). This is consistent with Phlm 18, where Paul recognizes his possible indebtedness in the case of Onesimus (and see also P.Grenf. II 67.18; P.Stras. I 32.10). On this reading, Rom 5:13b comes close to the sense of 3:20b: "through the law comes recognition of Sin."

e. Lit., "in the likeness of" Adam; BDAG, s.v. *homoiōma*.

f. Lit., "a right decree" or "right commandment," as in 2:26; 8:4, but that translation makes little sense here, since the act of grace does not lead to the decree. Presumably *dikaiōma* is chosen (perhaps unconsciously) for its conformity with the other words in context that end in *ma*; what is meant is the fulfillment of the decree or its result, righteousness (so also BDAG, s.v. *dikaiōma*).

g. Lit., "those who receive in life will reign," or "those who receive will reign in life." The phrase "in life" may be construed with either the participle ("those who receive") or the main verb ("will reign"). My translation amplifies "in life" to clarify its origin, which Paul will specify in 6:3–5.

h. Lit., "for rectification of life," rendered here as an epexegetical genitive, following Moulton 1908, 3:214 (see, e.g., 4:11; 6:4).

[5:12] Paul now takes up the question of how humanity came to be at enmity with God, having used the language of peacemaking and reconciliation in 5:1–11. In order to do that, he introduces the work of the twinned, mutually reinforcing powers of Sin and Death and their reign over all human beings (see the excursus below). These are not new agents in the letter, to be sure, since as early as 1:18–32 (and especially in 1:24, 26, 28) Paul has depicted the handing over of humanity to Sin's power and has declared that "they" were deserving of Death (see 1:32). In 3:9 he summarizes the situation succinctly with the assertion that all are "under the power of Sin." But 5:12–21 extends and intensifies those earlier comments in the form of a complex account of the kingdom established by the interlocked powers of Sin and Death and its overthrow by God's gracious initiative in the death and resurrection of Jesus Christ.[18]

It is through "one person" that Sin enters the world. Repeatedly, this passage refers to "the one" (vv. 12, 15, 16, 17, 18, 19) or "the one person" (vv. 12, 19), identified by the name Adam explicitly only in v. 14. As in 1 Cor 15:22, 44–48, Paul does not narrate the story of Adam (and Eve). Paul displays little interest in the story of Adam in and of itself, especially when compared with the elaborate retellings in the book of Jubilees (chs. 2–4) or the Life of Adam and Eve (LAE). Nothing here or later in Romans suggests that there is to be a restoration of humanity to its created state, certainly not its created glory. Humanity is granted "life," not restored to its Adamic state (Rom 5:17–18; 6:4). This "life" is consistent with 2 Cor 5:17 and Gal 6:15, where Paul writes about "new creation" rather than creation restored. In v. 12 the "one person" functions something like a doorman, the one who permits Sin to enter the world, and Sin in turn holds the door open for Death. Later in the passage "one person" becomes the means for comparing the actions of Sin and Death with those of God in Jesus Christ. For Paul, however, Adam is of little or no interest in and of himself.

The "one person" makes it possible for Sin to enter the world, and Sin in turn makes way for Death (v. 12a). That Death enters the world through Sin of course reflects the narrative of Genesis, according to which human death comes about as a result of the transgression of Adam and Eve. Yet as Paul

18. The difficulty of this passage is aptly reflected in the characterization of it by S. Lewis Johnson Jr.: "The terrain is wild, rugged, infested with exegetical booby traps, and dotted with the graves of interpreters who fell into them" (1974, 300).

reworks the story into one of Sin and Death rather than of Adam and Eve, Eve is altogether omitted.[19] There is a similarity in this sense to the Abraham "story" in ch. 4, in which Abraham plays only a minor role in God's story of promise.

Verse 12b turns to the all-encompassing consequences of the arrival of Sin and Death. Reversing the order of v. 12a, where Sin enters first and then Death, in v. 12b it is first Death that permeates to all people and then Sin. Preoccupation with the *eph' hō* ("so that"; see translation note c on v. 12) should not detract from perceiving the larger point: humanity became God's enemy because Sin and Death conquered the human world.

The interpretation of v. 12 invariably introduces the question of original sin, since the later development of that doctrine drew heavily on this verse. By contrast with Pelagius, who saw Adam's sin as setting an example that other humans followed but could have resisted (92), Augustine insisted that all humans were inevitably, invariably implicated in sin. Augustine mistranslated this verse (see translation note c on v. 12), and it is right to insist that Paul does not develop a doctrine of original sin; nevertheless, Augustine peered into the depths of this passage and understood the extent of Sin's reach into the whole of humankind. Without a grasp that "all" really does mean "all," there is also no need of a salvation that extends to all.[20]

[13–14] Observations about the reigning presence of Sin and Death reinforce Paul's dramatic recollection of the devastating penetration of Sin and Death into the entire world. First, he comments that Sin was already in the world before the arrival of the law (v. 13a), thereby reinforcing the chronology of v. 12. Then comes the statement that Sin is not recognized for what it is until the law is also present. This statement has caused considerable confusion, prompting explanations as unlikely as that Paul is referring to those who sin deliberately (Pelagius 93) or those who sin without having a specific, direct commandment as Adam did (Calvin 113). It is a mistake to try to smooth out all the bumps here, finding some meta-explanation that renders this claim compatible with all of the letter's other assertions about the law. Beginning with his first discussion in 2:12–29 and all the way through ch. 7, Paul makes a number of observations

---

19. The omission of Eve is noted as early as Ambrosiaster, who explains that Paul uses the masculine because the reference is to the whole of humankind rather than "a specific type" (96–97).

20. See the elegant discussion of the relationship between salvation and original sin in Ian A. McFarland 2010, especially 3–58. In addition, Benjamin Myers effectively demonstrates Augustine's profound grasp of this passage (2013). The implications of Paul's statement for unbaptized infants have long been debated (Sullivan 2011), but that question is something of a red herring so far as the text is concerned. The line Paul draws here is not between the baptized and the unbaptized but between the past in Adam and the present in Christ; Paul attributes salvation to God (1:16), not to baptism. Chapter 6 does introduce baptism, but it does so in order to address the life-giving consequences of God's action as that action is witnessed in baptism.

about the law, some of which are quite provocative (as in 3:19; 4:13–15; 6:14). These observations appear to be dropped into their context without development or explanation. They lead finally to the discussion in ch. 7, where Paul defends the law with the astonishing claim that, while the law itself is holy, Sin's power is such that it could make use even of the law.[21]

Verse 14 parallels v. 13, except that Paul now reinforces the presence of Sin's powerful partner, Death, rather than Sin itself. Death also ruled as a king, whether or not Sin was recognized as such. Paul cannot mean that Death no longer ruled after Moses, given the reality of human dying; instead, he implies that Death already ruled even before the law was given. That may be a clue to the second half of v. 14, the observation that Death ruled "even in the case of those who did not sin just as Adam did [or: did not sin in the likeness of Adam]." The point emphasizes Death's ruling power and also introduces "the one to come," which of course prompts the comparison between Adam and Christ in what follows. More important is coupling Death with the verb "rule as king." Later, in v. 21, Paul will speak of Sin's rule as a king, underscoring the notion that Sin and Death have formed a conglomerate that produces even more sin and death. That theirs is an illegitimate reign emerges at the end of v. 21, where Paul concludes that now grace reigns because of God's rectification, which in turn happens because of "Jesus Christ our Lord."

With the final phrase of v. 14, Paul identifies Adam as a "type of the one to come." Given the flexibility of the word *typos*, it is best not to force precision here, as if Christ becomes a restored or a new Adam. Adam is a type of Christ in a very particular sense: both of them affect all of humankind, one toward disaster and enslavement and death, the other toward grace and righteousness and life. To put it more sharply: what follows concerns the consequences of Adam's action and the consequences of God's action in Christ. Little or nothing is said about the figure of Adam as such.

Notably, the salvific actions of God remain off stage in vv. 12–14. One of the remarkable things about these verses is the absence of any reference to either God or Jesus until the final elusive phrase, "the one to come" (*tou mellontos*). The preceding discussion of the death of Jesus Christ in vv. 1–11 and the contrast between Adam's action and that of Christ in vv. 15–21 renders his silence during the arrival and conquest of Sin and Death over the cosmos even more dramatic.[22]

[15–17] Having identified a connection between Adam and Christ, Paul now turns first to *contrast* the consequences of their actions; the transgression and

---

21. Peter Leithart observes that this whole passage is dominated by a series of opposites (e.g., Adam/Christ, death/life), but for the law there is no opposite (2008, 263).

22. Jon Levenson describes this passage as "the unrelieved grimness of the old order, the order that 'reigned' from Adam to Jesus" (2003, 153).

the gracious gift are not alike.[23] In these lines Paul relentlessly elaborates the contrast between a single human act (the transgression of Adam) and the gracious gift of God (the obedience of Jesus). With vv. 18–19 Paul will compare Adam's action with that of Christ (transgression and right act; disobedience and obedience), but in these initial lines the focus is on the difference between a single human act that devastates and enslaves and a single divine act that rescues.

Both v. 15 and v. 16 open with statements of contrast, statements so terse that verbs must be supplied. Rendered literally:

> But not as the trespass, thus also the gracious gift. (v. 15a)
> And not as through the one who sinned, the gift. (v. 16a)

Adam's action is now represented by the single word *paraptōma* ("trespass"), and that action is contrasted with the single word *charisma* ("gracious gift"). "Trespass" is not frequently used by Paul outside of this chapter (4:25; 11:11–12; 2 Cor 5:19; Gal 6:1), but it works well here precisely because it reduces Adam to a single misdeed or misstep. In addition, Paul uses a variety of terms in this passage for individual actions ("transgression," "disobedience," and the verb "to sin"), all of which hammer home the point, and all of which seem to be individual instances of the activity of the power of Sin. *Charisma* typically refers to specific spiritual gifts (e.g., 12:6; 1 Cor 12:4), but here it refers to the single gift of Christ.[24]

The remainder of v. 15 explains the contrast between the human transgression and the divine gift by means of yet another contrast. Paul comments initially that by virtue of the "trespass," "many people died." This is only a slight restatement of the initial remark in v. 12 that Sin and Death entered the world and conquered all people through the act of "one person." Despite the use of *polloi* ("many"), Paul must mean that all died, since that is both what he has already said in vv. 12–14 and is empirically evident in the sense that all human beings die.

If the rest of the verse closely paralleled the first half, it would read, "Through the obedience of one, many lived." Verses 18–19 are constructed in this tightly parallel manner, but v. 15 is not. The focus instead is on God's grace and God's gift through Jesus, which abounded to many; the contrast is between one human transgression and the divine response. Unlike in the first part of the statement ("many people died"), the consequences for the "many" of God's gracious act are not yet stated, so intent is Paul on expressing God's gracious act as a counter to Adam's act.

---

23. The contrast does not mean Paul fears that the Romans will misunderstand and conclude that he is saying something negative about Christ (*pace* Cranfield 1:273), which seems rather unlikely.

24. *Charisma* also results in an effective homoioteleuton with the *-ma* ending of *paraptōma*. Similar repetition of words ending in *-ma* also occurs in v. 16.

The second negative contrast (v. 16a) closely restates the first: the effect of the act of the one who sinned is not the same as the effect of the gift. Again the contrast is between the human act and the divine gift. The language of "trespass" (*paraptōma*) is here replaced by the verb "sin" (*hamartanein*), and the noun "gift" (*charisma*) by a synonym (*dōrēma*), but these are minor variations on the same claim. This negative contrast is followed by two explanatory statements (v. 16b and v. 17), and here for the first time Paul begins to convey the consequences for humanity of God's gift, now in the language of righteousness, reception, and ruling.

Verse 16b contrasts the starting point of Adam's action with the starting point of the divine gift. The judgment derived from one action led to condemnation (and here there is an effective wordplay between *krima,* "judgment," and *katakrima,* "condemnation"). But the gift that derived from many trespasses led to righteousness. Paul is not saying merely that Adam and Christ had different starting points: Adam began with one sin; Christ began with all the sins between Adam and Christ. He is underscoring the fact that the divine gift that followed on many trespasses resulted in righteousness. Translating the second half of this statement parallel to the first results in this: "For the judgment that followed one act produced condemnation, but the gracious gift that followed many trespasses produced righteousness." It is almost as if Paul is claiming that trespasses *provoked* rectification, although he will reject that claim in 6:1–2.

Verse 17 again employs an argument from the lesser to the greater (as in v. 15 and earlier in 5:9–11), but this time the focus is explicitly on the question of who rules over humanity (Boring 1986, 269–92). The opening statement repeats exactly the opening of v. 15b ("since many people died through the trespass of one person"), but rather than "many people died," Paul writes that Death ruled as a king. Here his assumption comes to the surface: "many people died" *because* Death was ruler. The consequences of God's gracious act come into view with the second half of the verse, which picks up the terms of v. 15b (grace and gift) and anticipates the rule of those who receive these through Jesus Christ.

Not only does Death enter through the trespass of Adam, but Death ruled "through that same one." The "through" (*dia*) phrase seems superfluous, since Paul has repeatedly traced Death's rule to Adam, even at the beginning of the verse. Yet this "one" contrasts with the *dia* ("through") phrase in the second half of the verse, where "those . . . will rule in life through Jesus Christ."

The comment that many will rule comes as something of a surprise. Based on what has preceded, we anticipate a statement paralleling v. 17a—that is, as Death ruled, then grace or God will rule (a conclusion that comes finally in v. 21). Paul writes instead, "Those who receive the abundance of grace and the gift of righteousness [will] rule in . . . life." The notion that some human "they" will rule startles, given the earlier emphasis on the corrupt character of human life and its utter captivity (e.g., 1:24, 26, 28; 3:10–18) and the insistence on God's own power (e.g., 1:16). This promise of future rule anticipates ch. 6, with its reassurance of new life that is delivered from the disempowering grasp of Sin. It also anticipates the identification of believers as Christ's fellow heirs (8:15–17) and the declaration that "we" are supervictors (8:37).

Crucially, those who will reign are those who have *received from God*. Those who have been ruled over by Sin and Death will become rulers through God's agency. Also importantly, Paul never identifies the "they" here in such a way as to eliminate any category of human beings. What identifies the "they" who will rule is their reception from God and their rule, not their own achievement or any set limitations on the group.

Throughout this passage, no qualifier limits either the number of those who were caught up in the powers of Sin and Death or those who were released by God's grace. The only possible qualifier here is the word "receive" in v. 17, which reflects no *decision* made or action taken by human beings but merely underscores the fact of God's gift (see also 1:5; 3:24; 5:2). Interpreters sometimes argue but more often simply assume that the "all" refers only to the "all" who believe (e.g., Byrne 340; Dunn 1:295; Moo 366). That limitation undermines Paul's argument, however. Adam's act unites the whole of humanity in Sin and Death. If Paul then contrasts Adam's act with that of Christ but restricts the act of Christ to believers, his argument falls apart, implying that Adam's disobedience is more powerful than Christ's obedience, since Adam influences all people and Christ only some. Paul's argument moves in the opposite direction: Christ's obedience implicates the whole of humanity, despite the fact that only some experience the gift of faith in the present (and see the discussion of 6:1–11).

[18–19] Paul offers two further comparisons, this time cast in positive terms, and here the comparison is specifically between the actions of Adam (trespass, disobedience) and the actions of Christ (right action, obedience).[25] The actions of Adam and those of Christ are alike in the sense that both affect all of humankind. Verse 18 begins with what has become a refrain in the passage, "as the trespass of one." This statement would scarcely be translatable outside its argumentative context, since it has no finite verb. In context, however, its meaning is clear. The earlier language of "many" has yielded again to that of "all," and the terms of vv. 15–16 (grace, gift, etc.) are replaced with "righteous act." The gift to which Paul refers is in fact the righteous act of Jesus's obedient death, language he will use in v. 19. But here the contrast is between transgression and righteous act—a closer equivalent.

Verse 19 restates the contrast. Adam's disobedience produced "many" sinners, and Jesus's obedience produced "many" righteous. As earlier, "many" here

25. The comparisons in vv. 15 and 16 each begin with *ouk* ("not"), while those in vv. 18–19 are expressed positively.

necessarily means all, given that Adam's action led to the world-encompassing grasp of Sin and Death.

[20–21] Another comment about the law intrudes, in this case one that would surely perplex Roman Christians: the law "sneaked in" in order to increase the trespass. How is it that the law, which God publicly gave to Israel by the agency of Moses, can be said to have sneaked in? The verb Paul uses here occasionally occurs in military contexts (Polybius, *Hist.* 1.7.3; 2.55.3; Plutarch, *Publ.* 17.2), a fact that may reinforce the notion of power at work in this passage. Once again, the comment (which Paul himself has sneaked in) goes undefended and unexplained, since Paul will finally bring together these various statements in ch. 7 to address what it is that Sin has done to God's holy law.[26] The second half of v. 21 comes full circle to the defeat of the powers of Sin and Death. As Sin once ruled through Death or even together with Death, now God's grace rules through Jesus Christ.

This long series of contrasts could well have been accomplished more economically, but the sheer presence of such repetition and restatement signals the importance Paul places on the comparison. The last verse is perhaps the most important, with its claim that grace superabounded. Where Sin is excessive, grace is superexcessive. The implication is that God's grace has defeated Sin. If Sin ruled and now grace rules, that means grace has dethroned Sin. This is no friendly resignation from power in favor of another ruler, no mere reshuffling of priorities.

Here Paul pairs *charis* ("grace") with the same active verbs he has used of Sin and Death (see also 5:15).[27] He could as easily have said "Jesus Christ" or "God," since it is God's grace to which he is referring. It may be that he does so by way of underscoring the character of this conflict. God's triumph over Sin and Death is not conflict for its own sake but for the sake of humankind subject to cosmic bullies (see 8:31–39; 16:20). Those on the receiving end of this protective action receive it precisely as gift, which Paul has already established is done without regard to merit.

In 1:16 Paul identified the gospel as God's saving power for all who believe, and in 3:21–26 he connected that right-making power with the death of Jesus for all, since all have sinned. With this passage he spells out the universal extent both of human captivity to Sin and of God's redemptive action in Jesus Christ. Nothing in this passage calls for repentance and forgiveness; nothing here interprets Jesus as the embodiment of Israel; nothing here extends the

---

26. As Cousar observes, the point in v. 20 regarding the law is "that its intrusion into the human predicament did nothing to help. It made matters worse rather than better" (1995, 199). At least this is the specter Paul raises, although in 7:7–25 he will overturn it with his argument about Sin's role.

27. Elsewhere in Paul's letters *charis* takes active verbs only in 2 Cor 4:15 and 12:9.

covenant to include gentiles along with Jews. The contrast is between one world-encompassing event and another.

Excursus: The Powers of Sin and Death

The use of uppercase for Sin and Death in this commentary calls for explanation. From as early as 1:18 the letter has demonstrated a profound concern with what Paul first names *hamartia* in 3:9.[28] Humans ("they") refused to acknowledge God, which resulted in their being "handed over" (1:24, 26, 28). No one did what was right before God (3:10–18).

In 5:12 and continuing through ch. 8, however, the focus changes from human actions or inactions (e.g., 3:18, "there is no fear of God before their eyes") to the actions of Sin and Death. Repeatedly in 5:12–7:25 Paul refers to Sin and Death as the subjects of active verbs:

> Sin entered (5:12)
> Death also entered (5:12)
> Death already ruled as king (5:14)
> Death ruled as king (5:17)
> Sin increased (5:20)
> Sin once ruled as king through Death (5:21)
> Death no longer lords it over him [Christ] like a king (6:9)
> Let God arise to put an end to Sin's reign (6:12)
> Sin will not lord it over you (6:14)
> Sin, by staking out its base of operations through the commandment, produced in me [Paul] every desire (7:8)
> Sin sprang to life (7:9)
> Sin, staking out its base of operations through the commandment, deceived me [Paul] and even killed me (7:11)
> Sin—so that it might be apparent as Sin—through the good produced death for me, so that Sin through the commandment might grow sinful beyond all measuring (7:13)[29]

Customarily these statements are categorized as personification, a stylistic device Paul uses more frequently in Romans 5–8 than anywhere else (Dodson 2008, 120–21). That designation is accurate from the point of view of literary analysis, although it runs the risk of minimizing the claims Paul is making, failing to do justice to a central feature of the letter, to say nothing of Paul's interpretation of the gospel.[30]

---

28. Preoccupation with Sin/sin is more prominent in Romans than elsewhere in Paul's letters, although contemporaneous Jewish texts display considerable concern with the problem; see the important survey in Brand 2013.

29. Note also the use of Sin with the participle "living" in 7:17, 20, rendered "Sin lives" in my translation.

30. "Calling this 'personification' does not do justice to the apocalyptic worldview within which Paul is operating" (Jewett 374). De Boer is closer to Paul when he characterizes Rom 5–8 as "Paul's mythologizing program" (2013, 1–20).

From this series of statements, it emerges that Paul does not think only in terms of wrongdoing, although he can certainly refer to such instances, as he does with the words "transgression" and "trespass" in this passage and elsewhere with "sins" (e.g., 4:7; 7:5; 11:27; 1 Cor 15:13, 17; Gal 1:4). Sin is nothing less than a suprahuman power, one that takes advantage of Adam's transgression to become enslaver of the human world, even of Christ himself (6:10). Sin's power is such that it can make use of God's holy law to deceive and kill even the one who genuinely desires to live by that law (7:7–25). In the gospel event of Jesus Christ, God condemned Sin in the flesh of Jesus (8:3), which means that God has defeated Sin.

To say that Sin produces sinning may appear to separate both from the human, rendering humans as innocent victims who are forced around, little more than puppets. That is clearly not the case, especially considering Paul's reminder in 6:19 that "you" presented yourselves to Sin as its obedient slaves.[31] Yet Sin has taken over the person (7:7–25) such that escape is impossible without intervention. The human (whether individual or social) cannot break the power of Sin or sinning by repenting and undertaking new life. A glance at the early sermons of Acts illuminates the difference; Peter and the Lukan Paul call for repentance (e.g., Acts 2:38; 17:30), but Paul's letters neither call for repentance nor recall an earlier repentance prior to baptism.[32]

As Sin's powerful partner, Death also extends its grasp into the whole human world, even over Jesus Christ himself. Death is defeated in the case of Jesus, but its power continues to threaten (8:38). And the power Paul identifies as Death produces both physical death and a kind of death in life, reflected in the notion of human beings as Sin's slaves.[33] Already Paul has gestured in the direction of that death in life when he portrays humanity as weak, godless sinners at enmity with God (5:6–11). This notion of Death as God's enemy, which recalls 1 Cor 15:26, 54–57, stands in some tension with contemporary notions of death as natural, notions that exist also in Scripture (e.g., Ps 90:10; Sir 17:1–2; Eccl 12:7) and perhaps even in Paul (Phil 1:20–23). But this natural event signals that things are out of their intended order, that redemption is required (as in Rom 8:20–24).[34]

A number of additional questions about the origin and ontology of these powers arise at this juncture, questions Paul does not address. He is less concerned with those questions than he is with saying what Sin and Death do and how God has dealt with them in Jesus Christ. This lack of concern with questions of ontology may be somewhat analogous to his comments about God; Paul is not preoccupied with describing God's

31. Susan Eastman aptly identifies humanity as "both captive and complicit" (2017, 111)

32. The point of drawing attention to this particular silence in Paul is not to diminish the importance of repentance, which is amply represented elsewhere in the Bible. For Paul, nonetheless, human repentance does not suffice to break the problem of Sin and Death.

33. Here Paul anticipates Orlando Patterson's penetrating analysis of slavery as a kind of social death; that is, slavery separates the enslaved from personal history or community (1982).

34. As de Boer puts it, for Paul "bodily dying is not a 'neutral' or 'natural' process. . . . Rather, the *resurrection* of the crucified Christ *from the dead* has revealed that physical demise is a terrible offense, the annihilation of the human person by an alien, inimical power" (1988, 184–85).

ontology or attributes but with God's saving actions. Similarly, he is concerned about what Sin and Death produce, not about what or who they are.

A few places in the letters allow us to glimpse fragmentary answers to these questions, nonetheless. When ch. 8 invokes a series of things that might endeavor to separate human beings from God's love, the series culminates with the phrase "any other creature" (8:39), implying that all the opposing forces in the list are also among God's creations. From this we may infer that these powers are themselves derived, secondary; any independence from God is mere illusion. Finally, like other agents that work against God, Sin and Death will not be able to triumph over God's love.

Both 1 Cor 15:25–27, 54b–56 and Phil 2:6–11 help to confirm and extend this portrait. In the former text, Paul anticipates God's ultimate triumph, when Christ puts all things under God's feet. Finally, God will triumph over all God's enemies, the last of whom is Death, which is entangled with Sin (1 Cor 15:25–26, 56). Philippians 2:6–11 anticipates that triumph with the claim that "every knee" will bend and "every tongue" will acknowledge the lordship of Jesus Christ to the glory of God. Given the comprehensive character of this statement—including beings in heaven and on earth and under the earth—Paul appears to include all creation, including even the anti-God powers. Taken together, these passages rule out any sense that Sin and Death and other anti-God powers exist independently of God's creation. The dualism at work here is limited and temporal.

Adapting from work of Jeffrey Burton Russell, I suggest that these are ontological metaphors. More than figures of speech, they are attempts to convey a reality that exists beyond the confines of language, attempts to give expression to the profound captivity of human beings, a captivity that extends beyond the individual or even the corporate community to include all of creation (as in Rom 8:18–23).[35]

In a few places, Paul also employs the noun "grace" (*charis*) with active verbs and contrasts it with Sin and Death: grace "multiplied" (5:15, 20), grace "might rule as king" (5:21), grace "might grow" (6:1). Although "righteousness" (*dikaiosynē*) does not take active verbs, it is contrasted with Sin as the new place of Christian obedience (6:16, 18). Strict consistency might dictate that these terms also take the uppercase, alongside Sin and Death. There is a significant difference between these two sets of terms, however. "Grace" and "righteousness" rather clearly serve as synecdoches for "God." By using the term "grace" instead of "God," Paul highlights the unmerited nature of God's action in Jesus Christ (see above on v. 21). Similarly, by choosing to identify righteousness as the new location of Christian obedience, Paul draws attention to the altered situation of the baptized, in that they now serve God, the God who is righteous and has made them right as well (3:26). Sin and Death are not synecdoches for the activity of some other

---

35. Gaventa 2013b, 72–75; Russell 1977, 7–8. Addressing the same set of questions, Matt Croasmun invokes emergence theory (2017). On the implications of Paul's discussion of Sin for pastoral care, see Gaventa 2004a.

agent, or at least no other agent is named. They are aspects of creation, yes, but they are not ways of talking about some other agent.

6:1–11 Mutually Exclusive Locations

In W. H. Auden's "For the Time Being: A Christmas Oratorio," King Herod contemplates the implications of Jesus's birth and comments, "Every criminal will say, 'I like committing crimes. God likes forgiving them. Really the world is admirably arranged.'"[36]

With this line Auden reveals his comprehension of the logic of Rom 6:1. Paul has just insisted in 5:20 that the increasing grasp of the power of Sin means grace itself increases all the more, so logically it might follow that sinning actually enhances the strength and extent of God's reign. That logic only obtains, however, if Sin is identified with individual instances of wrongdoing (lowercase "sins") and grace with forgiveness. Paul does not make such an assumption, as 5:12–21 makes clear: Sin and Death are instead powers that rule over human life, powers that produce more sinning and more dying, and grace is God's active, life-giving intervention on behalf of humankind.

Romans 6 takes up the question of Auden's King Herod, perhaps because Paul's own teaching and preaching have prompted this reaction. Yet the response Paul gives in 6:1–11 has less to do with countering Herod's objection (i.e., moral license) than it does with demonstrating that Sin and God's grace are two different kingdoms with two different rulers. They are mutually exclusive locations. Those who have been baptized into Christ, united with Christ's own death, do not live in territory controlled by Sin. Paul introduces this point with his question in v. 2, the remainder of the passage serves to unpack his answer. Romans 6:1–11, then, amounts to a recasting of 5:12–21, focusing on the results of Christ's death for those who are baptized rather than on the actions of Adam and Christ. All humanity is implicated in the rule of God's grace, but not all presently receive its benefits.

Chapter 5 introduced the language of "life" into the letter, especially the new life that God brings about in place of the reign of Sin and Death (vv. 10, 17, 18, 21; earlier, see 1:17 and 2:7), and the contrast between life and death dominates in 6:1–11. Parallel claims that "we" died to Sin's power and now live, not in the realm of Sin but in that of God (vv. 1, 11) mark the opening and closing of the passage. This assertion of the new living arrangement is supported by an extended argument about death: first, death in baptism and transfer into new life (vv. 3–5); second, the way death with Christ destroys the rule of Sin (vv. 6–7);

---

36. Auden 1976, 394. The poem carries Rom 6:1 as an epigram, making Auden's dependence on Rom 6:1 both clear and deliberate.

and third, the coherence of death and new life with the defeat of Death and Sin in the resurrection of Jesus Christ (vv. 8–10).

More than earlier in the letter, the resurrection comes to the foreground here. The resurrection of Christ, who was himself under the power of Sin and Death (vv. 9–10), instigates the movement of the baptized from death to life. Not incidentally, Paul specifies in v. 4 that it is God's own glory that raised Christ from the dead.

The repetition throughout this section (as in 5:12–21) suggests its importance for Paul.

6:1 So, what does this mean? "Let's continue with sinning, so that grace might grow?"[a] 2 Of course not! Since we died to Sin's grasp,[b] how can we possibly still live there? 3 Or don't you understand? When we were baptized into Christ Jesus we were actually baptized into his death. 4 That means that, through baptism, we were buried with him into his death, so that as Christ was raised from the dead by the glory of the Father, we also might exist in newness, in life.[c] 5 For since[d] we have been united in a death like his,[e] we will certainly also be united to his resurrection.[f] 6 We know that our old self was crucified together with Christ,[g] so that the body that was governed by Sin[h] would be done away with and we would no longer be enslaved to Sin, 7 because the one who died has been released[i] from Sin. 8 And since[j] we died with Christ, we trust that we will also live with him 9 because we know that Christ, who was raised from the dead, is not going to die again: Death no longer lords it over him like a king.[k] 10 For the death he died, he died once only, death to Sin; but the life he lives, he lives to God. 11 So think of yourselves in this same way, as dead to Sin but living to God in Christ Jesus.

a. The quotation marks are supplied because Paul is imagining a misinterpretation of his previous comments (see below). Since the misinterpretation construes sin as an act rather than a power, "sinning" is here rendered in lowercase.

b. "Grasp" does not appear in the Greek but is supplied to reflect the notion of power at work in Paul's understanding.

c. The genitive is epexegetical (cf. "a sign—circumcision" in 4:11 and "rectification, that is, to life" in 5:18). The context suggests that Paul is talking about more than the renewal of life but about newness, bringing it closer to the "new creation" language of Gal 6:15 and 2 Cor 5:17.

d. Most often translated "if we have been united" (KJV, NRSVue, NIV), *ei* here has the connotation of "since," as it often does elsewhere (as in Matt 6:30; 1 Cor 9:11; see BDF §372; BDAG, s.v. *ei*; similarly, see Rom 8:10–11). "Our" unity with Christ (in v. 8 "our" death with Christ) is not a possibility Paul is exploring but a fact whose consequences he is exposing.

e. Lit., "to the likeness of his death," just as 5:14 refers to "those who sinned in the likeness of Adam" (i.e., "just as Adam did").

f. The second half of the verse is elliptical; lit., "we will be of the resurrection." The translation assumes that the *symphytoi* ("united to") of v. 5 governs the second half as well. The adversative particle *alla* (lit., "but") that introduces the apodosis joins the two clauses, underscoring its reality ("certainly"), as in 1 Cor 8:6; 9:2; 2 Cor 4:16; 5:16; 11:6 (see BDAG s.v.).

g. "With Christ" is supplied for clarity, on the grounds that the "crucified together" implies it. In addition, Paul has already indicated in v. 3 that "our" death is connected with Christ's own.

h. Lit., "body of sin," rendered here as a genitive of possession; cf. "body ruled by this Death" in 7:24.

i. Lit., "has been rectified," but *dikaioō* can have the sense of "made free," as in Acts 13:39; Sir 26:29; BDAG s.v.

j. See note d.

k. Paul's use of the verb *kyrieuō* (here "lords it over") is almost always negative, as in 6:14; 7:1; 2 Cor 1:24. See also Luke 22:25; Gen 37:8 LXX; Exod 15:9; Isa 3:12; 19:4.

[6:1–2] The opening question recasts the earlier statement of 3:8 ("Are we saying that we should do evil so that good may come?"). The question will return again in a slightly different form in 6:15: "Does that mean we should sin, since we aren't under law but under grace?" This question may suggest that Paul stands accused of promoting or permitting moral laxity, but there are problems with that assumption. If Paul has personally been accused of participating in or condoning immoral behavior, we would expect a direct, perhaps even fierce denial of the accusation, particularly in a context where he is unknown to many people and thereby even more subject to the whispers of others. Alternatively, he might offer straightforward ethical instruction such as that found in 1 Thess 4:1–12, or he might at least report that he offered such instruction to his congregations elsewhere. Particularly because he is writing from Corinth (see Rom 15:25–27; 16:21–23), where he has engaged very specific questions of Christian conduct, we would expect a forthright declaration about his practices and expectations if he thought his moral conduct or instruction were being called into question.

In the absence of such self-defense or ethical instruction, the question of v. 1 appears to play a different role. Rather than responding to critique, the question distorts the implications of 5:12–21 to make room for an emphatic restatement and amplification of that section. It is as if the bright but slightly resistant student in the back of the room, who has been waiting for an opportunity to find the crack in the argument, now pounces with a (willful?) misinterpretation of what Paul has said.[37] By transposing Paul's words about Sin's power into this

---

37. That analogy is consistent with understanding this and similar questions in Romans as employing the style of the diatribe.

absurd claim that Christians should promote sinning in order to promote grace, the question permits or even requires Paul to clarify further.

The question also marks a slight shift in the argument. Romans 6:1–11 turns away from the contrast between the actions of Adam and Christ and the rise and defeat of Sin and Death produced by those actions. Attention now falls on the results for the baptized of the triumphant power of grace (i.e., God's action in Jesus Christ), which liberates humanity from Sin and Death. The shift from third-person in 5:12–21 ("all," "every") to first-person plural signals that Paul now refers to those who already experience the reality of the universal Christ event.[38]

The emphatic "Of course not!" (*mē genoito*) in 6:2 introduces Paul's response in the form of a second question: "Since we died to Sin's grasp, how can we possibly still live there?" This contrast between Sin's toxic grasp and grace's empowerment for life runs throughout the passage, culminating in the declaration of v. 11 that "you" are "dead to Sin but living to God in Christ Jesus." The contrast sets the agenda for the letter through 7:6 as Paul patiently explores the incompatibility between life in Jesus Christ and death in the territory occupied by Sin and Death. It is impossible to live simultaneously in two places, both among the living and among the dead.

Paul is not saying that "we" *cannot* sin; if he held a perfected or perfectionistic understanding of humanity in Christ, he would scarcely find it necessary to include the moral exhortation that appears in 12:1–15:13 and elsewhere in his letters. To be sure, actual transgressions would offer a symptom of continuing in Sin's realm, but the question here is not so much whether "we" continue to do things that are wrong or abstain from good actions. The question concerns where "we" live, as becomes clear in what follows. If "we" are no longer God's enemies (see 5:19), then what are "we"? Whose kingdom is it, and whose side are "we" on?

[3–4a] Having said that "we died," Paul now explains in what sense that is so (vv. 3–4a) and then what consequences death has for life in the present (vv. 4b–8). The introduction of baptism may seem unusual, particularly if baptism is identified with washing for the forgiveness of sins (as in, e.g., Mark 1:4; Acts 2:38; Heb 6:2), but that interpretation of baptism ill fits Paul's comments here or elsewhere (although see 1 Cor 15:29).[39] Paul also seems unconcerned about offering instructions as to how baptism is to be carried out (as the author of the Didache will do a few decades after Paul's time, as in Did 7.1–4). For Paul, baptism is nothing less than incorporation into Christ himself, resulting

---

38. The logic of 2 Cor 5:18 is comparable: in Christ God is reconciling the entire world, but "we" are God's ambassadors.

39. As Tannehill observes, Paul's concern here is not primarily to offer his interpretation of baptism (1967, 7).

in the impossibility of remaining in the power of Sin (6:1). The assertion "We were baptized into Christ Jesus," then, means a change of lordship, consistent with what has been argued already in 5:12–21, the implications of which Paul will develop further in 6:12–23.

To this point, Paul's comments about baptism reflect his earlier letters, in which baptism means incorporation into Christ (Gal 3:27; 1 Cor 12:13), even entry into the single community that is Christ's body (Tannehill 1967, 23–24). Paul takes the argument a step further, however, by explicitly connecting baptism with Christ's death. This move departs from his earlier letters,[40] and the introductory formula "Or don't you understand?" may well signal that Paul knows this is an unusual move to make, one that has to be reinforced. How baptism is baptism "into his death" has to do not with the form of baptism (some equivalency between death and baptismal practice) but with the finality of the act for believers: it separates them from the lordship of Sin and Death and transfers them into the lordship of Christ by virtue of the fact of Jesus's death on the cross.[41] Baptism brings the cross's power to expression in the life of the baptized.

The lines that follow reinforce the connection between baptism and the death of Christ through repetition, as this more literal translation demonstrates:

v. 3a   We were baptized into Christ Jesus
v. 3b   into his death we were baptized
v. 4a   Therefore we were buried together with him
         through baptism into death.

Later elements of the passage further reinforce the claim that believers have died:

v. 5a   We were united in the likeness of his death
v. 6a   Our old self was crucified together
v. 7a   The one who died
v. 8a   Since we died

Verse 4a introduces a small but revealing variation on the repeated insistence that baptism into Christ is baptism into his death: "We were buried with him." At first glance, being "buried with" simply means being joined to Christ through baptism. Reflection on ancient burial practices suggests something more, however. While burial practices varied across the Mediterranean world for a range of reasons having to do with status, ethnic identity, and geographical location,

---

40. Mark 10:38 and Luke 12:50, however, do interpret Jesus's own death as baptism in a way that calls believers to radical identification with him.
41. Tannehill's discussion of this point remains crucial (1967, 21–34).

burial generally meant burial with family members. That expectation appears in Scripture (e.g., 1 Kgs 14:31; 15:24; 22:50) as well as elsewhere (Josephus, *Ant.* 10.48; *J.W.* 1.551; Herodotus, *Hist.* 5.5; Sabou 2005, 90–93), and it is reinforced by archaeological evidence (Hachlili and Killebrew 1983; Ubelaker and Rife 2011; Walbank 2005). Being buried with Christ, then, means not only being united to Christ Jesus but also being united to his "family," a family that Paul will later identify as the sons and daughters of God (8:14–16, 29–30).

The repetition of the prefix *syn-* in the lines that follow reinforces this connection between the baptized and Jesus: v. 5, *symphytoi* ("united"); v. 6, *systauroomai* ("crucified together"); v. 8, *syzaō* ("live with"). The repetition may also anticipate the bringing together of Jews and gentiles that Paul seeks to further with this letter: one sign of the gospel's work is the unity of Jew and gentile in praise of God (15:7–13).

The death to which Paul refers is very specifically Jesus's physical death on the cross. That death is no isolated event for Paul, however; it is nothing less than the working of the power of Death depicted in 5:12–21.[42] The connection between the physical death of Jesus and the anti-God powers comes to expression in 6:9–11, where Paul makes startling assertions implying that Sin and Death actually had Jesus himself in their grasp. Paul returns to this relationship in 8:32, where he writes that God did not withhold God's Son but handed him over (and see 4:25). Just as Sin produces sinning, Death can produce dying.[43]

[4b–c] With v. 4b, the connection between Christ's death and the death of believers in baptism yields to a connection between Christ's resurrection and the new life of believers. Paul introduces that connection with an elaborate statement about Christ's resurrection, namely, that "he was raised from the dead by the glory of the Father."

The resurrection of Christ is central to Paul's gospel, and he routinely attributes that event to God's action, even to the extent that God is identified as "the One who raised Jesus our Lord from the dead" (as in Rom 4:24; 8:11; 2 Cor 4:14; Gal 1:1).[44] Only here, however, does Paul comment that the resurrection takes place "by the glory of the Father." God's own glory figures importantly in the apocalyptic revelation of God's wrath in 1:18, since it is God's glory that humanity refuses to honor (1:21). In 3:23 the consequences of that denial are stated: humanity is removed from the presence of God's glory; in 5:2 one of the consequences of God's gift in Jesus Christ is that "we" are able to boast in

---

42. To be sure, the death of Jesus results from God's initiative (e.g., 3:25–26; 4:25; 5:6–8; 8:32), but the conflict between God and the anti-God powers provides the context for that initiative.

43. Simone Weil's essay on "force" or "power" in the *Iliad* offers an illuminating conversation partner for Romans at this point, as she explores the ways in which power consumes humanity, both the humanity of the temporarily powerful and that of its victims (2006).

44. There are exceptions, as in Rom 14:9 and 1 Thess 4:14. On the "naming" of God, see Watson 2006.

the "hope of God's glory" (and see 8:17–18). Only in 6:4, however, is God's glory said to *do* something.

By contrast with nonbiblical literature, where the word *doxa* ("glory") regularly conveys reputation (as in Josephus, *Life* 274) or even opinion (e.g., Plato, *Symp.* 202A), in the LXX the "glory of God" or the "glory of the LORD" concerns God's own presence, as in Exod 24:16: "The glory of the LORD came down upon Mount Sinai and the cloud covered it for six days" (see also, e.g., Exod 40:34; Lev 9:23; Ps 56:6 LXX; Ezek 11:23). More specifically, the "glory of God" (or of "the LORD") can also refer to God's presence in conflict, to God's triumph over enemies. The Song of Moses offers an excellent example:

> Your right hand, LORD, has been glorified in its strength.
> Your right hand, LORD, shattered the enemies.
> And by the size of your glory you crushed those who were hostile.
> You sent your wrath, and it devoured them like a reed. (Exod 15:6–7 LXX)

This passage is no oddity. Baruch promises Israel's exiles that the glory of God will save them from their enemies (4:24; 5:6, 7, 9). The Dead Sea Scrolls employ references to divine glory similarly (e.g., 1QH^a 11.33–37; CD^b 20.26), including instructions to community members to prepare banners for battle on which are inscribed the words "The Truth of God, the Righteousness of God, the Glory of God, the Justice of God" (1QM 4.6, 8; Gaventa 2014b).

When Paul claims that Christ was raised from the dead by the glory of the Father, then, he is saying something more than that there was a miracle of new or renewed life for one previously dead—more than, not other than. The resurrection is an act of divine power over against the powers that held Christ captive, namely, Sin and Death. The resurrection requires the very presence of God, who defeats God's enemies in order to reclaim the Son. The reference to God's glory, then, stands alongside the numerous other instances of conflict language in Romans (e.g., Gaventa 2013b).

Nothing less than God's powerful glory is required in order to remove "us" from the reign of Death and into "newness." The final clause of v. 4 states the result of Christ's resurrection for "us" in terms of newness that is life itself. A strict parallel with "Christ was raised" would be "we were [or will be] raised," but that statement only comes in v. 5, and even there it is somewhat oblique. Reasons for Paul's cautious wording lie as close as his dealings with Corinth, where assertions about the new life of believers apparently generated misunderstandings (as in 1 Cor 4:7–13).

Instead of claiming that "we" are already raised, Paul moves from Christ's resurrection to the newness in life of "us." At first glance, "we walk in newness" is a rather tepid claim, suggesting that incorporation into the death and resurrection of Jesus Christ means mere renewal or refreshment. Paul cannot, of course, claim that believers already fully share in Christ's resurrection, especially in view of abundant evidence to the contrary. But the phrase *en kainotēti zōēs* suggests something other than simply enhanced spirituality or a new lease on life. It is closer to Paul's use elsewhere of the language of new creation (2 Cor 5:17; Gal 6:15). This is not Adam restored to the time before his own disobedience, but a new humanity. Three successive statements elaborate on this move between death and life (vv. 5, 6–7, 8).

[5–7] Verse 5 restates the consequences of Christ's death for "us" in a slightly different way, by returning to the language of "our" death in vv. 2–3 and affirming that we were "united" in a death like his. Saying that "we" were united (*symphytoi*) with his death repeats what has already been said about the location of believers, their connection both with Christ's death and with one another.

Paul's claim that "we" were united in a death like Christ's employs the elusive word "likeness" (*homoiōma*). Paul uses the term later in 8:3 of Christ's being sent in the "likeness" (*homoiōma*) of human flesh, and in Phil 2:7 of Christ's being in the "likeness" (*homoiōma*) of humans. In both of those texts what Paul affirms is that Christ was actually a human being, even if he was also distinctly not just any human being. Similarly, in Rom 5:14 Paul refers to those who did not sin "in the likeness of the transgression of Adam" or "just as Adam did." The transgression was real, if not identical to Adam's in either nature or consequence. A similar logic obtains in 6:5: "We were united in a death like his." The believer's death at baptism, while real and transformative, is not death on behalf of others, as Christ's is said to be in 5:6, 8 and elsewhere; neither is it self-giving (as in Gal 2:20). The believer's death is also not physical, but the distinction between "spiritual" and "physical" misleads, at least to the extent that it conveys that the believer's death is somehow figurative, unreal, metaphorical. In Gal 2:19–20a Paul does not qualify the statement "I was crucified with Christ; I no longer live."

It is not only Christ's death to which "we" are united, since the end of v. 5 insists that "we" will also be united to his resurrection. Writing from Corinth, Paul is wary of prompting people to conclude they have already been raised from the dead. He is not at all wary, however, of insisting that belonging to Christ means that Christ's own triumph over death becomes the triumph of the believer as well. Paul does not linger over the future resurrected life, as his concern at this point is to articulate the regime change that has taken place and its present consequences. Nonetheless, this statement anticipates the striking words of assurance offered in 8:18–39 regarding the future awaiting God's children.

Verse 8 will economically restate v. 5, but between the two statements vv. 6–7 expand on the death "we" have experienced. Verse 6a begins by recasting v. 5a: "Our old self was crucified together with Christ." Literally the subject is "our former person" or "former human," making it possible that what

Paul has in mind is Adamic humanity, since he refers to Adam in ch. 5 as the *anthrōpos* (so 5:12, 19), but the "we" of 6:1–5 is not identical with Adamic humanity. Adamic humanity as a whole is scarcely crucified with Christ. The contrast of 5:12–21 is between the universal rule of Sin and Death through Adam's sin and the universal rule of grace through Christ's action, but that reign does not yet involve the whole of humanity in cocrucifixion. "Our old self" is also not simply a reference to the individual believer (contra Moo 396–97), for which we would expect the plural "persons" or "we." Instead, "our former person," "our old self," denotes the totality of prior life, viewed as a totality by the community of those joined together to Christ.[45]

The combination of "our old self" and "crucified together" intensifies preceding assertions about the death of believers by way of ushering in the important implications of v. 6a. The death of believers comes about for a purpose: so that the body governed by Sin would be done away with and "we" would no longer be enslaved to Sin. Neither language of the body nor language of enslavement has played a significant role in the letter up to this point, but both will do important work in chs. 7–8.[46] Shifting among various word groups is characteristic of this letter, but this shift is more than a stylistic quirk. The claim that the body was controlled by Sin, that it was released from enslavement, epitomizes in the strongest possible terms the human condition as depicted in 5:12–21.

The phrase "the body that was governed by Sin" refers to the person who is under Sin's ruling power. Rendering this as "sinful bodies" (CEV) feeds the assumption that Paul finds the human body—or flesh (*sarx*)—to be sinful in and of itself. That view is scarcely compatible with Paul's declaration that Jesus is from Israel's own flesh, to say nothing of the statements in 6:13 that believers should submit their own "limbs" (their very body parts) to God, and the summons in 12:1 to present their bodies to God sacrificially. "Body" instead refers to the whole person.

The existence of the human body during the reign of Sin and Death, however, was an existence under occupation. Sin ruled all human beings, thus becoming the possessor, so that "the body of Sin" is "the body that was governed by Sin." The destruction of this body is not, of course, physical, but it is nevertheless real as the grasp of Sin is being destroyed. Paul's assertion in Gal 2:19 closely parallels this one with its claim about cocrucifixion and Paul's declaration "I died." In both cases, what is at issue is showing why it is that "we" cannot possibly live under both Sin's reign and that of Christ.

45. That interpretation appears to be consistent with the way the phrase is used Eph 4:22 and Col 3:9.
46. "Body" (*sōma*) appeared in 1:24 regarding the dishonoring of the body and in 4:19 regarding the "death" of Sarah's body. The noun "slave" referred to Paul himself in 1:1 ("Paul, slave of Christ Jesus"), but neither that noun nor the related verb has appeared since that opening verse.

The final clause of v. 6 makes this interpretation of "body that was governed by Sin" explicit by stating its opposite: "we" are no longer enslaved to Sin. The harsh language of slavery will be much more prominent in the paragraphs that follow, but Paul has already prepared for it. Sin's lording it over humanity (5:17, 21) is scarcely an image that Paul or his auditors would experience as benign. Similarly, the relationship between slavery and death is well established. Not only is slavery physically violent, but it produces the death of the person by separating her from home, from family, from identity. It is not accidental that Paul's contemporaries regarded slaves as nonpersons, because in significant ways they had been separated from their lives.[47] That "we" were enslaved to Sin conveys the utter hopelessness of the human situation prior to the Christ event.

Excised from context, v. 7 might be confused for a gnomic utterance: "The one who died has been released from Sin." Claims to that effect do appear (e.g., Dunn 1:320–21; Jewett 404); the inclusion of such a general observation would be odd indeed, however, given Paul's earlier lengthy discussion of how all are under Sin. If natural death produces freedom from Sin, then there would be no need of God's action to liberate human beings, as nature would bring about the same result. The statement could refer to Christ himself, particularly in view of vv. 9–10, which place Christ's own life within the grasp of both Sin and Death. In context, however, the "one who died" appears to be a resumptive reference, taking up "our old self" from v. 6a.

[8–11] Verses 8–11 begin with a restatement of the death and future resurrection of the baptized but then move on to anchor that expectation in Christ's own death and life. Verse 8 largely summarizes the content of vv. 4 and 5: the baptized died with Christ, and in the future they will live with him. The slight difference here is the use of the verb "we trust" or "we believe" (*pisteuomen*) to introduce the apodosis: "Since we died with Christ, we trust that we will also live with him."[48]

The grounds for this trust are then articulated in vv. 9–10, in terms of both Death and Sin, recalling the partnership of these two in 5:12–21. Verse 9 opens with the claim that Christ's resurrection means he will not die again. This assertion does not implicitly contrast Christ's resurrection with that of others (Lazarus, e.g., contra Cranfield 1:313, Moo 402), as Paul never expresses interest in or knowledge about those miracle stories. The only comments he makes about resurrections other than that of Christ are about those who in the future will be raised together with Christ (as in 1 Thess 4:14–16; 1 Cor 15:12–57). When he

---

47. Orlando Patterson's classic study of slavery across centuries and cultures demonstrates, in the language of his title, that slavery is "social death" (1982).

48. A similar logic operates in Paul's early letter to the Thessalonians, where the reminder that "we believe Jesus died and rose" anchors his assurance that "we will always be with the Lord" (1 Thess 4:14, 17).

affirms that Christ will not die again, it is precisely because Death is no longer ruler over Christ, as Death had been ruler over all people (Rom 5:14). Verse 10 introduces Death's partner, Sin, with its assertion that Christ's death was a one-time event in which he died to Sin's power. His resurrection means that he lives to God, and therefore he is beyond the grasp of Sin and Death.

These statements are often passed over rather quickly, but they mark out crucial elements in Paul's Christology. Not only did Jesus Christ descend from the Davidic line (1:3), a bearer of Israelite flesh (9:4; and see Gal 4:4), but Jesus was under the grasp of Sin and Death (see also Rom 8:3). Christ entered fully into the human condition, the human condition as defined by Adam's disobedience and its consequences. Just as "all" humanity was ruled by the devastating partnership of Sin and Death, so was Christ. Christ too was subject to Sin's power and to Death's grasp.

Taking this claim seriously does not involve the question whether Christ himself committed sinful acts, a question in which Paul displays no interest. To be sure, 2 Cor 5:21 states that God "made the one who did not know sin to be sin on our behalf," but that statement is ambiguous. It can mean Christ did not know Sin's rule prior to his entry into human flesh, or it can refer more generally to Christ's "identification with sinful humanity" (Furnish 1984, 340). Concern about Christ's own sinlessness seems more consistent with Hebrews and its claims for the purity of Christ's sacrifice than with Romans (as in Heb 4:15 and 7:26–28).

Paul's concern instead is to locate Christ firmly within the world Sin and Death have entered and in which they have taken control (5:12; see also 8:4). It is within that world, dominated by Sin and Death, that conflict with these powers takes place.[49] God does not act as an isolated, external power, whose determination to defeat the enemy extends only to the launching of a drone attack from a safe distance. It is within the world of Sin and Death that Christ's action takes place. This is nothing less than a claim about the reality of the incarnation.

That reality implicates Christ in the vulnerability of the human condition. To enter the world controlled by Sin and Death means loss, powerlessness, and susceptibility to suffering. Similarly, the assertions in 4:25 and 8:32 about Christ's being "handed over" signal his vulnerability as a result of the incarnation.

Verse 10b epitomizes the defeat of Sin and Death with the pithy assertion that "the life he [Christ] lives, he lives to God." Paul does not elsewhere make such statements about Jesus's own resurrection, but they resemble the formulation regarding believers in 14:8 and the assertion he makes about himself in Gal 2:19–20 (an assertion that implicates others as well). Characteristic of Paul's understanding of the Christ event is that it means life "to God" or "for

---

49. "Christ died for this reason—to destroy sin and cut out its sinews," observed Chrysostom (*Homily* 11.2; PG 60:485–86; Burns 141).

God." Here he connects that life with Christ himself: "our" life with Christ, both present and future, comes about by virtue of Christ's own resurrected life with God. The contrast between this life with God and life under the rule of Sin and Death could scarcely be sharper (as Paul will elaborate in Rom 6:12–23). There is no question of a treaty giving the two sides shared power. There will be no consolidated government.

Verse 11 culminates this extended contrast between death to Sin and life with an important shift to the imperative mood (and see further in vv. 12–23). Paul addresses this directive to "you" with an emphatic pronoun: "Think of yourselves in this same way, as dead to Sin but living to God in Christ Jesus." Similar statements have preceded:

v. 2a	We died to Sin's grasp
v. 3	We were baptized into his death
v. 4a	We were buried with him into his death
v. 4b	We also might exist in newness, in life
v. 5a	We have been united in a death like his
v. 5b	We will certainly also be united to his resurrection
v. 6a	Our old self was crucified together with Christ
v. 8	Since we died with Christ, we trust that we will also live with him

What v. 11 introduces is not new information about the death and life of the baptized, but the call to "think of yourselves" in this new way.

In vv. 12–23 Paul will offer a series of admonitions that reflect this radical change of lordship, but prior to that series he offers what is tantamount to a new identity for the baptized. They are no longer the "dead in Sin's grasp" but are instead "living to God in Christ Jesus." Just as God has a new name (the One who raised Jesus from the dead), humanity has a new name—and therefore a new identity—as well. In the argument that follows, Paul will call believers by a series of names, including "slaves of righteousness," "children of God," and "coheirs of Christ." Consciously or not, Paul replaces the old identification with a new one, implicitly inviting his auditors into a life that is shaped by this new identity.[50]

It is customary to label this chapter as ethical instruction or exhortation (so, e.g., Fitzmyer 429; Dunn 1:305). Yet what Paul is arguing here is both less and more than ethical exhortation. It is less in the sense that there are no specifics

50. A suggestive conversation partner for this move is the climactic scene in the 2006 film *Blood Diamond*, in which a father searches for his son, a child forced into the role of slave-soldier. When the two meet, the son, captive to the world he has inhabited for years, points a gun directly at his father. The father addresses him, beginning with the words, "You are Dia Vandy of the Proumanday Tribe." The father goes on to recall the son's life before his capture and the love of the family that waits desperately for his return, in the hope that he can wrench his son back into life. Paul's prose lacks the cinematic drama of *Blood Diamond*, but the contrast he presents is even larger, involving, as it does, not restoration but new life.

here, no principles, no admonitions (and even those that follow in 6:12–23 are quite general).[51] Paul scarcely imagines that the baptized will avoid sinning (transgressing) altogether, although the passage was read that way by some of its earliest interpreters. Labeling this as ethical instruction misses the radical claims being made, both about Christ's own death and resurrection and that of believers.

This section is far more than ethical exhortation, concerned as it is with lives claimed fully and completely for God. Similarly, at a pivotal turning point, 12:1 urges the presentation of the whole person. The label *ethical exhortation* tends to minimize and routinize, asking after the bottom line. The claim Paul is making is more profound than can be captured in a series of moral urgings; instead, it involves the inhabiting of a new identity as people in Christ. They receive this new identity by virtue of Christ's own defeat of Sin and Death, and they anticipate the final realization of that triumph in and with their very bodies. They are by no means exempted from danger in the present time, however, as Paul hints in 6:12–23 and will unpack in 8:31–39.

6:12–23 No One Serves Two Masters

It is impossible to live both in the realm of Sin and in that of Christ Jesus, Paul has claimed in 6:1–11. The two territories are mutually exclusive, made so by God's powerful resurrection of Christ, an act that delivered Christ himself from the rule of Sin and Death. Baptism joins "us" to Christ's death, joins "us" to his burial, and grants "us" new life in the present and the promise of resurrection. This hopeful word is part and parcel of the hope for God's eschatological triumph. As we see in Rom 8, to say nothing of 1 Cor 15, resurrection locates the addressees firmly within the context of God's future. Hope is hope precisely because it is hope in God's future. The section concludes with v. 11, where Paul turns from first-person plural to second-person plural with the admonition that "you" should think of yourselves as having this new identity because "you" are not dead but alive.[52]

Sin and Death remain powerful, nevertheless, and the baptized have not escaped from the world.[53] They live in a world in which there are powers

---

51. Compare this passage with, e.g., 1 Thess 4:1–12 or 1 Cor 7:1–40.

52. Some scholars mark a new section with the question "What then? Does that mean we should sin?" in v. 15, which parallels 6:1 (e.g., Wilckens 2:33; Moo 422; Jewett 391). The advantage of beginning with v. 12 is that the notion of "presenting" the self for duty begins with vv. 12–14 and carries over into v. 16. Further, v. 11 concludes with the phrase "to God in Christ Jesus," recalling the final words in 5:11 and 5:21 (see also 6:23; 7:25; 8:39). In any case, the two sections are deeply interconnected; separating them is largely a matter of convenience for contemporary readers. Phoebe's auditors would not have noted a transition.

53. Paul is writing from Corinth (see 16:23), where it appears that some people have imagined themselves as impervious to the pull of wrongdoing (see, e.g., 1 Cor 2:14–3:4; 5:1–2). He may well

that actively work to separate them from God (see especially 8:35–39). That vulnerability may be glimpsed in 6:12–23, where Paul depicts the opposing powers with three conceptual domains:

> Rulership: reign, lord it over
> Slavery: slave, become a slave, obey (in a slavelike way)
> Military conflict: weapons, wages, perhaps also "handing over"

The intersection of these domains gives them considerable argumentative force. The Roman world knew all too well the capacity of rulers (whether heads of households or Caesar himself) for enslaving power. The use of military force was common, and a primary means of acquiring slaves was through warfare (with piracy as a significant alternative; Scheidel 2011).

This is the world Paul evokes in vv. 12–23, contrasting it at every point with the life of the baptized, who have been liberated (redeemed) from this enslavement and now belong to a different world:

> Rulership of God
> Enslavement to God
> Weapons for God

The apocalypse of God's saving power does not take place in the absence of conflict. The question in this passage is no longer who is in charge of the cosmos (as in 5:12–21), but what the triumph of God's glory in Jesus's resurrection looks like in the bodies of the baptized.

As before, there is considerable repetition in the argument, which would enhance its reception by Phoebe's auditors but which also suggests the importance for Paul of the point being developed. Something crucial is at stake in this passage that goes well beyond a simple response to the charge of moral indifference or even moral license. (Indeed, Paul's comment in vv. 14 and 15 would scarcely reassure his audience about his concern for the law, as ch. 7 evidences.)

6:12 Therefore, let God arise to put an end to Sin's reign[a] in your mortal body, ending obedience to the body's[b] desires![c] 13 And do not present your limbs to Sin any more[d] as weapons of wrongdoing, but present yourselves to God as people once dead and now living, and present your limbs to God as weapons of righteousness. 14 For Sin will not lord it over you, since you are not under law but under grace. 15 What then? Does that mean we should sin, since we aren't under law but under grace? Of course not! 16 Don't you know, when you present yourselves as obedient

---

have had the Corinthians in mind as he composed this section. Here and elsewhere, especially in 8:31–39, Paul makes clear that life remains "open to the attacks of the powers of the old dominion" (Tannehill 1967, 11).

slaves, you are slaves of the one you obey? Either you are slaves of Sin, yielding death, or slaves of obedience, yielding righteousness. 17 Thanks be to God—because you were slaves of Sin, but you became obedient from the heart to the imprint[e] of the teaching to which you were handed over, 18 and having been freed from Sin you became slaves for righteousness. 19 (I am speaking now about the human situation, because of the weakness of your flesh.) For as you earlier presented your limbs as slaves to impurity and to lawlessness yielding lawlessness, so now present your limbs as slaves to righteousness yielding holiness. 20 For when you were slaves of Sin, then you were free at least as far as righteousness goes. 21 And what fruit did you have back then? Things of which you are now ashamed, for the result of those things is death. 22 But now, having been freed from Sin and having been made slaves of God, you have your fruit for holiness, the result of which is eternal life. 23 For Sin pays its soldiers with death, but God's free gift is eternal life in Christ Jesus our Lord.

a. The third-person imperative (lit., "let Sin not reign") functions as a prayer for God's intervention, similar to that found in 3:4 (although with God as the subject of the imperative); Pss 7:7–10 LXX; 67:2–4 LXX; and often elsewhere (Marcus 1988, 389–90). When the phrase is rendered as "do not let sin reign" (as in NRSVue, NASB, NIV, NET), English-speaking audiences assume that the implied addressee is "you," but the parallels elsewhere suggest that the implied addressee is God.

b. Some early manuscripts read *autē* instead of *autou*, deleting the reference to the body's desires and construing the obedience as obedience to Sin rather than to desires (including 𝔓[46] D* F G). In addition, some manuscripts add *autē en tais* prior to "the body's desires," resulting in "obedience to Sin through the body's desires" (including C[3] Ψ K L P). The reading employed above (*tais apithymiais autou*) has solid evidence (including 𝔓[94] ℵ A B C*), and the others can easily be explained as harmonizations to the comment about obeying Sin in v. 16.

c. This translation construes the *eis* phrase, often rendered "so that you obey," less as a consequence of the preceding clause than as an implication or an explanation, following Wallace (1996, 592).

d. "Any more" reflects the difference between the present imperative (*paristanete*) and the aorist imperative (*parastēsate*).

e. Lit., the "form" of the teaching, but the word *typos* is used elsewhere of an impression such as that left by a ring upon a block of wax, as in Plato, *Theaet.* 192A, 194B; Philo, *Worse* 24.86; *Embassy* 31.210; *Spec. Laws* 1.20.106. (Gagnon 1993 offers numerous examples, and see further below.)

[12–14] "Therefore" at the outset of v. 12 is no vacant transition marker. Because the baptized have experienced death with Christ and now inhabit a new life with him, Paul is able to make imperative statements. To put the matter bluntly, admonishing the dead is unlikely to produce results. Even as Paul admonishes the living, however, he continues to locate his admonitions within the parameters established by God's actions. The baptized are not agents acting solely from their own resources.

The precise character of these early admonitions warrants careful attention. Verse 13 addresses "you" with two unambiguous imperatives ("do not present . . . but present . . ."), but those imperatives are surrounded by an invocation of God's power over Sin and a promise that Sin's reign will not succeed:

>   v. 12   Let God arise to put an end to Sin's reign in your mortal body
>   v. 14   For Sin will not lord it over you

These two verses control the instruction of v. 13. Similar juxtaposition of prayer and admonition appears elsewhere in Paul's letters. Later in Romans the admonition "welcome one another" introduces a rehearsal of God's action and a final prayer for God to fill the audience with "joy and peace" (15:7–13). First Thessalonians 5:23–24 follows a string of imperatives with a prayer for God's preservation of the addressees and concludes with a promise: "The One who calls you is faithful. God will do this" (5:24). In all these instances, ethical instruction assumes divine sustenance.

The prayer of v. 12 similarly invokes God's power as Paul prepares to exhort the Romans. He has just asserted that Death no longer lords it over (*kyrieuō*) Christ, who died to Sin's grasp (vv. 9–10). He now invokes God's power to bring an end to Sin's reign (*basileuō*, see 5:21) over the baptized as well. The use of a third-person imperative to call upon God is familiar from the Psalter:

>   Ps 7:7, 10 LXX   Arise, Lord, in your wrath . . .
>   *let the wickedness of sinners* be brought to an end.
>   Ps 67:2 LXX   Let God arise, and *let God's enemies* be scattered.[54]

Although Rom 6:12 differs in that God is not directly invoked, God's involvement has already been recalled earlier, especially in 6:4, where Christ's resurrection is said to be achieved by God's own glory.

Paul prays that Sin should not reign "in your mortal body." By contrast with Christ, who has died and will not die again, the bodies of the baptized continue to be subject to the limits of death. The fragility of the mortal body, the very fact that the body is mortal, in itself suggests that the imperative at the beginning of v. 12 needs to be read as addressed to God: only God would be capable of ending Sin's reign. Further, "mortal body" is one of several expressions in this passage that underscore the reality of the conflict involved ("limbs," "flesh"). It has to do with the concrete being of humans in the world.

---

54. Numerous additional examples appear in Marcus 1988, 389–90.

The remainder of this verse further depicts Sin's rule: it involves obeying the desires of the body. Verses 16–17 will repeat the language of obedience, providing a clue to its importance for Paul. He does not, however, spell out what obedience looks like in specific terms of attitudes or activities to be taken up or avoided. Obedience instead has to do with who one's lord is: Is it Sin or is it God?[55] The point comes to the surface a few lines below in v. 16: the one who is obeyed is the ruler. This association of obedience with an authority to be obeyed seems obvious enough, yet it may shed light on Paul's use of the word "obedience" elsewhere. In 1:5 he describes "our" vocation as that of bringing about the "obedience that comes from faith for the sake of his name," that is, the alignment with the gospel of God's Son (see also 10:16; 15:18; 16:19; [16:26]). Interestingly, "obedience" appears also in 2 Cor 10:5–6, where Paul depicts apostolic labor in martial terms.[56] First and foremost, Paul is not so much showing what obedience or its opposite looks like in the sense of offering concrete instructions; rather, obedience has to do with knowing on which side one serves.

That Paul refers to obedience "to its [the mortal body's] desires" sheds little light on the specific character of the desire, despite numerous efforts to pin it down as, for example, the desire for honor (Jewett 409). In 1:24, the only prior use of "desire" (*epithymia*) in the letter, God is said to have handed "them" over to "the desires of their hearts," an action that manifested itself in a number of results, chief among them idolatry. The desires "they" brought to life had to do precisely with withholding recognition from God, seeking to escape from God's authority, from the recognition of "their" status as God's creatures. Further, as 7:7–8 will demonstrate, warning about desire is evocative precisely because desire itself is voracious, regardless of its object.

In 6:14 Paul will assure the Romans of the reliability of God's lordship over Sin, but first he calls for their participation in God's realm. In this instance, however, instead of warning about specific vices and admonishing virtues, Paul again articulates the situation in terms of conflicting powers—that is, "your" obedience has to do with "your" alignment with one of the two sides in this conflict. No neutral territory exists; no one can opt out of this conflict. Two statements closely parallel one another, making the differences between them significant, as this more literal sketch indicates:

v. 13a	Do not	present your limbs anymore	as weapons of wrong to Sin
v. 13b	But	present yourselves	to God as living from the dead
	and	[present] your limbs	as weapons of righteousness to God

55. In the memorable language of Nancy Duff, "Ethics is not centered in knowing what is the good, but in knowing who is our Lord" (1989, 283).
56. See also 2 Cor 7:15; Phil 2:12; and Phlm 21. Only in Phlm 21 does "obedience" (*hypakoē*) suggest conforming to a particular expectation, in that case a request from Paul.

In both halves of v. 13, "you" are "weapons" (*hopla*), either of Sin or of God. With this term Paul indicates yet again that God is in conflict with a powerful entity known as Sin. The term *hopla* itself is overwhelmingly used of the physical materials employed in military campaigns, both in the LXX (e.g., 1 Sam 17:7; 2 Chr 32:5; 1 Macc 6:2) and elsewhere (e.g., Asclepiodotus, *Taktika* 5.1; 12.10–11; Sophocles, *Ant.* 115; Onasander, *Strategikos* 10.2; 12.1; 42.20–21; Josephus, *Life* 99; *J.W.* 1.76–77, 98). The word appears in a figurative sense in certain psalms, but those instances suggest, as Paul does, a God who fights on behalf of humanity (e.g., Pss 5:12 [5:13 LXX]; 35:2 [34:2 LXX]; 91:4 [90:4 LXX]).[57] Demosthenes uses *paristēmi* and *hopla* together for the putting forward (demonstrating) of armed force (*Cor.* 175.5; and see Asclepiodotus, *Taktika* 12.11).

The use of "weapons" further enhances the notion that v. 13 is an invocation of God's powerful intervention rather than an admonition for "you" to stop Sin's reign, since "weapons" exist for the use of any party in a conflict. Weapons do not themselves initiate or conduct the conflict. The combatants fight for control of humanity, rather than humanity initiating or conducting a conflict. No license can be found here for human beings to identify and declare their own war on God's enemies.[58]

Both sides of the present conflict also involve human "limbs" as weapons. "Limbs" is a fitting metonym for the physical body as a whole, but the specificity of the term is important. Just as Christ entered into human life in his body, even to the extent that he was himself ruled by Sin and Death (6:9–10), so also the change in human beings extends into the body in all its parts. It results in obedience, in their very body parts, in observable practice. That fact does not limit the claim but grounds it in the reality of physical life.[59]

While on both sides of the conflict "your" bodies are presented as weapons, there is also a stunning contrast between the two sides. On Sin's side of the battle, human bodies are "weapons of wrongdoing," and on God's side those same bodies are "weapons of righteousness." The *dik-* root connects these two terms *adikia* and *dikaiosynē*, and Paul has juxtaposed them earlier in 3:5a when he contrasted "our wrongdoing" with God's righteousness. The two appear

57. See Gaventa 2013b, and especially Ryan 2020 on the larger connections between Romans and the notion of the divine warrior in Israel's Scripture.
58. The language of slavery, rule, and warfare is inherently violent, which rightly disturbs contemporary readers of Romans. As the letter unfolds, however, it emerges that God's conflict, while powerful, is unconventional. It consists of the Spirit's intercession on behalf of weakness (8:26), gifting "everything" to "us" (8:32), mercy for all (11:32), identifying with the "weak" (15:1–6), and especially peace (16:20).
59. As John Barclay rightly observes, "Doomed to death, in a body that is bound by mortality, the believer is also the site of an impossible new life" (2013b, 66).

together with considerable frequency in Scripture and elsewhere.[60] In Romans, *adikia* functions as a comprehensive term for human wrong, whether done to God by the withholding of reverence (1:18) or to other human beings (1:29). *Dikaiosynē*, by contrast, refers to God's comprehensive activity in Jesus Christ of redeeming human life from the powers of Sin and Death. The weapons differ radically, then, because one continues to serve human wrong by way of being obedient to Sin, while the other serves God's saving act. Further, the weapons differ radically in their capacities. Sin's weapons are those who are still among the dead. The weapons offered to God are "yourselves . . . as people once dead and now living." God's weapons are those of people who have already been rescued from Death, people who in some limited sense already share in Christ's triumph, even as they wait for their own resurrection.

By combining the language of new life with that of weapons, Paul creates the unlikely image of a living weapon, not entirely unlike his later notion of a living sacrifice (12:1). The result strains the imagination, but it provides a crucial glimpse into Paul's understanding: the baptized are not the primary agents in this conflict; they are implements used by God, as previously they were implements used by Sin. But they are simultaneously alive ("new creation," 2 Cor 5:17 and Gal 6:15), and that life means they are anything but passive. It is not that they choose which side to be on (contra, e.g., Pelagius 98; Dunn 1:305; Moo 384–85), but the fact that they have been made alive means that they *can* serve.

That "you" are, in the present time, weapons either for Sin or for God indicates that the conflict continues. Christ died to Sin and Death, and they will not lord it over him again (Rom 6:9–10), but that does not mean Sin and Death have already been utterly defeated. They have not disappeared. Later, in 8:3, Paul will announce that Sin has been condemned in Christ's flesh, but he does not go so far as to claim that it has ceased to exist. The baptized remain vulnerable, inhabiting as they do a world in which Sin and Death, along with the other powers, attempt to separate them from Christ's lordship (8:31–39). This point is consistent with 1 Cor 15, where the resurrection stands as the determinative action that guarantees but does not yet constitute God's final triumph (15:23–28, 54–57).

With v. 14 Paul hints at this final triumph with a promise (cast as a future indicative): "Sin will not lord it over you." Sin cannot lord it over humanity because of the overpowering strength of God, that is, of God's action in Jesus Christ (5:21). Being "under grace" is to be under the protective reign of God's gift, just as being "under Sin" in 3:9 has to do with being under Sin's power.

---

60. See, e.g., Pss 7:17–18 [LXX]; 118:163–64 [LXX]); Pss. Sol. 4.24; 9.4–5; Xenophon, *Ages.* 11.3; Philo, *Heir* 43.209; *Spec. Laws* 2.26.141; Diogenes Laertius, *Lives* 3.104.

God's gracious rule will not permit Sin to triumph, although clearly Sin and other powers persist in their endeavors, as comes to expression in the remainder of the chapter. This statement anticipates 8:31–39, with its declaration that nothing will be powerful enough to separate "us" from God's love in Christ Jesus.

This word of assurance in 6:14 contains a surprising twist with the declaration that "you are not under law." In ch. 6 Paul has relentlessly contrasted Sin's role with that of Christ and God. In the past, the baptized lived in Sin's dominion, but they now live in the dominion of God. They were dead and now are alive. They were weapons of wrong, and now they are weapons of God's righteousness. Yet here the contrast between "then" and "now" is a contrast between "the law" and "grace," a contrast that implicitly aligns the law with Sin itself. Instead of contrasting the reign of God's grace with that of Sin, v. 14b insists you are not "under law."

This comment continues Paul's series of provocative remarks about the law. He announces that no one is rectified by law observance, that God's righteousness takes place apart from the law, only to acknowledge that the "law and the prophets" witness to God's righteousness (3:20–21). He insists that he establishes the law (3:31), but then rather quickly separates the promise to Abraham from the law (4:13). In 5:20 he attributes to the law an active role in increasing transgression. Studies of Romans are littered with attempts to wrestle all of these remarks into a systematic whole, but Paul is not writing a systematic essay. He is developing an argument and leading his audience along with him, even if by this point Phoebe's auditors may be scratching their heads. He will raise this question again and most shockingly in ch. 7, where it emerges that the problem is not the law at all but Sin, in that Sin has power sufficient to take over even the good and holy and right gift of God.

[15–18] Paul repeats the contrast between law and grace in a rhetorical question that recasts 6:1: "Does that mean we should sin, since we aren't under law but under grace?" As in 6:1, the question could reflect Paul's awareness that he has been suspected of undermining the law. As earlier, however, he offers no defense of his behavior or his ethical instruction or the conduct of his congregations. Implicitly, the question reflects the assumption that the law provides a protective barrier between humans and Sin, that those who live according to the law's guidance will be unlikely to sin. Paul does not address the question of the law's standing, deferring that problem to ch. 7. He instead presents a stark alternative, according to which "you" are slaves either of Sin or of obedience to God (v. 16). He thereby allows the hint to linger that being under the law is actually the equivalent of being under Sin, and it is exactly this conclusion that Paul will emphatically reject in ch. 7.

Instead of introducing a discussion of the role of the law, the question of v. 15 opens up a variation on vv. 12–14, this time cast in the language of slavery introduced in 6:6. Repeatedly these verses, continuing through the end of the chapter, employ language associated with slavery. That change does not so much shift the discourse from the martial arena or that of kingship to a new discourse on slavery but intensifies it, since the three are intertwined. The Roman Empire was established and extended by warfare, and military conquest was the single largest provider for the slave supply: the three sets of images are mutually reinforcing.[61]

This nexus of language having to do with conflict between God's power and that of Sin would be readily understandable to Paul's audience. Paul's auditors may hear echoes, as elsewhere in Romans, of the divine-warrior tradition (Ryan 2020). Some of Paul's auditors will have been quite familiar with Scripture, but they did not need Scripture to access slave language; slavery was ubiquitous in their world.[62] And the slavery language here ought not be separated from that of rulership or martial language. These are all terms of regime, domination, or power, and that implication would scarcely be lost on Paul's auditors.

This dense web of language further undermines the notion that the baptized volunteer for their service. At least as early as Pelagius, interpreters of Paul have identified this service with "freedom of choice" (Pelagius 98), but Paul says nothing about choosing or "enlisting" (Moo 384) as God's agents. It is God who brings "us" from death to life, thereby creating new agents who are able to "present" themselves.

Verse 16 returns to the language of "presenting" oneself found in v. 13, although instead of employing imperatives, Paul casts the language in diagnostic terms. "You" are slaves of the one to whom you present yourselves for obedience. Surprisingly, however, the contrast here is not between presenting the body's members as weapons either to Sin or to God, but obeying either Sin or obedience, presumably obedience to God:

Slaves of Sin	yielding death
Slaves of obedience	yielding righteousness

The shift results in the awkward notion that "you" are "obedient slaves of obedience." This may be Paul's understated way of responding to the anxiety that, apart from law observance, the baptized will persist in sinning, in disobedience,

---

61. Walter Scheidel comments that "merchants often followed Roman armies and bought up newly captured slaves on the spot" (2011, 296). In addition, slaves accompanied the military itself (Onasander, *Strategikos* 10.24; Josephus, *J.W.* 3.69–71; Tacitus, *Hist.* 2.87; Southern 2006, 224–25; Roth 1999, 90–91, 102–103, 107, 113). The two discourses, that of slavery and that regarding martial conflict, are interconnected, to say nothing of the brutal experiences of humans subjected to slavery.

62. John Goodrich questions the notion that Paul's use of slave language was influenced primarily or exclusively by Jewish tradition (2013). Establishing the percentage of slaves in the population is exceedingly difficult, as our sources are limited. One estimate for Italy as a whole places the total at 15 to 25 percent enslaved (Scheidel 2011, 287–89). For Paul's Roman audience, it can be safely assumed that slavery was ubiquitous (Edmondson 2011, 339).

although he may also be suggesting that genuine obedience is possible only for those who belong to Christ. As noted regarding the use of the verb "obey" in v. 12, however, the word largely serves in Paul's letters as a term of affiliation or allegiance (as in 1:5; 10:16; 15:18; 16:19). In addition, "obedience" here recalls the obedience of Christ in 5:19. The obedience of the baptized puts them in conformity with Christ.

In effect Paul declares, "Your obedience tells you whose slave you are." This is followed immediately by an affirmation of the Romans, so it is not at all a statement to be removed from context and used as a diagnostic tool, certainly not to diagnose the other and not oneself (see 14:1–11). Here the contrast is between enslavement to Sin, which leads to Death (again the two are intricately intertwined), and obedience, which leads to righteousness. The restatement here of slavery and its results is a little surprising on three counts. First, obedience stands where a reference to God or grace would be anticipated. Second, while the beginning of the verse identifies obedience as a marker that can go in either direction, now obedience is used in the positive sense only, as obedience to God (presumably). Finally, obedience leads to righteousness.

Paul provides no detailed description of the obedience he has in mind, but vv. 16–18 do provide a crucial hint about its character. First, the introductory "Thanks be to God" locates the responsibility for what has happened squarely with God. As in 7:25, Paul expresses praise or gratitude to God, thereby enacting within the letter itself the overturning of the thankless state of humanity described in 1:18–32 and again in 3:10–18. Perhaps he even anticipates that when Phoebe reaches this line the Romans will join their voice to hers in praise of God (Gaventa 2008a).

This word of praise in 6:17 suggests that Paul is not addressing libertinism within the Roman congregations themselves (either actual or suspected). They are, he declares, "slaves for righteousness" and no longer belong to Sin's powers. That does not mean they are beyond sinning, however, any more than the effusive language of glorification in 8:29–30 means they are beyond sinning. Chapters 12–16 provide ample evidence that Paul knows they remain vulnerable, even culpable.

In one sense, the terms Paul invokes as the grounds for thanksgiving are quite familiar by this point in his discourse:

v. 17a   You were slaves of Sin
v. 18   You were freed from Sin
          You were enslaved to righteousness.

However, Paul inserts a new expression:

v. 17b   You became obedient from the heart to the imprint of the teaching to which
          you were handed over.

Literally, "imprint of the teaching" is "form" or "type" of teaching (*typos didachēs*). This is not a phrase Paul uses elsewhere, and it is tempting to search for a specific body of teaching such as may be reflected in 16:17 with its warning against those who would mislead from the "instruction you learned" (see also Titus 1:9; Heb 6:2). Yet this is a distinctive formulation, especially when coupled with the statement that "you" were "handed over" to it. A revealing clue comes in the use of *typos* for an impression that is made on an object by something else, as when a sealing ring is pressed into warm wax. For example, Philo uses *typos* often of this sort of impression, when he writes that God "stamped" the minds of Jews as if using a "seal" to make "imprints of holiness" (*Spec. Laws* 1.5.30; and see also *Spec. Laws* 1.20.106; *Embassy* 31.211; and many other examples in Gagnon 1993). Drawing on that use for the term, "the imprint of the teaching" becomes a reference to formation. Having been freed from Sin, the baptized are handed over to be re-formed by "the teaching."[63] Taken in this sense, "the imprint of the teaching" resembles the "renewal of the mind" or "mindset" in 12:2. The content of the teaching remains unspecified, and it may be that this teaching is a variation on the term "gospel," as seems to be the case in 1 Cor 14:6, 26.

Taken together, vv. 17–18 encapsulate what the new life of the baptized looks like. The baptized have been freed from Sin's power by God's action, and they have been handed over for recasting, reshaping, as God's slaves. They are obedient "from the heart" in the sense that, having been claimed and reshaped by God, they are able to will this relationship.

Verse 18 marks the first time Paul has addressed the Romans as "freed" people, but the freedom Paul invokes is at odds with some notions of freedom popular among his contemporaries. For example, Epictetus and some other Stoics understood themselves as free in the psychological sense of being able to respond freely in any circumstance. A person cannot be compelled or forced in terms of her wishes or desires, since the person is or should be under her own control. The wise individual is able to restrain himself, to achieve genuine freedom on his own (e.g., Epictetus, *Diatr.* 1.17.21–27; 2.13.11; 3.22.45–49).[64] For Paul, by contrast, the human is always enslaved and at the same time always free: the question is not whether one is free or enslaved, but to whom or what one is enslaved and from whom or what one is freed.[65] Freedom in and of itself is not for Paul a preoccupation.[66] Further, Paul is convinced that genuine human

63. This expression resembles John Barclay's introduction of Bourdieu's notion of *habitus* into the discussion of Pauline ethics (2013b, 69–71).

64. And see Long 2002, 206–30; Lampe 2015.

65. Bob Dylan's "Gotta Serve Somebody" strikes close to Paul's understanding, as noted already regarding 1:1.

66. Galatians 5:1 appears to contradict this statement with its call to "stand firm" in the freedom to which "we" have been called. But the larger argumentative arc of that letter makes clear that this

freedom (freedom from Sin and for God) comes about by God's intervention in Christ Jesus. It is not an achievement of the philosophically astute or mature. In fact, the impossibility of human achievement of such freedom comes into view in 7:7–25, as the "I" laments its incapacity to do what it wills. How the philosophically astute might have responded to Paul's notion of freedom and slavery is one question. The response of those who knew the dreadful facts of slavery at first hand is another issue altogether.

[19–23] Verse 19a digresses as Paul calls attention to the character of his own remarks, describing them as speaking "about the human situation" because of the "weakness of your flesh." The language of slavery, dense both before and after this statement, has prompted the suggestion that he is apologizing for using an exaggerated and offensive analogy, which he knows to be exaggerated and offensive (e.g., Cranfield 1:325). That conclusion is unwarranted, given that Paul identifies himself unapologetically as Christ's "slave," not only in Gal 1:10; Phil 1:1; 2 Cor 4:5, but also in the opening words of this letter. In 1 Cor 7:21–23 he refers to Christians as simultaneously slave and free without offering any explanation for the terminology.[67]

Instead of being an apology, this aside draws further attention to what Paul is saying about the human consequences of God's action (Käsemann 182). That would be consistent with the use of the phrase *legein anthropina* in Plutarch, *Mor.* 13C ("What I am about to say has to do with human matters") and in Philo, *Dreams* 288 ("Why must we speak about things human?"). In other words, Paul acknowledges that he is repeating himself for the sake of making the human situation clear.

The explanation, "because of the weakness of your flesh," indicates that Paul has a very particular human situation in view. Rather than "weakness of flesh" in the general sense of human frailty, the personal pronoun in "*your* flesh" reflects Paul's focus on Rome itself. Later, in ch. 14, it appears that some among Roman believers imagine others to be weak while holding themselves to be immune to obligation, either to the food laws or to their neighbor's well-being.[68] He may anticipate that problem here by developing once more the implications of the resurrection of Jesus Christ for the baptized.

What follows in vv. 19b–23 again addresses two kinds of slavery, the slavery of the past and that of the present, this time by contrasting their consequences. In addition, however, Paul introduces the notion that each slavery was accompanied by a corresponding freedom. The "so now" of v. 19b and "but now" of

---

"freedom" is from slavery to things that are not God (4:8); it initiates a new form of obligation, one initiated by "crucifixion with Christ" and continued by "Christ who lives in me" (2:19–20). This is scarcely freedom in the sense of self-realization or self-actualization alone.

67. See also Luke 2:29; Acts 16:17.

68. Käsemann observes that weakness in this context is "defiance of the strong who would like to be free of all bonds and who thus protest against the apostle's exposition" (182).

v. 22 sharply separate the two periods, and a third such demarcation with the "but now" comes in 7:6.

Paul first recalls the slavery of the past, when "you presented your limbs as slaves to impurity and to lawlessness yielding lawlessness." With "impurity" (*akatharsia*), the scenario of 1:18–32 is again brought to mind, where Paul declares that God handed humanity over to impurity (1:24). And "lawlessness" recalls the question of 2:23 about the possibility that some Jews simultaneously boast about having the law while in fact they transgress it. It is that handing over to impurity (as a metonym for Sin itself) that has been overturned in the gospel.[69]

Now, however, having been delivered from that enslavement, and having been enslaved to righteousness instead (v. 18), the baptized can actually be admonished: "Present your limbs as slaves to righteousness yielding holiness" (v. 19). As earlier in this passage, *dikaiosynē* ("righteousness") is a shorthand reference to God's comprehensive act on behalf of humanity. The baptized become God's slaves, and that slavery produces "holiness." *Hagiasmos*, a relatively rare term, has to do with being set apart for God and for God's service (see, e.g., Judg 17:3; 2 Macc 2:17; 14:36; Sir 7:31; Amos 2:11; Ezek 45:4), as it does in 1 Thess 4:3–4, 7. Often *hagiasmos* is translated "sanctification," but that term has unfortunately acquired overtones of a process of growth that seems little in evidence here or elsewhere in Paul. In 1 Cor 1:30, Christ Jesus is said to have become "our wisdom from God," which Paul further identifies as "our righteousness and holiness and redemption." That passage provides a key to this one: all of these (including holiness in Rom 6:19) are acts of God in Jesus Christ.

This contrast between past and present is further explicated in vv. 20–23. First, vv. 20–21 recount the past, with its slavery to Sin and freedom from righteousness (that is, freedom from God). This amounts to a pithy summation of 1:18–32. When God handed humanity over, humanity was free for its own behavior but enslaved to Sin. Verse 21 then moves from this restatement to an explicit treatment of the consequences of that prior slavery. It had a certain fruit, a certain natural by-product. Paul does not specify what that "fruit" was but describes it as "things of which you are now ashamed," here echoing the statement in 1:27 about sexual activity that is shameful. The outcome of "those things" (note the distance maintained even in the pronoun) is death. There is a certain kind of freedom at work in humanity enslaved to Sin, but it is the wrong kind of freedom.

---

69. The language of lawlessness (*anomia*) is rare in Paul, appearing at 4:7 in a quotation from Ps 32:1 (31:1 LXX) and otherwise only at 2 Cor 6:14 as a descriptor of faithless people. "Impurity" and "lawlessness" appear together in charges against Israel (Ezek 22:5; 39:24; 1 Esd 1:47); the two are not exclusively identified with the conduct of gentiles; Wolter 1:400.

Paul does not linger over that last statement about death, so it is not clear whether he means a link between misdeeds and physical death (as in 1 Cor 11:29–30) or whether he means death in a more figurative sense. Given his earlier use of Death as a power that enters the world in the company of its toxic partner, Sin, it seems best to understand this as a reference to that same power. That is, the result of enslavement to Sin's power is the workings of Death, which would include both death within life as well as physical death. At 1:32 Paul concluded that "those who do such things" are worthy of Death, and here he restates that conclusion.

The *nyni de* ("but now") at the outset of v. 22 underscores the sharpness of the contrast between past and present, a contrast brought about by Christ's death and resurrection. Paul continues, repeating v. 18 almost exactly, although here substituting "God" for the earlier metonym, "righteousness." There is now different "fruit," a different result—holiness—already mentioned in v. 19. There is also a different outcome, the telos of "eternal life."

This passage echoes the comments in 2:6–11 about different behavior producing different judgments, but here the contrast is radically recast to reflect Paul's conviction that behavior follows from location. At this stage in the development of his argument, Paul does not contend that people choose their behavior or that they have control over their actions. Being enslaved to Sin produces the fruit of shame, and being enslaved to God produces holiness.

Verse 23 succinctly summarizes the argument about outcomes with a powerful contrast between the "wage" that Sin pays and the "gift" of God. The two halves of the verse parallel one another in structure, making the contrast between them quite stark:

The wage of Sin   is Death
The free gift of God   is eternal life in Christ Jesus our Lord

The "wage" Sin pays translates *opsōnia*, a term associated with the wages paid to soldiers as in 1 Cor 9:7 and widely elsewhere.[70] Sin pays its slave-soldiers with a wage; however, the wage they earn is Death. But God does not pay a soldier's wage. As Paul has already established in the case of Abraham, God does not offer a salary, for no one would be able to earn it (4:4). Instead, there is gift, *charisma*—namely, "eternal life in Christ Jesus our Lord." Although in 6:1–11 Paul carefully refrains from saying that "we" have been raised from

70. E.g., Luke 3:14; Aristeas 22; 1 Esd 4:56; 1 Macc 3:28; 14:32; Polybius, *Hist.* 1.66.3–5, 11; 1.67.2; 1.69.4, 8; 3.13.8; 3.25.4; 4.60.2; 5.30.5; 5.94.9; 6.15.5; 6.39.12; 11.25.9–10; 11.26.5; Diodorus of Sicily, *Bibliotheca historica* 31.14.1; 31.34.1; Dionysius of Halicarnassus, *Ant. rom.* 8.73.3; 15.3.3. This connection is made as early as Pelagius, who remarks, "One who does military service for sin receives death as remuneration" (100). The term can also be used of wages paid to domestic slaves (Goodrich 2013, 528–29).

the dead, or that we are already in the resurrection, he does announce here, as a promise, "eternal life in Christ Jesus our Lord."

The final phrase, "in Christ Jesus our Lord," separates Paul's notion of "eternal life" from a gift to an individual or to individuals. Life "eternal" is located firmly in the one who is Lord. Paul's repetition of reference to being "in" or "through" Christ Jesus is a hallmark of this section of the letter (see 5:11, 21; 6:11, 23; 7:25a; 8:39). Since this gift of life contrasts with the militant figure of Death (and its partner Sin), its location "in Christ Jesus" anticipates the completion of the triumph of God in Christ over death itself (8:39).

Paul is now poised to expand on this new life in terms of the activity of the Spirit, and he will do that in ch. 8. First, however, he will pick up his various provocative statements about the Mosaic law in a discussion that exonerates the law even as it dramatically depicts the capacity of Sin to make use of God's own holy law.

7:1–6 The Law No Longer Lords It Over You

It is one thing for Paul to say, in effect, "No one can live simultaneously under two regimes," when the regimes being juxtaposed are those of Sin and of God (as in 6:13, 16, 19–23). But within the discussion in 6:15–23, Paul has inserted another claim: "You are not under law but under grace" (6:15)—a statement that poses the issue of regime change in a provocative way, as it aligns grace with God and then law with Sin. If there are Roman Christians who connect God's benefits to observing the Mosaic law (possibly including those introduced in ch. 14 who continue with Jewish dietary practice), this claim will have come as a surprise. Paul now expands on that statement, first with a scenario that is inoffensive, even mundane, then with a series of comments that could well be inflammatory, preparing for the question of 7:7 ("Does it mean that the law itself is Sin?") and the lengthy answer that extends through the remainder of the chapter.

Because this passage continues the argument about regime change, the chapter division here is potentially misleading, as are scholarly analyses that show a new topic starting at 7:1.[71] To be sure, the disturbing claims about being released from the law as constraining agent prompt the argument in the remainder of the chapter. Romans 7:1–6 also introduces the terms "flesh" and "spirit" that do crucial work in ch. 8 (J. King 2017), where Paul unpacks life in the present time, when believers see God's deliverance on the horizon even as Sin and Death persist in their work. Yet 7:1–6 does continue closely on ch. 6 (Meyer 2004d, 67–68). It repeats a great deal of the vocabulary of 6:15–23

---

71. Nygren's commentary offers a prime example of this analysis, in which chs. 5, 6, and 7 are identified respectively as "free from wrath," "free from sin," and "free from the law" (191–349).

(Gieniusz 1993); it also grounds the argument about not living in two regimes simultaneously with a scenario drawn from common life.

A good deal of exegetical ingenuity attends the precise relationship between the scenario of vv. 2–3 and the text that follows from it. Is the woman's situation best understood as an allegory, a parable, an analogy, or an illustration? And is the scenario logically flawed, or have interpreters failed to understand it? The difficulty of the argument has been observed at least since Origen, who commented that in this passage "Paul seems to be moving between unmarked rooms through hidden passages" (*Comm. Rom.* 6.7; Burns 155). The interpretive challenge itself prompts readers (as it may have prompted Phoebe's auditors) to linger, in an effort to understand precisely what Paul intends.

7:1 Don't you know, brothers and sisters[a]—for I am talking with people who do know the law[b]—that the law lords it over[c] a person as long as she lives? 2 For example, a married woman is bound by the law to her husband while he lives, but if her husband dies, she is released from the law concerning her husband.[d] 3 This means that, while her husband lives, she is called an adulterer[e] if she becomes the wife of another man.[f] But if her husband dies, she is free from that law,[g] and she will not be an adulterer if she becomes the wife of another man. 4 This means, my brothers and sisters, that you also were put to death to the law through the body of Christ, so that you belong to another, to the one who was raised from the dead, so that we might bear fruit for God. 5 For when we were in the flesh, the sinful passions[h] aroused by the law were at work in our limbs, bearing fruit for Death. 6 But now we have been released from the law, dead to what held us, so that we serve as slaves to what is new, to the spirit, and not to what is obsolete, to the letter.[i]

a. Lit., "brothers," but Paul addresses both men and women in this letter. (See note above on 1:13.)

b. Translations usually render *ginōskousin nomon* (lit., "ones knowing the law") as "those who know the law" (KJV, NRSVue, NIV, NASB), which could imply reference to a specific group within the Roman congregations. Nothing in the Greek, however, suggests such a limitation. The assumption is that the audience knows the law.

c. "Lord it over" conveys the negative implication that seems to be at work here, as in 6:9, 14 (regarding Sin and Death) and also in 2 Cor 1:24 ("We do not lord it over your faith") and Luke 22:25 ("The gentiles' kings lord it over them"). In Rom 14:9, however, Christ is said to "rule over" the dead as well as the living, something Paul obviously understands to be positive.

d. The perfect tense of *dedetai* ("bound") and *katērgētai* ("released") is here understood as gnomic (so also BDF §349; Wallace 1996, 581).

e. As in v. 2, the future indicative *chrēmatisei* ("is called") is also used in a gnomic sense (as in 5:7; Wallace 1996, 571).

f. The construction here and above (lit., "to become for another man," *ginomai andri heterō*) is Septuagintal, as in Deut 24:2 (*ginomai andri heterō*) and in Lev 22:12; Num 30:6 (30:7 LXX); Ruth 1:13 (*ginomai andri*).

g. A few manuscripts (33, 629 and a few others) add *tou andros*, so that the phrase becomes "the law *of the husband.*" Although this phrase is not strongly attested, it probably reflects the sense of the text, the definite article in this case being resumptive (i.e., "that law I just mentioned"). Yet it may be that the move from the more specific "law of the husband" to "the law" serves Paul's argument, which will soon shift to "the law" in general.

h. Lit., "the passions of the sins" (*ta pathēmata tōn hamartiōn*), construed here as a genitive of content (Smyth 1956, §1323). The presence of the second article, which is not strictly necessary, underscores the character of these passions (BDF §269.2).

i. The genitives *pneumatos* ("spirit") and *grammatos* ("letter") are genitives of apposition (Cranfield 1:339).

[7:1] The opening question ("Don't you know, brothers and sisters?") draws attention to what follows (as also at 6:3) and is reinforced by the subsequent comment. People who know the Mosaic law should not have to be reminded that the law is in effect only while a person lives. Although Paul frequently addresses his letters to "brothers and sisters" (*adelphoi*; e.g., 1 Cor 1:10; 2:1; 3:1; 4:6; 2 Cor 1:8; Gal 1:11; 3:15; 4:12; Phil 1:12; 3:1, 13, 17), he has not done so since Rom 1:13. Numerous such instances will follow, marking places where he makes a particularly strong appeal.[72] In this instance, the nature of the appeal is not immediately obvious, since at least on the surface what he says in v. 1b could scarcely be contentious. The implications of the appeal, however, prove controversial.

Paul does not specify that the law they all know is Mosaic law, and indeed the comment seems a truism in the sense that no one who is dead is obligated to law, whatever its origin. The several comments Paul has previously made about the law clearly refer to the law of Moses (see especially 2:18; 3:19, 31; 4:13; 5:13; 6:14), however, and those comments in turn call forth the explanation here and in the remainder of the chapter. In addition, nowhere does Paul express a concern or reservation about observing Roman law; in fact, 13:1–7 might be hard to reconcile with any such reservation. His attention, here and elsewhere, is to Mosaic law.

That these people know the Mosaic law could, of course, mean that Paul addresses Jews at this point, as he later will address gentiles directly in 11:13. It could even imply that he imagines the Roman auditors to be predominantly Jewish. Yet there are numerous indications that the earliest gentile Christians in Rome and elsewhere came from the ranks of those who had already participated in the life of the synagogue (see the introduction), and they presumably were familiar with the law of Moses (as Luke assumes in Acts 15:21). Indeed, if

72. Romans 7:4; 8:12; 10:1; 11:25; 12:1; 15:14, 30; 16:17.

Paul's audience is dominated by gentiles, this statement amounts to a *captatio benevolentiae*, a flattering address designed to win the attention of the audience for what follows.

What Paul expects his addressees to understand is that "the law lords it [or rules] over a person as long as she lives." At first glance, this implies only that the law pertains to the living. Paul's wording, however, transforms an obvious point into something far more provocative. He writes that "the law lords it over" (*ho nomos kyrieuei*), thereby putting the law in the company of ruling figures of a malicious sort. Paul has earlier referred to the reign of Death (*basileuein* in 5:14, 17) and that of Sin (*basileuein* in 5:21 and 6:12; *kyrieuein* in 6:14), so to attribute "lording it over" to the law of Moses threatens to make the law guilty by toxic association even before Paul has introduced his analogy.

In addition, the phrase "the law lords it over" or "the law rules" (*ho nomos kyrieuei*) appears nowhere in the LXX (nor in Philo or Josephus). The phrase "the law of the Lord" (*ho nomos kyriou*) does appear over twenty times in the LXX (e.g., Exod 13:9; 2 Kgs 10:31; 1 Chr 16:40; Pss 1:2; 118:1; Isa 5:24; and see Luke 2:23, 24, 39), raising the possibility that Paul is playing on that phrase. While he will later speak of the "law of God" (Rom 7:25; 8:7) and the "law of the spirit of life" (8:2), at this point Paul continues his discussion of the impossibility of living under two regimes at the same time, and he will move from this statement to dissociate "us" from the lordship of the law of Moses.

[2] By way of illustrating the commonplace that the law obtains only during someone's lifetime, Paul offers a specific scenario involving marriage. There is a certain "slippage" (Watson 2000, 135) between v. 1 and v. 2, since v. 1 refers to the lifetime of an individual who is ruled by the law and v. 2 introduces the death of another party, the woman's husband. Taken on its own, however, this is a relatively obvious scenario. According to Mosaic law, marriage binds a woman to her husband for as long as he lives. Jewish women did not have the right of initiating divorce,[73] although Jewish men did have that prerogative (Deut 24:1–4).[74] In the event of the husband's death, however, a woman was free to marry again. Paul's formulation, "released from the law concerning her

73. Roman law permitted women to initiate divorce, at least under certain circumstances (Treggiari 1991, 435–61; Urbanik 2016). The difference between Jewish and Roman law is reflected in Josephus's account of Salome's divorce of her husband, Costobarus. Josephus reports that her action put her in conflict with Jewish law but then adds that she did not "follow her own country's law" (*Ant.* 15.259–60; Ilan 1996, 143). In 1 Cor 7:10–11 Paul does assume the possibility of a woman initiating divorce, but that appears to be a concession and comes with the stipulation that she remain unmarried or reconcile with her husband. A second marriage is not imagined. The two texts differ importantly in that 1 Cor 7 offers instruction to believers (presumably gentile believers) regarding marriage, and Rom 7:1–6 does not. Its function is illustrative rather than parenetic.

74. Deuteronomy 24:1 stipulates that a man may divorce his wife for "something objectionable," the meaning of which was disputed early in Jewish life (Sir 7:26; 25:25–26; Matt 19:3–9; Josephus, *Ant.* 4.253).

husband," will recur in v. 6, there applied to "us" and extended to include the law generally, not the specific law having to do with marriage.

Paul refers to the woman as *hypandros gynē*, literally, a "woman under a male." The adjective *hypandros* is rare, appearing nowhere else in the NT. Where it does occur, it does so in contexts where adultery is a perceived threat, as in Num 5:20; Prov 6:29; Sir 41:23; Polybius, *Hist.* 10.26.3; thus Paul's usage of this word could anticipate the possibility of adultery in v. 3 (so Rehmann 2000, 97–98). Its presence need not signal adultery so much as an emphatic indication of a woman's married state, however (Earnshaw 1994, 75–78). In addition, the *hypo* prefix suggests another possibility: that the woman is "under" the control of her husband because she is "under" the law. She is "bound to the law," just as the "you" of 6:14–15 were once "under the law." That is, the negative implication here concerns the problem of being bound to the law more than it does the woman's potential adultery. As long as her husband lives, the law lords it over her.

The second half of v. 2 confirms this interpretation, since what is said concerns the release of the woman from the law that binds her to her husband. Nothing here implies that she has done wrong or that she intends to do wrong. Her husband's death brings about her freedom, a point that coheres with v. 6, where "we" have been released from the law.

[3] Two implications follow from v. 2. First, a woman who has a living husband and who becomes the wife of another man will acquire the name "adulterer" (v. 3a). This point is particularly apt under Mosaic law, which did not allow women to initiate divorce (although see Mark 10:12). Second, if the husband dies, she is free to marry another (v. 3b). This last point is stated twice. Initially, in only a slight variation on the end of v. 2, she is "free from the law." The move from "law of the husband" to "the law" without further limitation may be important as Paul moves into vv. 4–6, where he offers no limitation to the freedom from the law. He then concludes that she will not be identified as an adulterer if she marries following her husband's death.

One advantage of this particular example is that it translates readily, since outside Jewish circles the same practice would obtain. Roman women could divorce their husbands, but a married woman who engaged in sexual relations with a man other than her husband was subject to severe punishment in the Roman world as a whole.[75] This part of the illustration is also not reversible, at least not in a Roman context, where fidelity in marriage was expected of women but not of men, and wives were admonished to tolerate their husbands' behavior.[76]

75. Situations varied significantly based on location, social situation, and period of time, and there are discrepancies between legal codes and actual practice. Treggiari reviews the evidence (1991, 262–319).

76. Plutarch, e.g., contends that a woman should not be angry if her husband engages in sexual relations with another woman, because that simply signals his respect for her in that he does not involve her in licentious activity (*Mor.* 140).

Yet Paul's emphasis does not fall on the potential of the woman for adultery but on the exclusive demand of the law. Should she go with another man while she has a living husband, she will acquire the name of adulterer.[77] But should her husband die, she is free. Despite the cultural assumptions regarding women and their sexuality, Paul presents this scenario as one in which the woman has a problem—namely, she needs to be rid of her husband. To be sure, that point should not be exaggerated; the name "adulterer" is scarcely neutral. Nonetheless, the scenario as Paul presents it prevents her from being called an adulterer and sets her free from her husband. At the very least, she is not criticized for her apparent but unarticulated desire to be free from the husband. Freedom from the husband is here presented as a good thing, anticipating the freedom "you" have to belong to another in vv. 4–6.[78]

On initial consideration this seems an odd choice to illustrate that the law governs a person only during that person's lifetime. Many more clear and direct examples might have been found—say, laws pertaining to offerings or to Sabbath observance. In addition, v. 3 is largely a restatement of v. 2, focused on the catastrophic results that would follow should the woman undertake to be married simultaneously to two men. That is exactly Paul's point, however. Marriage is an exclusive relationship, which is what Paul has been describing in ch. 6 and will continue with in vv. 4–6: people cannot belong both to the law and to Christ any more than a woman can be married to two men simultaneously.

[4] The illustration of vv. 2–3 serves as the basis for an analogy in which "you" (and later "we") are the ones who have been released from the law. And it is here that the innocuous statement of v. 1b and its equally innocuous illustration in vv. 2–3 become explosive, as Paul writes both that the law was the agent of Sin (v. 5) and that "you" or "we" died to the law (vv. 4, 6). Verse 4 makes the move that serves as the basis for what follows: "You also were put to death to the law through the body of Christ, so that you belong to another, to the one who was raised from the dead." Understanding the workings of the analogy is crucial, and it has often been argued that the analogy is a poor one (e.g., Dodd 103). But a schematic presentation reveals that the analogy works generatively by identifying "you" with both the husband who dies *and* the wife who is released from the law (Watson 2000, 135).

77. Wallace 1996, 571, cites Turner 1976, 86, who understands this future indicative as carrying an imperatival implication: "Let her be called." Such a translation ignores the context, which is not an instruction regarding sexual misconduct but an analogy. Wallace himself says the idea "is not that a particular event is in view, but that such events are true to life," with Rom 5:7 and Matt 6:24 as similar constructions (571).

78. Perhaps following this logic, Origen comments that the woman's new marriage is "far happier than the first" (*Comm. Rom.* 6.7; Burns 155).

v. 2a	Married woman	bound to living husband	by the law
vv. 2b	Married woman	released from law of husband	by death of husband
v. 3b	Married woman	free for another husband	by death of husband
	[You	bound to law	by unnamed agent]
v. 4a	You	died to law	by body of Christ
v. 4b	You	free for another, Christ	

This presentation deliberately omits v. 3a, the conclusion that the woman who takes a second husband while her husband lives will be called an adulterer, as that element is not applied to "you," at least not explicitly. As noted above, however, the conclusion that believers cannot simultaneously be under God's rule and under that of Sin/Death/the law has already been prominent in ch. 6 and is recapitulated in the woman's situation.

The bracketed element inserted between v. 3b and v. 4a articulates the unstated (suppressed?) element of the analogy. The analogy assumes that "you" were previously bound to the law. The agent or event that created that bondage remains unclear, but the argument leading up to this point suggests it must be Sin and Death as malevolent enemies of God. That is precisely why 7:7–25 needs to explain the relationship, affirming both that the law is God's (vv. 12, 22) and that Sin has managed to make use even of God's own law (vv. 11, 13).

What makes the analogy confusing initially is the multiple relationships in which "you" stand. The unstated assumption is that "you" are the married woman who is bound to the living husband and to the law, the one who is now free for a different relationship. "You" are also the first husband who died. As was the case in 6:1–11, Paul is articulating both the death and the new life of believers. Also as in 6:1–11, Christ's death and resurrection makes both "your" death and "your" new life possible.

The repetition of "brothers and sisters" at the beginning of v. 4 reinforces the connections between Paul and his audience, even as he moves to a point that may grate on the ears of some who listen while Phoebe reads. It was one thing to say that "you" died to Sin (6:11); it is another thing altogether to say that "you" died to the law of Moses.

This death to the law was brought about "through the body of Christ." For readers already familiar with Paul's letters, the phrase "body of Christ" elicits Paul's contention elsewhere that "we" are Christ's body, as in Romans itself (12:4–5) and especially in 1 Cor 12:12–27. That connotation cannot be excluded here, particularly considering the address of "brothers and sisters" and the subsequent assertion that "we bear fruit for God," both of which assume the interconnection of believers. Yet in what follows ("the one raised from the dead") as well as in 6:1–11, the emphasis has been on Christ's own death. The statement that "you also were put to death to the law through the body of Christ," then, connects "your" death to the death of Christ, but in graphic terms. It is Christ's physical body that brings about "your" release, just as earlier "your" limbs became weapons in God's battle (6:13). What is new in this passage is not that Paul is now transferring that language to the community, but that he is claiming Christ's death means release from the law itself. Small wonder that he must go on to explain what exactly he is saying about the law.

Death to the law means that "you" now belong to another, just as the once-married woman in vv. 2–3 is freed to be married to another man. The "other" to whom "you" now belong is identified here as "the one who was raised from the dead." This way of speaking of Christ reinforces the point that it is by virtue of him (and not the church as Christ's body) that "you" are released from the law. The claim that "you" died to the law and now belong to Christ epitomizes the regime change Paul has been eliciting since at least 6:1. It assumes that one may not belong both to the law and to Christ, recalling the radical assertion of Gal 2:19 ("Through the law I died to the law, that I might live to God"). On this point, Romans is no less radical than Galatians: the Christ event is all-encompassing, and one may not live in both regimes at the same time (Gaventa 2014c). Importantly, Paul does not say that "you choose" the other, Christ to whom "you" now belong.

With the final clause of v. 4, Paul shifts to the first-person plural: it is "we" who bear fruit for God. The language of "bearing fruit" (*karpophoreō*) further ties this passage to 6:12–23, which also concludes with a contrast between the "fruit" (*karpos*) produced by enslavement to Sin and the fruit produced by enslavement to God. The shift to first-person invites Phoebe's auditors to identify with Paul, but it also may be significant that Paul has already referred to the "fruit" he wishes to have at Rome (1:13) and now connects himself to them at the point where he is picking up this language again.

Despite the fact that the analogy is drawn from marital life, the *karpos* of v. 4 is not necessarily to be identified with the children brought forth by believers.[79] To begin with, Paul shifts at this point from the second-person plural to the first-person plural. More to the point, he has already used *karpos* in a general sense of ethical "produce" in 6:21–22, as noted above. And his comment in v. 5 about "bearing fruit" to Death is obviously not a reference to "persons." Further, while Paul speaks of himself in several contexts as the "mother" or "father" of his congregations (e.g., 1 Cor 3:2; 4:14–16; Gal 4:19; 1 Thess 2:7, 11–12), he does not in those settings employ *karpos* to refer to children in faith. The "fruit" imagined here is general rather than specific. Rather than specifying the character of the "fruit" anticipated, the notion that we "bear fruit" reflects

---

79. Jewett 434–35 sees the "fruit" as evidence that "you" belong to Christ in the sense of 2 Cor 11:2, where believers are presented as Christ's "pure virgin." However, Paul's use of *karpos* elsewhere does not support that argument, and the church as Christ's bride is quite removed from this text.

the integral relationship between living in this new regime and the conduct that follows from Christ's lordship. Life in the new regime is full human life, involving the entirety of embodied humanity. It cannot be restricted to a spiritual or intellectual portion of life.

In addition, "bearing fruit" is not something a plant does of its own volition or by its own determination; it results from the nature of the plant and its circumstances. That fact is reflected in the use of *karpophoreō* in the parable of the Sower, where some seeds produce an unimaginable harvest while others languish (Matt 13:23; Mark 4:20, 28; Luke 8:15).[80] For Paul, fruit bearing is a function of the neighborhood, or regime, in which one lives.

[5–6] The contrast between past and present returns in the contrast between "our" life when we were in the flesh and the "but now" that marks the beginning of v. 6. The contrast here both replays and transposes the contrast of 6:20–23. In both passages, "then" "we" produced deeds appropriate for death. And in both passages, "now" "we" have been released for a slavery that is positive and even liberating. Yet the terms used in 7:5–6 differ in revealing ways. To begin with, instead of belonging to Sin, here it is life "in the flesh" that is the problem. In addition, rather than Sin as the enslaving agent, here the law itself serves as a restricting agent from which "we" have now been liberated.

The introductory reference to "our" having been "in the flesh" announces a way of speaking about the distinction between the time before and after Christ ("when" in v. 5 and "but now" in v. 6) that has played no role in the letter to this point.[81] To live "in the flesh," as will become clear in 8:4–13, does not denigrate actual bodily existence. That should be clear already from the discussion in 6:13 and 19 of presenting one's "limbs" (*melē*) in God's service, to say nothing of the numerous indications of Christ's own physical existence (e.g., 6:1–11; 8:3; 9:5). Instead of a body-denigrating assertion, living "in the flesh" refers to a life restricted by merely human ways of thinking or assessing or acting (see especially 2 Cor 5:16–17; Gal 5:13–21). Consistent with the rest of the passage, there is no middle ground here: "we" exist on one side or another of this division. Life "in the flesh," for Paul, is life ruled by Sin and Death, as becomes clear in the remainder of v. 5.

At that time, Paul writes, "the sinful passions" were active in our "limbs" (see 6:13, 19). The language of "passions" recalls 1:26, with its solemn declaration that God "handed them over" to "dishonorable passions," there a metonym for Sin itself. These passions worked in "our" very members, the members (limbs)

80. The only appearances of *karpophoreō* in the NT outside Rom 7 and these Gospel texts are in Col 1:6, 10.
81. In Rom 1:3 and 2:28, "flesh" (*sarx*) refers to actual human flesh, whether the genealogical line of David or the physical act of circumcision, and in 3:20 "all flesh" is a conventional way of speaking of all humanity. The only other appearance of *sarx* prior to 7:5 is at 4:1, where it may also refer to a "merely human" way of thinking (see translation note on 4:1).

that were formerly described as "weapons" for impurity and lawlessness (6:19), to bear fruit for Death. What Paul means by "bearing fruit" for Death might well be captured in the vice list at the end of ch. 1 as well as in the catena of 3:10–18; those actions and attitudes serve the powers of Sin and Death.

"Sinful passions," literally "the passions of the sins," is an unusual construction for Paul, for whom *hamartia* typically appears in the singular.[82] As translation note h on v. 5 indicates, this is likely a genitive of content: the content of the passions Paul refers to here is "sins." While moralists among Paul's contemporaries shared his concern about the passions, for them passions out of control were a sign of bad personal development, that is, bad character (e.g., Epictetus, *Diatr.* 2.18.8–26; Seneca, *Ira* 2.12.4; Cicero, *Tusc.* 5.20; Stowers 1981, 46–49; Long 2002, 27–28, 215–20). For Paul, the passions are problematic insofar as they are sinful.

Paul further characterizes the sinful passions as "aroused by the law" (literally, "through the law"). This continues the provocative comments about the law that have littered Paul's argument up to this point in the letter. He has already written that God's rectifying act comes apart from the law's action (3:19–21), that the promise to Abraham is not connected to the law (4:13), and even that the law produces wrath (4:15) and that its arrival increases disobedience (5:20). Now the law is associated directly with Sin in "our" very bodies. And the "now time" of v. 6 is the time when "we" have been released from the law by virtue of dying to its captivity.

The result is that "we" are slaves to what is new, to the "spirit," and not to what is obsolete, to the "letter." Chapter 2 contrasts the "spirit" and the "letter" by way of explicating a difference between what is obvious and what is not obvious, but here the contrast serves to distinguish what is obsolete from what is new. Once again, Paul insists on the radical difference between "then" and "now." By introducing "spirit," which has played little role in the letter up to this point (1:4, 9; 2:29; 5:5), Paul prepares for its important role in ch. 8. *Gramma* ("letter") appears to be a metonym for the law, and its use here prepares for the quotation of a specific law in v. 7.

With delicious understatement, Calvin introduces this passage with the remark that Paul's earlier comments about the law "might have given rise to many other [question]s" (137). Yet this passage scarcely resolves the difficulty. Although it is noteworthy that Paul does not declare that the law itself died,[83] the radical character of this passage has discomforted some of Paul's interpreters, who fear the specter of antinomianism. Calvin, for example, is quick

---

82. The only other instances of the plural of *hamartia* in Romans are in 4:7 and 11:27, both of which are scriptural citations.

83. Contrast Ambrosiaster, however, who commented that "the law is said to be dead when its authority expires" (124).

to insist that the law is not "abrogated in regard to the Ten Commandments, in which God has taught us what is right and has ordered our life, because the will of God must stand forever." Release from the law is not release from "righteousness which is taught in the law, but from the rigid demands of the law and from the curse which follows from its demands" (139).[84] In a similar vein, Cranfield contends that the passage "has to do with the Christian's freedom from the law as condemning" (1:332).

Such distinctions may be helpful for general reflection on the place of the law in Christian life, but they find no support in this passage. Paul's audience instead hears a shocking alignment of the law of Moses with the realm of Sin and Death. That problem, in turn, prompts the remainder of the chapter.

So the question at the end of this passage is about the regime to which the law belongs. Paul has put the law on the same side of the line as the anti-God powers, in company with Sin and Death. Already he has said that "you are not under the law," and he does not say that the law itself died. Neither does he say that Sin died. It is not that Sin and Death and the law are dead, but that their power has been broken.

7:7–25 Sin's Invasion of the Holy, Right, and Good Law

Is Paul identifying the law of Moses with Sin itself? That question has been lurking since 3:31, and finally it comes into full view. Paul has come perilously close to making that identification in the preceding lines, which name the law as the agent that arouses "sinful passions" and declare that "we" have been set free from the law. In addition, being "under the law" and being "slaves of Sin" appear in worrisome proximity to one another in 6:12–23. The question can no longer be postponed, although curiously it turns out that the answer to the question about the law provides Paul with yet another—and final—occasion for exploring the destructive workings of Sin.[85]

The remainder of the chapter constitutes a single if complex unpacking of Paul's initial *mē genoito*: "Of course not!" Here he explains with some care how Sin can make use of the law without the law itself being identical to Sin or inherently sinful. The problem is instead that Sin has weaponized even the holy law of Moses to take "me" captive. And "weaponized" is not an exaggeration, as the language Paul uses of Sin continues the martial imagery of chs. 5–6.

---

84. These comments, of course, reflect Calvin's distinction among the various "uses" of the law (1960, 2.7.6–12).

85. The word *hamartia* appears thirty-seven times in Rom 5–7, and it appears five times in the opening lines of ch. 8 (vv. 2, 3, 10), but then only twice in the remainder of the letter (11:27; 14:23). The verb *hamartanein* is far less frequent, appearing in 2:12 (twice); 3:23; 5:12, 14, 16; 6:15.

Identifying the discourse as concerned with addressing the relationship between Sin and the law makes it possible to approach the much-vexed question of the "I" of Rom 7 from a fresh direction.[86] The "I" plays an important role in the discourse, but the "I" is not the focus of the discourse or the reason for its appearance.

At least since the time of Augustine, who notoriously changed his position on the question, interpreters have quarreled over the identification of the "I" in this passage.[87] Readers across the long history of interpretation have assumed that the *egō* is Paul himself, yet they have quarreled fiercely over whether this *egō* is Paul before or after his conversion (often referred to as the "unregenerate" or the "regenerate" Paul).[88] A third avenue of interpretation was proposed already by the earliest commentators, namely, that Paul employs a stylistic device through which he gives voice to the position or experience of another. Ambrosiaster writes that "by pretending to speak about himself, the apostle is making a general point" (129). The remarks of Chrysostom (*Hom. Rom.* 12; *NPNF*[1] 11.427), Pelagius (102), and Origen (*Comm. Rom.* 6.9–10; Burns 170) similarly assume that Paul is giving voice to the experience of someone else. That suggestion reemerged in the early twentieth century and has in turn led to a range of new interpretations, including prominently the notion that Paul is using "speech in character" (*prosopopoeia*) to articulate a situation that is not his own (at least not exclusively his) but that of another, imagined conversation partner.

Following on the awareness that Paul's central preoccupation in this discussion is with Sin and its power to use even God's own holy law, and that this is the culmination of an extended discussion about Sin's doings, the "I" should be interpreted in view of the larger context in the letter.[89] Attending carefully to the context undermines a narrowly autobiographical reading. Since Paul has been developing an argument about the universal grasp of Sin and Death and

86. This point was demonstrated ably by Paul W. Meyer in a landmark essay on Rom 7 that influences my reading of this passage (2004d).

87. Proposals for the identity of the character range widely. Reviews of the history of interpretation may be found in Schelkle 1956, 242–47; Cranfield 1:342–47; Hultgren 681–91.

88. The quotation marks around "regenerate" and "unregenerate" signal discomfort with such terms, given the fact that the letter itself undermines such distinctions (Meyer 2004d, 61–67). Further, since the entire letter is written in light of the revelation of Jesus as God's Son (1:3–4), even if Paul were trying to describe the experience of the "unregenerate" he would necessarily be doing so from the point of view of the "regenerate." This is a bit like trying to distinguish "preresurrection" from "postresurrection" materials in the Gospels; all of them are written from the perspective of the resurrection.

89. As Moses Stuart observed, "The question concerning chap. vii.5–25 is not, whether it be true that there is a contest in the breast of Christians, which might, at least for the most part, be well described by the words there found; but, whether such a view of the subject is congruous with the present design and argument of the apostle" (463; quoted in Meyer 2004d, 57).

their overturning by God in the Christ event, stopping to reflect on his own experience either prior to or following the apocalypse of Jesus Christ would seem to be a jarring move at this point. In addition, there is little indication elsewhere in his letters that Paul struggled with his conscience in a way that any autobiographical reading of 7:7–25 requires (note especially Phil 3:2–11). That is not to say that Paul himself is removed from the account of the "I."[90] The "I" is part of the rhetoric of the passage, part of what makes it work its way so powerfully into the mind of readers and hearers even today, though without being the focus of the passage (Gaventa 2013c, 78).

Rather than an "authentic transcript of Paul's own experience" (Dodd 108), Rom 7 reflects the final step in the discourse about Sin and Death. Paul first moved from accusations against the nameless "they" of 1:18–32 to arguments about Sin's role with the whole of humanity (3:9–20; 5:12–21). With 6:1–7:6, he brings the argument closer to the audience, with the "we" who once belonged to Sin as its slaves but who have now been liberated by God's action. The use of the singular "I" marks the final movement. In other words, Paul's relentless argument spirals down one last time.

The speaker here resembles the speaker of the lament psalms, now transplanted into the landscape of the cosmic conflict between God and the powers of Sin and Death. That speaker invites the audience to come further into the conflict by identifying with the situation of the "I" (Gaventa 2013c).

Having limned the work of Sin in the experience of the "I" who endeavors only to observe God's holy law, Paul will turn in Rom 8 to address the new life of those God has liberated from Sin's death-dealing grasp.

7:7 So, what does this mean? Does it mean that the law itself is Sin? Of course not! But I did not know Sin except through the law. For I did not know desire until the law said, "Do not desire." 8 And Sin, by staking out its base of operations through the commandment, produced in me every desire. For without the law Sin is dead. 9 I was alive then, without the law, but when the commandment arrived, Sin sprang to life, 10 but I died. And the commandment—the commandment that was meant for life—this turned out to be the death of me.[a] 11 For Sin, staking out its base of operations through the commandment, deceived me and even killed me through the commandment. 12 So the law itself[b] is holy, and the commandment is holy and right and good.

13 Does this mean that the good became death in my case? Of course not! But Sin—so that it might be apparent as Sin—through the good

90. The pronoun may not "yield details about Paul's personal life," yet that does not mean that the pronoun is "purely fictive" (so Meyer 2004d, 60).

produced death for me, so that Sin through the commandment might grow sinful beyond all measuring. **14** For we know that the law is spiritual, but I am fleshly since I have been sold under the power of Sin.

15 I do not understand my actions. What I want to do is not what I actually do. Instead, I do what I hate. **16** Since I do[c] what I do not want to do, I agree that the law is good, **17** but I perceive that I am no longer the actor. Sin is, and Sin lives in me.

18 Now I know that nothing good lives in me, in my flesh. For willing the good is near to me, but doing the good is not. **19** I do not do the good that I want to do, but the evil that I do not want—that is exactly what I do! **20** And since I do[c] what I do not want to do, I perceive that I am no longer the actor. Sin is, and Sin lives in me.[d]

21 Therefore what I find concerning the law[e] is this: that while I can will to do the good, evil is close to me. **22** I rejoice in the law that is God's in my very self, **23** but I also see that there is a second law in my limbs, and that second law does battle with the law governing my mind and is taking me prisoner by means of Sin's law, the law that lives in my own limbs. **24** I am utterly miserable![f] Who will deliver me from the body ruled by this Death?[g] **25** Thanks be to God through Jesus Christ our Lord!

So I am a slave to God's law in my mind, but to Sin's law in my flesh.

a. More lit., "this was found to be death in my case." The translation retains the force of the Greek in a more idiomatic style.

b. "The law itself" reflects the *men* ("on the one hand"), which implies a contrast between the law's holiness and the activity of Sin.

c. The *ei* here is most often translated as a conditional "if," but *ei* can carry the notion of "since," as in 1 Thess 4:14; Rom 6:8; 15:27 (BDF §372.1; BDAG s.v.). That translation indicates the relationship among the clauses; because the "I" observes this gap between desire and action, the "I" can perceive the underlying problem, which is the colonizing power of Sin.

d. This translation of vv. 15–20 brings out the parallels and emphases of these lines, but it strays from a more literal rendering.

e. This instance of *nomos* is customarily translated as "I find it to be a law" (NRSVue) or some similar expression, on the assumption that in this instance *nomos* refers to a principle (see NASB, NIV, KJV). The arguments adduced in BDAG s.v. *nomos* for "principle" are forced, however; tellingly, LSJ s.v. offers several glosses for *nomos*, none of which is "principle" or its equivalent. That implication is unlikely in a passage that has been discussing God's own law (*nomos*) at length and with such care. Instead, *nomos* here is an accusative of respect, hence the translation above (so Meyer 2004d, 76; cf. Rom 10:5; 1 Cor 9:25; Wallace 1996, 204).

f. Customarily rendered "Wretched person that I am!" (NRSVue), the translation above is more colloquial.

g. Taking the Greek genitive "of this death" as a possessive of "the body."

[7:7] Following a pattern begun at 3:1, Paul's imagined conversation partner offers a conclusion that follows logically from Paul's argument: Is the law itself to be identified with Sin? Once again the rejection is immediate: "Of course not!" For those who have listened to Phoebe reading the letter, especially if they have heard reports undermining Paul's proclamation of the gospel, the question may have pressed itself hard. And the reaction—"Of course not!"—seems at odds with what has just preceded in 7:1–6, just as 3:2 seems at first glance a contradiction to 2:17–29.

The explanation is initially straightforward and in keeping with previous observations about the law: "I did not know Sin except through the law." This assertion lightly recasts earlier statements that have pointed in the same direction. At 3:20 Paul concludes his discussion of human sinfulness with the claim that law observance does not provide the solution to human captivity; it does not rectify. Instead, "through the law comes recognition of Sin." Closest to 7:7 is 4:15's assertion that "where there is no law there is no transgression." And in 5:13 Paul argues that although Sin was already in the world before the law arrived, Sin "is not recognized without the law." In all these instances Paul makes an obvious assertion—there is no breaking a law if the law is not present—that creeps toward the frightening association of the law with Sin.[91]

Verse 7 differs from these earlier statements, however, in that Paul reiterates the claim and, as he does so, introduces a specific commandment: "Do not desire." He then repeats the statement (slightly reworded) with a very specific commandment, the first two words of the final command of the Decalogue in Deut 5:21 LXX and Exod 20:17 LXX. The abbreviated wording understandably opens numerous interpretive possibilities for his choice of this particular commandment. Because the commandment begins with the desire for the neighbor's wife (although not in the Hebrew of Exod 20:17) and Paul has just raised the possibility of adultery in the marriage analogy of 7:1–6, sexual desire seems pertinent.[92] Paul does not specify sexual desire, however, and that is likely too limited a focus for the passage. The larger philosophical and cultural context offers ample evidence of a concern about desire run out of control, both sexual and otherwise (e.g., 4 Macc 2:1–3:6; Philo, *Contempl. Life* 61; Epictetus, *Diatr.* 2.1.10; 2.18.8–9; *Ench.* 15; Dio Chrysostom, *Or.* 1.13; 3.34; Stowers 1994, 46–52).

More can be said about this prohibition, both in the context of the Decalogue and in the context of Paul's argument. Standing as the culmination of the

---

91. In the preface to the second edition of his Romans commentary, Barth observed that Paul is always "on the brink of heresy" (13). The category of "heresy" may be anachronistic, but the observation is nonetheless pertinent.

92. In addition, 1 Thess 4:3–5 suggests that Paul was especially concerned about the sexual behavior of gentile converts, and Rom 1:26–27 plays on Jewish assumptions about promiscuous behavior among gentiles (see comment on 1:26–27).

Decalogue, the prohibition against desire is emphasized through repetition of the verb and elaboration of the proscribed objects of desire (P. Miller 2009, 389).

> Neither shall you covet your neighbor's wife. Neither shall you desire your neigh-
> bor's house, or his field, or his male or female slave, or ox, or donkey, or anything
> that belongs to your neighbor. (Deut 5:21 NRSVue; similarly Exod 20:17)

Further, the prohibition of desire or covetousness is substantially connected to all the prior commandments. That seems obvious in the case of murder, adultery, theft, and lying, all of which arise from desire that has run out of control. It is also true of the first commandment, however, since the anxiety to possess what belongs to the other is deeply related to mistrust of God's provisions for human life (P. Miller 2009, 406–8).[93] In the context of the argument Paul is developing in this letter, the prohibition against desire recalls 1:18–32, with its castigation of "those people" who refuse to acknowledge God properly, who refuse to acknowledge their own creatureliness, and whom God in turn hands over to their own desires, making them captives of Sin itself (vv. 24, 26, 28).

Bearing in mind this enlarged sense of the prohibition, "Do not desire" does not refer to a specific moment in Paul's own experience or to the arrival of the law as an obligation for the Jewish male come of age. Earlier in the letter the law's arrival is identified with the giving of the law of Moses to Israel (5:13), and later Paul will enumerate the giving of the law among the benefits of Israel (9:4). The law is indisputably associated with Israel. Yet Paul has also indicated that all people, both Jew and gentile, are accountable for their actions (2:6–11) and that God made clear the obligation of the human to acknowledge God (1:18–20). In other words, the workings of Sin that Paul is about to depict are not exclusive to Jews but obtain for gentiles in equal measure. In addition, the aggression of Sin does not remove the "I" from responsibility. The "desire" that Sin produces with the help of the law is a genuine desire, and it can be all-consuming, which is exactly why it is a particularly compelling commandment for Paul to cite here. The "I" that is overtaken by Sin is nonetheless "I"; it willingly cooperates in its own colonization.

[8] Verse 7 has scarcely offered a satisfactory answer to the question about the law. To be sure, Paul has vehemently denied that the law is to be equated with Sin, but he has also repeated and elaborated his earlier claim that the law produces knowledge of Sin. Verses 8–12 continue to unpack the relationship between Sin and the law, and here the account shifts attention back to the workings of Sin.

---

93. Philo, *Spec. Laws* 4.15.84 LCL identifies desire as "the fountain of all evils" (so also in *Decalogue* 28.142–153; 32.173). Similarly, Apoc. Ab. 24.10 connects desire with "every kind of lawlessness." See also Jas 1:15.

Having already introduced the handing over of humanity to Sin in 1:18–32 and the enslavement of all people under Sin in 3:9, and having narrated the devouring power of Sin and Jesus's victory over it in chs. 5–6, Paul returns one last time to examine the workings of Sin.[94] Once again (as in 5:12–13, 20–21; 6:12, 14) Sin becomes the subject of a string of active verbs:

v. 8   Sin, by staking out its base of operations . . . produced
v. 9   Sin sprang to life
v. 11   Sin, staking out its base of operations . . . deceived me and even killed me
v. 13   Sin . . . produced death for me, so that Sin . . . might grow sinful
v. 17   Sin lives in me (repeated in v. 20)

This aggressive language reflects the understanding that Sin is at war with God and that humanity is caught in the conflict, a scenario that culminates in 8:31–39.[95]

Already in v. 8 the subject of the sentence, in terms of both grammar and substance, is Sin. Now Paul goes beyond his earlier observations that Sin is *recognized* as Sin because of the law's command. Far more troubling, Sin uses the commandment and through it produces "every desire." The intensifying "every desire" menaces without clarifying, since the point here is not to define what "every desire" might look like but to capture the terrifying regime of Sin.

Sin uses the commandment by "staking out its base of operations" through the commandment. The noun *aphormē* occurs in a significant range of texts referring to the pretexts, resources, or even staging ground for a military battle (Thucydides, *Hist.* 1.90.2–3; Polybius, *Hist.* 3.69.8–9; Philo, *Flaccus* 5.35; 7.47; Dionysius of Halicarnassus, *Ant. rom.* 5.5.3; 6.25.3; Onasander, *Strategikos* 42.6.15).[96] In light of the conflict language elsewhere in this passage, this way of articulating the relationship between Sin and the law (the commandment) reflects Sin's hostile intent. Sin, weaponizing the commandment, produces "every desire."

The pithy formulation of v. 8b concludes in stark terms that, without the entry point provided by the law, Sin is dead. This comment stands in some tension with 5:13, which explicitly claims that Sin was already in the world, even without the law. The context suggests that what Paul means is not that Sin does not exist without the law but that Sin is rendered powerless without the law. With this statement the law becomes something more than a pretext or means

94. The further references in 8:2, 3, and 10 serve as part of a transition to Paul's discussion of the Spirit's role in the present. References to Sin (or sins) in 11:27 and 14:23 are similarly subsidiary to this extended discussion.

95. Notably, regarding this passage Ambrosiaster repeatedly connects Paul's comments about Sin with the work of the Devil (129–32).

96. See also Gal 5:13; 2 Cor 11:12–15; 1 Tim 5:14; 3 Macc 3:22; Martyn 1997a, 485, 492–95; Gaventa 2013b, 64–65; Ryan 2020, 173.

of access for Sin's activity; it becomes fuel for the functioning of Sin's work within the human being.

[9–10] Verses 9–10 once again narrate Sin's use of the law, this time turning up the rhetorical volume. The "I" is emphasized through the use of the emphatic pronoun *egō* instead of being contained within the inflected verb form, as is more normally the case. Further, the life of the *egō* is contrasted with the death of Sin by the conjunction *de*, sometimes left untranslated. A wooden translation clarifies the contrast:

> For without the law Sin is dead (v. 8b)
> *but I* [*egō de*] was living then, without the law (v. 9a)

This is the first of several such contrasts appearing in the lines that follow:

> Sin sprang to life (v. 9b)
> *but I* [*egō de*] died (v. 10)
> the law is spiritual
> *but I* [*egō de*] am fleshly since I have been sold under the power of Sin (v. 14)
> But . . . I am no longer the actor [*nyni de ouketi egō*]
> Sin is, and Sin lives in me (vv. 17, 20)

The "I" becomes the subject of two parallel statements: "I was living," and then "I died." The first "I" statement, "I was living," is followed by a recasting of v. 8. Now the law "comes," presumably meaning that the law comes into the world (as in 5:13), and therefore Sin springs to life and produces death (v. 10).

"I died" is followed by an explanation: the commandment was intended for life, but its result was death. Paul's syntax here is unmistakable: literally, he writes, "the commandment, for life; it, for death." Such a statement, taken by itself, once again opens the path toward a damning interpretation of the law (as earlier in 3:19, 27; 4:15; 5:13; 6:14). Yet shortly Paul will make his most unequivocal declaration about the law's goodness (v. 12) and once again reject the conclusion that the law itself produces death (v. 13).

This death of the "I" contrasts with that of Gal 2:19, where the "I" that dies is crucified together with Christ and then lives for God. In Rom 7:10 the death of the "I" is produced by enslavement to Sin. The logic is that of slavery (recall 6:17), which alienates enslaved persons from their world and produces social death (Patterson 1982, 5 and passim).

[11] First, however, v. 11 summarizes Sin's actions with Paul's most vigorous depiction so far of Sin's role. Repeating the opening phrase of v. 8 that Sin took the commandment as a base of operations, Paul also repeats the assertion that Sin worked through the commandment.[97] Then he continues: Sin

---

97. There is an inconsequential difference in word order; in addition, v. 8 is introduced by *de* ("and," "but"), and v. 11 by *gar* ("for," "since").

"deceived me and even killed me through the commandment" (v. 11). These are strong declarations. In ch. 5 Paul writes that Sin and Death entered the world (5:12) and that they ruled like kings over the world (vv. 14, 20–21). Chapter 6 acknowledges the enslaving power of Sin (6:6, 14, 18). Now Rom 7:11 specifies the actions as deception and murder, and the target of this activity is no longer the cosmos as a whole (5:13) but the individual "I."[98]

[12] Paul will expand on the aggression of Sin in vv. 13–20, but for now he returns to the opening question of whether the law itself is Sin (v. 7), offering the unambiguous response: "So the law itself is holy, and the commandment is holy and right and good." The introductory *hōste* ("so," "therefore") signals that the claims about the law follow from what has preceded, although Paul has not made an argument about the properties of the law as such. He has instead asserted the law's use by Sin, which makes space for this conclusion that goes well beyond dissociating the law from Sin, associating it instead with God. Just as the writings are said to be holy (1:2), the people God has called are holy (1:7), and God's spirit is holy (5:5), the law is also holy.

For Paul, the law's goodness is conferred and guaranteed by virtue of God's creation and bestowing of the law (see also 9:4), rather than by virtue of its observably true and beneficial content (Hayes 2015, 1–4).

With this direct assertion of the law's holiness, Paul departs from his disparaging comments in Galatians, where the law is said to have been delivered to Israel through the work of angels and by a messenger (3:19). There he made little attempt to exonerate the law or to moderate his position, insisting that the law was not able to give life (Gal 3:21) and that Scripture confined "all things" under Sin, implying that the law itself was among those things (Gal 3:22–23). Echoes of these claims appear in Romans but are more carefully nuanced (see, e.g., Rom 3:19–20 and 8:2), especially in 7:12, where the goodness of the law is affirmed without qualification. Paul may have modified his argument in response to sharp reactions that prompted further reflection (Tobin 2004, 70–78), yet it remains doubtful that Paul's fellow Jews would have found the discussion satisfying. Despite this vigorous claim that the law is holy, Paul still presents the law as associated with Sin, and he still distinguishes the law from the promise made to Abraham (4:13–14).

The effect of vv. 7–12 is less an exoneration of the law than an extension of Paul's argument about Sin. However holy, right, and good the law is, Sin has had the power to take the law as its own weapon.[99] With vv. 13–20, the terror of that observation comes to expression.

---

98. The repetition of the "p" and "t" sounds in *exēpatēsen* ("deceived") and *apekteinen* ("killed") enhances the effect.

99. See Gaventa 2016a. Given the minimal and elusive comments Paul makes about the law following this chapter (8:2–4, 7; 9:31; 10:4–5; 13:8–10), it does not seem that he has changed his

[13] Verse 13 returns to the question of v. 7 but recasts it, transposing the terms "law" and "Sin" with "good" and "death." Sin and Death/death have been associated closely since Paul linked them in 5:12, and already death has been invoked in vv. 8, 10, and 11. The substitution of "good" for "law" reflects the affirmation of v. 12, his assertion that the law ("the commandment") is indeed good. Yet using the more general term "good" for "law" has the effect of intensifying the discussion, avoiding as it does any hint of criticism of the law itself. The answering *mē genoito* ("Of course not!") again emphatically rejects the implication that it is the "good" that brings about "death" for "me."

The remainder of v. 13 displays Sin's action as a power grab. Paul restates his earlier claim that Sin made use of "the good" (instead of "the commandment" as in vv. 8–9, 11), but this time in an expanded form that pays little attention to the law as such and a great deal of attention to Sin's own aggression. Sin acted, working through the good to bring about death (recalling v. 8) in order that it might be recognized as Sin. This statement imputes volition to Sin in that Sin wants to be acknowledged for its power.[100] The remaining clause ("so that Sin through the commandment might grow sinful beyond all measuring") extends that willfulness: Sin becomes excessively sinful by use of the commandment. The portrait in ch. 5 of the growth of Sin's regime is here recalled by reference to its specific use of the commandment—the holy and right and good commandment (7:12)!—to make itself even more powerful.

Paul's earlier remarks about the law have prompted this question (as in v. 7). The answer he gives, however, has more to do with Sin than with the law. Sin's quest for power is not to be stopped even by the commandment of God, since Sin has become more powerful than God's law. The lines that follow demonstrate how Sin acted for its own voracious purposes.

[14] If Paul's only concern in this passage is to rescue his view of the law from misunderstanding, he could stop with v. 13. He has affirmed the

---

conviction about the actual practice of law observance from Galatians (and see Rom 14:14, where he identifies with those who are convinced that the dietary laws have been overturned). Instead, he has moderated his presentation, perhaps because he is unknown to most of the Roman audiences, which leads him to proceed with caution. After 9:4 nothing more is said of the law except in 9:31; 10:4–5; 13:8–10. Despite the concession in 9:4 that the giving of the law is among the blessings of God to Israelites, nothing at all in the remainder of chs. 9–11 suggests that Israel is identified with the law. The statement in 10:4 is notoriously ambiguous, as is 13:8–10 (see further below on each of those texts).

100. In what appears to be an attempt to avoid the implication that Sin itself has agency, Cranfield (1:354–55) attributes the action here to God, making God the subject of both *hina* clauses, but that interpretation overlooks the pattern of Sin's actions, both here and in chs. 5–6. God is nowhere named here as an agent and will not be until 7:25a. To be sure, Paul later insists that Sin and other powers aligned against God will ultimately be subject to God's triumph (see 8:31–39; 11:32 [to which Cranfield appeals, 1:355]; and 16:20), but that does not diminish the active role of Sin in this passage and elsewhere.

goodness of the law and has disentangled it from association with Sin, or at least he has tried to do that. In that case, however, the question arises why he continues in vv. 14–25a along lines that are in some respects similar. Tracing the argument closely, it seems Paul is not content to say that Sin has made use of the law for its own ends. Sin has not just used the law but has colonized the "I," and it is here that Paul's strongest language emerges. He takes a further step, claiming that Sin has actually produced a kind of split within the law, producing a law that is God's and another law that belongs to Sin (v. 25b; Meyer 2004d, 75).

Verses 14–20 show how it is that Sin becomes excessively sinful, even in the case of the "I" who knows the law, who delights in it and wishes to follow it. Like the speaker of Ps 119, the "I" knows that the law is spiritual and good (vv. 14, 16) and wants to observe the law. Unlike the speaker of Ps 119, however, the "I" finds observance to be impossible (Gaventa 2013a).

With v. 14 the verb tense changes from aorist to present, raising the possibility that the shift to present tense marks some particular historical moment. What is seldom observed, however, is that the shift in tenses does not begin with the "I" statement of v. 14b but with the preceding statement, "We know that the law is spiritual."[101] The shift to present tense *eimi* ("I am fleshly") conforms to that initial use of the present tense. In both cases the point is not to document a particular historical moment but to vivify the discourse. As Paul proceeds not simply to assert that Sin works through the law but also to depict its actions, the first-person account in present tense brings the argument closer to the audience.

Verse 14 opens with a gnomic claim: "We know" that the law is spiritual (recalling the depiction of the law in v. 12 as "holy and right and good"). The law is understood to be spiritual, but the spiritual law stands in contrast to the fleshly "I": "I have been sold under the power of Sin." Paul can and does speak of human flesh in neutral terms, as when he refers to bodily ailments (2 Cor 12:7; Gal 4:13–14) or when he speaks of corporate humanity as all "flesh" (Rom 3:20). The fleshly body is not inherently bad. Paul also speaks of "flesh" in negative terms, when flesh is ruled by Sin, as is the case in this passage (and see especially 8:3–9, where being "in the flesh" becomes shorthand for being "under Sin").[102] What Paul has affirmed in 3:9 about all—Jews and gentiles alike—he now affirms again, signaling that the problem that really needs to be under discussion is Sin rather than the law itself. However spiritual the law is, it has not counteracted the enslaving power of sin.

---

101. The preceding assertion about the law in v. 12 has no finite verb; translations supply the "is": "The law is holy and the commandment is holy and just and good" (v. 12b; similarly v. 7a).

102. Ambrosiaster comments on Rom 7:18, "[Paul] does not say—as it seems to some people—that the flesh is evil, but rather that what dwells in the flesh is not *good* but sin" (135).

And enslavement is in view. Although the Greek *pipraskein* ("to sell") appears in a range of texts, it is regularly and widely associated with the selling of humans into slavery, frequently in the context of battle.[103] Consistent with the conclusion of 3:9 that all are "under Sin," the "I" is under the power of Sin as slave master.[104]

[15–20] Exactly what enslavement under Sin looks like unfolds in an extensive statement that twice culminates with the despairing remark "Sin lives in me." It is one thing to be owned or occupied; it is yet another to have Sin dwelling in one's very being.

Sorting out the relationships among the law, Sin, and what the "I" wants and does not want, does and does not achieve, poses a challenge. The presentation below depicts the repetitions and relationships:

Observation	v. 15a	I do not understand my own actions.
Explanation	v. 15b	What I want to do is not what I actually do.
	v. 15c	Instead, I do what I hate.
Conclusion	v. 16a	Since I do what I do not want to do,
	v. 16b	I agree that the law is good,
	v. 17a	but I perceive that I am no longer the actor.
	v. 17b	Sin is, and Sin lives in me.
Observation	v. 18a	Now I know that nothing good lives in me, in my flesh.
Explanation	v. 18b	For willing the good is near to me, but doing the good is not.
	v. 19a	I do not do the good that I want to do,
	v. 19b	but the evil that I do not want—that is exactly what I do!
Conclusion	v. 20a	And since I do what I do not want to do,
	v. 20b	I perceive that I am no longer the actor.
	v. 20c	Sin is, and Sin lives in me.

The initial observation of a conflict between willing and acting (v. 15a) introduces this painful account of the experience of being "sold under the power of Sin." An explanation follows (v. 15b–c), in which "I" specifies the inability to do what is desired and the inevitability of doing what is abhorred. This explanation leads to a conclusion: this pattern of not doing what is wanted means that even though the "I" affirms the law's goodness (v. 16b), that is not enough to

---

103. See, e.g., *Il.* 21.40, 58, 78, 102; *Od.* 14.297; 15.387, 453; Ps 104:17 LXX; T. Zeb. 4.10; T. Jos. 1.5; Diodorus Siculus, *Bibliotheca historica* 4.31.5; 26.20.2; Josephus, *Ant.* 14.313, 321; Philo, *Joseph* 41.247; *Spec. Laws* 4.4.17; Onasander, *Strategikos* 35.2; Plutarch, *Sol.* 13.2; Epictetus, *Diatr.* 4.1.7; 4.1.116. Not surprisingly, given the strong association between defeat in war and enslavement, a number of these passages concern people enslaved in the aftermath of war. This association further reinforces the conflict scenario at work here.

104. Jewett rightly notes that the exact expression "sold under Sin" appears nowhere else in Greek texts before Paul and later appears only in Christian texts influenced by this verse (461). This distinctive formulation reflects Paul's earlier conclusion in 3:9 as well as Gal 3:22.

produce right conduct *because* the "I" is not in her own control. Instead, "Sin lives in me."[105]

Verse 18a follows logically from v. 17. If Sin lives within "me," then v. 18a must also be the case by virtue of Sin's colonizing actions. Nothing good lives within "me," within the flesh. Having earlier used "the good" as an alternative expression for "the law" (v. 13), Paul maintains that substitution here: it is not the good (the law) that lives "in me," but Sin. The point is not an ontological discussion or even a moral discussion about the character of the human body, but a consideration of the awesome power of Sin that invades both the law and the human person. It displaces the law as it colonizes the person.

Verses 18–20 repeat the logic of vv. 15–17, beginning with the general observation that nothing good lives within the human. Verses 18b–19 restate v. 15b–c, this time labeling what the "I" wants as "good" and what the "I" actually does as "evil."

The conclusion is exactly the same as in v. 17: Because "I" see the discrepancy between what "I" want and what "I" actually produce, "I" understand finally that I am not under "my" own control (v. 20b). Instead, Sin is in control. Sin is living within "me." Sin has become parasitic upon "my" life.

Lines from this passage resemble commonplaces found elsewhere in Paul's intellectual world. As early as Euripides's *Medea*, the distraught mother who anticipates murdering her own children announces that she knows the wrong of what she is about to undertake, but wrath (*thymos*) has overwhelmed her will (1078–80). Ovid's Latin interpretation of Medea in *Metamorphoses* casts her speech in this way:

> But some strange power draws me against my will.
> Desire persuades me one way, reason another.
> I see the better and approve it,
> but I follow the worse. (7.19–21 LCL; see Tobin 2004, 234–35)

This dilemma appears in philosophical discussions as well. Epictetus contends that Medea is mistaken in thinking that the death of her children is to her benefit; if only she understood the situation rightly, she would not commit the act (*Diatr.* 1.28.7–9). Others teach that the problem is not one of knowledge but passions run out of control, particularly rage (see Seneca, *Med.* 380, 916–19, 951–53, 988–89; so also Galen, *Hippoc. et Plat.* 3.3.13–22). Similarities exist between these discussions and individual elements in Paul's discourse,

---

105. Stendahl identifies this as "the rather trivial observation that every man knows that there is a difference between what he ought to do and what he does" (1976, 93). For the person who affirms the life-giving character of God's law, however, like the "I" in this passage, this is anything but a trivial observation.

particularly vv. 15–16 and 18b–19 (Stowers 1994, 260–64, 269–72; 1995, 198–202; Tobin 2004, 228–36).

Those similarities are limited, however. They cease when observation of human behavior yields to analysis as to its cause. For the philosophers, the problem exists within the human character, and the question is how to arrive at control of one's behavior (Nussbaum 1994, 439–83). For Paul, the problem is not with human reason or the passions but with the human's occupation by an outside force. Twice the "I" interprets the inability to conform willing and doing with the conclusion "Sin lives within me."

This colonized "I" contrasts sharply with the "I" of the Psalter. The speaker of Ps 119, for example, expresses a delight in the law that echoes in Paul's declaration that the commandment is "holy, right, and good" and the law "spiritual" (e.g., Ps 119:63, 94, 162). The speaker of Ps 119 also exudes confidence in the ability to keep the law (see vv. 69–70, 78, 87, 141, always with *egō* in LXX), while the "I" of Rom 7 can only delight in the law without being able to observe it (Gaventa 2013c).

The power of Sin, introduced in 3:9 and then narrated in terms of its grasping entry into the world in 5:12–21, is not simply repeated here in ch. 7 but articulated in horrifying terms: "Sin lives in me" (vv. 17, 20). Sin's domination is not observed at arm's length but experienced in parasitic terms. It cannot be avoided or defended against, since it lives within the person.[106] To say that Sin colonizes the human person is not at all an exaggeration, given Paul's use of the verb *oikeō* ("lives") in this passage.

To be sure, in Gal 2:20 Paul remarks that "Christ lives in me," but both the contexts and the verbs differ. The affirmation that Christ "lives" (*zaō*) refers to Christ's own actual life, as the verb *zaō* applies to all living things, including plants and animals (LSJ s.v.). Further, in Gal 2 the life the "I" lives is one of trust occasioned by the loving act of Christ (2:20). In Romans, by sharp contrast, the assertion that Sin "lives in me" employs the verb *oikeō* and connotes living in a particular space: people live in a particular house or a people occupy a territory (LSJ s.v.). The life the "I" lives is disempowered by the colonizing *oikeō* of Sin.

[21–23] Paul turns from the consequences of Sin's power in the "I" to its consequences for the law itself, taking the argument a step beyond his earlier claim that Sin had made use of the law. Now he will speak of *two* laws, one that is God's and is recognized by the "I," the other that is Sin's and does battle with the "I." He begins by restating vv. 15–16, 19–20: it is possible to will to do the

---

106. Orlando Patterson concludes his landmark study of slavery with the claim that it is best understood as "human parasitism," a condition that reflects the complex mixture of domination, dependence, and exploitation involved in slavery. He notes that the customary designation of the slave owner as "master" can mask the brutality of slavery, because "master" also refers to "master" artists or teachers or authorities (1982, 334–42).

good, yet evil lies close at hand. Actually, the wording slightly recasts those statements, and the reworking is revealing. The earlier versions consistently take the first-person singular: "What I want to do is not what I actually do," and so on. The restatement in v. 23 locates *to kakon* ("evil") as the subject. Evil lies close at hand, like the predator it is.

Verses 22–23 then introduce the distinction between two laws, the law of God and "another" law, not to be reduced to a principle or norm of experience (see translation note e on v. 21) but an actual fracture in the law. The first is and remains God's own (v. 22). This is the law in which "I take delight." The word *synēdomai* ("take delight") is a hapax legomenon in the NT and is not in the LXX, but the notion of rejoicing or delighting in the law is certainly to be found in the psalms (as in 118:14, 111, 162 LXX). Elsewhere the "inner" person is contrasted with the "outer" person, as in 2 Cor 4:16 and Eph 3:16. Here the phrase captures Paul's earlier language about "wanting" (v. 15) and "willing" (v. 16), and it anticipates the reference to "my mind" in v. 23. Within the depths of the self, the "I" delights in God's law.

The "I" also sees a second law (literally, "another" law), named toward the end of v. 23 as "the law of Sin." What Paul has been saying about Sin's use of the law is encapsulated in this brief phrase. "The law of Sin" is the law insofar as it has been taken over by Sin for its own purposes (see also 8:2). This is the law at work "in my limbs," that is, the law that produces the actions depicted in vv. 15–20, the inability to do the good and the compulsion to do wrong. When Paul instructs the Roman congregations to present "their limbs" to God, he refers to those limbs as "weapons" (6:13, 19), and that martial imagery returns here regarding the body parts in which this "other" law is at work. The law "does battle" with "the law governing my mind," that is, God's law. And the law of Sin "is taking me prisoner." It is that law, he repeats, that lives in "my" members. The end of v. 23 recasts the claim of vv. 17 and 20b: Sin is "in my own limbs."

Taken on their own, these are astonishing statements about the law. Yet they are substantively connected with two crucial elements in the letter that stretch back to 1:18. First, the language of conflict that began with 1:24, 26, 28 and has recurred regularly returns here when Sin is said to make use of the law for the purposes of doing battle with every good thing that is within "me." Sin uses even the law to make "me" a prisoner of war. This conflict language will culminate in ch. 8, with Paul's assertions about God's victory over these enemies.

Second, this is the climax in Paul's relentlessly recurring account of Sin that stretches all the way back into the first chapters of the letter. The account began with gentile sinning (1:24, 26, 28) and then yielded to a declaration of Sin's power over all people (3:9), a power from which "we" are delivered (chs. 5–6). Now it is revealed that Sin has made use of, indeed has made captive, even the good and holy and right law of God. To be sure, the result is a defense of the law, but it is far more than that: it is an exposé of Sin's imperial reach.

[24–25a] The captivity of the "I" to Sin produces the outcry "I am utterly miserable!" Trapped between delight in God's law and enslavement to Sin's law, the "I" perceives the need for deliverance, deliverance that must come outside the self rather than from individual resolution or determination or education. Ernst Käsemann's observation that, for Paul, "anthropology is cosmology *in concreto*" is entirely pertinent here (1971a, 27): the cosmic conflict between God and anti-God powers is experienced in the daily lives of human beings. Later in the letter the cosmic triumph of Christ is also played out in daily living (as in 12:1–15:13). The two are not mutually exclusive.

"Who will deliver me from the body ruled by this Death?" What the "I" sees is a life (the body) ruled by Death, referred to here as "this" Death. The cry for rescue employs *rhyomai*, a verb often used in the LXX in contexts in which God is rescuing Israel from its enemies (e.g., Exod 6:6; 14:30; 2 Sam 12:7; Mic 4:10; Isa 44:6). In Ps 17, the "I" is made to be "miserable" by the ungodly (16:9 LXX) and cries out for God's deliverance (16:13 LXX; Gaventa 2013c). The rescue required in Rom 7 is not from external enemies, however, but from "the body ruled by this Death" (see translation note g on v. 24). The body is the locus of the conflict, or at least it is one locus of conflict. And Death is still very much a power here, making it likely that Paul has in mind the body as ruled by Death.

Verse 25a offers only the briefest of answers to the question "Who will deliver me?" but it is an answer consistent with Paul's argument throughout the letter, and one that anticipates the direction of Rom 8. Rescue comes through the gift of "God through Jesus Christ our Lord." This phrase continues the pattern established in 5:11, in which points of summation are punctuated by reference to "Jesus Christ our Lord" (5:11, 21; 6:11, 23; 8:39). Yet "punctuated" understates the invocation, because these are acknowledgments of the profound action God has taken in Jesus Christ. Most of ch. 7 makes no reference to God or Jesus Christ (until this point, the only references are in v. 4 and v. 22), which has the effect of highlighting this word of praise.[107]

Following the doxological tone of v. 25a, the final half verse of this chapter sounds a jarring note as the expression of gratitude yields to yet another summation of the split within the law. The "I" declares that it serves both God's law (with thought, intent) and Sin's law (with action). Suggestions that this puzzling statement arises as a gloss fail for lack of any supportive manuscript evidence (e.g., Bultmann 1947, 197–202; Jewett 456–58, 473). Proposals that the two halves of v. 25 were reversed (Dodd 114–15) are likewise convenient but not convincing. My translation sets v. 25b apart as a separate paragraph, which is an attempt to present it as transitional. It summarizes the diagnosis of vv. 14–24a

---

107. See above on 1:25 for a discussion of interjections of praise and doxology in Romans; see also the introduction.

by way of introducing 8:1, the announcement of the end of condemnation.[108] The result is that the end of ch. 7 and the opening of ch. 8 are linked together by repetition and variation.[109]

Situation	I am utterly miserable! Who will deliver me from the body ruled by this Death? (7:24)
Response	Thanks be to God through Jesus Christ our Lord! (7:25a)
Situation	So I am a slave to God's law in my mind, but to Sin's law in my flesh. (7:25b)
Response	Now there is no condemnation for those in Christ Jesus. (8:1)

The "I" cries out for deliverance from life ruled by Death. Even though the "I" desires to observe God's law, enslavement to Sin remains a fact. Liberation comes about only through God's action in Jesus Christ, an action that results in the declaration "No condemnation!" That declaration and its consequences take us deep into ch. 8, with its exposition of life in the Spirit.

However difficult it is to keep track of Paul's argument in Rom 7, it is clarifying to notice the difference from Galatians, where his disparaging remarks make no effort to exonerate the law. Here, by contrast, Paul's emphatic response to the question of whether the law itself is Sin (v. 7) is and remains "Of course not!" He adamantly rejects the implication of his own statements earlier in the letter (to say nothing of his remarks in Gal 3). Just the same, the remainder of the letter shows remarkably little interest in the law, especially when discussing God's dealings with Israel in chs. 9–11.[110]

Paul's thinking appears to have shifted, to have penetrated further, so that he sees Sin's role in taking humanity captive and making use of the law to do that. Indeed, Sin's action is such that it captures the law itself, making use of the law to further undermine even the best desires of the human and finally producing a split within the law (Meyer 2004d, 75).

Despite lively debates in Paul's own time about the Mosaic law, it seems unlikely that his argument would have satisfied many of his Jewish peers, who would have suspected Paul of rejecting tradition (as evidenced independently in Acts 21:28). Similar readings by Christians over the long history of reflection on this text have produced interpretations that find fault with Judaism as a religion or Jews as a people. Such readings entirely miss the point of the chapter, which has to do with the power of Sin to corrupt *even* that which is good, *even* God's own law. In other words, it is not law observance or the content of the

---

108. The persistence of the "I" here is the only reason for not attaching 7:25b to 8:1.

109. Here I am influenced by Bruce Longenecker's identification of these verses as an instance of "chain-link" transition (2005, 88–93; see also J. King 2017).

110. Despite the assertion that the law is among God's gifts to Israelites (9:4), the reference to the law in 10:4 is notoriously and perhaps deliberately ambiguous (see below and Gaventa 2016a).

law that makes for wrongdoing, as when interpreters speak of "legalism" or a narrow Jewish piety or concern for "boundary issues." Paul's concern is with the ability of Sin to take captive even the best of human plans and intentions, among which he includes the law precisely as *God's holy commandment*.[111]

8:1–17 Liberation by the Spirit

Paul has twice announced the implications of God's action in Christ Jesus in terms of breaking humanity out of the powerful grip of Sin and Death (5:1; 6:1–7:6). Now, having reached the bottom of the spiral (Keck 1995, 25–26) with its depiction of Sin's ability to make use even of the holy law of God, to inhabit the body of the person, to bring about a fissure in the law itself (7:7–25), Paul shifts to describe what God's liberation looks like, first in the case of the addressees (8:1–17) and then in a larger, cosmic context (8:18–39). Much that is said here has been anticipated earlier, but Paul now develops those earlier hints about life in the Spirit.

Language about the Spirit has been sparse up to this point in the letter, but it dominates this chapter.[112] At 5:5 Paul wrote of God's love "poured out into our hearts through the Holy Spirit that has been given to us" (see also 1:4, 9; 2:29), and now he depicts what it means, what it looks like, when the Holy Spirit is poured into "our" hearts. That consideration is by no means simply abstract or theoretical; the Spirit figures significantly in Paul's understanding of the ongoing conflict between God and anti-God powers (see especially 8:6), as the Spirit stands on the side of "us," interceding for "us" (v. 26).

Although the second half of ch. 8 demonstrates that "we" have scarcely escaped from the harm inflicted by powers opposed to God (to say nothing of 9:1–15:13), with 8:1–17 Paul sketches the new identity of "us," those who are no longer at enmity with God, those who have been grasped by God's Spirit, who no longer fear enslavement. The new name is "children of God," children who are confident in their inheritance, who cry out to God in eager expectation. The significance of the Spirit's intervention comes into view in the expressions employed in this passage for those whom it inhabits: the Spirit's presence means life and peace (v. 6); the Spirit's occupation of the human brings dead bodies to life (v. 11); the Spirit makes children for God from those marked by Sin and Death (v. 14); the Spirit means adoption into God's household (vv. 15–17).

Understanding the Spirit of God as mediating God's presence and empowering God's agents appears already in numerous Jewish texts (e.g., Ps 51:11;

---

111. It is in this sense that Karl Barth's reading of Rom 7 as a critique of "religion" is on target (Barth 241–42 and passim), and "religion" in this case means Christianity fully as much as it means Judaism.

112. The word *pneuma* appears in Romans thirty-four times, twenty-one of which are in ch. 8.

Isa 11:2; 44:3; Ezek 36:26–27). What is distinctive in Paul's usage (and that of other early Christian texts) is the relationship assumed between the Spirit and Jesus Christ (Feldmeier and Spieckermann 2011, 225–26).

8:1 Therefore, now:[a] no condemnation for those who are in Christ Jesus.[b,c] **2** That is because the law under the power[d] of the Spirit that yields life[e] in Christ Jesus freed you[f] from the law under the power of Sin and Death. **3** Given that the law was powerless because it was weakened through the flesh,[g] God, by sending his own Son in the likeness of flesh ruled by Sin and to deal with Sin, condemned Sin in the flesh **4** so that the right decree of the law might be fulfilled by us, who do not live conformed to mere flesh but conformed to the Spirit.

5 For those conformed to flesh[h] side with[i] the flesh, but those conformed to Spirit side with the Spirit. **6** For the mindset of the flesh is death, but the mindset of the Spirit is life and peace. **7** So then, the mindset of mere flesh is at enmity with God; it does not submit to God's law, since it is not able to do that. **8** For those who live in the realm of mere flesh are not able to please God.

9 But you, you[j] do not live in mere flesh but in the Spirit, since[k] God's own Spirit inhabits you. But if someone does not have the Spirit of Christ, this one does not belong to Christ. **10** And if Christ is in you, the body may be dead because of Sin, but the Spirit means life because of righteousness. **11** And if the Spirit of the One who raised Jesus from the dead inhabits you, the One who raised Christ from the dead will also make even your mortal bodies alive through the Spirit that inhabits you.

12 So then, brothers and sisters, we are not obliged to the flesh, which means to live conformed to flesh, **13** since if you live conformed to flesh, you are going to die; but if by the Spirit you put to death the actions of the body, you will live. **14** For those who are led by God's Spirit, those are God's sons and daughters.

15 For you did not receive a spirit of slavery to fear again. Instead you received a spirit of adoption by which we are able to cry out, "Abba! Father!" **16** The Spirit itself confirms[l] our spirit; we are God's children. **17** And if we are children, then we are also heirs. We are God's heirs and also coheirs of Christ, since we suffer together that we will also be glorified together.

a. A few manuscripts (D* sy[p]) omit *nyn* ("now"), perhaps reflecting wariness that Paul's declaration would encourage moral laxity by removing fear of a final accountability.

b. Some manuscripts (A D[1] Ψ 81 365 629) insert the words *mē kata sarka peripatousin* ("who do not live according to the flesh"); others (ℵ[2] D[2] 33[vid] 𝔐 ar sy[h]) add that phrase and also *alla kata pneuma* ("but according to the Spirit"). Both appear to be attempts to qualify Paul's categorical declaration of noncondemnation by making Paul's descriptive language in vv. 4–8 into an ethical requirement.

c. The translation reflects the Greek, which has no verb, highlighting the importance of this declaration. Cf. 2 Cor 5:17: "So if someone in Christ: new creation."

d. Following the fissure in the law in 7:23 ("a second law"), here *nomos* exists in two forms, one controlled by Sin and the other by the Spirit (Meyer 2004d, 76; Martyn 2003, 579–81).

e. Lit., "spirit of life in Christ Jesus," understood as a genitive of purpose or direction, as in Rom 8:36; Gal 2:7 (BDF §166; Wallace 1996, 100–101). Throughout the translation of this passage, uppercase "Spirit" refers to the agent of God or Christ, lowercase "spirit" to the human spirit.

f. *Hēmas* ("us") appears in a couple of manuscripts (Ψ bo); and *me* ("me") in several (A D 1739ᶜ 1881 𝔐 lat sʰ sa), but the reading *se* ("you" singular) is both well attested (א B F G 1506* 1739* ar b syᵖ) and unexpected, making it easily understood why the other two readings arose as correctives.

g. The initial clause is a nominative/accusative absolute that stands in apposition to the main verb (Moule 1968, 35; Porter 1999, 91); the circumstance in which God acts is that of the law's powerlessness, but the focus here is on God's agency of sending and condemning.

h. *Kata sarka*, "according to flesh," can refer to physical life (as in 1:3; 9:5), but in Paul it can also mean having merely human values or ways of thinking and behaving (as in 1 Cor 1:26; 2 Cor 1:17; 5:16; 10:2, 3; 11:18). Translating it as "conformed to flesh" demonstrates the constraints imposed by the realm of mere flesh. The parallel phrase *kata pneuma* is translated accordingly.

i. Lit., "they think the things of the flesh," but *phroneō ta* appears to be idiomatic for "to side with" someone or "to belong to" someone's cause.

j. The emphatic *hymeis* is rendered here by means of the doubled address.

k. *Eiper* is often translated "if" (ESV, NIV, KJV), but it can mean simply "since" (as in NRSVue), acknowledging the fact that the Spirit of God does live "in you." Verse 9a, along with vv. 15–16, suggests that "since" is the better alternative; see also 3:30; 8:17; 1 Cor 8:5; and perhaps 1 Cor 15:15. That is to say, this is a logical rather than a conditional use of *eiper*.

l. Because of the *syn* prefix *symmartyrei* is often translated as if the Spirit testifies or witnesses *together* with our spirit, as in both NIV and NRSVue, but the function of the prefix in the case of *symmartyreō* is to intensify the verb rather than to indicate partnership between the Spirit and "our" spirit (see BDAG s.v.; Euripides, *Frag.* 319; *Hipp.* 286; Sophocles, *Phil.* 438; du Toit 2010).

[8:1–2] The terrifying recognition by the "I" that there are two laws—the law of God that is "holy and right and good" (7:12) and the other law that has been seized upon by Sin itself (7:23)—and that these two laws are both at work in "me" has already prompted a cry for deliverance and a confession of dual enslavement (7:24b). Perhaps Phoebe's auditors in Rome expected to hear a declaration of condemnation and a demand for repentance. Instead, they hear that there is no such verdict; indeed, they are reminded of their liberation.[113]

This announcement is far removed from the language of cool reflection on an abstract problem; it bears instead the marks of an announcement about an event: "Now: no condemnation . . ." It is tempting to identify 8:1 as the lifting of a death sentence, but what Paul writes instead is that there is no such death sentence. At 2:1 and 14:23 Paul refers to specific instances in which individuals condemn themselves by their actions, but the condemnation of 8:1 recalls the more ominous and universal use of condemnation (*katakrima*) in 5:16 and 18, where the condemnation of all humanity follows on Adam's act of disobedience. That handing over (1:24, 26, 28) of humanity to the powers of Sin and Death no longer exists "in Christ Jesus."

The modifier "those who are in Christ Jesus" stipulates both the extent of the nonjudgment and the change in focus that marks this chapter, which explores the results of God's action for life in the present. The phrase appears here for the first time in Romans. The locative sense it carries, the sense that people have been moved from one realm into another, appears as early as 6:3 with the notion of being baptized "into Christ Jesus" and united in his death and resurrection. Curiously, nothing is said here about faith as a qualifying factor. The language of faith has slipped off the screen and will not return until the end of ch. 9.[114] Nonetheless, *pistis* as trust or reliance on God's action in Jesus Christ is at the heart of what it means to be "in Christ" (as in 1:16; 3:22; 5:1).[115] The phrase "in Christ Jesus" also recalls the action that made possible the declaration of no condemnation. Together with "now," the phrase signals the advent of a radically new human situation "in Christ Jesus."

The opening declaration is followed in v. 2 by a restatement of 5:12–21 focalized on the two laws in the lament of 7:7–25. The two laws have a place in God's liberation of humanity from its slavery. On the one hand, there is the law that is possessed by Sin and Death. This law, which is good and holy and right, having its origin in God, has nevertheless become the tool of Sin and Death, has actually been taken in hand by Sin and Death (Meyer 2004d).[116] But the other law is in the possession of "the Spirit that yields life in Christ Jesus," and this law liberates.

---

113. Käsemann rightly contends that 8:2 "sets all that follows under the heading of liberation" (215).

114. *Pistis* ("faith" or "trust") last appeared at 5:1 and next appears at 9:30.

115. The *pistis* implicit in the notion of being "in Christ Jesus" scarcely resembles the anemic concept of *pistis* as an individual's assent to certain propositions about Jesus.

116. The long history of Christian misrepresentation of all things Jewish makes it necessary to notice again that Paul does not criticize Jewish attitudes toward the law or even the law itself (despite some earlier comments of a provocative nature, as in 3:20; 4:13; 5:13; 6:14). He contends instead that Sin is so powerful that it can take captive *even* God's holy law.

Much is compressed into the phrase "the law under the power of the Spirit that yields life in Christ Jesus."[117] Reference to life most immediately contrasts with the reference to the "law under the power of Sin and Death," but the Spirit is associated with life at several points in the discussion that follows: the Spirit's intention is to produce "life and peace" (v. 6); the presence of Christ means that the human spirit is alive because of righteousness (v. 10). Comprehending Paul's discussion of the Spirit is exceedingly challenging, but this verse introduces important facets of the Spirit's work that will unfold throughout this chapter.[118] The Spirit is associated with Christ or God as a powerful agent. That agent is actively involved in human lives in the context of the conflict between God and anti-God powers in that the Spirit liberates "you" (and see also vv. 5–7). And the Spirit comes to be known through experience in that it produces life (and see also vv. 15, 26–27).

Tangled up in Paul's distinction between two laws, readers may skip over the remainder of the sentence, but it is crucial: there has been an act of liberation. Associated frequently elsewhere with the redemption of slaves and prisoners (e.g., Thucydides, *Hist.* 1.124.3; 8.15.2; Polybius, *Hist.* 16.13.1; T. 12 Patr. 11.1.5; Philo, *Embassy* 155; Plutarch, *Sull.* 18.5), the verb *ēleuthērōsen* ("freed" or "liberated") characterizes this as an event in the conflict between God and the anti-God powers.[119] Here Paul unpacks the redemption he announced as early as in 3:24 or even 1:16: the saving act that is the gospel comes into human lives as liberation.

The object of this liberative act is the singular "you," which comes as a surprise, since "you" in Paul is most often plural (as in the immediate context, 8:9–11). The "I" that has dominated 7:7–25 makes this switch to second-person even more puzzling, yet that "I" provides the clue for understanding the

117. This instance of *nomos* is among those often understood as a principle or pattern of some sort rather than the Mosaic law, but Paul is unlikely to introduce a significantly different use of the word immediately following his careful discussion of the relationship between Sin and the law. Martyn observes a disturbing interpretive tendency to take Paul's negative uses of the word *nomos* as references to Mosaic law while identifying his positive uses of the word as principles or abstractions (2003, 577).

118. Among the challenges to any discussion of the Spirit are at least the following: the distinction between human spirit and what Paul will call "God's Spirit" or "the Spirit of Jesus Christ"; the entanglement of Paul's language with discussion of the Trinity; and of course the imprecise character of any discussion of spirit that bleeds over into descriptions of personality, energy, or temperament—particularly in an era that wants to distinguish spirituality from religion. As Paul Meyer notes, this latter difficulty cuts across ancient philosophical and religious traditions (2004a, 117).

119. BDAG s.v. distinguishes *eleutheroō* in the "spiritual" sense from its use in political contexts, and such a distinction is warranted in the few appearances of the verb in Epictetus (*Diatr.* 3.24.67–68; 3.26.39; 4.1.114; 4.7.17). Paul's use is of course "spiritual" in the sense that the Spirit has a role in it, but the dense language of conflict that surrounds this passage implies that Paul is not thinking of the Spirit's liberation in a restricted way, as when it is limited to personal salvation, for example.

pronoun here. Having completed the speech of the "I" who so compellingly voices the enslavement produced by Sin's malicious use of God's good law, Paul turns to address that same "I" with a word of liberation: Now God's action in Jesus Christ has freed you.[120]

[3–4] Verses 3–4 explain how the liberating event took place. Verse 3 opens with an observation about the law's disability, and v. 4 closes with a claim that the law's right demand is fulfilled. The action is not accomplished by the law, however; the law has not changed. Nor is the action that of humans, except in the secondary sense that humans live from the Spirit's empowerment. Central to this liberating event is God's condemnation of Sin through the sending of God's own Son.

The claim that the law is *adynaton* ("powerless") recalls the depiction of Sin's horrifying seizure of the law for its own ends (7:7–25). Paul claims that the law was rendered powerless by the flesh, although the agent at work in ch. 7 is Sin rather than flesh (though see 7:18, 25). This shift in nomenclature anticipates the discussion that follows, which contrasts life "in the flesh" with life "in the Spirit." More to the point, life "in the flesh" is yet another way of referring to human life as it has been taken captive by Sin's power.

The description of the law as "powerless" may seem hyperbolic given that *adynatos* is often understood to invoke the more limited notion of weakness rather than powerlessness (e.g., Rom 15:1; Joel 4:10 LXX; Job 36:15 LXX; Plato, *Hipp. maj.* 296a; Lysias, *Epitaphios* 2.73). But *adynatos* can connote powerlessness (BDAG s.v., LSJ s.v.; e.g., Herm. *Mand.* 11.19 [43.19]; Diogn. 9.6; Herodotus, *Hist.* 5.9; 6.16; Aristotle, *Ath. Pol.* 49.4), and the question of power lies at the heart of this letter, having been introduced as early as 1:4 with reference to Christ's resurrection. Paul declares in 1:16 that the gospel is God's own power (*dynamis*), and 4:21 recalls Abraham's confidence that God is powerful (*dynatos*) to complete what has been promised. Assurance about God's power to protect "us" from any other power culminates the argument of ch. 8 (vv. 38–39). God's powerful intervention comes about in a context in which Sin has decimated the law's power.

The statement of God's action takes the auditors deep into Paul's understanding of the gospel.[121] The initial participial clause describing God's action

120. Again, this is not to exclude Paul himself from those addressed. Far from limiting the range of addressees, the "I" is a rhetorical device that makes the analysis more vivid and powerful. The "you" of 8:2 does the same. As Susan Eastman puts it, "We may hear each person addressed as individual—you, and you, and you" (2013, 103).

121. There is a shift here between v. 2, which identifies "the Spirit that yields life in Christ Jesus" as the agent, and v. 3, which identifies God as the agent. The fact that Paul can say both these things without sensing the need to explain their relationship to one another suggests that for him these agents are intertwined. His assumption of the interconnection between God and the Spirit is such that he can move from one to the other without explanation.

draws on what is likely an early Christian interpretation of the life of Jesus: God sent Jesus, God's Son. That conviction appears not only here and in Gal 4:4 but elsewhere, including Mark 9:37; Matt 10:40 // Luke 10:16; John 4:34; 5:36; 13:20; 1 John 4:9–10. In common with Gal 4:4–7, Rom 8 affirms that Jesus entered into human life, that he did so to secure redemption for humanity, that the Spirit enables "us" to cry out to God, and that "we" become heirs of God, God's children.

Yet the assertion of Gal 4:4 that Christ was "born of a woman" is more neutral than the assertion that the Son was "in the likeness of flesh ruled by Sin." "Likeness" (*homoiōma*) misleads if it opens the door to notions that limit the Son's participation in human life, since the controlling element in the phrase is Sin rather than likeness (Blackwell 2011, 127; Paulsen 1974, 59). To the contrary, Paul is asserting the reality of the Son's humanity (see above on "likeness" in 5:14 and 6:5). The Son becomes flesh and, as such, is fully part of the human condition of enslavement to the powers of Sin and Death.[122] This is a shocking statement, unless earlier statements are reckoned with seriously—statements both about Sin as a power and also about Christ himself.[123] In 6:9 Paul claims that Death no longer rules over Christ, because when he died he died to Sin. But that the Son was "in the likeness of flesh ruled by Sin" means that Christ was subject to Sin's power. For all those who live after Adam, which is to say for all humanity, that is the only flesh that exists prior to the death and resurrection of Christ.

The reason for sending the Son follows: God sent the Son "to deal with Sin" (*peri hamartias*). This slight prepositional phrase summarizes God's intervention to defeat Sin as that intervention has been unpacked throughout much of the first seven chapters of Romans. God acts in Jesus Christ in order to deal with Sin.[124] The final phrase makes this clear: God condemned Sin in the flesh. The verb is crucial; there is no condemnation for those in Christ Jesus *because* God has condemned Sin "in the flesh." The phrase is ambiguous; it could refer either to the territory ruled over by the flesh (see vv. 5–7) or to the flesh of Jesus Christ. Probably both senses are in play. It is the death of Jesus, his very fleshly

122. As Robert Tannehill observes, this is "not merely a general affirmation of divine intervention but an affirmation of the Son's identification with humanity in its situation of need" (2007, 227). In the words of Dietrich Bonhoeffer, "God took on the whole of our sick and sinful human nature, the whole of humanity which had fallen away from God" (2001, 214).

123. At least this statement is shocking for those who expect Paul to affirm Christ's sinlessness, but Paul does not seem interested in that question, except perhaps for 2 Cor 5:21, and even there the point seems to be Christ's identification with sinful humanity.

124. *Peri hamartias* appears in the LXX as a "sin offering," but that nuance is inappropriate here, where Sin is not removed but condemned. Even in the LXX the phrase is often best translated simply as "for sin" (Breytenbach 1993, 73–75). In Lev 5:6, for instance, the phrase *peri hamartias* modifies the animal presented to the priest, who then makes an offering resulting in sin being removed. *Peri hamartias* describes what is brought "for sin."

death, that defeats Sin (see especially 6:10). But Jesus's flesh also participates in the realm of the flesh.

Sin is actually condemned not just in the sense that God judges it to be guilty, but that God takes action to bring about Sin's defeat. To condemn (*katakrinein*) elsewhere is associated with destruction, and that nuance appears to be at work here as well (e.g., Herodotus, *Hist.* 7.146; Xenophon, *Apol.* 7; Dan 4:37a LXX; Sus 53; Josephus, *Ant.* 10.124). Paul has already touched on this point with his claims about the superabundance of grace in ch. 5 and especially in the argument of 6:10 that Christ died to Sin once and will never again do so.[125] It is, of course, this death to Sin and defeat of Sin that ushers in the work of the Spirit, which Paul takes up shortly.

Verse 4 moves to the result of this condemnation of Sin: it takes place so that the right decree of the law can be fulfilled. Paul does not dwell on the content of this *dikaiōma* or the decree of the law. Further complicating matters, following this passage (and see v. 7), the letter pays scant attention to the law. The few comments Paul makes about *nomos* later in the letter are notoriously elusive. In 9:31 he will write that Israel pursued something called the "law of righteousness," and in 10:4 that Christ is the *telos* (the end or the goal) of the law. The only other reference to the law comes in 13:8, 10, where Paul asserts that love fulfills the law. This paucity of discussion about what it means to fulfill the law's right decree implies that Paul is not especially concerned with offering a revised version of Mosaic law to be followed in Christian communities.[126] His concern, rather, is for clarifying Sin's use of the law and Sin's defeat, which he has done. He turns now to contrast living under the reign of Sin and Death with living under Christ's reign. Here he employs the language of flesh and Spirit/spirit by way of transitioning into a lengthy discussion of the Spirit's role of giving and sustaining life. The identification of "us" as the ones who live conformed to Spirit rather than to flesh marks the transition to that discourse.

This invoking of those who live according to the Spirit parallels the phrase "in Christ Jesus" in v. 1: those who are "in Christ" are the ones who live aligned with the Spirit rather than with mere flesh. The flesh–Spirit/spirit dichotomy has already surfaced in ch. 7, but here it returns and will dominate the discourse

---

125. Writing of the "sending" of the Son in Gal 4:4, Martyn comments that sending means "redemption has come from outside the human orb. For Paul, to say that God *sent* his Son is to say that God *invaded* the cosmos in the person of Christ" (1997a, 407). "Invasion" language is disturbing, but the context of the language of condemnation and the martial language that pervades Rom 5–8 demonstrate that it is fitting for Paul's discourse. Humanity's plight is such that only intervention from the outside can be effective.

126. See further the discussion of Rom 14:1–23, which is hard to reconcile with the notion that Paul wanted to establish some new or revised notion of the law, especially when he insists that the reign of God is not about food or drink.

through 8:13, at which point Paul shifts to language drawn from the arena of the family (although there as well the Spirit is at work).[127]

Life in the Spirit is the backbone of this passage, recurring in various forms in vv. 4, 9, 11, 13, and 14. The repetition of reference to living keeps this passage from being abstracted as a theoretical discussion about some imagined essential differences between flesh and spirit. In addition, the shift to the present tense shows that Paul here undertakes to interpret what life looks like in the present time for those who have been grasped by God in the gospel of Jesus Christ, who live in anticipation of God's impending triumph over all God's enemies.

[5–8] Paul shifts to the present time, in which some people are "conformed to flesh" and others "conformed to Spirit." The present tense is significant, marking as it does the life-giving change God's Spirit brings about in those conformed to Spirit, a change addressed in vv. 9–17. The present tense also leaves open the possibility that those "conformed to flesh" will be joined to the ranks of those "conformed to Spirit." The "all" of 5:18 and 11:32 leaves that possibility open, as does the global reference of 8:19, since even those "conformed to flesh" yearn for deliverance. At the very least, these are not timeless distinctions between two different types of human beings. Nor do the present differences invite Paul's auditors to view their status triumphantly (as will be clear in 11:13–24). The chasm separating these two conformities reflects the size of God's deliverance rather than some moral or intellectual achievement by human beings.

The Spirit/spirit–flesh distinction is first explored negatively, with attention to the flesh side in vv. 7–8, and then positively, with attention to the Spirit in vv. 9–11. Initially the distinction is made between ways of thinking or perceiving as those indicate alignment with or against God's Spirit. Paul uses both the verb *phroneō* and the related noun *phronēma*, words that can be used of those who are partisans, even of those who serve on the same side in a political or military conflict, and not simply as a reference to thinking in similar ways.[128] In Herodotus, for example, the verb is used in reference to those who sided with King Apries (*Hist.* 2.162) and later to the Greeks who battle on the side of Xerxes (7.102). In 1 Maccabees, when Alexander Epiphanes makes Jonathan high priest, he writes that Jonathan should "take our side," using *phroneō* (10:20). Josephus similarly refers to Herod's supporters as "those who think like Herod," again using *phroneō* (*Ant.* 14.450).[129] The assertion of v. 7 that the

---

127. Here as elsewhere, being conformed to flesh does not mean that flesh per se is a bad thing; for Paul, conformity to flesh is shorthand for captivity to Sin and Death.

128. To be sure, *phroneō* does not always suggest partisanship; it can reflect thinking that has a particular character (as in 12:3, 16) or thinking that favors a particular action (as in 14:6, although there may be a partisan tinge in that instance).

129. See also Aristophanes, *Pax* 640; Xenophon, *Hell.* 6.3.14; 7.4.40; Demosthenes, *Cor.* 18.161; *3 Philip.* 56; Diod. Sic. 20.35.2; Esth 8:12b LXX; Cranfield 1:386. In all these cases, *phroneō* ("think") is paired with *ta* (lit., "the things of") as here in vv. 4–5.

mindset of the flesh is at enmity with God reinforces the possibility that Paul has partisanship in mind, contrasting partisanship with "flesh" and partisanship with "Spirit" (recalling Gal 5:16–18). As in 5:10, life outside the action of God in Jesus Christ is life at war with God: "We were enemies."

Life at war with God is identified with Death (v. 6a), recalling the partnership of Sin and Death in 5:12–21. Conformity to the Spirit is life, death's opposite, but it is also here identified with peace. Already the letter greeting has introduced peace (1:7), and it appears in 2:10 as one characteristic of the comprehensive rewards for those who do the good and in 5:1 as a description of those who have peace with God through Jesus Christ (and contrast 3:17). That is the way in which peace happens: it comes about through God who is identified as the "God of peace" (15:33; 16:20).

Three additional statements in v. 7 unpack this partisanship with flesh. First, those in partnership with flesh are not submissive to the "law of God," that is, the law in God's hands (as in 8:2a). This recalls 7:7–25 with its impassioned comments about the "I" and its fleshly inability to act according to God's good law. The second statement should also not be surprising: not only is one who is in league with flesh unsubmissive to God, but such obedience is impossible. As 7:7–25 has demonstrated, this is not a matter of repentance or a change of the human will but sheer inability. Verse 8 then interprets this claim in other terms: those who are "conformed to flesh" are not able to please God. Here Paul has wandered far from the demand attributed to Peter that people repent and do God's will (Acts 2:38; 5:31; see also 13:38). For those conformed to flesh, action that is pleasing to God is simply impossible.

With 12:1–2 the reversal of this statement will come into view: those who are conformed to the Spirit, those who have received God's mercies, are admonished to make their entire lives an offering that pleases God, and that action is possible only because of the Spirit's arrival.

[9–11] Verse 9 returns to the statement Paul has already made in vv. 1 and 4, this time directly addressing the audience, employing the emphatic pronoun "you" (plural): "You, you do not live in mere flesh but in the Spirit, since God's own Spirit inhabits you." Where 7:17, 20 described life under the occupation of Sin, now life occurs under the occupation of God's own Spirit, using the verb *oikeō* in both places. This stunning contrast between occupations epitomizes the liberative act of the God who condemned Sin in the flesh of Christ.[130]

A significant difference between Paul's descriptions of the two occupations is that, while he evokes in painful terms the occupation of the "I" by Sin (the inability to do what is desired, the identification of the good but the captivity to wrongdoing), the Spirit's occupation comes to expression in terms that are both

---

130. "*Christ in us* is therefore both the place where we are deprived of our liberty and the place where we receive it" (K. Barth 286, ital. orig.).

communal and nonspecific. The Spirit means life (vv. 10–11), the Spirit leads (v. 14), the Spirit enables calling on God as Father (v. 15), the Spirit is a witness to "our" adoption, the Spirit intercedes (v. 26). How the Spirit's occupation is experienced remains unstated, precisely because it is Spirit and manifests itself in a limitless and uncontrolled range of places and actions.[131]

Verse 9b frames the Spirit's occupation in terms of its absence and what that signifies: "If someone does not have the Spirit of Christ, this one does not belong to Christ." The notion of having the Spirit is misleading if it is understood in a possessive sense, especially as Paul has just spoken about the Spirit's occupation. Having the Spirit here is a shorthand reference to being occupied by the Spirit. The emphasis falls on the Spirit rather than on the person or the possession of the Spirit (K. Barth 273).

Notably, Paul shifts from the expression "Spirit of God" to "Spirit of Christ" without distinguishing between them (as in vv. 2–3). Debates about the Trinity and its relations lie well beyond Paul's time and outside his awareness, but his claims about the Spirit's activity tie it intimately both to Christ and to God the Father. However such expressions might come into play in discussions of the Trinity, Paul's discussion is focused on the emphatic declaration that having Christ's Spirit means that one belongs to him.

Verses 10b–11 expand on this existence in Christ, occupied by Christ, aligned with God's actions (going back to the partisan language of v. 7). Here Paul recasts the language of 6:3–5, connecting Christ and the baptized, this time inflected through the work of the Spirit (vv. 10a, 11a) on the human spirit. The construction of v. 10b is both significant and potentially confusing. Translated woodenly, Paul writes:

| On the one hand | body | dead | because of Sin |
| On the other hand | Spirit | life | because of righteousness |

The two halves parallel each other syntactically, with one revealing difference: the adjective "dead" is not followed by the adjective "living" but by the noun "life." That prompts translators rightly to understand the "spirit" referenced here as the divine Spirit (as in vv. 9, 11, 14), as in NRSVue, NIV, KJV, ASV, CEB, ESV. The contrast Paul makes at this juncture is not between two forms of human life, one dead and one living, but between Sin's occupation of the human, rendering the human dead (as in 7:24), and the Spirit's occupation, which produces life because of God's rectifying act in Jesus Christ. Verse 11 unpacks this terse claim in just that way. The occupation of the Spirit of God means nothing less than bringing life from the dead.

---

131. The Johannine Jesus expresses the point more succinctly: "The Spirit blows where it wills" (John 3:8).

The human situation is now radically altered: life reigns instead of death; God's own Spirit lives in you.

Twice Paul identifies God by reference to the resurrection. God is "the One who raised Jesus from the dead" and then "the One who raised Christ from the dead." Paul employs slight variations on this phrase in 4:17, 24; 10:9; 2 Cor 1:9; 4:14; 1 Thess 1:10; Gal 1:1 (see also Acts 3:15; 4:10; 13:30; Eph 1:20; Col 2:12; 1 Pet 1:21). Together with "the God and Father of our Lord Jesus Christ" (Rom 15:6; 2 Cor 1:3), "the One who rectifies the ungodly" (Rom 4:5), and the like, such expressions name God in Paul's letters, in place of more traditional epithets such as "God of Israel" or "God of Abraham" (Gaventa 2022e).

However important the resurrection of Christ is in Paul's understanding of God, that event is not an end in itself. The assumption of v. 11 is that whatever has happened to Christ is also to happen to "you." It is not simply that God, Christ, and the Spirit are connected with one another, but "we"/"you" are also connected with them. God can and will do for humanity what has been done in the case of Christ.[132] Paul has already made claims about the future life of believers, life generated by Christ's own resurrection (5:10; 6:11). Eventually he will extend that claim to the part of Israel currently hardened (11:15; Linebaugh 2013b, 217). But already that resurrected life is anticipated in the Spirit's activity, as Christians exist, even in the present, out of that future. They live "ahead" of themselves (Ziegler 2018, 78).

This comes about, Paul repeats, "through the Spirit that inhabits you." Although Paul elsewhere anticipates the resurrection of believers (Rom 6:4–11; 1 Cor 6:14; 15:12–19, 51–53; 2 Cor 4:14; Phil 3:10–11), only here does he identify the Spirit as the agent of resurrection. In 6:4, however, Paul identifies Christ's own resurrection as having taken place through the "glory of the Father." And 1 Cor 6:14 states that it occurred through God's power. These instances in which Paul couples the verb *egeirō* or *zōopoiēsō* with *dia* in the genitive ("raise through the agency of" or "make alive through the agency of") are closely related, in that all of them identify the resurrection itself with divine power. In particular, the "glory of the Father" connotes not just God's presence and action, but God's presence in situations of conflict (see above on 6:4; Gaventa 2014b). The Spirit's powerful agency, then, extends well beyond that of making individual lives (or even communities) spiritual. It has to do with liberation from the power of Death itself.[133]

The plural "you" does not diminish the significance of this claim for individual lives any more than the singular "I" of 7:7–25 excludes the colonization

---

132. As Käsemann observes, "Paul only speaks of the resurrection of Christ in connection with, and as the beginning of, the resurrection of the dead in general" (1971b, 55).

133. Does the Spirit's agency in resurrection apply to the resurrection of Jesus Christ itself (so Hill 2015, 159–63)? The text does not yield a clear answer to that question, even if it does convey the intimate relationship among God, Jesus, and the Spirit in their workings on behalf of "you."

of Sin from corporate life. The emphasis lies on the Spirit's indwelling, an activity that will be explored in the lines that follow.

[12–14] "So then, brothers and sisters" draws attention to the urgent claim that follows: "we" are not under obligation to the realm of the flesh. The terminology of obligation is new in this passage, although Paul used it in 1:14 of his obligation to preach the gospel. Here the positive side of obligation remains unexpressed, as it is the negative side Paul is concerned to elaborate.

The structure of the argument is important:

v. 12   We are not obliged to the flesh, which means to live conformed to flesh,
    v. 13a   if you live conformed to flesh,
           you are going to die;
    v. 13b   if by the Spirit you put to death the actions of the body,
           you will live.
v. 14   Those who are led by God's Spirit, those are God's sons and daughters.

Paul begins a series of parallels only to deviate from the logical conclusion in revealing ways. Following v. 13a, "if you live conformed to flesh, you are going to die," the natural parallel would be "if you live conformed to the Spirit, you will live." With the phrase "by the Spirit," however, Paul interjects his assumption that only with the Spirit's assistance is it possible to triumph over the "actions of the body," which is to say, a life lived in conformity with merely human values and expectations. Verse 14 repeats this emphasis: it is those who are led by God's Spirit who are God's children.

This line culminates the contrast begun in v. 4 between life *kata sarka* and life *kata pneuma*. There are "two possibilities of human existence" (Cranfield 1:394), yet Paul's contrast sits at some distance from Deut 11:26–28 or 30:15–20, texts that address their audience with choices to be made, with the language of possibility. Paul has repeatedly demonstrated that there is no escape from life in the flesh apart from God's action in Jesus Christ. In addition, life in the Spirit is "possible" not because humans freely choose it but because they are chosen (see especially 8:28–30 and the language of calling in 1:1, 7, and elsewhere). What v. 15 will affirm is that you "received," not that you "chose" from a menu of options.

As often elsewhere, Paul insists on the integrity of what later would be referred to as "faith and life," yet his comments about "life" or behavior remain at a very general level. No specific actions are either commanded or proscribed. Even when he shifts to more extended treatment of particular questions in 12:1–15:6, the argument begins by assuming that those in the Spirit are enabled to discern God's will (12:2). The work of these lines in ch. 8 is less to give ethical instruction than to reidentify Roman believers by new names, relocating them in a cosmos that remains under siege, as comes to explicit expression in the final lines of the chapter. That reidentification and relocation carries with it new behavior, to be sure. It involves the entire person (12:1–2), which is taken up into a new identity, a new location, through the Spirit's work.

The final phrase of v. 14 introduces the expression "son of God" (rendered above as "sons and daughters of God"). The gender-specific reference to "son" shows the relationship of those in Christ to Jesus Christ as God's Son, although it seems clear that Paul has in mind both female and male offspring.[134] Even before the explicit reference to relationship to Christ, this introduction of the phrase "son of God" implies a profound relationship to Christ, since Paul has consistently referred to Jesus as God's Son (1:3, 9; 5:10; 8:3; and later in 8:29, 32). It also reflects God's history with Israel, in that Deut 14:1 addresses the Sinai generation: "You are sons of the Lord your God." This name, epitomizing the new human situation, is explicated in the lines that follow.

[15–17] As Paul explains what it means to be God's sons and daughters, the contrast between flesh and Spirit/spirit at last falls away. From this point, language of Sin and Death appears infrequently and does not again stand center stage, as it has done almost since 5:12. The spiral of Sin has ended, replaced by a depiction of God's victory in human life and, indeed, in all of creation (vv. 19–22).

Verse 15 opens with "For you did not receive a spirit of slavery to fear again." This seems an odd thing for Paul to say, given that he identifies himself as Jesus Christ's slave in 1:1 and that he admonishes the Romans to present themselves as slaves of righteousness in 6:19 (and see 6:16, 22; cf. also 1 Cor 7:22; 2 Cor 4:5; Gal 1:10; Phil 1:1). The fact that this is an abstract noun, "slavery" rather than the noun "slave" (so also in 8:21; Gal 4:24; 5:1), scarcely makes for a satisfying explanation. Instead, the phrase needs to be considered as a whole: "a spirit of slavery to fear again." The fear Paul evokes is that associated with slavery to Sin that necessarily produces Death (as in 6:15–23).[135]

Instead of a spirit of fear, the spirit "you" received is that of adoption. Although Paul's Scriptures include ample evidence of Israel being referred to as God's firstborn (Exod 4:22; Jer 31:9 [38:9 LXX]) or God's son (Deut 8:5; 14:1; 2 Sam 7:14; Ps 2:7; Prov 3:12; Isa 43:6; Mal 3:17), the language of adoption is absent.[136] Roman evidence is another matter altogether, for Roman males could and did legally adopt males largely as a way of securing the family

---

134. Similarly, Paul applies female terminology to males as well as females in the lines that follow, when "we" are said to be in labor (8:22–23).

135. The connection between fear and slavery coheres with Orlando Patterson's wide-ranging study of slavery, which demonstrates the deep patterns of power, domination, and fear that are at the heart of slavery (1982).

136. *Huiothesia* does not occur in the LXX, not even in texts such as Exod 2:10, where Pharaoh's daughter takes Moses into her household, although it does appear when Philo (*Moses* 1.19) and Josephus (*Ant.* 2.232) discuss the event (Heim 2017, 130–34).

line and property.[137] This complex of evidence strongly suggests that while Paul's language may be informed by his understanding of God's relationship to Israel, that understanding is inflected through Roman practice and would likely be understood through that practice (Heim 2017, 112–47). (This point will return in 9:4, where "adoption" is said to be among God's gifts to the Israelites.)

Introducing the language of adoption means the slavery to righteousness advocated in 6:15–23 is not simply an exchange of masters, a mere substitution for the prior slavery to Sin. Instead, slavery to righteousness is simultaneously adoption into the household. Paul's rhetorical change of register from fear-inducing slavery to adoption goes to the heart of the Spirit's role. Release from slavery to Sin does not produce the freedom to do as one pleases; through the agency of the Spirit, release from slavery produces relationship with God, a relationship that moves the child to cry out, "Abba, Father!"

Rare in Paul's letters, the verb *krazō* occurs in a parallel statement in Gal 4:6 and in Rom 9:27, where Isaiah is said to "cry out" over Israel. Crying to God (*krazō*) is a regular feature of the psalms, where it often has to do with deliverance (as in Pss 3:4 [3:5 LXX]; 18:6, 41 [17:7, 42 LXX]; 22:2, 5, 24 [21:3, 6, 25 LXX]; 107:6, 13, 19, 28 [106:6, 13, 19, 28 LXX]). Elsewhere "crying out" rarely appears in contexts where one human calls out to another (e.g., Gen 41:55; Judg 1:14; Tob 2:13). Overwhelmingly, "crying out" appears in contexts where people are seeking deliverance in a situation of distress (Judg 3:9, 15; 1 Macc 9:46; Job 30:20; Hos 8:2; Mic 3:4; Joel 1:14; Hab 1:2; Isa 19:20). Especially in view of the reference to suffering beginning in v. 17, the implication seems to be not simply that "we" cry to God as "Father," but that the Spirit enables "us" to cry to God for rescue.[138]

This notion that the Spirit enables speech (here indirectly, through the Spirit given) coheres well with the Gospel tradition in which Jesus promises that his followers will be given speech when needed by the Spirit (Mark 13:9–11; Matt 10:18–20; John 14:26; 15:26–27). Similarly in Acts, the Spirit fills believers at Pentecost, their speech having been prompted by the Spirit (2:4; and see 6:10; 19:6). The particular speech Paul invokes is the cry to God as "Abba." Joining this transliteration of the emphatic Aramaic "Father" with the Greek translation *ho patēr*, Paul underscores the cry (so also in Gal 4:6).[139] Attention

137. According to Heim (2017, 118–19), Greco-Roman sources consistently use *huiothesia* to refer to "adoptive sonship" and never use it to "express the sonship of a natural or biological son."

138. The insistence that *krazō* refers to ecstatic speech seems a reasonable one in view of both some uses of the verb (as in Ps 4:4 LXX; Mark 5:5; 9:26; Matt 27:50; Acts 16:17; so Jewett 498), and evidence of Spirit-filled worship elsewhere in Paul's letters (as in 1 Cor 14:6–19), although Hultgren wisely notes that gentile Christians would at some point have been taught the Aramaic term "Abba" (314).

139. Jeremias's argument that "Abba" is a childlike address, the equivalent of "Daddy," has been discredited (Barr 1988a; 1988b).

has been lavished on the Abba cry in an effort to discern its possible relationship to Jesus's address of God (Mark 14:36; R. Brown 1993, 1:172–75). What is often neglected meanwhile is the way in which crying out to God as Father overturns the devastating conclusion of 3:19. There Paul declared every mouth closed in the face of human refusal to acknowledge God (3:10–18, which in turn recalls 1:18–32; Gaventa 2008b). Here, giving evidence of the Spirit's liberative empowerment, the adopted child opens the mouth to call upon God as Father.

Verse 16 provides the implication of the cry: the Spirit itself witnesses that "we" are God's children (this time using the gender-inclusive *tekna* rather than *huios*). Not only is the cry to God the result of the Spirit's activity, but the cry in turn gives evidence of "our" place in God's household.[140] Paul knows the need to test spiritual gifts (1 Thess 5:21) and the temptation to misinterpret them as possessions rather than gifts, but those cautions in no way undermine his perception about the Spirit's role. The initiative has come from God, who takes "us" into God's household, and it returns to God in the cry of recognition. This is not an act of self-identification of one who bellows "*I* am God's child," but of one who experiences God's benevolent intervention.

The rhetorical chain of v. 17 unfolds the implications of adoption, as God's children become heirs, who in turn are coheirs of Christ. Since adoption in the Roman world largely served to secure heirs, this is not a startling move (Heim 2017, 215). It intensifies the familial language already at work in the passage, language that makes explicit what is implicit in being "buried together" in baptism; being buried together is already a familial image (see on 6:3–4). It culminates in 8:29, which identifies Christ as the firstborn of many.

The final phrase of v. 17 makes clear that being coheirs of Christ involves the fullness of Christ's action: "since we suffer together that we will also be glorified together." Being a member of the household involves "us" in all that belongs to God's family. Although Paul does not linger over the details of Jesus's suffering, he acknowledges it, as when in 15:3 he writes that Christ did not please himself. Here the frank admission of suffering, both the suffering of Christ and that of God's children, marks the transition to v. 18 and the discussion there of the suffering of the present time.[141] Suffering does not have the last word, however, as Paul anticipates the "apocalyptic revelation of God's sons and daughters" in v. 19 with the claim that "we will also be glorified together" (and see 5:2).

Familiarity with Romans may cause contemporary readers to overlook a simple question: Why has Paul lavished such attention here on the Spirit? At

---

140. As in Gal 4:6–7, this is primarily an indicator of a changed relationship: no longer slave but son.

141. This reference to suffering stands out all the more, given that Paul is writing from Corinth, where suffering is scarcely extolled by the community (see, e.g., 1 Cor 4:8–10).

Corinth, the discussion of the Spirit emerged in response to boasting about spiritual gifts, and in Galatians Paul invoked the Spirit as evidence that faith does not arrive by means of law observance but through experience of the Spirit (Wedderburn 2004, 149–54). Those challenges do not appear to be in play in Romans. Instead, as Paul instructs the Romans on life in the present—that is, life in Christ—which is freed from Sin but not yet freed from this age, this discussion of the Spirit locates and empowers believers in the new era.

Here Paul is very far from a privatistic or triumphalistic notion of the Holy Spirit as the agent who doles out spiritual attributes to individual believers. To begin with, the familial language (including the reference in v. 12 to "brothers and sisters") connects believers to one another even as they are themselves profoundly related to Christ through the activity of the Spirit. Moreover, as becomes clearer in the lines that will follow, the Spirit's activity is part and parcel of the conflict between God and anti-God powers in that the Spirit produces evidence of God's ongoing action. The "militant" spirit (Ziegler 2018, 72) comes to the fore in the lines that follow.

8:18–30 In the Mean Time

The first half of Romans 8 describes those who are "in Christ Jesus," moving from their liberation from Sin (vv. 2–3) to the indwelling of the Spirit (Spirit of God, Spirit of Christ) to their new life as God's children (adopted, heirs, coheirs with Christ). With v. 17 Paul takes an odd turn, however. Just as he has settled in to exalted language about those who are "in Christ Jesus," he introduces the language of suffering. The audience may anticipate a depiction of their coming glory, but Paul instead plunges back into the struggles of the present time. As he does so, he writes of creation (all of creation), of the Spirit's intervention, and of God's action in advance, at every turn sparking intense discussion exegetically, theologically, and hermeneutically.

Here the cosmic—that is to say, the world-encompassing—character of the letter comes into clear view. Earlier references to all humanity, to Abraham's inheritance of the world, and to Sin's entry into the world demonstrate that the actions of God in Jesus Christ encompass more than individuals. Now the cosmic horizon of those actions comes into full view in the groaning of all creation, which conveys its urgent need for deliverance and its anticipation of God's deliverance.

The shared plight of all creation prompts Paul's extended comments about the role of the Spirit and of God. In vv. 19–24 the grammatical subject is creation or the subset of creation identified as "we," but beginning in v. 26 the subject is the Spirit or God and their provision for "us." The Spirit is at work in the present, interceding with God on "our" behalf. Further, God's actions have a history, in that God has already and is even now providing what is good for

God's children, beginning with the Son (vv. 28–30). To affirm that these lines take place "within the larger life of God" (Hultgren 325) does not mean that they are an abstract reflection on a distant deity; to the contrary, even in the "inner life of God" provision is already made for the care of God's creation. Verses 31–39 will demonstrate that this care is needed because God's children remain under attack.

Precisely because of the statements concerning creation, this passage has generated a great deal of interest as a potential resource for addressing the ecological crisis. It makes excellent sense that interpreters have turned to this passage in search of an environmental imperative, given the urgent need for humanity to alter its relationship to the planet and all of its inhabitants. That is a laudable endeavor, even if careful attention to the text shows its limitations.[142] Paul could scarcely foresee the careless destruction of the earth's resources in the last two centuries, to say nothing of the spiraling consequences that destruction has set in motion. All the same, the shared plight of all creation, both human and nonhuman, in this passage does convey the value of all creation to God.

This passage has also prompted a number of proposals about the influence of particular texts from Israel's Scriptures. The creation language leads some interpreters to see Gen 3 in the background (Dunn 1:470; Wright 596; and Wolter 1:510–11).[143] Exodus motifs have also been proposed for this passage, particularly in the language of groaning and redemption (Keesmat 1999, 97–135). The attention to creation prompts suggestions that Paul is drawing on prophetic texts, especially Joel 1–2 (Braaten 2006) and Isa 24–27 (Moo 2008). All of these motifs may be in play here, without any single motif dominating. In such a highly evocative passage it should come as no surprise that Paul draws (perhaps even unconsciously) on a range of available imagery.

8:18 For I hold the sufferings of the present time not worth considering in view of the coming glory that is to be apocalyptically revealed[a] for us.[b] 19 For creation's eager expectation yearns for the apocalyptic revelation of God's sons and daughters[c]—20 for creation was subjected to futility not freely but because of the one who subjected it[d]—in hope 21 that creation itself will be freed from its slavery to decay into the freedom of the glory of God's children.

22 For we know that all creation groans together and is in labor together until now. 23 Not only that, but we, we who already have the first fruit of

142. See Horrell, Hunt, and Southgate 2010, 63–86, 238–47 for a review of the extensive literature as well as astute assessment of the issues involved.

143. On the tenuousness of the connection to Gen 3, see Horrell, Hunt, and Southgate 2010, 75, who draw attention to the repetition of *katapheirō* ("corrupt") in Gen 6:12–13 and suggest there may be a broad reference to the entire sweep of Gen 1–11.

the Spirit, even we ourselves groan as we yearn for adoption, the redemption of our body.[e]

24 For we were saved in hope, but hope that is already seen is not actually hope, since who hopes for something already seen? **25** But since[f] we hope for something we cannot see, then we yearn for it persistently.[g]

26 Similarly, the Spirit also helps in our weakness. We do not know even what to pray for, not as we should know,[h] but the Spirit itself pleads with unutterable groans. **27** And the one who searches hearts knows the Spirit's thinking, since the Spirit intercedes with God on behalf of the saints.

28 And we know that for those who love God, God assists them in everything for the sake of the good,[i] for those who are called according to God's purpose. **29** Since those whom God knew in advance, he decided in advance would be shaped in the likeness of his Son, so that the Son would be the firstborn among many brothers and sisters. **30** And the ones he decided upon in advance he also called; and the ones he called he also rectified; and the ones he rectified he also glorified.

a. See 1:17, 18. "Apocalyptically revealed" is awkward, but it has the advantage of signaling that something more than mere uncovering of information is involved. As becomes clearer in the lines that follow, Paul refers to an event, not simply to a disclosure.

b. The translation understands *eis* here as direction or purpose. The future glory happens "for us," a statement Paul will unpack with vv. 28–30. The alternative translation "to us" obscures numerous elements in the passage that depict this future as God's action on behalf of God's children.

c. Lit., "sons," but "sons and daughters" better reflects the gender-inclusive nature of the Roman congregations; see the women's names in the greetings of 16:3–16, to say nothing of the role of Phoebe as interpreter of the letter (16:1–2).

d. Following Duncan's proposal (2015) that v. 20 is an aside, apart from the final phrase "in hope," which modifies the yearning and expectation of v. 19 (see the similar combination of hope and longing in v. 25; Gal 5:5; Phil 1:20). This change of punctuation avoids the implausible suggestion that God is the agent of hoping and recognizes the secondary contribution of the verse to the argument.

e. The singular "body" here reflects the Greek singular *sōma*. Although singular nouns can be used for plural referents (i.e., the distributive singular; Moulton 1908, 3:22–24), the examples normally given for Paul's usage of the distributive singular are questionable. Especially in the case of *sōma*, Paul appears to distinguish between "bodies" (as in, e.g., 8:10; 12:1) and the corporate "body" (8:23; 1 Cor 6:19, 20; 2 Cor 4:10).

f. Lit., "if" (*ei*), but the context implies that "we" do in fact hope for something unseen. This is a logical rather than a conditional use of *ei* (see also 8:31).

g. The customary translation "patience," found in KJV, NRSVue, and NIV, is tepid as a rendering of such vast yearning (so Jewett 521, who suggests "perseverance" as a "less attitudinal" term than "patience").

h. As Cranfield (1:421) rightly notes, the object of "pray" is "what" (*ti*) rather than "how." *Katho dei* further modifies the verb "pray"; hence, the translation repeats the "we" to draw attention to the depth of Paul's comment.

i. The Greek is ambiguous and can be rendered literally either as "all things work together" or "he works all things together." The fact that a few manuscripts supply *theos* ("God") demonstrates an early desire to resolve the ambiguity ($\mathfrak{P}^{46}$ A B 81 sa). The translation reflects an exegetical judgment that God is the agent, since God is the agent in the remainder of this passage; it would seem odd if the initial statement were not consistent with that fact. In addition, already in vv. 26–27 the Spirit is the agent working on behalf of human beings.

[8:18] Paul opens by drawing attention to what follows: "I hold" or "I consider."[144] As in other places where Paul comments on eschatological events (1 Thess 4:13–18; 1 Cor 15:20–28), questions arise about the basis for his remarks. (Is Paul implicitly claiming a special revelation? Has he arrived at the comments that follow through reflection on his own?) He does not pause for comment about sources, instead moving quickly to the central concern of the remainder of the chapter: the present time, with its experience of suffering and its confidence in God's redemption. Already in ch. 5, to which this passage has numerous connections, he has said, "Let us boast also in our afflictions" (*thlipsis* rather than *pathēma*), and later in this passage he refers to groaning (8:22–23, 26) and weakness (v. 26), all of which seem to have these "sufferings of the present time" in view.

The question immediately raised for contemporary readers, although likely not for Paul's first audience, is what these sufferings might be and what the causes might be. The unspecified character of the remark is consistent with the several other contexts in which Paul refers to sufferings, usually in a general sense as here (2 Cor 1:5; Gal 5:24; although see the reference to Christ's sufferings in Phil 3:10). While he does not specify the nature or causes of the sufferings, the care lavished on this passage, together with its crucial location in the argument, suggests that Paul addresses something of existential importance. This is not an abstract discourse on suffering offered in prospect of the ills that attend creation. The list of situations in v. 35 may offer possibilities (poverty, violence), and the presence of slaves within the Roman congregations suggests numerous contexts for suffering (see on 16:3–16).

It is worth noting that Paul describes these sufferings as "of the present time," literally, "the now time." Already in Romans, Paul has marked his discourse with *nyn/nyni*:

---

144. This is the only time Paul uses the verb *logizomai* in first-person singular in Romans (elsewhere see 2 Cor 10:2; 11:5; Phil 3:13).

3:21   But now, without the law's involvement, God's righteousness has been made plain
3:26   As a demonstration of God's righteousness at the present time
5:9   Therefore, even more now since we have been rectified through his blood
5:11   Our Lord Jesus Christ through whom now we have received reconciliation
8:1   Therefore, now: no condemnation for those who are in Christ Jesus

(See also 6:19, 21–22; 7:6.) "Now" in these instances is an identifiable point in time, between the resurrection of Jesus and the final triumph, but it is more than a chronological reference.[145] The "now time" is that life time reclaimed by God in the death and resurrection of Jesus.

Paul's initial statement about these "now time" sufferings is a bold one: they are "not worth considering in view of the coming glory that is to be apocalyptically revealed for us."[146] At first glance this seems dismissive of sufferings, but the discussion that follows shows Paul by no means dismisses suffering. Rather than dismissing it or admonishing passivity, he puts suffering in what he takes to be its proper context, a context that is located temporally, cosmically, and theologically.[147]

Until this point in the letter, "glory" has referred to God's own glory rather than to any human glory.[148] In an important sense, however, even here God's glory is in view, since what Paul has said in vv. 14–17 is that the glory "we" have derives from God and from sharing in the glory of Christ.[149] That point is underscored in v. 30, where the list of God's actions for humans culminates with the claim that God glorified them. The circular character of this glory comes to expression in Rom 15:7–13, with its claim that Christ "welcomed you, for the glory of God" (15:7).

The claim that glory is "apocalyptically revealed" recalls the lines early in the letter, with their declaration of the revelation of God's righteousness and wrath (1:17–18; cf. 2:5).[150] Unlike those apocalypses, however, which

---

145. To be sure, in 7:17 "now" indicates the result of the previous analysis and lacks any clear notion of time. In 15:23 and 25, "now" simply refers to Paul's upcoming visit to Jerusalem and then Rome (although it is evident that he sees those plans as part of the unfolding of the gospel).

146. As Ann Jervis puts it, "Afflictions have a present tense, they do not have a future" (2007, 121). This connection between an arduous present and future glory or divine triumph also appears, e.g., in Dan 7:21–27; 12:1–3; 4 Ezra 13.14–59; Jub. 23.22–31; 2 Bar. 25–30.

147. The logic here recalls 2 Cor 4, where Paul also contrasts present hardship with future glory. There, however, the focus is largely on apostolic hardship (understandably so in the context), and no connection is made to the rest of creation.

148. On the possible exception of 3:23, see the discussion above and Gaventa (2014b).

149. See K. Barth 1957, II.1.666–77, on the way God's glory overflows into humanity.

150. English cannot do justice to the alliteration that begins with *apokalyphthēnai* ("apocalyptically revealed") in v. 18 and includes *apokaradokia* ("eager longing"), *apokalypsis* ("revelation"), and *apekdechetai* ("wait") in v. 19.

are already underway (present tense), located in the "now time," this one is described as *mellousan*, yet to be revealed.[151] The lines that follow underscore the future character of this glory, yet they stop short of depicting it, by contrast with 1 Thess 4:13–18 and 1 Cor 15:20–57, both of which depict the triumphant return of Christ.

The glory is "for us." What follows is no abstract, disengaged analysis of suffering. This is not a study of its origins or its nature. Paul writes for the sake of the community of those grasped by the gospel, and here he locates that community in its struggling present as well as in the future God has already put in place. (Note the aorist tense of the verbs in vv. 29–30.) In a similar move, he will later assert that Scripture was written "for our instruction" (15:4). In neither case is the "for us" claim one that excludes the outsider, as should be evident from his concern for the whole of creation in what follows, to say nothing of his concern for "all Israel" in chs. 9–11.

[19–21] These three verses are connected by their common subject, *ktisis* ("creation").[152] (Creation [*ktisis*] continues to be the grammatical subject even in v. 22, but the disclosure formula at the beginning of that verse connects it tightly to what follows.) Grammatically, the subject of the opening statement is the vivid noun "eager expectation" (*apokaradokia*), with "creation's" as its possessive genitive. It is creation that longs, that was subjected, that will be freed. By beginning with "eager expectation," Paul intensifies the statement that follows.[153]

What exactly does Paul include in the term "creation" (*ktisis*)? Dispute about that question is almost as old as the letter itself.[154] At a minimum, this *ktisis* refers to all nonhuman creation (a position widely advocated). That would follow a pattern of usage for *ktisis* found elsewhere in Jewish literature (e.g., Wis 2:6; 5:17; 16:24; 19:6).[155] In addition, the claim that creation itself mourns

151. This expression is awkward, as Moulton notes (1908, 3:350), comparing it with the similar word order in Gal 3:23. He suggests that there may be "a stereotyped phrase" in each case: "the coming glory" or "the coming faith."

152. The discussion of vv. 19–25 draws on Gaventa (2007b, 51–62), although with some modifications, especially regarding v. 20.

153. The noun *apokaradokia* appears in the NT or the LXX only here and in Phil 1:20, there also in an eschatological context. The related verb *apokaradokeō* likewise does not appear in the LXX or NT, but it does appear in Polybius in martial contexts (*Hist.* 16.2.8; 18.48.4; and 21.36.3) and once in Josephus in reference to waiting for a battle to commence (*J.W.* 3.265). This is a very small sample, to be sure, but it may underscore the urgency of Paul's language.

154. The most widely advocated proposals are these: creation includes everything that is not human; it refers to nonhuman creation together with unbelievers but not believers; it refers only to nonbelieving humanity but excludes nonhuman creation. For the history of interpretation as well as additional bibliography, see Reumann 1973, 98–99; Cranfield 1:413–14; Dunn 1:464–65; Christoffersson 1990, 13–46; Blowers 2013; Tyra 2014, 2019.

155. E. Adams 2000, 178. The personification of various elements in creation also occurs or is implicit in a number of passages, including Isa 44:23; 49:13; 55:12–13; Pss. 64:13–14 LXX; 97:7–9 LXX (Horrell, Hunt, and Southgate 2010, 73).

or is in labor recalls prophetic language regarding the mourning of the earth and its devastation (Joel 1:10, 18–20; Isa 24:1–6; Jer 4:23–25).

Yet Paul's notion of *ktisis* encompasses human as well as nonhuman creation. In 1:18–32 Paul accuses humanity of idolatry, charging that "they" made images of human beings, birds, four-footed animals, and reptiles and substituted those images for the glory of God (1:23). Just a few lines later he refers back to this accusation with the words "they venerated and worshiped the created [*ktisis*] instead of the Creator" (1:25). This charge places human beings within creation itself, because humans are included in the list of images used in counterfeit for God. The origin of humanity's enslavement to Sin lies in its refusal to understand itself as made by God, a point summarized in 3:10–18 with the charge that no one fears God. (This claim reappears in 8:20, which describes creation's subjection as unwilling. Humanity did not wish to be subjected; in fact, humanity rebelled against its rightful place as creature.) "Creation" (*ktisis*), every earthly thing that is not God, encompasses both human and nonhuman life, all of which eagerly awaits the culmination of God's redemptive action.

Human creation includes both believers and nonbelievers, all of whom participate in creation's shared longing. To be sure, Paul will soon separate the groaning of "us" believers, setting it apart from that of creation as a whole, because the longing of believers is an informed longing, a longing enriched and assisted by the Spirit. It is longing just the same.

In addition, nonbelieving humans also groan together with the whole of creation. They may be unaware of their groaning, just as the whole of humanity is oblivious to the reign of Sin and Death in the aftermath of Adam (5:12–21) and does not understand itself to be the weapon of Sin (6:12–23). What Paul sets before his audience is the world as he understands it *post-Christum*, not a confession offered by various parties. As Paul perceives the cosmos in the light of the Christ event, the whole of creation is groaning.

This understanding of creation as inclusive of all things, human and nonhuman, coheres with Paul's statements elsewhere. The lengthy argument of chs. 9–11 engages Scripture to voice the impossibility of understanding God's own wisdom and knowledge and concludes with "Because from him and through him and to him are *all things*" (11:36). The unity of everything in relationship to God appears also in 1 Cor 8:6, further underscoring the connection between humanity and the remainder of creation. And the "all" (*pas*) of v. 22 reinforces the inclusive connotation of "creation" in this passage, since "all" in Romans so often refers to all humanity (see, e.g., 1:5, 7, 8, 16; 2:9–10; 3:9, 12, 19, 23; 5:18; 11:32, 36; 15:11).

Drawing attention to humanity's groaning does not imply that nonhuman creation is thereby of less interest to Paul or that nonhuman creation does not play a serious role in this text. On the contrary, the shared longing of all of creation—human and nonhuman alike—signals the importance of the longing itself as well as the extent of the crisis Paul is calling up before his audience. All of creation stands together as it anticipates the completion of God's action. The significance of Paul's concern here for the whole of creation is not only exegetically defensible but theologically compelling. Without it, redemption threatens to become redemption *from* the world rather than redemption *of* the world—the whole world (Beker 1980, 181).

Does this "creaturely solidarity" mean that Paul thinks of creation as inherently good, as in those interpretations of the passage that conjure up the eschatological restoration of nonhuman creation (Tyra 2014, 254–55)? Paul is not anticipating a restoration of paradise, or at least such language is absent from the passage. Yet neither does Paul reflect a material dualism according to which there is evil in creation itself. The concern here is not with evaluating the inherent goodness or evil of creation but with asserting its shared life in relationship to God. To be sure, it is difficult to imagine that Paul would have regarded anything God made as inherently evil, precisely because God made it.

What all of creation longs for together is the "apocalyptic revelation of God's sons and daughters." The expression "God's sons and daughters" comes into Romans at 8:14, where it refers explicitly to those who are being led by God's Spirit, who receive a spirit of adoption and who are God's children and fellow heirs with Christ.[156] It is easy to assume an identification between these "sons and daughters" in v. 19 and those referred to a few lines earlier. Yet that identification does not do justice to the fact that Paul insists they are to be *apocalyptically revealed*, which opens up the possibility that this group might be distinguished from (and larger than) the group introduced earlier in the chapter.

Several other factors point in the same direction, namely, that the "future apocalypse of the sons [and daughters] of God promises the rectification of all who are called to be God's sons and daughters, including those who are not yet included in the category 'Christian'" (Eastman 2002, 266). Any easy supposition that the "sons and daughters" can be identified narrowly will find itself troubled just a few lines later when Paul identifies the Israelites, without qualification, as those upon whom God has conferred "adoption" (*huiothesia*, 9:4). In addition, in 11:26 Paul will announce what he identifies as a mystery, which is that "all Israel" will be saved, reinforcing that point with the assertion that God's "gifts and calling" to Israel are "irrevocable" (11:29). In other words, the "we" who know about the longing of creation and who have the first fruit of the Spirit are among God's children, but the present "we" are not the only ones to be apocalyptically revealed. At a minimum, attempts to limit the identification of God's sons and daughters to the narrow circle of believers run the risk of assuming in advance what God will bring about.

---

156. The word *huios* appears earlier in the letter, but only in reference to Jesus Christ as God's Son (1:3, 4, 9; 5:10; 8:3).

The aside of v. 20 (see translation note d) identifies the reason for creation's longing, for "creation was subjected to futility" (*mataiotēs*). This subjection comes about at the initiative of God, since only God would be able to subject creation. The futility or meaninglessness here ascribed to creation recalls the situation of 1:21, where humanity "becomes vacuous" (*mataioō*) in its thinking. It is not humanity alone that suffers this condition but the rest of creation as well.

The statement that creation was not subjected "freely but because of the one who subjected it" underscores God's action. When translated as "not of its own will" (NRSVue) or "not by its own choice" (NIV), *ouch hekousa* prompts confusion about whether creation has a will of its own and can in turn generate misunderstanding regarding the identity of creation in this passage. The term *hekōn* often appears paired with its opposite, *akōn*, as it does in 1 Cor 9:17, where it draws attention to a contrast between doing something freely and doing it under compulsion.[157] That pairing suggests that reading the phrase in v. 20 as a comment about creation's own will is mistaken. Instead of drawing attention to the disposition of creation, the phrase draws attention to the one who *subjects* creation, namely, God.[158] What this aside in v. 20 does is describe the subjection and reinforce the notion that creation was *acted upon* by God.

The final phrase in v. 20 ("in hope") marks the end of the aside and returns to the longing of creation, prompting the explanation of creation's hope in v. 21. Paul now recasts what he has been saying about God's liberating act on behalf of humanity in terms of the whole of the cosmos. God's handing over of humanity (1:24, 26, 28) was simultaneously the handing over of all creation; by the same token, the liberation of humanity anticipates the liberation of all creation.[159] Along with humanity, which is a small portion of creation, the whole of creation will be freed (as believers are freed in 6:18, 20–23; 8:2, 15).

This freedom is from "slavery to decay into the freedom of the glory of God's children." The "decay" (*phthora*) or corruption of nonhuman creation appears in Isa 24:1–6, prompting the suggestion that Paul has in mind especially this passage (Moo 2008, 85). But elsewhere in the LXX, human decay or death comes into view, as in Ps 103:4 (102:4 LXX); Jonah 2:6 (2:7 LXX); Wis 14:12, 25. Perhaps more to the point, Paul's usage of the term elsewhere always has human death or decay in view (1 Cor 15:42, 50; Gal 6:8). The decay to which Paul refers is not simply environmental ruin; neither is decay limited to one aspect of creation but refers to all of it. By the same token, the anticipated freedom of creation means more than simply bringing about an end of decay

---

157. See BDAG, s.v. *hekōn*; LSJ, s.v. *hekōn*; and especially Rickert (1989) on the range of connotations.

158. Note also the role of God as subjecting agent in 1 Cor 15:27–28 and Phil 3:21.

159. Kraftchick (1987) draws attention to the reversal of Rom 1 in Rom 8.

or death, since Paul contrasts decay with "the glory of God's children." More than mere continuation of life is at issue in this anticipation of future glory.

[22–23] Verses 18–21 are couched as Paul's own understanding ("for I hold"), but with "for we know" in v. 22, Paul shifts to first-person plural as he prepares to restate the longing of creation, this time singling out the specific longing of "us." The addition of "all" (in "all creation") intensifies the language used in vv. 19–21 and recalls Paul's frequent use of *pas, pantes* earlier in the letter (e.g., 1:7, 8, 18; 2:9,10; 3:19–20). Creation is said to "groan together" and to be "in labor together." The second of these verbs (*synōdinō*) belongs to a word group regularly used of the anguish of childbirth, as in Mic 4:10 LXX; Isa 13:6, 8 LXX; Jer 6:24 LXX. This notion of the birth pangs occurs frequently in apocalyptic texts (as in 1 En. 62.4; 2 Bar. 56.6; 4 Ezra 4.42; 1QH^a 11.6–8; Mark 13:8; Rev 12:2; see Gaventa 2007b, 32–34, 56–57). Although the first verb (*systenazō*, "to groan together") and words related to it are not usually associated with childbirth, the related noun *stenagmos* does refer to the groaning of childbirth in Gen 3:16 LXX, and it appears paired with "being in labor" in Jer 4:31 LXX. It is not too much, then, to conclude that both "all creation" in general and "we" in particular are in the process of giving birth, confirming creational solidarity. "Until now" at the end of v. 22 continues the letter's insistence on the "now time" and intensifies the childbirth image by its implication of extended labor.

Verse 23 further highlights the notion of laboring and longing with its focus on "us," that is, those who already have the first fruit of the Spirit. Far from saying that the children are *not* part of creation's longing, v. 23 highlights that longing. Even the fact that "we" possess the first fruit (or perhaps precisely *because* of that possession), "we" long right along with (and indeed as part of) the rest of creation. If creation is imagined as an orchestra performing this work of longing, "we" are a featured section of the orchestra, not a different orchestra or the performers of a different composition.

This "we" has the first fruit (*aparchē*) of the Spirit. The genitive "of the Spirit" introduces a mild ambiguity, because it can convey either the source of the first fruit (genitive of origin) or the nature of it (genitive of apposition). Both senses are present earlier in the chapter, where the Spirit is the liberating agent (8:2), is in possession of believers (8:9), indwells believers (8:11), but believers have also received a spirit of adoption (8:15). Probably both senses are invoked here: the first fruit "we" receive is from the Spirit, but it also is a gift of spirit, the contents of which will be hinted at in the lines that follow. Notably, in Paul's Scriptures these first fruits are the firstfruits of harvest given *to* God *by* humans (Exod 23:19; Deut 18:4; 26:2; Sir 7:31). Here, by contrast, the firstfruits are what humans receive from God or God's Spirit (Jewett 518). The logic resembles Rom 3:25, where Paul asserts that God put forward Christ as the cover. Rather than humans building the temple at God's instruction, in Romans it is God who puts Christ forward as the holy place.

However powerful the first fruit of the Spirit, it does not exempt "us" from groaning "as we yearn for adoption, the redemption of our body." As often in this letter, Paul wrenches the argument away from the expected next step. Logically, what should have followed the discussion of groaning together in childbirth is the birth of a baby. Instead of a birth, however, there is adoption.[160] By shifting the image from that of birth, which would emphasize human agency, to that of adoption, which emphasizes human reception, Paul once again underscores God's initiative.[161] It is God who brings about adoption (8:15; 9:4).

The phrase that immediately follows underscores divine agency as well as deepening the rhetorical surprise: adoption is identified as "the redemption of our body." The language of redemption, as in 3:24, underscores the prior enslavement of all creation ("slavery to decay," v. 21). That redemption is of "our body," the singular signaling the unity of creation. God's redemptive action in Jesus Christ is not confined to the human world but has repercussions for all the created order.

[24–25] With v. 26 Paul will turn to the role of the Spirit in the present time of birth pangs, but first he comments on the hope that characterizes this period of longing. "For we were saved in hope" constitutes a terse restatement of the longing Paul has attributed to "all creation" and specifically to "us." The expectation he has been describing means "we" live in a sense of hope, which for Paul is not mere wishing or optimism but confident expectation.

Verses 24b–25 make the seemingly mundane point that hope is about the future; hope is not about what can already be verified by experience. Paul returns to a statement of expectation, repeating the verb "yearn" (*apekdechomai*) used in v. 19 of creation as a whole and in v. 23 of believers in particular. This time, however, the expectation is accompanied by *hypomonē* ("persistence"). Paul replays the vocabulary of ch. 5, where he wrote that *thlipsis* brings about persistence, and persistence character, and character hope. Here the addition of persistence simply signals that "we" wait, expect, long for something that we know lies ahead. Taken together, these lines also prepare the audience for what Paul will say regarding the current activity of the Spirit (vv. 26–27) as well as regarding the all-encompassing care of God (vv. 28–30).

[26–27] A significant shift takes place at v. 26, where the Spirit becomes the subject of the action. Already in v. 23 the shift from birth imagery to that of adoption and redemption signals the role of God in fulfilling this longing; humanity of its own does not give birth. The remainder of the passage turns to

---

160. This rhetorical turn will be less obvious in contemporary practice, where adoptive parents may well wait for the birth of the child they will adopt. In the Roman world, however, adoption had little to do with the rearing of small children, structured as it was largely to provide adult heirs.

161. Human beings do not remain in a state of sheer passivity, as becomes clear in 12:1–2 and is anticipated in 6:12–23. On this point, see de Boer (2022, 169), who corrects an overstatement of mine on this question (2007b, 56).

the role, first, of the Spirit (vv. 26–27), then of God (vv. 28–30), both in and beyond the "sufferings of the present time." Verses 31–39 will then make clear that the context of the birth pangs is one of ongoing conflict. Although defeated in the resurrection of Jesus, the anti-God powers have by no means finally surrendered their struggle for God's creation.

The notion that vv. 24–25 explicate the confident expectation of vv. 22–23 is underscored by v. 26, which begins with "similarly" and then moves directly to the intercessory actions of the Spirit. "Similarly" connects what Paul is about to say concerning the Spirit with what has preceded, but the connection between the Spirit's intercession and the end of v. 25 is vague at best. Understanding the movement of the argument here requires setting aside vv. 24–25, taking them as an elaboration on vv. 22–23, so that vv. 26–27 explore what it means to have the "first fruit of the Spirit."

The Spirit helps, Paul writes, "in our weakness." He does not comment on the nature of this weakness, leaving it unspecified, as are the "sufferings" of v. 18. This abbreviated way of referring to the ongoing human condition (as in 6:19) locates believers in their present sufferings *and* in hope. Even those who have been adopted, who have the first fruit of the Spirit, have *only* that first fruit: they remain in need of assistance.[162]

The weakness of the present time comes to expression as Paul indicates how the Spirit helps: "We do not know even what to pray for, not as we should know." Given Paul's claims elsewhere that he prays for the congregations "always" or "without ceasing" (1 Thess 1:2; Phlm 4), his instruction about prayer in the context of worship assemblies (1 Cor 12:12; 14:13–15), and especially his urgent appeal that the Romans pray with him for his upcoming journey to Jerusalem (15:31; see also his requests for prayer in 1 Thess 5:25; Phlm 22), this remark comes as a genuine surprise. This frank admission of the inadequacy of prayer underscores the limited character of the first fruit of the Spirit, however strengthening that may be.

The limitation is countered by the action of the Spirit, which "pleads with unutterable groans." The end of v. 27 explains that these groans, unavailable to human beings, are in fact intercession on behalf of the saints. However persistent and urgent and necessary human prayer may be, humans require assistance from the Spirit. Believers may have the Spirit within them (8:9b, 11), but the Spirit also remains "external, praying on their behalf" (Hultgren 325). The Spirit's "groans" need not be available or understandable, since God knows the heart and "knows the Spirit's thinking." This is a discourse of comfort,

---

162. Paul's use of *astheneia* and related terms depends very much on the context. In 5:6 he comments on Jesus's death "while we were still weak," as if weakness lay only in the past, although in 14:1 he admonishes welcoming "the one who is weak in faith," a reference to certain groups of Christians.

locating the needs of believers not in their own energies alone but in the relationship of God and the Spirit: "The entire emphasis is on God, the life of God, from start to finish" (Hultgren 325–26). The Spirit does not intercede because God requires persuasion, as becomes clear in the following verses with their extensive depiction of God's prevenient care for humanity. A few lines later Paul will also write that Jesus intercedes (v. 34), there in the context of continued threats posed by anti-God powers.

[28–30] Paul now moves to a powerful statement of assurance based on God's all-encompassing care, having placed the current sufferings in the context of all creation's longing, and again in the context of the Spirit's intervention. Verse 28 opens with "we know that for those who love God," marking out the section and underscoring shared understanding. The love of God persists in and through the profound longing, the hopefulness, and the first fruit (vv. 19–27). Those who love God are those to whom the Spirit has given this love (5:5), and shortly Paul will affirm that they have been "called according to God's purpose." In other words, while this human love for God is real and active, it too is among God's gifts.

Those who love God find that "God assists them in everything for the sake of the good."[163] Paul does not specify what this statement means, leaving room for various interpretations that reduce Paul's claims to pablum. Given the context, "everything" sweeps both backward and forward. The sufferings of v. 18 that introduce this entire section are part of the "everything," but closer to hand is the assurance of vv. 26–27 that the Spirit intercedes and of vv. 29–30 that God has already acted on behalf of God's people. "Everything" God does is for good.

That "those who love God" do so as a result of God's own initiative comes to expression with the additional phrase "those who are called according to God's purpose." This recalls the opening lines of the letter, with Paul's identification of both himself and the Romans as people who have been called (1:1, 6–7), and also to God's calling into being in 4:17, but it also anticipates the emphasis on calling and purpose in Rom 9. A similar expression in 9:11 characterizes the selection of Jacob prior to birth as an instance of God's purpose, and 11:28–29 applies to all Israel the language of "beloved" and "called."

The chain of vv. 29–30 amplifies the calling (notice the connecting "since" [*hoti*] at the beginning of v. 29):

| The ones he knew in advance | he also determined in advance |
| And the ones he determined in advance | those he also called |

---

163. *Panta* ("everything") introduces an alliterative string that extends through the beginning of v. 30: *panta*, *prothesin* ("purpose"), *proegnō* ("knew in advance"), *proōrisen* ("decided in advance"), *prōtotokon* ("firstborn"), *pollois* ("many"), *proōrisen*.

| And the ones he called | those he also rectified |
| And the ones he rectified | those he also glorified[164] |

The first two verbs ("knew in advance," "determined in advance") introduce and control what follows: the calling, rectifying, and glorifying of God's children has been decided in advance. Distortions of such an argument are easy to come by, as is evident in some misreadings of Paul's notion of election. Considered in the light of chs. 9–15, however, these verbs are powerful signals. Among Paul's claims about Israel is that God has not rejected his people, "the people whom he knew in advance" (11:2), and culminating that long section is the assertion that God's "wisdom and knowledge" are not accessible to the likes of human beings. Later still Paul will urge the audience not to think too much of its own opinions (12:3, 16) and not to arrogate to itself the role of judge (14:1–12). Taken together, these seem important indications that these assertions about God's foreknowledge are ways of removing speculation from the likes of human beings.

The three verbs that follow (called, rectified, glorified) then interpret what it is that God's knowledge accomplishes. All of them go deep into the fabric of the letter. God has called the Romans as well as Paul himself (1:1, 7). God has rectified (3:21–26; 5:5, 9). And God has glorified (8:16–17), reversing the previous situation of being removed from God's own glory (3:23), a glory active in the resurrection of Jesus (6:4).

Intruding into the chain of God's actions, perhaps governing or at least interpreting it, is the statement that those God determined in advance would be "shaped in the likeness of his Son, so that the Son would be the firstborn among many brothers and sisters." Perhaps nowhere in Paul's letters does he more powerfully associate the new human being with the Son than with this claim that they become shaped to his own likeness (though see 2 Cor 3:18). Earlier in Romans he identifies baptism as dying with Christ that produces living with Christ (6:1–11), and in 8:17 he identifies believers as Christ's siblings who suffer with him and who will be glorified with him, but here they take on his very likeness.

Christ is explicitly identified as the firstborn among these brothers and sisters, which places all the other brothers and sisters in relationship to him. A further implication of this insistence that Jesus is the firstborn of the brothers or sisters will appear in 9:1–5. The Israelites are said there to be the recipients of adoption, and from their physical descent emerges the Christ. Yet if he is the "first," they are his younger brothers and sisters, which is to imply that their identity follows from his own, rather than the other way around.

The several verbs with the *pro-* prefix ("in advance") invite reflection on time: When exactly did God act? In some theological interpretations, notably that of Karl Barth (1957, 145–94), this prefix prompts the notion that God's

---

164. Translated somewhat literally for the sake of displaying the formal parallels.

action is pretemporal, that this is God's eternal election. Caution is in order, however, as Paul uses several verbs with this prefix in Romans, all of which refer to some prior action without specifying when that action took place (1:2, promised beforehand; 1:13, planned beforehand; 9:23, prepared beforehand; 9:29, said beforehand; 15:4, written beforehand). Perhaps more to the point, distinguishing between events that take place within history and those that take place in the eternal life of God is not customary in Paul.

Read in context of Paul's remarks about the subjection of all creation, these claims about God's prior action have the effect of putting that subjection in its rightful place. The subjection happened in the past with consequences that extend into the present, but with vv. 29–30 Paul locates God's redemptive action prior to subjection. The subjection always had this outcome in view. Verses 31–39 will carry that logic further, reassuring Paul's Roman auditors that no opponent has the power to separate humanity from its rightful Lord.[165]

In effect, with these lines Paul grasps the Roman Christians and lifts them out of their own time so that they are able to glimpse both what God has done and what God will do on their behalf.[166] It is only partially visible in the present, but God has already marked them out as siblings of the firstborn, Christ. It is from this vantage point that he can move to the provocative reassurance of vv. 31–39.

Although the language focuses on the gifts bestowed on those who are called, it surely is significant that Paul never specifies who is "in" and who is "out" of God's care. Indeed, nothing is said here of those on the outside. The emphasis remains on the verbs characterizing God's all-encompassing action. Paul's point is less to construct a wall of separation than to emphasize that whatever is happening (the "everything" of v. 28) happens within the realm of God's oversight.

The passage ends as it began, with reference to both glory and suffering. Nothing here suggests that suffering is not real or is to be ignored or denied; instead, Paul extends the context of suffering in the solidarity of the whole of creation, and he lifts up the role of the Spirit as sustainer. Verses 31–39 will further contextualize suffering by identifying it as part of an ongoing struggle, a struggle God will win on behalf of God's creation.[167]

---

165. As Ziegler astutely observes regarding 8:29–30, God's "'effectual calling' forges a powerful heuristic connection between the faith-creating work of the Spirit, its origins in eternal election, and its telos in the rectification and glorification of creatures in Christ" (2018, 77). Caution regarding the modifier "eternal" does not undermine the rightness of this comment.

166. Compare Richard Bauckham's suggestive comment that the Seer of the Apocalypse and his readers are "taken up into heaven in order to see the world from the heavenly perspective. . . . The effect of John's visions, one might say, is to expand his readers' world, both spatially (into heaven) and temporally (into the eschatological future)" (1997, 7).

167. As Emerson Powery contends, these lines combine groans and praise: "The combination of groans and doxology should characterize the human response to a world in which other elements of the created order also groan and praise. . . . So, Paul encourages us to groan on!" (2004, 322).

8:31–39 Trash Talk

In the face of suffering and the longing of all creation (8:18–19), Paul has extolled both his confident hope in future redemption and the sure signs of God's care, already evident in the present work of the Spirit. Now he evokes the situation of God's children as secure in that powerful care even as they continue to be under attack by forces that would wrench them from their rightful place.

A series of questions (vv. 31, 33a, 34a) structures the passage, in which Paul first demands to know who might work against God's children (vv. 31–36) and then exults in the certain failure of those same agents. The initial question sets the tone: Who is against? Two more questions then summon up a legal proceeding: Who will accuse? Who will condemn? The questions that follow (vv. 32, 33b, 34bcde) move away from the courtroom and into the language of conflict. With the final question (v. 35a), the methodical activity of a courtroom proceeding falls away and raw conflict comes into view: What will separate? This final question and the answer in vv. 38–39 assume that agents exist who actively seek to separate God from God's people.

The passage distills crucial elements in chs. 1–8. The claim that God is "for us" echoes the announcement of 1:16 that the gospel is God's saving power, and the statements about God's handing over of the Son to death, of the Son's resurrection and intercession, recall much of 3:21–26; 5:1–11; and 8:28–30. That "we" suffer in the present time refers back immediately to 8:18–30. That there is resistance to God's salvific activity, both human and larger than human, replays 1:18–3:20 as well as 5:12–6:23. In concentrated fashion, these lines perform again much of the first half of the letter—constituting its peroration.

The reperformance is rhetorically powerful. In addition to the series of questions, it includes two lists (hardships in v. 35, powers in vv. 38–39); a synopsis of Christ's death, resurrection, and its effects; and an evocative citation of Scripture. Although assessing the effect of this passage on first-century audiences is beyond the powers of the commentator, it is hard to imagine that Phoebe's auditors remained unmoved. Its persistence in Christian worship, especially funeral liturgies, reflects the enduring power of this passage.

8:31 So, what shall we say about these things? Since God is for us, who is against us?[a] **32** God did not withhold his own Son but handed him over for all of us. How will he not graciously give us—together with Christ—everything?

33 Who will bring an accusation against God's elect? Will it be God who accuses, the one who rectifies?[b]

34 Who[c] will condemn us to death?[d] Will it be Christ Jesus[e] who condemns, the one who died—rather,[f] the one who was raised, who also is at God's right hand, who also intercedes for us?

35 What will separate us from Christ's love for us?ᵍ Will it be affliction or anguish or persecution or hunger or nakedness or hardship or the
sword? 36 As it is written, "On your behalf we are being put to death the
whole day long; we are regarded as sheep for slaughter." 37 But even in all
these circumstancesʰ we are supervictorsⁱ through the one who loved us.

38 For I am convinced that neither death nor life, neither evil angelsʲ
nor rulers, neither things that are present nor those to come, neither powers, 39 neither height nor depth, nor any other creature exists who will be
powerful enough to separate us from God's love in Christ Jesus our Lord.

a. As is the case with a number of other instances of "if" (*ei* or *eiper*) in the letter
(see above on 8:9), this one is logical rather than conditional; hence the translation
"since."

b. The Greek can be either a declarative statement, "It is God who justifies," as in
NRSVue, NIV, and NET, or a question, as is reflected above (and in Fitzmyer 533;
Jewett 531). Given both the larger context, which moves toward a declaration that
nothing can separate, and the fact that the list of potential separating agents in v. 35b
is clearly a rhetorical question ("Will it be any of these things?"), it seems best to
take both v. 33b and v. 34b also as questions, the answer to which is obviously no.
The words "who accuses" have been added to make the relationship to v. 33a clear,
as also below in v. 34.

c. Construed as two questions, as in v. 33.

d. *Katakrinōn* can be either present or future, but the latter seems preferable given
the fact that the rest of this series of "who" questions is future (vv. 33, 35; as well as the
verb in v. 39; so also BDF §351.2.)

e. Manuscript evidence is nearly evenly divided between "Christ" (e.g., B D K) and
"Christ Jesus" (e.g., 𝔓⁴⁶ᵛⁱᵈ ℵ A C F). Ehrman proposes that *Iēsous* was added under
pressure from gnosticizing interpretation (1996, 152), but "Jesus" could easily have been
omitted in harmonization with v. 35.

f. *Mallon* is sometimes rendered as "more than" (NET, NIV, CEB), presumably
under the influence of the several *pollō mallon* phrases in 5:9, 10, 15, 17. Where there
are two verbs or verbal forms, however, *mallon* typically does more than contrast the
two. It substitutes the second for the first, as in 14:13: "Let us stop deciding about one
another but decide this instead [*mallon*]" (see also 1 Cor 5:2; 6:7; Gal 4:9; Matt 10:6,
26; Mark 5:26; but cf. 1 Cor 14:1, 5). See also BDF §495 (3), which identifies this as
an instance of epidiorthosis, that is, a corrective that intensifies what has been said
previously.

g. Lit., "the love of Christ." Out of context, the phrase could refer either to "our" love
of Christ (objective genitive) or to Christ's love of "us" (subjective genitive). While Paul
does refer to humans loving Christ or God (as just lines earlier in 8:28), in this context,
where the topic statement is "God is for us," it seems highly unlikely that Paul has now
shifted viewpoints to limn the power of human love for Christ.

h. Lit., "in all these things," but the reference back to the list of circumstances in
v. 35 seems clear. The "in" (*en*) here is ambiguous; it might be construed instrumen-
tally as "through all these things," in the sense that they are a means to victory, but that

interpretation does not cohere well with Paul's earlier remarks about suffering. Paul acknowledges the fact of suffering and connects "our" suffering to that of Christ, but to say that "we" conquer by means of these things is another matter altogether.

i. Jewett rightly suggests "supervictors" (549), which reflects the heightened claim Paul is making and, as Jewett notes, anticipates the warning against being "super-minded" in 12:3.

j. *Angelos* is most often translated "angel," but in this as in a number of other contexts, the sense is clearly of beings who disobey God or do harm in some way (as in 1 Cor 11:10; also Matt 25:41; 2 Pet 2:4; Jude 6; Josephus, *Ant* 1:73); hence the translation "evil angels."

[8:31] Once again Paul employs the question *ti oun eroumen* ("So, what shall we say?"), yet this time he is not introducing a false conclusion (as in 3:5; 6:1; 7:7; 9:14) but gathering up what he has said previously in order to address "these things." "These things" recall the sufferings introduced in 8:18 and alluded to variously in what follows. Yet they may also include the actions of the Spirit (vv. 26–27) and of God (vv. 28–30). Both the universal longing for deliverance *and* God's comprehensive care are in view.

Although this instance of the question "What shall we say?" does not introduce a false conclusion, it does nonetheless stand in continuity with its predecessors. What is rejected is not the notion that more sinning means more grace (6:1) or that the law itself is Sin (7:7), but the possibility that any agent can conquer God's people.

The startlingly direct question of v. 31b stands as the central motif of this passage, perhaps of the entire letter. It is difficult to render Paul's Greek here in intelligible English, as the question consists of two parts, each of which has a simple subject (God, who) and a prepositional phrase (for us, against us), and neither of which has a verb. A literalistic rendering would be: "If God for us, who against us?"

It is unimaginable to Paul that God is not "for" us.[168] This succinct comment epitomizes the letter to this point and anticipates what follows in chs. 9–11. God's power for salvation (1:16) is precisely the manifestation of God's being "for" us. God's love comes to expression in Christ, who died "for us" (*hyper hēmōn*; 5:8). The Spirit intercedes "for" (*hyper*) the holy ones (8:27), just as Paul will shortly say that Christ intercedes "for us" (v. 34; and see 10:1). These are all actions that demonstrate God's being "for" us.

This brief but powerful synopsis of the gospel coheres with other significant voices in the biblical witness. Giving thanks for rescue from enemies, the psalmist exults:

---

168. Distortions of this statement into assertions that God is on "our side" in human conflicts, whether personal or ecclesial or national, amount to a gross misappropriation of the passage, which asserts God's determination that humanity is to live under God's rightful lordship.

With the LORD on my side I do not fear.
What can mortals do to me?
The LORD is on my side to help me;
I shall look in triumph on those who hate me. (Ps 118:6–7 NRSVue)

Similarly, Pss 23:4b and 56:9 insist that no harm can come to the speaker because God is "with me," as does Isa 8:8, 10 (cf. Matt 1:23; 28:20). Closer still to the formulation of Rom 8:31 is Sir 4:28: "God will do battle for you" (*hyper sou*).

For Paul, in common with many of these texts, this claim that God is "for us" counters the recognition that there are other powers operative in the world. "Who is against us?" (*kath' hēmōn*) is a clear expression of opposition. In Rom 11:2 Elijah is said to have interceded with God "against Israel" because of Israel's conduct and his own abandonment. First Corinthians 4:6 warns the addressees about inflating themselves "against the other," and 1 Cor 15:15 identifies the claim that there is no resurrection as preaching "against God" (see also 2 Cor 13:8; Gal 5:17). The stark opposition of being "with us" or "against us" recalls Jesus's assertion that those who are not "with" him (*met' emou*) are "against" him (*kat' emou*; Matt 12:30//Luke 11:23; but cf. also Mark 9:40// Luke 9:50).

Following this terse opening question, Paul unpacks both sides. First, he explains what it means to say that God is "for us," in v. 32 focusing on God's actions and in v. 34 on the Christ event, Christ's role. He also explains what he means by the question of who (or what) can be "against us." This is achieved through a crescendo of questions (in vv. 33, 34, 35), each of which begins with the interrogative *tis* ("Who?" or "What?"), as does the leading question in v. 31 (in neuter form, *ti).* The questions culminate in a list of events and then of powers that might stand behind those events.

[32] As evidence that God is "for us," Paul introduces a single event: God's act in handing Jesus over to death. Paul does not invoke God's action in creation or God's history with Israel, however important those actions are elsewhere in this letter. What it means to say that God is "for us" is condensed to God's action with God's own Son, as it is through that lens that Paul now interprets both creation and Israel's history.

Three distinct verbs characterize this divine action "for us":

God did not withhold
God handed him over
God will graciously give us

Largely because of the first verb, "withhold" (*pheidomai*), this verse has long been connected to Abraham's readiness to comply with the divine demand for the sacrifice of Isaac in Gen 22, which the angel characterizes to Abraham with these words: "You did not withhold your beloved Son from me" (22:12, 16 LXX).[169] There are limitations to this connection, however, especially since Abraham's readiness to follow God's command is not the equivalent of God's initiative. In addition, if Paul had been deliberately invoking the sacrifice of Isaac, it is hard to understand why he would have omitted the descriptor "beloved." The verb *pheidomai* ("withhold") does connect the two texts, but that is not a rare word, appearing frequently in reference to the sparing (or not) of lives in conflict settings. Deuteronomy 7:16 LXX, for example, instructs Israel not to withhold any of those (*ou pheisetai*) who are given over for destruction by God. Elsewhere it is Israel itself that is not withheld, as when 2 Chr 36:17 LXX recounts how the Chaldean king "did not spare" *(ouk epheisato)* any of the young men.[170] This usage of *pheidomai* in the context of battle occurs as early as Homer (*Il.*15.215; 21.101; 24.158; *Od.* 9.277; 22.54; LSJ s.v.), as well as in Paul's near contemporary Josephus (*J.W.* 1.352; 4.82, 197, 310; 6.345; *Ant.* 14.480; 18.359; 19.141; *Ag. Ap.* 2.213).

In some cases, as in Rom 8:32, "withhold" is paired with "hand over" (*paradidōmi*), the second action attributed to God (e.g., 1 Sam 24:11 LXX; 2 Chr 36:17 LXX; 1 Esd 1:50 LXX; Zech 11:6 LXX). This action recalls Rom 4:25, with its claim that Jesus was "handed over for our transgressions," which in turn echoes Isa 53:12 LXX. *Paradidōmi* in Rom 8:32 is regularly translated as "gave up" (NRSVue, NIV, NET, CEB), which has the effect of melding the second and third verbs (*charizomai*, "graciously give") and construing the two together as a sacrificial act. Yet *paradidōmi* often concerns turning someone or something over to a third party, particularly in a conflict situation, often military.[171] In ch. 1 Paul argued that humanity's rejection of God prompted God to "hand over" (*paradidōmi*) humanity to impurity, dishonorable passions, and an unsuitable way of thinking, which serve as metonyms for Sin itself (see above on 1:24–32).

Taken together, these actions of withholding and handing over place Paul's statement about Jesus's death within the arena of conflict. As God once handed humanity over to Sin and Death, so in the cross God handed Jesus over to another agent. As divine warrior, God hands Jesus over to the unnamed powers that hold humanity captive, precisely in order to defeat those powers.[172] Paul does not name those powers here, but he has already named them in 6:9–10, writing that Death "no longer lords it over him [Christ] as king" and that Christ experienced "death to Sin." Sending the Son in human flesh, subject to Sin and

169. This interpretation goes back at least as early as Irenaeus (*Against Heresies* 4.5.4).

170. See also 1 Sam 24:11 LXX; 2 Sam 18:5 LXX; 21:7 LXX; Ps 77:50 LXX; Pss. Sol. 13.1 LXX; 17.12 LXX; Zech 11:6 LXX; Isa 13:18 LXX; Jer 28:3 LXX; Ezek 20:17 LXX. See further Gaventa 2007a, 135–36.

171. See above on 1:24–32 for numerous examples across a wide band of Greek texts, especially the LXX; and see Gaventa 2007b, 113–23.

172. On Paul's use of the divine warrior motif in this passage, see Ryan 2020, 183–90.

Death, handing the Son over to Sin and Death in the cross, God both defeats God's own enemies and liberates captive humanity because Sin and Death cannot hold Christ captive.

Crucially, God's handing over is "for us" (*hyper hēmōn*). Paul offers as evidence for this opening claim that God is "for us" this singular act rather than a longer recital of God's creative and sustaining action. It is this phrase that leads into the third statement, the future claim about God's expected gifts. The evidence of God's past actions indicates what the future will bring; since God has not withheld but handed over God's Son, God will "graciously give us . . . everything." Paul uses the verb *charizomai* ("graciously give") of God's gifts a few times elsewhere (1 Cor 2:12; Gal 3:18; Phil 1:29; 2:9; Phlm 22; of human acts of forgiveness, see 2 Cor 2:7, 10, 13), but nowhere else as a sweeping claim about the comprehensive gifts bestowed on God's people. Here it recalls the triumph of grace over Sin and Death in 5:12–21. Not only are "we" no longer God's enemies (5:10), no longer subject to Sin (6:2), but "we" live in the realm of God's gracious power, and "we" anticipate the time in which God will give "everything." This giving has already happened, but its culmination lies ahead, at an event Paul does not pause to depict.

The phrase "together with Christ" is ambiguous. The question, rendered woodenly to demonstrate word order, is "How not also with him everything to us will he give?" By virtue of its position, "together with Christ" might point back to the first part of the verse, suggesting that God has given Christ in the crucifixion and will later give everything else in addition to Christ. Alternatively, "together with Christ" may complement "us," as in "How will God not give us everything together with Christ?" where Christ is corecipient. The former makes sense of the immediate context, while the latter builds upon the relationship Paul has just posited in vv. 29–30 (and see v. 17) between Christ and believers. Selecting one nuance over the other is not necessary and may undermine the richness of the divine advocacy Paul seeks to articulate.

[33–34] The questions of vv. 33–34 cast any potential opposition to God's people in the context of legal proceedings, since *egkaleō* often appears in contexts involving prosecution (e.g., Acts 19:38; 23:29; Josephus *Ag. Ap.* 2.137–38; BDAG s.v.). The repetition of *k* sounds (in *egkalesei, kata, eklektōn,* and *dikaiōn*) sharpens the harshness of the question, which is not simply who accuses God's elect but who would dare to do such a thing. After all, "God's elect" are God's own, so that accusing them would be tantamount to accusing God. A similar turn of phrase in 11:1 ensures that the answer to the question "Has God rejected God's people?" is "Of course not!" They are God's people, just as here they are God's elect.

In the LXX, "elect" in the plural often refers to Israel, as in 1 Chr 16:13; Tob 8:15; Pss 88:4; 104:6, 43; Isa 65:9, 15, but it can also identify those chosen for specific tasks, as in Judg 20:15; 1 Sam 26:2; 1 Chr 9:22; 1 Macc 9:5.

Christian texts early on apply it to faithful followers of Jesus, as in, e.g., Matt 24:22, 24, 31; Mark 13:20, 22, 27; 2 Tim 2:10; 1 Pet 1:1; Rev 17:14. Paul uses the adjective only here and in Rom 16:13 in reference to "Rufus, elect in the Lord." In 1 Cor 1:27 he uses the related verb *eklegomai* to describe God's selection of those who are unlikely objects of God's calling. Often, however, he speaks of God as calling human beings, as he has just done in v. 30 and will do again in 9:7 (in a citation of Gen 21:12 LXX), using the related verb *kaleō*. Paul himself is "called" to be an apostle (1:1), believers in Rome are among those "called" (1:7), and Isaac is called into being (4:17; 9:7). In common with these passages, the "elect" are such as a result of this action by God rather than by virtue of their own qualifications.

The absurdity of bringing charges against God's elect is only magnified by the question that follows in v. 33b: "Will it be God who accuses, the one who rectifies?" The answer to that question is so obvious that the negative *mē genoito* is not needed. By identifying God here as "the one who rectifies," Paul returns to the announcement of 1:16 identifying the gospel as God's power through which God's righteousness is revealed and the development of that claim particularly in 3:21–26 and 5:1–21. Those who have been rectified (5:1) need have no fear of accusation. Naming God as "the one who rectifies," Paul recalls Isa 5:8 LXX: "The one who rectified me draws near; who is the one who is judging me?"

Verse 34 recasts the question, this time with Jesus Christ as the potential agent of condemnation: "Who will condemn us to death? Will it be Christ Jesus who condemns, the one who died?" The rhetorical volume increases here; rather than simply accusing, the imagined opponent condemns to death. In addition, the imagined opponent is named the condemning one, just as God is named the rectifying one (v. 33). With the language of condemnation, Paul returns to the declaration of 8:1–3 that there is no death sentence against those who are in Christ and that in Jesus's own flesh God condemned Sin. Paul compounds the absurdity with the question that follows: Will the condemning one be Christ Jesus? Yet another article-plus-participle construction renders this also a name, "the one who died" versus "the condemning one."

To this point, the identification of Christ formally parallels that of God in the preceding verse: God who rectifies, Christ Jesus who died. What follows this initial identification, however, dramatically increases the volume on Paul's argument. Not only is Christ "the one who died," but "rather, the one who was raised, who also is at God's right hand, who also intercedes for us." At first glance, nothing in this formulation startles, given the manifold ways in which Christian traditions claim that Christ died, was raised, and was elevated. Yet each of these phrases modifies Paul's comments elsewhere concerning the events following Jesus's death, and those modifications play a role in the assurance he offers about the relationship between Christ and "us."

To begin with, the insertion of "rather" (*mallon*) between death and resurrection is unique in the Pauline letters. Paul makes numerous references to the death and resurrection of Jesus. Some of those references are quite brief, as when 4:24 asserts that "[God] raised Jesus our Lord from the dead" (also 8:11; 10:9; 14:9; 2 Cor 5:15; Gal 1:1; 1 Thess 1:10; 4:14), while others are more elaborate (as in Rom 6:8–10; 1 Cor 15:4, 12–16, 20; 2 Cor 13:4). In all these instances, death and resurrection are distinguished, the distinction being inherent in the acts themselves, but only here does he explicitly contrast them.

The insertion of *mallon* could even be understood, however wrongly, as not just overturning but erasing the crucifixion. Such a denigration of the significance of Christ's death is inconsistent with Paul's views, as the letters elsewhere offer evidence. The apparent denigration here, however, serves to emphasize what follows in stark terms: Christ was raised, and that resurrection is an act of divine power. What Paul presses into service with the help of the surprising *mallon* is the sheer power of the resurrection. The remaining two assertions of v. 34 confirm that understanding of *mallon*.

First, Christ "also is at God's right hand," another indication that power is the operative notion in this verse. Paul does elsewhere either assert or imply that Christ is currently in heaven (see Phil 3:20; 1 Thess 1:9–10; 4:16; perhaps also Rom 10:6; Phil 2:9), but nowhere else does he explicitly place Christ at "the right hand of God." Doing so, Paul shows the triumph of God in raising Christ from the dead and elevating him (as also in Rom 1:4), but he does more than that. He also interprets that elevation as triumph over God's enemies.

The OT regularly associates God's right hand with power, particularly power in overcoming enemies of Israel, as when Moses celebrates God's victory over Pharaoh:

> Your right hand, O LORD,
>   glorious in power—
> your right hand, O LORD,
>   shattered the enemy.
> . . . .
> You stretched out your right hand;
>   the earth swallowed them. (Exod 15:6, 12 NRSVue)

Employing the notion of God's right hand similarly, Isaiah has God speak words of assurance to Israel in the face of the nations:

> Do not fear, for I am with you,
>   do not be afraid, for I am your God;
> I will strengthen you; I will help you;
>   I will uphold you with my victorious right hand. (Isa 41:10 NRSVue)

By far the most extensive use of this terminology comes in the Psalter (17:7; 18:35; 20:6; 44:3; 48:10; 60:5; 63:8; 78:54; 98:1; 108:6; 109:31; 110:1; 118:15–16; 138:7), where it invokes God's saving power, often in the form of God's victory over enemies of Israel. As is widely acknowledged, the specific text in play in Rom 8:34 is Ps 110:1:

> The LORD says to my lord,
>   "Sit at my right hand
> until I make your enemies your footstool." (NRSVue)

Paul turns to this text also in 1 Cor 15:25, and other early Christians similarly understood it in relation to Jesus (Matt 22:44; Acts 2:34–35; 1 Cor 15:25; Eph 1:20; Col 3:1; Heb 1:3, 13).

Citing Ps 110:1 serves to show Christ's elevation, but that elevation is not elevation for its own sake, a straightforward change of status. The concluding line of Ps 109 also depicts the work of God on behalf of God's people:

> For he stands at the right hand of the needy,
>   to save them from those who would condemn them to death.
> (109:31 NRSVue)

The remainder of Ps 110 abounds with language of conflict and divine triumph:

> The LORD sends out from Zion your mighty scepter.
> Rule in the midst of your foes. (110:2 NRSVue)

> The Lord is at your right hand;
>   he will shatter kings on the day of his wrath.
> He will execute judgment among the nations,
>   filling them with corpses;
> he will shatter heads
>   over the wide earth. (110:5–6 NRSVue)

Phoebe's auditors need not have been familiar with the entire psalm to catch the nuance, given the numerous instances in which Israel's Scriptures associate God's right hand with power over enemies. Yet any who did know the psalm, especially in its context, could well have grasped its strident reassurance that God would not surrender them to their enemies. In Romans, the enemies are not peoples arrayed against Israel, but larger-than-human enemies, as becomes clear in vv. 35–39. This is kingly language,[173] but the setting of the kingly language is not the court at leisure; rather, the king is in battle mode.

The final distinctive element of this christological statement is the claim that Christ "intercedes for us." Christ takes on the role earlier ascribed to the Spirit

---

173. Jipp 2015, 196; Ziegler 2018, 35–51.

in 8:26–27. Both of them intercede, the Spirit by completing human prayer and Christ by advocating in the face of those who would bring any charge against God's people. Exactly how the intercession of the Spirit and that of Christ are logically related does not trouble Paul as he makes these powerful pastoral claims. The move from the end of Ps 109 regarding God's deliverance of those in need to the opening of Ps 110 seems especially apt. The conclusion is unavoidable: if the resurrected, empowered, interceding Christ is "for us," then enemies of whatever sort will be defeated.

Verses 32 and 34 combine to give a powerful statement of the gospel as Paul understands it, drawing on events introduced earlier, including righteousness (v. 33), condemnation (as in 8:1–3), the death and resurrection of Jesus (e.g., 1:4; 5:10; 6:4), and intercession (8:26–27). God handed over God's own Son to enemy powers on behalf of humanity. And Death did not triumph, since Christ was raised; he is even at God's right hand, the place of power, and he intercedes on behalf of humanity.[174]

[35–37] The third and final question raises the rhetorical volume once again, both in the introductory question and in the list of possibilities that forms the follow-up question. More than the possibility of being accused (v. 33), more even than the possibility of being condemned to death (v. 34a), the possibility of being separated from Christ's love is the ultimate terror. This prospect threatens to undo the work Paul has limned throughout chs. 5–8. Christ's singular obedience introduces the reign of God's grace that places humanity out of the reach of Sin and Death. Baptism into Christ transfers the human from the power of Death into life, making humanity fellow heirs with Christ, the firstborn of God. The specter of being separated from Christ's love is the specter of being separated from all that sweeping depiction of deliverance.

Paul can and does speak of God's love without further explication, as when he addresses the letter to those in Rome who are God's beloved (1:7) or when he concludes 2 Corinthians invoking the "God of love" and the "love of God" (2 Cor 13:11, 13). When he gives specificity to God's love, however, he connects it with the death of Jesus, particularly identifying it as the reason for God's intrusive action in the cross. Galatians 2:20 is perhaps the closest parallel to this passage, where Paul writes that "the Son of God loved me and handed himself over for me." Similarly, 2 Cor 5:14 directly links Christ's love with his death on behalf of humanity. Romans 5:8 couples God's love with his action in Jesus Christ "while we were still sinners," demonstrating that God's love is no mere favoritism limited to the pious but a commitment that acts fiercely to overcome humanity's sinfulness, even humanity's enmity (see 5:10).

174. Calvin captures this verse well: Anyone "who desires to condemn us after this must kill Christ Himself again. But Christ has not only died, He has also come forth as conqueror of death, and triumphed over its powers by His resurrection" (185).

In the second question, Paul parades a host of events that might defeat the power inherent in this love. Instead of the earlier, absurd suggestion that God who has made things right might be the accuser or that Christ who is the risen, victorious intercessor might be the condemning judge, the circumstances proposed in v. 35 derive from lived experience. This catalog of hardships has parallels, both elsewhere in Paul's letters (1 Cor 4:11–13; 2 Cor 6:4–5; 11:23–30; 12:10) and in other ancient writers (e.g., Seneca, *Marc.* 18.8; Dio Chrysostom, *Or.* 16.3; Philo, *Virtues* 5; Fitzgerald 1988, 47–116; Hodgson 1983). Paul adapts his lists to suit the individual setting, here beginning with the general "affliction or anguish" and concluding with the most specific reference to the violence of "the sword."

"Affliction" (*thlipsis*) already features in 5:3 as a circumstance that does not defeat those who stand in "this grace" because God's love enables them to endure, even to hope. Paul elsewhere recalls circumstances of his own apostleship as characterized by affliction (2 Cor 2:4; 4:17; 6:14; Phil 1:7; 1 Thess 3:7) and acknowledges the afflictions of others who wait for God's final deliverance (Rom 12:12; 2 Cor 1:4; 2:4; Phil 4:14; 1 Thess 1:6; 3:3). In a similar way, 2 Cor 4:8; 6:4; and 12:10 speak of the anguish (*stenochōria*) of apostolic labor, without presenting details.[175]

By contrast with the general terms "affliction" and "anguish," "persecution or hunger or nakedness" summons up raw deprivation. In 2 Cor 11:23–25 Paul includes beatings among his experiences, offering no further details. As is all too obvious, both in the past and at present, persecution need not be systematic or official to produce terror; it need not include physical violence to be terrifying. "Hunger" and "nakedness" graphically ensure that the hardships Paul evokes are not confined to personal angst or worry (see 1 Cor 4:11; 2 Cor 6:4; 11:27).

The list concludes with "the sword," injecting violence into the list again without specifying any details of that violence. Given the several connections between this list and 2 Cor 11:23–28, the experience of suffering at the hands of local authorities may be in view. Paul uses this same word again only in 13:4, where he characterizes the authorities as bearing the sword for good reason, that is, to punish those who do wrong. Clearly he knows that "the sword" can be used to persecute as well as to bring about good (and see its use in the Gospels, e.g., Matt 26:47–55; Mark 14:43–48; Luke 21:24; 22:36–38, 49–52; John 18:10–11). Taken together, the list brings to life those situations that threaten to separate "us" from Christ's love without offering a particular account. Attempts

---

175. The pair "affliction and anguish" has appeared already in Rom 2:9, where Paul contends that punishment for evildoing falls on "the Jew first and also the Greek" (and see Deut 28:53, 57; Isa 8:22–23; 30:6). It may be that Paul regards even that punishment as penultimate, especially in light of Rom 11:32. While the "us" in 8:31–39 is restricted to those who already have been taken up by the love of Christ, that circle has no fixed boundary, certainly not a boundary created by human beings.

to connect individual items in this list with specific moments in Paul's work or with experiences among the Romans are unlikely to be productive.

The sword at the end of v. 35 anticipates, perhaps even summons up, the psalm text that follows, which begins with the image of continual dying. We are being put to death, all day long (see 1 Cor 15:30–31):

> On your behalf we are being put to death the whole day long;
> we are regarded as sheep for slaughter. (Ps 44:22 [43:23 LXX])

That citation of the psalm is paired immediately with a sharply contrasting statement: "But even in all these circumstances we are supervictors through the one who loved us" (Rom 8:37).

After opening with a recollection of God's powerful deliverance of Israel from affliction, the psalmist laments the suffering of God's people, explicitly pointing to God as the agent responsible for their suffering. Beginning with "You have rejected us and shamed us," the psalmist itemizes God's betrayal:

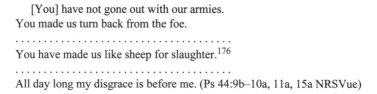

> [You] have not gone out with our armies.
> You made us turn back from the foe.
> . . . .
> You have made us like sheep for slaughter.[176]
> . . . .
> All day long my disgrace is before me. (Ps 44:9b–10a, 11a, 15a NRSVue)

Psalm 44:22, Paul's citation, brings together and repeats elements of this long complaint about God's "somnolent disregard for his people's suffering" (Hays 1989, 58) before the final lines of the psalm call on God for deliverance:

> Rise up, come to our help.
> Redeem us for the sake of your steadfast love. (v. 26 NRSVue)

In the context of Romans, however, Paul suppresses the accusations against God. He has named circumstances that cause suffering, not agents (although see below on Rom 8:38). Not only does the quotation omit those accusations, but nothing in Paul's discussion suggests that God is the cause of human suffering. The psalmist's "on your behalf" lays the blame at God's feet, but here the phrase becomes the equivalent of "for us" in the preceding lines; "we" are the objects of these torments because we are God's children. God handed Jesus

---

176. The psalms and the prophets frequently identify the people of Israel as God's sheep (Pss 78:52; 95:7; 100:3; Isa 40:11; Jer 50:6; Ezek 34:15, 22; Mic 2:12), an analogy that Christian texts early on appropriate (Matt 10:6; Mark 6:34; John 21:16; Heb 13:20), although it appears nowhere else in Paul's letters.

over (v. 32), but it is not God who wields the sword or brings about hunger or persecution. It is not God who "regards us" as nothing more than sheep to be slaughtered.

If Paul suppresses the psalmist's accusations against God, beginning in v. 37 he intensifies the notion of God as warrior on behalf of God's people. With the contrastive statement of v. 37, Paul implicitly answers the psalmist's lament (Ryan 2020, 189–90). The psalmist urges God to rise up, to "redeem us for the sake of your steadfast love," to which Paul responds, "But . . . we are supervictors through the one who loved us."

The *alla* ("but") opening of v. 37 abruptly redirects the discourse. No longer described as subjected to death, treated as animals to be massacred, "we are supervictors." The present tense is significant in that "we" are at one and the same time sheep for slaughter *and* superbly victorious. The simultaneous imagery of death and life recasts in dramatic terms the language of ch. 6, in which "we" are simultaneously dead to Sin and alive to Christ.

The rare verb *hypernikaō* does not appear elsewhere in Paul, and its usage here may reflect a widespread aphorism attributed to Menander, which warns that being victorious is well and good but being a "supervictor" is not. A "supervictor" appears to be someone who utterly destroys the opponent, a tactic of dubious wisdom in military contexts (Menander, *Sent. Byz.* 419; *Sent. pap.* 9. r.7; *Mon.* 1.299; Jewett 549; Rance 2008). Paul does not shy away from the verb, but he tempers potential excesses with the additional words "through the one who loved us." This clause places a limit on the human agents; "we" are victors through and only through the one who loved us, so the victory is not "ours," as is abundantly clear in the context. While the victory is actualized through human agents (Macaskill 2013, 241), those human agents are the agents of another. Second, the "supervictory" does not decimate human populations; it is instead a conquering of "these things," these circumstances, produced by agents to be named in v. 38.

Reference to the love of Christ circles back to the opening question of v. 35: What can possibly separate "us" from Christ's love? It also anticipates the end of the chapter, which invokes the love of God in Christ Jesus.

[38–39] The questions have ended. Although the questions themselves repeatedly demonstrate that God is "with us," Paul takes one further step. He responds to every question with a final exclamation of the impossibility that any merely created thing might separate "us" from God's love in Christ Jesus. Verse 35 has itemized adverse situations in which separation might occur; now vv. 38–39 list the agents and circumstances that produce the situations (Byrne 277).

Paul moves from first-person plural ("we are supervictors") to first-person singular ("I am convinced"). He will continue to speak individually through the opening lines of ch. 9 (although there with the emphatic *egō*). This shift represents personal conviction, to be sure, but more than emotional commitment is at work. As he asserts in powerful fashion that no one and nothing can undermine God's relentless claim on God's people, Paul moves to "I" speech to invite the audience to join in, to identify with the "I" (see on 7:7–25).

The list itself consists of four paired terms, interrupted by the single term "powers" and culminated by "any other creature," as follows:

death	life
evil angels	rulers
things present	things to come
powers	
height	depth
any other creature	

The list alternates between circumstances and agents. Evil angels, rulers, powers, and "any other creature" are all agents of some sort, while death and life, present and future, height and depth are all circumstances or settings. Movement back and forth between the two creates a comprehensive presentation of human life under continual assault.

Although earlier in Romans Death itself is an agent, one that establishes its reign over human life (5:12, 17, 20–21), paired with "life" it is a circumstance (as also in 8:6; 1 Cor 3:22; 2 Cor 4:12). In the immediate context "death" refers to the circumstances that produce daily death, death-dealing in the midst of life.

The second pair, evil angels and rulers, designates figures with capacities beyond those of humans, agents who seek to do harm. Evil or disobedient angels appear in a range of texts (1 En. 6; Jub. 5.1–11; Matt 25:41; Rev 12:9; Jude 6), often traced back to the hubristic "sons of God" in Gen 6:1–4. Just as angels may be benign or rebellious, rulers (*archai*) may be benign (Rom 13:3; Luke 12:11; Titus 3:1) or may also represent a threat to God's rule. First Corinthians 2:6 names the "rulers of this age" as the ones who put Jesus to death. First Corinthians 15:23–26 anticipates God's final victory over every ruler and every authority and power (*dynamis*), including them among God's enemies. Similarly, the Philippians hymn anticipates that "every knee," whether in heaven or on earth or under the earth, will acknowledge Christ's lordship (2:10).

The third pair, things present and things to come, returns to the circumstances glimpsed in the first pair: "death" and "life." In 1 Cor 3:22, Paul similarly joins the present and the future to death and life. Although in that context he is elaborating on the things that belong to those who are in Christ, the notion of comprehensiveness obtains in both places. "Things to come" may hint at eschatological judgment but is better understood as a sweeping comment about time: nothing at any point in this life can produce separation from God.

As already noted, the agent identified as "powers" stands without an accompanying partner, although it is joined with others in 1 Cor 15:24 where, as here, it refers to some otherwise unspecified transcendent power (and see Eph 1:21; 1 Pet 3:22). Standing alone, "powers" calls attention to the play on words that will follow, since in v. 39 Paul introduces the related verb *dynamai* to capture the lack of power in the face of God's love. The contrast extends well beyond this passage, however, as Romans has from the beginning identified the Christ event with God's own power (as in 1:4, 16, 20; and see 9:17). To single out other "powers" here is to recall where real power resides.

The final pair, "neither height nor depth," may be astronomical terms, "the domain of many transcendent forces" (BDAG, s.v. *hypsōma*), but given their association in this passage with life and death, present and future, they may more generally refer to place. No agent or event—no matter where it originates or where it takes place—can bring about separation from God.

Standing alone, the final item is "any [*tis*] other creature." This phrase may seem to be the Pauline equivalent of "and so on and so forth," but it is no mere throwaway. The addition of "other" (*hetera*) interprets everything in the list as creation, as *mere* creation. Paul never pauses to identify the ontological status of any of God's enemies, but the implication is that all of them—all these agents and all these circumstances—are created. What these enemies seek is to separate "us" from "God's love in Christ Jesus our Lord."

With this dramatic passage, Paul culminates the conflict language that has been at work in the letter since his initial declaration that the gospel is a matter of God's powerful salvation (1:16). The purpose of that power is rescuing humanity not simply from unbelief or from malformed belief but from powers in the cosmos that actively seek to separate humanity from its rightful Lord. "Actively seek" is no overstatement; this passage is mere posturing if Paul does not himself believe that there are agents in the universe working to undermine God. The fact that he does not elaborate on their origin or their actions does not lessen their reality.

Paul is by no means alone in this conviction. The notion that God is in conflict with other powers appears elsewhere in Paul's letters, as in 16:20 and in 1 Cor 15:24–28, and similar convictions appear in Col 2:14–15 and Heb 2:15, to say nothing of the Apocalypse. Paul's earliest interpreters took the language seriously. Ambrosiaster, for example, writes of Rom 8:38–39 that these are "all things which are inflicted by the devil in order to capture us" (167). Chrysostom similarly makes reference to the devil and concludes that "neither the tyrant nor the people nor the battle array of demons nor the devil could prevail over the apostles" (*Hom. Rom.* 15.4; Burns 216).[177]

---

177. Powery adds "not ecclesial traditions, not societal mores, not economic disenfranchisement, not the dissolution of affirmative action" (2004, 322).

As rich as this passage is, there is a striking omission that bears noticing. Although 8:31–39—possibly all of 8:18–39—is routinely described as eschatological, nothing in this passage directly references the *parousia* or the final victory of God.[178] First Thessalonians 4:13–18 anticipates in vivid detail the triumphant return of Jesus and his reception of his own people (see also 1:10; 2:19; 3:13; 5:23). First Corinthians 15 anticipates God's victory and the resurrection of all. Given the extended discussion of suffering and anticipated redemption in Rom 8:18–30, and given the insistence in vv. 38–39 that nothing will separate God's people from God's love, it seems obvious that Paul would conclude this passage with some explicit anticipation of Christ's return. Elsewhere in the letter there are hints that he does anticipate a return and an accounting (13:11; 14:10–12; perhaps also 2:6–10), but here there is a strange silence. The reason for that silence may lie just on the other side of the wholly artificial chapter division: God's triumph in Jesus Christ is incomplete—indeed, it is inconceivable—apart from Israel, the people God created and sustains and from whom God also will not be separated.

---

178. This point is made by Esler (2003b, 260–67), for whom this serves as evidence that eschatology is a mistaken category in reference to Paul.

Romans 9:1–11:36
"All Israel"

Even giving a name to the issue that drives these chapters is challenging: Is it the fact that most Jews do not recognize in Jesus of Nazareth the Messiah of God? Or is it instead the possibility that God has proven fickle with respect to the promises to Israel? Perhaps Paul's concern lies with the arrogance of gentile Christians who condescend to Israel. Given the conclusion of this section, with its repeated insistence on God's provision for all (11:26–32) and its warning against pretending to know God's plans (11:20, 25, 33–36), another potential concern lies with the false claim to understand God's mind. All of these issues are in play in this rich argument. But reading these chapters in close proximity to the end of ch. 8, with its triumphant declaration of God's present provision for and future redemption of all creation, suggests that the overarching question is where Israel belongs in God's eschatological victory.

Superficially, this section of the letter appears to be self-contained. It opens with a personal oath punctuated by doxology (9:5) and closes with yet another doxology (11:36). It can be read as a single unit without reference to the remainder of the letter. Not only that, but a reader could easily move from the end of ch. 8 to the beginning of ch. 12 without noticing a gap. Or at least a reader outside the first century could do so, as the history of interpretation confirms. But the appearance of a self-contained unit is deceptive.[1]

Skipping over chs. 9–11 could well undermine the letter as a whole. Paul has announced at the outset that the gospel is for Jew and Greek (1:16), and he will close the body of the letter with a reminder that Christ welcomed both the circumcised and the gentiles (15:7–13). The final lines of the letter body express Paul's anguish over his anticipated sojourn in Jerusalem (15:16, 30–33), an anguish associated with the resistance he fears he will encounter there. However self-contained the argument may *appear* to be (and there are many connections back

---

1. An earlier generation of scholars read Rom 9–11 as additional to the main argument of the letter (Sanday and Headlam 225) or a mere "practical" problem (Lietzmann 89). C. H. Dodd opines that chs. 9–11 stand alone (Dodd 1932, 148). In more recent decades the tendency has been to attach an outsize importance to this passage, as when it is identified as the climax of the whole argument (Witherington and Hyatt 244) or "the very center" of the letter (Grieb 2002, 87). Neither extreme accounts adequately for the letter as a whole.

to chs. 1–8, as will become clear), Rom 9–11 plays a crucial role in this letter. Here Paul attends to two words in relationship to one another: the "word of God" in Israel's Scripture (9:6a) and the urgent apocalyptic "word" of the Christ event.

And this is a rich argument. Paul draws on Scripture more densely than anywhere else in this or any other of his letters (see Wagner 2011, 155–57), but he does not always read Scripture in a predictable way. He teases his auditors, leading them to the brink of the conviction that Israel has been rejected, only to reject that conviction out of hand. He nudges the audience to conclude that the problem is Israel, only to attack his largely gentile audience for their arrogance—a concern that persists in later chapters of the letter (see 12:3, 16; 14:10). Landing prematurely on any individual statement is costly, as some earlier comments are reframed and even subverted later on. That characteristic holds throughout Romans, but it is perhaps especially true here.[2]

Apart from the opening and closing (9:1–5; 11:33–36), there are few clear divisions within this section. In what follows, the series of "What shall we say?" questions and disclosure formulas ("Therefore I say," "I do not want you to be ignorant") have been used to mark new divisions, since those questions and formulas indicate a desire to grasp the attention of the audience while moving it from God's creation of Israel to a consideration of Israel's current position of divinely generated fracture, and then to a disclosure about Israel's future.

9:1–13 The Calling Into Being of Israel

Paul turns in 9:1 to what seems to be a new concern, but the continuity between the end of ch. 8 and the beginning of ch. 9 is quite clear. To begin with, he continues to speak in first-person, and emphatically so. More substantively, the insistence that no power and no situation can bring about separation from God's love in Christ Jesus ushers in the question of Paul's own kin, the Israelites. Is it possible that Israel can be cut off from God?

How this question has been raised Paul does not specify. He later issues strong warnings to those gentile auditors who may think they have displaced Israel, or at least part of Israel (11:13–22), which could mean that their presumption prompts this extended reflection. It is also clear that his upcoming trip to Jerusalem arouses anxiety (15:30–32), which might in turn provoke this lengthy engagement.

However the question has come to Paul, his answer begins with a general statement about God's gifts to Israel (9:1–5), a statement that expands

2. This way of navigating the chapters is preferable to the judgment that Paul does not know at the outset of ch. 9 what he will write at the end, that he is discovering his argument as he moves through it (Grieb 2002, 92). The care with which the letter as a whole is constructed undermines that theory, to say nothing of the evident importance Paul attaches to the letter.

in vv. 6–13 into a history of Israel's creation. This is an idiosyncratic history, however, by virtue of its insistence on God's creation without reference to Israel's goodness, faith, obedience, or even potential. That insistence on God's creation sets the tone for the argument that follows.

> **9:1** I am telling the truth in Christ. I am not lying. My conscience confirms me[a] in the Holy Spirit when I say **2** that great grief and constant pain fill my heart. **3** Honestly, I myself could even pray to be cut off from Christ for[b] my brothers and sisters, my physical kinfolk. **4** They are Israelites. Theirs is the adoption and the glory and the covenants and the giving of the law and the service and the promises. **5** Theirs are the fathers, and from them is the Christ, physically speaking, the one who is over all—God be blessed forever.[c] Amen!
>
> **6** Now it is not that God's word has failed, since it is not[d] the case that all of those who are from Israel constitute[e] Israel. **7** Neither is Abraham's offspring the same thing as all Abraham's children, but "through Isaac will your offspring be called." **8** That is, the children of the flesh do not constitute God's children; instead, the children of the promise are regarded as offspring. **9** For this is the word of the promise: "About this time I will come and Sarah will have a child."
>
> **10** Not only that, but the same thing is true of Rebekah also.[f] She became pregnant with twins from a single sex act with one man,[g] Isaac our father. **11** And before they were born or had done anything whether good or bad—so that the electing purpose might remain God's, **12** not from actions but from the one who calls—it was said to her, "The greater will serve the lesser."[h] **13** As it is written, "Jacob I loved, but Esau I hated."

a. See the translation note on 8:16. The prefix *syn* in *symmartyrousēs* functions to intensify the verb rather than to indicate partnership.

b. *Hyper* can be understood as "in the place of" or "instead of" rather than simply "for." In that case, Paul's wish is to be substituted for Israel in the divine judgment. But that substitutionary move is not necessitated by the Greek. In 8:27, 31, and 34, *hyper* with a genitive of persons means simply "for" or "on behalf of" (see also 10:1; 15:30).

c. The translation of v. 5 is highly contested; see below for discussion.

d. The negative *ou* here is generally taken with the "all" (*pantes*) that follows, but construing it as negation of the entire statement better reflects the parallels with vv. 6a and 7a. Paul similarly negates entire statements at several points in the letter (2:13, 28; 7:15, 19; Gaventa 2010, 259).

e. Lit., "are Israel," understood here as "being" in the sense of "being what makes up" or constitutes Israel. This avoids introduction of "really" or "truly" as descriptors of Israel and is more consistent with Paul's emphasis on God's act in bringing Israel into being.

f. The words "the same thing is true of" have been added by way of explicating how the phrase "not only that, but" connects v. 9 with v. 10.

g. More lit., "from the sexual emission of one man." Paul is explicit here, rejecting the possibility that the twins might have separate fathers.

h. Verses 11–12 are quite awkward, and the dashes in the translation reflect that awkwardness. The long opening clause is a genitive absolute ("and before they were born or had done anything whether good or bad") that introduces a *hina* clause with "the purpose" (*prothesis*) as its subject before the main verb arrives at last in v. 12, *errethē* ("it was said").

[1–3] The depth of Paul's concern comes to expression already in these opening lines, especially when they are read in close connection to the soaring conclusion of ch. 8. Verse 1 consists of three separate asseverations of the reliability of what follows:

> I am telling the truth in Christ
> I am not lying
> My conscience confirms me in the Holy Spirit

Although Paul elsewhere uses individual expressions similar to each of these statements (2 Cor 1:12; 7:4; 11:3; 12:6; Gal 1:20), nowhere else do all of them appear together. The fact that these other expressions of truthfulness occur in Galatians and 2 Corinthians, letters in which Paul's authority is under attack, may underscore the severity of Paul's concern here.

Parallel references to Christ and to the Holy Spirit at the end of the first and third affirmations heighten the effect of this complex declaration, motivating the audience to accept what Paul is about to say. Yet more is at work here than sheer pathos. By locating himself in Christ and in the Holy Spirit, Paul connects what he is about to say with his sweeping language in ch. 8 regarding the love of Christ and the working of the Spirit. Paul does not speak some "truth in Christ," as if there were two truths, one belonging to Christ and one that is outside Christ. (There are no "alternative facts.") He speaks as one who is in Christ.[3] Locating himself "in Christ" and his conscience "in the Holy Spirit," Paul identifies himself from the outset of this discussion as one who belongs to Christ and the Spirit. That location is primary for Paul, as is clear in the first words of the letter ("slave of Christ Jesus"). It has primacy even over his physical relationship to Israel, and it is from that location in Christ that he considers the relationship between God and the Israelites, his kin.[4]

The truthfulness Paul insists on concerns the pain and grief in his own heart. He employs the noun here translated "grief" (*lypē*), and a related verb (*lypeō*),

3. This is a prime instance of the *encheiristic* ("in the hands of") use of "in Christ" identified by Teresa Morgan (2020, 85).

4. Theologically there is an interesting parallel between this primacy of Christ over physical family and Gospel sayings about rejecting the family in order to follow Jesus, as in Mark 10:29–30.

most often in 2 Corinthians concerning his fraught relationship with believers there (e.g., 2 Cor 2:1–5 [7x], 7; 6:10; 7:8–11 [8x]; 9:7); elsewhere the terms appear only in Rom 14:15; Phil 2:27–28; 1 Thess 4:13). *Odynē* ("pain") is a hapax legomenon in Paul's undisputed letters (although see 1 Tim 6:10). Here the terms come together with modifiers that make the entire statement more dramatic, although even this declaration pales in comparison with what follows in v. 3. Paul now announces that he could wish for himself ("I myself") to be cut off from Christ for the sake of "my brothers and sisters, my physical kinfolk."[5] The severity of this declaration becomes clear in view of Paul's announcement of anathema elsewhere on those who do not love Jesus (1 Cor 16:22) and those who preach "another" gospel (Gal 1:8).

Yet just a few lines earlier Paul has declared, in language that leaves little room for ambiguity, that nothing can separate "us" from God's love in Christ Jesus. The contrast between that insistence and the present statement of Paul's own desire can scarcely be accidental, even if the verbs differ. This thing that is impossible—to be separated from Christ—Paul claims is possible for himself to desire.[6] This notion of impossibility is not confined to Paul's own standing, for it will soon emerge that Rom 9–11 abounds in impossibilities: the impossible birth of children, the impossible callings of God, the impossible (temporary) reversal of Jew and gentile, and finally the impossible greatness of God's mercy.[7]

With the end of v. 3, the reason for this outpouring comes into view: "my brothers and sisters, my physical kinfolk." Given Paul's ubiquitous use of familial language to construct or at least to support the connections among believers (as in, e.g., Rom 1:13; 7:1, 4; 8:12, 29), the term *adelphoi* does not initially signal the topic at hand. Gentiles are also addressed as "brothers and sisters" (e.g., 1 Cor 1:10; 2 Cor 1:8; Gal 1:11; 1 Thess 1:4). It is with *syngenoi* ("kinfolk") and *kata sarka* ("physical") that the source of this outpouring of anguish comes into view. What precisely prompts Paul's profound concern he does not stipulate. Earlier in the letter he rejected the deduction that the faithlessness of some Jews undermines God's own faithfulness (3:3), and that way of putting things provides a clue to Paul's undertaking in these chapters.

[4–5] The kinfolk are "Israelites." Paul rarely uses this term, which appears again in Rom 11:1 and otherwise in Paul's letters only at 2 Cor 11:22.[8] The

---

5. The line recalls Moses pleading with God on behalf of Israel, asking to be blotted out of God's book in favor of Israel's forgiveness (Exod 32:32; Wagner 2002, 52), although there are no verbal connections between the two passages.

6. Wayne A. Meeks identifies this rightly as an "impossible vow" (2002, 214).

7. Note Karl Barth's frequent use of "impossible possibility" when commenting on Romans (e.g., 75, 79, 138, 202, 282, 381).

8. Outside of Paul's letters, "Israelite" appears in the NT only in John 1:47 as Jesus identifies Nathanael as "the Israelite in whom there is no guile," and several times in the speeches in Acts (Acts 2:22; 3:12; 5:35; 13:16; 21:28).

choice of "Israelites" rather than "Jews" (as earlier in Rom 1:16; 2:9–10, 17, 28–29; 3:1, 9, 29) is consistent with the discussion of Israel that follows as well as with the historical gifts to Israel itemized in the remainder of this verse. Its use conveys linkage to Israel in its relationship to God. In addition, unlike "Jew," which is used by insiders and outsiders alike (e.g., Mark 7:3; Acts 10:22; Plutarch, *Ant.* 3.1; *Oth.* 15.5; Epictetus, *Diatr.* 1.11.12–13; BDAG s.v.), "Israelite" is a designation Jews use of themselves (e.g., John 1:47; Acts 2:22; Josephus, *Ant.* 3.189; BDAG, s.v. *Israēlitēs*).

Immediately Paul describes Israelites with a list of things that are "theirs." A single relative pronoun links the first six items to the Israelites: adoption, glory, covenants, giving of the law, service, promises. The connection between each of these items and the Israelites is significant, although in several cases the route is a circuitous one. The introductory word, "adoption" (*huiothesia*), places the emphasis from the outset on God's initiative; adoption reflects a decision and action by the adopted parent. Identifying Israelites as adopted is peculiar, since the term does not appear in the LXX, although Israel is referred to as God's "son(s)" on numerous occasions (e.g., Exod 4:22; Deut 8:5; and see Heim 2017, 251–320). The use of "adoption" rather than "sonship" places the Israelites alongside those adopted in 8:15, 23, and all of them (Israelite and non-Israelite) follow from Christ, the "firstborn," the "Son" (8:29, 32), even as Christ comes physically from them (v. 5).

The five items that follow adoption are also gifts from God to Israel. That "glory" belongs to the Israelites requires specification. It is not, in the first instance, human glory, although there is a glory bestowed by God (as in 8:17, 18). In Romans "glory" has largely been associated with God's own glory, as in the reference in 1:23 to the "glory of the immortal God," and 6:4 where Christ is said to have been raised from the dead by the "glory of the Father." This is consistent with notions of divine glory in Israel's Scriptures, where God's glory is God's presence (e.g., Exod 15:6–7; 24:16; Ps 56:6 LXX; Isa 30:27–33; Bar 4:24; 5:6–7, 9; see Gaventa 2014b, 32–34; and see above on 6:4). The "glory" of the Israelites, then, is the presence of God with and among them.

"Covenants" (*diathēkai*) is unusual for its use in the plural, and the plural could simply be an instance of homoioteleuton, since the other Greek words in this series all end with "a," "ia," or "ai." Nonetheless, Israel's history includes several covenants: with Noah (pre-Israel in the strict sense but narrated in Israel's story; see Gen 6:18; 9:9), with Abraham (Gen 15:18–20), and with Moses (Exod 31:16–18; 34:10). Paul may have all of these in view, as all are bestowed at God's initiative and all of them mark the course of God's dealings with Israel (and see the covenant language at Rom 11:27).

"Giving of the law" appears only here in Paul (cf. 2 Macc 6:23; 4 Macc 5:35; 17:16; Josephus, *Ant.* 3.287; 3.320; Philo, *Abraham* 1.5; *Moses* 2.2). As with *diathēkai*, the choice of *nomothesia* may result from homoioteleuton, which the more predictable *nomos* ("law") would have interrupted. Yet the substitution again highlights the fact that the law Paul has identified as the "holy and right and good" law (7:12) is also God's gift. Emphasizing the giving of the law at this point (as distinct from the law itself) not only underscores the rich giftedness of Israel but undercuts any notion that the law is inherently problematic.

"Service" (*latreia*) and the related verb "serve" (*latreuō*) refer particularly but not exclusively to cultic service (1:9, 25; 12:1; Phil 3:3). In the LXX, the obligation of worship may not be best described as a gift, but it is an obligation placed upon Israel by God rather than an option Israel selects (e.g., Exod 3:12; 4:23; 23:25; Deut 6:13; 7:4, 16; 10:12, 20; Josh 22:5). There are dire warnings against the service of other gods (e.g., Deut 4:19; 5:9; 2 Chr 7:19).

The final word in this sequence, "promises" (*epangeliai*), further underscores the divine direction of this series, since promise is obviously and explicitly identified with God's action. In Rom 4, promise characterizes God's interaction with Abraham and his offspring (4:14, 16, 20, 21; and see 9:8). Later, in the culmination of the letter, Paul identifies the arrival of Jesus Christ as confirming God's promises to Israel's ancestors (15:8).[9] The language of promise does not appear in Genesis, but Paul is not alone in the NT in interpreting the relationship between God and Israel as one marked by divine promise (see, e.g., Acts 2:39; 7:17; Heb 11:9, 11).

The symmetry created by the extended use of homoioteleuton ends with v. 5. By way of drawing attention to what follows (Moo 564; Jewett 566), a resumptive "theirs" (*hōn*) introduces "the fathers," and "from them" (*ex hōn*) introduces "Christ, physically speaking." Only one such father has been mentioned to this point in the letter, Abraham, who is identified as the father of both the uncircumcised and the circumcised (4:11–12). In the lines that follow, however, other specific fathers in Israel's line will be identified (vv. 6–13). Perhaps more important, in 11:28 Paul will insist that the hardened portion of Israel remains beloved because of "the fathers," and in 15:8 he will identify Christ's ministry with confirming the promises made to "the fathers." By identifying "the fathers" as one of the attributes of Israel, Paul again underscores the giftedness of Israel. He will spell this out in the lines that follow: Abraham and Isaac are not Israel's fathers by virtue of their own actions but by God's gift.

Since Christ is not described as "theirs" but as "from them" in a physical sense, the possibility arises that Paul is arguing against those Jews who do not recognize Jesus as the Messiah of God (so, e.g., Barrett 178; Cranfield 2:464;

---

9. See below on 15:8. While the promises in Gen 15:1–11 include children and land, here by contrast the promises are identified solely with Christ. The stunning language of Gal 3:16, in which Paul identifies the seed of Abraham as the singular Christ, is not far away.

Moo 565; Jewett 566–67). Christ would then be *from* but not *of* Jews, from them only by virtue of his birth. The language connects as well as separates, however; Christ is physically an Israelite (as also in 1:3), even as he is also "over all" (Gaventa 2016b, 246).

The translation of the remainder of 9:5 has divided exegetes for centuries. The statement about Christ can be read in at least two ways. One possibility is as follows:

> . . . the Christ physically speaking, who is God over all, blessed forever. Amen!

In this translation, the concluding doxology stands in apposition to Christ, identifying him as God. The alternative rendering inserts a period between the reference to Christ and the concluding doxology, as follows:

> . . . the Christ physically speaking. May God who is over all be blessed forever. Amen!

Since the earliest manuscripts generally do not provide punctuation, either reading is possible. The first is the most natural way of construing the syntax, in which the reference to "who is God" (*ho ōn . . . theos*) follows immediately on "the Christ" (see the similar syntax, without reference to Christ, in 1:25; 11:36; Gal 1:5; 2 Cor 11:31; Fitzmyer 549). Syntax is not the only argument in favor of this construal, however. Having just commented on the flesh, the human descent of Christ, reference to his relationship to God would make the passage more consistent with 1:3–4. In addition, Paul does elsewhere place Jesus in an exalted role, as in Phil 2:6–11, where he is said to have given up the "form" of God and to have been given "the name above every name," which would be the divine name. Moreover, Paul's references to God frequently identify God so closely with Jesus Christ that God is not known apart from Christ (as in Rom 4:25; 8:11; Watson 2006).[10]

This widely commended translation creates some difficulties, however.[11] Paul does identify Christ closely with God, but he nowhere else directly names him God. No other doxology in Paul's letters is ascribed to Christ. Even assuming Paul would call Christ "God," the question remains whether he would do that at this point in this letter. As he takes up the fraught discourse about God's dealings with Israel (and the gentiles), it would be ill-advised for Paul baldly

---

10. Among those who adopt the view that Christ is the subject of the doxology are Cranfield 2:464–69; Fitzmyer 548–49; Wright 629–31; Jewett 367–68; and Gathercole 2017, 118–22.

11. Those who understand the doxology as separate from the reference to Christ include Käsemann 259–60; Wilckens 2:186, Lohse 269–70; Hultgren 353–55. For additional proposals and the history of interpretation, see Cranfield 2:465–66; Metzger 1973; Carraway 2013, 15–18.

to identify Christ as God.[12] The "Amen!" that follows invites Roman auditors to join in, to lend their assent to the doxology, so that Paul can begin the long journey to 11:26. Does he really want to set the teeth of his auditors on edge at the very beginning, especially when he is about to narrate a rather peculiar version of Israel's history? Paul does challenge his auditors at a number of points, as with the shift to accusation at 2:1, the insistence that "we" were weak, ungodly sinners in 5:6–11, and especially the challenge to gentile arrogance in 11:18–19, but it is hard to see why he would insert this direct challenge at this juncture in the letter.

The translation above seeks middle ground by inserting a dash between "the one who is over all" and "God," leaving interpretation to the ear of the audience. In fact, resolving this ambiguity has very little consequence for understanding the argument Paul is undertaking (Keck 229), despite the vigorous discussion it has generated and even its potential significance for understanding Paul's Christology. On either reading, Paul has firmly identified the Christ as biologically connected to the Israelites, and on either reading the Christ is one of the gifts God has bestowed on the Israelites. In addition, on either reading, the doxology, one of several in the letter (also 1:25; 11:36; 15:33), invites the auditors to join in Paul's praise for all God's gifts. Paul presumably hopes that the auditors in Rome will also listen generously to what comes next.

[6–9] The recital of God's gifts to Israel introduces the declaration of v. 6a: "It is not that God's word has failed."[13] Between the doxology and the suggestion that God's word *might* be thought to fail stands the situation Paul confronts, namely, the relationship between the Israel of God and the God who raised Jesus Christ from the dead. Routinely and rightly identified as the thesis of the whole of Rom 9–11, "God's word" connects Rom 1–8 with the implications of those chapters for Israel. "God's word" (*ho logos tou theou*) recalls the "sayings of God" in 3:2 (*ta logia tou theou*), likely a general reference to Scripture. Yet 9:6a does not refer to Scripture in isolation from the Christ event, as the reference to Christ in v. 5 makes clear.

As evidence that God's word has not failed, Paul writes, "It is not the case that all of those who are from Israel constitute Israel." Most English translations and interpretations take the negation (*ou*) to apply to the initial phrase (*pantes hoi ex Israēl*)—hence, "not all those who are from Israel." A few, however, construe the *ou* with the second phrase (*houtoi Israēl*), reading "these are not all Israel" (Piper 1993, 48; Bell 2005, 210). But the negation may be taken with the statement as a whole, as seems to be the case earlier in 2:13, 28; 7:15, 19.

---

12. Munck contends that Jews in the audience would have found a doxology addressed to Christ offensive (1967, 33), but gentiles who have frequently visited in local synagogues might not have been much more sympathetic.

13. This discussion of vv. 6–13 is anticipated by Gaventa 2010.

That construal produces this: "For it is not the case that all those who are from Israel [i.e., Israelites by birth], these people are [i.e., they constitute] Israel." What the negative *ou* produces is less significant than the translation of the words *houtoi Israēl* (literally, "these Israel"). This second reference is customarily understood to refer to the "true" or "faithful" or "spiritual" Israel, as in the NRSV rendering that "not all Israelites truly belong to Israel."[14] The assumption at work in such additions is that Paul already makes use in 9:6 of the distinctions he will make later between "the election" (11:7) and "the rest" or between the "part" and "all" of Israel (11:25–26). In ch. 11 Paul makes such a distinction and does so explicitly; there is a *division* (in Paul's time) within Israel, but in 9:6b a different point is under construction, which is that the only Israel that exists is the one God brought into being through promise and call.

Everything that follows depends on clarity here: Paul's point is that Israel ("those who are from Israel") does not make itself, does not construct Israel. Although Israel is composed of the descendants of a particular family line and is in that sense biological, its origin is not in the first instance biological because its creation and sustenance come from God. Paul does not here or elsewhere distinguish between genuine and false Israelites. Even in the highly polemical situation of 2 Cor 11:22, Paul does not succumb to the temptation to undermine the claims of his opponents on this point; he shares with them the names "Hebrew," "Israelite," and "descendant of Abraham."

Paul begins a concise history of Israel in v. 7, but it is a peculiar version of that history, especially when compared with versions found elsewhere in contemporaneous literature. Wisdom of Solomon 10:1–11:14, for example, extols Wisdom's actions in the face of Israel's history of righteousness and of wrongdoing. Hebrews 11 chronicles the faith of the ancestors in each generation. The Stephen speech in Acts 7 reports on obedience and also on rebellion. Neither extolling virtue nor criticizing vice, Paul attends exclusively to God's calling.

Verse 7a reiterates the distinction of v. 6b, but this time by referring to the "offspring of Abraham" (*sperma Abraam*). Since here "all the children" (*tekna*) are distinguished from the "offspring," it is possible that Paul is drawing attention to God's choice of Isaac in preference to Ishmael. The citation of Gen 21:12 LXX introduces a different emphasis, however—that of calling: "Through Isaac will your offspring be called."

The "calling" of Abraham's offspring brings in a term that reappears frequently in this brief narration of God's dealings with Israel—that of God's call

14. Note the addition of "truly" or "really" in the commentaries of Barrett 179; Fitzmyer 558; Hultgren 360; and the addition of *wirklich* in the German commentaries of Schlier 289; Lohse 270. Cranfield writes of "Israel within Israel," identifying this as "the company of those who are willing, obedient, grateful witnesses to . . . grace and truth" (2:474). More succinctly, Fitzmyer identifies this group as "the Jews of faith" (560). Tobin puts the matter colloquially: "Not all Israelites are the real thing" (2004, 327).

(vv. 7, 12, 24, 25, 26). Paul has introduced calling in connection with Israel's history already in 4:17, when he describes Abraham's trust of "God, who makes the dead live and who calls into being that which does not exist."[15] In the context of Rom 4, it is the promise of Isaac and of future children for Abraham and Sarah that Paul identifies as nothing less than calling into existence, an act of creation, a point he elaborates by reference to their age (4:19). This notion of God's creating, God's calling into being, is in turn consistent with other creation motifs in Romans, notably in 1:18–32 and in 8:18–25. Coherent with these earlier passages, then, the point of the citation of Gen 21:12 in Rom 9:7 lies in God's *creation* of offspring through Isaac and less in the *choosing* of Isaac over Ishmael, Hagar's child, who is never mentioned.

Verses 8–9 interpret this creative act as one of divine promise. To be sure, Paul does distinguish between groups of children (*tekna*). Yet this identification of the groups is telling; rather than distinguishing the children of flesh from children of *spirit*, which might be expected especially in view of the long discourse on flesh and spirit in 8:3–11, Paul distinguishes flesh from *promise*. Further, he identifies the specific promise in language drawn from Gen 18:10, 14—the promise that the aged and barren Sarah, the one who dares to laugh at God's word, will give birth to a son. In Genesis, as here in Romans, emphasis falls on the promise, God's act of bringing a son into existence, and only secondarily on the choice of one of Abraham's sons rather than the other.[16]

[10–13] God's action is implicit in vv. 7–9, but with the recounting of Rebekah's motherhood, God's action becomes explicit: "The electing purpose [is] God's." Opening with Rebekah's name rather than that of Isaac is striking, given that immediately prior to this reference the focus is on Abraham's offspring. Sarah enters the text only with the promise cited from Gen 18:10, 14. Similarly, in Rom 4 Abraham is the focus of the discussion; reference to Sarah appears only in the context of Abraham's reflection on the seeming impossibility of God's promise (4:19).[17] By contrast, this recollection of the calling of Jacob begins through a focus on Rebekah.[18]

Verse 10 not only begins with Rebekah's pregnancy, but it does so in language that draws attention to the single sexual act that produces the twins.[19]

---

15. Language of calling is otherwise scarce in Romans, appearing only in 1:1, 6, 7; 8:28, 30. See also 1 Cor 1:26–28 with its reference to God's selection of "the things that did not exist."

16. Note also that in Rom 9, by contrast with Rom 4, Paul makes no reference to Abraham's trust.

17. Sarah is referred to by name elsewhere in the NT only at Heb 11:11 and 1 Pet 3:6.

18. Otherwise mention of Rebekah is curious, since she is never referred to in the Bible outside of the Genesis account, although there are references to her in Jubilees (e.g., 19.10, 13, 16; 23.4), the Testaments of the Twelve Patriarchs (T. Levi 6.8; T. Naph. 1.9), Testament of Jacob (2.6), the DSS (4Ql frag. 3.1), and in Joseph and Aseneth (1.8).

19. This point is observed as early as Augustine, who comments that Paul spoke "with utmost care" with the words "by a single sexual union" (*Div. quaest. Simp.* 1.2.3; Burns 224).

Rather than write that Rebekah "conceived" (*syllambanein*, as in, e.g., Gen 4:1; 25:21; Luke 1:24), Paul uses *koitē*, "bed," which figuratively refers to sexual intercourse, specifically to sexual emission (e.g., Lev 15:4; Num 5:13; BDAG s.v.; LSJ s.v.). By contrast with some fraternal twins, such as Castor and Pollux, who have different fathers, Jacob and Esau share a single father.[20] Having established this point, in v. 11 Paul abruptly changes focus from Rebekah to the twins, specifying that they have not yet been born; further, they have done nothing at all, neither good nor ill. Here Paul overlooks Gen 25:22–23, which recounts the twins' struggle in Rebekah's womb and her lament, together with the divine response which Paul does quote in v. 12.

The reason for Paul's odd specificity about the twins' conception and gestation comes into view with the end of v. 11. This happened "so that" the "electing purpose" might remain that of God alone. Reference to either God's purpose *or* God's act of election would have made the point, which Paul reinforces by use of both words (as in 8:28). Verse 12a takes the matter further still with the additional phrase "not from actions but from the one who calls." "From actions," literally translated as "from works," might be regarded as a shorthand for works of the law (as at 3:27; so Dunn 2:542; Wright 637); however, Paul is not contrasting the law with faith but with divine action. The contrast has to do not with the law but with whether the initiative is that of a human being or of God (see Watson 2016, 189).

Evidence for God's initiative comes in the form of two citations of divine speech. The first is explicitly said to be addressed to Rebekah, declaring that the older twin will serve the younger one (Gen 25:23), a violation of primogeniture. Paul follows this citation with one that puts the selection in stark terms: "Jacob I loved, but Esau I hated" (Mal 1:2–3). Here for the first time reference is made to the one not chosen, a reference that prompts the question of v. 14 regarding God's justice.

Paul's emphasis on God's role in this decision coheres with the Genesis account, in that God's choice is revealed to Rebekah before she gives birth. Both Jewish and later Christian interpreters demonstrate their discomfort with this report, however. The renarration in Jubilees attributes the action to Abraham rather than God, aligning Abraham and Rebekah in their favoritism toward Jacob (19.15–25; 22.10–20). Philo contends that God knows in advance the actions that will later reveal the relative merits of Jacob and Esau (*Alleg. Interp.* 3.88–89; Richardson 1999, 26–94). According to Ambrosiaster, God's action

20. According to mythological tradition, Castor and Pollux, the Dioscuri (mentioned in Acts 28:11), are the sons of Tyndareus and Zeus, respectively. While rare, it is biologically possible for twins to have two different fathers. That possibility seems to drive Theodoret's emphatic comment underscoring Paul's emphasis, "She conceived both children at the same time from this one father" (*Commentary* 9.9–13; Burns 223). Alicia Myers's study of mothers in the NT suggests this line of observation (2017).

reflects God's foreknowledge of their worth (75; similarly Pelagius 116; and Chrysostom, *Hom. Rom.* 16.10; *NPNF*[1] 11.463).[21] By contrast with his contemporaries and in contradiction to his own later interpreters, Paul explicitly denies any difference between the twins in terms of their character, and nothing in Romans suggests that God acts out of prior knowledge as to their faith or faithful deeds. In Paul's telling, God chooses because God chooses, a point that reverberates in the chapters that follow. First, however, Paul will indirectly acknowledge the problem faced by Jubilees and Philo, among others: Where is the justice in God's actions?

9:14–29 The Peculiar Mercy of God

"Jacob I loved, but Esau I hated." The starkness of the formulation propels Paul forward into a question about God's injustice (or wrongdoing) that is answered in terms of God's mercy and God's freedom. Paul continues to review Israel's history, this time in the persons of Moses and especially Pharaoh, before shifting abruptly in v. 24 to the present time ("us").[22]

The initial question and response regarding God's justice (vv. 14–18) are followed by a question about the possibility of human resistance (vv. 19–21), which produces a strong defense of God's purpose (vv. 22–23), both in the case of "us" (Jew and gentile who have been called, vv. 24–26) and in the case of Israel as a whole (vv. 27–29).

This is no abstract argument about divine attributes. The passage is dense with voices of Scripture that speak concretely about God's dealings with Israel. Already in v. 12 a divine word is spoken to Rebekah. Now God speaks to Moses, Scripture speaks to Pharaoh, God's voice is heard in Hosea, Isaiah cries out over Israel. In all these voices, as well as in the use of the familiar scriptural imagery of potter and clay, Paul hears of God's freedom to create, to shape, to harden, and to rescue God's people.

9:14 So, what does this mean? There isn't wrongdoing on God's part, is there?[a] Of course not! 15 For God says to Moses, "I will have mercy on whomever I have mercy, and I will have pity on whomever I have pity." 16 So then, God's choice depends[b] not on the one who wills it nor on the one who strives for it[c] but on the one who is merciful, namely, God. 17 For Scripture says to Pharaoh, "I raised you up for this reason, so that I might demonstrate my power in your case and so that my name might

21. See further Parmentier 1990 and Payne 1990.
22. I have written on this passage elsewhere (Gaventa 2010, 263–68), but this discussion modifies that work in some significant ways, particularly regarding the opening question in v. 14 and the translation of vv. 22–23.

be declared in all the earth." 18 So then, God has mercy on whom God wills, and God hardens whom God wills.

19 So you will say to me, "Why does God still place blame? Since who can resist God's will?" 20 You there,[d] who are you that you presume to answer back to God? Does the thing that is made respond to its maker, "Why did you make me like this?" 21 Doesn't the maker of the pot have the authority to shape from his lump of clay either a valuable vessel or one for mundane use[e]?

22 And what concern is it of yours[f] if God wanted to demonstrate his wrath and make known his power, and for that reason God brought forth vessels of wrath with great persistence, vessels prepared for destruction, 23 so that he might make known the wealth of his glory on vessels of mercy prepared for glory? 24 Those vessels of mercy[g] are the ones he also called, us, not only from Jews but also from gentiles, 25 as it says even in Hosea:

> I will call the one who is not my people my people
> And the one not my beloved beloved.
> 26 And in the place wherever they will be called,[h]
>   "You are not my people,"
> There they will be called sons and daughters of the living God.

27 Now[i] Isaiah cries out over Israel,

> Even if the number of the sons and daughters of Israel was as
>   the sand of the sea, a remnant will be saved,[j]
> 28 for the Lord will be at work upon the earth, fulfilling and
>   completing his word.

29 And just as Isaiah said before,

> Unless the Lord Sabaoth had left us offspring,
> we would have become like Sodom and would have been made
>   like Gomorrah.

a. The translation reflects the introductory particle *mē*, which anticipates a negative answer to the question. The translation also follows the Greek order by placing "wrong-doing" (*adikia*) toward the beginning of the question.

b. Some phrase is required to complete this sentence fragment, which reads more literally, "therefore not of the one willing nor of the one running but of the one being merciful, God." Translations often supply "it depends not" (KJV, RSV, NRSVue, NIV), leaving "it" unspecified, but the context indicates that the divine choice is the subject here.

c. Lit., "running," here in a figurative sense, as in 1 Cor 9:24b; Gal 2:2.

d. See 2:1. Lit., "O man" or "O human," but "you there" is more idiomatic.

e. Lit., "a vessel for honor" (*eis timēn*) and one for dishonor (*eis atimian*), yet dishonor suggests something quite negative (as in 1:26), while the analogy has to do with pots that have different functions. See similarly 1 Cor 12:23, with its contrast between body parts that are valued (the eyes) and those that are thought to be of less importance (the feet).

f. Verses 22–23 constitute a lengthy protasis (subordinate clause) for which there is no apodosis (main clause). In fact, the protasis continues even into v. 24. The introductory question ("What concern is it of yours?") is supplied so as to produce a complete English sentence. The confrontational character of the introductory question follows from the previous lines, with their challenge of human prerogatives to resist God's action.

g. Grammatically, the relative pronoun *hous* could refer to both sets of "vessels" in vv. 22–23, but the use of the language of "call" (*kaleō*) makes that interpretation highly unlikely. For Paul, "calling" language consistently refers to calling into faith, service, even calling into existence. First Thessalonians 4:7 is a possible exception, but the notion of a calling to impurity is immediately rejected, so the exception confirms the rule in that case.

h. Following the reading of 𝔓⁴⁶ F G etc., rather than *errethē autois* ("it was said to them") in ℵ A D K L P Ψ etc. "They will be called" might reflect assimilation to the same verb at the end of this verse (Jewett 588), but it seems more likely that *errethē autois* represents scribal conformity to Hos 2:1 LXX.

i. *De* can be construed as an adversative ("but"), as in Moo 629 and Jewett 598, but given that vv. 25–26 concern at least some Jews, vv. 27–28 seem to mark a shift in attention rather than a contrast.

j. English translations routinely supply "only," as in "only a remnant will be saved," despite the fact that the text has no adverb (e.g., NRSVue, CEB, NIV; see Hays 1989, 68, 206n68).

[14–18] The citations in vv. 12b–13 name the subject directly: God's calling is God's calling. The question of v. 14 then follows naturally: Is God unjust in following this action without taking merit into account? The issue is urgent because Paul has couched the choice as determined solely by God's decision, by contrast with other interpreters of Israel's history who impute to God foreknowledge of the twins' character or some other grounds for action (see above on 9:10–13). In addition, of course, the strong wording of v. 13 ("Jacob I loved, but Esau I hated") forces the question of v. 14.

Despite Paul's adamant response to the question ("Of course not!"), he scarcely answers it in the lines that follow. Paul continues his odd history of Israel, this time through the pair of Moses and Pharaoh (in place of Jacob and Esau). Paul's handling of the two figures is similar in form:

> Introduction of Moses/Pharaoh (vv. 15a, 17a)
> Quotation from Scripture (vv. 15b, 17b)
> Interpretive conclusion (vv. 16, 18)

This parallel treatment reflects Paul's point: what is important in each case is what God does through the human agent.

Verse 15, God's address to Moses, comes from Exod 33:19 LXX, the larger context of which is Israel's shocking construction and worship of the golden calf (Wagner 2002, 52; Barclay 2010a). Yet the divine declaration occurs not when Moses intercedes for Israel's forgiveness (32:30–35) but later, when Moses pleads with God for God's presence. The mercy Moses receives, and Israel along with Moses, is that of God's continued presence. Further, the exchange is marked by God's declaration that Moses is not able to see God; that is, Moses is not able to know God's ways. That context in Exodus may be in play in 9:15, in that humanity is not able to know God's mind as God has mercy. In other words, what Paul finds weighty in the biblical event is God's intent to be present with Moses (and Israel) rather than Israel's disobedience. If so, what Paul has in view with "mercy" is God's continuing presence rather than forgiveness as such, or at least the two are combined.

Paul's comments about Pharaoh in v. 17 reinforce that understanding, but first comes the conclusion drawn from the statement to Moses: God's action has nothing to do with human planning or human exertion but only with God, who is here named as God-who-has-mercy. The connection back to v. 12 is clear. Nothing about God's action either in the selection of Jacob or in the merciful presence of God with Moses (and thereby Israel) depends on human agency. The quotation's reference to mercy is carried over into v. 16, where Paul describes God as "the God who is merciful," introducing language that features prominently in ch. 11.

Verse 17 brings the second human agent into the picture, namely, Pharaoh. With no introduction, Paul cites a divine word addressed to Pharaoh in Scripture: "I raised you up for this reason, so that I might demonstrate my power in your case and so that my name might be declared in all the earth." The quotation is drawn from Exod 9:16 LXX, although with some slight yet significant modifications:

> And you were preserved for this reason, that I might demonstrate my strength in you and so that my name might be spread in the whole earth.

Instead of "you were preserved," however, Paul writes, "I raised you up." Going well beyond the claim that God protected Pharaoh's life, in Paul's rendering Pharaoh comes into existence for God's purposes (no less than did Isaac or Jacob). In addition, Paul employs a different word for strength or power. Where Exod 9:16 asserts that God demonstrates his power (*ischys*), Paul employs another noun, *dynamis* (see Rom 1:16, 20; 15:13, 19).

Exodus 9:16 speaks to Pharaoh but, especially with these modifications, it speaks beyond Pharaoh to the "now time" of Paul. Not only is the outworking of God's power on evidence elsewhere in Romans, but the dissemination of God's name in the whole earth anticipates the summation of the letter in 15:7–13. The claim that Pharaoh is the instrument of God's power also anticipates 9:22, where the vessels of wrath have the purpose of making known God's power. The final phrase, "all the earth," does appear in Exod 9:16, but here it is especially important, since *pas* ("all") recalls the universal horizon of Romans (Tobin 2004, 331). As Paul depicts Christ's welcome of Jew and gentile alike "for the glory of God" (15:7), he looks forward to the shared praise of God's name by all people (15:9). In several ways, then, Exod 9:16 speaks to Pharaoh, but it speaks beyond Pharaoh into the gospel Paul announces to the Romans.

Paul draws the pertinent conclusion ("so then," *ara oun*) from the quotation (v. 18). While God has mercy on those he chooses (repeating v. 15), God also hardens those he chooses. Pharaoh is the quintessential figure with a hardened heart. In Exodus and elsewhere, the hardening of Pharaoh's heart is attributed both to God and to Pharaoh (as in Exod 4:21; 9:34–35; 10:1; 13:15; see also 1 Sam 6:6). This shared responsibility for Pharaoh's disobedience lives on in the history of interpretation (McGinnis 2012). Paul, by contrast, has nothing whatever to say about Pharaoh's resistance to God's will.[23] In this account, Pharaoh is no more the author of his hardening than Isaac and Jacob are of their birth.[24]

[19–21] A second set of questions, this one by an imagined interlocutor ("you"), pursues the implications of God's dealings with Pharaoh. If God's mercy and God's hardening alike have no relationship whatever to human action, then how can God hold humans accountable? The questions in vv. 19–20—"Who can resist God's plan?" "Who are you?"—already indicate how Paul will answer.

The opening words of Paul's response to this imagined interlocutor indicate its importance, since "you there" draws attention to what follows (just as the same address did at 2:1, 3; Job 40:4b–6; see Wagner 2002, 56–57). The utter inconceivability of responding to God not only has precedents in Scripture but sets the stage for 11:33–36. Paul does not there cast the issue as daring to question God, but he does reiterate the inaccessibility of the divine mind and the utter inadequacy of human thought. Crucial to grasping Paul's argument in Rom 9–11 (and elsewhere) is the recognition that God's ways are not subject to human judgment.

By means of explaining why "you" may not resist God's will, vv. 20b–21 depict the relationship between God and the human with a simple, direct analogy that has a rich history in Jewish literature. First, "Does the thing that is made respond to its maker, 'Why did you make me like this?'" Paul's answer follows

23. Contrast Cranfield (2:485), who identifies Pharaoh as "the type of those who resist God—as the prefiguration of that disobedient Israel which is now opposed to the gospel." Paul, however, identifies him only as one to whom Scripture speaks.
24. Karl Barth (352) rightly observes that "Moses and Pharaoh are interchangeable."

Isa 29:16, although the image of the potter and the clay appears in a wide range of texts.[25] Here that language serves as a pointed reminder that God is Creator and God decides what becomes of creation.

Verse 21 expands and reinforces, lest there be any confusion, this time putting the question from the standpoint of the Creator (as v. 20 couches it from the standpoint of the created thing). The artisan has the authority to make a pot that is valuable, worthy, even priceless—and one that is not. Paul is clear that the artisan works with "his" (*autou*) lump; even before the artisan begins, the formless clay is his possession.

The comparison itself is familiar, but Paul makes distinctive use of it. He goes well beyond the insistence that God made Israel (as in 9:6–11) to comment on the intention of God's work. A vessel is made either to be prized or to be ordinary. One vessel may be an extravagant creation as in "an elegant decanter for wine" (Jewett 594), while another is nothing more than a "chamber pot" (Dunn 2:557). Presumably, however, all sorts of vessels are intended to serve in some way; the artisan does not make vessels simply to toss them away.

More to the point, nothing is said to suggest that the pots have thought or behaved in any way that determined their use. Given the analogy, the notion of earning one's reward is absurd. That small and obvious point trips up any attempt to identify the pots in Paul's analogy with particular people or peoples. This is not a description of a human personality or will, which would seem to be utterly clear by now given Paul's declarations. It is a statement about the prerogative of the Creator, whether the potter or God.

Important connections exist between this argument—its substance if not its vocabulary—and that of 1:18–32. What drives 9:19–21 is the contention that God is the Creator of humanity, that God has the prerogative to do what God wills, and that the human is not entitled to question God's designs. That is substantially what Paul means when he opens 1:18–32 with the claim that God is known from what God has made and that humanity has put in God's place things that are not God. The same conviction appears immediately following, in 9:22–23, where the vocabulary of wrath and power and patience and glory replays the language of 1:18–32.

[22–26] The difficulty of translating vv. 22–23 (see translation note f on v. 22) reflects its content, which is a densely compacted question implicitly challenging any human presumption to second-guess God's desires and actions. Understanding this question requires noticing the relentless attention to God's actions:[26]

---

25. E.g., Ps 2:9; Isa 45:9; 64:8; Jer 18:1–6; Sir 33:7–13; Wis 15:7–17; 1QS 11.22; 1QH[a] 9[1].23; 12[4].30.

26. As Michael Wolter (2017, 42–43) notes regarding these verses, "Paul is not interested in the human beings and in the question of who has to expect 'wrath' and who 'glory,' but what is at issue is only God."

v. 22 God wants to demonstrate and to make known
       God brought forth
v. 23 [God wants] to make known

These divine actions reinforce key motifs in chs. 1–8. The making known of God's power importantly recalls 1:16–17 (as well as 1:4, 20; 4:21), as the demonstration of God's wrath recalls 1:18 (see also 2:5, 8; 3:5; 4:15; 5:9). The letter has often referenced God's glory (1:23; 3:7, 23; 4:20; 5:2; 6:4) and will do so again in 11:36 and 15:7. The "vessels of mercy" intended for glory echo earlier anticipations of the eschatological glory of humanity (2:7, 10; 8:18, 21).

Attention to this primary concern with the action of God goes a long way toward locating properly Paul's treatment of the two sorts of "vessels." The term itself is ambiguous (Hanson 1981, 433–34). It can refer to an object in and of itself, in which case these "vessels" are themselves the recipients of God's action. "Vessels" can also refer to the instrumental use of an object, as in the analogy of v. 21, where the pots serve either precious or mundane purposes (see also Acts 9:21, where Paul himself is the instrument). In this case they are "brought forth" by God, as in Jer 27:25 LXX ("The Lord opened his treasury and brought out his instruments of wrath" [*ta skeuē orgēs autou*]). God acts with endurance or persistence (BDAG, s.v. *makrothymia*) rather than with patience for the objects themselves, and they are used for the purposes of destruction rather than being the objects of destruction.

On either translation, Paul goes on in v. 24 to identify the vessels of mercy as "us." He notably refrains from putting names or identities to the "vessels of wrath," leaving a gap readers are eager to fill, as the commentary tradition makes clear (e.g., Wilckens 2:202–3; Dunn 2:568; Wright 642). Phoebe's auditors may have wanted to do that as well, and it is even possible that Paul exploits that desire in his argument in Rom 10, where Israel as a whole is presented as tripping over the stumbling stone (9:30–32), ignorant of God's righteousness (10:3), and disobedient and resistant (10:21). Ironically, however, the very act of attempting to identify the vessels of wrath violates the argument Paul has made about wrath and mercy as divine prerogatives.

To be sure, v. 24 does identify the vessels or instruments of mercy as "us," marking a dramatic leap from Israel's early history (Isaac, Jacob, Esau, Moses, Pharaoh) to the present time. This seamless shift from past to present recalls 4:24, where Paul's narration of God's dealings with Abraham abruptly yields to God's dealings with "us." It also anticipates 15:4, where Paul will write that whatever was written beforehand was written for "our" instruction.[27]

---

27. These interpretive moves reflect Linebaugh's claim that "Paul's hermeneutic is eschatological" (2013b, 194).

The "us" called in the present (Paul's present) are both Jews and gentiles ("from Jews" and "from gentiles"). What Hosea "says" combines language drawn from Hos 2:25 LXX and 1:9b LXX, but with important modifications. Here the language of "call" is intensified, since Paul supplies "I will call" (*kalesō*) where Hos 2:25 LXX reads "I will say," and also has "they will be called" instead of "it was said to them" from Hos 2:1 LXX.[28] These changes in call language place the citation alongside Rom 4:17 and 9:6b–13, where Paul writes of calling into being things that did not exist, the calling into being of Israel. Now, however, gentiles are among those "called."

In addition to this intensified call language, applied to Jew and gentile alike, Paul's text replaces the language of mercy from Hos 2:25 LXX with the language of love. That seems an odd change, given the "vessels of mercy" in v. 23 as well as the mercy language of vv. 15–16. It may be, however, that "love" connects back to the quotation of Mal 1:2 LXX in v. 13: "Jacob I loved, but Esau I hated" (Wagner 2002, 82–83). In that case, Paul is asserting that even God's own sharp declaration of rejection and acceptance, the rejection of Esau and the acceptance of Jacob, is susceptible to overturning, because God is free to love whomever God wills.

Gentiles are not the only ones addressed in vv. 25–26, however. The inclusion of Jews here reiterates that Jews no less than gentiles are among those who are "vessels of mercy." Jews also are addressed as the "not my people" who are called "my people," "my beloved." Neither Jew nor gentile is part of this group by birth, even if they are Jew or gentile by birth.

[27–29] Paul's use of the words of God from Hosea is remarkable for their identification of gentiles among the sons and daughters of God, but they are also remarkable in that Paul applies them to some from among the Jews. "Some" is not "all," however. Implicitly if not explicitly, Paul has returned to the anguish that opens this chapter (9:1–3) and has raised the specter that much of Israel remains outside those lovingly addressed in vv. 25–26. Perhaps they are even to be identified with the "vessels of wrath." Verses 27–28 speak into that horror with words that Isaiah "cries out" on Israel's behalf.

The speech of vv. 27–28 comes largely from Isa 10:22–23 LXX, with the addition of "the number of the sons and daughters" drawn from Hos 1:10a LXX.[29] In Isaiah as here, the statement anticipates destruction. But it also affirms the salvation of a remnant, a notion to which Paul will return in 11:5 (although with a different but related Greek word, *leimma* rather than *hypoleimma*, as here). Both elements stand, and Paul provides no clue as to their relationship to each other.

28. See the extended discussion in Wagner 2002, 78–89.

29. For detailed comparison of Paul's text with that of the LXX and MT, see Wagner 2002, 95–100. It appears that Paul replaces "the people of Israel" with "the number of the sons and daughters of Israel" (see Hos 1:10 LXX) by way of linking this citation with the end of v. 26.

What he does provide in v. 28 (from Isa 10:22–23) is a declaration of God's action. God will put God's word into effect fully and completely. Unlike Isa 10:23 LXX, which refers to "the whole inhabited world" (the *oikoumenē*), Paul calls up God's action "on the earth" (and see Isa 28:22b LXX). Just as Pharaoh came into existence to spread God's name on "all the earth" (by God's hardening of him), now God's word takes place across the earth. If there is a slight ambiguity to vv. 27–28, there is none to v. 29, which Isaiah "said before" in a speech drawn from Isa 1:9 LXX. To say that Israel would have been "like Sodom and . . . Gomorrah" calls up its utter destruction.[30]

Yet God has left a remnant, a seed, anticipating the discussion of the remnant and the remainder in ch. 11, where both the remnant and the remainder play a role in the salvation of "all Israel" (11:26). God has also left a seed. Given the parallels between vv. 27–28 and v. 29, the two may be identical; seed and remnant may both anticipate Rom 11. In Rom 4:13, 16, 18 *sperma* is a physical seed, the offspring of Abraham, although even that offspring results from God's action, as also in 9:7–9. Romans 1:3 identifies Christ as from the "seed of David," however, and Gal 3:16 identifies Christ as the single seed of Abraham, raising the possibility that the ancient Christian identification of the seed as Christ is not altogether fanciful (Ambrosiaster 187; Origen, *Comm. Rom.* 7.9; Burns 241). On either interpretation, it is God's action that produces the seed, and it is God who will use that seed to bring about Israel's redemption.

The opening question of v. 14, whether God has been unrighteous, has been answered in terms of God's mercy. That mercy has been extended to "us," but the somber character of vv. 27–29 raises the terrifying possibility that much of Israel lies beyond God's mercy. Paul will overturn that conclusion in ch. 11, and he has already paved the way for that outcome here (with mercy, seed, remnant)—and not least with his overarching insistence going back to vv. 6–13 that Israel is God's creation. Before he does that, however, Paul needs to account for vv. 27–29. What has happened to Israel that would prompt Isaiah's lament?

9:30–10:21 Cornerstone Becomes Stumbling Stone

The preceding lines evoke a disturbing situation of Israel under judgment and in desolation. Despite the opening account of God's creation of Israel (9:6–13) and the claim that Jews are among those whom God has called (v. 24), devastation dominates the cries Paul draws from the words of Isaiah (vv. 27–29). The pressing question of how this disaster has come about is addressed in 9:30–10:21. It is not simply that God generated this crisis, although Paul does indeed imply that in 9:33. Paul also wants to show specifically that God's action in Jesus Christ lies at the heart of this crisis.

---

30. As in, e.g., Gen 19:24; Deut 29:23; Amos 4:11; Jer 23:14; Matt 10:15; 2 Pet 2:6; Jude 7; Philo, *Dreams* 1.85.

Links between this passage and chs. 1–8 are numerous as Paul returns to the language of righteousness, faith, and salvation announced in 1:16–17, explicated in 3:21–26, and extended in 5:12–21 in connection with the death and resurrection of Jesus Christ. The return of this language in the context of God's dealings with Israel (and gentiles) is revealing. What Paul has to say about Israel's present and future is said through the Christ event. As Paul sees it, Christ is nothing less than the starting point of Israel's story (Gaventa 2016b).[31]

Locating this discussion in time proves crucial. Paul's use of the aorist tense (see vv. 30–32; 10:3) permits readings of this passage as a critique of Israel across its history, resulting in conclusions that he is arguing against a tendency to "legalism" (Cranfield 2:512) or to "national pride" (Dunn 2:595–96; 2006, 358; 2007, 111). But the fact that Paul refers to events with the past tense does not mean those events lie in the long sweep of Israel's history. Neither is Paul investigating a sustained pattern of Jewish failings. Instead, he is referring to the immediate past, to the situation of Israel in the context of the "now time" action of God in the death and resurrection of Jesus Christ (1:3–4, 16–17). That much is clear when the opening line (9:30) describes gentiles who overtook righteousness even if they were not seeking it. That reference must be to the immediate past and present, to the gentile mission, which means that the parallel description of Israel in v. 33 (and all that follows) also has to do with the present time, or the immediate past.[32] As noted in the introduction to chs. 9–11, the confident cry of 8:31–39 produces a question: What place does Israel have in God's final victory?

Curiously, throughout this passage Paul writes of Israel as a single unit. It is Israel as a whole that pursues the "law of righteousness," Israel that has tripped, Israel that has zeal for God without recognition. Apart from the possible exception obliquely signaled in 10:16 ("not all have obediently heard"), this passage throughout refers to "Israel" (9:31; 10:19, 21) or "they" (10:1–3). Suppressed for now is the notion of a seed (9:29), a remnant (9:27; 11:5, 7). The effect of this move is to induce the question of 11:1: Has God rejected God's people? Rhetorically, Paul tempts the audience into exactly the arrogance he later warns about in 11:13. Not unlike 1:18–32 and 3:10–18, Paul is laying a trap for his auditors.

However much Paul's concern with Israel is in the forefront, God's dealings with gentiles also come into play. Not only have gentiles arrived at a righteousness they did not seek (9:30), but in 10:11–13 Paul returns to the claim that

---

31. Putting the same point somewhat differently, Jonathan Linebaugh (2013b, 205) observes that "for Paul, history's temporal beginning is not its hermeneutical beginning."

32. Since that is the case, employing this passage to construct a critique of Judaism as such is already a distortion, quite apart from the abominable legacy of Christian polemic against Jews and Judaism.

there is no distinction between Jew and Greek (1:16; 3:22), that God enriches everyone who calls upon him. The chain argument of 9:14–15 applies to Jews and gentiles alike.

The passage opens with the stunning image of a race God has rigged so that Israel will trip and fall (9:30–33). Understanding that event requires understanding Israel's ignorance about Christ, who is God's righteousness (10:1–4). A remarkable exegetical move reinforces this claim (10:6–8), which in turn prompts conclusions about the lordship of Christ over all and the salvation of all who call upon Christ's name (10:9–13). The passage ends by first commenting on how it is that people come to call upon the name of the Lord (10:14–17) and then returning to the crisis of Israel's response (10:18–21), forcing the question that opens ch. 11.

9:30 So, what shall we say? Astonishingly,[a] gentiles, who were not running after righteousness, nevertheless won righteousness, namely, the righteousness that is from faith. 31 Meanwhile, Israel, which was running after the law of righteousness,[b] did not reach that law. 32 Why did this happen? Because Israel's race was not from faith but as if the race could be run on actions.[c] They tripped over the stone that causes stumbling, 33 just as it is written:

> "Look! I am placing in Zion a stone that causes stumbling and
>   a rock that gives offense,
> and the one who believes in it will not be put to shame."

10:1 Brothers and sisters, my own[d] heart's desire and my petition to God is for their salvation. 2 For I testify concerning them that they do have zeal for God, but their zeal is without recognition. 3 For since they do not know God's righteousness and they seek instead to establish their own righteousness,[e] they do not submit to God's righteousness. 4 For the end of the law is Christ, who brings about righteousness for everyone who believes.

5 For Moses writes regarding the righteousness from the law,

> "The one who does these things will live by them."

6 But by contrast,[f] the righteousness from faith speaks this way:

> "Do not say in your heart, 'Who will go up into heaven?'"

That means to bring Christ down.

Or 7 "Who will go down into the abyss?"

That means to bring Christ up from the dead.
8 But what does it say?

"The word is near you—it's in your mouth and in your heart."

That means the word of faith that we preach. 9 Because if you confess with your mouth that Jesus is Lord, and you believe with your heart that God raised him from the dead, you will be saved. 10 For with the heart he is believed, resulting in righteousness, and with the mouth he is confessed, resulting in salvation.

11 For Scripture says, "Everyone who believes in him will not be put to shame." 12 For there is no distinction between Jew and gentile. For the same one is Lord of all, enriching all who call on him. 13 For everyone who calls on the name of the Lord will be saved.

14 Now the question is, how will they call on him if they do not believe? And how will they believe in him if they have not heard about him? And how will they hear apart from someone preaching? 15 And how will they preach if they have not been sent? As it is written, "How timely[g] are the feet of those who proclaim good things."

16 But not all have obediently heard[h] the gospel. For Isaiah says, "Lord, who believed our report?" 17 So faith comes from the report, and the report through the word of Christ.

18 But I ask, have they not heard? Indeed, they have heard:[i] "Their voice has gone out to all the earth and their words to the ends of the inhabited earth."

19 But I ask, did Israel not know? In the first place Moses says,

"I will provoke you with a nonpeople, and with a foolish people,
    I will enrage you."

20 And Isaiah dares also to say,[j]

"I was found among[k] those who did not seek me. I became present to those who did not ask for me."

21 And he says regarding Israel,

"The whole day long I stretched out my hands for a people who disobey and contradict."

a. The adverb does not appear in the Greek but is added here to capture the surprising, even offensive, state of things Paul is describing.

b. Despite the appearance of "the righteousness based on the law" in the NRSV, or "the law as a way of righteousness" in the NIV and other such variations in English translations, the order is "the law of righteousness" (as in NRSVue).

c. Lit., "not from faith but as from works." The opening and concluding clauses are added to complete the sentence.

d. The untranslated particle *men* draws attention to the subject in cases such as this one that report on the speaker's emotional or intellectual state (BDAG s.v.).

e. *Dikaiosynē* ("righteousness") is omitted in several manuscripts (including A B D P), but it does appear in 𝔓⁴⁶ ℵ F G and others. Haplography probably accounts for the omission (so also Jewett 606), although it may also be that a scribe supplied the obvious referent of "their own."

f. *De* could be and sometimes is read as a simple conjunction, but the fact that Paul goes on to elaborate on righteousness connected with Christ and with faith and says nothing further about keeping the law suggests that the connotation here is contrast rather than harmony. The phrase "by contrast" is intended to make that nuance explicit. (See Sprinkle 2008, 168–73 for a review of the discussion; his own view is that contrast is intended.)

g. Generally translated "beautiful" (as in KJV, NRSVue, NIV, among many others), *hōraios* often refers to timeliness, ripeness (see LSJ, s.v., BDAG, s.v., Hultgren 376; Dunn 2:621–22; Fitzmyer 597). Reference to the timely arrival of Christ-preaching seems consistent with the letter's preoccupation with the "now time" (as in 3:21).

h. *Hypakouō* refers to obedience, but the *akouō* root recurs in v. 16b–18 with "report" (*akoē*) and "hear" (*akouō*), suggesting that hearing is already at work in v. 16, in this case a hearing that results in obedience.

i. Supplying "they have heard" to reflect the emphatic character of Paul's response.

j. Lit., "Isaiah dared and he spoke," but understood here as an instance of hendiadys (Wagner 2002, 205).

k. The preposition *en* ("among") appears in NA²⁸ only in brackets, reflecting the editors' view that it is uncertain. It appears in a few major manuscripts (𝔓⁴⁶ B D* F G) but is omitted in many more. Nonetheless, its omission may well reflect harmonizing with Isa 65:1 LXX, since the inclusion of *en* has "absolutely no basis in the LXX text tradition" (Wagner 2002, 206).

[9:30–33] The preceding verses have depicted a world turned upside down: some gentiles are included in the people God has called, and Isaiah's words conveying Israel's devastation have become reality. The question of v. 30 is inevitable: What can anyone say to this strange state of affairs? By way of explanation, Paul resorts to language suitable for the athletic arena: running (*diōkein*), winning (*katalambanein*), reaching a goal (*phthanein*). Gentiles are not even running the race, yet they arrive at the goal. Israel is running but never arrives at the goal.[33] The verbs are those used in Phil 3:12–16, where Paul

---

33. Campbell cleverly describes the situation as one in which the "spoils have gone not to the athletes but to the spectators" (2009a, 790), but it is not clear that the gentiles are even spectators; they do not seem cognizant of the very race they have won. At a more substantive level, the remarks

speaks earnestly of his own striving, but here they are turned into a parody of the athletic contest.[34]

What gentiles have won, Paul specifies, is righteousness that comes "from faith" (v. 30). As often elsewhere, "faith" for Paul is shorthand for that Christ-generated faith in Jesus Christ (e.g.,1:5, 8; 3:28), faith in God as the one who raised Jesus from the dead (e.g., 4:24). That Paul intends faith in Christ becomes explicit in 10:8–9. By contrast with these gentiles, Israel was in pursuit—vain pursuit—of what Paul here terms *nomos dikaiosynēs* (v. 31). Paul uses this phrase nowhere else, which is probably why English translations strain against it.[35] In context the phrase seems positive, suggesting that Israel is pursuing the law as it is interpreted by righteousness or perhaps the law that produces what is right. Israel, by contrast with gentiles, has been in pursuit of what is good, yet Israel did not achieve it. Far from condemning Israel's stance, Paul seems to be applauding it. Again, Paul refers to "Israel" here as a single entity, with no hint of the division implicit in 9:24 or the split between remnant and remainder in 11:7.

Verse 32 asks the obvious question, which is how this can be the case, and answers with an elliptical "because not from faith but from works," rendered above as "Because Israel's race was not from faith but as if the race could be run on actions." This terse expression cannot be detached from its argumentative context and generalized into an accusation about "works righteousness." Instead, it addresses the specific question of why Israel does not recognize Jesus of Nazareth as its Lord, the Messiah of God. Read in that way, "not from faith" is not a reference to some general Jewish failure to trust or rely on God, much less a disposition to legalism or misplaced confidence in national boundary markers. Instead, the faith in view here is the reliance on Christ exposed throughout the letter, as will become clear in the opening of ch. 10. This pursuit of righteousness has failed because it is not faith in Jesus Christ. It is "from works"; that is, it is based on their own activity, a notion excluded earlier, in 9:12.

Paul's explanation of this inverted race is already strange, but with his further explanation at the end of v. 32 things turn stranger still: "They tripped over the stone that causes stumbling." When he turns to Scripture to explain what that assertion might mean, he draws two passages together in an explosive way. Much of the citation comes from Isa 28:16 LXX, which reads as follows:

Paul makes about his own experience in Phil 3 echo this passage, since Paul depicts himself as having been overcome.

34. Campbell rightly observes that Paul "is twisting the normally heroic discourse [of the contest] into a farce" (2009a, 790).

35. The phrase appears only in Wis 2:11 with strikingly different connotation: "Let our might be our law of right" (NRSVue).

Look, I set in the foundations *of Zion a stone,* a precious, chosen, valuable cornerstone for its foundation, and *the one who believes in it will not be put to shame.*[36]

In place of the stable image of "cornerstone" in the LXX, however, Paul inserts "a stone of stumbling," a phrase found in Isa 8:14, along with "rock," there described as "fallen" rather than "rock that gives offense." In other words, Paul has taken a text associated in its Isaianic context with the building of something solid, with security and stability, and transformed it into a trick God is playing on Israel, actually inducing Israel's fall. First Peter 2:6 also draws upon Isa 28:16 but retains the language of cornerstone and associates it with Jesus (and see Matt 21:42), which makes Paul's transformation of the statement even more surprising, at least to readers familiar with those texts.

Paul does not specify the identity of the stone, a move that has tripped interpreters no less effectively than God's purported tripping of Israel.[37] Some scholars identify the stone with the law (including Meyer 1980, 64; Keck 245), others with the gospel (e.g., Gager 1983, 252; E. Johnson 1995, 230), many others with Christ (e.g., Cranfield 2:510–12; Fitzmyer 579; Jewett 613; Hultgren 381–82). Paul cites Isa 28:16 just a few lines later (Rom 10:11), where the identity is explicit: it is Jesus Christ as Lord, already introduced by the series of references to Christ in 10:4–9. In this initial context, however, the identity remains ambiguous (Wagner 2002, 156; N. T. Wright 1991, 244), which reinforces the trick God is playing. The ambiguity contains a touch of verisimilitude as well, since tripping over any rock begins as a not-knowing—not seeing the object, not recognizing the peril, not understanding what lies in the path.

The ongoing discussion of the rock's identity should not eclipse the eschatological character of this passage, which itself becomes an occasion for interpretive stumbling. That the believer "will not be put to shame" recalls the opening lines of the letter, in which Paul declares that he is "not ashamed of the gospel," which is God's power bringing about salvation. As noted in the discussion of 1:16, Paul's use of pride and shame language in connection with the gospel often has an eschatological location, as in 5:2 and 15:17 (and see 1 Thess 2:19, which explicitly connects pride with the parousia). The Jesus tradition similarly contains warnings to those who are ashamed of Jesus that he will be ashamed of them in judgment (Mark 8:38//Luke 9:26; cf. Matt 10:33).

[10:1–4] Again Paul's anguish comes to expression, underscoring his initial comments in 9:1–5. The introductory "brothers and sisters" (*adelphoi,* literally "brothers") places Paul alongside the audience (as in, e.g., 7:1; 8:12; 11:25; 12:1)

---

36. Italics represent exact borrowing from the LXX, with the slight difference that the LXX has "put to shame" in the aorist subjunctive rather than the future indicative.

37. For the notion that God has tricked Israel, see Meeks 2002, 212–13.

while he unpacks the elliptical comments of the preceding lines. Israel has "zeal" for God. No doubt is expressed here about the sincerity of Israel's zeal, just as 9:31 insists that Israel has been running after the law of righteousness. Although the word *zēlos* can refer negatively to zealous partisanship (13:13; 1 Cor 3:3), Paul also uses it positively of zeal for the good (2 Cor 7:11; 9:2; 11:2).

The problem is not with zeal as such but with zeal that is "without recognition," zeal that is uninformed or misled. The same noun appears in Rom 1:28 when Paul characterizes the human refusal to acknowledge God as God (and see 3:20). As 10:3 explicates this flawed zeal, it emerges that the problem is not that Israel refuses to acknowledge God (as in 1:28 regarding the gentiles), but that they seek to establish their own righteousness rather than submit to that of God. That "righteousness" is the key term here becomes clear in the repetition:

> They do not know God's righteousness
> They seek instead to establish their own righteousness
> They do not submit to God's righteousness
> The end of the law is Christ, who brings about the righteousness of
> everyone who believes

Verses 5–7 will return to the contrast between righteousness associated with the law and that associated with faith in Christ, already alluded to in 9:30–31. The righteousness associated with faith in Christ is an event, announced in 1:17 and depicted again in 3:21–26: God acts to make right through the death of Christ, which overturns the powers of Sin and Death. This is no generalized critique of Israel's nationalistic disposition or some supposed moral flaw, but a specific comment grounded in the gospel events.

Verse 3 repeats the charge of ignorance, explaining it by asserting that "they do not submit to God's righteousness." This is manifestly a charge of resistance to God (as will recur in 10:21), but it also defies any notion that Paul's concern is limited to a single act of belief or an isolated moment. To "submit" is to recognize and be ruled by God's order, to recognize that "Jesus is Lord." That is a statement of faith, but it is more significantly an acknowledgment of lordship.

This framework makes it possible to contextualize the deeply contested statement in v. 4, that Christ is the *telos nomou*. The debate revolves around the possible implications of *telos*, since it can connote either the "end" as in the termination, or the "end" in the sense of completion or goal, so that Paul may be saying either that Christ marks the termination of the law or that Christ marks its fulfillment, its goal.[38] In Heb 7:3, for example, Melchizedek is said to have

---

38. For review of the debate, see Badenas 1985, 7–37; Oegema 1998, 222–30; Wolter 2:108–10. It is not only Paul whose work provokes such confusion. After publishing his famous work *The End of History and the Last Man,* Francis Fukuyama repeatedly found that people took him to mean "termination" when he meant "target" or "objective" (cited by Joe Klein in "Francis Fukuyama

neither beginning nor *telos,* end of life, but Jas 5:11 refers to the *telos* of the Lord, which must be purpose or goal rather than end in the sense of termination. In addition to the ambiguity of the Greek word, the difficulty is that the debate too often takes upon itself the full weight of establishing Paul's understanding of the Mosaic law.

Ironically, the content of Rom 10 has very little to do with the law, apart from the peculiar reference above to the "law of righteousness" (9:31). Instead of being the center of Paul's comments, the phrase *telos nomou* is driving toward the end of the verse. Christ is the law's *telos* in that Christ is bringing about righteousness for everyone who believes. The reference to faith then serves to usher in the discussion about faith and rectification that follows.

Although Paul is not making a definitive statement about the law of Moses, what he does say warrants attention. To begin with, Paul has little to say about the law in this lengthy section of the letter addressing God's dealings with Israel, particularly in ch. 11 dealing with Israel's future. If the law is not Israel's stumbling point (at least not once Paul reaches 10:11, with its repetition of Isa 28:16), neither is the law an identifier of Israel. At no point in the remainder of this complex examination of God's dealings with Israel does Paul again connect Israel with the law. The interpretation of Scripture Paul offers in 10:5–8 separates Israel from the law by connecting Israel to Christ. Chapter 11 will contend that Israel is now divided, that Israel will be saved when the deliverer comes. Nowhere in these chapters does Paul connect Israel's future to the law, either to its observance or to its termination (Gaventa 2016a). This in itself is a radical move, given the well-known identification of Israel with the law of Moses.

Once again the reference to Christ in v. 4 underscores the observation that the entire discussion in ch. 10 is misunderstood when read as a generalized analysis of Israel's zeal for God or the lack thereof. It is instead a discussion about Israel's current rejection of the gospel claim that Jesus is Lord. Righteousness is not simply justice or rightness before God; rather, it is God's righteousness in Jesus, as becomes explicit in vv. 5–8.

[5–8] Paul's remarkable interpretation of Scripture continues in these verses, in which the earlier contrast between God's righteousness and human righteousness (v. 3) gives way to a contrast between the law's righteousness and that of faith. Already Paul has reduced the hardening of Pharaoh to a one-sided divine action, placed gentiles alongside Jews as Hosea's "no people" who have become "my people," and transposed the founding rock into a stumbling stone. Here, however, he takes what is arguably his most radical exegetical step, reading "Christ" in the very places where Deuteronomy reads the keeping of the commandment.

---

and Yascha Mounk Wonder, Is Democracy Finished?" in *New York Times Book Review*, Sunday, June 3, 2022, p. 12).

Moses enters briefly to write about the law's righteousness. What "Moses writes" concerning the law comes from Lev 18:5 (only insignificantly altered): "The one who does these things will live by them."[39] The reversal of every element in this statement drives Paul's argument forward (through v. 13). That reversal comes in the form of a pesher-like interpretation of lines drawn from Deuteronomy:

> Deut 9:4 LXX: Do not say in your heart, . . . "Because of my righteous acts the LORD led me out to inherit this good land."
> Deut 30:12 LXX: Who will go up into heaven for us and bring it [the commandment] down for us? And hearing it we will do it.
> Deut 30:14 LXX: The word is very near in your mouth and in your heart and in your hands to do it.

"Who will go down into the abyss?" does not appear in Deut 30:12–14, although similar references to the abyss appear elsewhere (e.g., Job 38:16; Ps 32:7 LXX; Isa 51:10).

By contrast with the law's righteousness about which Moses writes, the righteousness that comes from faith speaks for itself. Although Paul elsewhere refers to the "righteousness of [or from] faith," this is the only time he places the prepositional phrase first, literally rendered "the from faith righteousness." The shift of position is consistent with the emphasis throughout on *pistis*, shorthand for the Christ event.

In addition, the righteousness that stems from faith in Christ is not about "doing these things." Deuteronomy 30 has to do with keeping the law, with doing the law, but Paul has suppressed both the response, "We will do it," in 30:12 and the claim that the word (of the commandment) is near to "your" hands to be done in 30:14. Unlike Lev 18:5's promise regarding the one who "does" the law, the righteousness of faith is not about human action (Sprinkle 2008, 182).

Most important, in Paul's interpretation the subject is not the law but Christ. Reference to the law or human action is suppressed here, because it is Christ who is brought down from heaven, Christ who is brought up from the dead, and the word about Christ that is near.[40] Given the widespread importance of Deut 30, this shift amounts to a radical "rereferentialization" of the text.[41] Conforming the argument to the gospel declaration about Jesus's origin and his resurrection from the dead (as in v. 9 below) likely accounts for the insertion

---

39. See also Gal 3:12, where Paul similarly contrasts the law and faith.

40. "Paul's glosses actively suppress the wording of the scriptural text, rather than simply filling gaps" (Watson 2016, 312).

41. "Rereferentialization" is David Lincicum's helpful expression (2010, 156). See further his discussion of the widespread influence of Deuteronomy in Second Temple Judaism (passim).

of "Who will go down into the abyss?" in place of Deut 30:13's "Who will go across for us to the other side of the sea?"[42]

With v. 8 Paul introduces Deut 30:14 concerning the nearness of the "word." His major change (as noted above) is to elide "in your hands to do it." What is "near" is no longer the law; instead, picking up "word" (*rhēma*) from Deut 30:14, Paul introduces "the word of faith that we preach." The universal urgency of that proclamation becomes the focus of vv. 9–13.[43]

[9–10] That "faith" is metonymy for the gospel itself is reinforced in vv. 9–10, where Paul elaborates on the "word of faith that we preach" and its redemptive character. The "mouth" of v. 8 generates "if you confess with your mouth," and the "heart" generates "[if] you believe with your heart." The objects of those two actions are mutually interpretive:

> Jesus is Lord
> God raised him from the dead

Here as elsewhere, Paul does not frame faith in terms of belief that Jesus is to be identified as the Messiah of God, although that identification is presupposed in the lines above and ubiquitously elsewhere. Instead, he frames faith in terms of power, both God's power in the resurrection and Jesus's implied power as resurrected Lord (see "Son of God in power" in Rom 1:4; 14:9; cf. also 1 Cor 15:23–28; Phil 2:9–11).

The declaration that "Jesus is Lord" appears several times in Paul's letters. In 2 Cor 4:5 similarly "Jesus Christ is Lord" provides a synopsis of "what we preach." The central character of the identification of Jesus as Lord comes to expression also in 1 Cor 12:4, when Paul insists that only by means of the Holy Spirit does anyone confess Jesus as Lord. Importantly, the Philippians hymn culminates with the anticipation of an eschatological and universal confession that Jesus Christ is Lord.

Faith in turn yields righteousness, salvation (v. 10). That assertion lends itself all too readily to reductionistic notions of faith as intellectual assent or to claims about the necessity of "really" believing "in one's heart" (Cranfield 2:527). Such unfortunate interpretations have the result of shifting attention away from the lordship of Christ and onto the human agent, even though Paul is quite clear in

---

42. On the incarnational logic in this passage, see Capes 2007.

43. These several points at which Paul elides references to action require contextualization. Paul does not dispute the importance of human action, as will be apparent in chs. 12–15. What Paul disputes is the ability of human action to deliver humanity from its state of entrapment in Sin and Death. This is the case he argued in 1:18–5:21, culminating in the exposure of the reign of Sin and Death in 5:12–21. From Paul's vantage point in Christ (speaking in Christ, 9:1), he perceives that the human situation is not remedied even by doing the law, although the law is holy and right and good (ch. 7). What humanity (both Jew and gentile) needs is liberation from this captivity.

what follows that faith stems from God's own act of sending, to say nothing of the role of the Spirit in bringing faith about (e.g., 5:5; 8:14; 1 Cor 12:4).

[11–13] Isaiah 28:16 returns, having been quoted already in 9:33b; here it both authorizes and summarizes vv. 8–10. At this point, however, the ambiguity about the identity of the rock has disappeared as the "him" is explicitly identified with Jesus (v. 9). In addition, Jesus is "Lord of all" (cf. Acts 10:36); he enriches those who call on him (see 2 Cor 8:9; Phil 2:6–8); calling on his name results in salvation (quoting Joel 3:5 LXX). All of these claims, but particularly the citations from Isaiah and Joel, associate Jesus directly with God (Cranfield 2:529; Rowe 2000). Although Paul does identify Jesus as God's agent (the Son who is sent, the Son raised from the dead), he also can and does associate Jesus directly with God. If God's name is now "the One who raised Jesus our Lord from the dead" (4:24), by the same token Jesus is publicly confessed as "Lord of all."[44]

In addition to these striking claims about Jesus, vv. 11–13 emphasize the inclusive character of the "one" who believes. Paul has added "everyone" (*pas*), which appears neither in v. 33b (except in some harmonizing manuscripts: 33 1739 Ψ 𝔐) nor in Isa 28:16 LXX.[45] That "everyone" recalls the "everyone" of Rom 10:4 and is reiterated in the lines that follow:

> There is no distinction between Jew and Greek
> Lord of all
> Everyone who calls on him (twice)

This repeated emphasis on the universal grasp of the gospel reflects the fact that Paul's concern in these chapters is not for Israel alone. Already he has stipulated that God has called some gentiles (9:24–26) and that gentiles arrived at righteousness without even trying (9:31). Now he reiterates the letter's early insistence that the gospel is for all people. Strikingly, by way of demonstrating the universal extent of the gospel, he draws on Joel 3:5, a text in which "all" means all of Israel, with not a gentile in sight. As in Rom 9:25–26, a text originally addressing Jews now addresses both Jews and gentiles, at least in Paul's hearing of the gospel.

And it is the gospel Paul discusses here. The connections to chs. 1–8 are extensive, reaching back all the way to 1:1–17, with its claims about the resurrection of the Son of God in power and the universal grasp of Jesus's saving lordship. Romans 3:27–31 is also replayed here, in the insistence that there is no distinction, that there is one God, one Lord of all. This relationship to chs. 1–3

---

44. Rowe astutely refers to "the mutual interweaving of subjects (Jesus and God)" in this passage (2000, 144).

45. "This is a crystal-clear example of a deliberate modification of the text by Paul" (Wagner 2002, 169).

underscores the claim that Paul's comments in this chapter pertain to the present time, the "now time" of the gospel. They are not a criticism of Judaism per se, whether by means of an accusation of legalism or ethnocentrism. It is from the point of view of God's present action that Paul perceives both the universal power of Sin and Death and the universal grasp of Jesus's lordship.

[14–15] Insistence on the universal reach of Christ's saving lordship prompts urgent concern for preaching and responsiveness to preaching. In the chain argument of vv. 14–15, Paul traces faith itself back to its origin in God's sending act. The unspecified nature of the third-person plural "they," following as it does on the insistence on the universal extent of the gospel ("there is no distinction"), includes both Jews and gentiles. Paul will turn to comment on Israel, and in surprising terms, in v. 19, but at present the "all" of vv. 11–13 obtains.

The chain opens by taking up the language of Joel 3:5: "How will they call on him if they do not believe?" Although in the preceding section faith, confession, and calling on the name appear in parallel statements, here distinctions come into view. Since calling on is said to derive from faith, calling on and believing cannot be the same act. In Joel 3:5 and often elsewhere in the LXX, calling on the name of the Lord refers to prayer in the context of worship (e.g., Gen 12:7; 13:4; 26:25; Pss 104:1; 114:4 LXX; and see Estes 2016, 24, 26–33). That nuance may be at work here also, connecting this statement with the emphasis on worship elsewhere in the letter. Paul traces human captivity to Sin and Death to its origin in human refusal to acknowledge God as God, the primary act of worship (1:18–23; 3:10–11). God's rescue of humanity is then evidenced in crying out to God (8:15) and in acts of worship and praise (15:9–12).

The second question, "How will they believe in him if they have not heard about him?" introduces an external agent; worship and faith begin with hearing a word from someone else. The remainder of the chain, culminating in the citation of Isa 52:7 in v. 15b, only intensifies this shift in the direction of an external origin for faith. The third question, "How will they hear apart from someone preaching?" takes the logic a step further, since no one can hear the news of God's action in Christ apart from public speech. And the fourth question, "How will they preach if they have not been sent?" moves the question of agency back yet another step. No one can believe apart from hearing (i.e., having the word given them), and no one can preach unless sent to do so.

Paul draws on Isa 52:7 to convey the urgency of this action. Where Isaiah depicts the single *euangelizomenou*, the "one" who proclaims, Paul has the plural *euangelizomenōn* (cf. Nah 2:1), bringing the citation into line with the plural reference to preachers in Rom 10:8. Also, Paul has abbreviated Isaiah's description of what is announced, omitting the place of reference (on the mountains) and condensing "of the one who proclaims a report of peace, of the one who proclaims good things," to "those who proclaim good things." The effect is to focus the citation on the timeliness (see translation note g on v. 15) of the agents of good news, the ones who have been sent. In addition, those who recognize the language of Isa 52 and its context have further reason to associate this text with urgency, because the passage calls up the image of the Lord's victorious return to the people (Ryan 2020, 201, 221–22).

[16–17] The sharply adversative *alla* ("but") of v. 16 interrupts this depiction of the arrival of messengers and the expectation that they will be heard: "But not all have obediently heard the gospel." In contrast to the "all who call on him" and "everyone" in vv. 12–13, "not all" signals a change of direction.

Yet another citation from Isaiah (53:1 LXX) follows closely on the passage just cited. This time, however, the citation is introduced with "Isaiah says," rather than "as it is written." In the brief question "Lord, who believed our report?" Paul finds his own conclusion: faith comes through a report. By distinction, however, this report is "through the word of Christ." For the reader who knows Isaiah's words in their context, the Servant Song comes to mind and the long history of Christian interpretation of that passage. Yet it is hard to imagine that auditors in Rome knew Isaiah well enough to hear the question ("Who has believed our report?") as a cue announcing the fulfillment of the Servant Song.[46]

[18–21] With the double assertion "But I say" (*alla legō*) at the beginning of vv. 18 and 19, Paul expands on vv. 16–17 for their present implications: "Not all have obediently heard the gospel." Once again he does this by means of Scripture. Having said that faith comes through hearing, he asks, "Have they not heard?"—formulating the question such that the answer is obvious even before he quotes Ps 18:5 LXX with its elegant claim that "all the earth" and "the ends of the inhabited earth" must have heard "their voice," "their words." Hearers of the letter who are familiar with the Psalter may recall that Ps 19 (18 LXX) celebrates creation as unmistakable witness to God's power and glory. The "voice" and the "words" of the quotation are those spoken by the heavens, taken up by Paul into the "word of Christ." The larger context of Ps 19 resonates with the accusations of Rom 1:18–32 that "they" refused to acknowledge God.

With the question of v. 19, Israel comes into view, and again the question presupposes the answer: "Did Israel not know?" The three texts that follow explain what it is that Israel should have known, and each anticipates Paul's argument in ch. 11 about what God is doing and will do with Israel (and the gentiles). Paul first introduces the voice of Moses in Deut 32:21 LXX: in the face of Israel's idolatry comes the declaration that God will incite Israel with those on the outside. But Paul omits the initial announcement of God's own jealousy over Israel's provocation and cites only God's intent to provoke Israel by means of another people, a nonpeople. This becomes a focal point of the

46. See the discussion in Hays 1989, 63; Wagner 2002, 178–80, 334–35.

argument in ch. 11, that God is using Israel's rejection of the gospel in order to save all. (Note the change from "them" in the LXX to "you" in Romans.) Having said in 10:2–3 that Israel did not know, now Paul claims that they should have known this from Scripture (Wagner 2002, 188).

Next the voice of Isaiah returns, with two statements Paul labels as "daring." Whether the text of Isaiah is itself daring is one thing; Paul's treatment of it certainly is. Taking two statements from Isa 65:1–2, both of which address Israel, Paul quotes both but separates them so that one speaks about gentiles and the other about Israel (Wagner 2002, 212–23).

What Isaiah dares to add to the voice of Moses is not just that God will provoke Israel by means of the nonpeople, but that God will be found among those who are not looking. This citation of course recalls 9:30, with its declaration that the gentiles who do not pursue righteousness are the ones who have nonetheless arrived at it (although note also Rom 3:11, which includes Jews among those who do not seek God). Israel should have known all of this, since it is found in Israel's Scripture. Verse 21 introduces the very next line in Isaiah (65:2), again specifying that it pertains to Israel. Paul shifts the phrase "all day long" from its position mid-sentence in the LXX to the beginning, drawing attention to God's persistence before characterizing Israel's rejection.

In these lines, Paul consistently depicts Moses and Isaiah as speaking now: "Moses says," "Isaiah dares also to say," "[Isaiah] says regarding Israel." Paul hears these voices in the present (Wagner 2002). Not only do they speak in the present, but they speak about the "now time," in which "the slave of Christ Jesus" comes to grips with the relationship between his own people and Jesus who is Lord of all. Unlike the Stephen speech in Acts 7, which posits a continuity across the generations in Israel's resistance to God's will (note especially Acts 7:51–53), Paul writes about a present crisis without parallel in Israel's history (the introduction of Elijah in 11:2–4 notwithstanding). Nothing else in Rom 10 can be construed as a diagnosis of an ongoing problem within Israel. The time is now.

Rhetorically, the net effect of this passage is to force the question of 11:1: "It's not that God has rejected God's people, is it?" Beginning with the stunning notion of God tripping Israel and culminating with the picture of recalcitrant Israel, the argument drives toward the possible response, "God has rejected God's own." And again, the language of 10:21 assumes that Israel as a whole is in rebellion.

Theologically, the net effect of this entire passage (9:30–10:21) is that of placing Christ at the center of the relationship between God and Israel. While the ordering of gifts in 9:4–5 might be understood to locate Christ as the culmination of God's dealings with Israel, even one in a series of gifts, here more is being said. God has tripped Israel with Christ. Christ is already close at hand, in no need of being ushered into the human sphere. Christ is Lord of all people.

The news being brought by God's messengers is about that same Christ. Israel's crisis is Christ-generated.

11:1–10 God's Division of Israel

The possibility that the "word of faith" has generated a rupture between Israel and God has come to agonized expression in chs. 9 and 10. After recalling God's creation of Israel through Abraham and God's prerogative to deal with Israel however God wishes, Paul invokes the words of Isaiah in 9:27–29 to limn the possibility of utter disaster. Chapter 10 accounts for the disaster by depicting the event of Christian preaching as a crisis: God has tripped Israel by placing the gospel in its path. Israel should have understood but has refused to do so, despite God's continual overture.

The cumulative effect of these chapters is to force the question of 11:1: Has God rejected Israel? Paul's emphatic "no" ushers in his contention that God has brought about a temporary division within Israel (11:1–10). Just as Elijah was ignorant of God's actions to preserve Israel (vv. 2–3), those in the present (Paul's present) who think God has rejected Israel are unaware that God has divided Israel (vv. 4–10). The remainder of the chapter will address the intent of that division and anticipate its ultimate, eschatological healing.

11:1 Considering all this,[a] I say, "It's not that God has rejected God's people,[b] is it?" Of course not! For I also am an Israelite, from the seed of Abraham, the tribe of Benjamin. 2 God has not rejected his people, the people he knew in advance.

If you think that he has,[c] don't you know in the case of Elijah what Scripture says, how he pleaded with God against Israel?

3 "Lord, they killed your prophets, they tore down your altars,
and I alone am left and they want my life!"

4 But what does the divine response say to him?

"I have left for myself seven thousand men who have not bent
the knee to Baal."

5 It is the same way at the present time: there is a remnant by election through grace. 6 And if that election is by grace, then election is not[d] from actions, since then grace is not grace.

7 What then? What Israel seeks, this it did not achieve. Now the election[e] achieved it, but the rest were hardened. 8 It is just as it is written,

God gave them a confused spirit,[f]
eyes that do not see and ears that do not hear, until this very day.

9 And David says,

"Let their table become trap and net
and stumbling block[g] and retaliation for them.

10 Let their eyes be darkened so that they do not see,
and bend their backs always."

a. Lit, "therefore" (*oun*). "Considering all this" indicates that the question of 11:1 arises not just from the immediately preceding lines but from all of chs. 9–10.

b. A few manuscripts read "his inheritance" ($\mathfrak{P}^{46}$ F G b) rather than the well-attested "his people." Despite some argument for this reading on the grounds that it is the more difficult reading, and that a scribe substituted "people" under the influence of v. 2 (Given 1999, 91–92), the variant probably reflects assimilation to Ps 93:14 LXX (Jewett 630). Further, the repetition of "his people" serves Paul's rhetorical purpose, as suggested by 11:13, 18–19.

c. The introductory particle *ē* may be translated simply as "or," but "if you think that he has" reflects the repetition of v. 1a in v. 2a and the possibility that some auditors may indeed think God has severed relations with Israel, a possibility underscored in 11:18–24.

d. Although *ouketi* can mean "no longer" with reference to time (as in Rom 6:9; John 14:19), it does not necessarily carry a time reference. It can reflect a logical inference, as in Rom 7:17, 20 and here (BDAG s.v.). In Paul's view, election is either by grace or by works; there is no middle option or compromise between the two.

e. Usually translated "the elect" or "the chosen" ones (as in NIV, NRSVue), but this is the same abstract noun used in v. 5 above (and see 9:11; 11:28; 1 Thess 1:4). BDAG evidence for the translation of this word as a reference to chosen people rather than to election itself is unconvincing, since the only other instance in the LXX, NT, or Apostolic Fathers when *eklogē* refers to a discrete group is 1 Clem 29.1. Presumably, translators opt for "the elect" in order to make for a tidy parallel with "the rest," but this awkward contrast between "the election" and "the rest" further enhances Paul's emphasis on God's role. However *eklogē* is translated, there is no reference to the number included, contrary to the implication found in some translations: CEV, "only a chosen few"; GNT, "only the small group"; NLT, "a few."

f. Lit., a spirit of stupefaction or confusion. The translation assumes that the genitive is one of quality (Smyth 1956, §1320).

g. Most English translations include the indefinite article before the words "trap," "net," and "stumbling block" (e.g., CEB, NASB, NIV, NRSVue). That is not necessary, however, and the omission makes for a more forceful malediction, which seems to be the point, both in the psalm and in Paul's reading of it.

[11:1–2a] The question of v. 1 may be inevitable, given Paul's argument in the preceding chapters, but the answer appears well before the customary "Of

302   Romans 11:1–10

course not!" The introductory *mē* sets up the question for a negative answer ("It isn't the case, is it?"). In addition, by affirming that this is "God's people," that the people Israel belong to God, Paul hints at the abiding character of the relationship. When Paul does explicitly answer the question in v. 2a, he does so by repeating the question almost verbatim. (In Greek even the word order is the same, with only a different negative word, *ou* rather than *mē*.)

Is this a living question among Paul's addressees in Rome or even among his circle in Corinth? Given its formulation, which resembles some earlier questions in the letter that are likely more argumentative than existential (as in 6:1, 15; 7:7), it is difficult to be certain. Paul has not been to Rome, which makes deducing anything of the attitudes of Roman Christians a precarious exercise (see the introduction). Yet in just a few lines he will issue a sharp warning to gentiles against arrogance with respect to Jews (11:13–25), suggesting at a minimum his concern that some gentiles may have concluded that God's favor has passed to them.

The possibility of God's rejection of Israel has many precedents. First Samuel 12:22 and Ps 93:14 LXX are often adduced as parallels, although in both texts the statement is cast in future tense and attributed to the human speaker rather than to God ("The Lord will not reject"). In 1 Sam 12:22, Samuel assures the people that the Lord will not reject them, even though they have been asking for a king (although note that the passage concludes with a warning that they will be swept away if they persist in disobedience). Many other passages reflect the possibility of divine rejection, and the contexts vary considerably. In some cases God announces that he will reject the "remnant"—namely, Judah (2 Kgs 21:14; 23:27; 2 Chr 35:19 LXX)—or prophets announce that God will reject the people at least temporarily (Hos 9:17; Jer 7:29; Lam 2:7; 3:31; 5:22; Ezek 5:11). In the context of lamenting Israel's defeat, the psalms often claim that God has rejected the people (e.g., Ps 44:9–12 [43:1–13 LXX]; 60:10 [59:12 LXX]; 74:1 [73:1 LXX]). Psalm 94:14 (93:14 LXX), by contrast, reassures the people of God's presence with them during their oppression by the powerful (see vv. 4–7).

What makes Paul's reassurance in Rom 11:2a striking is his addition of the phrase "the people he knew in advance," which does not appear in 1 Sam 12:22 or Ps 93:14 LXX or in any other "rejection" passages.[47] The phrase recalls Paul's earlier reference to foreknowledge in Rom 8:29–30, where God's foreknowledge is also connected with calling and rectifying. It is also connected with being shaped in the likeness of God's Son. It is not far-fetched to make that connection to Christ here as well, given the reference to Christ in 9:5 and especially 11:26, which places the salvation of "all Israel" in the context of the "deliverer" who comes "from Zion."

---

47. *Proginōskō* appears in the LXX only a few times, all of which are in Wisdom of Solomon (6:13; 8:8; 18:6).

Some commentators read the reference to foreknowledge as restricting the reassurance to a portion of the people (including Pelagius 124; Calvin 239). Grammatically, however, the phrase applies to the people as a whole, not to a portion of it, since the relative pronoun has as its precedent the entire people (*laos*) rather than some portion. More to the point, Paul does not qualify God's foreknowledge.

Between the question of v. 1a and the forceful response in v. 2a, Paul introduces himself as evidence of God's nonrejection. The language is emphatic: *egō Israēlitēs eimi* ("*I* also am an Israelite"). This statement alone would have been sufficient to make the point, but Paul underscores it with "from the seed of Abraham, the tribe of Benjamin." Self-disclosure is rare in Paul's letters (although see 2 Cor 11:22; Phil 3:5), and yet this is the third time he has appealed to his own place in or passion for Israel in these chapters (9:1–3; 10:1). Despite his depiction of Israel as "they" in ch. 10, Paul is anything but removed from the situation under discussion.

[2b–6] For further evidence that God has not rejected Israel, Paul introduces an exchange between God and the prophet Elijah, following Elijah's flight from the fury of Jezebel. A lengthy introduction presents the quotation ("what Scripture says") as something the audience should already know. Remarkably, Paul recalls that Elijah was pleading with God against Israel (*kata tou Israēl*). This depiction distorts the story in 1 Kings, where Elijah laments his own predicament and complains about Israel's desertion, but he does not intercede against Israel (1 Kgs 19:10, 14). If Paul does have 1 Sam 12:22 in mind ("God has not rejected his people"), he may also have in mind the words of Samuel that immediately follow: "It would be a sin against the Lord for me to cease praying for you." This action also contrasts Elijah with Paul's prayer for Israel (10:1), with the Spirit's pleading on behalf of "us" (8:26–27), and with Christ's pleading for "us" (8:34). Even before Elijah speaks, Paul signals that there are problems; presumably that means anyone at Rome or elsewhere who has concluded that God has rejected Israel is also making a significant mistake.

Paul's introduction to the speech betrays Elijah's error, and the introduction to the divine response lays bare the gap between Elijah's view and that of God.[48] The introductory "but" (*alla*) sets the stage. Another quotation from 1 Kgs 19 follows, this time introduced as "What does the divine response say?" Instead of the customary reference to Scripture speaking or to a human agent (Isaiah, David, Moses), this time the speech is explicitly said to be divine. The word *chrēmatismos* is used only here in the NT, although the related verb occurs in

---

48. The words Elijah speaks in v. 3 draw from both 1 Kgs 19:10 and 19:14 (LXX). There are a few modifications, most of which are insignificant. It may be important, however, that Paul inserts the vocative "Lord" at the outset, which underscores Elijah's complaint before God.

situations involving divine disclosure (e.g., Matt 2:12, 22; Luke 2:26; Acts 10:22; Heb 8:5; but see Rom 7:3).

The words of the divine speech modify the narrative of 1 Kings in a small but revealing way. In 1 Kgs 19:15–18 God directs Elijah to proceed with the anointings of Hazael and Jehu as kings of Aram and Israel respectively, and with the anointing of Elisha as prophet in Elijah's place. Paul omits those instructions, moving directly to what he finds relevant: "I have left for myself seven thousand men who have not bent the knee to Baal." In the LXX (although not in the Hebrew), the voice tells Elijah, "You will leave" seven thousand males (*andres* in both texts), but Paul alters it to "I have left for myself." In the LXX, these men are apparently to be identified by Elijah, but in Romans it is God who has already identified them, and they belong to God ("for myself").[49]

That the relationship of the seven thousand to God is the salient point is reinforced in vv. 5–6, as Paul turns to the present time. He has earlier referred to this "now time," *nyn kairos* rendered literally, as the time of God's rectifying humanity through Jesus's death (3:26) and the time of suffering (8:18). Reinforced by several other references to "now" (e.g., 5:9, 11; 6:19, 21; 8:1), they suggest more than a mere historical marker of the present by comparison with "back then." The "now time" is the time inaugurated by the death and resurrection, the time of the Christ event.

The remnant exists in the "now time." Here Paul terms the remnant a *leimma*, a word related to the *hypoleimma* of 9:27 (quoting Isa 10:22). The notion of the remnant varies across Jewish texts, referring sometimes to a fragment of Israel that is threatened with destruction (e.g., 2 Kgs 21:14) and other times to the fragment that becomes the core of a restored Israel (e.g., Isa 11:10–16).[50] As noted above, 1 Kgs 19:18 LXX identifies the remnant with the faithful, although Paul's interpretation of that event emphasizes God's role. For Paul, the salient feature of the remnant is that it is elected by grace.

Whatever its background, Paul does not linger to qualify or quantify the remnant apart from the crucial point that the remnant is *kat' eklogēn charitos*: it came into being by God's election through grace. The wording is redundant, since either noun would make the point. Yet Paul is not content even with that redundancy, amplifying it in v. 6: it happened through grace, not actions, since grace then would not be grace. It is crucial to see Paul's emphasis here on God's initiative: this remnant exists not by its own faithfulness but by God's decision and action. Further, the contrast between grace and (human) action may

---

49. "The refusal to bend the knee to Baal therefore implicitly represents the content of divine deliverance and not its basis" (Seifrid 2000, 161).

50. Ronald Clements warns against imagining a "fixed concept" or doctrine of the remnant in the Second Temple period, comparing ideas of remnant to that of messiah in their flexibility. In both cases there is a "vital image, or guidelines, by which a great variety of scripture passages could be understood and related to the later condition of Judaism" (1980, 118).

have struck Paul's contemporaries as peculiar, perhaps even offensive, since many would have assumed that gifts (in this case, divine grace) were reserved for those whose character and action warranted them (Barclay 2015, 39–45, 209–38). For Paul, however, no one warrants God's grace (3:21–24), placing all the emphasis on God's electing action.

[7–10] "What then?" (11:7) moves to a further implication. It does not suffice to say that there is a divinely created *remnant*; there is a divinely created *division* within Israel. Returning to the argument of 9:30–10:21, Paul writes, "What Israel seeks, this it did not achieve." Consistent with that earlier discussion, "Israel" here again refers to the entirety of the people God created.

With the two *de* clauses at the end of v. 7, however, Paul posits a split within Israel:

> Now [*de*] the election achieved
> But [*de*] the rest were hardened

It is crucial to see that the split is *within* Israel: nothing here suggests that "the rest" cease to be part of Israel. They clearly belong, which raises the question of v. 11 about their future, their place within God's purpose for the whole of Israel.

The phrase "the election" singles out not the individuals but the divine act. That the election "achieved" is virtually tautologous, since the election is God's. Of the contrasting group, "the rest," Paul asserts that they "were hardened." The passive verb reinforces the quotation from Deut 29:3 that follows: the hardening is God's act no less than is the election.[51] Here it is useful to recall the introduction of Pharaoh in 9:18, where God is said to harden Pharaoh's heart (*sklērynein* rather than *pōroun*, as here). Pharaoh's hardening is connected with the enhancement of God's glory, which at least introduces the possibility that the hardening of "the rest" will also serve God's purposes.

Verses 8–10 comment on this group, "the rest," through two scriptural citations; the first explains God's hardening (v. 8), and the second pronounces a puzzling malediction (vv. 9–10). Verse 8 draws largely from Deut 29:3 LXX, although recast in more emphatic terms. Where Deut 29:3 LXX observes, "God did not give you a heart," Paul claims that God *did* give, and what God gave was a "confused spirit" (Isa 29:10 LXX). By contrast with the gracious, empowering spirit/Spirit at work in Rom 8:10–11, this spirit disables "the rest." They have unseeing eyes and unhearing ears (cf. also the use of Isa 6:9 in Mark 4:12; John 12:40; Acts 28:26).[52]

---

51. Translations that attribute the hardening to human stubbornness or willfulness misconstrue the Greek, as when the CEB reads "others were resistant" or the CEV "were stubborn."

52. Representing bodily difference as a symptom of God's disfavor is deeply troubling, and no less so for being widespread in Scripture and beyond. It may be useful as a counter to recall that,

The speech of David, taken largely from Ps 68:23–24 LXX, dramatically reinforces the contention that "the rest" are unable to hear and see God's Christ because of God's own action. Here, however, the tone is less observational than maledictive; that is, this is not so much a report on the status of "the rest" as a divine pronouncement that brings about their impairment. Some of the language echoes Paul's earlier report about Israel. The stumbling stone recalls 9:33, God's tripping of Israel, and the reference to darkened eyes repeats v. 8. The final line ("bend their backs") evokes helplessness that fits with stumbling around, unable to see what lies ahead.

Exegetes have long puzzled over the reference to "their table," at times producing vicious interpretations. For example, Pelagius connects this table with the one "where they rejoiced at the death of Christ, while they ate the Passover" (126). Identifying the table with Scripture, Origen wrote that "Scripture becomes a snare for them when they read what has been prophesied about Christ" (*Comm. Rom.* 8.7; Burns 267; see Cranfield 2:551–52 for additional suggestions). Given that Paul is citing Ps 68:23–24 LXX, the presence of "table" may merely reflect its integral place in those lines. There is, however, an additional possibility: in Rom 14, Paul does take up a conflict produced by differences over food practices, presumably communal food practices. And there again is *skandalon* in his warning against causing the brother or sister to stumble (14:13).[53] If there is a connection between the two texts, this indirect reference to eating anticipates the warning of ch. 14 against allowing eating to become a trap. Nevertheless, the word "table" (*trapeza*) does not occur in Rom 14, and the dispute about food practices would not pertain to the people Paul here labels "the rest."

The conclusion appears to be that God may indeed save a remnant but that he will destroy "the rest." That would be an understandable conclusion, especially for anyone acquainted with what follows in Ps 68:29:

> Let them be wiped out from the book of the living,
> and do not let them be enrolled among the righteous.

Even without that knowledge, the implication of vv. 7–10 appears to be that although some have been chosen, the remainder are under a curse that will not be lifted ("until this very day," "always"). The question of v. 11 is entirely apt. Once again Paul has led Phoebe's auditors to a conclusion he will sharply reject.

---

for Paul, all humans are dis-abled apart from God's decisive action in Christ, as evidenced by the first half of Romans.

53. This possibility was suggested by Minear, although he is more emphatic than the evidence allows: "The issues of ch. 14 are clearly visible here in Paul's choice of citations from scripture" (1971, 79).

11:11–24 Faltering Is Not Falling

Movement from the lesser to the greater (*qal wahomer*) structures this passage; more important, movement from lesser to greater signals the theological argument, which contrasts the present situation of "the rest" of Israel with the future riches of gentile as well as Jew. Paul opens with claims that the future inclusion of "the rest" of Israel—the part not currently identified as "remnant"—will produce "abundance" or "riches" for gentile and Jew alike (v. 12). He closes with the assertion that those branches that "naturally" belong to the olive tree can readily be grafted in again by God (v. 24). In both cases, "how much greater" (*posō mallon*) marks the comparison (Tobin 2004, 362). Paul furthers the comparison with the contrasts in vv. 15–16, where the present state of "the rest" is contrasted with the future (first fruit, lump; root, branches). The mystery disclosed in 11:25–32 is anticipated already here.

This rhetorical strategy resembles that of Rom 5, the only other passage in the letter to make use of *qal wahomer* argument. The connection between the two passages is both rhetorical and substantive. In 5:1–11 Paul contrasts the present and future consequences of God's action in Jesus Christ. In 5:12–21 Paul contrasts Adam and Christ: one disobeys and thereby brings Sin and Death into the world, while the other obeys and brings not only grace but the overthrow of Sin and Death. In both cases the assumption is that God's action not only overturns the present situation but does so to excess. That same notion of God's excessive intervention is at work in 11:11–24: the present state of "the rest" is not simply an opportunity for gentile deliverance but contrasts with their future "fullness" and God's capacity to include Jew and gentile alike. Whether the present is described positively as peace with God (5:1) or the reign of grace (5:20), or negatively as the division of Israel into "the remnant" and "the rest" (11:7), Paul anticipates a future in which God's reign is exponentially greater than the present.

Within this logic of excess, the beginning of v. 13 ("I am talking to you gentiles") jolts the reader to attention. Presumably these words also captured the attention of Phoebe's auditors, gentile and Jew alike. Paul has allowed the audience to assume that the problem he is addressing has to do solely with Israel's situation before God, an assumption reflected in all too many discussions of Rom 9–11. It now emerges that Paul also has in his sights gentile arrogance in the form of a presumption to know God's intention for "the rest" of Israel. The argument Paul makes here concerns not simply Israel's disobedience or even God's relationship to Israel but also gentile arrogance.

11:11 Considering all this, I ask: The rest haven't faltered so that they fall,[a] have they? Of course not! But it is through their trespass that salvation comes to the gentiles so as to provoke them.[b] 12 Now if their trespass is wealth for the world, and their defeat is wealth for the gentiles, how much greater will be the wealth produced by their fullness?

13 Now I am talking to you gentiles: since I am myself a gentiles' apostle,ᶜ I glorify my service, 14 if somehow I might provoke my flesh and I might save some of them. 15 For if their rejectionᵈ means the reconciliation of the world, what could their welcome be but life from the dead? 16 And if the first fruit is holy, the whole lump is holy. And if the root is holy, the branches are holy.

17 Now if some of the branches were broken off, and you, a wild olive shoot, were grafted in among the restᵉ so that you share the root—namely, the richness of the olive treeᶠ— 18 do not boast over the branches! Since if you boast, you are in the wrong,ᵍ because you do not support the root but the root supports you. 19 So you say, "Branches were broken off so that I might be grafted in." 20 Well said.ʰ They were broken off in faithlessness, but you yourself stand in faith. Do not be presumptuous, but fear. 21 For if God did not spare the natural branches, God will certainly not spare you. 22 Consider, then, both the goodness and the harshness of God. On those who fell, there is harshness, but on you, God's goodness, if you continue in that goodness, since you also could be cut off. 23 And as for them, unless they continue in faithlessness, they will be grafted in, because God is able to graft them in again. 24 For if you were cut off from your natural place in a wild olive tree and unnaturally grafted into the cultivated tree, how much more readily will those who naturally belong be grafted in to their own olive tree?

a. "Faltered" and "fall" reflect the alliteration of vv. 11–12. "P" sounds recur in *eptaisan* ("faltered") and *pesōsin* ("fall"), which then recur in the lines that follow with *paraptōmati, parazēlōsai, paratōma, ploutos,* and *plērōma*. In addition, there is homoioteleuton in the series *paraptōma, hēttēma,* and *plērōma*.

b. Most often translated as "provoke to jealousy" (KJV) or "make Israel jealous" (NRSVue) but simply "provoke" or "irk" is also possible, as in Ps 37:1, 7–8. If this language is influenced by Deut 32:21 LXX, which Paul has already quoted in 10:19, there also "provoke" seems a reasonable translation, given its parallel in the line that follows: "I will enrage you with a senseless people."

c. "I am myself" reflects the emphatic *egō*. "A gentiles' apostle" is odd, but it displays Paul's unusual word order (BDF §474, 4), which highlights his role among gentiles.

d. Significant debate attaches to the translation of *apobolē*, which may be either "loss" or "jettisoning" (LSJ s.v.). The question is whether Paul refers to the loss experienced by "the rest" (through their misstep) or to their rejection by God (as in vv. 7–8). Jewett (680) and Fitzmyer (612) contend for the former on the grounds that Paul has already indicated God has not rejected Israel, but that is to neglect both the remnant of vv. 1–5 as well as the action of God in vv. 7–8. The second "their" ("their welcome") does not appear in the Greek but is inferred from "their" in the first half of the verse and logically required by the parallel. Paul has in mind a very particular welcome, not hospitality in general.

e. Lit., "in them," resulting in the odd suggestion that the wild shoots were grafted in *among* the branches that were broken off. Presumably Paul means that "you" were grafted in among the remaining branches.

f. Lit., "the root of the richness of the olive." The awkwardness of this phrase generated a complex textual tradition. Some manuscripts insert a *kai* between "the root" and "the richness" (e.g., ℵ² A D¹ L P), while others omit "the root" altogether, yielding "the richness of the olive tree" (e.g., 𝔓⁴⁶ D* F G). The decision of NA²⁸ is preferable, based on ℵ* B C Ψ, since it seems likely that this awkward expression was smoothed out rather than that an earlier, more straightforward expression was modified. The translation construes "the richness of the olive tree" as appositional, describing the character of the root.

g. Although "you are in the wrong" does not appear in the Greek, it is clear from the context that this is the implication of v. 18b.

h. LSJ, s.v. *kalōs*; there may be a note of condescension, perhaps even irony at work here: "Well, good for you," or "How nice for you."

[11–12] The introductory question of v. 11 closely parallels that of 11:1: "Considering all this, I ask" draws attention to what follows, the Greek particle *mē* anticipates a negative answer, and the response once again is "Of course not!" (*mē genoito*). What has changed is the subject. Instead of the possibility that God has rejected God's people (by implication, the whole of Israel), Paul inquires about "them," presumably referring to "the rest" as in vv. 8–10 and suggesting that the current situation might be irreversible.

The question follows logically on the preceding lines, particularly given the time references ("until this very day" in v. 8 and "always" in v. 10) that convey the finality of the division in Israel. For anyone familiar with Ps 68 LXX, cited in vv. 9–10, the likelihood of the irreversibility is increased, as the psalmist goes on to plead:

> May their camp be deserted;
>   and in their tents let no one live.
> . . . .
> Add lawlessness to their lawlessness
>   and do not let them enter into your righteousness.
> Let them be wiped out from the book of the living;
>   let them not be written down among the righteous. (Ps 68:26, 28–29 LXX)

The physical imagery of vv. 8–10—closed eyes, unhearing ears, and bent backs—produces the consequences of vv. 11–12. Those impaired in vision, hearing, and stance are more prone to misstep and to falls, at least in Paul's view.[54]

54. On the problematic assumptions at work here about what it means to be able-bodied, see above on 11:8–10.

The language of physical movement also connects these lines with the earlier depiction in 9:30–31, in which Israel runs a race it cannot win, while gentiles win a race they do not even enter.

In neither case is there actual competition between Israel (or "the rest" of Israel) and gentiles, however. Paul turns the competitive image upside down: rather than triumphing over one another, the faltering of "the rest" leads to gentile salvation, and the salvation of gentiles provokes Israel in ways that remain unspecified. The race turns out to be for mutual benefit rather than for competitive victory.[55]

While it is tempting to cast about for specifics to verify or undermine Paul's claims in v. 11, uncertainty abounds as to how the faltering of "the rest" leads to gentile salvation or how gentile salvation is provocative to "the rest." To be sure, Luke's account of Paul's labor provides several occasions when Jewish resistance to Paul's preaching prompts him to go instead to gentiles (Acts 13:46; 18:6; 28:28), but gentile reception does not seem to usher in Jewish responsiveness, and Paul's letters offer little evidence to confirm or correct such a strategy. The language of provocation recalls the citation of Deut 32:21 in Rom 10:19, but neither passage specifies how exactly Israel is provoked or what follows from that provocation. Instead, Deut 32 continues with a veritable litany of the divinely inflicted consequences Israel should expect for its disobedience (Deut 32:22–27).

Rather than specify the provocation, Paul introduces in v. 12 the *qal wahomer* logic that dominates this entire passage and reflects his conviction that present events do not disclose the future situation of "the rest" of Israel. Three clauses make up the verse:

v. 12a   Now if their trespass is wealth for the world,
v. 12b   and their defeat is wealth for the gentiles,
v. 12c   how much greater will be the wealth produced by their fullness?

With the initial clause, the trespass of "the rest" is wealth for "the world." In Romans, Paul has frequently referred to "the world" (*kosmos*) in the sense of the entire human population, particularly drawing attention to the creaturely character of that population (1:8, 20; 3:6, 19; 4:13; 5:12; Gaventa 2011a, 266–69; E. Adams 2000, 151–94). The implication appears to be that "their trespass" is abundance for both Jew and gentile alike, although how that takes place remains unstated.

Verse 12b intensifies the logic slightly, since "they" have not simply taken a misstep but are defeated. Now it is no mere "trespass" or misstep but a "defeat,"

---

55. Susannah Ticciati helpfully develops a noncompetitive interpretation of the jealousy motif in these chapters (2012).

a more ominous possibility and one with undertones of rejection. The noun *hēttēma* is rare, but the passive of the related verb *hēttaō* appears in the LXX, frequently in the context of military defeat (e.g., Isa 13:15; 30:31; Jer 31:1; 2 Macc 10:24).

Verse 12c signals that the present is not the final word regarding Israel's division. Far from concluding that "the rest" have failed and that failure is permanent, their "fullness" will be even greater. What that fullness means must wait, however, since v. 13 takes a surprising turn.

[13–16] The numerous questions vv. 11–12 produce must wait, as Paul pivots to address "you gentiles." Following a chain of several questions introduced with "I say" or "we say," this direct address to "you gentiles" is startling. The opening lines of 7:1 address those who "know the law," but without the second-person "you" that calls out a portion of addressees.[56] Despite multitudinous depictions of Rom 9–11 as concerned with "God and Israel" or even "Israel's unbelief" or some such, this direct address to gentiles prompts the suspicion that Paul's long discussion about God and Israel has an immediate cause in gentile believers. The specific problem comes into view only with v. 18, but this direct address puts the audience on alert.[57]

The second half of v. 13b also is unusual for its appeal to the character of Paul's ministry. The statement takes emphatic form with "I am" (*eimi egō*), and Paul's "title" follows the unusual order *ethnōn apostolos*, frontloading the gentile audience of his apostleship (see also 1:5). When he refers elsewhere to his work among gentiles, as in 1 Thess 2:16 and Gal 2:7–14, he does so defensively. Here the concern is not with *Jewish* resistance to gentile mission, however, but with *gentile* misunderstanding of Israel's future.

The phrase "gentiles' apostle" sets up the main clause: "I glorify my service." Early in the letter Paul traces human captivity to Sin back to human failure to glorify God (1:21), a charge that is reinforced with the assertion that humanity knew of God and, later, that humanity "exchanged" God's glory for that of created beings (1:23). Abraham is singled out for giving glory to God in 4:20. As the body of the letter draws to a close, Paul will pray that all Roman believers "together with one voice . . . glorify" God (15:6; and see 15:9). To glorify Paul's ministry is exceptional. The closest parallel appears in Gal 1:24, where Paul reports that the Judean congregations "glorified God in me," that is, glorified God because of what had happened in Paul's life.[58] Almost certainly

---

56. Romans 12:3 is comparable grammatically in that it combines "I speak" with "you" in the dative, but in that instance the audiences in Romans are being addressed as a whole ("everyone among you"; and see Phlm 19).

57. On the place of gentiles in Roman audiences, see the introduction. See on 1:6 regarding the oddity of using "gentile" in direct address.

58. To be sure, Paul uses *doxazein* in 1 Cor 12:26 for the honoring of a member of the body, which opens up the possibility that in Rom 11:13 he means simply that he respects his vocation (as

this is a way of acknowledging (as he says emphatically in 1:1) that the ministry comes from God; beyond that, it may invite the Roman auditors to join in giving glory to God.

Apostleship to the gentiles is not for the gentiles alone. Any exclusivist understanding of Paul's work crashes into v. 14: "if somehow I might provoke my flesh and I might save some of them." While Paul's work is among the gentiles, his hope is to contribute to the salvation of "the rest" of Israel. As above, Paul does not linger over the nature of that provocation, and speculation about how envy of gentile salvation prompts the faith of "the rest" of Israel is cut off as Paul moves on quickly to the results (in vv. 15–16) rather than to the process. Instead of lingering over the mechanics, Paul speaks of the people: "my flesh" rather than "Israel" or "the rest" conveys Paul's own involvement in this question.[59]

Given Paul's overwhelming pattern of attributing salvation to God, the clause "and I might save some of them" is unexpected. Yet in 1 Cor 7:16 he refers to the possibility of a wife saving her husband, and in 1 Cor. 9:22 of his adaptability, which he hopes will lead some to salvation. "Some" reflects a modest expectation of his own apostleship, not a modest expectation for the salvation of "the rest" of Israel, as is evident from the lines that follow (to say nothing of 11:26, 32).

Verse 15 continues the contrast from lesser to greater introduced in v. 12:

Their rejection   reconciliation of the world
Their welcome   life from the dead

"Rejection" here refers back to the divine hardening and its consequences, which, as Paul has already indicated, produce "abundance" for the world. Although the word "rejection" (*apobolē*) is a hapax legomenon in Paul (appearing elsewhere in the NT only in Acts 27:22), here it stands as a one-word summation of vv. 7–10. The remainder of this verse resides deep within Paul's interpretation of the gospel, especially in Romans. "Reconciliation" recalls 5:10, which characterizes the work of Christ's death as reconciling God's enemies ("us") to God (and see 2 Cor 5:18–20). "Welcome" anticipates Paul's summary in Rom 15:7 of the nature of Christ's own *diakonia*: "Christ welcomed you for the glory of God."

The comparison between present rejection and future welcome culminates in the phrase "life from the dead." The phrase ably sums up the consequences of Christ's resurrection for believers (see the repeated expressions in 5:21; 6:4,

in "I take my assignment seriously"; BDAG s.v.). Given the context, however, with its thorough grounding in God's action, to say nothing of Paul's own insistence that his calling is from God (1:1), it seems likely that he is also praising God for his assignment.

59. Paul's flesh language here recalls the contemporary idiom of "having skin in the game."

22–23; 8:6), even if Paul does not elsewhere employ this precise wording.[60] Paul is revealing his expectation that God will not abandon "the rest" of Israel, but he also reveals that he learns about Israel's eschatological future from the events of the gospel.[61] What is anticipated with "life from the dead" would only be possible by virtue of miracle, not by virtue of human belief. To understate considerably, human conviction does not produce life from the dead.

Verse 16 bridges these claims about the gospel's extravagant grasp of "the rest" and the more explicit warning to gentile believers in vv. 17–24. It is conventional to connect this analogy to the first offering referred to in Num 15:17–21 (see the marginal notes to NA[28]), but Paul's wording does not match that scenario. The "first fruit" or first bit of a loaf set aside for the priests is holy, but that first bit does not make the rest of the loaf holy (see also Lev 23:20; Ezek 44:30; Gordon 2016, 357). Paul's argument appears to be more aligned with his logic in 1 Cor 5:6, that whatever pertains to a portion of dough pertains to the whole of it, and whatever is said of the root of a tree is said of the whole of it. These statements serve to emphasize the implicit promise of vv. 12 and 15, namely, that "the rest" of Israel will finally not be separated from the remnant (the first fruit, as in Rom 16:5; 1 Cor 16:15). The present divided state of Israel does not predict or control the future.

[17–21] The relationship between root and branches in v. 16b yields to a lengthier warning to "you" (now in the singular rather than the plural of v. 13) about the peril of condescension to "the rest." In vv. 17–21 three different "if" clauses introduce dire consequences: the "if" at the beginning of v. 17 leads to "Do not boast over the branches" in v. 18a; the "if" in v. 18b leads to "Do not be presumptuous, but fear" at the end of v. 20; and the "if" at the beginning of v. 21 introduces the possible result: God may not spare you.

Paul now identifies "the rest" as "some of the branches." "Some" (*tines*) is indefinite; it seems to imply a small number (as in 3:8 and Gal 1:7), although Paul's own argument in chs. 9–11 presupposes that a majority were among the "some."[62] The discrepancy prompts suggestions that Paul is being diplomatic (Fitzmyer 614) or euphemistic (Dunn 2:672). What is overlooked in that urge to conform the text to expectation is that Paul is not concerned here with an accurate description of the branches that have been excised. His concern is with "you," those who have taken it upon themselves to judge others. If Paul does not specify the size of the group named as "some," that seems consistent with the vagueness of 11:7 regarding the numerical distribution of "the election" and

---

60. *Zōē* ("life") appears more often in Romans than in any other Pauline epistle.

61. Along similar lines, Linebaugh comments, "Israel's present and future are reimagined around the rejected and resurrected Christ" (2013b, 218).

62. Admirably, Calvin comments that "some of the branches were broken, not that the whole of the top of the tree was cut off" (249–30).

of "the rest." Both "some" and "you" are the subject of passive verbs: some of the branches were cut out; you were grafted in. Alike they have been acted upon by another, which in context can only be God.

The analogy regarding the root and branches of an olive tree generates interpretive dispute around several questions, including the scriptural images that shape Paul's use of the comparison, the agricultural practices implied together with Paul's knowledge of them, and the intended identity of the "root."[63] Paul's Scriptures refer to the olive tree frequently, most often literally (e.g., Deut 8:8; 28:40; 2 Kgs 18:32; Neh 8:15). In metaphorical references, the righteous speaker identifies as a "green olive tree" (Ps 52:8), or the faithful one is promised children like the abundance of an olive tree (Sir 50:10). In some cases Israel itself is an olive tree, as in Hos 14:6 and Jer 11:16, although to strikingly different purposes. The range of usage, as well as the ubiquity of olive trees in the Middle East, makes the introduction of the olive tree into the text understandable, but the same factors also make it perilous to connect Paul's comments to a single passage or a single usage.

Paul's depiction of grafting a wild shoot into a cultivated tree prompts questions about actual practice. A near contemporary of Paul, Columella, wrote extensively about the cultivation of trees in *De res rustica* and *De arboribus*. In one passage, he describes what appears to be a therapeutic treatment for unproductive olive trees, by which the tree itself is rejuvenated through the insertion of a "green slip taken from a wild-olive tree" (*Rust.* 5.9.16). Yet nothing in Rom 11 suggests that Paul understands the tree itself as needing rescue (as distinct from certain branches; contra Baxter and Ziesler 1985). In addition, Columella elsewhere describes grafting at some length, which seems to be distinct from this process of rejuvenating an unproductive tree (*Rust.* 5.11; Esler 2003a).

Other ancient texts reflect a practice directly contrary to Paul's language: cultivated shoots are grafted into wild trees, not the other way around. Theophrastus recommends grafting cultivated slips into wild trees and explicitly warns against the opposite strategy (*De causis plantarum* 1.6.10). Theophrastus was writing in the third century BCE, which might undermine his relevance. Yet several of Paul's early interpreters, including Ambrosiaster (209), Augustine (*Enarrat. Ps.* 72.2; Burns 275), and Pelagius (129), comment that Paul has reversed standard practice. Augustine explains, "We never see a wild olive grafted onto a cultivated olive tree. For whoever did such a thing would find nothing but wild olives."

---

63. Attempts to make the root-and-branches language of v. 16 align closely with the more extended allegory of vv. 17–24 end up in exegetical contortions. The comparison of v. 16 concerns the wholeness of the loaf or that of the plant, while the root-and-branch analogy of vv. 17–24 serves a different purpose. A similar use of catchwords in transition occurs with "what is owed" in 13:7 and "owe nothing" in 13:8.

This reversal of normal practice may be deliberate (so Esler 2003a), in keeping with Paul's strategy elsewhere (see e.g., on 9:25; 10:5–8). The lack of verisimilitude should not be overinterpreted, however; Paul will shortly opine that the branches that have been cut off can be grafted back into the tree, a prospect so wildly unrealistic as to suggest that Paul is scarcely concerned with agricultural practice, not even with the intentional undermining of agricultural practice. In both cases, that of the initial engrafting and that of the return of the missing branches, Paul's picture is contrary to nature, consistent with his depiction of gentile believers in v. 24 (as well as in 9:25–26, 30). God can accomplish this unnatural act, which rules out any gentile boasting (as he will shortly emphasize in v. 18).

God's engrafting means that "you" now share "the root." The identification of Christ as the "root of Jesse" in 15:12 (via Isa 11:10) may be anticipated here; indeed, Origen insisted that it is Jesus Christ alone who is the root (*Comm. Rom.* 8.10; Burns 273; and see Khobnya 2013 for a recent endorsement of this view). That interpretation has some merit, especially given Paul's notion of Christ as the "firstborn" (8:29) and the *aparchē* ("first fruit") in 1 Cor 15. If Paul thinks along these lines, however, it seems odd that it does not appear elsewhere. His dominant ecclesial image is that of the "body of Christ" (Rom 12; 1 Cor 12:12–31; cf. Eph 3:6; 4:12) rather than the olive tree (Käsemann 309).

A more widely held view is that the root is the patriarchs, a position taken as early as Pelagius (127), Chrysostom (*Hom. Rom.* 19.16; *NPNF*[1] 11.490), and Augustine (*Enarrat. Ps.* 72.2; Burns 275). The patriarchal root of Israel is an attractive proposal, one that would be at home in Luke's Gospel (1:55, 73) and the book of Acts (3:13; 7:2). Yet this notion that the patriarchs uphold Israel as well as the engrafted gentile branches does not sit at all well with the history Paul produces in Rom 9:6b–13, which resolutely insists that Israel came into existence and continues to exist only as a direct result of God's action. Even in Rom 4 Paul emphasizes God's promise to Abraham, not the obedience of Abraham itself.

A better suggestion is that the root is the promise to Israel or the election of Israel, a suggestion found already in Ambrosiaster ("the hope of the promise," 209) and recently revived by Barclay (2015, 550–51, 575). This interpretation makes sense in light of the promise language that follows in 15:8, not to mention 4:14–16, 20; 9:4, 8. Importantly, it has the advantage of reflecting Paul's continued emphasis on divine activity—the God who makes the promise—while maintaining the connection with the particular history of Israel.

Paul identifies the root in terms of its richness, an association found also in Judg 9:9 and T. Levi 8.8. In a way that loosely resembles Paul's language here, Philo connects the richness of the earth with God's gifts (*Migration* 101; *Posterity* 123; cf. *Unchangeable* 178). In the present context, "richness" underscores the language of excess throughout the passage, particularly that of "wealth" in v. 12.

The gentile "you" addressee "shares" the root—literally, "has become a sharer" (*synkoinōnos*). The implication of that term, as well as what follows through v. 24, is that the two types of branches remain distinct. Nothing here indicates that the gentile branches become the natural branches or that the natural branches cease to exist. What they share is the root, the divine promise. They are not separate, connected as they are by the same root, but neither are they dissolved into one another. That point seems to be reinforced in vv. 25–32, and it bears importantly on the discussion of "all Israel" in v. 26.

The extended "if" statement of v. 17 with its lengthy analogy yields to a terse, clear imperative in v. 18a: "Do not boast over the branches." Paul has been preparing for this warning since the startling direct address in v. 13, "Now I am talking to you gentiles." Everything in between has led to this imperative, the first since 6:19. Paul's understanding of his vocation, the expectation he has for the mission, the analogy of root and branches—everything has come together in this terse directive against boasting over the branches, "the rest" of Israel.

Verses 18b–20 amplify the directive by imagining the gentile boast itself and undermining it, before issuing a second imperative in v. 20b. In diatribe style, Paul presents the boast: "Branches were broken off so that I might be grafted in." The personal pronoun "I" (*egō*) reinforces the inflected verb, drawing attention to the boast. The implication is that "I" am somehow special by virtue of the reduction of others. The implication is tantalizing: the "I" does not boast of accomplishments but of the loss experienced by others. A notion of the zero-sum game is at work in the claim of the "I": "We cannot both be upheld by the root, so *they* were taken out for *my* benefit."

A contemporary English rendering of Paul's response of "Well said" might be the sneering "How nice for you!" Verse 20a takes the imagined claim to superiority and recasts it: "They were broken off in faithlessness, but you yourself stand in faith." This enigmatic statement is unpacked in vv. 22–24. Paul now moves quickly to a second imperative: "Do not be presumptuous, but fear." In context, the warning against presumptuousness clearly refers to gentile boasting over "the rest" of Israel. A few lines later Paul will attempt to forestall the presumed cleverness of those who suppose that they know God's will. Such concern about presumptuousness will return in 12:16, as part of a general warning about false claims to human knowledge, and it seems to play a role also in the discussion of 14:1–15:13, although the language there differs.

The appropriate gentile response to being grafted into the tree of promise is fear because, as v. 21 bluntly reminds the audience, God, who did not spare the branches that belong, will certainly not spare those that are unnatural (i.e., gentiles). The warning about gentile condescension toward "the rest" of Israel is serious. The lines that follow reflect the expectation that God's final victory will leave no one behind (to say nothing of 8:31–39), but that does not diminish the warning about gentile arrogance, a warning all too often cast aside in the history of Christian discourse and action.

[22–24] The transitional *ide oun* ("Consider, then") marks a slight change in the discussion and invites the audience's attention. Paul continues to discuss the relationship between gentiles and "the rest" of Israel, now with more focused attention to God's own "goodness" and "harshness" rather than to the perils of gentile boasting. This shift leads directly into the climactic announcement in vv. 25–32 of the divine "mystery" that is underway.

Paul invites attention to God's "goodness and harshness" in relationship to the two groups. The parallel presentation quickly gives way to a more extended concern with "the rest" of Israel. First comes a close parallel summarizing the present situation:

v. 22b	On the ones who fell	harshness
	on you	goodness of God

A second statement anticipates possible consequences for each party, but here what is anticipated is a change on each side, a disastrous change for "you" but a hopeful change for "them":

v. 22c	If you continue in that goodness	since you could be cut off
v. 23a	Unless they remain in faithlessness	they will be grafted in

The emphasis on God's role is already implicit here, since it is God's goodness in which "you" persist, not human action or conviction.[64]

That implicit word quickly becomes explicit with the end of v. 23: "God is able to graft them in again." The assertion that God is able or, more literally, powerful (*dynatos*) for this task returns the audience to the very opening of the letter, where the risen Christ is said to be publicly revealed as "Son of God in power" (1:4). The gospel itself Paul identifies as "the power of God" bringing about salvation. Chapters 5–8 identify the working out of that power in the death and resurrection of Jesus, with its defeat of Sin and Death. That same power provides the warrant for Paul's confidence that God can even graft in branches that have been cut out, branches for which there would otherwise be no hope.

To be sure, Paul's words imply a change on the part of "the rest." "Unless they remain in faithlessness" bears the possibility that they will remain in faithlessness. Yet v. 24 makes clear that Paul expects God's power to prevail (Gathercole 2017, 131). This is not an abstract promise of restoration, offered

---

64. As Ross Wagner observes, "It is not insignificant from a pastoral perspective that Paul exhorts them to hold fast to God's goodness rather than to keep believing. The focus remains on God and not on an introspective obsession with one's spiritual 'temperature'" (2002, 274).

with the notion that it may be accepted or declined. Paul fully anticipates the salvation of Israel he will announce in v. 26. God has already removed wild olive branches from their natural place and grafted them in where they do not belong. How much easier will it be for God to graft in again those who naturally belong?

In addition to preparing for the "mystery" of vv. 25–32, this final instance of *qal wahomer* radically undermines any theory of limited good as applied to God's own goodness. The root, which is God's promise, supports all. There is no notion that "the rest" of Israel is displaced forever or that only a limited number may enter.

11:25–36 "All Israel Will be Saved"

The logic of divine excess that characterizes 11:11–24 culminates in the disclosure of a mystery: God will save "all Israel." By identifying Israel's salvation as a "mystery," a term drawn from the realm of apocalyptic discourse, Paul locates this particular mystery in the power of God apocalyptically expressed in the events of the gospel (1:16–17).

As elsewhere, however, that gospel is not for Israel alone. Once again Paul draws attention to the role the divine hardening of part of Israel plays in bringing about salvation of gentiles. Further, Paul announces the mystery itself in order to prevent the audience from drawing its own conclusions, spinning its own webs of speculation. The destructive possibility of gentile arrogance has not been left behind.

The disclosure of Israel's salvation is not an end in itself, however. Just as Paul introduced ch. 9 with doxology, he concludes ch. 11 with doxology. Verses 33–36 celebrate God's inaccessible wisdom, implicitly acknowledging that eschatological redemption lies beyond human understanding.

25 Now I do not want you to be uninformed about this mystery, brothers and sisters, since then you might rely on your own thinking.[a] A hardening has come upon part of[b] Israel until the fullness of the gentiles comes in, 26 and in this way[c] all Israel will be saved. As it is written:

> The deliverer will come from Zion
> to turn ungodliness[d] away from Jacob.
> 27 And this will be[e] my covenant with them
> when[f] I take away their sins.

28 As far as the gospel is concerned, they are enemies[g] on your account, but as far as the election, they are beloved on account of the fathers, 29 since the gifts and the calling of God are irrevocable. 30 Just as then you were rebellious to God but now you have received mercy through their

disobedience, 31 so now they have been disobedient through the mercy given you[h] so that they also now[i] may receive mercy. 32 For God has shut up all in disobedience, that God might have mercy on all.

33 Oh, the depth of the abundance and wisdom and knowledge of God.
How incomprehensible are his judgments,
and how inscrutable are his ways.
34 For who has known the mind of the Lord
or who became his counselor?
35 Or who made a gift to him,
and was given a gift by him in exchange?
36 Because from him and through him and to him are all things.
To God be glory forever. Amen!

a. *Para* ("on your own") is omitted by several early manuscripts ($\mathfrak{P}^{46}$ F G Ψ *et alia*), and a few others substitute *en* ("among"; A B 630), but the changes are negligible.

b. *Apo merous* ("in part") may qualify either the hardening ("a partial hardening") or Israel ("a part of Israel"). There seems nothing partial about the present hardening, however, given Paul's description of it in vv. 8–10 as resulting in utter incapacity. In addition, "a part" is consistent with reference to "the rest" (v. 7) and "some" (v. 17).

c. "And in this way" renders *kai houtōs*. Although the phrase may reference time ("and then") rather than manner (Van der Horst 2000), manner is more consistent with the argument earlier in this chapter, to say nothing of Paul's outright rejection elsewhere of eschatological timetables (1 Thess 5:1–11). It is one thing to anticipate the nearness of God's victory and another altogether to presume to control God's calendar.

d. Lit., "ungodlinesses," since *asebeia* appears here in the plural, but the distinction in meaning is slim, and the plural makes for awkward English.

e. The Greek has no verb, so some form of the copula is needed. I have supplied "this will be" rather than "this is" in deference to the future implication of "when I take away" in the following line.

f. *Hotan* can be rendered either "when," in the sense of a particular event, or "whenever," as a reference to a frequent action. Paul most often uses the word with respect to single events (as in 1 Cor 13:10; 15:24–28 (4x); 16:2–5 (3x); 16:12; 2 Cor 10:6; 1 Thess 5:3; Goodrich 2016, 15), and that is the most reasonable implication here.

g. Although the adjective *echthros* can mean either "hated" or "hating" (BDAG s.v.), in Paul it consistently appears as a substantive, "enemies," as in Rom 5:10; 12:20; 1 Cor 15:25, 26; Gal 4:16; Phil 3:18.

h. Scholars often construe the phrase "through the mercy given you" (*tō hymeterō eleei*) in relation to the closing verb "that they also now may receive mercy" (e.g., Cranfield 2:582–85; Fitzmyer 627; Wright 694) rather than as here, where it is attached to the earlier verb "they have been disobedient." While there are instances in which words precede *hina* ("in order that"; e.g., Acts 19:4; 2 Cor 2:4; BDAG s.v.), in those cases the sense is quite obvious. Here, by contrast, "through the mercy given you" would be placed not immediately following the *hina* but after the verb several words later.

Construing "through the mercy given you" with "they were disobedient" is more natural syntactically, and it makes sense in the context. See further Jewett 710; Wolter 2:221.

i. The manuscript evidence is divided on the presence of *nyn* ("now"). "Now" appears in important early manuscripts, including ℵ B D*·c, but it is also absent from a number of important manuscripts, including 𝔓⁴⁶ A D¹ F G. The translation includes "now," on the grounds that scribes might have deleted it by way of remedying the perceived implication that "the rest" of Israel is "now" receiving mercy (so also Jewett 694; Metzger 1971, 527). This decision is by no means obvious, however, as "now" might have been added to enhance the parallelism between the two clauses of v. 31 (Hultgren 415; Wolter 2:202). (A few manuscripts also read *hysteron*, "later," but that reading is not well attested and even more obviously intends to remedy the perceived problem.)

[25a] The declaration that "I do not want you to be uninformed" is the first transition since 9:6 made without a question:

9:14   So, what does this mean? There isn't wrongdoing on God's part, is there? Of course not!

9:30   So, what shall we say? Astonishingly, gentiles, who were not running after righteousness, nevertheless won righteousness, namely, the righteousness that is from faith.

11:1   Considering all this, I say, "It's not that God has rejected God's people, is it?" Of course not!

11:11   Considering all this, I ask: The rest haven't faltered so that they fall, have they? Of course not!

This departure in form signals early on that what follows is no longer simply another stage in the argument but its culmination. Paul has moved from God's creative activity in bringing Israel into existence, to the hardening of Israel, to the salvific role of Israel, to concern about gentile arrogance. The division in Israel has not yet been resolved, however; nor has the eschatological triumph of God's word been displayed (9:6a).

The opening statement, "Now I do not want you to be uninformed about this mystery, brothers and sisters," draws attention to what follows, just as at 1:13 and elsewhere (see 1 Cor 10:1; 12:1; 2 Cor 1:8; 1 Thess 4:13). Only here and in 1 Thess 4:13 does Paul follow that declaration by specifying the consequence of ignorance. Concerned with death in the community, 1 Thess 4:13 addresses inappropriate grief. Romans 11:25, however, addresses inappropriate speculation. Consistent with several remarks in the preceding lines, Paul is aware that gentile believers (and perhaps Jews as well) may attempt to second-guess God's intent for the remainder of Israel.

In other contexts Paul writes positively about human thought, at least as that thought has been taken captive by the Spirit (e.g., 8:25) or granted by God (e.g., 12:3; 15:5). There is a role for differing judgments (as in 14:6 and Phil 3:15). Paul's concern is not with intellectual activity as such but with the realistic possibility that people would confuse their own suppositions (perhaps those suggested above in vv. 18–20) for God's intent (and see vv. 33–36). This would represent a lapse into what he earlier calls thinking *kata sarka*, thinking that is preoccupied with merely human values.

By contrast with such constricted thinking, Paul announces "this mystery," technical terminology for information that is divinely revealed. This term locates his comments firmly in the realm of apocalyptic thinking (as in, e.g., Dan 2:18–19 LXX, T. Levi 2.10; 1QpHab 7:1–5; 1 En. 41.1; 103.2; 4 Ezra 10.38; 2 Thess 2:7; Rev 1:20; 10:7; 17:5, 7; see R. Brown 1968; Bockmuehl 1990; Wolter 2005, 171–91). Elsewhere in Paul "mystery" can refer to special teaching reserved for the wise (1 Cor 2:2, 7; 4:1; 13:2; 14:2), although that mystery also is associated with apocalyptic (A. Brown 1995, 113–14). In 1 Cor 15:51 "mystery" appears in an unambiguously apocalyptic setting: "Look, I am telling you a mystery: we will not all sleep but we will all be changed."[65]

In this context in Romans, "mystery" locates Israel's future in the workings of God. Consistent with the argument throughout Rom 9–11, Paul contends that Israel is God's creation and has always belonged to God; therefore, Israel's future also belongs fully to God. What Paul will say about the mystery remains fragmented and elliptical, since inherent in the very concept of mystery is its impenetrability. While Paul claims the capacity to make the mystery known, he does not claim to understand it fully (consistent with 1 Cor 13:12), as the conclusion of the chapter will acknowledge and even celebrate. Any such claim would render Paul himself the target of his own warning against relying on his own thinking.[66]

Paul says nothing as to the source or means of his knowledge of the mystery. Based on the scriptural citation in vv. 26b–27, some interpreters conclude that Paul has arrived at this knowledge through scriptural study and reflection (e.g., Dahl 1977, 152; Bell 1994, 126–27). Other interpreters contend that Paul is the recipient of direct revelation (e.g., Wilckens 2:254; Dunn 2:678–79). Answering that question lies beyond the exegete's grasp, as the text is less concerned with how Paul arrived at the mystery—how it came to him—than with its origin and its promise.

[25b–26a] The remainder of v. 25 reinforces the current situation: part of Israel has been hardened at present. This information is not new—it does not constitute the mystery—since it restates 11:7, where Paul first refers to the

---

65. See below on Rom 16:25, which references the "the revelation of the mystery." There are significant text-critical concerns about that passage, however.

66. As Samuel I. Thomas puts it, "The term 'mystery' itself entails a denial of access to its meanings; it often denotes things not understandable by human imagination, things—in Elliot Wolfson's words—that are beyond 'the spot where intellect falters before its own limit'" (2009, 1).

distinction between "the election" and "the rest."[67] With considerable irony, the language of "hardening" associates this group with Pharaoh, whom God is said to have "hardened" in 9:18 (employing there the verb *sklērynō* rather than the noun *pōrōsis* as here). That troublesome association between Pharaoh and even a portion of Israel does not end in hardening, however; in both cases the divine act of hardening has a salvific purpose. Just as Pharaoh's hardening was done in order to save Israel and glorify God's name, so the present hardening of a portion of Israel has the purpose of saving gentiles for the glorification of God's name.

The hardening of "the rest" of Israel is not permanent but temporary, as is clear with *achri hou*, "until the fullness of the gentiles comes in." Earlier in ch. 11 it is the fullness of Israel Paul refers to (v. 12), but here it is the fullness of gentiles who "come in." Numerous passages in Paul's Scriptures anticipate gentiles entering Jerusalem for the worship of God (e.g., Pss 22:27; 86:9; Isa 2:2–4; 56:6–8; 60:3; 66:18; Jer 16:19; Mic 4:2; Zeph 3:9; Zech 8:20–23; Tob 13:11). Importantly, none of these passages see the "entry" of gentiles as an entry into the people of Israel in the sense that gentiles are amalgamated into Israel. (That fact itself undermines interpretations of "all Israel" below as inclusive of gentiles.) Most of them imagine gentiles streaming into Jerusalem, a feature Paul passes over. The "entry" that is significant for Paul is entry into the worship of God (which is confirmed by 15:6–13 and elsewhere in the letter).

What follows in v. 26 is thus the conclusion toward which Paul has been driving and which he will now expand. This division of Israel has taken place, which in turn sets in motion the entry of gentiles into the worship of God. The culmination of these events is what Paul identifies as the mystery: "all Israel" will be saved.

"All Israel," a seemingly straightforward phrase, has generated a discussion that is anything but straightforward.[68] Drawing on the imagery of the olive tree in vv. 17–24 and the notion of gentile "entry" in v. 25, some interpreters understand "all Israel" as a reference to the totality of believing Jews and believing gentiles (e.g., Augustine, *Civ.* 21–24; Burns 282–83; Wright 689–90) or with a restored Israel and believing gentiles (Staples 2011). This interpretation is fatally flawed, however. What the natural and unnatural branches of the olive tree share is sustenance by means of the root, the divine promises to Abraham (see above on 4:16; 11:17), and gentile "entry" is into shared service of God rather than into a people. Further, nowhere in chs. 9–10 or anywhere else in Paul's letters does "Israel" function as a synonym for the church (unless it does in this passage).[69]

---

67. This statement does not contradict 9:6–13, as there Paul is not talking about a division in Israel but about the creation, the calling into being, of Israel, one Israel.

68. Goodrich 2016 and Zoccali 2008 offer helpful overviews of the debate.

69. To be sure, "the Israel of God" in Gal 6:16 has routinely been read as a reference to gentile and Jewish believers together; however, see Eastman 2010 for an important corrective.

Conceding that "all Israel" refers exclusively to Jews, other scholars have seen in "all Israel" an Israel comprised only of the faithful, which in this context would mean those Jews who confess faith in Jesus as the Messiah of God (e.g., Merkle 2000; Zoccali 2008). According to this view, 9:6–13 serves to introduce the notion that there has always been a "real" Israel and a "false" one. If, however, 9:6–13 has to do with the creation of Israel rather than the identification of a "real" and a "false" Israel (see above on 9:6–13 and Gaventa 2010, 259–60), then this interpretation falls. More to the point, since 11:7 Paul has had in view a division within Israel, a division between the remnant and the remainder, a division brought about by God. To be sure, these branches have been cut out, but v. 24b anticipates that God will indeed regraft them.

The remaining option, and by far the most straightforward, is that Paul means what he says: "all Israel" refers to the totality of the Jewish people, the historic people God created with Abraham and sustained in every generation. Israel's relationship to itself is no longer disrupted (Glancy 1991, 202), because God restores "the election" and "the rest" to one another and, more importantly, to God.

Most interpreters would agree with this position, although there is a lingering dispute over the extent of "all." Some commentators contend that "all" means Israel as a whole, not every single individual (Moo 737–38; Hultgren 420). The phrase appears frequently in the LXX, and on numerous occasions it is quite clear that "all" does not equal "every." When the Deuteronomist writes that "all Israel shall hear and be afraid," the expectation is that punishment inflicted on wrongdoing will serve as a deterrent for all, but it is scarcely likely that "all Israel" participated in the stoning of Achan (Josh 7:25). The Mishnah anticipates that "all Israelites have a share in the world to come" but immediately follows that statement with a list of exceptions (Sanh. 10:1–6). Nonetheless, Paul does not stipulate exceptions, and the use of *pantas* in the plural ("all [people]") in v. 32 weighs against this limitation (as might also the comparison of Christ and Adam in 5:12–21, since the comparison assumes that all humanity is implicated *both* in Adam's sin and in Christ's obedience).[70]

Reflection on the scope of "all Israel" should not deflect attention from the culminating word *sōthēsetai* ("will be saved"). The agent is undoubtedly God, consistent with Paul's usage elsewhere in Romans (5:9; 8:24; 9:27; 10:9, 13; but see also 11:14). The statement goes no further into the circumstances Paul anticipates, yet refraining from speculation is extremely difficult. It seems

---

70. Another question that might be ventured is whether Paul's reference is synchronic or dia-chronic—that is, does it include "all Israel" at the time of the parousia, or across time? If Paul is aware of those two possibilities, he makes no reference to them (nor to gentiles across time). First Peter 4:6 may be concerned about the possibility of taking the gospel to the dead, but Paul's letters give no evidence of that concern (apart from, possibly, 1 Cor 15:29).

unlikely that he expects this salvation to come through the widespread impact of Christian preaching, despite his references to apostolic labor in 10:15 and 11:14, since that conventional means would scarcely warrant the language of mystery (so Hultgren 419). Instead, Paul anticipates the salvation of "all Israel" at the eschatological return of Christ (so also, e.g., Cranfield 2:577; Bell 1994, 144; Hofius 1990, 37). To begin with, vv. 26b–27 anticipate the parousia and the arrival of the deliverer. That arrival supplies the eschatological moment the audience might well have anticipated at the end of ch. 8, where it is suppressed in order to take up the question of God and Israel.

Reading these verses eschatologically then places them alongside Paul's expectation about the return of Jesus in 1 Thess 4 and 1 Cor 15. As those passages indicate, Paul regards that return as a triumphant act of God. The language of the Philippians hymn (borrowed in turn from Isa 45:23) provides a hint about its public character:

> At the name of Jesus
> every knee will bend,
>> that of heavenly and earthly and beneath-the-earth beings
> and every tongue will confess that Jesus Christ is Lord to the glory of God the
> Father. (Phil 2:10–11)

In other words, for Paul, the parousia amounts to an undeniable, self-evident enactment of the relationship of Jesus Christ to God. It is different in character from "now time" actions of human proclamation that elicit or fail to elicit faith (as in Rom 10:14–15 or 11:14). There is no need for a human *apostolos* when the presence of the living Lord elicits acknowledgment.

[26b–27] Paul now turns again to Isaiah, drawing most of the citation from Isa 59:20–21, supplemented in the last line by a few words from Isa 27:9. The larger content of Isa 59 is especially pertinent, for immediately before the lines cited the prophet depicts God as a warrior clothed with armor of righteousness, a "helmet of salvation" and "garments of vengeance." It is this divine warrior who comes as deliverer in 59:20–21 (Ryan 2020, 226–27). Whether the auditors will draw the connection is far from certain; however, Paul's own knowledge of the context from which he is quoting seems undeniable, given that he has drawn on Isa 59 already in the relentless catena of Rom 3:10b–18.

The deliverer in the context of Romans is Jesus himself, just as Paul celebrates the Thessalonians for their anticipation of the arrival of God's Son, "the one who is delivering us from the coming wrath" (1 Thess 1:10). To be sure, Paul can also refer to God as deliverer (2 Cor 1:10), as well as God acting through Jesus for deliverance (Rom 7:24–25). In this particular instance, however, a distinction is made. God is the speaker ("this will be my . . . when I take away") who announces the coming of the deliverer, who can only be Jesus Christ.

A slight change appears with the phrase "from Zion" (*ek Siōn*) which in the LXX reads "on behalf of Zion" (*heneken*). The shift of preposition, likely introduced by Paul himself (Wagner 2002, 284–86), reverses the direction of Isaiah's text. Rather than coming on behalf of Zion, the redeemer comes out of Zion. Although in Paul's Scriptures "Zion" often refers to Jerusalem itself (1 Kgs 3:15; 8:1; 2 Kgs 19:21, 31; Pss 13:7; 47:3, 12; 50:20; Amos 1:2; Mic 3:10, 12; Joel 3:16; Zeph 3:16; Zech 9:9—all LXX), Paul evinces little interest in the city geographically but only in reference to its people (e.g., Rom 15:25, 31; Gal 1:17–18). In some instances, however, Zion refers to the Jewish people as a whole (Isa 51:16; Zech 2:10 [Heb. 2:14]), just as "Washington" or "New York" may refer to residents of a location instead of a geographical spot. That may be the case here. In that sense, the deliverer comes from the people of Israel (reinforcing the original statement in 9:1–5).[71]

While the second line ("to turn ungodliness away from Jacob") follows Isa 59:20 LXX word for word, it also radically reinterprets those words. Isaiah anticipates the redemption of Israel from the godless nations, but for Paul the ungodliness is that of "Jacob," that is, Israel itself. To be sure, the line on its own is ambiguous, but Paul's introduction of v. 27b (drawn from Isa 27:9) eliminates that ambiguity (Linebaugh 2013b, 222).

This move recalls Paul's initial declaration in 1:18 of God's wrath against "all ungodliness" of humanity. In the context of ch. 1, couched in the language of Jewish apologetics, this seems to be a castigation of gentile ungodliness, but 2:1–3:9 amply involves Jews in "all ungodliness," culminating in the catena of 3:10–18 with its conclusion that "there is no fear of God before their eyes." Further, Paul associates Abraham with ungodliness (4:5), and in 5:6 he says that Christ died for "us," identifying "us" with "the ungodly." This line from Isaiah, then, recalls what has been an important thread in the letter, namely, the gospel's power to deal with resistance to God. For Paul, it is not particular to the hardened "rest" of Israel to be ungodly. "We" were ungodly, a "we" that includes not only gentile but Jewish auditors and indeed Paul himself.

Verse 27a continues the direct citation of Isa 59:21, introducing the word "covenant" (*diathēkē*), which has appeared in the letter only at 9:4, in the list of God's gifts to Israel. Again in keeping with that passage, the anticipated covenant is one God creates in this singular act of taking away sins through the deliverer who is to come. That is to say, this covenant will come into being eschatologically through God's redemption.

Here the citation from Isa 59 breaks off, and v. 27 concludes with a phrase drawn from Isa 27:9 LXX: "when I take away their sins." In Isa 27:9, however,

71. Paul's only other reference to Zion is in 9:33, where he cites Isa 28:16: "I am placing in Zion a stone." In that instance the reference is geographical, but it simultaneously refers to the people who are being tripped.

"sin" is in the singular. Given Paul's routine use of "sin" in the singular and often as the power Sin (e.g., Rom 3:9; 5:12, 20; 6:6, 12, 22; 7:11, 13, 17, 20; Gal 2:17; 3:22), this choice is puzzling. Assuming that the change is his own, which seems likely (Wagner 2002, 283), the plural may simply reflect pressure from the plural of "godlessnesses" in v. 26. It could also have in view the particular acts of sin associated with "the rest" in their hardened state.

The cumulative effect of this citation is to locate the salvation of "all Israel" in the triumphant return of Jesus, the anticipated deliverer. He is himself a child of Israel ("from Zion," as also in 9:4 and 1:3). Interpreters occasionally draw attention to the relative paucity of reference to Jesus Christ in chs. 9–11, but that infrequency of direct reference can be misleading if it is assumed that these chapters bracket out a role for Christ. The "deliverer" of 11:26 is crucial, to say nothing of the role of Christ in 9:5; 10:4, 7.

[28–32] These penultimate verses amount to a terse summary of ch. 11, perhaps of the whole of chs. 9–11. Having announced the mystery of Israel's salvation, *all* Israel's salvation, Paul now tersely restates the mutuality between Jew and gentile. In this instance, however, the impulse of the text is less to confront gentile arrogance than to declare God's unchanging commitment to Israel in the sharpest of terms. Following each statement about the standing of "the rest" in relation to gentiles, Paul announces God's commitment to redemption.

First, vv. 28–29 reflect on the current state of "the rest" (the *loipoi* of 11:7) This is not Israel as a whole, which is not mentioned and would not be identified as "enemies." Verse 28 depicts them from contrasting angles, although it quickly becomes clear that the two angles are not of equal valence. The two halves of v. 28 are tight parallels, as this wooden rendering demonstrates:

With respect to the gospel	they are enemies	on account of you
With respect to the election	they are beloved	on account of the fathers

Understanding this potentially devastating claim that "they are enemies" requires returning to 5:10, where in the extended comparison between Christ and Adam, Paul characterizes "our" reconciliation to God as having taken place "when we were enemies." That assertion anticipates the *synkrisis* of Adam and Christ, which reveals the triumphant reign of Sin and Death brought to an end in the death and resurrection of Jesus (note 6:3–23). To be an "enemy" indicates being allied with the continuing influence of Sin and Death in the world.

Paul depicts "the rest" of Israel as God's enemies "on your account," in the sense already examined earlier in ch. 11: God has hardened "the rest" in a move that makes space for gentiles. This point is introduced in 11:11–12, it is again touched on in 11:15, it lies beneath the grafting analogy in vv. 17–24, it has been stated explicitly in v. 25, and it will be stated once more in vv. 30–31. This is simply the most shocking form of the statement, declaring that these are presently God's enemies "on your account," that is, for the sake of God's action on behalf of Phoebe's gentile auditors.

This shocking statement is not the final word, however, since the second half of v. 28 examines "the rest" from the point of view of "the election." Paul describes them as "beloved on account of the fathers." On its own, that phrase might suggest that the fathers somehow warranted God's love, but Paul's use of the language of calling in 4:17 regarding Isaac argues against this, since in that context an immediate connection is made between Isaac's birth and the resurrection of Jesus. Perhaps more to the point, 8:28–29 connects God's calling with God's Son. So as with "as far as the gospel," "as far as the election" has to do exclusively with God's action on behalf of human beings, in this case Israel. Just as in 5:10, however, these "enemies" are not permanently God's enemies.

In fact, these "enemies" are at the very same time also "beloved." The tight parallel to v. 28a is important. In the same way that "on your account" refers to God's action and says nothing about the merits of "you," "on account of the fathers" likewise has nothing to do with the merits of the fathers. It is not that "you" acted in a way that warranted God's use of "the rest" of Israel for salvation; neither did "the fathers" act in a way that warranted God's love of "the rest."

Verse 29 makes this point explicit: the reason they are beloved "on account of the fathers," according to v. 29 (note the *gar* or "since"), is that "the gifts and the calling of God" are unchangeable. To reiterate, what makes them beloved is God's gift and call. God may have played tricks on Israel (9:30–33), and God may be using Israel in ways that are unexpected, but God is nevertheless trustworthy—not predictable, but trustworthy (Gaventa 2007b, 149–60, 202–5). God's gifts and calling are not contingent on Israel's response.

"Enemies" and "beloved," the paired titles of v. 28, are grammatically equivalent, but they are not eschatologically identical. "Beloved enemies" is not a permanent position that renders "the rest" as tragic figures. To the contrary, the "beloved" are those to whom God's "gifts and calling" are unshakeable.

A second sequence of tight parallels appears in vv. 30–31, recasting the language of "enemies" and "beloved" into that of disobedience and mercy. The use of emphatic pronouns "you" and "they" reinforces the contrasts, and the contrast between "then" and the repeated "now" conveys the immediacy of these events. The following wooden representation depicts the parallels:

Just as	you	then	disobeyed God	
and	you	now	have received mercy	by their disobedience
thus also	they	now	disobeyed	by your mercy
that	they	now	might receive mercy[72]	

72. See Siegert 1985, 174–75 for a more detailed analysis of the rhetoric.

The dative phrases mechanically rendered above as "by their disobedience" and "by your mercy" are elliptical, although the context renders them relatively clear. The "disobedience" of the rest of Israel, a disobedience set in motion by God's hardening, is both specific and generative. As is clear from the reference to the gospel itself, this disobedience has to do with the Christ event; it is not a sweeping claim about Jewish disregard over time. Similarly, Paul anticipates that the mercy shown to gentile believers will usher in God's mercy to the whole of Israel. "The rest" of Israel are instrumental in the mercy shown to gentiles, and the gentiles are also instrumental in the mercy shown to "the rest" of Israel.

Paul concludes this long discussion of God in relation to Israel—and the gentiles—by enlarging this statement about shared disobedience and shared mercy in v. 32. The agency of God is explicit: it is God who confines all and God who shows mercy to all. In addition, no longer is the realm of action restricted to "you" gentiles and "those" unbelieving Jews. Now it is "all" whom God has confined in order to show mercy.

This terse, direct sentence pulls together the long argument of chs. 9–11. From the perspective of the twenty-first century, Paul's logic seems convoluted at worst, opportunistic at best. But that would be a significant misreading, since v. 32 is not simply the result of Paul's argument about Israel but an epitome of the entire letter. The long exposition of human rebellion against God culminates in 3:9 with the claim that "all" are under the power of Sin, both Jew and gentile, before turning in 3:21–31 to recall God's redemptive action in Jesus Christ for all, Jew and gentile alike. Romans 5:12–21 extends that argument by contending that Adam unleashed the rule of Sin and Death in the world, a devastation overcome with equal ferocity in the death and resurrection of Jesus. With the double "all" of v. 32, Paul invokes that narrative once again.[73]

To be sure, construing this "all" as "all people without qualification" appears to trip over earlier statements in the letter. The opening lines announce God's salvation "for everyone who believes," a stipulation repeated in 3:22 and extended in 10:9–13. Those apparent limitations may instead be acknowledgments of the peace (5:1), the new life (6:4) currently enjoyed by those already called to faith. In 11:25–32 the scenario is eschatological, anticipating the salvation of all when in fact every knee is bowed (Phil 2:10). Even so, at present Paul grieves, precisely because much of Israel is not caught up in the hope and joy of the gospel (9:1–2).[74]

---

73. To declare the universal horizon of Paul's language is not to endorse universalism as a doctrine, since any such claim goes beyond the text (esp. in view of vv. 33–36). To underscore the universal horizon of the gospel is simply to acknowledge that God's love cannot be constricted by human reflection.

74. Note Goodrich's wise objection to the vacuous notion that hope and grief cannot coexist (2016, 11).

[33–36] It is not unusual to refer to 11:25–32 as the conclusion of Rom 9–11, but that designation overlooks the actual ending of these chapters, which is not the eschatological salvation of all Israel or even the anticipation of divine mercy for all. Paul's comments on God and Israel (and the gentiles) culminate with this extended word of praise that follows immediately on v. 32 without introduction or transition.[75]

This "thundering chorus of scriptural voices" (Wagner 2002, 301) reflects a wide range of Jewish wisdom and apocalyptic texts (e.g., Job 5:9; Sir 1:1–10; 18:4–6; Wis 17:1; 2 Bar. 14.8–10; 1 En. 93.11–14; 1QH 15.26–32). Verse 34 quotes Isa 40:13 LXX, and v. 35 paraphrases Job 41:3. The language of v. 36 recalls Stoic sentiments (e.g., Marcus Aurelius, *Meditations* 4.23) as well as passages in Philo (*Cherubim* 125–27).

Scholars often categorize these lines as a hymn, citing its organization in three strophes (vv. 33, 34–35, and 36), the use of triads (riches and wisdom and knowledge, the three questions of vv. 34–35, and the three prepositional phrases in v. 36a), the repetition of pronouns for God, and the concluding doxology (Bornkamm 1969, 106–8; Deichgräber 1967, 61–64; Gloer 1984, 115–32). Some regard it as a synagogue hymn Paul thought appropriate to the context (E. Johnson 1989, 164–74), while others regard it as having been significantly modified (Jewett 713–14) or perhaps composed by Paul himself (Moo 759).

While the commonalities with other Jewish texts are indisputable, and while Paul may have known these lines or found them together elsewhere, the more compelling question is not where Paul found these lines but what they do here.[76] Pelagius saw in them Paul's praise for the mystery that had been revealed to him, yet Paul makes no claim here about his own knowledge. Among the texts adduced as similar to this passage is 1QH 15.26–32, which celebrates God's singular standing and judgment:

> Who is like you, Lord, among the gods?
> Who is like your truth?
> Who, before you, is just when judged?

Curiously, however, these lines are preceded by specific claims that the speaker has been the recipient of God's revelation:

> I give you thanks, Lord,
> because you have taught me your truth,

---

75. On the importance of doxology in Romans, see Gaventa 2008a, 2008b.
76. What Karl Barth wrote of v. 36 seems apt: "If Paul simply borrowed the formula, why is it that the theory of borrowing provides no more than an utterly superficial explanation of what he has actually done?" (423).

you have made me know your wonderful mysteries,
your kindness with sinful men.[77]

Although Rom 11:25 assumes that Paul has been the recipient of revelation, he does not lift that fact up for celebration. More to the point, there is a gap between the specific mystery to which Paul refers in v. 25 and the sweeping depiction in vv. 33–36. What has been revealed to Paul is vastly significant, but it is nonetheless a fragment of God's "abundance and wisdom and knowledge." As 8:19–22 indicates, even the salvation of all Israel is only a fragment of the cosmic horizon of God's redemption.

Numerous elements in these lines recall important elements in the letter. The question of abundance recalls the abundance gentiles ("the world") have received through the faltering of "the rest" of Israel, as well as God's own abundance of mercy in 9:23 (and see 2:4). The elaborate recognition of the vastness of God and the impossibility of human knowledge contrasts with the refusal of humans to acknowledge even the sliver of God's reality that is made known to them (1:18–32). The celebration of God's otherness also recalls 8:18–30, where Paul speaks to a present time of suffering fueled by the confident hope that God's intended future for creation is inexpressibly larger than humans can imagine or express. The "everything" or "all things" of 8:28 return here in the claim that "all things" are from, through, and for God (Tobin 2004, 378–79; and see 1 Cor 8:6).

Whether or not these verses were already a hymn before the writing of this letter, in this context they undoubtedly serve a hymnic function in their full-throated summons to the Roman auditors to join in celebration of the glory of God, both hidden and known. With the "Amen!" Phoebe may once again elicit the praise, the endorsement, the agreement of the Roman auditors to all that Paul has said about God's dealings with Israel and with the gentiles.

In keeping with commentating tradition, I have taken positions above on a number of questions, including the referent of all Israel and the eschatological implications for all people. But vv. 33–36 draw a veil across all of that, reminding all Paul's readers—both ancient and modern— that no one knows God's mind. It is one thing to announce that the action of God in Jesus Christ for the reclamation of humanity from Sin and Death has begun and that God's action in no way undermines God's commitment to the historic people Israel. It is another altogether to draw up a timetable or claim to know how and when God's triumph takes place. It would be odd indeed for Paul to assert that he has the "plan" in full, and odder still for Paul's interpreters to assert their control over the text.

77. The translation is that of Martínez (1996, 344–45). Tobin finds this passage to be an especially apt parallel to 11:33–36 (2004, 377–78).

What can be said with confidence is that Paul has now addressed the question left open at the end of ch. 8: Can humans accomplish what is impossible for anti-God powers? Can they separate themselves from the love of God in Christ Jesus? Specifically, does the "us" of that passage include all of Israel? In his extended response to the question, Paul not only affirms God's relationship to Israel, but he also once again recasts the question into a question about—or a confrontation with—gentile Christian presumption to know God's will.

Romans 12:1–15:13
Grasped by the Lordship of Christ

Having summoned the Roman congregations to cry out "Amen!" in response to the incomparable wisdom and work of God, Paul now takes up the lives of those human bodies in the one body, the body of Christ.[1] That statement requires qualification, of course, since Paul has already and repeatedly identified the auditors by their relationship to Christ. In 1:6 he addresses them as those Jesus Christ "called," in 5:1–11 as those reconciled to God by the death of Jesus Christ, and repeatedly in chs. 6–8 as belonging to Christ through death and new life. But beginning with 12:1 and continuing through 15:13 he examines specific aspects of—and challenges to—that shared life in Christ.

It is customary to describe this as the ethical section of the letter, a distinction that is of only limited helpfulness. Often the term "ethics" references specific issues, such as environmental ethics or sexual ethics or racial ethics. Alternatively, we may think of a systematic program of ethics, such as the virtue ethics of Aristotle or Kant's categorical imperative. Paul is engaged in neither of those forms of ethics, even if he does have particular issues in view and has convictions that drive his responses.[2] In addition, referring to this as the "ethical" section of the letter promotes the notion that Paul has dispensed with theology and now offers instruction based (or not) on that theology (conventionally termed the "indicative" versus the "imperative"). The situation is far more complex, far more radical. For Paul, assertions about God's action are assertions about God's claims on human life, human behavior. And every assertion about human action reflects convictions about God.[3]

Referring to this as the "ethical" section of the letter does have one advantage, however. It may invite readers to recognize the substantial gap between

---

1. The heading of this section was suggested by Käsemann's comment that justification is "manifested as the grasping of our lives by Christ's lordship" (323).

2. "Having convictions" misrepresents Paul to the extent that it conveys something highly rational. It is shorthand for the impact of the apocalyptic revelation of God's power in Jesus Christ. Put more concisely, for Paul, "ethics is not centered in knowing what is the good" or in conforming to a set of rules and regulations, "but in knowing who is our Lord" (Duff 1989, 283).

3. An excellent example appears in 1 Cor 11:17–34, where Paul locates the crises surrounding community meals as violations of Christ's table.

the vast mystery of God Paul lifts up in 11:33–36—to say nothing of the immensity of God's work in the bulk of chs. 1–11—and the puny expectations of humans, even those who have perceived God's mercies. However daunting Paul's call to "present your bodies" may be, it scarcely warrants notice alongside the God who justifies the ungodly even to the extent of handing over God's own Son (4:5, 25; 5:6; 8:32).[4] After all, the question of 11:35, "Who made a gift to [God]?" is rhetorical; no one could do such a thing.

Yet Paul assumes he is addressing an audience that, as a result of God's act in Jesus Christ, can both recognize and respond to an ethical demand (Martyn 2008, 180–82). Unlike humanity enslaved to Sin and Death, reduced to the role of weapons for Sin and incapable of doing what is right, this audience can be urged to genuine love (v. 9). Having been removed from Sin's lordship, placed under that of Christ, and having received the Spirit, the audience is free for extravagant service to God and to one another. The result of baptism is "newness, life" (6:4) that is lived out in community. It is driven by the Spirit, it lives out of the Spirit's gifts (8:11), it shares adoption with Christ himself (8:16–17, 28–30).

Recipients of such gifts can be called to service, as chs. 12–15 make clear. But recipients of such gifts simultaneously remain capable of wrongdoing. Whatever Paul means by naming "us" as God's children, conformed to the image of his Son (8:29), he does not mean that God's children are impervious to danger, error, wrongdoing. Had he entertained such notions, chs. 12–15 would have been superfluous. This new life, enlivened by the Spirit of God and shared in the body of Christ, remains susceptible to attack, as the end of Rom 8 recounts, with its list of agents and circumstances contending for power.

The introductory summons of 12:1 reflects the same urgency that characterizes the first eleven chapters of the letter. The "but now" (*nyni de*) of 3:21 and 6:22 reemerges in the warning about "this age" (12:2), to say nothing of the stark apocalyptic language of 13:8–14 and the reminder about final judgment in 14:10–11 (and perhaps also 12:19). Time has been gathered up, as Paul puts it in 1 Cor 7:39 (A. Brown 2018). In such a context of time made critical by God's action, there is no reason to hoard up gifts and every reason to spend liberally on one another (12:5, 10, 16; 13:8; 14:13, 19; 15:7, 14) and on all people (12:17–18; 13:7).

Following this summons, with its depiction of life as radical sacrifice, the remainder of the chapter promotes an understanding of that life in terms of shared generosity made possible by divine gift and characterized by love. Romans 13:1–7 addresses interactions with governing authorities, followed by a call to watchful love in 13:8–14. In 14:1–15:6, the most developed discussion

---

4. This seems to be the insight driving Karl Barth's lengthy reflection on the problem of ethics in his Romans commentary (424–29), on which see Gaventa 2023.

and perhaps the goal of the entire section, Paul addresses problems created by clashing understandings of food laws. The entire unit as well as the body of the letter culminates in 15:7–13 with its doxological summation.

The issues addressed in this portion of the letter are diverse. Paul offers no comprehensive treatment of topics. But neither are the topics addressed simply random. By comparison with similar sections of 1 Thessalonians and 1 Corinthians, for example, there is no reference to idolatry and scant attention to sexual misconduct.[5] The lengthy discussion of food practices in ch. 14 suggests that this is a particularly pressing problem, and numerous points in ch. 12 appear to anticipate that discussion.

12:1–8 Present Your Bodies

With 12:1–2 Paul sets the stage for all that follows through 15:13 by characterizing the new life of believers as given over to God. Verses 3–8 draw on the notion of the one body of Christ to discourage arrogance and to depict the abundant use of the gifts received by the community.

Stylistically, terse statements dominate the chapter, such as "Bless those who harass you," and "Rejoice with those who rejoice, weep with those who weep." To be sure, vv. 3–8 constitute a single lengthy sentence, but that sentence is marked by the staccato effect of short phrases piled on top of one another. (Similarly, the depiction of authentic love in vv. 9–13 consists of a series of short phrases.) This literary feature may well reflect the fact that much of the content is traditional, as some statements have close parallels in other Pauline letters (S. Kim 2011, and see below). Individual admonitions would have been familiar to those acquainted with the Jesus tradition, Stoic moral philosophy, or Jewish wisdom literature (W. Wilson 1991, especially 92–148). The use of numerous terse statements could also have had an impact on Phoebe's auditors in Rome. Following on Rom 9–11, with its twists and turns of logic and its convoluted sentences, the concise language of ch. 12 may have been received as a refreshing change.

Another feature in this passage may also reflect the situation at Rome, namely, the multiple appeals to authority. Foremost is the authority of God (12:1), following which Paul invokes his own authority as the recipient of apostolic grace (v. 3), and he ends the chapter with an invocation of Scripture that "the Lord speaks" (v. 19). These appeals to authority usher in instructions that

---

5. Romans 13:13 does refer to sexual misconduct, but only briefly. Of course, Paul has introduced same-sex relations in 1:26–27 as evidence of the "handed-over" state of humanity, but he offers no instruction about it either there or here. One of the category mistakes interpreters make regarding that passage is to treat it as ethical instruction instead of as a narrative of human rebellion and captivity.

are frequently more evocative than prescriptive, however, sketching the character of gifted life in the one body of Christ rather than issuing specific commands such as are found in 1 Thess 4–5. This feature of Romans may reflect Paul's tentative situation as he addresses groups largely unknown to him, but it is also consistent with the language of 12:2, which attributes to the Romans the capacity to discern God's will, a capacity that contrasts sharply with the incapacity on evidence in chs. 1–8 (see above on 1:18–32; 3:25; 7:14–25; 8:7).

12:1 So I urge you by God's mercies, brothers and sisters, to present your bodies as a sacrifice that is living, holy, and pleasing to God.[a] That is your reasonable[b] service. 2 And do not be shaped by this age, but be transformed by the renewal of the mind so that you discern God's will for you,[c] the good and pleasing and fully mature.[d]

3 For by the grace given me, I say to everyone among you not to think bloated thoughts beyond what is right to think but to think sober thoughts, as God has assigned to each a measure, namely, faith.[e] 4 For as we have many parts in one body but all the parts do not have the same function, 5 in this same way the many of us are one body in Christ, meaning that we are each parts of one another,[f] 6 having differing gifts[g] according to the grace given us—if prophecy as it corresponds to faith,[h] 7 if service in service,[i] if the teacher in instruction, 8 if the comforter in comfort,[j] the giver in sincerity, the leader in eagerness, the compassionate in gladness.[k]

a. English translations often treat this as a "living sacrifice" that is also holy and pleasing (e.g., KJV, NRSVue, NIV), but nothing in the Greek warrants doing so, as all three modifiers stand together in juxtaposition to "sacrifice" (Cranfield 2:600; Wolter 2:251).

b. *Logikos* is often translated "spiritual" (RSV, NRSV, NASB), a word that limits the range of an act that is all-encompassing. Following a suggestion of Betz, Jewett takes it as worship that "conforms to reason" (730), which appears to make worship subservient to human rationality (an understanding in sharp conflict with Paul's language in 1 Cor 1:20–21). Instead, this is "reasonable" service (KJV, NRSVue) in the sense that it conforms to the expectations established by God's mercies (cf. Epictetus, *Diatr.* 1.16.19–21; what is fitting or rational is that the human praises God).

c. "For you" is supplied to clarify that "God's will" refers to the divine will for this community, as in 1 Thess 4:3; 5:18, 2 Cor 8:5; and numerous references to God's will related to apostolic service (Rom 1:10; 15:32; 1 Cor 1:1; 2 Cor 1:1). The modifiers "good and pleasing and fully mature" are consistent with that understanding.

d. "Fully mature" is preferable to the conventional translation of *teleios* as "perfect" (e.g., KJV, NIV, NASB), since Paul consistently employs *teleios* to refer to maturity in faith (1 Cor 2:6; 13:10; 14:20; Phil 3:15).

e. *Metron pisteōs* is construed here as a genitive of apposition, following Cranfield 2:613–16 and Cranfield 1962. The letter displays a fondness for this construction, as in "a sign—circumcision" in 4:11 (and see also 5:18 and 6:4). Taking the phrase as "a measure of faith" in the sense of a quantity or portion of faith wrongly construes it as an introduction to v. 4, instead of as a modifier of the infinitive clause preceding it (so Dunson 2011, 36).

f. *Melē* is often translated "members," which in English is a somewhat dated term for body parts that has the advantage of connoting the figurative "membership." Yet *melos* refers to parts of the human body (BDAG s.v.), as in the "limbs" of 6:13, 19; 7:5, 23, and the more graphic translation "parts" does better justice to Paul's imagery.

g. Verses 6–8 continue the sentence begun at v. 4, because *echontes* ("having") is a nominative participle modifying the *esmen* ("we are") of v. 5. The gifts that follow describe the "we" of the body in Christ (see Berding 2006).

h. Lit., "according to the analogy of faith."

i. The translation retains the awkward "service" of the Greek rather than conforming this abstract noun to the series of participles that follows ("the one teaching" etc.). The pressure to tidy up the list is evidenced already in a few manuscripts that substitute "the one serving" for "service."

j. *Parakaleō* and *paraklēsis* could equally well be translated "exhort" and "exhortation," but since those connotations are already present in "prophecy" and "teaching," the role of comfort seems preferable here.

k. Although sometimes treated as imperatives (KJV, NIV), these brief phrases are all dependent on the indicative statements of vv. 5–6 describing the parts of the body of Christ and their mutual belonging (as in NRSVue).

[1–2] The opening words, "So I urge you by God's mercies, brothers and sisters," signal not simply the transition to but also the significance of Paul's admonitions. The initial word, *parakalō* (urge, appeal, comfort), appears here for the first time in Romans, although later Paul will use it when he appeals to the Romans for their prayers in support of his fraught journey to Jerusalem (15:30) and again in 16:17 as he warns about the dangers of false teaching (and see, e.g., 1 Cor 1:10; 4:6; 2 Cor 6:1; 1 Thess 4:1). Here, as in those later instances, the tone is one of urgency.

The *oun* ("so" or "therefore") locates what follows in relationship to what has preceded, but how far back does *oun* extend? For someone who has just read of God's final mercy for all (*eleeō*; 11:32) and who may recall the earlier citation of Exod 33:19 regarding divine mercy and hardening (9:14–18), the reference to "mercies" (*oiktirmos*) leaps off the page. This association could incline toward a narrow view of the connection (i.e., to construing the *oun* as referring only to chs. 9–11), given that "mercy" language does not appear earlier in the letter. However, in what follows there are several connections—both verbal and substantive—with earlier portions of the letter, extending all the way back to ch. 1. More to the point, it would be shortsighted to imagine that Paul's references to "mercies" in chs. 9–11 are unrelated to the gracious acts of God earlier in the letter.

Through God's comprehensive mercies, then, Paul urges the Romans "to present your bodies," recalling his earlier admonition in 6:13:

And do not present your limbs to Sin any more as weapons of wrongdoing, but present yourselves to God as people once dead and now living, and present your limbs to God as weapons of righteousness.

In ch. 6 the context is the conflict between God and anti-God powers, most particularly Sin and Death. By virtue of his resurrection, Christ himself is no longer subject to these powers and has brought about human redemption and new life (6:6–11). The presentation of "limbs," of "yourselves," puts the addressees at God's disposal in this ongoing conflict (cf. 1 Macc 1:35; Prov 22:29; Dan 7:10).

The admonition here in 12:1 differs, but it is not unrelated to that of ch. 6. Now the context is that of worship, as Paul urges the presentation of "your bodies" as a sacrifice.[6] The combination of "present" and "sacrifice" renders the liturgical context unmistakable (as in Diodorus Siculus, *Libr.* 3.72.1; Lucian, *Sacr.* 13; Josephus, *J.W.* 2.89; BDAG, s.v. *paristēmi*). Paul urges the Romans to offer up their "bodies" (*sōmata*), which for him connotes the entire person (see above on 1:24; 6:6). Significantly, these bodies are no longer ruled by Sin and Death (as in 6:6, 12; 7:24; 8:10); to the contrary, they are made holy in the sacrifice (and see 8:30).

This notion of presenting the self sacrificially, particularly when accompanied by the description "living," suggests to some that Paul intends a polemic against Jewish sacrificial practice: rather than offering dead animals, Paul is urging the sacrifice of living humans (e.g., Dunn 2:710; Edwards 282). Here the long history of Christian anti-Judaism lingers. To begin with, Paul does not elsewhere contrast sacrifice "in Christ" with other sacrifices; nor does he anywhere else polemicize against temple practice. Indeed, Luke's account of Paul's work depicts him carrying out sacrifice in Jerusalem (Acts 21:26). In addition, sacrifice was widely practiced in Mediterranean religions; if Paul's aim were to polemicize here (which seems unlikely and unsuitable to the context), his polemic might as easily be directed to non-Jewish customs, given the distance between his Roman audience and the Jerusalem temple.

Instead of polemicizing against Jewish sacrificial practice, Paul is radicalizing that central act. Three modifiers follow on "sacrifice": "living," "holy," "pleasing to God." Significantly, these bodies are no longer ruled by Sin and Death (as in 6:6, 12; 7:24; 8:10); instead, they are living, recalling the claims of 6:1–5, 9–11. They are also holy, a claim that has already been made (1:7; 6:19, 22), but one that acquires a deeper resonance here in the context of sacrificial language. Sacrifices belong to God; they are rendered holy by virtue of being offered up (as in Lev 19:8; 27:9–10; Philo, *Spec. Laws* 1.221–22). To identify

---

6. In an apparent allusion to 6:13, Chrysostom comments on 12:1 that *paristēmi* is the word used for the supplying of warhorses: "And thou too hast presented thy members for the war against the devil, and for that dread battle-array" (*NPNF*[1] 11.497).

this sacrifice as "pleasing to God" further confirms its rightness, as when Paul identifies the gifts of the Philippians in support of his work as a sacrifice that is "pleasing to God" (Phil 4:18; and see 2 Cor 2:14; T. Levi 3.6).

All these modifiers apply to the sacrifice itself, which consists of "your bodies." Since "body" refers to the whole person, that person necessarily includes the physical human. It is the body that is presented, not only the mind or the spirit. (This point stands counter to the popular misconception that Paul has disdain for the human body; see above on 6:6.) This is what constitutes "reasonable," or fitting, service. Here service to God that is appropriate or fitting is the handing over of the whole self. This all-encompassing act of worship contrasts sharply with the withholding of worship in 1:18–32, to say nothing of the enslavement of the human in 6:12–14. When Sin rules in the body, only Sin can be pleased.

Following directly on the doxology of 11:33–36, with its celebration of the capaciousness of God's wisdom and God's ways, the language of sacrifice continues this notion of God's otherness, in terms of God's holiness. The sacrificial animal—in this case the human—becomes God's own, becomes holy (as in Lev 19:8; 27:9–10; and see Philo, *Spec. Laws* 1.221). The body once ruled by death (6:12; 8:11) becomes holy in this act.[7]

Verse 2 consists of two imperatives, parallel in form, followed by a purpose clause:

Do not be shaped   by this age
but be transformed   by the renewal of your mind

English translations sometimes suggest that there is a wordplay between the two verbs (using "conformed" and "transformed," as in KJV, NASB, NIV, NRSV), but there is not. Yet in substance there is a relationship in that each word, *syschēmatizō* and *metamorphoō*, has to do with molding or forming (BDAG s.v.)

The first imperative takes the negative: do not be shaped by this age. Most of Paul's references to "this age" appear in the Corinthian correspondence (1 Cor 1:20; 2:6–8; 3:18; 2 Cor 4:4; and see Gal 1:4), where the phrase seems to be a comprehensive term for those attitudes and values that are merely human in contrast to God's own way of seeing and valuing. "This age" has its own rulers or gods who were at work in the crucifixion of Jesus (1 Cor 2:8) and who create unbelief instead of faith (2 Cor 4:4). Along with the admonitions in Rom 6:12–14, the implication of this admonition is that those who have been

---

7. Donald Juel observes that the baptism of Jesus and the rending of the temple veil in Mark both disrupt the status quo in that God no longer remains at a safe distance but intrudes into the human sphere (1994, 34–36). In this different context, Paul may reflect a similar notion, that the demarcation of sacred from profane has been breached.

redeemed by God's action in Jesus Christ, who have been freed for new life, nonetheless remain susceptible to the pull of "this age." The agents identified in 8:38–39 are still at work, even if their failure is both begun in the resurrection of Jesus and confirmed by the power of God's Spirit.[8]

The second admonition states things positively: "Be transformed by the renewal of the mind." A strict parallel between the two imperatives would have produced "be transformed by the new age" or "the age to come." Although Paul never uses that phrase (J. Davies 2021), his letters nonetheless evince an expectation of Jesus's triumphant return and resurrected life for humanity, suggesting a new age (most explicitly in 1 Thess 4:13–18; 1 Cor 15). The curious absence of this particular phrase may stem from a concern to avoid the triumphalist thinking on display in Corinth (see especially 1 Cor 4:6–8), the community from which he writes. People who think they have already arrived at "the age to come" can be dangerous, as Paul has experienced.

What Paul urges instead is "the renewal of the mind." In 1:28, as part of the apocalypse of God's wrath, Paul declared that God had "handed over" rebellious humanity to an "unsuitable way of thinking," an act that produced a relentless list of misdeeds on the part of humanity. The mind of the "I" in 7:23, enslaved to Sin, is able to perceive what is right but not able to complete it. Now, however, the mind has been renewed, having been liberated from its enslavement. This is a reference, then, to the newness of life brought about through baptism (6:4).

Renewal of the mind is not an end in itself, however; it is not mere self-improvement but has as its goal "that you discern God's will." As with renewal of the mind, this comment directly reverses the account of human captivity Paul sets out in the early chapters of the letter, where the human refusal to "approve" God (*dokimazō*) triggers the handing over of humanity. In addition, in 2:17 the one who calls herself a Jew is taunted with accusations of wrongly believing that she knows God's will and is able to examine (*dokimazō*) what is important based on the law.

Now, by means of God's mercies in the Christ event and being re-formed by renewal of the mind, "you" are able to discern God's will, which Paul goes on to identify as "the good and pleasing and fully mature." No abstraction, "God's will" refers to what God wants for these communities, or so parallel references to God's will suggest (see especially 1 Thess 4:3; 5:18; and also, e.g., Rom 1:10; 15:32). Both "the good" and "the pleasing" figure importantly in the instructions that follow, although this admonition prepares particularly well for ch. 14, where the one who is in Christ is "pleasing to God" (*euarestos*) and "approved by" (*dokimos*) human beings (v. 18).

---

8. "Since the whole world lies in the power of the evil one, we must put off all that is of man, if we would truly put on Christ" (Calvin 265).

[3] A sacrificed person and a renewed mindset could be invoked to address any number of specific problems or issues, but Paul quickly focuses on one in particular, namely, the problem of arrogance. He then takes up the body of Christ image, which indicates both *that* there is interrelationship *and* that all relationship in the community is through Christ. He will return again to the possibility of bloated self-regard in v. 16. All of this suggests, as noted earlier, that although many individual statements in this chapter have counterparts elsewhere, Paul's introduction of them prepares specifically for the major problem he will address in ch. 14.

Verse 3 opens with a tight formal parallel to v. 1:

| v. 1 | I urge you | by the mercies of God | to present |
| v. 3 | I say to . . . you | by the grace given me | not to think |

As he shifts to specific manifestations of the renewed mindset, the life given over to God, Paul again begins with a formal declaration, in this case "I say to you" rather than "I urge you." Instead of "by the mercies of God," appeal is made "by the grace given me." And the "grace given me" invokes Paul's vocation, which, as in 15:15–21, is a solemn responsibility to the gospel. Far from drawing attention to his own speech (there is no emphatic pronoun *egō* here), this phrase directs the responsibility for Paul's speech elsewhere, to the same God whose mercies he invoked in v. 1 and whose scriptural voice he will cite in v. 19.

In place of the simple "you" of v. 1, Paul's speech is addressed to "everyone among you," a pleonastic expression signaling the importance of what follows. More than rhetorical emphasis is at stake. The plural verbs and pronouns of vv. 1–2 reflect a corporate notion of worship and transformation (see especially Jewett 727), but the hubris of individuals can disrupt community life. Paul's response to the Corinthian community, in which a man has a sexual relationship with his father's wife, confirms that he is very much aware of this problem ("A little leaven leavens the entire lump," 1 Cor 5:6).

A series of four infinitives supply what it is that Paul is "saying" to them. A literalizing translation demonstrates the wordplay:

Not *to think beyond* what is necessary *to think*
but *to think* in order *to think soberly*.

Phronein ("to think") is used twice, accompanied by *hyperphronein* ("to think in a bloated way," "to be arrogant") and *sōphronein* ("to think in a sober or sensible way"). A simple "think in a sober way" would have sufficed, and the elaboration provides a clue that this particular concern is at the forefront in Paul's consideration. The possibility (or reality) of gentile arrogance has already come to expression in ch. 11, and the inappropriate valuation of one's own thinking will return in ch. 14.[9]

The conclusion to v. 3 recasts this language about thinking appropriately: the thought appropriate for each person has to do with the "measure" God has granted, namely, faith. This statement bookends the beginning of the verse; as Paul himself speaks through God's gift, in this case a reference to his own vocation, each person thinks as God has assigned. Such an expression could lend itself to the notion of greater and lesser conviction handed out by God (as in, e.g., R. Longenecker 926), but that notion scarcely fits the context, which addresses the more general question of appropriate thought, in anticipation of the discussion of *charismata* in vv. 4b–8.[10]

The impact of this admonition about hubris comes into view in vv. 4–5. The health of the whole community is at stake when individuals ("everyone among you" and "each" in v. 3) think in a way that is bloated. Verses 4–5 return to an analogy Paul used at greater length in 1 Cor 12, in which the members of the community are understood as the parts of a single body. This metaphor would likely have been familiar to Paul's addressees, as it appears in a wide variety of texts, often applied to the *polis* as a single body in relation to its parts. For example, Epictetus advises individuals of the *polis* not to act like "a detached unit, but to act like the foot or the hand, which . . . would never exercise choice or desire in any other way but by reference to the whole" (*Diatr.* 2.10.4; LCL). Philo writes of the whole *ethnos* as "a single body" (*Spec. Laws* 3.131), and Josephus describes the rebels at Masada infecting the whole nation, as "in the body when inflammation attacks" and "all the members catch the infection" (*J.W.* 4.406).[11]

These few illustrations demonstrate that the topos was highly flexible in its application, and Paul himself employs it differently here than in 1 Corinthians. The pressing concern for unity in 1 Cor 12 prompts a lengthy discourse, in which some body parts lament their insignificance, while others boast of their importance. In Rom 12, however, the analogy appears only briefly, largely by

9. I have often wished that Paul had been more evenhanded on this point, admonishing also those who think too little of their own judgments (as perhaps he does in 1 Thess 5:14). The one-sidedness of the instruction further suggests its importance in Paul's assessment of the situation in Roman congregations.

10. Goodrich (2012) contends that *pistis* here is the "trusteeship" assigned each person, further emphasizing the connection between v. 3 and the discussion of *charismata* that follows in vv. 6–8, but that would mark a dramatic shift in Paul's use of *pistis* in this letter. In addition, had Paul wanted to signal the assignment of specific roles here, he might have used *oikonomia* or *oikonomos* (so Porter and Ong 2013, 102). To be sure, in 2 Cor 10:13 Paul employs *merizō* and *metron* in reference to apostolic labor, but without *pistis* and in the clear context of a boundary dispute with other Christian teachers.

11. Further examples, explication, and bibliography appear in Mitchell 1992, 157–64; Wolter 2:267.

way of affirming the diversity of functions within the singular body, which is itself "in Christ."

[4–8] Verses 4 and 5 open with straightforward parallel statements about a body and its parts, both of which closely resemble statements in 1 Cor 12:

> v. 4a   As we have many parts in one body (cf. 1 Cor 12:12)
> v. 5a   In this same way the many of us are one body in Christ (cf. 1 Cor 12:20)

The consequences of this oneness of the body's parts come to expression in vv. 4b and 5b:

> v. 4b   but all the parts do not have the same function
> v. 5b   meaning that we are each parts one of another

As will shortly become clear in vv. 6–8, the "one body in Christ" is the locus of a variety of gifts, each of which serves others in the body. If Paul does not linger over the notion of the unity of the members of the body as he does in 1 Cor 12:13–27, he nonetheless addresses a single body, while simultaneously addressing each of its parts.[12] And the parts are not all the same; there is no pressure toward uniformity or sameness, not even in the notion of shared body parts (v. 5b). Indeed, vv. 6–8 will celebrate and encourage those differences (and see 1 Pet 4:10–11).

Grammatically, v. 6 extends v. 5, since the participle "having" modifies the "we" of v. 5, and that extension continues through v. 8, "having differing gifts according to the grace given us." The affirmation of difference in gifts reinforces the "many" in vv. 4–5. In addition, there is "one body in Christ," which means there is one source of the gifts. Paul names it as "grace" or "gift" (*charis*), just as Paul's own work results from "grace," locating both inside the gift of the gospel itself (e.g., 3:24; 5:2; and especially 5:15–16; 6:23; 11:29).

When Paul takes up specific gifts in vv. 6b–8, English translations sometimes shift toward the imperative:

NIV   We have different gifts, according to the grace given to each of us. If your gift is prophesying, then prophesy in accordance with your faith.

CEB   We have different gifts that are consistent with God's grace that has been given to us. If your gift is prophecy, *you should prophesy* in proportion to your faith.

Nothing in the Greek calls for that shift, however, since these are not the imperatives (or hortatory subjunctives) they are often represented to be. Instead, they

---

12. "Paul speaks emphatically here not simply to the community as a corporate entity, but to each member of the Roman congregations" (Eastman 2014, 120).

are descriptions of the gifts that characterize the body of Christ, and Paul lifts them up to elicit, to create, to instruct, rather than merely to admonish.

This suggestion finds reinforcement in the presentation of the gifts, the first four of which are introduced by *eite* ("if" or "whether"):

> if prophecy
> if service
> if the one teaching
> if the one comforting

The next three retain the phrasing (definite article plus participle) of "the one teaching" and "the comforter," but the *eite* drops out, so that anyone reading the letter aloud might gather speed toward the end of the list:

> the one sharing
> the one ruling
> the one showing mercy

The particular gifts Paul invokes are unsurprising, representing an array of community needs. The first, prophecy, is qualified by an unusual expression, rendered more literally as "according to the analogy of faith." Although *analogia*, which appears nowhere else in the NT, is frequently understood as "in proportion" to the individual's faith (Sanday and Headlam 356–57; Dunn 2:727–28; Jewett 747; BDAG s.v.), in that case Paul might easily have written "with faith," making this phrase consistent with the several that follow (in/with service, teaching, etc.). A stronger lexical option is "in agreement with" or "in correspondence to" (LSJ s.v.; Hultgren 449), implying that prophecy is responsible insofar as it corresponds to "faith," in this sense to the gospel itself. This rendering brings the phrase closer to the "measure, namely, faith," in v. 3. Further, it coheres with Paul's comments about prophecy elsewhere. In 1 Thess 5:20–21 he warns against rejecting prophecy, only to add "but test everything." Further, the lengthy discussion of prophecy and other gifts in 1 Cor 14 elevates prophecy precisely because of its capacity to upbuild the community (14:5, 29–33). "As it corresponds to faith" joins those other texts, which recognize both the contribution of prophecy and the need to subject it to scrutiny.

The remainder of this list reflects preoccupations on evidence elsewhere in Paul's letters. Paul has already characterized his own work as *diakonia* ("service") in 11:13, and he will identify both Christ and Phoebe with the term *diakonos* (15:8; 16:1). Reference to teaching occurs with less frequency, although Paul refers to his own teaching role in 1 Cor 4:17. He urges the Thessalonians to "comfort" one another in the face of grief (1 Thess 4:18; 5:11). Romans opens with Paul's desire to "share" with the addressees and, by implication, to receive from them as well (1:11; and see 1 Thess 2:8). He refers to leaders only here and in 1 Thess 5:12, where the concern is for how they are treated by those in their care. Elsewhere in Paul's letters mercy is associated entirely with God (e.g., Rom 9:15, 18; 11:30; Phil 2:27), although importantly human mercy is among the beatitudes in Matt 5:7.

Early in his commentary on Rom 12, Karl Barth writes that Christian exhortation can never be reduced to demand, since "it is the demand that grace should come into its own" (428). That language elegantly epitomizes these opening lines, where Paul anticipates with some specificity how God's mercies and God's gifts overflow into human lives. He is nonetheless well aware that grace does not always manifest itself in human behavior, as will become clear in the verses that follow.

12:9–21 Love in Christ's Body

Instructions about life in the one body of Christ continue, although a shift occurs at v. 9. Paul has been discussing the generous exercise of diverse gifts by individuals who together make up the one body (prophecy, teaching, etc.), but in v. 9 he takes up those characteristics and practices that should mark the whole of the community (rejoicing, praying, etc.). Introducing the section is the overarching concern with love: "Let love be authentic." That general guideline is interpreted by the warning about shunning evil and holding on to good (v. 9b), and restatement of this concern with good and evil marks the end of the section (v. 21; and see 13:3–4).

Numerous parallels to individual statements appear in a wide array of sources, ranging from Paul's own letters to other early Christian texts, Jewish wisdom texts, and philosophical writings.[13] In other words, much here resembles conventional ethical instruction. Even that way of putting the matter is misleading, as if Paul had a library of teachings before him and randomly pulled some from one shelf and some from another. Paul's selection and presentation reflect his own concerns, including those of dealing with enemies (whether inside or outside the community) and hubris (as already noted in 11:13–24; 12:3).

English translations generally obscure the fact that only a few standard imperatives appear in this passage (in vv. 14, 16b, 19–21); instead, Paul moves back and forth from participles to imperatives. Since the imperatives provide the framework around which the remainder of the discourse is organized, the translation locates paragraph shifts accordingly (see translation notes b and i on vv. 9 and 16 and the discussion below for specifics).

---

13. Those interested in exploring parallel texts will find the commentaries of Jewett (758–79) and Wolter (2:276–305) especially helpful, in addition to Walter Wilson's important study (1991). The focus of this commentary remains on the shape and rationale for Paul's own discourse, rather than on his possible sources, which are extensively discussed elsewhere.

12:9 Let love be authentic.[a] For us that means shunning what is evil but holding on to what is good,[b] 10 loving one another with familial love,[c] honoring one another more than ourselves,[d] 11 not withholding eagerness, being fired up in the Spirit,[e] serving the Lord,[f] 12 rejoicing in hope, enduring in suffering, persisting in prayer, 13 sharing in the needs of the saints, pursuing hospitality to the stranger.

14 Bless those who harass[g] you. Bless and do not curse. 15 Rejoice with those who rejoice, weep with those who weep.[h]

16 That means[i] thinking together with one another, not thinking presumptuously but being associated with the marginal.[j] Do not rely on your own thinking.

17 It also means not repaying anyone evil with evil, but attending to what is good before all people, 18 and—so far as it is possible on your side—being at peace with all people, 19 not enacting judgment yourselves, beloved, but yield to the wrath of God.[k] As it is written, "Judgment belongs to me. I will repay," the Lord says. 20 "But if your enemy is hungry, feed him; if she is thirsty, give her drink. For when you do this, you heap coals of fire on their heads." 21 Do not be conquered by evil, but conquer evil with good.

a. The initial statement has no verb, consisting only of *agapē* and *anypokritos* (lit., "love authentic"), so in another setting it might be rendered as a simple declaration: "Love is authentic." What follows in vv. 10–21 is more than descriptive, however, especially when the imperative verbs of vv. 14, 16, 19–21 are taken into account. *Anypokritos* is frequently rendered "sincere" (NIV, CEV) or "genuine" (RSV, NRSVue, ESV), words that connote the attitude or affect of the one loving. "Authentic" better fits the context, which incorporates actions as well as attitudes.

b. A series of participial clauses follows (interrupted by the adjective *oknēroi* in v. 11a), again without a finite verb, and all of these clauses appear in nominative plural. These are usually translated as simple commands (e.g., KJV, NIV, NASB, NRSVue). Some grammars identify them as imperatival participles (Wallace 1996, 650), while others are more guarded (Turner 1976, 4:89; BDF §468.2). The origin and existence of imperatival participles is much disputed; for a review of the discussion, see Porter 1989, 270–77. Moulton (1908, 1:17–83) locates it among other regular substitutes for the imperative that developed in Greek over time, but Daube argues for Semitic origins (1964; see also W. Davies 1980, 130–33; and esp. Kanjuparambil 1983). Yet both the variety of formulations within this section and the possible relationships among them are obscured when they are rendered as simple commands. For that reason, I have retained the participial connotation. Since in context the plural refers to the "we" of v. 5 (or possibly the "you" of the audience), I have supplied "for us" to reflect that connection with the larger argument. Jewett translates similarly, although his discussion on this particular point is a bit indecisive (755, 759–90).

c. Lit., "with brotherly love."

d. The verb *proēgeomai* most literally refers to preceding or leading (BDAG s.v.), so the translation of Cranfield reads, "Prefer one another in honour" (2:632–33).

e. As often elsewhere, the Greek "spirit" here could be either the individual's spirit (as in NRSV and NIV) or the Spirit of God (as in Jewett 755; Moo 788). Given Paul's emphasis on the Spirit's empowerment elsewhere (5:5; 8:23; 14:17; 15:13), the latter is preferable, as also in Acts 18:25 (Gaventa 2003, 264).

f. A few early manuscripts (D*·c F G) read "the time" (*kairō*) rather than "the Lord" (*kyriō*), almost certainly a scribal error. (Metzger 1971, 528, and Jewett 755 offer differing but plausible explanations.)

g. In view of the general character of the statement, "harass" seems preferable to the more typical "persecute," which connotes official action in a way that "harass" may not. Although the narrative of Acts sometimes assumes the existence of what might be called official persecution, as when Paul receives authorization from authorities in Jerusalem to pursue Christians in Antioch (9:2), and Paul's letters also provide some indications of official action (2 Cor 11:23–25), it is not clear that Paul has in view here authorized actions.

h. Both "rejoice" and "weep" are infinitive in form, used here imperatively (as also in Phil 3:16; Luke 9:3; see BDF §389; Smyth 1956, §2013).

i. Another series of participles begins here, prompting the inclusion of "that means" to signal the shift. The slight disjuncture created by "that means" reflects the abruptness in the text. See below on v. 9 for further discussion.

j. *Tapeinos,* "low," can refer either to thoughts that are low or humble (as in Matt 11:29; 2 Cor 10:1), or to people who occupy lowly positions (as in Luke 1:52; Jas 4:6). A contrast between presumptuous and humble thought cannot be ruled out, but in a passage with some similarities to this one, Paul urges concern for those who occupy marginal places in the community (1 Thess 5:14). Further, a contrast between arrogance and treatment of the lowly may reflect the influence of Prov 3:34 LXX (as in Jas 4:6; 1 Pet 4:5).

k. "Of God" does not appear in the Greek, but the definite article is anaphoric (Moulton 1908, 3:173), suggesting that this particular wrath is to be identified with God's wrath earlier in the letter (esp. 1:18; 3:5; 9:22). Further, the citation that follows explicitly connects judgment with God.

[9–13] The call for authentic love both introduces the section and characterizes the behaviors that follow as manifestations of love. Earlier Paul has claimed that "God's love [for us] has been poured out into our hearts through the Holy Spirit that has been given to us" (5:5), strongly suggesting the origin of this authentic love in the Spirit (as in Gal 5:22), to say nothing of God's loving act in the sending of the Son (and see 5:8; 8:35, 39).[14] Elsewhere Paul frequently associates love with the life of the community (as in 13:8–10; 14:15; Gal 5:13; and especially 1 Cor 13:1–14:1). What this love looks like comes into view in the lines that follow.

---

14. Bertschmann (2014, 156) rightly comments that love is "as much or more an empowering divine presence than a single virtue."

The use of participles here and in vv. 16–19 warrants further reflection. Setting aside the question of antecedents for using the participle as an imperative (see translation note b on v. 9), it is noteworthy that Paul himself does not use participles in similar treatments in 1 Thess 5:12–22 or Gal 5:13–6:10.[15] Some have attributed the participles to Paul's use of an earlier source (Daube, Talbert), but even if he is drawing on a source, he is quite capable of modifying it, reformulating those participles as imperatives. It seems more likely that he employs these participles diplomatically, preferring the less direct mode of exhortation in this unusual epistolary situation in which he writes to a number of Christian groups, none of which is of his own founding. In addition, the brevity of the phrases, the absence of finite verbs, and the use of asyndeton may generate interest among auditors.[16]

That is not to deny or diminish the ethical direction of the passage, particularly in light of its many parallels with contemporaneous ethical instruction. The declaration "This is who we are" functions to invite, to solicit, even to create identification and conformity.[17] Such a strategy is at work already in Rom 6, especially in the description of the auditors as "dead" to Sin and "living" in God through Jesus Christ. A similar strategy may be seen at 8:17, which aims to strengthen the auditors by declaring their identity in relationship to God and Christ (and see 8:28–30). There is more than one way to elicit behavior.[18]

The paired participles that form the second part of v. 9 (shunning what is evil, holding on to what is good) interpret the notion of authentic love in an elemental form, the distinction between good and evil (see Ps 97:10; Amos 5:14–15). Verse 21 will replay the contrast in the form of a direct admonition: "Do not be conquered by evil, but conquer evil with good" (and see also 12:17; 13:3–4). Although it may be assumed that this distinction is available to common sense (Bertschmann 2014, 157), Paul has already identified "the good" with God's will, something that is available to those who have been transformed (12:2). More to the point, the depiction of humanity having been handed over to an

---

15. Talbert 1969, 84. W. Wilson (1991, 158) notes two exceptions to Talbert's claim that Paul does not use the imperatival participle: Gal 6:1b and 2 Cor 8:24. However, a number of early manuscripts (e.g., ℵ C D¹) have an imperative in Gal 6:1b instead of the participle, perhaps indicating early discomfort with the ambiguity of the participle.

16. David Alan Black (1989, 6) remarks that Paul here "repeatedly stabs the ears of his audience with a rapid barrage" and cites Quintilian (*Inst.* 9.3.50), who commended asyndeton when speaking with vigor.

17. Contemporary claims that "this is *not* who we are" have become fraught in recent years in North America, where they have the capacity to minimize or even dismiss acts of hatred as aberrant. In other contexts, as I think intended here, such claims can promote the formation of communities that embody genuine love.

18. Walter Wilson notes that wisdom literature, to which he links much of this passage, "relies less on authoritative command than on the cogency of [its] advice and the persuasiveness of [its] argument" (1991, 163).

adokimos mind (1:28) suggests that Paul does not have great confidence in human discernment apart from the gospel. An exception may be found in the "I" of Rom 7, who has the capacity to know the law and to long to do the good, but of course that speaker finds herself unable to do the good, even when it is identified and desired.

The paired statements (again participles) in v. 10 share the reference "one another." The first connects the *agapē* of v. 9 with nothing less than family love (and see 1 Thess 4:9; Heb 13:1; 2 Pet 1:7). Again an important contrast is at work, since the characteristics of humanity handed over in 1:18–32 include the "heartless," with *astorgoi* as a negative formulation of the *philostorgoi* ("loving") depicted here. *Philadelphia* elsewhere generally refers to love within the family (as in 4 Macc 13:23, 26; 14:1), but here it extends to the fictive family of the community. Given the importance of family in the Roman world, this is a powerful statement. In his treatise on brotherly love, Plutarch admonishes those who hold others in more esteem that their own brothers (*Mor.* 479D). While Paul is not diminishing the importance of love within the biological family, he is interpreting and encouraging love within the body of Christ as a form of family love.

If the first half of v. 10 urges the community to the intimacy of family love, the second half urges the more visible act of honor.[19] In 13:7 Paul will instruct the Romans to fulfill expectations in the public arena by paying taxes and giving respect and honor as it is due (and cf. 1 Pet 2:17). At this point, however, he speaks not of what is due to an office but presumably what is due to everyone within the circle of "one another."

The first two clauses of v. 11 complement one another. "Eagerness" (*spoudē*) was earlier attached to leadership (v. 8), but now it serves as a warning against withholding from corporate life. Given the admonitions against laziness (again *spoudē*) in Jewish wisdom literature (see, e.g., Prov 6:9; 20:4; 31:27; Sir 22:1–2; 37:11), the connotation may be stronger than mere "withholding" conveys. In 1 Thess 5, which resembles this passage, Paul encourages care for those who are disorderly, "small souled," and "weak" (v. 14), and he may have in mind those whose investment is minimal. By contrast with such indolence, he evokes for the Romans a life "fired up in the Spirit."[20]

"Serving the Lord" seems a bit out of place, given that the entire chapter might be characterized as service to the Lord, to say nothing of the chapters that follow. It may stand as a companion to the preceding reference to the Spirit. At

19. Admittedly, "public" and "private" realms were less distinct than in contemporary Western experience. The distinction here is between the realm of the family and that of the polis.

20. The phrase "fired up" came to the foreground of American public life for its recurrent role in Barack Obama's first presidential campaign. In his memoir *A Promised Land*, he describes its origin in a 2007 rally in Greenwood, South Carolina, where Edith Childs called out to the room, "Fired up! Ready to go!" (2020, 97–98).

the conclusion of the letter, Paul will warn against people who "are not serving our Lord Christ but their own belly," suggesting both that "the Lord" in v. 11 'is Christ and that for Paul this phrase aptly names those "in Christ" (and see 14:18). A few lines below, however, "the Lord" is certainly God, given the citation that follows.

The remaining participles in vv. 12–13 have numerous counterparts elsewhere in the NT, reflecting a shared sense of their importance. Jesus instructs the disciples to rejoice that their names are written in heaven, and characters in Acts frequently rejoice in response to the gospel (e.g., 5:41; 8:39; 11:23; 13:48). Paul urges rejoicing in 1 Thess 5:16, as well as Phil 3:1 and 4:4. To rejoice "in hope" almost certainly connotes resurrection hope, since hope is closely correlated with resurrection both in Paul's letters (1 Cor 15:19) and in Acts (e.g., 23:6; 24:15; 26:6). The notion that suffering is inevitable, particularly suffering that arises from commitment to the gospel, appears across a wide range of NT texts (e.g., Matt 13:21; Mark 13:19, 24; John 16:33; Acts 14:22; 2 Cor 1:4; Rev 1:9). Reference to prayer is ubiquitous in the NT, but the notion of persisting in prayer figures prominently in Luke's depiction of the early community in Jerusalem (Acts 1:14; 2:42; 6:4; and see Col 4:2). That same Lukan depiction characterizes the community as sharing its resources as needed (Acts 2:45; 4:35). *Philoxenia*, hospitality to the stranger, is urged in Heb 13:2, but its value appears in writing as early as Homer and was essential to the work of Paul and others in the early Christian movement (and see Acts 28:1–10).

Such associations between these admonitions and other early Christian texts (including Paul's own letters) ought not obscure their connections within the logic of Romans. The early lines of ch. 5 connect eschatological hope directly with suffering: "Let us boast also in afflictions, knowing that affliction produces endurance." The same association recurs in the forceful midsection of ch. 8 (although employing the word *pathēma* rather than *thlipsis*). Paul will later urge the Romans to pray along with him for deliverance as he takes the offering "for the poor among the holy people" (15:26, 31–32). In addition, prominent in the letter closing is the request to offer hospitality to the stranger in the form of the deacon Phoebe. It seems clear that these lines, however familiar they may be from contemporaneous ethical instruction, appear here with specific intent.

[14–15] The final Greek word of v. 13 is *diōkontes*, which sets up a startling repetition, since the verb allows for both the pursuit of hospitality (v. 13b) and unwelcome pursuit by others (as in v. 14a). The move is made more abrupt in Greek, because it opens with the first unambiguous imperative of the passage: "Bless . . . bless . . . do not curse."[21]

---

21. In isolation, *eulogeite* could be either indicative or imperative, but the *mē* introducing *katarasthe* marks it an imperative, thus resolving the ambiguity.

Most commentators posit a shift at v. 14 from comments about relationships internal to the congregations to relationships with those on the outside (e.g., Edwards 300; Moo 780; Hultgren 457). Commands to bless the "harassers," warnings against returning evil for evil, and scriptural quotations concerning relations with enemies fit comfortably into that interpretation. In addition, there is evidence of that interpretation at least as early as Chrysostom (*Hom. Rom.* 22.14; *NPNF*[1] 11.506).

Yet some factors complicate this assumption. To begin with, vv. 15–16 do not fit smoothly into the rubric of "attitudes to outsiders." Perhaps rejoicing and weeping appropriately (v. 15) could be applied to dealings with outsiders, but the warnings of v. 16 against arrogance and relying "on your own thinking" replay earlier statements about appropriate and inappropriate thought in v. 3, which are clearly addressed to internal community life (and see 11:25). If vv. 14, 17–21 concern relationships outside the community, then vv. 15–16 constitute a strange digression. Further, ch. 14 at least raises the possibility that there are deep disagreements about the continuing importance of conforming to Jewish food law and other practices, disagreements that produce mutual judgment and rejection (14:4, 10, 13). Finally, the conclusion of the letter finds Paul warning against troublemakers who may mislead the Roman auditors (16:17–20), and those troublemakers appear to come from within Christian circles.

In addition, in 1 Thess 5:15 Paul warns against repaying evil for evil, and he does so immediately following instructions about dealing with people who inhabit the margins of the community. Elsewhere some Jewish warnings about vengeance assume conflicts among members of the group addressed rather than between the group and "outsiders." For example, Lev 19:18 instructs, "You shall not take vengeance or bear a grudge *against any of your people*, but you shall love your neighbor as yourself" (NRSVue, ital. added). At Qumran this instruction is taken up explicitly in the context of the members of the community (CD 9.2–5; and see 1QS 10.17–18).[22] Ambrosiaster reflects this possibility when he writes that Paul "prohibits proper punishment not only for one's inferiors, but also for one's equals and superiors. In other words, we should not seek to be avenged against a brother who perhaps sins against us" (231).

The most important factor in favor of understanding vv. 14, 17–21 as addressing dealings with outsiders may come within the text, when v. 17 assumes that evil has been done and especially in the citation of Prov 25:21, which identifies the perpetrators as enemies. Admittedly, Paul writes in 1 Cor 15:25 of God's enemies, he asks the Galatians whether he has become their enemy (4:16; see also 5:11), and he refers to other followers of Jesus as "enemies of the cross" in Phil 3:18. Those letters address congregations familiar with him, however,

22. See Yinger 1998 for further discussion of these and additional texts.

letters in which he must defend himself. It is far more difficult to imagine Paul, in this particular letter, in which he will later urge generous action toward the brother for whom Christ died, characterizing fellow believers as enemies.

Taken together, these various considerations make it far from obvious which groups are intended by vv. 14, 17–21. Perhaps v. 14 introduces "outsiders," who then return more emphatically in vv. 17–21, or perhaps there is a difference between the "harassers" (insiders?) and the "enemies" of vv. 17–21. This very ambiguity, the fact that the text can be read either way, could itself be significant. Paul may be less concerned with separating insider from outsider than are most of his interpreters. (See above on 8:29–30.) That seems entirely consistent with the insistence of 5:6–10 that God acted for "us" when we were "weak . . . ungodly . . . sinners . . . enemies." That formative knowledge motivates Paul to work toward strengthening the bonds of this community, all the while cognizant that God's love acted when "we were enemies" (Gaventa 2007b, 143–46; Hubbard 2016).[23]

Whoever the "harassers" may be, whether internal or external, the admonition to bless rather than curse has an important parallel in the Jesus tradition. In Matt 5 Jesus announces a blessing on the persecuted (v. 10) before instructing the disciples to pray for those who persecute them (v. 44; and see Luke 6:27–30). Paul may have known this as a saying from Jesus, although in that case it is hard to understand why he does not attribute it directly to him. In 1 Cor 4:12 he applies this attitude to himself and his coworkers ("When reviled, we bless; when harassed, we endure") as part of his warning to the Corinthians about their own arrogance, a connection that may be at work in Rom 12 as well, given the caution about arrogance in v. 16. The repetition of the verb "bless" underscores the positive action of blessing.

Verse 15, as noted earlier, does not follow easily on a teaching about outsiders, but if v. 14 has to do with internal strife (along the lines of ch. 14), the admonition to rejoice and weep in harmony with others might serve to demonstrate what blessing harassers could look like. The second half of the verse ("Weep with those who weep") repeats the substance if not the exact wording of Sir 7:34: "Do not withdraw from those who weep, but grieve with those who grieve." Shared celebration and shared mourning create bonds. By the same token, those who are bound together are likely to respond in just this way. Paul makes a similar observation in 1 Cor 12:26 in the context of community conflict: "If one body part suffers, all the body parts suffer together; if one body part is glorified, all the body parts are glorified together."

---

23. Hubbard's discussion of this passage in connection with Rom 5:6–10 appears in the context of a rejoinder to the claims by Engberg-Pedersen (2000) and Thorsteinsson (2006) that Paul restricts his concern to those within the Christian community by contrast with concern for love of all humanity in Stoic texts.

[16] Verse 16 returns to the concern for appropriate thought that figured prominently in 12:3 (as well as in 11:20, 25). Three participial phrases open the verse, which culminates in a prohibition:

> . . . thinking together with one another,
> not thinking presumptuously
> but being associated with the marginal.
> Do not rely on your own thinking.

The first phrase urges unity in thought, a value Paul underscores decisively in 15:5–6, where shared thought is further identified as being conformed to Christ Jesus and having as its goal the glorification of God "with one voice." This same instruction occurs in 2 Cor 13:11; Phil 2:2; 4:2, but without the additional elaboration that signals something of its importance.

Paul sharply distinguishes the second and third phrases (note the conjunction *alla*, "but"). The second phrase, worded negatively, warns against presumptuousness or arrogance. Concern with presumptuous thought has already appeared in 11:20, the only other time Paul uses the word *hypsēlos* ("exalted," here rendered "presumptuous"), and there he attributes it to gentiles who dare to imagine that they have replaced the natural branches of Israel (or at the very least Paul imagines they may be doing such a thing).

By contrast, the third phrase urges association with the *tapeinoi*, the "lowly" or "marginal." Whether Paul has in mind some specific group of individuals is difficult to say. Avoiding arrogance and its consequences will be more readily available for those who seek out the marginalized than for those who worry about their own proud thoughts, or perhaps the logic should be reversed: those who are not absorbed in their own thoughts are more available to be of service to the marginal.

With the final clause, "Do not rely on your own thinking," Paul inserts another clear prohibition. This one replays 11:25, where Paul announces the mystery of God's salvation of Israel in order to prevent the audience from engaging in disastrous speculation. The warning recalls that of Isa 5:21 about those who are wise in their own eyes, although Prov 3:7 is closer in that it combines the warning about arrogance with turning from evil, an association replicated in vv. 17–21. Once again, Paul reflects traditional instruction, but such traditions could well have come to mind precisely because he feared certain tendencies at Rome (and see below on ch. 14).

[17–21] Extended attention to dealing with evil holds together the final verses of the chapter. Having written largely about "holding on to what is good," Paul now turns to the shunning of evil (v. 9). Verse 17 opens these lines with the contrast between evil (*kakos*) and good (*kalos*), and v. 21 closes with another contrast between evil (*kakos*) and good (*agathos*). Once again a series of participles, the final series in this chapter, culminates in an imperative: "Yield to the wrath of God."

Following the initial warning against doing evil in exchange for evil (recalling Prov 20:22), Paul offers a positive description: "attending to what is good before all people" and "being at peace with all people," if it is possible from "your" side (and see Heb 12:14). The shift here to "all people" distinguishes this section from the earlier concern with upbuilding "one another." Being concerned for good for all people recalls the universal grasp of the gospel announced repeatedly in the letter (1:5, 16; 3:22–23; 5:12–21; 11:26, 32). Recipients of God's peace when they themselves were enemies of God (5:1, 10), the Roman auditors are summoned to enact that peace with all people. The qualification "so far as it is possible" acknowledges that no one has the power to make peace unilaterally. Having himself sustained physical attack (2 Cor 11:24–27), Paul comments here from experience.[24]

What they can do unilaterally is refrain from enacting judgment. With the final participle at the beginning of v. 19a, the emphasis changes: "Not enacting judgment yourselves," instead, "yield to the wrath of God" (see translation note k on v. 19). Paul's language sharply undercuts any notion that judgment about good and evil belongs to the addressees. Separating "not enacting judgment" from "yield to the wrath of God" is the clear adversative *alla* ("but"). The instruction itself takes the form of a clear imperative, and that imperative in turn is underscored by a scriptural citation identified as divine speech ("the Lord says").

The instruction against enacting judgment echoes Lev 19:18, which forbids human vengeance within Israel and is followed by a positive command: "You shall love your neighbor as yourself." Paul does not here call for love, either of neighbor or of enemy, but of course this passage does not contain the whole of Paul's instruction about life in the body of Christ. Instruction continues in 13:8–10, which does explicitly command love of one another and love of neighbor.

At this point, rather than following the lines of Lev 19 with a positive admonition about love, Paul transposes the discussion to a forceful reminder that the role of enacting justice belongs to God alone. Even those who are being renewed such that they know God's will (12:2) are not equipped to enact God's justice. That is God's prerogative.[25]

"Yield to the wrath of God" reminds the audience of Paul's earlier assertions about the working of God's wrath (1:18; 2:5, 8; 3:5; 4:15; 5:9; 9:22), and the

---

24. This interruption of the cascading phrases may be instructive in pastoral situations. To take a single but important example, women experiencing domestic abuse frequently are admonished to remain with abusive husbands on the basis of the household codes of Eph 5:22–24 and Col 3:18. Such advice assumes that wives can keep the peace on their own (among many other problematic assumptions). At the very least, pastoral care needs to remember that it is not always "possible with you."

25. Bertschmann sees in v. 19 an opening for Christians to identify and "denounce concretely experienced evil" (2019, 291).

citation of Deut 32:35a emphatically underscores the point.[26] Paul will return
to this notion of divine prerogative in 14:10–12, where he will insist that the
Romans not judge one another because they all are accountable to the judgment
of God. The language used in the two passages differs. In ch. 14 the judgment involved is identified as criticism; in this passage the language is that of
enacted judgment (often translated "vengeance," although see Ochsenmeier
2013, especially 365). The point is not simply that God is the best avenger of
wrong, but that God alone is able to discern and evaluate behavior (perhaps
recalling 11:33–36).

The claim that God is the only proper agent of enacted justice does not end
the matter, however. With v. 20, Paul introduces specific instructions about
actions to take in place of distorted human attempts at enacting justice. The
citation follows Prov 25:21–22a LXX, while leaving off v. 22b with its promise
of divine reward (on which see below). Far from enacting justice on the enemy,
the appropriate response is to provide for the enemy's needs.

The third line of this citation has proven to be as dense as the burning coal
it invokes. Debate focuses on whether Paul regards this explanation ("*for* when
you do this") to mean that piling coals on the head of the other is itself punishment or whether it induces repentance. Both interpretations have ancient and
modern proponents (reviewed in Martens 2014). Yet focus on implications
for "the enemy" is otherwise missing from vv. 17–21, which have as their
concern the Christian rather than what happens to the enemy (Martens 2014,
291). More to the point, given that Paul has just written that enacting judgment belongs to God, it seems strange indeed to propose that this is meant to
be punishment.

One possible reason Paul retains this puzzling line from Prov 25:22 is an
association he makes elsewhere between "fire" and eschatological accountability. First Corinthians 3:13–15 anticipates that "fire" will disclose and test
apostolic labor, destroying products that are faulty but saving the "builder."
Possibly it is the "fire" of eschatological accountability that prompts Paul to
include this line (Martens 2014, 300–303). This association is helpful, although
it needs to be held lightly, given that Paul's focus throughout is on the addressee
and God rather than on consequences for the enemy.

Verse 21 concludes this section by reframing and intensifying v. 17a. If
evil *is* returned for evil, then evil has won. Not only has God's authority been
usurped by the human agent, but the human is conquered. Augustine's observation seems close to Paul's reasoning: "Do you want to overcome evil with
evil? To conquer malice with malice? There will be two wicked people, both
of whom have to be overcome" (*Serm.* 302.10; Burns 313).

---

26. Here Paul's citation more closely conforms to the Hebrew than to the LXX, but exactly the
same wording appears when Heb 10:30 quotes this passage.

The way to combat evil is with "the good," reinforcing "clinging to the good" in v. 9 and anticipating the distinction Paul will make in 13:3 between good and evil action. He makes no reference here to the death of Christ, but Ambrosiaster may not be far from Paul's assumption at this point when he writes that "one who appears temporarily to be conquered by evil in fact conquers evil; indeed, even the Savior conquered evil in this way, when he did not resist" (Ambrosiaster 232).

The apparent eclecticism of this section, with its shifting grammatical formulations and its numerous parallels to other ancient texts, should not obscure Paul's concerns for upbuilding the community, for extending care to those outside the community, and for leaving to God—whose ways are unfathomable (11:33–36)—the execution of judgment. All of those concerns need to be kept in mind when turning to ch. 13, since reading that passage out of context continues to pose massive risks.

One concern notably absent here is any sense of divine reward for the doing of good, in contrast to the wisdom tradition, which assumes that God will reward those who do what is right (W. Wilson 1991, 196). The language of reward and punishment found in 2:5–9 has disappeared. The doing of good is simply what is called for *and* what is called forth when "grace come[s] into its own" (K. Barth 428).

13:1–7 Rulers Also Belong to God

These seven verses rank among the most difficult in a letter that overflows with interpretive challenges. A major reason for their difficulty is the burden imposed by the widespread, varied, and often pernicious use of this passage. We always read with our interpretive predecessors, whether or not we are aware of their influence. No one takes up a text innocently, and interpretations of this particular passage have a sustained and often troubling history that shapes readers and their responses. Although this commentary has not lingered over the history of interpretation of Romans, in this case it is unwise to turn to the text without acknowledging the long struggle to interpret it.[27]

And it is a long struggle. Even the earliest allusions to this passage already qualify it by recasting it ever so slightly. Polycarp responds to the proconsul's demand for a defense with the statement, "We are taught to render all due honor to rulers and authorities appointed by God, *in so far as it does us no harm*" (*Mart. Pol.* 10.2; LCL [Ehrman 1996]; ital. added). Defending Christians charged with impiety, Theophilus writes, "I will pay honour to the emperor

---

27. My own earlier work on this passage appears in Gaventa 2017a, where there is some further discussion of the history of interpretation. And see Schelkle 1952; Zsifkovits 1964; Wilckens 3:43–74; Lategan 1992, 2012; Miyata 2009; Krauter 2009; Cassidy 2010; Vásquez 2012.

not by worshipping him but by praying for him. . . . He is not God but *a man appointed by God not to be worshipped* but to judge justly" (*Autol.* 1.11 [Grant 1970]; ital. added).[28]

At least as early as Origen, readers of Romans sought to limit the claims of this passage by pairing it with other texts. Often, as in the case of Origen, Acts 5:29 was introduced into the discussion: "We must obey God rather than human beings."[29] Ambrosiaster looked to Mark 12:17 // Matt 22:21 // Luke 20:25: "Give to the emperor the things that are the emperor's, and to God the things that are God's" (235–36). More recently, Karl Barth, who wrote about Rom 13 on several occasions, put the passage alongside Rev 13 with its depiction of Rome and Rome's rulers as sea monsters (1954, 97).

While some have wanted to limit the passage, others have weaponized an absolutizing reading of it. Hitler's Germany and apartheid-era South Africa come to mind readily enough, but two centuries earlier, educator and activist Elizabeth Dawbarn urged Clara Neville to remain in England rather than emigrate to the United States on the grounds of the loyalty to rulers imposed by Rom 13 (Dawbarn 1794; Sancken 2012). More recently, United States attorney general Jeff Sessions memorably invoked Rom 13 in an attempt to quell criticism of President Donald Trump's actions at the Mexican border. It is also revealing that the same individuals or groups can invoke this passage in one context while tacitly ignoring it in another, as when pastor Robert Jeffress, who had publicly connected President Barack Obama with the antichrist, later invoked Rom 13 to insist that President Trump had the authority to bomb North Korea.

Quite apart from this complex history, numerous challenges arising from the passage itself make it difficult to gain interpretative leverage. Paul's announcement that everyone should "submit" to the governing authorities arrives with no fanfare. The transition from the end of ch. 12 is abrupt, and no word of introduction hints at the reason for Paul's comments (by contrast, e.g., with 7:1; 1 Cor 8:1; 1 Thess 5:1). Here the focus is on a single issue, for which Paul provides an extended argument, by contrast with the numerous topics introduced in Rom 12. In addition, no parallels to this passage elsewhere in his letters provide points of comparison or possibly supplement understanding.

A further puzzle posed by this passage is the extent to which it appears to contradict what Paul has said earlier in the letter about the *inability* of the human to do the good. The first half of the letter depicts the human being as subject to the power of Sin, unable to do what is right, producing evil even when desiring

28. These and other of the earliest allusions to or citations of Rom 13 are discussed by Wendell Willis, "Romans 13 in Patristic Interpretations" (an unpublished paper made available by the kindness of the author).

29. Origen, *Comm. Rom.* 9.27. Burns (314) observes that all the early commentators tried to nuance Paul's comments in some respect.

the good (see above on 3:10–18; 5:12–21; 7:7–25). Yet Rom 13 claims that rulers both know and serve the good (although see below for qualifications of those claims), an optimistic assessment hard to reconcile with Paul's insistence in chs. 1–8 that all human beings are subject to the power of Sin (see Gaventa 2017a for further discussion of this point).

Some scholars have taken these peculiarities as indications that the passage was not part of the letter originally but was inserted by a later editor (e.g., Barnikol 1961; Walker 2001). Such arguments have not won wide acceptance because no manuscript evidence supports a version of the letter without this passage. Another strategy of accounting for the passage is to contend that Paul is speaking with irony (Carter 2004) or, more popularly, that this is a "hidden transcript," a public document whose subversive meaning is accessible to believing insiders but veiled from others (N. Elliott 2008, drawing on J. Scott 1990). Yet Paul did not write Romans for a larger audience, but only for those in Rome who are "called to be saints" (1:7), so there is little reason to imagine a need to conceal meaning from outsiders (Barclay 2011, 382–83; Robinson 2021).

This reminder about the letter's audience can provide an important curb against some egregious interpretations. Paul does not appear to be addressing the authorities themselves, who stand outside the passage as a third party. His instructions aim to shape the behavior of the addressees, who are believers, rather than their rulers. That means this is not a treatise on rulership, as is Seneca's *De clementia,* which purports to advise the emperor Nero on the differences between a tyrant and a good ruler.[30] Treating Rom 13 as an address to rulers can promote the presumption that God sanctions any and all action by rulers. Far from providing rulers with unrestricted authority, however, Paul's assertion that God puts authorities in place means that all their authority is derivative and is subject to withdrawal, recalling what he has already said about Pharaoh in 9:17.

Chapter 12 suggests an orientation for approaching this passage. Paul's goal throughout ch. 12 appears to be the strengthening of the vulnerable Roman communities of faith. To some extent that is the case for the whole letter, but it seems particularly clear in ch. 12 (and again in ch. 14), where he is preoccupied with the ways believers engage with one another and encourage one another. If strengthening and protecting are Paul's major concerns in the preceding passage and again in the one that follows, then 13:1–7 may also reflect his fear that Roman auditors will imperil themselves and one another, in this instance by resisting rulers (whether local or otherwise), particularly by their refusal to pay taxes (see below on vv. 6–7).

---

30. Interestingly, this point was recognized by Queen Elizabeth I, whose *Sententiae* on rulers opens by citing Rom 13, only to follow the quotation with warnings drawn from other texts about foolish and unjust rulers. In other words, she looks to other sources for wisdom about her own role. (The text is available in Mueller and Scodel 2009, 331–94.)

Attending to the structure of this passage is of critical importance. It opens with a call for submission, which is repeated in v. 5:

> Every person should submit
> That is why it is necessary to submit

Between these two imperative formulations, vv. 1b–4 provide an extended defense of the imperative. Prominent in the defense is an insistence on God's role, but that insistence is coupled with an emphasis on fear:

> Rulers are a cause for fear not to good work but to evil
> You don't want to fear?
> If you do evil, then fear

This extended admonition culminates in the specific instructions of vv. 6–7, introduced by *dia touto* ("for this reason"). For those who bring to their reading centuries of argumentation focused on vv. 1–5, vv. 6–7 seem to be an afterthought, but the *dia touto* makes it clear they are crucial. Verses 1–5 justify the admonition, but vv. 6–7 explain why the admonition is necessary, even if the particular circumstances—the details regarding tribute and taxes—remain unstated, known to Paul and presumably his Roman addressees and thus assumed rather than expressed.

13:1 Every person should submit to the ruling authorities,[a] because there is no authority except the authority that comes from God, and those that exist were placed there by God. 2 Therefore, someone who rejects[b] the authority resists the placement[c] of God, and those who do resist will bring judgment upon themselves, 3 because the rulers are a cause for fear not to good work but to evil.

You don't want to fear the authority? Then do what is good, and you will have their[d] praise, 4 because the authority is God's servant for you, meant for good.[e] But if you do evil, then fear, because he does not carry the sword without a purpose, because he is God's servant who punishes, meant for wrath for the one who does evil. 5 That is why it is necessary to submit, not just because of that wrath[f] but also because of conscience.

6 For this reason, then, pay your taxes,[g] because the authorities[h] are God's ministers, persistent in this matter. 7 Pay everyone what is owed—whether tribute to the tribute agent,[i] tax to the tax agent, respect to the one who is owed respect,[j] or honor to the one who is owed honor.

a. Several manuscripts, including $\mathfrak{P}^{46}$ D* F G, read, "Submit to all the governing authorities," omitting the noun *psychē* and substituting *pasais* (dative plural) for *pasa* (nominative singular). Given early evidence of struggles to understand this text, the changes are more consistent with early scribal error (Cranfield 2:656) than with a desire to make the instruction more emphatic (contra Jewett 780).

b. The Greek *antitassomenos* ("who rejects") echoes and inverts the earlier command in v. 1 for submission (*hypotassesthō*). Order is in play in both cases, whether submitting to it or undermining it.

c. Another wordplay on the *tass-* stem in which *diatagē* ("placement") replays *tetagmenai* ("were placed") from v. 1.

d. Lit., "its" praise, since the pronoun is feminine, governed by the abstract feminine antecedent *exousia*, but the agents distributing praise or wrath are human.

e. The translation construes *eis* as purposive, both here and at the end of the verse, "meant" for good, "meant" for wrath.

f. Lit., "the wrath," but this resumes the reference to wrath in the preceding statement.

g. In form the verb *teleite* ("you pay") might be either indicative or imperative, but the context favors the imperative, making v. 6a consistent with the imperative in v. 7. Although *gar* (here indicating an inference: "then") does not frequently introduce an imperative, there are examples of such (see, e.g., 1 Cor 1:26; Eph 5:5; Heb 12:3; Job 8:8; 11:4; 4 Macc 5:13; 16:5; Philo, *Alleg. Interp.* 3.158; Josephus, *Ant.* 7.220; Wolter 2:319–20). The combination here reflects the emphatic character of Paul's instructions.

h. "The authorities" is supplied for clarity, since it is the agents rather than the taxes that are God's servants.

i. The Greek is far more elliptical, as in "to the one the tribute, the tribute," but this translation reflects the sense of the Greek, in that every agent (*pasin*) is to receive what is obligated to that agent. English translation cannot do justice to the interesting repetition of sound here, with the *ph* of *phoros* ("tribute") repeated in *phobos* ("respect") below, and the *t* of *telos* ("tax") repeated in *timē* ("honor") below.

j. Although *phobos* ("respect") is the same word as *phobos* ("fear") in v. 3, the context dictates a different translation.

[1a] The opening instruction is abrupt, as noted above, and the inherited chapter division intensifies that impression by inserting a gap between this text and what precedes. Paul regularly moves to a new topic or question with some obvious transitional marker, such as "since" or "therefore" (as in, e.g., 1:18; 3:1; 8:1), and readers expect the same pattern here. A number of such transitionless statements characterize ch. 12, however, making the asyndeton simply another feature of this section of the letter (12:9a, 9b, 14, 15, 18, and 13:8; although 14:1 differs). By distinction from ch. 12, however, Paul now offers a sustained argument that includes warrants and consequences. That development of the argument may reflect the fact that Paul is concerned with protecting the Roman congregations from danger of some sort; language of "fear" is prominent. He has not, however, finished with his concern about their internal relations, as becomes clear especially in ch. 14.

"Every person" (*pasa psychē*) encompasses all, leaving no room for exceptions. The admonition that follows addresses all believers in Rome, without differentiating by ethnicity or status (as is the case in Paul's only other use of this phrase, 2:9, where it concerns universal accountability). The "every person" may even include those outside the community as well as those on the inside (so

Furnish 2005, 80), although the context makes it clear that Paul is instructing Roman believers in particular rather than the world at large.

All are to "submit" to the ruling authorities. The verb *hypotassesthai* has to do with recognizing or conforming to an order or a placement (as do several of the words that follow), as when Ephesians enjoins believers to "submit" to one another and invokes the submission of the church to Christ before instructing that wives should "submit" to their husbands (Eph 5:21, 24). While the verb *hypotassō* is distinct from that for obedience (*hypakouō*), submission very often implies obedience. When seventy followers of Jesus, upon their return from a successful mission, report that the demons "submit" to them (Luke 10:17, 20), some sort of obedience inheres in recognizing the superior status of the human agents.[31] In 1 Cor 15:25–28, Paul anticipates God's final triumph as the time when Jesus will "submit" or subject everything under God's feet, a final ordering that signals the defeat of all opposition to God and presumably implies obedience.

In this context, obedience is qualified in an important way, however, since Paul will immediately claim that it is God who puts the authorities in place. That action by God is something more than a simple chain of command in which God's place is higher than that of the governing authorities and their places higher than those of the addressees. God is not only the one who orders these things; God is the one to whom real obedience is owed (1:5; 5:19; 6:16–17; 10:16; 15:18; 16:19; and perhaps 16:26).[32] The pertinent issue is the qualitative difference between what is owed to God and what is owed to the governing authorities. One of the dominant motifs of Rom 1–8 is the refusal of human beings to give God what is rightfully God's: gratitude, praise, worship, respect, awe (1:18–32; 3:10–18). It is that withholding of what rightfully belongs to God that sets in motion God's handing over of humanity to the devastating grasp of Sin and Death. Nothing similar to that demand for recognition and praise of God, that recognition of the relationship between Creator and created, is in play in Paul's call for submission in ch. 13. Early interpreters such as Polycarp and Theophilus were right to distinguish respect for the authorities from worship of them. What Paul means by "submission" comes to expression in vv. 6–7 in the language of taxes and honor, pragmatic forms of submission that are greatly removed from obedience to God.

The phrase "ruling authorities" is frustratingly vague, as it permits no identification of particular officeholders and thereby also no obvious limitations. The introduction of the term *archontes* ("rulers") in v. 3 does not clarify matters,

31. See also, e.g., 1 Chr 22:18; Pss 17:48 LXX; 36:7 LXX; 59:10 LXX; Plutarch, *Pomp.* 64.3.
32. Romans 6:12 and 16 appear to be exceptions to this observation in that both refer to obedience to "desire" or to "sin." Yet those exceptions serve to reinforce Paul's understanding that genuine obedience is obedience to God. Paul's other letters also frame obedience in relationship to God (2 Cor 7:15; 10:5–6; Phil 2:12). Philemon 21 is an exception in that obedience there refers to obedience to Paul's own request (and also the non-Pauline Col 3:20, 22; Eph 6:1, 5).

since in 8:38 "rulers" are paired with "angels," presumably indicating suprahuman agents. Similarly, 1 Cor 2:6–8 identifies the "rulers of this age" who put Jesus to death, suprahuman powers that act through human agents. This pattern has occasionally given rise to the hypothesis that the "authorities" and "rulers" here are the same suprahuman agents at work in 8:31–39 and elsewhere (especially Cullmann 1950, 97–113), but the subsequent commands about the payment of tribute and taxes make it clear that Paul has human rulers in mind, and it is scarcely imaginable that Paul would enjoin respect for the "rulers of this age."

The lack of specificity likely suggests that Paul refers to a range of officials with whom members of the Roman congregations are apt to come in contact. Neither "authority" (*exousia*) nor "ruler" (*archōn*) appears to be a technical term for any particular office or set of offices. These terms are also not synonyms for "government" in the modern sense of a comprehensive system that regulates major aspects of life for residents, which is why it is unlikely that Paul has the larger phenomenon of Rome itself in mind here. What vv. 6–7 suggest is that the authorities Paul has in view are specifically those concerned with taxes and levies, perhaps especially at the local level. The Acts of the Apostles offers glimpses of that network of local officials who make sure that Roman power is protected (e.g., Acts 16:35–40; 18:12–17; 22:22–29).

Whoever these "ruling authorities" may be, they are external to the congregations Paul addresses. Unlike 12:14–21, where there is some uncertainty whether the "harassers" and the "enemy" are within the congregations, here nothing suggests the authorities are among the addressees. To the contrary, the fact that there is no instruction addressed to the authorities argues against their being included. These are outsiders in the sense that they are not among those Paul addresses in the letter, but Paul is confident that they are not outside God's grasp (again, 5:6–11 is pertinent: no one lies beyond God's reach). They are not "other" to God, so they cannot be "other" to God's people either.

[1b–3a] The second half of v. 1 initiates a series of reasons for submission, constructed as a sequence of *gar* ("because") clauses and culminating in v. 5, which replays the initial imperative. Paul offers two interrelated reasons for submission: first, God has put authorities in place; second, not submitting to them has fearful consequences.

First, Paul claims that any authority that exists is *hypo theou*—it is "by" or "from" God. He amplifies this assertion slightly with the additional comment that any authorities that exist have been put in place by God; that is, they have been set up by God. This statement is coherent with the accounts of Israel's history offered by Paul's Scriptures, however puzzling it may seem in its context because of its abrupt introduction and its lack of parallel elsewhere in Paul's letters. From the identification of Saul to a reluctant Samuel forward into Israel's history, God is the one who installs rulers. In addition, some wisdom texts affirm God's role in placing rulers in power, as when Prov 8:15–16 claims that kings rule by divine Wisdom, although there the implication seems to be that their own right work is credited to Wisdom rather than that they are installed by Wisdom. Wisdom of Solomon 6:3–4 states that rulers receive their power directly from God, although that claim is immediately followed by warnings to rulers against wrongdoing (vv. 5–11). Paul is not referring to Israel's kings, to be sure; the complicated narrative of Israel's history simply indicates that there is precedent for associating God's will with governing authorities.[33]

Although Paul does not elsewhere discuss authorities in a way that would shed light on this passage, he does briefly discuss one authority in particular: the Egyptian he identifies simply as "Pharaoh" (Rom 9:17).[34] The introduction of Pharaoh is itself remarkable, since the passage otherwise attends to Israel's ancestors rather than to crises in Israel's history. Importantly, what Paul says about Pharaoh is entirely about God's dealings with him. Just as God "loved Jacob" but "hated Esau" (9:13), a choice made while they were still in Rebekah's womb and for no reason other than God's decision, God also put Pharaoh in place for no reason other than God's will. Paul quotes Exod 9:16 LXX:

> Scripture says to Pharaoh, "I raised you up for this reason, so that I might demonstrate my power in your case and so that my name might be declared in all the earth."

Here the voice of Scripture and that of God ("I") address Pharaoh together. They announce not just that God "preserved" Pharaoh (*dietērēthēs*, Exod 9:16 LXX), but that God "raised him up" (*exēgeira*). God brought Pharaoh into being for a reason. Further, although Exodus attributes the hardening of Pharaoh's heart both to God and to Pharaoh (Exod 4:21; 9:34–35; 10:1; 13:15; and see 1 Sam 6:6), here God alone hardens the heart of Pharaoh. Further, God acts for the enhancement of God's own power and name (see above on 9:17–18 for further discussion).

If God's treatment of Pharaoh provides a glimpse of the thinking behind 13:1–2, then "there is no authority except the authority that comes from God" is quite far from implying approval of the actions of the governing powers.

---

33. See also Josephus, *J.W.* 2.140. There are also qualifications to the tradition, as when 1 En. 46.5 warns that God will overturn the reign of kings who do not praise him and acknowledge that their kingdoms come to them from God. In Acts 12:20–23 Luke depicts the dramatic fall of Herod Agrippa I in just such terms: when he failed to reject the acclamation of himself as a god, "an angel of the Lord struck him down, and he was eaten by worms and died" (v. 23, NRSVue).

34. Reference to David does occur at 1:3, where Jesus Christ is said to be his descendant, and David is invoked as speaker of the psalms quoted in 4:6 and 11:9. While 1:3 does have royal connotations, the primary implication of that reference to David is that Jesus Christ is born of Jewish flesh. In any case, Paul does not identify David as someone put in place by God, by contrast with Pharaoh in 9:17.

Particularly in view of emerging association between the emperor and divinity, as exemplified in Augustus's *Res gestae,* Paul's insistence that the authorities are God's appointees could be perceived as a demotion. In other words, in the context of the first century, Paul is arguing that any human authority is inherently derivative and subordinate. Further, all human authority exists for God's own purposes. That is not to say that authorities *intend* to fulfill God's purposes; nothing Paul says about Pharaoh suggests that the Egyptian ruler thought of himself as God's agent or desired to obey God's command. In addition, nothing here stipulates that good inheres in the authority of Pharaoh as such, either by virtue of his birth or his actions.

With v. 2, Paul returns to his opening instruction about submission to the authorities, this time lodging it in the order established by God. Attempts to undermine the governing authorities are the equivalent of resistance to God and will be punished. Paul continues to draw on words that emphasize order. Verse 1 appealed for being "ordered under" and for the placement of "order" by God, and in v. 2 the one who resists goes against the order of God. Yet it is especially important to see what Paul says and does not say. He does not equate the authorities with God who puts them in place, but he locates them in God's act of ordering things.

This does not mean that order itself is inherently good, however. Interpreters sometimes seize on this "ordering" language, as if Paul were elevating order itself as a principle. Dunn, for example, connects order here with both nature and "divine reason." He goes on to comment that "such orderliness is part of the creative purpose of God" and that "a society needs constraints in order to ensure 'the good'" (2:771; see also John Chrysostom, *Hom. Rom.* 23; *NPNF*[1] 11:513; Erasmus 347). Paul is not addressing the needs of society as a whole, however; neither is he commenting on God's purposes in creation. Further, while appeals to the necessity of order in society are understandable and the need for order is reasonable, appeals for "order" can also be treacherous, as such appeals too often favor groups who hold and maintain power for their own purposes. What one group regards as order another may well experience as oppression (Stringfellow 1978, 55–63).

This appeal to God's ordering culminates in a threat about judgment that awaits those who resist God's order. What content that judgment takes on remains unspecified, although later there is reference to the sword, implying physical harm (v. 4). Instead of expanding on the character of judgment, Paul introduces its source: the rulers themselves. In this passage, judgment and wrath (vv. 4–5) refer to the actions of the ruling authorities, by contrast with the instructions given the addressees themselves (as in 12:19 and 14:3–5, 10, 13) and also by contrast with references to divine wrath (1:18; 2:1, 8; 12:19).

The introduction of judgment opens the door for the extended discussion about fear that continues through v. 4. With v. 3a Paul reintroduces the language of good and evil he employed earlier in 12:17, 21, but this time with respect to fear of rulers. So long as one does "the good," there is nothing to fear; it is only when one does evil that one need fear. This fear, as with judgment and wrath, is distinct from the fear (also *phobos*) that is appropriate awe in response to God, both in Paul and elsewhere in Scripture (e.g., Neh 5:15; Ps 33:12 LXX; Prov 1:7; Isa 11:3; 2 Cor 7:1). In 3:18 Paul draws on Ps 35:2 LXX to lament the absence of awe before God (*phobos*). Here, by contrast, fear is the appropriate response for wrongdoers, since they face punishment. As with judgment and wrath, this term takes on a specific resonance in this context.

[**3b–5**] Paul elaborates this warning regarding fear, beginning with the question "You don't want to fear the authority?" Two parallel statements contrast possible behaviors, the outcome of each, and the reasons supporting those outcomes:

Do good	you will have praise	because he is God's servant for you, for good
If you do evil	fear	because he does not carry the sword without a purpose
		because he is God's servant who punishes for wrath, for the one who does evil

The notion that good conduct generates praise from authorities appears elsewhere (e.g., Xenophon, *Oec.* 9.14; Demosthenes, *Or.* 20.154; Polybius, *Hist.* 6.14.4–5; Velleius Paterculus, *Hist. rom.* 2.126.3; Philo, *Embassy* 7; Wolter 2:315). It is nevertheless odd to find Paul espousing this principle, since it seems to run contrary to his own experience. At least 2 Cor 11:24–25 reflects instances when Paul was not praised but punished by authorities, except in that passage the authorities clearly did not find his behavior a reflection of "the good."[35] More to the point, this appeal places a value on human praise that stands in some tension with Paul's own earlier evaluation of praise from God rather than humans (Rom 2:29; and possibly also 1 Cor 4:5; Gal 1:10), although that tension may be modified by the larger claim that God orders the authorities.

The contrasting statement opens with "if you do evil," a slight alteration of the parallel to the previous "do what is good," weighted toward the expectation that the addressees will not in fact commit evil acts. What follows is a single word announcing the ominous outcome: "Fear." (Colloquially, "Be very afraid!") Having said that rulers are not a reason for fear, having asked whether the audience wishes *not* to fear, Paul now announces that evildoers in fact should fear.

---

35. As Steven Friesen puts it, "When [Paul] composed these lines he had scars on his body from unjust floggings by rulers and authorities" (2007, 2:641).

This admonition is followed again by the claim that the authority is God's servant, but first Paul inserts "for he does not carry the sword without a purpose." Far from merely balancing out the preceding reference to praise in exchange for good, this vivid image summons the prospect of physical harm. It also recalls 8:35, where "the sword" takes its place alongside other threats to God's people, including famine and nakedness. Not surprisingly, "the sword" (or sword-bearing) as a reference to the official use of force appears in a range of contemporary texts, ranging from papyrus references to officials who "bear the sword" (*CPJ* 2.152.5; P.Tebt. 2.391.20; Jewett 795) to Seneca's advice to Nero to be the kind of ruler who prudently keeps his sword sheathed (*Clem.* 1.3) to Philo's anticipation of the sword punishing evildoers (*Rewards* 147) to Epictetus's scorn for those who have guards with swords (*Diatr.* 1.30.7; and see Acts 12:2; 16:27).

For a second time Paul identifies the authority as God's *diakonos*, God's servant or emissary (see below on 16:1). Initially that servanthood is identified in general terms with bringing about "the good" (v. 4a). Here, however, servanthood is more closely linked with punishment. It is not just that the authority exists to prevent wrongdoing or to avoid evil (as in 12:9); rather, the authority is the agent of judgment in the case of wrongdoing. More to the point, in v. 4a the action of the authority is "for you," but here it is "the one who does evil" (v. 4b). Associating authority with punishment (*ekdikos*) collides with Paul's earlier counsel against enacting judgment in 12:19, where punishment is God's responsibility. The scenarios Paul addresses differ, since ch. 12 concerns someone who is perpetrating evil against or within the community, while 13:4 warns those within the community about the consequences of wrongdoing, specifically wrongdoing that involves responsibilities to those in authority.

In both cases, whether praising the good or punishing wrongdoing, the authority is said to be God's *diakonos*, God's servant or agent. Verse 6a will refer to authorities, or at least some of them, as *leitourgoi*, another term for an agent or servant. These are both terms Paul applies to himself (e.g., 15:16; 1 Cor 3:5; 2 Cor 6:4) as well as to Phoebe (Rom 16:1) and others (e.g., Phil 1:1; 2:25). Christ himself is said to have become a *diakonos* in Rom 15:8. It is tempting to attach status claims to at least some of these instances, particularly in light of later respect for the office of deacon, but that is to miss the point. A *diakonos* is the agent of another (see below on 16:1, where Phoebe's identification in this role becomes the subject of scholarly dispute). Far from elevating the authorities, Paul's comments locate them as "only" servants, put in place and subject to God's will.[36]

36. That Christ is "merely" a *diakonos* in this sense may provoke protest, particularly in view of Paul's calling him "Son of God in power" (1:4) and of his exaltation in 8:34. Yet those claims sit alongside the notion that God sent him (8:3), that he did not please himself (15:3), and elsewhere

An additional nuance may be involved here, at least on the assumption that the authorities Paul has in view are local or regional officials, as argued above. While Paul is not writing about "Rome" as such or about "the empire," these authorities are agents of Rome, put in place by Rome, or more generally in service of Rome. (Again, the accounts in Acts provide examples, such as 16:19–23; 17:5–9; 25:6–12.) To observers who have not been grasped by the gospel, they are agents of Rome. But that is not how Paul frames them; for Paul, they are God's.

Having provided these words of explanation loaded with references to fear, in v. 5 Paul repeats the opening instruction about submission, this time with the insistent "it is necessary." Two *dia* ("because of") clauses qualify the instruction: "because of wrath" and "because of conscience." The first epitomizes what has just been said about the possibility of punishment. The second *dia* clause, however, introduces a new element, that of conscience (*syneidēsis*), adding an internal motivation to the external motivation for which he has been arguing (so rightly Jewett 798). This appeal to conscience is a bit startling, coming as it does without introduction or explanation.[37] In the context of this entire section of the letter, introduced by 12:1–2, however, conscience presumably refers to awareness that has been formed by God's mercies and the renewal of the mind; in other words, conscience also is part of the *sōma* that is offered up to God.

[6–7] To this point, of course, no specific behavior has been invoked that might warrant either praise or punishment (a feature of the text that has encouraged those who wish to find support for their own demands for obedience). With vv. 6–7, however, the situation changes as Paul takes up a prominent feature of civic governance, namely, taxation. The elaborate introduction to this specific instruction again makes it likely that this is the problem Paul has had in view throughout the passage. He has been preparing for this instruction. It is still difficult, however, to reconstruct the situation prompting Paul's response. Noting on literary grounds the emphasis on taxation and respect is not the same as discerning the reasons for that emphasis. As often elsewhere when considering the historical context of the letter, the fact that Paul has never been to Rome complicates any hypothesis, since it is difficult to discern what he actually knew about Rome.

Regarding taxation itself, several stipulations are important. To begin with, the complex tax system existed in order to serve the needs of the emperor and his power. According to Dio Cassius, Julius Caesar had observed a century earlier that rulers needed two interrelated things in order for their realms to

---

that he is the one *through whom* God's triumph comes (1 Cor 15:24). Paul does not seem to find the two sorts of assertions to be in contradiction.

37. This sudden appeal to conscience recalls 1 Cor 11:16, where, having argued from the ordering of creation, Paul abruptly adds a reference to what is being done in other "churches of God."

thrive: an army and money (*Hist. rom.* 42.49.4; cited in Günther 2016, 1). However reliable that attribution, it does match the workings of Roman taxation, which existed in order to enhance the standing of the emperor. (The gospel saying "Give Caesar what belongs to Caesar and God what belongs to God" seems to reflect this understanding, that the tax went to "Caesar"; Mark 12:17 // Matt 22:21 // Luke 20:25.)[38]

In addition, the tax system favored residents of Rome and Roman citizens, who were not subject to the tribute tax to which Paul refers in vv. 6–7. The tribute (*phoros*) specifically acknowledged the status of the provinces as territories ruled by Rome (Günther 2016, 2; Coleman 1997, 310). Some individuals in Rome, among them Prisca and Aquila (16:3), however, would have been subject to the tribute since their legal residence for taxation purposes was elsewhere (Acts 18:2; 1 Cor 16:19; Coleman 1997, 313). Perhaps more significant, the tax (*telos*) Paul mentions was levied on an extensive range of goods and services, and from this series of taxes Roman citizens and residents would not have been exempt (Suetonius, *Cal.* 40; cited in Günther 2016, 3).

Some historical evidence suggests that unrest over taxation increased in the mid to late 50s CE. Tacitus's account of Nero's reign reflects anger arising from the greed of tax collectors as well as from the fact that actual tax regulations were kept secret from the public, thereby understandably arousing suspicion (*Ann.* 13.50–51; see also Suetonius, *Nero* 44.1–2).[39] Paul may have been aware of this unrest and concerned about the possibility of Roman auditors being swept up into action that would prove injurious to them. Given both fragmentary evidence and Paul's own distance from Rome, it is wise not to lean heavily on any particular reconstruction; it is enough to observe that Paul is concerned about some specific violation having to do with the paying of taxes.

Verse 7 also instructs the audience to give respect (*phobos*) and honor (*timē*) as obligations to those to whom they are due. Although Paul has just lines above written that authorities are not a reason for fear (*phobos*), here he advocates for *phobos*, obviously with a different nuance. The respect and honor (*timē*) advocated here reflect a much larger culture of distributing honor (and withholding it), but at the same time they round out the passage. Having emphasized the payment of taxes, Paul adds two other obligations. As put in place by God, these authorities warrant respect and honor.

---

38. This fact already distinguishes Roman taxation from any modern system, in which taxation is generally *intended* to enhance the corporate good rather than to enhance the power and wealth of an individual.

39. Philo's comments about the cruelty both of rulers and of tax agents, while not addressed to residents of Rome, underscore the difficulty experienced as a result of Rome's aggressive measures (*Spec. Laws* 2.92–94; 3.159–162; 4.218). However, see Rathbone (2008, 260–67) for cautions about relying on the accounts of Tacitus and Suetonius.

Questions about this passage persist, particularly questions about what appears to be resistance to taxes and fines.[40] Yet some points emerge with clarity: Paul's instructions recognize the governing structures of his day, but they do so in measured language. To be put in place by God is to be God's own servant after all—nothing more. The authorities are to be obeyed, as otherwise there could be fearful consequences. Paul advocates the paying of taxes and respect as required.

A glimpse back at the end of Rom 11 and the opening of Rom 12 will reveal stark differences with these instructions. In 11:35 Paul asked (employing the language of Job), "Who made a gift to [God], and was given a gift by him in exchange?" The clear answer is "No one," since no one could possibly engage in mutual giving with God. No one can possibly give God all that is owed. In Rom 13, however, it is simply assumed that the obligations are such that they can be fulfilled. This obligation is manageable, and it is expedient that the Romans meet the obligation in order to prevent serious consequences for the communities.

The relationship between this passage and the end of Rom 12 is also illuminating. There, although Paul writes of blessing the one who "harasses" and of caring for "the enemy," it proves difficult to identify the culprits. It is not even clear whether they are believers or outsiders (see above on 12:9–21). The governing authorities are almost certainly "outsiders" in the sense that they are not part of Paul's audience; they are not among the community of faith. They are not enemies, however, which is an important distinction. Paul emphasizes the need to respect them, but he does not attribute to them authority in and of themselves, a distinction often lost in the history of grappling with this text. In keeping with the rest of the letter, Paul implicitly undermines the urge to divide the world into "we" and "they." Even the governing authorities are treated as part of God's creation rather than outside God's authority or realm.

This passage poses a significant challenge to anti-imperial interpretations of the letter. That is not to say that the gospel supports the empire, whether the empire of Rome or any other. Nor does it mean that Paul would align himself with the empire's claims. His letters have villains of a different sort in mind, however, as 16:20 anticipates with God's crushing of Satan.[41] Sin and Death and their numerous allies (8:31–39) may make use of any number of "rulers of this age" (1 Cor 2:6–8), but the emperor and his cronies remain God's creation. As Paul moves seamlessly to the obligation of love and the urgency of the

40. As Leander Keck observes (325), Rom 13 remains "more successful in thwarting a convincing explanation than the experts" have been in finding one.

41. There is no "glorification of political power" nor "any attempt at making it into a mythology or demonic force" (Käsemann 1969a, 203).

present time (13:8–14), this instruction about acknowledging the ruling powers shrinks to its rightful size. The governing authorities are installed by God and remain God's servants, not the other way around.

It is the failure—sometimes willful failure—to recognize that way of prioritizing things that makes this passage perennially vulnerable to misuse.

13:8–14 Love in God's "Now Time"

From the language of obligation and debt that concludes 13:1–7, Paul turns to an altogether different debt, that of love—love that fulfills the law, particularly love expressed by those who, having themselves been claimed by Jesus Christ, know what time it is, the time of salvation, of daylight, of being wrapped up in Christ.

Two distinct sections stand side by side. The first, vv. 8–10, addresses the obligation of love, which Paul identifies as fulfilling the Mosaic law; the second, vv. 11–14, addresses the eschatological nearness of salvation. They are not joined together in a conventional way (e.g., by *gar* or *de*), which makes it possible to treat them separately, as commentators often do (e.g., Jewett 804–28; Wolter 2:329–45). In addition, some scholars also hold that vv. 11–14 draw upon an ancient baptismal liturgy (following Schlier 395–97), which further reinforces notions of their distinctiveness.

Yet there is also good reason for reading the two sections together. To begin with, a grammatical connection joins the two, which supports holding them together (see translation note e on v. 11). More to the point, together they occupy a transitional space between two extended discussions of particular issues— respect for the ruling authorities (13:1–7) and community conflicts focused on observance of food laws (14:1–15:6)—and each section (13:8–10 and 13:11–14) bears importantly on both issues. Beyond that, the two sections are mutually interpreting. On its own, vv. 8–10 could be construed as exalting love in relationship to the law or perhaps for its own sake. By virtue of the apocalyptic urgency—the christological urgency—of vv. 11–14, however, the instruction about love takes on a specific location. Love is not a vague humanistic principle, a good in and of itself—at least not for Paul; instead, it exists in a christological context. Correspondingly, the instruction on love prevents vv. 11–14 from being perceived as permission to absent oneself from life in the present. People who understand the obligation of love for others will be less likely to neglect the needs of those around them out of preoccupation with the impending eschaton. In addition, a community that elevates love for the "other," the "neighbor," will not misconstrue the "weapons of light" and putting on the Lord Jesus Christ as license to harm other human beings (reinforcing 12:14–21). At least in substance, then, these two sections belong together and interpret each other.

13:8 Owe nothing to anyone except to love one another,[a] since the one who loves the other[b] fulfills[c] the law. 9 For the Decalogue's instructions,[d] "Do not commit adultery," "Do not murder," "Do not steal," "Do not desire," and any other commandment, are summed up in this saying: "Love your neighbor as yourself." 10 This love does not produce evil for the neighbor. Therefore, the fulfillment of the law is love.

11 And especially[e] since you know what time it is, that the hour is already here when you[f] should wake from sleep, because now salvation[g] is nearer us than when we began to believe.[h] 12 The night has passed, and the day has come near. Therefore, let us cast off[i] the works of darkness and put on the weapons of light. 13 As in the day, let us live decently. That means not with riotous feasts and drinking bouts, not with promiscuous sex[j] and indecent behavior, not with conflict and jealousy. 14 Instead, put on the Lord Jesus Christ and make no plans concerned for the flesh, plans that serve only fleshly desires.[k]

a. The definite article preceding "love one another" simply marks out that phrase as a substantive and does not require translation, although it might be rendered "except you owe the debt to love one another."

b. Grammatically this clause is ambiguous. Instead of "the one who loves the other," it might be translated "the one who loves has fulfilled the other law" (as advocated by Marxsen 1955, 230–37). Paul does refer to "another" law in the context of Rom 7, but there he is discussing the terrifying situation in which God's one law has been fractured by Sin's occupation (see above on 7:23). However, when he uses *heteros* ("other") independently, he most often does so to refer to persons (as in, e.g., Rom 2:1, 21; 1 Cor 3:4; 10:24; Gal 6:4). More telling, he never employs the verb "love" (*agapaō*) without an object (Thompson 1991, 125).

c. Lit., "has fulfilled" the law, but treated here as a gnomic perfect (Meyer 2004b, 211) or an empiric perfect (Smyth 1956, §1948). It states a general principle rather than conveying a completed event.

d. The definite article introduces this series of prohibitions (lit., "the 'Do not . . .'"). Since it is obvious that these prohibitions come from the Decalogue, the phrase has been supplied (as in de Boer 2011, 343).

e. *Kai touto* (lit., "and this") is used adverbially by way of drawing attention to what follows—hence "and especially" (BDAG s.v.; BDF §290, 5; see 1 Cor 6:6, 8; Eph 2:8).

f. The manuscript tradition is divided between *hēmas* ("us"; $\aleph^2$ D F G L etc.) and *hymas* ("you"; $\aleph^*$ A B C P etc.). The difference is a single letter, and any distinction in pronunciation could have been undetectable (as is the case also in Rom 5:1; 14:8, 19; see Wolter 2:337). Possibly an earlier "you" was altered to "us," as it made for consistency with the first-person expressions that follow, although there is a parallel shift between first-person in v. 12 and second -person in v. 14. I have opted for "you," as it seems more likely that a scribe would have conformed the pronoun to the "we" that follows than that a scribe would have disrupted the consistency.

g. While "our" (*hēmōn*) can modify salvation, so that it is "our salvation" that has come nearer (NIV; Jewett 816; Moo 834), "salvation is nearer to us" is the stronger translation (NRSVue, NASB, REB, ESV; Cranfield 2:679, 681). Paul's use of the possessive "our" typically follows rather than precedes the word being modified (e.g., Rom 1:4; 3:5; 8:16; 1 Cor 2:7; 10:11; 15:14; 2 Cor 1:7), although important exceptions occur (Phil 3:20; 2 Cor 8:24; 1 Thess 2:19). In addition, the only time Paul uses a personal pronoun elsewhere to modify "salvation" is in Phil 1:28, yet textual variants render even that instance uncertain (and see the reflexive pronoun "your own" with "salvation" in Phil 2:12). Further, while the LXX does use the expression "our salvation," it never appears with "our" preceding "salvation," but always following (as in, e.g., Ps 17:3, 36; 4 Macc 9:4; Isa 25:9).

h. Lit., "we believed," but the aorist here is inceptive, referring to the beginning of faith.

i. A number of early manuscripts read *apothōmetha* ("let us put away"; ℵ A B C D¹ etc.), which is followed in NIV and NRSV. Fewer manuscripts read *apobalōmetha* ("let us cast off" or "throw away"; 𝔓⁴⁶ D*² F G), but *apobalōmetha* is a hapax legomenon in Paul's letters, and *apothōmetha* appears in some parallel NT passages (Eph 4:22, 25; Col 3:8; Heb 12:1; Jas 1:21; 1 Pet 2:1). Those factors make *apobalōmetha* the more difficult reading and therefore preferable (so also Jewett 816; Wolter 2:337; followed by NRSVue).

j. *Koitais* ("promiscuous sex") is the plural of *koitē*, which refers to sexual intercourse or sexual emission (as in Rom 9:10). In context, the plural implies sex that is out of control, just as Paul does not warn against eating and drinking as such but against excessive festivities.

k. *Eis epithymias* (lit., "to desires") attaches rather loosely to the remainder of v. 14b, which follows a standard construction ("make a plan for something"; BDAG s.v.).

[13:8–10] The passage opens by inverting the language of obligation in v. 7: instead of "Pay everyone what is owed," Paul writes, "Owe nothing to anyone, except to love one another." Although vv. 1–7 have as their goal the protection of the community from danger and therefore the meeting of imposed obligations for paying taxes and honors, genuine obligation lies elsewhere. Paul may be employing wording associated with monetary debt (e.g., Matt 18:28; Luke 16:5; BDAG, s.v. *opheilō*), but the obligation he introduces here is of a different sort.

Verses 8b–10 elaborate on this obligation by intertwining love with the law. The opening and closing statements constitute an inclusio that depicts and reinforces the relationship:

v. 8b   The one who loves the other fulfills the law
v. 10b   Therefore the fulfillment of the law is love

Any slight unclarity about which law Paul has in view dissolves with the citation of elements from the Decalogue in v. 9: "Do not commit adultery," "Do not murder," "Do not steal," "Do not desire." The wording follows Deut 5:17–21 and Exod 20:13–17 LXX, but Paul has omitted the commandment against lying, and he has condensed the prohibition against desire by eliminating the various specifications attached to it (the neighbor's wife, house, etc.). This leaves a prohibition against desire itself (as in 7:7; and see below, v. 14).[42] Similar abbreviations of the Decalogue appear elsewhere, however, making it unlikely that significance attaches to the details of this abbreviation (see, e.g., Luke 18:20; Jas 2:11).

With "any other commandment" Paul invokes the remainder of the Decalogue and possibly the rest of Mosaic law. All of it he finds encapsulated in a single statement drawn from Lev 19:18: "Love your neighbor as yourself." The same instruction appears in Gal 5:14 and Jas 2:8 as well as in the Jesus tradition (Matt 5:43; 22:39; Mark 12:31; Luke 10:27).[43] As with earlier similarities to the Jesus tradition in Rom 12, it may be that Paul is influenced by the Jesus tradition, yet he does not identify Jesus himself as the source, by contrast with 1 Cor 7:10. The role of Jesus Christ in these chapters is central, as in 12:5; 13:14; 14:9; 15:3, but with the possible exception of 15:3, he is not identified as a teacher.

Paul shares with other early Christian writers this emphasis on love as a characteristic of the community, notably John 13:34–35; 15:12–13, 17; 1 John 3:7–20. He has written about it in similar terms in Gal 5:13–14 and more expansively in 1 Cor 13. Phoebe's auditors will not have been familiar with Paul's other correspondence, however, much less the Johannine corpus. They will likely hear this instruction in light of what the letter has already said, most recently in ch. 12, where "let love be authentic" stands over all of vv. 9–21 (Keck 329). That passage in turn interprets what has been said earlier in the letter about love, specifically, the love of God. Romans 5:5 referred to the love of God being poured into "our" hearts. Love is simply not possible for humanity under the power of Sin (the various behaviors in 1:18–32 and 3:10–18 might be regarded as its antithesis); it comes about when God's love for humans overflows into human existence. Any inclination to imagine that the only love that matters is love between God and human individuals collides with these texts, however, where love becomes the community "rule" (12:9–10) and fulfills the law (13:9–10).

Initially v. 8a calls for love of one another, the "one another" (*allēlos*) replaying the language of mutuality in 12:5, 10, 16. In both cases, addressing

---

42. There is a minor difference in the ordering of prohibitions, as Paul follows the order of Deut 5 MS B (murder before theft), by contrast with Exod 20, which places theft before murder.

43. Notably, Gal 5:13–14 does not associate love with obligation, as Rom 13:8 does, a difference that may confirm the sense that Paul refers to obligation largely by way of transition from 13:6–7 to this new topic.

gatherings in Rome, Paul focuses on love within those groups. Verse 8b takes things in a slightly different direction, however, referring to "the one who loves the other" (*heteros*). The language changes again in vv. 9b–10, with the citation of Lev 19:18, which commands love of the "neighbor" (*plēsion*). Interpreters differ over whether "the other" extends love beyond the community, with some finding that Paul refers to individuals "who are different from us" (Moo 830) and others that this instruction addresses the community alone (Jewett 813).[44] Since he is addressing particular communities at Rome, it seems fair to suppose that his concern here is for these people in relationship to one another. We have already seen, however, that the boundaries around this community (or communities; see the introduction and on 16:3–16), are permeable (as reflected in 12:13–21). More to the point, the love "God poured into our hearts" (5:5) is precisely love for those who are weak, ungodly, sinners at enmity with God (5:6–10). Given the reach of God's own love, it is difficult to imagine that Paul regards love "for one another" to end at the proverbial church door.[45] Again, the best evidence of what Paul means by loving the neighbor comes in 12:9–21, where love is depicted in specific acts of caring for others.

Paul reinforces concern for the neighbor in v. 10a: "Love does not produce evil for the neighbor." That statement is likely an instance of *litotes*, since love can scarcely be reduced to the avoidance of evil (as is clear in 12:9–21), but the wording aptly summarizes the four prohibitions cited in v. 9a, as each of them is harmful to the neighbor (and see 1 Cor 13:4–7). In addition, this way of putting things—the avoidance of doing evil to the neighbor—anticipates the discussion in ch. 14, where Paul will prioritize concern for the welfare of other believers over the assertion of one's own prerogatives. Destroying "the work of God" and causing the brother or sister to fall (14:20–21) could well serve as examples of producing evil for the neighbor.

If the letter as a whole makes clear what Paul means by love, both God's love for humans and humanity's practice of love for one another, it is far less clear what Paul wants to convey about the law. The language of fulfilling the law presupposes that the law warrants fulfillment; there would be no need to mention the law in this particular context if Paul were in fact disregarding or undermining it (as he denied early on; see 3:31). To speak of the law's fulfillment (*plērōma*), however, is not the equivalent of saying that the law is "done" (as with *poieō* in 2:13–14 or *prassō* in 2:25).[46] If Paul does not say that the

---

44. The appearance of "neighbor" (*plēsion*) in 15:2, where Paul is addressing conduct within the assemblies in Rome, could count in favor of a narrow reading of 13:8–9, although nothing in that passage restricts concern to the boundaries of the believing community.

45. One might be forgiven for hearing in this debate an echo of the question of Luke 10:29.

46. On this distinction, see Barclay 1988, 135–42; Westerholm 1988, 201–5; 2004, 435–37; and the discussion in de Boer 2011, 345. And see above on 8:4, where there is a similar ambiguity.

law has come to an end when love is practiced, he also does not say that love constitutes the keeping of the law.

A related ambiguity surrounds Paul's assertion that the law is "summed up" (*anakephalaioō*) by Lev 19:18. That text appears elsewhere, as noted above, in summaries of the law. Matthew 22:36–40 pairs it with the first commandment (love of God) as the two great commandments on which "the whole law and the prophets depend."[47] Luke 10:27–28 also pairs Deut 6:5 with Lev 19:18, adding the stipulation "Do this and you will live." Paul, by contrast, does not identify love of neighbor as an entry point to the entirety of the law. Neither does he claim that love offers a path to new life or salvation, something he identifies with the death and new life of baptism into Christ (6:1–11). That the law is "summed up" again recognizes the law's significance while not necessarily prioritizing it.

Even with these ambiguities of expression, taken on its own this brief passage might be construed as evidence that Paul derives his ethic from and centers it on *nomos* (as in Schreiber 2012, 117). The surrounding context, however, presents a serious challenge to that notion. This passage marks the last reference to *nomos* in Romans and the first time Paul has employed it since the notorious claim in 10:4 that "Christ is the end of the law." That slim fact warrants reflection.[48] More to the point, the long discussion of ch. 12 makes no appeal to the law. In ch. 14 Paul not only does not appeal to the law but instead appears to undermine it with his claim that "the reign of God does not consist of eating and drinking."[49] Whatever role the law plays in this text, it does not serve as the source of Paul's instruction elsewhere in chs. 12–15; nor does it stand as an identifying mark of the new community. It is instead to Christ that Paul appeals, especially in 12:5; 13:14; 14:9; 15:3, 5–6.[50]

The ambiguity in Paul's treatment of the law forces two questions: Why even bother to introduce the law? And why do so at this point in the letter? It may be that he knows, or fears, that he is suspected of undermining the law, although such a conclusion is by no means obvious. Read in context, this passage reinforces the emphasis on active love in 12:9–21. Perhaps more importantly, it

---

47. Later Jewish texts provide such summaries as pedagogical elements that offer an entry point into the study and observance of torah, something on evidence neither in Paul nor in the Gospels (see Donaldson 1995).

48. As noted earlier, Paul concludes his lengthy discourse on God and Israel (and the gentiles) without further reference to the law (see above on 10:4 and Gaventa 2016a), effectively writing of Israel's future without connecting that future to law observance.

49. While later interpreters may have found it convenient to separate ethical from cultic regulations, that convenience overlooks the significance of dietary practice for many first-century Jews.

50. To be clear, this is not to claim that Paul has ceased to be a Jew or that he has become anti-Jewish, but it is to notice how radically his understanding of God's action in Jesus Christ now shapes his thinking.

prepares for the difficult discussion in ch. 14, where Paul elevates the requirements love imposes even as he tacitly undermines a significant element of the law by aligning himself with those who regard the food laws as having been abrogated. In that argument, love in the form of respecting the qualms of fellow believers may in fact observe certain elements of the law in practice even while undermining them in theory (see below on 14:17).

[11–14] These lines are easily overlooked, overshadowed as they are by the more accessible discussion of love in vv. 8–10 and the extensive treatment in ch. 14 of conflicts in (or among) the assemblies. Here Paul returns to the foreground the apocalyptic character of the life he sketches in these chapters. Already in 12:1–2 the notion of nonconformity to "this age" has prepared the stage. In addition, the reference to future divine judgment in 14:10–12 reiterates the lordship of Christ, and the language of rejoicing in 15:9–13 anticipates the fulfillment of Christ's "welcome" in the rejoicing of Jew and gentile alike. Apocalyptic elements do not merely whisper in this passage—they shout, locating the lives of those who are called solidly in the realm of the future that already shapes the present.

Paul moves from the obligation to love to the urgency of the time with the clause "especially knowing what time it is." The subject of this knowledge is the "we" who believe, who cast off works of darkness in favor of light's weapons, who even put on Christ himself. Paul shifts to second-person address in vv. 11b and 14, but this introductory phrase assumes a shared knowledge on the basis of which he can make his appeal. It locates Paul and his audience together in time and sets the tone for what follows. It also tacitly acknowledges those others who do not know, although Paul does not linger over that difference.

What "we" know, Paul writes, is the "time," and time references saturate these few verses. Some such references are obvious: "time," "already," "hour," "now," "night," and "day." In addition, because the language of darkness and light conveys the experience of night and day, it also is a reference to time.[51] By extension, "wake from sleep" is also time-related language. "When we began to believe" suggests a time when "we" did not believe, further reinforcing the preoccupation of this passage with time and the urgency of Paul's remarks.

Knowing the time—even the hour—means that "you should wake from sleep." This contrast between sleep and wakefulness appears earlier in 1 Thess 5:6; it also occurs in the gospel tradition (Mark 13:35–37 // Matt 24:42, 44). Wakefulness is urgent because (*gar*) salvation is near "now." In this letter, "now" (*nyn, nyni*) has often functioned to call attention to the new situation in place by virtue of God's intervention in Jesus Christ. "Now" marks the

---

51. This obvious association can easily be lost for readers who, given artificial illumination, no longer experience night as unavoidable darkness. That loss in turn opens the door for distorting this imagery into language about skin color, a move to be rejected in the strongest terms.

rectifying act of God in the crucifixion of Jesus (3:21), which takes place in the "now time" (3:26; also 8:18; 11:5, 30). "Now" humans have received reconciliation through Jesus Christ (5:11), and "now" they have been moved from one lordship to another, from that of Sin to that of God (6:19, 21–22). There is "now" no condemnation for those in Christ Jesus (8:1). Paul also uses "now" simply to refer to a present situation (15:23, 25), but the frequency with which he associates "now" with reference to gospel events is notable.

The "now" of v. 11 is specifically the present in which salvation has drawn near to "us." Whatever has already happened, salvation is not accomplished, or at least it is not completed. It is not something humans "have" at all, but something that moves toward the present (as does "the day" in v. 12a). Similarly urgent claims appear in the gospel tradition, attached to the reign of God (Mark 1:15; Matt 4:17). Elsewhere in the NT, Heb 10:25 asserts that the "day" is coming near, and 1 Pet 4:7 that the "end" (*telos*) has come near, while Jas 5:8 explicitly claims that the parousia of the Lord has come near.

Paul does not explicitly name the parousia, however. Unlike 1 Thess 2:19; 3:13; 4:13–18; 5:23, and 1 Cor 15:23–28, Romans never explicitly addresses the parousia of Jesus. In 8:18–39 Paul takes his audience to the brink of that event, anticipating the glory of the future and assuring them that nothing has the power to separate "us" from God's love. Just where one might expect some depiction of Jesus's triumphant return, however, Paul suspends that line of thought, taking up instead the extended treatment of God's dealings with Israel (and the gentiles) in chs. 9–11. In 11:26–32 he again anticipates the fulfillment of God's saving act, but reference to the parousia is still muted (perhaps "the deliverer," 11:26), and he turns instead to doxology (11:33–36) and paraenesis (12:1–15:6).

That "salvation" has come near recalls the opening of the letter with its announcement about God's saving power (1:16–17). The gospel, for Paul, simply *is* God's power bringing about salvation through the death and resurrection of Jesus Christ. In other letters, Paul writes of God rescuing from "the present evil age" (Gal 1:4) or of Jesus "delivering us from impending wrath" (1 Thess 1:10). Paul does not depict the arrival of salvation in detail, as the point in Rom 13 is neither to comfort (as in 1 Thess 4:14–18) nor to reassure his Roman auditors of the power of God (as in 1 Cor 15), but to magnify for them the emergency conditions in which they now live.

Verse 11 ends with a somewhat unusual reference to belief or trust: "when we began to believe." Although he does elsewhere employ the inceptive aorist with the verb "believe" (e.g., 10:14; 1 Cor 3:5; 15:2; Gal 2:16), only here does Paul draw attention to the beginning of faith with the adverb "when" (*hote*). Time is marked from that point, from when "we" believed, although faith is itself a by-product of God's intervention in Christ, as in 2 Cor 5:16, where "our" altered epistemology results from the death of Christ for all. By gauging the nearness of salvation according to the time "when we began to believe," gospel events that happened to "us," Paul emphasizes the implications for "us." In addition, with the use of first-person plural, Paul maintains his place alongside the Romans, calling them to look with him at what is happening.

Verse 12 recasts the claim about the nearness of salvation into the realm of night and day:

v. 11b   *Salvation is nearer* us than when we began to believe
v. 12a   The night has passed, and *the day has come near*

Salvation and the day are both said to draw near, although the grammatical expressions differ. That juxtaposition of salvation and day in turn exerts pressure on understanding what Paul means by "day" here. "Day" has clear associations with the prophetic notion of the "day of the Lord" as the day of judgment (as in, e.g., Isa 13:6, 9; Ezek 13:5; 30:3; Joel 2:1, 11, 31; Amos 5:20). Paul does use that language elsewhere (1 Cor 5:5; 2 Cor 1:14; 1 Thess 5:2), and in Romans he refers to a day of accounting in 2:5, 16 (and see 14:10). Yet this passage does not anticipate judgment as such; it instead invokes the day as the time of salvation in which Paul and the Romans *already live* (similarly to 2 Cor 6:2, with its citation of Isa 49:8).

Taken together, these two statements suggest that when "we" began to believe, "we" lived in the night. The call to "cast off the works of darkness" reinforces that suggestion, since it presupposes that those "works" threaten. In the context of Romans, this notion is scarcely surprising, given the argument of 1:18–5:21. If God acts to rectify weak, ungodly sinners who are God's own enemies (5:5–10), it cannot be surprising that Paul identifies those same people (including himself: "we") as having been clothed in the works of darkness.

With v. 12b Paul moves to the implications of this impending crisis. The contrast between the first and second halves of this statement is revealing:

> Let us cast off the *works* of *darkness*
> Let us put on the *weapons* of *light*

Contrasts between darkness and light characterize many premodern traditions, so it is not at all surprising to find them in Jewish traditions as well. Associations of God and God's blessings with light, evil or enemies of God with darkness, appear extensively in Israel's Scriptures (e.g., Ps 43:3; Isa 9:2; 42:6; Zech 14:7), other Second Temple literature (e.g., 1 En. 41.8; 92.4–5; 108.11; 1QS 1.9–11; 2.16; 3.13, 20–22; 1QM 1.1–17; 3.6, 9; 13.16; Philo, *Creation* 33; *Alleg. Interp.* 3.167; *God* 3), and elsewhere in the NT (e.g., Luke 16:8; John 3:19–21; 1 Pet 2:9; Rev 22:5), including Paul's own letters (1 Thess 5:4–5, 8; 2 Cor 6:14).

If the contrast between darkness and light is unsurprising, the parallel contrast between "works" and "weapons" is surprising. Darkness and light might both produce "works" of some sort, but Paul disturbs the parallel with "weapons" instead. Works associated with darkness, of course, recalls ch. 1 with its extensive list of vices. Importantly, the works there are also produced by darkness, at least in the sense that the behavior Paul describes is produced after humanity has been "handed over" to "unsuitable passions" and "dishonorable thinking" (1:26, 28). That handing over originates with human refusal to acknowledge God as God (1:18–23), to be sure, but the specific actions or works he describes are those produced by the handed-over humans.

By contrast with the works produced by darkness, Paul urges the Romans to put on "weapons of light." In 6:13–23 Paul identifies the addressees themselves as weapons (*hopla*), previously the weapons of Sin but now weapons of God for righteousness. Now the addressees are themselves to take up weapons, but they are the weapons of light. The language closely resembles 1 Thess 5:8, which also links life in the day (light) with being wrapped up in the armor of faith (cf. Eph 6:10–11, 14). The notion of putting on armor is a familiar one elsewhere as well (e.g., Herodotus, *Hist.* 7.218.2; Isa 59:17; Wis 5:17; T. Levi 8.2; Josephus, *Ant.* 7.283; Philo, *Embassy*, 97). The *hopla* here appear to be defensive weapons that serve to protect against the vices depicted in v. 13b; perhaps better, they serve as defenses against the darkness itself.

Reflection on Paul's use of darkness and light language in comparison with literature from Qumran may prove useful. In 1QS 1.9–11 a distinction is made between the "children of light" and the "children of darkness," the latter of whom are to be hated (and see 1QS 2.16; 3.13). In a similar vein, the Treatise of the Two Spirits contrasts the work of the Prince of Lights with that of the Angel of Darkness (1QS 3.20–22). More graphically, the War Scroll depicts a future battle between the sons of light and those of darkness (1QM 1.1–17), in which God will "exterminate all the sons of darkness" (13.16). In preparation for this battle, members of the community are to write slogans on their trumpets, including the words "God's battle formations for avenging his wrath against all the sons of darkness" (1QM 3.6 [Martínez and Tigchelaar 1997]).

Paul shares in the dualistic perspective of these texts, although there are revealing differences. For those Jews who produced the Treatise of the Two Spirits and the War Scroll, a sharp line exists between two groups—a line marked by conflict and enmity, even destruction. For Paul, the second group can only be inferred.[52] He invokes the difference between night and day to urge action in the present rather than to inculcate hatred toward the outside. As we have seen elsewhere in the letter, he is far more preoccupied with articulating what God has done and will do on behalf of humanity, even all humanity

---

52. Paul does comment on those who belong to the night and darkness in 1 Thess 5:5, yet he follows that comment with an admonition that the community seek the good both for one another and for all people (5:15).

(11:32), than he is with castigating outsiders. Those who understand that they themselves were once God's enemies (5:10) are less likely to see other humans as their enemies.

Verse 13 provides limited specificity to Paul's instructions: "As in the day, let us live decently." "Day" here, continuing the language of light that precedes it, simply means a time when actions would be visible (under the all-capturing eye of the surveillance camera). The previous reference to the arrival of the day of salvation might suggest completed eschatological life is in view, but Paul does not anticipate what life will look like following the parousia. Slender phrases in Rom 6:8; Phil 1:23; and 1 Thess 4:17 convey a longing to be united with Christ, but they do not carry with them an appeal to live "decently" (*euschēmonōs*; see 1 Thess 4:12; 1 Cor 14:40). Here that decency or propriety is defined largely by its opposites in the verse that follows. Having sketched in ch. 12 the character of life in Christ, here Paul alludes to it only briefly.

Verse 13b itemizes some actions that might well be classified as works of darkness: riotous feasts, drinking bouts, promiscuous sex, indecent behavior, conflict, and jealousy.[53] These "works" are standard elements of vice lists (Gal 5:19–21; 2 Cor 12:20–21; Eph 4:19; 1 Pet 4:3). The fact that Paul concludes the list with two "works" that directly bear on communal disputes may be deliberate, given the content of ch. 14 (and see 1 Cor 3:3, where concern about ecclesial fractures opens the body of the letter).

By contrast with these works of darkness, in v. 14 Paul again calls on the Romans to "put on" (*endyō*), but this time the object is not weapons (as in v. 12) but "the Lord Jesus Christ." This is a striking image, because "put on" appears regularly with clothing (e.g., Mark 1:6; 15:20), with weapons (as above), and with attributes or virtues (e.g., 1 Cor 15:53; Luke 24:49). But reference to "putting on" a person is unusual.[54] Importantly, Gal 3:27 employs the verb "to put on" of baptism as the point when "you put on Christ," and several scholars identify this passage with early baptismal liturgy (e.g., Schlier 395–97; J. Kim 2004, 135–36), but the phrase is significant beyond its reminder of baptism. In a remarkable exposition of this statement, Chrysostom compares it with a saying of his own time about being "wrapped up" in another person, connoting love and constant devotion (*Hom. Rom.* 24; *NPNF*[1] 11.520).

With the final words of v. 14, "make no plans" that cater to the desires of the flesh, Paul lumps together the vices itemized in v. 13b. Such behavior offers evidence of a mindset oriented toward "the flesh." Notably, in 1:24 humanity

---

53. Ambrosiaster characterizes those feasts as "extravagant banquets which are thrown with a contribution from all the participants or are put on by each of the comrades in turn" (239). That interpretation may indicate that Ambrosiaster understands such feasts in associational terms. On customs around meals in associations, see Kloppenborg 2019, 209–44, 399–409.

54. In Dionysius of Halicarnassus, *Ant. rom.* 11.5.2, reference is made to someone who "puts on" Tarquinius, but in that instance the individual is impersonating Tarquinius.

is characterized by desires of the heart that are oriented toward themselves and away from God. Humanity is rendered incapable of resisting such desires.[55] In the "now time" of the Christ event, to engage in such behavior is to live as if the "now time" had not begun.

If the urging to "put on Christ" is unusual syntactically, it nonetheless ought not come as a surprise, given that Paul makes multiple appeals to Christ in this part of the letter. Believers are "in Christ," which governs the way they understand their relationships both to him and to one another (12:5–21). They belong to the Lord Jesus Christ and eschatologically will stand before his judgment (14:8–12). They have obligations to those for whom Christ died (14:15). They are to treat one another as Christ treated them (15:1–6), in the hope that they will share a mindset marked by Christ Jesus (15:5). However much elements in these chapters resemble ancient moral philosophy or other Jewish writings, what holds them together in Paul's presentation is the fact of Jesus Christ— more specifically, the immediacy of God's apocalypse in Jesus Christ.

Perceiving the role of the Christ event in this section of the letter helps contextualize Paul's remarks about the law in the preceding lines. Love fulfills the law, and that is good; nothing Paul writes here critiques the law. Nonetheless, the law does not shape Paul's instruction.[56] To the contrary, it is Christ who shapes it. In this way, Paul is preparing for the delicate controversy to be taken up in ch. 14. There again he will write no word against the law. He will not even use the term *nomos*. Instead, he will appeal to the lordship of Christ and the necessity of caring for other members of the community, even to the extent of sacrificing one's own prerogatives. And when he writes that the "reign of God" is not about diet, because the one who serves Christ pleases God, the law appears to have been eclipsed.

Commenting effectively about vv. 11–14 is exceedingly difficult. It is one thing to sift the imagery in vv. 11–14, unpacking references and tracking their usage elsewhere, but Paul is not simply opening an apocalyptic toolbox in order to frighten his auditors into compliance. Instead, he is grasping for words to convey something that lies beyond any human articulation—that the final triumph of God has arrived at the threshold.[57] It has opened the door. Not only that—it has thrust open the doors and windows and is on its way into a world

55. Paul's concern about inappropriate desires was widely shared, as ably documented by Stowers, although Paul's remedy is scarcely mastery of the self (1994, 46–52).

56. Sanders astutely observes that Paul does not offer a positive instruction about precisely how much feasting and eating is permitted; that is, Paul is not writing an early Christian halakah (1983, 119).

57. In a public reading decades ago, Toni Morrison was asked about her writing process. She extended her arm and remarked (as I recall), "The words you want are always over *there*, just out of reach." That is a struggle for all writers, but it is especially apt when commenting on a passage of this sort.

that simultaneously groans (8:22) and clings to the way things are (13:11–14). *That* is where "we" live, breath sharply drawn, poised for what comes next.

14:1–12 Differences over Dinner

"Welcome the one who is weak in faith" introduces a discussion of commensality that extends through 15:6, although that way of putting the subject already distorts things. As important as questions of dining partners and menu items were in the Roman world,[58] more important for Paul is upbuilding the groups in relationship to their rightful Lord. Paul has been preparing for this discussion throughout chs. 12–13. The initial claim that there is "one body" in Christ (12:4–5) returns here, as does the exhortation to be wrapped up in Christ (13:14), since it is the Romans' shared relationship to Christ that funds this passage. In addition, Paul's warnings about thinking too highly of oneself (12:3, 16) prepare for the instructions in this passage, particularly in the questions of 14:4, 10. His claim that love fulfills the law (13:10) may also play a role, since it respects the law while at the same time framing the law in terms of love, particularly love of the neighbor (note 15:2).

Paul's comments make it difficult not to inquire about the situation at Rome, and commentators have done so at least since Origen (*Comm. Rom.* 9.35). Yet it is equally impossible to achieve the precision we would like because Paul himself is indirect. Not having been to Rome and not having the established relationships that permit him considerable latitude elsewhere, he needs to proceed with care. That indirectness prompts some interpreters (notably Karris 1991) to conclude that Paul addresses a general concern rather than a particular situation at Rome, but the sheer extent of this discussion weighs heavily in favor of a specific problem at Rome, as most contemporary scholars agree.

Agreement that Paul has a specific situation in view is more widespread than agreement on the precise nature of the situation.[59] It seems clear that some among the Roman addressees are convinced they must (continue to) observe Mosaic dietary law (including certain days of fasting), while others are convinced that they do not need to do so. Such disputes matter little when people consume their daily meals, or even when small groups of similarly inclined believers gather, but the problem becomes acute when groups come together in a larger assembly and the host determines the menu (as in 1 Cor 10:27). That would especially be the case if there were Jews who experienced pressure from other Jews because of their association with Christian circles (Barclay 1996a, 291, 298–99).

---

58. The literature on this topic is extensive. See Smit 2007 for a convenient collection of both primary and secondary literature.

59. For reviews of this debate, see Cranfield 2:690–96; Reasoner 1999, 1–23; Toney 2008, 1–42.

Notably, although the dispute arises from varying relationships to Mosaic law, Paul does not identify these as Jewish or gentile groups, although elsewhere in the letter he repeatedly refers to Jews and gentiles or Greeks (e.g., 1:16; 2:10; 3:9). In addition, he does not hesitate to single out gentiles for direct address when he thinks the circumstances warrant (11:13, 17–24). This may mean that disagreement does not fall along strictly ethnic lines. After all, Paul himself is a Jew, and he explicitly says in 14:14 that no food is impure. It could also mean that he is reluctant to identify the dispute with ethnic difference lest he ignite or exacerbate ethnic tensions (so Grieb 2002, 127).

The designations Paul does use are quite revealing, and they provide a strong indication of what he hopes to achieve. Initially, he refers to the "one who is weak in faith," but not to the strong until 15:1. Along the way he identifies them as the Lord's household slaves, brothers and sisters, the "one for whom Christ died" (v. 15), "the work of God" (v. 20), and "the neighbor" (15:2, cf. 13:9). All these designations derive from the gospel, reflecting their relationship to God's action in Jesus Christ. That relationship, rather than either ethnic identification or relationship to Mosaic law, is prior and determinative in Paul's treatment of the subject.

Paul opens by questioning his auditors' right to judge one another, invoking the power and prerogatives of God (14:1–12). The evenhandedness of vv. 1–12 gives way in vv. 13–23 to a warning that those who are confident about eating anything can in fact undermine the faith of others. The conclusion (15:1–6) redefines power, real power, in terms of Christ's own behavior and culminates in a prayer-wish that locates all parties together in the worship of God. These are not three distinct sections but are closely interconnected, separated in the commentary only for convenience of presentation.

14:1 And welcome the one who is weak in faith, but not for disputes over debated matters. 2 One person has faith sufficient to eat everything, but the one who is weak eats only vegetables.[a] 3 The one who eats everything must not disdain the one who does not eat, and the one who does not eat must not judge the one who eats, for God has welcomed her[b] into the household. 4 After all, who are you to be judging the household slave of another? She will stand or fall before her own Lord. And she will stand, because the Lord is powerful enough to make her stand.

5 One person assesses one day as different from another, but another assesses every day the same. Let each person be convinced in his own mind. 6 The one who is intent on the particular[c] day is such in the Lord; and the one who eats, eats in the Lord, for he gives thanks to God. Also, the one who does not eat does not eat in the Lord, and he gives thanks to God. 7 This is the case because none of us lives to himself and none dies to himself, 8 so if we live, we live to the Lord, and if we die, we die to the

Lord; so whether we live or whether we die, we belong to the Lord. 9 It is for this very reason that Christ died and lived again,[d] that he would be Lord both of the dead and of the living. 10 You, why do you judge your brother or sister? Or you, why do you disdain your brother or sister? For all of us will stand before God's[e] judgment seat. 11 As it is written, "As I live, says the Lord, before me every knee will bend and every tongue will praise God." 12 Therefore, each of us will give a self-account to God.[f]

a. A few manuscripts read the imperative form *esthietō*, "let him eat" ($\mathfrak{P}^{46}$ D* F G), rather than the indicative "[he] eats." Although the imperative variant has claim to be the more difficult reading, upending the careful parallel statements, it is not widely attested and may reflect influence from the imperatives in v. 3 (Cranfield 2:701).

b. "Him" in Greek, but altered here to make the scope of the households visible, consistent with the names in 16:3–15.

c. "Particular" is added to make clear that Paul's comment concerns the one who observes rather than the one who regards all days as equal.

d. Several variants replace "Christ died and lived again," as in "Christ died and was raised" (F G 629) or "Christ died and was raised and lived again" (including $\aleph^2$ D Ψ), but none is widely attested, and the desire to smooth out the unusual "lived again" is obvious.

e. A number of manuscripts replace "before God's" with "before Christ's" (including $\aleph^2$ C^2 Ψ), apparently under pressure from the preceding statement that Christ is Lord of both dead and living.

f. The phrase "to God" is included by $\aleph$ A C D^2 Ψ and other manuscripts, but it is also omitted in a number of manuscripts (including B F G). Although it is difficult to imagine why scribes would have deliberately excised the phrase, it could have resulted from homoioteleuton, given the presence of the same words, *tō theō* ("[praise] God"), at the end of v. 11.

[14:1] Nothing at the beginning of this verse indicates a major transition in the argument. There is no "So I urge you" (as in 12:1) or "Now, brothers and sisters, I myself am confident" (as in 15:14) that would signal to auditors a shift of focus. Auditors may hear the *de* ("and") in 14:1 as a connection to the preceding statements, and that connection with "putting on" Christ is important for approaching this passage.

"Welcome the one who is weak in faith" obviously addresses those outside that group, those often and problematically referred to as "the strong." (Paul does not refer to "the strong" until 15:1, and even then there is no reason to think "the strong" is a fixed designation for a particular group, whether a self-designation or otherwise.) Even this initial address hints that it is those who are *not* weak who most need instruction (as Paul sees it), a point confirmed by vv. 13–23. Importantly, neither here nor anywhere else in the passage does Paul admonish "the weak" to change their dietary practices or encourage them to strengthen their faith, although he does insist that both sides refrain from judgment.

The end of v. 1 warrants attention: people are not to be welcomed for the purpose of debate. Already this phrase hints at Paul's concern. A positive explanation of welcome emerges in ch. 15, but here a serious warning is sounded against those whose welcome is contingent and condescending, whose outstretched hand offers a syllabus for the instruction of the brother or sister. Welcoming people only to argue with them does not constitute genuine welcome.

Paul does not yet specify what he means by the "weak in faith," which must be learned from the context, although perhaps Phoebe amplifies.[60] Elsewhere it is the context that suggests its implications. In 1 Thess 5:14 the weak are associated with the disorderly and low in spirit, while in 1 Cor 8:10–11 the weak in conscience are susceptible to harm from those who consume food that has been sacrificed to idols. Romans 4:19 describes Abraham as not weakening in his confidence (*pistis*) about God's promise of a child, while 5:6 claims that Christ died "while we were still weak."

[2–4] The opening admonition to those who are not weak now falls aside, and vv. 2–12 address both sides with parity. Parallel statements in vv. 2–3 describe the disputes at Rome and offer initial instructions, followed in v. 3b by a theological warrant and in v. 4 by a challenge to their (presumed) behavior, reinforced by further theological explanation.

v. 2	One person has faith sufficient to eat everything	but the one who is weak eats only vegetables.
v. 3	The one who eats everything must not disdain	and the one who does not eat must not judge,

v. 3b   for God has welcomed her.

v. 4   Who are you to be judging the household slave of another?
She will stand or fall before her own Lord.
And she will stand,
because the Lord is powerful enough to make her stand.

The contrast in v. 2 between "everything" and "only vegetables" provides a glimpse, however limited, into the conflict. There are those who eat *panta* ("everything") and those who eat only vegetables. The latter may be a hyperbolic reference to those so concerned about violating Jewish law that they severely restrict their diets, although there is evidence that substantiates just such practice (as in Dan 1:8–16; 2 Macc 5:27; Josephus, *Life* 14; cf. also Jdt 12:1–2;

---

60. Gäckle suggests that Phoebe, Prisca, and Aquila are familiar with Paul's understanding of weakness and thus can explain it, distinguishing it from a negative Stoic interpretation (2005, 447–48).

Add Esth 14:17). The phrase about eating "everything" also warrants attention, for it may convey more than disregard for Mosaic dietary practice. Eating "everything" would not sit well in a culture for which dietary moderation was a virtue.[61] In addition, for Jews, eating "everything" hints at the excess attributed to gentiles, who were thought to worship anything and to engage in sexual relations with anyone (Rom 1:18–32; Wis 13–15).

Paul does not label these eaters as strong, but he does say that they "have faith" or they "believe" they may eat everything. The combination of the verb *pisteuein* ("believe" or "trust") with an infinitive appears nowhere else in Paul's letters, since he normally employs the verb for trust or confidence in God or God's actions (e.g., 1:16; 4:17; 1 Cor 15:11; Gal 2:16). As the argument proceeds, it appears that this is a shorthand expression for those whose faith is not tied to dietary law, by comparison with those whose faith remains entangled with dietary law (Barclay 2013b, 194).

Verses 3b–4 begin Paul's response: neither side is to judge the one on the other side, because "God has welcomed her." With this compact phrase, replayed in 15:7 as the welcome of Christ "for the glory of God," Paul epitomizes the gospel's anthropological implications as an event of welcome. The salient feature of both the eaters and the abstainers is not that they either eat or abstain but that God has already welcomed them. By implication, what is *not* important is this difference over dietary practice.

The implications of God's welcome emerge sharply in v. 4: "Who are you to be judging the household slave of another?" The terminology here is not *doulos* (as in 1:1; 6:19–20) but *oiketēs*, specifically a household slave (BDAG s.v.; LSJ s.v.). Consistent with the notion that the problem here is one of hospitality when the communities gather, Paul spins out the analogy of the household. In this case the real householder is God, not the human host of the meal.

This continued use of slavery imagery reflects the world in which Paul lived, where slavery was ubiquitous, even as it deeply offends contemporary notions of human dignity, to say nothing of violating biblical understandings of God's love of humanity. As elsewhere, this is Paul's attempt to articulate the relationship humans have to God, reflecting his own conviction that no human is ever free from the influence or power of another party (note 6:20–23; Gaventa 2015). Ironically, however, this statement simultaneously undermines the notion of the human householder's rights.[62] If God is the householder—the real householder—then the owner is not; he or she is

---

61. Sandnes lists some twenty-eight Greek terms for gluttony, which is impressive in and of itself, as he notes (2002, 36). Moreover, eating within limits, with restraint, was identified as a virtue (e.g., Epictetus, *Diatr.* 1.13.1; Epicurus, *Sent. Vat.* 59; *Ep. Men.* 130–31; Galen, *San. Tu.* 6.14 [449K]).

62. I am grateful to Rodney Kilgore for this observation.

relegated to subservience alongside others, leveling the relationship of slave and human householder.

The remainder of v. 4 elaborates this notion of God as householder. The individual stands or falls before her own Lord. The notion of God as one's own Lord is striking, recalling Paul's use of "my Lord Jesus Christ" (Phil 3:8) and "my God" (e.g., 1:8; 1 Cor 1:4; 2 Cor 12:21). Here Paul implicitly contrasts that person's Lord with other possible lords (such as fellow believers). Paul immediately assures his auditors: she will stand *because* God is able to make her stand. If the notion of "standing" earlier in Romans is that of remaining firm or finding oneself in a certain place (as in 5:2 and 11:20; cf. 1 Cor 15:1; 2 Cor 1:24), here it takes on a sense of standing in the face of threat (as in Eph 6:13–14; Ps 35:13 LXX). Verse 12 will anticipate that everyone gives an account to God, but the assurance offered here is profound: God is able to sustain (and see 1 Thess 5:23–24). The threatening language of 2:8–9 undergoes a significant alteration here, where the individual's eschatological future is no longer determined by that person's behavior. An account will be given, but God is able to make that one stand. This anticipation of divine accountability categorically excludes any ground for judging others.

[5–10] As noted above, these verses replay and expand on the statements in vv. 2–4. First, Paul offers straightforward observations about behavior; second, he interprets the behavior theologically; and finally, he presses again the question about judgment.

v. 5   One person assesses one day as different   but another assesses every day
       from another . . .   the same.

       Let each person be convinced in his own mind.

v. 6   The one who is intent on the particular day is
       such in the Lord;
       and the one who eats, eats in the Lord,   for he gives thanks to God.
       Also, the one who does not eat does not   and he gives thanks to God.
       eat in the Lord,

       v. 7   None of us lives to himself and none dies to himself.
       v. 8   If we live, we live to the Lord, and if we die, we die to the Lord.
              Whether we live or whether we die, we belong to the Lord.
       v. 9   It is for this very reason that Christ died and lived again,
              that he would be Lord both of the dead and of the living.

       v. 10 You, why do you judge your brother or sister?
              Or you, why do you disdain your brother or sister?
              For all of us will stand before God's judgment seat.

Verse 5 introduces a new element in the controversy, namely, the observance of particular days. Paul quickly returns to the discussion of eating, making it likely that these are days of fasting, although no certainty is possible.[63] At any rate, Paul appears to assume they will understand what he means and simply adds, "Let each person be fully convinced in his own mind." This notion—that it matters how one regards one's own actions—already seems to undermine the expectation that there is a right and wrong stance on the dispute, anticipating Paul's later comments about the dangers of prompting people to act against their convictions (vv. 14, 23). This statement also anticipates Paul's later affirmation of the "eaters." If what matters is that someone believes she is right in her dietary practice, then the action itself (or lack of action) is irrelevant. Paul slips this comment in without further elaboration. Personal conviction matters, but more than personal conviction is at stake, as becomes obvious.

Verse 6 again describes two different patterns of behavior, as previously in v. 2, but this time the differences in behavior are explicitly identified as actions "in the Lord." One person observes days (of feasting), one eats, one does not eat, and all of them are said to act "in the Lord" and to "give thanks to God." Large seams of this letter are hereby invoked: the initial charge against humanity includes the claim that humans did not give thanks to God (1:21), so this assertion that both sides *do* thank God is crucial. They were baptized into Christ (6:3–4) and now inhabit one body in him (12:4–5). Whatever they do is done in the Lord, not simply eating and abstaining but the whole of life and death.

From the single issue of diet, Paul shifts in vv. 7–9 abruptly to the whole of life and death, declaring that all of life and death are "in the Lord." A certain unintended irony is at work here, as vv. 5–6 minimize the dispute, but vv. 7–9 suddenly transpose the discussion into the realm of life and death. The point, of course, is that the whole of life belongs to God. That life belongs to God is fundamental to biblical understandings of the world, but it is particularly appropriate to Romans, since 1:16–17 announces God's saving power in the gospel events, and 1:18–32 discloses humanity's determination to belong to itself rather than to God the Creator.

What Paul has in view in Rom 14 is not creation as such, however, but the death and resurrection of Christ. With the words "for this very reason," v. 9a introduces the terse gospel summary, "Christ died and lived again." Elsewhere Paul uses the language of resurrection (*egeirō*), as in 1 Cor 15:3–4; Rom 4:24–25, and the slight variation to "live" (*zaō*) reflects Paul's shaping of the formula to the present context. "Our" life and death belong to the Lord because he died and lived.

---

63. Margaret Williams presents evidence of fasting on the Sabbath by Roman Jews (2004), which is one candidate for the "day" to which Paul refers.

Verse 9b makes the point explicit: "that he would be Lord both of the dead and of the living." The order "the dead and the living" reverses that of vv. 7–8, as it follows the order of Christ's own death and resurrection. More than literary repetition is at work here, however. This ordering recalls ch. 6, with the baptismal move from death in Sin to life in Christ. The death and resurrection of Christ bring about this lordship, in that they defeat Sin and Death itself (see 6:6–11). This text participates in that apocalyptic claim about the rulership of the world. In other words, v. 9 recalls, however tersely, God's action in Christ to rescue the world from its captivity to Sin and Death.

Verse 10 parallels v. 4, again with the emphatic pronoun "you." Here Paul turns to the familial language of "brother" instead of the language of household slave, giving the indictment a more personal sting. It is one thing to judge another person, another to judge a brother or sister. There is no cause to judge or disdain, since all people will stand before God's judgment seat. The general "stand or fall" in v. 4, which references the eschatological accountability of the other, is now the judgment seat before which all of "us" stand (*bēma*; and see 2 Cor 5:10 for the judgment seat of Christ). Anticipating that the brother will be judged requires also anticipating that "we" will be judged.[64]

[11–12] The passage concludes by repeating the assertion of v. 10 about eschatological accountability, but a citation from Isa 45:23 LXX introduces that assertion:

As it is written, "As I live, says the Lord, before me every knee will bend and every tongue will praise God."

The introductory words, "As I live, says the Lord," do not appear in Isa 45:23 LXX, however. They are instead a standard introduction that appears widely in Scripture (e.g., Num 14:21, 28; Deut 32:40; Isa 49:18; Jer 22:24; Ezek 5:11; see Wagner 2002, 337). The fact that the introduction is conventional seems to numerous interpreters to confirm the identification of the "Lord" in v. 11 as God. God is named as the object of praise and the one to whom an account is given, which may mean that "the Lord" of the introductory formula also is God (so, e.g., Cranfield 2:710; Moo 864; Wolter 2:367).

Yet the identification of "the Lord" in v. 11 as God is not as straightforward as it seems. To begin with, this is the only time Paul includes the formula "As I live, says the Lord," despite its widespread usage elsewhere and despite Paul's extensive engagement with Scripture in Romans.[65] In addition, the statement

---

64. A comment of Bonhoeffer on the Sermon on the Mount seems apt for Rom 14:4, 10 as well: "If the disciples judge, then they are erecting standards to measure good and evil. But Jesus Christ is not a standard by which I can measure others. It is he who judges me and reveals what according to my own judgment is good to be thoroughly evil" (2001, 171).

65. The phrase also appears nowhere else in the NT.

"as I live" (*zō*) recalls the earlier distinctive reference to the resurrection of Christ as "he lived," again using *zaō* (v. 9), a relationship observed as early as Ambrosiaster (245; M. Black 1972, 8; Wagner 2002, 338). Christ's death and resurrection here mark his rule over both the dead and the living. All of this strongly suggests that the Lord who speaks in v. 11 is actually Christ. The result is arresting: "Before me every knee will bend and every tongue will praise God." This line then coheres well with Phil 2:10–11, where every knee bends at Jesus's name and every tongue confesses his lordship to the glory of God. More to the point, this line underscores both the lordship of Christ and the glorification of God, two central preoccupations of the letter.

Paul returns in v. 12 to the notion of final accountability, this time casting it even more directly than the "all" of v. 10: "Each of us" will give a "self-account"—more literally, an account about himself or herself. Any notion that accountability is for "other" people fails here with Paul's emphasis on "all" and "each" (Moo 864–65). That insistence sets the stage for the appeal in vv. 13–23. In addition, giving a self-account differs somewhat from the similar discussion of accountability in 2:1–11, 16, where God judges human actions and human hearts. Here no specific standard of judgment is named, but the individual is liable to give an account. That slight alteration may reflect Paul's understanding that the addressees have received the renewed mind that enables discernment (as in 12:1).

To this point Paul has dealt with the quarrel in an evenhanded way. The two sides—eaters and abstainers—both act so as to serve God. What matters is the lordship of Christ, which obviates any human lordship, and accountability to God excludes judgment of one another. If all of life and death, death and life, belongs to God, then there is no ground for judging others. Verses 13–23 will deftly alter this tactic, however, by arguing against the behavior of the eaters, while simultaneously endorsing their point of view.

14:13–23 The Danger of Being Right

The first half of ch. 14 approached the dispute about food (about shared meals) with an even hand: no one is in a position to judge, because everyone is accountable to God. That strategy of addressing both parties in the same way falls to the side in the second half of the chapter, where Paul aligns himself with the eaters—no food is unclean—while warning them against harming others through their actions. It is not enough, then, simply to tolerate difference; since believers belong to one another in Christ (12:4–5), they are obligated to pursue peace and upbuilding (14:19).

At first glance this is an eminently practical approach to the dispute, founded in the claim about Christ's lordship in vv. 1–12. That pragmatism ought not obscure the danger Paul identifies, however. When he attributes to the eaters the

capacity to harm, even to destroy others—the very ones for whom Christ died—
he implies that those eaters constitute a significant threat. There is more than a
hint of hyperbole here. It is hard to imagine that, if pressed, Paul would affirm
that human beings can destroy others eschatologically, particularly in light of
his earlier assertion in v. 4 that the Lord is the one who will make the other
stand. Yet the hyperbole exposes Paul's conviction that believers are obliged
to upbuild those "for whom Christ died" (v. 15), the "work of God" (v. 20).

Three instances of "so then" (therefore, *oun*) introduce three sections in the
passage. The first lines bridge from vv. 1–12 to the new stage having to do
with the potential to harm (vv. 13–15), the second section identifies concessive
behavior by the eaters as an act of faithfulness (vv. 16–18), and the third section makes Paul's views explicit: believers should not engage in practices that
will harm others (vv. 19–22a). The blessing and warning of vv. 22b–23 round
out the chapter.

14:13 So then let us stop deciding about[a] one another but decide this
instead—not to place before your brother an occasion for stumbling or
offense. 14 For I am utterly confident[b] in the Lord Jesus that there is
nothing that is impure in itself. But to the one who regards something
as impure—to that one it is impure. 15 So if through food your sister is
injured, you are no longer living by the norm of love. Do not through your
food destroy that one for whom Christ died.

16 So then do not let your good become disreputable, 17 for the reign of
God does not consist of eating and drinking, but righteousness and peace
and joy through the Holy Spirit. 18 For the one who serves as a slave to
Christ in this way is pleasing to God and approved by human beings.

19 So then let us pursue the things that make for peace and the things
that produce mutual upbuilding. 20 Do not, because of food, tear down
the work of God. To be sure, everything is clean,[c] but it is wrong for the
one who eats because of a stumbling block put in place.[d] 21 It is good not
to eat meat, not to drink wine, and not to do anything else that causes
your sibling to stumble. 22a As for your faith, which you have turned in
on itself,[e] have that faith before God instead.

22b Blessed is the one who does not judge himself for what he decides.
23 But the one who disputes[f] is condemned if he eats, because he is not
acting out of faith. And everything that does not come from faith is sin.[g]

a. *Krinōmen* is rendered here as "deciding about" rather than "judging" (14:4, 5, 10)
in order to bring out the wordplay in this verse.

b. Lit., "I know and am confident," construed as hendiadys and rendered idiomatically.

c. Interestingly, ℵ² adds the words "to the pure," moderating Paul's argument to mean
that things are pure for those who are themselves pure.

d. More lit., "through an occasion for stumbling." Considerable ambiguity attends this prepositional phrase, which could refer either to the wrong done by the one who eats because of the influence of others or to the wrong done by the one whose eating in the presence of others causes them to stumble. Given the repetition of v. 14a that immediately precedes, it seems likely that this statement repeats v. 14b with its claim that food will be impure to the one who believes it to be such.

e. Customarily translated as "the faith that you have, have as your own conviction before God" (NRSV), but I have construed *kata seauton* (lit., "according to yourself") in opposition to the *kata agapēn* (lit., "according to love") in v. 15 and the *kata Christon Iēsoun* (lit., "according to Christ Jesus") in 15:5. It is not a matter of keeping one's faith private (something that ill accords with Paul's letters) but of faith that is turned in on itself (Gaventa 2011b, 10).

f. Widely translated as "doubts" (KJV, NRSVue, NIV, etc.), the verb *diakrinomai* is better translated as "disputes" (Spitaler 2007; Schliesser 2012; and see above on 4:20). To be sure, when *diakrinomai* is used with the meaning "dispute," a dative phrase normally identifies the other party in the argument (BDAG s.v.), but here the context provides that other party, at least implicitly. Taking *diakronomai* as "dispute" also has the advantage of making accessible the inclusio with "disputes" in 14:1 (Spitaler 2009, 59–61).

g. Some manuscripts place the doxology of 16:25–27 here, but that inclusion is poorly attested.

[13–15] The opening clause, "So then let us stop deciding about one another," continues the first-person plural from the preceding lines ("all of us will stand," "each of us"). With the second clause, "but decide this instead," Paul shifts to second-person address. The effect is to place the addressees on notice that a demand is about to be made of them, a demand that goes well beyond the toleration urged in vv. 1–12.

What Paul instructs is that "you" should not "place before your brother an occasion for stumbling or offense." This statement confirms that the dispute concerns shared meals, particularly those shared when several smaller groups come together, as noted earlier. The menu of a single household or a homogeneous unit would not constitute a difficulty for others (Barclay 1996a, 291). What an eater or her household consumes on their own, in isolation from a larger gathering, might give the abstainers pause, but it would not likely entrap them in the way depicted here.

Whatever the situation, the language Paul uses is provocative. When discussing God's dealings with Israel and the gentiles in chs. 9–11, Paul drew on Isaiah to contend that Israel tripped on a stumbling stone put in place by God (see Rom 11:9). That action is one of a series of divine actions bent toward Israel's eschatological salvation, but while God has that freedom to trip Israel (note 9:14–15), when humans take it upon themselves to trip others, they produce disaster (Gaventa 2011b, 7–8).

The opening words of v. 14 announce Paul's conviction "in the Lord Jesus" that no food is inherently unclean. The phrase "in the Lord Jesus" can refer to

Paul's own situation in the sense that he himself is in the Lord Jesus (6:3), just as he is in the body of Christ (12:5) and has put on Christ (13:14). The phrase could also refer to the way he arrives at this conviction, whether through a special revelation or by virtue of a teaching from Christ (so Thompson 1991, 184–99). Given that the Jesus tradition contains a similar statement about food purity (Matt 15:11, 17–20; Mark 7:15, 17–23), it is possible that he means he has been taught in some way, although the formulation here differs from the places where Paul specifically refers to sayings of Jesus (as in 1 Cor 7:10) or to the reception of tradition (1 Cor 11:23; 15:3). Whatever its referent, the phrase "the Lord Jesus" firmly locates what Paul is about to say in the present time, the "now time" of God's action in Jesus.

"Nothing is impure in itself" unmistakably refers to Jewish food laws, as is evident both from the context and from the association of the term *koinos* elsewhere with impurity (Mark 7:2, 5; Acts 10:14; 11:8; 1 Macc 1:47, 62). Although this assertion would surely find assent among the eaters at Rome, it may well have been startling to the abstainers. While there was likely a range of Jewish practice regarding food laws, Paul's assertion contradicts the instructions of formative passages such as Lev 11:1–23 and Deut 14:3–21.

Isolated from its context, "Nothing is impure in itself" could be construed as a critique of Jewish practice in a longitudinal sense, that is, a considered denial that the food laws ever had legitimacy. This is where the phrase "in the Lord Jesus" plays an important role, as does the introduction of "reign of God" in v. 17. Because of the intervention of God in Jesus Christ, the situation has changed (see Marcus 1999, 1:457, on Mark 7:19).

Having opened with this strong affirmation of the position of the eaters, Paul now prepares for instructing them: something is impure if someone regards it that way. Here he replays his own comments from 1 Corinthians to the effect that what matters is the perception of the one for whom this is a problem (1 Cor 8:7–12). Notice that whatever Paul means by v. 14c—"to that one it is impure"—he does not linger there. Paul perceives the damage that can come to those who act against conviction. At the same time, he is not analyzing the inner workings of the abstainer but warning the eaters about the danger of their liberty.

Verse 15 makes that danger explicit: if the eaters indulge their freedom, invoking their conviction that no food is impure, the eaters may do real harm to the abstainers. It is not difficult to imagine a scenario: a meal at which the host (from among the eaters) serves items that are proscribed by Mosaic law and thereby pressures the abstainers into a choice. Whatever that choice may be, it causes injury. Either the abstainer refuses the host's offerings and violates hospitality, or the abstainer eats and commits what she regards as a serious offense against God—or against the Jewish community.[66]

---

66. Jewish law offers provisions for addressing purity violations (Lev 5:1–13; Sanders 1992, 214–17, 222–30), which makes it unlikely that those who ate what they regarded as impure thought

Paul does not parse that grief or injury, because his concern is to prevent such an occasion. Instead, he continues to address the "eater," the one with whom he himself agrees. Such conduct means that "you are no longer living by the norm of love." Given what Paul has said about love in these chapters (see on 12:9; 13:8–10), this is a powerful indictment. What orients this passage is the question of whether the person is aligned with love, which is to say with Christ Jesus (see 15:5), or only with their own liberty (as in 14:22).

This indicative statement yields to a warning about what the norm of love requires in this instance: "Do not through your food destroy that one for whom Christ died" (v. 15b). Paul intensifies his rhetoric in two important ways. First, in place of the passive description of the "brother" as being grieved, he writes the imperative "destroy," making it clear that the agent of harm is "you" and that the harm is severe. Second, he renames the "abstainer." Instead of "the weak" (v. 2) or even "the brother" (v. 13), he refers to "that one for whom Christ died." The identifying characteristic of this individual (or group) is not food habits or even relationship to you (brother), but the fact that this is a person for whom Christ died. The connection between Christ and the abstainer is now expressed in intimate terms, making it impossible for the eater to turn away, to "other" the one with whom she disagrees.

This appeal to Christ's death on behalf of the fellow member of the community replays the earlier discussion of Christ's death on behalf of "us," when we were weak (5:6–8). The implication of identifying the other in this way is that the other person's life has a value that must not be destroyed. (And, of course, that category—the one for whom Christ died—is all-inclusive.)

How exactly the brother is destroyed Paul does not specify,[67] but with this warning Paul introduces a peculiar tension with other elements in the letter (McCruden 2005, 239). Just a few lines earlier he has written that the Lord is able to make that one stand and will do so, regardless of differences about food (14:4). Repeatedly he attributes saving power to God (e.g., 1:16; 3:21–26; 11:32). Most emphatically, the closing lines of ch. 8 affirm that nothing in creation can separate humanity from its rightful Lord. How is it, then, that anyone can destroy a fellow believer? Presumably, Paul anticipates that his words will intercede, and his Roman auditors will come together (as celebrated in 15:1–13), averting this disaster.

---

they were destroying themselves by so doing. Perhaps Paul anticipates that the abstainer who eats impure food under duress will experience a sense of alienation from fellow Christians, even from Christ himself who has produced this alienation. The logic might run as follows: If I eat what I should not eat and I believe that God is unhappy with me for that reason, am I not also cut off from Christ by that?

67. Disputes about whether this is eternal destruction (e.g., Gundry Volf 1990, 85–97; Schreiner 710) are beside the point and overlook the prior claim that God is able to make people stand. The debate imputes the power of salvation to the individual's faith and then imputes the power of damnation to the fellow believer, which is to distort the letter severely.

[16–18] The second "therefore" follows directly on v. 15: "So then do not let your good become disreputable." In the "now time" of Jesus Christ, no food is impure, and consuming it is acceptable, even "good," but the unloving, destructive practice of that "good" can bring disrepute onto the community. The text offers no specifics, and Paul's physical distance from the situation plays a role. Possibly he fears that the devastation to the abstainers will alienate other Jews and undermine the work of proclamation.

Verse 17 again signals Paul's agreement with the eaters: as no food item is inherently impure, similarly the reign of God does not consist of eating and drinking. Elsewhere Paul introduces the "reign of God" to refer to eschatological life, which is not "inherited" by the unethical (1 Cor 6:9–10; Gal 5:21) or indeed by "flesh and blood" (1 Cor 15:50). In other instances, however, there are indications that the "reign of God" has already begun. First Corinthians 4:20 polemically connects signs of the "reign of God" with "power" rather than with "word," that is, with the deeds Paul performs rather than with the impressive rhetoric of others. Later Paul anticipates that, at the end, Christ will hand the reign over to God, which presupposes that Christ already reigns at present (1 Cor 15:24–25; and see Rom 8:34).

In Romans the phrase *basileia tou theou* ("reign of God") appears only here, but the issue of who reigns has been present in the letter almost since the outset, where Paul identifies Christ with resurrection power (1:4) and the gospel itself as God's own power (1:16). Crucially, ch. 5 limns the power of Sin and Death, toxic partners who "ruled" over all humankind in the wake of Adam's disobedience, prior to their defeat through the "rule" of grace in the death and resurrection of Jesus Christ (5:14, 17, 21; 6:12). That reign provides confidence for Paul's addressees, who are called to action based on their location within the power of God.

This statement might have produced widespread agreement, since no one would have baldly identified God's rule as coterminous with eating and drinking, yet as it stands it may nevertheless unsettle the priority given to dietary practice in Jewish identity. One thing widely recognized about Jews was their avoidance of pork, a habit that was also regularly lambasted by gentiles.[68] This avoidance was especially striking in Rome, where pork was both popular and available.[69] Therefore, while Paul's statement is innocuous on the surface, it may nonetheless discomfort those who would abstain from pork and other nonkosher foods.

68. E.g., Juvenal, *Sat.* 6.159–60; 14.98–99; Plutarch, *Mor.* 669D. Feldman provides a convenient survey of the primary texts (1993, 167–70); see also Rosenblum 2010, 96–100.

69. Tribute and taxes sent to Rome from elsewhere meant that pork was more readily available there than elsewhere (A. King 1999, 171, 189). It was also among the most common meats used in sacrifices (Rosenblum 2010, 97). In general, however, meat of any kind was not a regular feature of most people's diets (Garnsey 1999, 16–17).

Verse 17b offers an alternative statement about God's reign. It consists of "righteousness and peace and joy through the Holy Spirit." These three terms nicely capture the letter's treatment of the gospel's work in human life. Not only is the gospel identified with righteousness as early as 1:17 and 3:21–26, but 5:1–11 ties God's rectifying act to the peace with God that humans are called to celebrate because of "our Lord Jesus Christ." Peace and joy figure prominently in the prayer wish of 15:13, to say nothing of the instruction to pursue peace in 14:19 (and see 12:18). All of this takes place "through the Holy Spirit," a brief reference that stretches back to Paul's discussion of the work of the Spirit in 8:8–17, 26 and forward to 15:13.

A tiny shift in vocabulary between these two halves of v. 17 is also revealing: earlier Paul has spoken of food and drink, but here the language is of "eating" and "drinking." That change in vocabulary shifts the topic from the items on the menu to the act of consuming them. The rule of God is not about either the freedom to consume whatever someone wishes *or* the obligation to refrain from eating. Even though Paul's addressee throughout this section is the eater, the abstainer could also find herself challenged here.

Based on this reminder of God's reign, v. 18 completes the section with a contrast to v. 16. If the result of destructive behavior by the eaters is that their own freedom ("your good") brings about disrepute, the behavior Paul urges is both pleasing to God and approved by human beings. This statement deeply echoes ch. 12, with its concern for doing what is acceptable to God's will (12:2) as well as serving Christ (12:11). There is a slight ambiguity in the phrase "in this way" (lit., "in this"). While it could refer to the specific compromise Paul is advising, the *gar* ("for," "because") connects the statement back to v. 17; being a slave to Christ is itself serving righteousness and peace and joy in the Holy Spirit.

[19–22a] The final section begins as a positive statement (by contrast with the "not" in v. 13 and the "no longer" in v. 15). Paul urges that "we" should pursue "the things that make for peace and the things that produce mutual upbuilding." Given the context, it might be tempting to regard "peace" in this sentence as the absence of strife among human beings, the absence of conflict in this community (or series of communities); indeed, that human peace is not to be excluded (especially in light of 12:18). Yet throughout the letter "peace" is associated with God as its giver, as in the formulaic greeting of 1:7, the granting of peace as an eschatological gift in 2:10 and 5:1, the prayer of 15:13, and the characterization of God as the God of peace in 15:33 and 16:20. Peace is also said to be a gift of the Spirit (8:6). Pursuing the "things that make for peace," then, is acting in a way that conforms to the peace God has brought about in Jesus Christ and through the Spirit (and in contrast to ways of destruction). The second half of v. 19 moves toward the particular situation, the "upbuilding" of one another. This image is one Paul has used in 1 Corinthians also (e.g., 8:1;

10:23; 14:3–5), and it is especially apposite here following the notion of the household and preceding the phrase "work of God."

Having appealed for the eaters to base their behavior on the peaceful upbuilding of the whole number of believers, v. 20 recasts the earlier points of vv. 15b and 14 respectively. Instead of "that one for whom Christ died" (v. 15b), now it is "the work of God" (v. 20a) that is jeopardized. Both expressions identify the "other" party in theological terms, earlier the death of Christ and now God's "work." Whether that "work" refers to the individual, as in v. 15, or the community itself, it is God's own work that is in jeopardy. Paul could hardly give the situation a more frightening cast than this one. If the refusal to acknowledge God brings about God's wrath (1:18), what would be the consequences of destroying God's own work?

Verse 20b then replays the striking statement of v. 14, with "everything is clean" instead of "nothing is impure in itself." Once again Paul affirms the stance of the eaters, now using the very word, "everything" (*panta*), that earlier designated the diet of the eaters (v. 2). He affirms their principle, and then he follows up with a strong adversative (*alla*): but it is actually wrong for those who eat solely to demonstrate their own vaunted principles.

With v. 21 Paul makes the implications of this instruction clear: it is good to avoid meat and wine and anything else by which "your sibling" falls. Agreeing with the eaters does not mean endorsing their current practice. When believers gather, the eaters should observe kosher law so as not to do harm to their brothers and sisters. The specification of meat probably refers to pork (see above), and wine may be suspect because of the general anxiety around gentile food, although precise reconstruction will continue to elude interpreters. The point is clear enough: a meal with severe restrictions is more appetizing than harm to a sister or brother.

Paul concludes his address to the eaters with another direct word to "you": "As for your faith, which you have turned in on itself, have that faith before God instead" (v. 22a; and see translation note e). In this way he labels the conduct of the eaters as reflexive in that it is turned in on itself rather than directed toward Christ or God. This characterization coheres with the warning that they are not walking in love (v. 15b) and anticipates the prayer for agreement aligned with Christ in 15:5. The problem with the eaters is not their conviction but the way they prize their conviction, turning it in on themselves, more than the health of the community.[70]

[22b–23] Since v. 13 Paul has been addressing the eaters, as it is their behavior that threatens to undermine others. With the macarism of v. 22b, however,

---

70. Karl Barth astutely characterizes this chapter as a "warning to all who find themselves in entire agreement with what has been said and are persuaded that their own opinions have been fully confirmed" (502).

he returns to the language of quarreling and judging that opened the chapter, language addressed to both sides of the dispute. The depiction of one who does not "judge himself for what he decides" is somewhat opaque, to be sure, but it may recall the earlier observation that both those who eat and those who abstain do so in honor of the Lord (v. 6). By contrast, there is not blessing but condemnation for the one who "disputes," recalling the disputes of v. 1. Disputing is not an act born of faith, since the one eating (whatever the menu) acts with the goal of convincing or convicting someone else. That is, such eating is not in honor of the Lord but in honor of one's own convictions. This could apply both to those who eat everything and to those who abstain, because people on both sides can be eating out of a disordered need to be right.

For this reason, Paul can characterize the behavior that is not "from faith" as sin. However concerning as an isolated statement, it captures the importance Paul attaches to this entire discussion. Table practice that is bent toward quarreling rather than toward honoring the Lord is self-aggrandizing and is a manifestation of sin (even Sin?) itself, since it threatens the body of Christ.

The opening lines of ch. 15 will transpose this conclusion into a positive key by introducing Jesus as a paradigm of behavior that ushers in the glorification of God. Paul has carefully prepared for that move by reminding both sides of the dispute that they are each and every one accountable to Jesus Christ, by renaming the parties from "other" to "the one for whom Christ died," and by warning of the dire possibilities of valuing one's own judgment more than the well-being of the whole.

15:1–6 Strength for Upbuilding

This brief passage rounds out Paul's treatment of the community conflict with an evocative description of strength modeled on the strength of Christ. Paul has moved from invoking Christ's lordship (14:9), to his death for others (14:15), to the need to serve him (14:18). Now he presents Christ as the paradigm of genuine strength (15:3) as well as the criterion for community reflection (15:5).

This passage also anticipates 15:7–13, particularly with its comment on Scripture's instructive power (v. 4) and on the shared glorification of God (vv. 5–6). The blessing of vv. 5–6 submits the conflict to God's power and provides a transition to the doxological summation of 15:7–13. That doxology is crucial, as it locates the larger discussion in its proper context. The welcome extended to others (14:1; 15:7) is important, but it is not an end in itself, as Paul will make clear in vv. 7–13.

15:1 Now we who are strong are obliged to bear the weaknesses of those who are not strong and not to please ourselves. 2 Let each of us please the neighbor for the good, for upbuilding.[a] 3 For even Christ did not please himself, but as it is written, "The insults of those who insult you fell on me." 4 For whatever was written previously, it was written for our instruction, that through the endurance and the encouragement that come from the Scriptures^b we might have hope. 5 And may the God of that same^c endurance and encouragement grant you harmonious judgment^d that accords with Christ Jesus, 6 so that together with one voice you might glorify the God and Father of our Lord Jesus Christ.

a. Two different prepositions (*eis* and *pros*) are both rendered "for," as they seem to be used in parallel.

b. The preposition *dia* ("through") appears twice, so the Greek may be rendered "through the endurance and through the encouragement that comes from the Scriptures," detaching "endurance" from "Scripture" (as in NIV and NRSVue). Since Paul associates God with both in v. 5, however, it seems more likely that he also associates both with Scripture (as in NKJV).

c. The addition of "that same" reflects the judgment that the definite article introducing God's "endurance and encouragement" is resumptive of those same features in the preceding verse.

d. More woodenly, "that you might think the same thing with one another." "Judgment" reflects the decision that the specific thought Paul refers to here is the thought about food and days in 14:5–6.

[15:1–2] For the first time in this treatment of the conflict between eaters and abstainers, Paul refers to the "strong" (*dynatoi*) and those who are "not strong" (*adynatoi*). Given that he has just been addressing those with whom he agrees—the eaters—and urging them to take care lest they destroy others, presumably the "strong" are these same eaters. That is, the development of Paul's instructions to this point suggests that "we who are strong" are those who do not follow Jewish food law.

Yet things are a bit more complex than they at first appear. Because Paul has not previously identified anyone in these groups as "strong," himself included, the label is unattached. It might refer to anyone who wishes to be thought strong.[71] The most obvious connection is to the eaters, since they are the ones whose behavior needs to be modified; nevertheless, the use of "we" also invites the abstainers to hear themselves included. At the very least, even if this direct speech addresses the eaters, it may nudge others toward that ethic of not pleasing oneself. In other words, strength, as Paul sees it, is not to be identified with

71. Similarly, Hultgren suggests that all of Paul's audience would have thought themselves included among the strong (524). Reasoner (1999, 218–20) and especially Jewett (876) connect this terminology with Roman cultural understandings of social and political standing, and 1 Cor 1:26 does use "the strong" (*hoi dynatoi*) with that connotation, associated as they are with the "well-born." Elsewhere, however, Paul can speak of himself as "strong" by virtue of his weakness— strong through Christ's power (2 Cor 12:9–10)—and that sense seems better fitted to this context.

either eating or abstaining. It has to do with the willingness to "bear the weaknesses" of others.

What such "bearing" looks like Paul does not say, although the larger context demands something more than mere tolerance (as in 14:1; 15:7). Paul amplifies this notion of strength with the notion of pleasing others rather than by specifying the character of these "weaknesses" or the identities of the two groups. "We" are obliged not to please ourselves but to please "the neighbor for the good, for upbuilding" (v. 2). Elsewhere in his letters Paul occasionally demeans pleasing other humans in favor of pleasing God (Gal 1:10; 1 Thess 2:4), but he also endorses the notion that spouses seek to please one another (1 Cor 7:33–34). More to the point, in 1 Cor 10:33 pleasing others is contrasted with self-aggrandizement and lifted up as a means of serving salvation for all.[72]

Here the one to be pleased is "the neighbor." This term also, like "the strong," does not appear in ch. 14, and it may further invite both sides of the dispute to consider their behavior. Importantly, in 13:9–10 Paul quoted Lev 19:18, "Love your neighbor as yourself," and amplified that with "This love does not produce evil for the neighbor." Now that general notion of neighbor love takes on specificity in the context of the food dispute.

Pleasing others is done "for the good, for upbuilding." Paul's earlier concern with conquering evil with good (12:21) recurs here.[73] As in 1 Cor 14:3–5, 12, 17, 26, "upbuilding" refers to the community's life, not simply to the development of the individual. (Contrast the individualistic translations of the NIV and NRSVue.) Yet the two—the individual and the corporate—are both involved, since the community will scarcely be amplified without individuals (and a destructive individual can damage the community), and the community in turn shapes individuals.

[3–4] What it means to act for the neighbor Paul unpacks in vv. 3–4 by appeal to Christ and to Scripture: "For even Christ did not please himself."[74]

---

72. George Eliot's character Adam Bede recalls Rom 15:1 and then says, "There's a text that wants no candle to show 't. 'T shines by its own light" (1959, 50). At that early stage of the novel, Bede is acknowledging, perhaps even celebrating, his own strength. He knows himself to be possessed of a strong back and the ability to assist those around him who might be thought weak. Adam Bede's strength may well have invited nineteenth-century readers to admire him, a working man known in the community, one who earns the respect of the local gentry. The long arc of the novel will teach him another kind of strength, however, one much closer to the strength that does not need to please itself. (My attention was drawn to this passage by a comment in Cranfield 2:731.)

73. That reference further complicates the question whether 12:14–21 refers to "insiders" or "outsiders" (see above on that passage). The language of "good" here also recalls the lament of the "I" in 7:7–24, who sees what is good but is unable to do it. By contrast, Paul now assumes that the addressee can work for the good.

74. In Romans, Paul refers to "the Christ," combining the definite article with *Christos* in the nominative case and without the name Jesus, only here, in 9:5, and in 15:7 (elsewhere, only in 1 Cor 1:13; 10:4; 11:3; 12:12).

At first glance, the observation that Christ "did not please himself" appears a strange act of understatement, especially in view of Paul's frequent reference to Christ's death (as recently as 14:9, 15). Presumably the preceding injunction influences the choice of words. With this reminder of Christ's own action, however understated, Paul forges a tight, unavoidable connection between that action and what he asks of "the strong." Further, the appeal to Christ rules out any appeal to one's own freedom or privilege. If "the Christ," Lord of both the dead and the living (14:9), did not exercise his prerogative to please himself, no space remains for "the strong" to demand that their own desires be gratified.

Paul follows this observation with a citation from Ps 68:10 LXX: "The insults of those who insult you fell on me."[75] The fact that the citation is in first person encourages the identification of the speaker as Christ (so Hays 1993), who becomes the object of those who revile God. Yet the introductory formula is "as it is written," not "as Christ said," by contrast with various points when Paul has evoked the words of Isaiah or David or even God (e.g., 9:15, 27, 29; 10:19; 11:9). That difference makes the "I" at least slightly ambiguous.[76] In the same way that the psalmist's "I" is now spoken by Christ, that "I" also invites those who would be genuinely strong to align themselves with Christ and to see their own situation as analogous to his (comparable to the "we" of v. 1). Taking on the weaknesses of others becomes their way of taking on the insults that fall on him. Given the evidence of Roman scorn for Jewish food laws (see above on 14:13–23), it is not hard to imagine that those who voluntarily observe those practices in deference to others would incur such ridicule, perhaps especially gentiles who align themselves with Jewish practice.[77]

Paul moves from this invocation of Christ's own action to a comment about Scripture (v. 4), which was written earlier "for our instruction." At a minimum, this statement furthers Paul's argument by underscoring the applicability of the psalm text: it spoke then and it speaks now.

Paul does not simply claim that Scripture teaches, however. Instead, he writes that Scripture was written "for our instruction." This remark recalls 4:23–24, which asserts that the words of Gen 15:6 apply both in the case of Abraham and in "our" own. Unlike 4:23–24, however, 15:4 makes no reference to an earlier addressee, and at least one possible implication of this statement is that Scripture *only now* has its proper addressee. In that sense it resembles 1 Cor 10:11: "on whom the ends of the ages have come." Such an assertion can do considerable wickedness, as it would were it lodged in a polemical context

---

75. Paul has already quoted this psalm in 11:9, although there not in reference to Christ.

76. The referents of personal pronouns shift, depending on the speaker; see above on Rom 7 and Gaventa 2013a, 79–81.

77. This suggestion is similar to that of Barclay, that the psalm text is "refracted through a double lens" (2011, 55).

by way of contrasting "our Christian" interpretation of Scripture with that of "those" other people, or insisting that Israel's Scripture has no place except as part of an eventual Christian Bible. The context here is not polemical, however. Instead, the force of this comment about Scripture is eschatological, in keeping with the letter's repeated reminders of the "now time" (as in, e.g., 3:21; 5:9; 8:1, 18; 13:11).

The eschatological force of "written for our instruction" comes into focus with the second half of v. 4, since "hope" is for Paul frequently connected with eschatological expectation. First Thessalonians 2:19 explicitly identifies the Thessalonians as Paul's own "hope and joy and crown of boasting" before the Lord Jesus when he comes. Again, 1 Thess 4:13–18 differentiates the community's response to death from that of those "who have no hope." Similarly, 1 Cor 15:19 ridicules the notion that anyone "hopes" in Christ for this life only. While less explicit, references to hope earlier in Romans also associate it with eschatological expectation, as in boasting "in our hope for the coming of God's glory" (5:2; and see 8:20, 24–25).

If eschatological hope is the goal of Scripture's instruction, it comes about through "endurance" and "encouragement." These are probably not qualities inherent in Scripture, especially in light of v. 5a, which associates both endurance and encouragement with God. They are, instead, characteristics of life in Christ that come through Scripture's instruction. These are characteristics Paul lifts up elsewhere also, as when 5:3 asserts that affliction produces endurance (see also, e.g., 2:7; 8:25) and when 12:8 identifies encouragement as among the spiritual gifts (see also, e.g., 1 Cor 14:3).

Notably, Paul never directly instructs the Romans about how to resolve the conflict over shared meals, even though he has commented on and around it at length. At the conclusion of 1 Cor 8–10, by contrast, he finally gives some specific directions (10:25–28). (Indeed, one reason for the extensive scholarly debate about the situation addressed in Rom 14 is the absence of such detail.) Context matters: he does not have the relationship with these gatherings that would allow him to speak directly into the setting. More than sheer pragmatism is at work, however. Paul has already implied in 12:1–2 that they have received renewed minds that are able to discern God's will, and in 13:14 he has urged them to wrap themselves up in the Lord Jesus Christ. With that understanding, he leaves them to address the situation.[78]

Taken together, vv. 3–4 invoke both the action of Christ and the words of Scripture as loci from which the Romans may act. At the same time, by drawing attention to Scripture's importance, Paul prepares for what he is about to do in vv. 7–13. There he will conduct a chorus of Israel's voices in celebration of the

---

78. This conclusion is consistent with Horrell's observation that Paul's is an "other-regarding ethic with a specifically Christological shape" (2015, 190).

final and inclusive glorification of God through the work of Jesus Christ. By elevating Scripture at this point, Paul readies his hearers for the word that is to come.

[5–6] Paul closes this long instruction with a prayer reinforcing what he has been saying, even as it turns the addressees over to God's care. Paul does not expect the Romans to be able to reach agreement out of their own resources. The prayer opens by calling on "the God of that same endurance and encouragement." Given the repetition of this language from v. 4, it appears that Scripture does not bestow these gifts on its own but as by-products of God's abundance. As elsewhere, Paul identifies God in terms of God's activity with and for God's people, as in 15:13, which calls on the God of hope, and 15:33, which calls on the God of peace (see also 16:20; 2 Cor 13:11; Phil 4:9; 1 Thess 5:23). If Scripture teaches endurance and comfort, they nevertheless originate with God (and see 2 Cor 1:3).

What Paul asks specifically is that God grant them "harmonious judgment that accords with Christ Jesus." Concern for agreement within the community occurs in several other letters (e.g., 1 Cor 1:10; 2 Cor 13:11; Phil 2:2; 4:2), and Paul already introduced it in 12:16, probably anticipating this lengthy discussion of a point on which there was considerable disagreement. The final words of the verse serve to make this agreement something far different from the lowest common denominator or even a lofty community concord. What Paul seeks for them is agreement "that accords with Christ Jesus." This enlarges on his appeal to Christ in v. 3, identifying Christ not only as a paradigm of behavior that pleases the neighbor (Meyer 2004b, 215) but as the central criterion of the community's reflection. Shared thought that conforms to Christ Jesus stands in tension with the faith Paul has described in 14:22 as turned in on itself. Here Paul comes close to the substance of 2 Cor 5:16 (there formulated negatively), where he identifies the thought of the "now time" as no longer conformed to the merely human (*kata sarka*; Martyn 1997b, 89–110).

As important as this shared judgment is, Paul's prayer does not end with v. 5. The purpose clause (*hina*) introducing v. 6 identifies an ultimate goal that lies well beyond agreement, even agreement that forms itself according to Christ. The final goal is shared glorification of God by a "chorus of psalmists" (M. Scott 2014, 93).[79] Verses 7–13 will extend the language of worship to Christ's redemption of Jew and gentile alike.

With this prayer for shared doxology, Paul draws together a thread that begins in 1:18–32, where the presenting problem of humanity (at least gentile

---

79. The notion of a single voice united in worship occurs in Dan 3:51 LXX and 2 Chr 18:12 LXX, as does "together" (*homothymadon*; Jdt 9:12; 13:17; Wis 10:20; Acts 1:4; 2:46; 4:24). In addition, "voice" translates *stoma*, the same word used in 3:19 where Paul concluded—based in part on the psalmist's complaint that "their mouth is full of cursing and bitterness" (3:14)—that the law "speaks" in order to close "every mouth."

humanity) is its refusal to glorify or give thanks to God (1:21). In Paul's view, part and parcel of being human is to glorify God, and this refusal sets in motion the disastrous consequences that follow. The catena of 3:10–18 extends that argument, concluding that no one seeks God or fears God. Chapter 4 singles out Abraham as the exception, the one who did glorify God (4:20). By virtue of their adoption, believers are able to cry out to God as Father (8:15). God is glorified for God's dealings with Israel (11:36).

To be sure, Paul's treatment of the conflict bears within it the unspoken danger of suppressing difference, a concern that has come to the forefront of discussion in recent decades (Horrell 2015).[80] Despite his explicit statement that both groups serve God with their behavior (14:5–6), and even despite urging the eaters to respect the qualms of the abstainers, Paul's claim that no food is unclean aligns him firmly on the side of the eaters. Nonetheless, the sameness Paul valorizes in 15:5–6 has less to do with actual practices than it does with a shared attitude toward the other and toward Christ.

This passage not only concludes Paul's discussion of this particular issue but moves toward 15:7–13. There he will recast this prayer for doxological unity into a larger context, responding not to a specific dispute about practice but to the relationship between Jew and gentile in light of God's action in Jesus Christ.

15:7–13 Welcomed by Christ for the Glory of God

In this passage Paul builds on the discussion begun in 14:1, at least in the sense that the emphasis on welcome and on the work of Christ for diverse groups continues here. Yet it quickly becomes apparent that the "welcome" Paul admonishes extends beyond the specific disputes that gave rise to 14:1–23. "Welcome" encompasses the eschatological welcome all have received from Christ and for God's glory. Here the unity of Jew and gentile through God's grace produces unity in praise and glory. Indeed, the unity of Jew and gentile is brought about for the larger goal of God's glory. Now the corrupt worship that characterized the human in 1:18–32 has been replaced by a new creation in which—by virtue of the "shoot of Jesse"—all together join in the praise of God. The culminating prayer of v. 13 makes sense for just this reason.

---

80. That statement reflects a shift in hermeneutical perspective. A generation ago, in conversations about this passage, I regularly heard complaints that the abstainers (aka "the weak"), by curtailing the stance of the strong, could always impede progress. That was especially a concern for discussions around the ordination of women or LGBTQ+ persons. Now the objection is not that the strong are hemmed in by the weak but that the weak are condescended to or even suppressed by the strong, forced into conformity. Wisdom may lie in avoiding such analogical applications and looking instead to the larger motivations at work here, namely, the insistence that all are serving God, the concern for not harming one another (other regard), and shared thought that is conformed to Christ.

These lines also prepare for the discussion of Paul's own work in 15:14–33, especially his ambitious plan to take the gentile offering to Jerusalem before going on to Rome and then to Spain. By extolling Christ's work on behalf of Jew and gentile, Paul clears a space for his urgent request of prayer in support of his trip to Jerusalem (15:30–32).

In overall structure this passage resembles 15:1–6. Both passages open with an admonition (vv. 1–2, 7), followed by an appeal to the action of Christ (vv. 3a, 8–9a), evidence from Scripture (vv. 3b–4, 9b–12), and a prayer (vv. 5–6, 13). Here Jew ("circumcision") and gentile are named, something that differs from ch. 14, even though Jewish food laws were under discussion. That change reflects the likelihood that the dispute is not entirely along ethnic lines, especially given that Paul himself is a Jew who agrees with the eaters. Perhaps more important, identifying the groups as Jewish and gentile in ch. 14 would mean identifying Jew and gentile by the quarrels that divide them. Here, by contrast, Paul will identify them by their shared glorification of God and their shared confidence in God's benefits.

15:7 So welcome one another, just as Christ welcomed you,[a] for the glory of God. 8 For I declare that Christ has become a servant of circumcision for God's truth, in order to confirm the promises made to the ancestors,[b] 9 and so that the gentiles might glorify God for God's mercies.[c]
This is just as it is written,

"For this reason I will confess you among the gentiles
    and I will praise your name."

10 And again it says,

"Rejoice, gentiles, together with God's people."

11 And again,

"Praise the Lord, all you gentiles,
    and let all the peoples praise him."

12 And again Isaiah says,

"There will be a shoot of Jesse,
    one who rises to rule the gentiles,
    and in him the gentiles will hope."

13 Now may the God of that hope fill you with all joy and peace in believing, so that you abound in hope through the power of the Holy Spirit.

a. A number of ancient manuscripts read "us" (*hēmas*), including B D* P, rather than "you" (*hymas*), which appears, e.g., in ℵ A C D¹ F G. Evidence for the latter is stronger (Metzger 1971, 536), but the difference is minimal, since Paul knew that he himself had been welcomed (Phil 3:2–11; Gal 1:11–17; 1 Cor 15:8–9).

b. Lit., "fathers" (*paterōn*), but rendered "ancestors" on the assumption that Paul refers to the Israelites in general (as in Rom 9:4), which would of course include Sarah and Rebekah (9:6–13).

c. The awkward transition at the beginning of v. 9 generates a significant debate about translating these lines. There are three major possibilities:

1. The introductory "I declare" statement governs v. 8b and v. 9a separately, resulting in "For I declare that Christ has become a servant of circumcision on behalf of the truth of God. . . . And [I further declare] that gentiles should glorify God for God's mercy" (as advocated by, e.g., Cranfield 2:742–44, although he takes the conjunction *de* as adversative). This rendering is defensible grammatically, but it involves a lengthy separation of v. 9a from the introductory "I declare." More to the point, on this translation, gentile glorification of God is severed from any action of Christ, something that seems to conflict both with v. 7 and with much else in the letter.

2. The phrase "Christ has become a servant" governs all of vv. 8b–9a, with "Christ" as the subject of both verses and "the gentiles" understood as an accusative of respect (Wagner 1997): "For I declare that Christ has become a servant of circumcision on behalf of the truth of God, in order to confirm the promises made to the ancestors, and [a servant] with respect to the gentiles on behalf of God's mercy in order to glorify God." The strength of this translation is that it puts the two *hyper* ("on behalf of") clauses in parallel and permits an easy transition to v. 9b if one assumes that Christ is the speaker of the psalm (Hays 1993). But the identity of the speaker is not necessarily Christ, and while it seems consistent with Christ's welcome "for the glory of God" to say that Christ glorifies God, in 15:6 Paul has just written that "together with one voice you might glorify God." In other words, the argument about who gives glory to God may support either construal of the grammar. In addition, the argument for an accusative of respect at the beginning of v. 9 ("with respect to the gentiles") seems forced.

3. "Christ has become a servant of circumcision for God's truth" is followed by two infinitive phrases in parallel, the first with Christ as subject, the second with gentiles as subject. This translation is reflected above (and see, e.g., Jewett 892–93; Moo 888–89, 892–93; NRSVue; NIV). Grammatically this appears to be the most defensible rendering, even though it does not construe the two *hyper* clauses as parallel. The shift of subject from Christ to gentiles is only a problem if v. 9b is assumed to be from the mouth of Christ, which is not necessarily the case. This translation also has the advantage of connecting both the confirmation of promises and gentile glorification of God to Christ's servanthood without slighting the role of Christ for Israel by making it merely a step on the way to the gentile glorification of God.

[7–9a] The same imperative appears here as in 14:1 (*proslambanesthe*), marking a substantial connection between the two passages. There, however, the admonition is to welcome those who are weak in faith; here, all are admonished to "welcome" one another.

With v. 7b Paul moves to the reason for his admonition, which simultaneously summarizes the theological argument undergirding 14:1–15:6: "Christ welcomed you for the glory of God." The phrase "for the glory of God" modifies both verbs; that is, both the imperative "welcome" and the indicative statement of Christ's own "welcome" are for the purpose of glorifying God. At the very least, the "welcome" that Christ offers is for God's glory, so the "welcome" Paul exhorts needs to be of the same sort. This verse provides a clue to the whole section, in that it involves a human action learned from Christ's own action, and it also has to do not only with human reconciliation but also with God's glory.

Reference to God's glory recalls an important thread in the letter. Central to Paul's indictment of humanity is the claim that "they" did not glorify God (1:21). For that reason they were removed from God's glory, which is to say God's own presence (3:23), although in Christ they even boast "in [the] hope for the coming of God's glory" (5:2). In 6:4 Paul wrote that Christ's resurrection came about through God's glory. In all these places, glory has to do with the very presence of God (Exod 24:16; 40:34; Lev 9:23; Ps 56:6 LXX [57:5 MT]; Ezek 11:23), a presence often manifested in conflict, specifically in triumph over God's enemies, as in Exod 15:6–7; Hab 3:1–19; Bar 4:24; 5:6–9; 1QH^a 11.33–36; CD^b 20.26; 1QM 4.6, 8 (see above on 6:4 and Gaventa 2014b). To say that Christ welcomed humans for God's glory is to say that God is to be praised, but it specifically invokes praise for God's triumph. The catena that follows reinforces this point by anticipating the shared praise of God.

Following the introductory statement "I declare," which draws attention to what follows, vv. 8–9 expand on the action of Christ, showing what Paul means by Christ's welcome. First, Christ has become a "servant of circumcision for God's truth." Both the nouns "servant" and "circumcision" are unusual. Elsewhere Paul refers to Christ as a servant (*diakonos*) only in Gal 2:17, and there he introduces the term in order to deny it: Christ is not a "servant of Sin." Further, the designation "servant of circumcision" rather than "Israel" or "the Jews" is notable, particularly given that reference to circumcision has not appeared since the discussion of God's dealings with Israel in ch. 4. (Circumcision is not listed among the gifts of God to the Israelites in 9:4–5.) The graphic expression resembles the similar contrast between "circumcision" and "gentiles" in Gal 2:7, 9, where Paul reports the division of labor between himself (to the gentiles) and Peter (to the circumcision). In addition, if "circumcision" is a derogatory term (Marcus 1989), the claim that Christ became a "servant of circumcision" identifies this servant with those who are known in the wider world through this demeaned physical act.[81]

In addition, Christ is a servant of circumcision "for God's truth." In 3:4, while discussing the benefits of circumcision, Paul introduced God's truthfulness, which prompts the suggestion that what Paul invokes here is God's covenant faithfulness (Käsemann 385). That is not the only reference to truth in the letter, however. "God's truth" appears prominently in 1:25 (and see 1:18) as a marker of what is ostensibly the presenting accusation against gentiles. There Paul plays on a familiar Jewish accusation about gentile idolatry, charging gentiles with suppressing the "the truth about God." (It turns out, of course, that Jews share in this same captivity to Sin.) To identify Christ as "a servant of circumcision for God's truth," then, is to connect Christ's servanthood for Israel with the overturning of human rejection of God.

Christ's servanthood has a dual purpose: to confirm the promises of the ancestors and so that gentiles would glorify God for God's mercies (see translation note c on v. 9). While these expressions differ, and do so in ways that cohere with God's differing histories with Jews and gentiles, at the same time there is considerable interplay between the two. Israel receives God's promises (as in 9:4–5), but gentiles also are included in the promises, in the sense that they are—as uncircumcised—among the children promised to Abraham (4:13–17). By the same token, God's mercies extend to both Jews and gentiles, or at least that seems to be the implication of 9:23–24 and 11:32. In effect, this statement encapsulates the gospel's astonishing character not only of welcoming the other but of welcoming the other on terms that are unexpected, and for God's own glory.

[9b–12] The familiar introduction "just as it is written" (*kathōs gegraptai*; see also, e.g., 1:17; 2:24; 3:4; 8:36) connects the opening statement to the catena of vv. 9b–12. Given the proximity of the reference to gentiles in v. 9a as well as the several references to gentiles within the catena, the introductory phrase may be construed as tying the catena tightly to v. 9a, that is, to gentiles. In the verses that follow, however, Paul has selected texts that reference not only gentiles but gentiles and God's "people" (Israel) together.

In addition, the first three texts in the catena all bear on thanksgiving to God or the glorification of God. For example, Paul might have taken up the language of Isa 49:6 LXX (as in Luke 2:32; Acts 28:28) to identify Israel (or Christ) as a light

---

81. Only Jewish males are circumcised, but women are nonetheless implicated, given that Jewish women would usually marry only those circumcised (Barclay 1996b, 411–12). Garroway (2012a) proposes that the translation should be "agent of circumcision" in that Christ establishes faith as "intangible, genital" circumcision, which allows gentiles to become part of the covenant with Abraham. But that proposal assumes Paul is concerned here only with gentile inclusion, a proposal that founders on the several references to the *laoi* in the catena of vv. 9–12, as noted above.

for gentiles. Alternatively, Isa 55:5 LXX anticipates the nations (gentiles) turning to Israel, acknowledging God's glorification of Israel. Instead, the catena emphasizes not only gentile inclusion or the unity of Jew and gentile but their shared praise of God.

The four citations are joined together by repeated introductions: "as it is written," "and again it says," "and again," "and again Isaiah says." For those gathered to hear Phoebe read the letter, these brief introductions may have had a kind of staccato effect.[82] This presentation differs from that found in 3:10–18 or 11:33–36, where texts come together seamlessly, creating the impression that Paul is quoting a single text. The fact that Psalms, Deuteronomy, and Isaiah are all represented here also may underscore the importance of what is said, as Paul summons the multiple voices of his Scriptures as witness to the glorification of God by Jew and gentile alike.

The first citation (v. 9b), "I will confess you among the gentiles and I will praise your name," comes from Ps 17:50 (LXX), the only alteration being the omission of the direct address "Lord" following "gentiles."[83] The "I" here resumes the "for I declare" of v. 8, as it is Paul who initiates this praise of God among the gentiles.[84] "I will confess your name among the gentiles" serves as a pithy encapsulation of Paul's apostolic labor; it also aligns well with Paul's self-reference in priestly terms in 15:16. As elsewhere in the letter (see on 7:7–25), however, the "I" may well invite auditors to join in praise, especially as they have now experienced several expressions of praise and interjections of "Amen!" (as in 9:5; 11:33–36), of which this passage is the culmination.

The citation appears at the conclusion of a psalm that celebrates God as the divine warrior who has secured triumph over the speaker's enemies. The superscription of Ps 17 LXX attributes the psalm to David himself, and the psalm concludes with reference to David and his descendants as king. God is the "deliverer," the "stronghold," who carries out a fierce battle on the speaker's behalf. God trains the speaker for war and secures the speaker's victory. Auditors familiar with the psalm might well connect this line with the conflict language earlier in Romans (e.g., 6:13; 8:31–39; and see the introduction). Even

---

82. "And again" appears similarly in 1 Cor 3:20; Heb 1:5; 2:13; 10:30, although in shorter passages.

83. This omission could reflect Paul's understanding that Christ himself is the speaker. However, Paul has just indicated that the goal of this praise is the glorification of God (vv. 7–8), so praise in this instance is praise directed to God rather than to the Lord Jesus (Paul's frequent designation, as in e.g., 1:4, 7; 6:23; 13:14; 14:14).

84. "Paul places himself in the role of the eschatological agent whose task is to initiate the crescendo of praise" (Jewett 895). Hays (1993, 123–24) proposes that the "I" here is Christ himself, as also in 15:3, but that is not a role into which Paul casts Christ elsewhere (see Kujanpää 2019, 281). To be sure, Paul's emphasis does not lie with the identity of the speaker but with the content of the citations (Keck 1990, 93).

apart from taking the whole of the psalm into account, however, the quotation summons important features of Romans, including the notion of calling on the name (10:12–13; 14:11) and the ubiquitous concern about the gentiles (e.g., 1:5, 14; 3:9, 29–30; 10:12; 11:13).

Verse 10 calls out, "Rejoice, gentiles, together with God's people!" "God's people" (*laos*) is a clear reference to Israel, as earlier in 10:21–11:2.[85] The line, an exact quotation of Deut 32:43 LXX, comes from the Song of Moses, which celebrates God's defeat of God's enemies. In Deuteronomy those are human enemies (see especially vv. 39–42). In the context of Romans, however, where God has made peace with human enemies (5:10) and will later be identified with peace (16:20), the enemies who are defeated are suprahuman (Sin and Death in 5:12–21; the numerous figures and situations in 8:31–39). It is by no means obvious that hearers would recognize in this brief statement the entirety of the Song of Moses, however. Most immediately, the relevance of this line is its image of gentiles rejoicing together with Israel.

Rejoicing continues in v. 11 with the quotation of Ps 116:1 LXX.[86] As in the previous line, here again the gentiles and the "peoples" join together in praise. The repetition of terms from v. 10 means that "all the peoples" here still refers to Jews (despite the shift to the plural and the parallelism of the psalm itself; Kujanpää 2019, 287; Wagner 2002, 286). This united praise of God continues the emphasis on the unity of Jew and gentile and the right acknowledgment of God in praise and thanksgiving. Suggestively, v. 2 of the same psalm refers to God's mercy and God's truth, which connects it tightly with Rom 15:8–9. For those familiar with the psalm, this connection reinforces the grounds for shared praise.

Isaiah has the last word in the catena (v. 12), which is unsurprising given that his voice has assisted Paul throughout this letter (hence Wagner's image of Isaiah and Paul "in concert"; 2002, passim). Paul's text follows that of Isa 11:10 LXX, although importantly Paul omits the phrase "in that day." Whether or not that omission was deliberate, it marks an important distinction between Isaiah's words and Paul's hearing of them. For Isaiah, this "shoot of Jesse" comes in the future; but for Paul, the "shoot of Jesse" has already come. This reference to the Davidic line reaches back to Rom 1:3, where Paul first identifies Jesus Christ as David's offspring. Not only has that offspring "arisen" (*anistēmi*) in the sense of coming on the scene, but Jesus Christ has "arisen" in that he has been raised from the dead; Paul uses *anistēmi* of resurrection in 1 Thess 4:14,

---

85. Outside of this passage and 10:21–11:2, in Paul *laos* appears only in 9:25–26; 1 Cor 10:7; 14:21; and 2 Cor 6:16, all of which are scriptural citations.

86. There are slight alterations from the LXX. It reverses the order of the opening admonition, reading "Praise the Lord, all the nations," where Paul's order is "Praise, all the nations, the Lord." In addition, the LXX puts the second "praise" command in second-person ("[You] praise") rather than third ("Let them praise").

16 (cf. Eph 5:14). The resurrection means that this offspring of Jesse "rules" the gentiles and that they find hope in him. Although Paul does not use this precise expression elsewhere, Isaiah's words serve to restate Paul's own claims about Christ's reign, as in his depiction of Christ's place at "God's right hand" (Rom 8:34; and see 1 Cor 15:24–25). It is because of that reign that gentiles have hope.

Hope itself is eschatological for Paul. That is clear as early as 1 Thess 1:3 and 2:19, where he refers specifically to hope in the day of Christ's return, and in 1 Thess 4:13, where he refers to unbelievers as those who have no hope. By contrast, one characteristic of those who have been rectified by God's faith-giving acts in Jesus Christ is their hope for God's glory (Rom 5:2). Hope suffuses Paul's contrast of present agony and future redemption in 8:18–24.

This final citation connects the catena tightly to Christ, reinforcing Christ's relationship to circumcision (Jesse), to resurrection, and to the hope of the gentiles. The reference to gentile hope anticipates 15:25–32 and Paul's concern that the gentile offering might be rejected there in Jerusalem.

With these four citations, joined by the insistent repetition of "and again," Paul makes good on the claim that Scripture was written for our instruction (15:4). He finds in Scripture the fact of Jew and gentile together, their shared glorification of God, and their relationship to Christ's welcome and to God's final triumph.

[13] Paul has followed the opening admonition with a reminder of Christ's action, reinforced by multiple passages of Scripture invoking praise of God shared by Jew and gentile. Now he concludes with prayer (paralleling the function of vv. 5–6). The movement is revealing, suggesting as it does that this united praise, this welcome of one another, is nowhere possible apart from God's gift. Yet the prayer goes beyond the one found in vv. 5–6, where unity in doxology is central. Paul now prays for the fullness of God's gifts during the present time, the time of waiting in hope and expectation (8:18–24).

Repeating the word "hope" from the quotation in v. 12, Paul here describes God as "the God of that hope," a naming of God that joins his earlier identification of God as the God of endurance and comfort (15:5; and see "God of peace" in 16:20). He prays specifically for joy and peace, both of which are hallmarks of the behavior he urges in ch. 14. Paul admonishes those who confidently eat anything and everything to pursue peace (14:19; note the contrast with 3:17, where no one knows peace). In addition, he characterizes the reign of God as one of righteousness and peace and joy in the Holy Spirit (14:17). That connection between the divine reign and peace should come as no surprise, given Paul's association of it with eschatological blessing (2:10) and with the arrival of that blessing in the present (5:1).

Joy has already appeared in 14:17 as a feature of God's reign (along with righteousness and peace), and in 15:32 Paul anticipates arriving in Rome with

joy. Elsewhere it figures importantly as a spiritual gift (Gal 5:22) and a characteristic of those who have been grasped by the gospel (1 Thess 1:6; 3:9;
Phil 1:25; 2 Cor 8:2). Here as well, Paul associates joy and peace with believing
or trusting. Perhaps because it is difficult to describe or subject to analysis, joy
seldom comes to the surface in exegetical discussions, but for Paul it appears
to be a cherished by-product of God's intervention in Jesus Christ. It is not too
much to suggest, then, that this joy and peace give rise to the very rejoicing he
has been depicting and anticipating in the catena.

Paul closes with yet another expression of hope, that "you abound in hope
through the power of the Holy Spirit." Already Paul has said (with Isaiah) that
gentiles hope in Christ (the "shoot of Jesse," v. 12). And he has identified God
as the God of hope (v. 13). Now hope comes "through the power of the Holy
Spirit." If Paul does not spell out the relationship of the Spirit to Christ and God
as later believers will feel the need to do, he nevertheless acknowledges here
and elsewhere the place of the Spirit in actualizing God's presence (recalling
especially 5:1–5).

Taken together with the remainder of the letter, 15:1–13 simultaneously
differentiates and joins Jews and gentiles. By referring to circumcision and
the promises, Paul calls up the particular relationship of Israel to the God who
created and has sustained it, differentiating Israel from gentiles. Yet they are
joined together in Christ's work in that both receive from those promises, both
need God's mercy, both need God's truth. And most especially, both share in
the glorification of God and in the joy and peace of the gospel.

Notably, nothing here hints that Israel qua Israel has come to an end. Nothing
indicates that gentiles are now part of Israel itself (further undermining interpretations of 11:26 as having to do with the church, Jew and gentile). To be sure, in
1 Cor 12:2 Paul comments on a time when "you" (Corinthians) were gentiles, as
if the addressees have ceased to be gentiles, but that comment is something of a
Pauline oddity and likely signals Paul's association of gentiles with the worship of multiple gods. Here the two groups, circumcision and gentiles, remain
distinct while sharing profoundly in the gifts of God's action.

By drawing attention to these interrelated distinctions, Paul prepares for the
second half of the chapter. There he will comment on the letter he has written
before turning to the work that lies before him, but that work becomes concrete
in the gentile offering, an offering that Paul anticipates with evident anxiety.

Romans 15:14–16:23[27]
Closing the Letter

In 15:7–13 Paul has exulted in the ultimate outcome of the gospel. Having been welcomed by Christ Jesus, gentiles and Jews welcome one another for God's glory. The language of hope that repeatedly marks the conclusion of the passage ("the gentiles will hope," "the God of that hope" "you abound in hope through the power of the Holy Spirit") strongly recalls and reinforces the eschatological expectation at the end of ch. 8 as well as elsewhere in the letter (e.g., 11:26–27, 32; 13:11–14; 16:20).

Paul now begins the lengthy closing of the letter, although formally the letter body extends through 15:33. First, he locates the letter as an event in his own vocation (15:14–21) before turning to his plans for the immediate future, plans that are deeply connected to the relationship between Jewish and gentile believers (15:22–33). He then locates the letter more immediately, first by commending Phoebe, whose work will be at the heart of the letter's reception (16:1–2). He then asks his addressees (her auditors) to greet one another by name, greetings that serve to knit disparate groups together (16:3–16). A brief set of warnings introducing a word of assurance of God's victory over Satan (16:17–20) precedes greetings from Paul's companions in Corinth (16:21–23). The closing benediction (16:25–27) likely comes from a later hand.

15:14–21 The Letter in Retrospect

What Paul writes in 15:14–33 about his own work and his immediate plans has its home within Paul's larger eschatological conviction, in that there is an urgency to his work in general and specifically in Jerusalem, Rome, and Spain. This passage (vv. 14–21) locates Paul's letter to the Romans within a recapitulation of his vocation, cast here in liturgical imagery. Many elements in this section echo elements of the letter opening, a feature of ch. 15 noted as early as Chrysostom, who repeatedly draws attention to the way the "end" of the letter recalls and replays the introduction (*Hom. Rom.* 29; *NPNF*[1] 11.542–43).

15:14 Now, brothers and sisters, I myself am confident about you, confident that you yourselves are full of goodness, having been made complete with all knowledge and enabled also to counsel one another. 15 Despite that confidence[a] I have written you quite boldly, in part by way of reminding you, because of the gift given me by God 16 that I should be a servant of Christ Jesus among the gentiles, serving the gospel of God as a priest would, so that the offering the gentiles have made[b] would be acceptable, made holy by the Holy Spirit.

17 Therefore in Christ Jesus I have this[c] reason for boasting so far as God is concerned, 18 for I dare to speak only of what Christ has brought about[d] through me for the obedience of the gentiles—in word and work, 19 by the power of signs and wonders, by the power of the Spirit of God,[e] such that I have completed the gospel of Christ from Jerusalem and around[f] as far as Illyricum. 20 For[g] this reason I prize the honor of proclaiming the gospel where Christ has not been named, so that I do not build on the foundation of another, 21 but as it is written:

> Those to whom he has not been announced will see,
> and those who have not heard will understand.

a. "Despite that confidence" takes the opening *de* as an adversative that introduces a qualification to Paul's statement of confidence in v. 14.

b. Although "offering of the gentiles" is routinely understood to be the gentiles themselves (i.e., an objective genitive or even a genitive of apposition), it may well be a subjective genitive referring to "the offering the gentiles have made," whether of themselves (as in 12:1) or of financial support (as in 15:26–27). See Downs 2008, 146–57.

c. The article preceding *kauchēsis* ("reason for boasting") is resumptive.

d. The translation smooths out the awkward wording of "for I do not dare to say anything of the things which Christ has not brought about."

e. "Spirit of God" appears in some manuscripts (including $\mathfrak{P}^{46}$ ℵ D[1] L P Ψ) and "Holy Spirit" in others (including A D[*.2] F G 33). Both options have ample attestation, and the difference is negligible. "Of God" is slightly preferable because that is a phrase used in Romans only at 8:9, 14, and Holy Spirit could easily reflect assimilation to 15:13 and 16. One manuscript, B, reads simply "spirit," without any modifier.

f. *Kyklō* could refer to the region around Jerusalem, but more probably it calls up the extent of Paul's travel (BDAG, s.v.).

g. Verse 20 continues the sentence beginning with "I dare" in v. 18. Here it is treated as a new sentence for the sake of clarity.

[15:14–16] In lines without parallel elsewhere in his letters, Paul concludes the letter body with reflections on writing the letter, and that in the context of his vocation.[1] The passage opens with direct address to "brothers and sisters" (last

1. Elsewhere he does refer to some specific element in a previous letter (e.g., 1 Cor 5:9, 11), defend a previous comment (e.g., 1 Cor 2:3, 9; 7:12), or indicate that he is physically writing his name (Gal 6:11; Phlm 19), but nowhere else does Paul remark on a letter in retrospect as he does here.

used in 12:1) and an emphatic statement of confidence. Not content with "I am confident about you" (*pepeismai . . . peri hymōn*), Paul supplies an emphatic "I myself" and an equally emphatic "yourselves," raising the rhetorical volume to draw attention to what immediately follows, the content of Paul's confidence. They are "full of goodness," "complete with all knowledge," able even to "counsel one another." It is striking that Paul uses the combination "full of" (*mestoi*) and "complete" (*peplērōmenoi*) here and nowhere else except in 1:29, where he writes that "they" are "filled up with" all sorts of evil acts and "full of" other evil acts. Similarly, in 8:8 he writes that those who are "in the flesh" are "not able" to please God, but here the hearers are addressed as "enabled" to counsel one another. However unintentional, this repetition indicates a radical sense of what changes in human beings from their captivity to Sin and Death to their newness of life in Christ.

This effusive statement of confidence may well be a *captatio benevolentiae*, intended to keep Roman auditors at Paul's side as Phoebe reads this final portion of the letter. Similar expressions of confidence in his addressees occur elsewhere, always where Paul's confidence seems more rhetorical than factual (2 Cor 2:3; Gal 5:10; and Phlm 21). In addition, the goodness, knowledge, and counsel Paul attributes to them here scarcely match the content of the letter that has preceded, given its extensive treatment of God's action in Jesus Christ. Had Paul actually regarded the Roman audience as full of knowledge, he would scarcely have needed to write so long a letter. Further, the opening thanksgiving of Romans is striking for its lack of specificity, perhaps because Paul is not at all convinced of their goodness, wisdom, and readiness to counsel one another. This declaration resembles 1 Cor 1:4, where Paul celebrates the gifts bestowed on the Corinthians only to launch into a massive correction of their use of these gifts in the letter that follows.

Having secured their attention, Paul comments on his writing of the letter, an act that again is unusual. Typically, when Paul comments on writing to congregations, he does so to remind them of some specific instruction (1 Cor 5:9, 11) or to defend something he has written in a previous letter (2 Cor 2:3, 9; 7:12). Here, by contrast, he admits that the letter is a bold move, undertaken in part by way of "reminding" them. It strains credulity to imagine that Paul really thinks the letter is simply a reminder, given both its extent and the pains he takes over its content. Instead, this seems a variation on the rhetorical "you know" that introduces new material or at least new implications (e.g., 1 Thess 4:2, 5:2; 1 Cor 12:2). To the extent that the letter is a reminder, it recasts the gospel the auditors have received in order to make memory of what God has done to rescue humanity from Sin and its associated powers, to give new life, and to unify Jew and gentile (see the introduction; Gaventa 2009).

This bold act of writing comes about by means of grace, "because of the gift given me by God." The clause recasts 1:5 ("through whom we received grace and apostleship"), where Paul also describes his vocation as a gift. The two clauses that follow in v. 16 convey the particular results of Paul's gift: first, that he is a servant for the gentiles, and second, that the offering of the gentiles might be acceptable.

The language Paul uses for himself is striking. He has referred to tax agents as *leitourgoi*, God's public servants (13:6), and elsewhere he identifies Epaphroditus as a *leitourgos*, a servant of Paul's own need (Phil 2:25), but he does not employ the term for himself elsewhere. Nowhere else does he refer to his labor as priestly service, language that is reinforced by the "offering" terminology that follows. These lines also recall the letter's opening, even as they recast it. There Paul identifies himself as a slave and an apostle (1:1); here he is a priestly servant. There his gift is one of bringing about "the obedience that comes from faith" (1:5); here he is concerned with the holiness of the gentile offering.

The phrase "serving the gospel of God as a priest would" warrants closer examination. The verb *hierourgeō*, a hapax legomenon in both the NT and the LXX (apart from an alternate reading at 4 Macc 7:8), refers to doing priestly service. When it takes an accusative object, that object is the object being sacrificed (as in the lambs of Josephus, *Ant.* 3.237; cf. 5.263; 11.110; Philo, *Spec. Laws* 1.177). Here, by contrast, it is the gospel that is being served.

In v. 16a, then, Paul's self-identification is liturgical, and that imagery continues in v. 16b with "the offering the gentiles have made." Such a statement is susceptible of an anti-Jewish interpretation, according to which Paul is proposing to displace animal sacrifice or service in the Jerusalem temple, but such polemics are out of keeping with the context. Instead, by identifying himself and the gentiles with liturgical language, Paul continues the focus on worship, prominent as early in the letter as 1:21, 25 (and see Gaventa 2008a, 2014b).

Verse 16b then identifies the goal of Paul's service as the acceptability and sanctification of the "offering the gentiles have made." Literally, Paul writes of the "offering of the gentiles," and most interpreters, stretching back at least as early as Chrysostom (*Hom. Rom.* 29; *NPNF*[1] 11.543), take this to be a reference to the gentiles themselves as the offering Paul makes. The NASB makes that view explicit by translating, "that my offering of the gentiles may become acceptable." Yet it is unclear in what sense Paul himself makes an offering of the gentiles. More to the point, at a key moment in the letter Paul has admonished the Romans to present themselves as a living sacrifice (12:1), which implies that they are the ones who make the sacrifice. To be sure, 12:1 employs *thysia* rather than *prosphora* as in 15:16b, although the two are found together in the LXX (Ps 39:7; Dan 3:38; Sir 34:19; 1 Esd 5:51). Further, construing this offering as one made *by* the gentiles, the phrase once again bookends the opening of the letter, with its reference to the obedience that comes from faith (1:5). As Paul brings about gentile obedience (see also 15:18), he also brings about gentile offering.

An additional implication of taking the offering as one the gentiles make is that it anticipates the discussion of the collection later in the chapter. The body of the letter culminates, after all, in a request for prayer that the gentile offering might be received in Jerusalem (vv. 30–33; and see Downs 2008, 147–56).

The offering the gentiles have made is said, by God's grace (since the word governs all of v. 16), to be acceptable, sanctified by the Holy Spirit. In the first instance, Paul refers to divine acceptance, as the words immediately following concern Paul's own reasons for confidence before God. Yet his anguish over the collection's acceptability in Jerusalem may not be far from his mind (v. 31). Divine and human acceptance are intertwined in this case, because the offering the gentiles make is the result of God's own gift, regardless of whether those in Jerusalem see it as such.

Further, the Holy Spirit has a role in making the offering holy. Notably, these final lines of the letter contain numerous references to the Spirit (14:17; 15:13, 16, 19, 30), more than any since Paul's extensive discussion in ch. 8. The Spirit is active not only in initiating believers into their adoption and interceding for them (8:12–16, 26) but also in making their offering holy.

[17–19] Because of the grace given Paul ("therefore" links v. 17 to what has preceded), he has a reason for boasting. That reason is, first of all, said to be "in Christ Jesus." As in 5:2, 11, the boasting Paul has earlier abjured (2:17, 23; 3:27; 4:2) is both acceptable and even desirable in Christ, since boasting here is not about Paul's own accomplishments but arises from his place in Christ (cf. 12:5). Second, Paul's reason for boasting is "so far as God is concerned." Although Paul elsewhere refers to "boasting in God" (*kauchasthai en tō theō*; 5:11) and "boasting before God" (*kauchasthai enōpion tou theou*; 1 Cor 1:29; and cf. 1 Thess 2:19), here the boasting is "so far as God is concerned." Boasting can carry an eschatological connotation, as in 5:2, 11 and especially in 1 Thess 2:19 (the "crown of boasting" at the parousia), but here boasting "so far as God is concerned" designates the character of the boast differently. The following verse makes clear what Paul has in mind, which is to distinguish Christ's work from Paul's work apart from Christ.[2]

Paul's boast is simultaneously an inversion of boasting, although different from the parody of boasting found in 2 Cor 12–13. Paul claims that he has reason to boast, but his boast is doubly qualified. It is both "in Christ Jesus" and "so far as God is concerned," such that Paul is not in fact boasting of himself.

The more detailed statement of vv. 18–19 extends this point. What Paul dares to say is confined to what Christ has done through him "for the obedience

---

2. Read in a society determined to restrict God to the sphere of religious or spiritual activity, this phrase might suggest that Paul has in mind a distinction between things governed by God and those not governed by God. Even the most cursory reading of Paul's letters should undermine that supposition. Moreover, given the way the gods permeated the ancient world, Paul was far from alone in such a supposition.

of the gentiles." These accomplishments he summarizes without explanation: "in word and work, by the power of signs and wonders, by the power of the Spirit of God." The first two terms appear together in 2 Cor 10:11: "Let that sort of person understand that whatever we say [*logos*] when away through a letter, we will do [*ergon*] when present." *Ergon* elsewhere characterizes endeavor on behalf of the gospel, both Paul's (e.g., 1 Cor 3:13–15; 9:1; Phil 1:6) and that of others (1 Cor 15:58; 16:10). And one of the numerous uses of *logos* in Paul's letters is as a near synonym for the gospel (e.g., 1 Cor 1:18; 14:36; 2 Cor 2:17; Gal 6:6). Taken together, "word and work" function as a synecdoche for apostolic life.

"By the power of signs and wonders" startles, given that Paul has not referred to such events in the letter, and elsewhere he expresses some disdain for those who expect signs (1 Cor 1:22). In Acts, the phrase occurs repeatedly, however, beginning with Peter's quotation from Joel 3 in 2:19 (e.g., 2:43; 4:30; 5:12; 6:8; 15:12). There "signs and wonders" evoke the power at work through the apostles and other Christian preachers, power that signifies the inbreaking of the "last days" (Acts 2:17). Paul uses the phrase only once elsewhere, in 2 Cor 12:12, where it is also paired with power (*dynamis*), although in that instance the term is plural.

The third phrase summarizing Christ's work in Paul is "by the power of the Spirit of God." Here Paul leaves behind the paired items to repeat his emphasis that it is the Spirit that achieves these things. The Spirit works not only to make the offering holy (Rom 15:16) but in the apostles themselves. The several references to the Spirit in this chapter (vv. 13, 16, 19, 30) recall and expand the claim in 8:5–17, 26–27 about the Spirit's work of giving life, adopting, and interceding.

The result of this apostolic activity (*hōste*) is that Paul has "completed the gospel of Christ from Jerusalem and around as far as Illyricum." This apparently straightforward assertion is anything but straightforward. To begin with, the combination of "complete" (or "fulfill"; *plēroō*) with "gospel" is distinctive (as is the earlier combination of *hierourgeō* with "gospel" in v. 16). Paul writes of proclaiming the gospel (2 Cor 11:4; Gal 2:2; 1 Thess 2:9), making it known (Gal 1:11), being unashamed of it (Rom 1:16), but not of completing it. Especially given questions that arise from the place names themselves, Jerusalem and Illyricum, he may be suggesting that he represented the gospel in this wide geographical sphere, not that he himself introduced it in every place.

Even that geographical observation is odd, since Paul himself rarely notes the nature and extent of his travels, much less the circumstances.[3] What he means by the selection of these two place names as geographical markers for his work is even more opaque. Pairing Jerusalem with Illyricum is odd, given that

---

3. A travel agenda appears in 2 Cor 1:15–16; 1:23–2:2, where the focus is on his reasons for not already having visited Corinth again. In 2 Cor 12:14 he does invoke his own difficulties in travel.

one is a city name, the other the name of a province.[4] The pairing does result
in a minor instance of alliteration (*Hierousalēm* and *Hillyrikon*), however, so
that the sounds of the names themselves enhance the large scope of the labor.[5]

Despite its unquestioned importance in the Gospels and, indeed, in the life
of Jesus, Jerusalem seldom appears in Paul's letters. That curiosity is consistent with Loveday Alexander's observation that cities "scarcely exist on the
Pauline mental map except as locations for churches" (2005, 101). Her insight
is confirmed by his few references to Jerusalem (in Gal 1:17; 2:1; 1 Cor 16:3),
the allegory of Gal 4:25-26 being an exception. He surely begins the arc of this
brief geographical report with Jerusalem by way of anticipating his upcoming
journey and his deep fears about his reception there (15:25-33).

The name Illyricum, a hapax legomenon in the NT, is more puzzling. It is
the Roman name for a region on the eastern side of the Adriatic, and it does not
include cities associated with Paul's mission (apart possibly from Dalmatia;
2 Tim 4:10). Perhaps Paul introduces the name because it would be known to
the Romans (Fitzmyer 714). The province would have stood just beyond Macedonia and Achaia (see v. 26 below), suggesting another possible explanation:
Paul may think of Illyricum as just beyond his furthest reach to date, making it a
rhetorically effective name for expressing the gospel's extent.

[20–21] In this expansive journey representing the gospel, Paul claims, "I
prize the honor." The verb itself (*philotimeomai*) can refer to public or civic
service (BDAG s.v.), but it need not be limited to that sphere. It is used by
Philo and Josephus for being especially eager for something (e.g., Josephus,
Ant. 5.290; 7.64; Philo, *Decalogue* 60; *Spec. Laws* 4.74). The sense here seems
to be simply that Paul desires to do what he is called to do (as in 1:15). Specifically, Paul's desire is to preach the gospel where Christ has not been named,
not to build on another's foundation. This, of course, echoes his comment in
1 Cor 3:10 that he is like the builder who lays a foundation on which another
builds (and see 2 Cor 10:15-16).

The specific formulation "where Christ has not been named" introduces a bit
of unclarity, as Paul does not elsewhere refer to "naming" Christ. Minimally,
he might refer to the sheer act of proclamation, quite apart from results (Jewett
915). In view of the several ways this passage recalls and recasts the letter's
opening, he may be specifying what is involved in apostleship "among all the
gentiles . . . for the sake of his name" (1:5; and see also 9:17; 10:13).

---

4. Loveday Alexander observes that using the regional name is itself unsurprising, as "regional
names also predominate in Paul's travel plans and in his rare moments of autobiography" (2005,
100). She also observes that Paul is not at all reticent about using Roman designations: "He has no
qualms about a strategic approach that mirrors the Roman attitude to its conquered territories" (101).

5. BDAG, s.v. *Illyrikon* compares Paul's remark with saying "from Dallas, Texas, all the way
to Anchorage, Alaska," but the mismatch of categories makes it closer to "from Dallas all the way
to Alaska."

Paul reinforces this assertion with the letter's final citation from Scripture, this time from Isa 52:15 (LXX). In the immediate context the citation authorizes the taking of the gospel to those who have not yet heard, places "where Christ has not been named." Once again, Paul employs a passage that in its own literary and historical context addresses Israel, but the word he hears in it concerns gentiles in the present (as in 9:25–26; 10:19–20; Wagner 2002, 333–36). These two verses appear to stand in some tension with the opening of the letter, where Paul announces his plan to preach the gospel in Rome (1:15). Given that *euangelizesthai* is consistently used by Paul for announcing something new, not for subsequent instruction (see above on 1:15; Dickson 2005; Gaventa 2009), the implication is that Paul understands the Romans still to be in need of the gospel, at least in some sense. That conclusion coheres with the content of the letter, which extends well beyond a simple act of self-introduction or defense of Paul's practice of gentile inclusion. As Paul sees it, the Roman believers have not yet received the gospel in its entirety; as a result, he begins his proclamation with this letter.

The Isaiah citation concludes Paul's retrospective remarks about the letter, its relationship to his vocation, and the character of that vocation. With v. 22, he turns to his upcoming travel, once again recalling the opening lines of the letter.

15:22–33 The Letter in Prospect

Having articulated the letter's place in his own vocation in 15:14–21, in the final verses of the letter body Paul introduces his immediate plans. Initially he recalls his desire to be in Rome before going on from Rome to Spain (vv. 22–24). Verses 25–29 then announce the startling news that he will first go well out of his way in order to deliver the collection to Jerusalem. The significance—and the dangers—attached to this visit to Jerusalem occupy the final section, which concludes with an urgent prayer (v. 33).

Prominent in these lines is Paul's sense of the profound web connecting believers across geographical and ethnic lines. Believers in Macedonia and Achaia mark—perhaps even make—that web concretely with their financial support. Paul anticipates that this gentile support and the connection it represents may be rejected in Jerusalem, as he himself may be rejected. The Roman audience is not left to one side as mere spectators to Paul's plans, however, since Paul asks for their prayerful support and does so in terms strong enough to disclose the depth of his worry.

15:22 Therefore, I have many times been kept from coming to you. 23 But now that I have no place remaining in these regions where I have not taken the gospel,[a] and since I have desired for many years to come to you, 24 as I go to Spain I hope that I can visit you as I make my way there and be sent on my way there by you after I have first benefited from your company for a while.[b]

25 But now I am going to Jerusalem by way of serving the holy ones there. 26 For Macedonia and Achaia were pleased to establish a certain fellowship[c] for the poor among the holy people in Jerusalem,[d] 27 both because they were pleased to do so and because they are their debtors. For since[e] the gentiles have fellowship with them in spiritual matters, they are also obliged to serve them in physical matters. 28 When I have completed this task and have sealed this fruit over to them, I will go to Spain by way of you. 29 And I know that when I do come to you, I will come with the fullness of Christ's blessing.

30 So I urge you, brothers and sisters, through our Lord Jesus Christ and through the love of the Spirit, that you contend along with me[f] through prayers to God on my behalf, 31 that I might be delivered from the disobedient in Judea, and that my service for Jerusalem might be acceptable to the holy ones, 32 so that I can come to you with joy and through God's will be refreshed among you.

33 May the God of peace be with all of you. Amen![g]

a. The words "where I have not taken the gospel" are added for clarity, assuming that v. 23 follows on the statement in v. 20 regarding Paul's priority.

b. Verses 23–24 are syntactically awkward, consisting of a string of participial clauses only loosely modifying the finite verb *elpizō* ("I hope"). That awkwardness likely prompted the addition of the verb phrase *eleusomai pros hymas* ("I will come to you"), found in ‭א‬[2] 33 104 and elsewhere.

c. Most English translations have "contribution" (ESV, KJV, NIV) or "resources" (NRSVue) or even "money" (CEV) instead of "fellowship." However, elsewhere the term *koinōnia* regularly refers to an association or fellowship, rather than concretely to a contribution for an association or fellowship (e.g., 1 Cor 1:9; Gal 2:9; Polybius, *Hist.* 5.351; Plato, *Resp.* 371b5–6), which strongly suggests that fellowship is the connotation here as well (see Peterman 1994; Jewett 928–29).

d. Lit., "the poor of the holy ones." This could be rendered as a genitive of apposition, so that it is translated "the poor, namely, the holy ones," but most interpreters concur in translating it as a partitive genitive, as above (see esp. Keck 1965, 1966).

e. Lit., "if" (*ei*), but here indicating a supposition, as in 6:8; Matt 6:30; and elsewhere (BDAG, s.v. *ei*, 3).

f. *Synagōnizomai* is a hapax legomenon in the NT and LXX, but in other ancient literature it refers to assisting someone, and occasionally specifically to assisting in a contentious situation (as in Thucydides, *Hist.* 5.109; Plato, [*Alc. maj.*] 119e; Josephus, *Ant.* 5.183; 17.220; Philo, *Flaccus* 13.111). Given the context, in which Paul expects opposition, and the earlier martial language in the letter (as in 7:23; 8:35, e.g.), it is reasonable to assume that Paul's usage also reflects a contentious situation.

g. "Amen" is omitted by 𝔓[46], in all likelihood because it (and 1506) inserts the doxology of 16:25–27 at this point. The same passage appears following 14:23 in numerous manuscripts (including A L P Ψ). The fact that these lines move around in the manuscript tradition is among the several reasons for regarding them as a later addition to the letter. (See below on 16:25–27.)

[22–24] By way of concluding the letter body, Paul turns from his retrospective account to anticipate the challenges that lie ahead, now that he has "no place remaining in these regions." Once again, as in vv. 19–20, the desire to take the gospel where it has not been introduced governs his itinerary, or at least it governs the way he reflects on that itinerary.

The distinctiveness of these lines in the context of Paul's letters should be noted. Although he does often make reference to travel plans, those comments largely concern the addressees directly (as in 1 Cor 4:18–19; 16:2–9; 2 Cor 1:15–16, 23; 12:14; 1 Thess 2:17–20; Phlm 22). Here Paul takes time to spin out both a more detailed itinerary and some reasons for it, presumably because of the challenge the Jerusalem detour poses, both in Jerusalem itself (vv. 25–33) and in the understanding of the Roman addressees (vv. 22–24).

Verse 22 opens this section by observing that Paul has often been prevented from traveling to Rome. As in 1:13 he does not name the circumstances that have previously made the journey impossible (by contrast with 1 Thess 2:18) but moves quickly to assure the Roman auditors of his desire to come to them. Paul repeats this desire:

v. 22   He was prevented from traveling to Rome (by implication, he wanted to do so)
v. 23   He has wanted to go to Rome for many years
v. 24   He hopes to see the Roman Christians

He will reinforce this desire again in vv. 28–29 and yet again in v. 32.

No reasons explicate this desire, and the "but now" that opens v. 23 marks it as urgent. It is possible Paul sees Rome itself as important because of its sheer political power, although such a valuation would sit oddly alongside his radical relativization of merely human values elsewhere (most notably 2 Cor 5:16–17). Other possibilities include his sense that the assemblies in Rome are important because they are well known elsewhere (as in 1:8), his perceived need to defend his views from misinterpretation by others (Tobin 2004, 73–76, 102–3), and his desire to receive significant material support for his work in Spain (Jewett 87–89). The only reason he provides here is that Rome is a stopping point for his venture to Spain, though he gives no specifics identifying his hopes for Roman support. Importantly, in 1:15 he indicates his desire to preach in Rome itself, a desire that sits well alongside the remarks of vv. 20 and 23 about going into new territory only if Rome itself is understood to be new territory. The letter, as v. 15 indicated, is only a reminder "in part"; it may also begin Paul's preaching in Rome if the letter itself is regarded as proclamation.[6] Verse 24 expresses the general hope of being supported but without any specific indication what that support might be.

[25–29] To travel from Paul's current location in Corinth westward to Rome and then again westward to Spain is entirely reasonable. What Paul announces in v. 25 is anything but reasonable: "But now I am going to Jerusalem."[7] An eastward detour of over 700 nautical miles scarcely signals the importance of Rome for Paul's plans, and Paul's awareness of the awkwardness of this news could account for his repeated reassurance of his wish to be in Rome.

Paul immediately states the reason for this outrageous detour: he is going to Jerusalem in service of the "holy ones" there, using an expression (*hoi hagioi*) he regularly uses for those who would later be termed Christians (e.g., Rom 1:7; 8:27; 1 Cor 1:2; 6:1; Phil 1:1). The verb *diakoneō*, here translated as "by way of serving," can be used of service in numerous forms (e.g., 2 Cor 3:3; 8:19–20; Phlm 13; as well as Mark 1:31; Luke 8:3; Acts 6:2, among many others). Here that service takes the form of a fund, generally termed "the collection," that gentile assemblies are sending to poor Christians in Jerusalem.

The collection features prominently in Paul's work, as is evident from his comments elsewhere. He gives instructions for its gathering and delivery in 1 Cor 16:1–4, and he provides an extensive theological rationale for it in 2 Cor 8:1–9:15.[8] It has provoked a complex of historical questions, including the chronology of Paul's work and letters, various possible comparanda in the Roman world (patronage, associations, the temple tax), and the socioeconomic status of believers in Rome and elsewhere; and none of these issues can be addressed adequately here.[9] For present purposes, what is important is understanding that the collection does occupy Paul across much of his labor, that it involves concrete human need as well as the relationship of Jew and gentile created by God in the gospel, and that Paul perceives it as sufficiently important that he risks his life for it (Wan 2000, 192).

That Macedonia and Achaia are named as donors aligns well with 2 Cor 8:1–9:15, and once again Paul uses the names of regions rather than local assemblies (Alexander 2005, 100). Taken together, Macedonia and Achaia suggest a geographical sweep to the collection that serves Paul's purposes in conveying the importance of his task. (This is similar to saying "the United States" has entered

6. Here I assume again that *euangelizesthai* refers to initial introduction of good news, not further instruction or admonition of those already within the assembly of faith. See above on 15:20, as well as on 1:15 (see further Dickson 2005; Gaventa 2009).

7. Curiously, Luke puts these same words ("I am going to Jerusalem") in Paul's mouth in his Miletus speech (Acts 20:22), but the combination of *poreuomai* with *eis* indicating destination is entirely idiomatic (e.g., BDAG, s.v. *poreuō*).

8. Galatians 2:10 demonstrates concern for the poor that Paul shared with believers in Jerusalem, but it is probably not identical with the Jerusalem collection (B. Longenecker 2010, 157–206).

9. For a concise review of the discussion, see Downs 2008, 3–26.

into a treaty rather than "Washington" or even "the current administration.") Despite the uncertainty regarding the Corinthian contribution on evidence in 2 Cor 8–9, his reference to Achaia implies that they did in fact contribute.

Paul does not specify what the need is, although he identifies the recipients as "the poor" among believers. In Acts the prophet Agabus announces a famine in Judea (11:27–30), and Josephus also writes about famine in Judea around this same time (*Ant.* 20.51–53, 101). There need not have been any particular crisis, however, given the extent of vulnerability across the Roman world. Paul's audience at Rome would have understood that widespread vulnerability without requiring further explanation.[10] In other words, Paul does not need to specify the causes for poverty, because most people understood that any loss of health or income could leave them destitute, and they would have recognized the vulnerability of others. In addition, by drawing attention to the specific circumstances of the poor, Paul might have been inviting shame on the recipients.[11]

Paul identifies the collection as a "certain fellowship for the poor." The money becomes then not simply a means of addressing physical need—although it is that, given the word "poor" and the reference to physical needs in what follows. But to "establish a certain fellowship" is to do something more. It is to construct or offer a connection. Fellowship implies a sharing—even a dignity—to this gift that is revealing.[12] It suggests a belonging to one another in the body of Christ (12:4–5). The danger Paul anticipates in vv. 30–32 may have its origin precisely in the fact that the collection conveys this mutual belonging of Jewish and gentile communities. With that claim Paul may go well beyond what is tolerable for at least some Christians in Jerusalem.[13] Verse 27 opens with the same two words as in v. 26, "because they were pleased" (*eudokēsan gar*), underscoring the voluntary nature of this gift, even though Paul turns immediately to obligation language, which the remainder of the verse explains in terms of a mutual exchange. The two expressions are not at odds with one another. Paul has identified himself in ch. 1 both as compelled to apostleship (1:1) and as eager to carry it out (1:15).

---

10. Barclay captures the situation ably: "A wide range of common events could create a crisis for a household, and the vast majority of the ancient population, urban and rural, lived no further than two such crises away from destitution, most much closer to the brink than that [including Paul himself]" (2023, 245).

11. Barclay 2023, 1; citing Luke 15:16; 16:3; *CIL* IV 9839b; as well as Welborn 2015, 189–243.

12. Underlying this sentence is recent work that understands the collection not as an act of philanthropy by those with a surplus of resources but as an exchange among people of limited resources. See especially Downs 2016, 17; Schellenberg 2018; for a later period, Buell 2008.

13. Turning this point another way, Jouette Bassler astutely observes that Paul is collecting funds for people who reject his interpretation of the gospel, people who might otherwise be identified as his enemies (1991, 113).

With v. 27b Paul specifies the nature of the fellowship that is shared. The gentiles now share "in spiritual matters," so they are obliged to share with "the holy people in Jerusalem" in physical matters as well. Since there is spiritual fellowship, there ought also to be physical fellowship. It is important not to be reductionistic here, either by isolating spiritual from physical matters or by enumerating specific Jewish and gentile contributions. (A rough comparison may appear in 1:3–4, where Jesus Christ is identified both physically and spiritually; those features of his identification are not competing with one another.) The point is not who brings what gifts to the body, but that Jews and gentiles share in both realms, making the fellowship total (as in the bodies that are presented in 12:1). In addition, Paul's indirectness here ("physical matters" rather than "resources" or "funds") may serve to respect the dignity of poor Jerusalemites.

It is important to be clear what the collection does and does not signal. It does signal the mutuality of Jew and gentile in the Christ event, both mutual giftedness and mutual responsibility. Paul does not hereby dissolve the line between Jew and gentile (by contrast with the author of Ephesians, for example, for whom the "dividing wall" of separation has been broken down; 2:14–15). Jews remain Jews who share in matters of spirit and flesh. Gentiles remain gentiles who share in matters of spirit and flesh. Nothing indicates that the gentiles in Macedonia and Achaia are now Jews or quasi-Jews. They remain gentiles, and it is precisely *as gentiles* that they are in fellowship with Jerusalem's Jews.

Neither does the collection represent some priority attached to Jerusalem itself, either the Jerusalem leadership or the geographical location. Strikingly, Paul mentions no individuals (by contrast with Gal 2:1–10) and writes nothing about fulfilling an obligation made previously. In fact, had the collection arisen from fulfilling an obligation or signaling loyalty to Jerusalem leadership, it would scarcely have generated the anxiety on evidence in Rom 15:30–32 (Downs 2008, 35–36). Moreover, neither here nor elsewhere does Paul attach the significance to Jerusalem itself that is found in other early Jewish and Christian texts (e.g., 11QTemple; Ezek 40–48; Luke 24:47; Acts 1:4; Rev 21). What Paul finds important are fellow Jewish believers in Jerusalem, that is, Jerusalem in relationship to Jesus Christ.

Verse 28 begins by anticipating the outcome of the visit to Jerusalem, here cast in positive, confident terms (see vv. 30–31 for a less optimistic presentation). Paul expects that he will "complete" this service to the saints by "sealing" this "fruit" to them. The image of "sealing" appears elsewhere as an expression for a secured transfer of goods (BDAG, s.v. *sphragizō*; Jewett 931–32). Paul takes care to ensure that there are no grounds for suspecting malfeasance when it comes to the collection (1 Cor 16:3–4; 2 Cor 8:16–24). When this has been handed over, Paul says that he will go through Rome to Spain, coming "with the fullness of Christ's blessing." Presumably, that confidence in Christ's approval looks both backward (to Jerusalem) and forward (to Rome and Spain).

[30–33] The confidence about Jerusalem expressed in vv. 28–29 recedes here, giving way to Paul's direct and dramatic plea for prayers on behalf of his work and his person. Although he does elsewhere ask for prayer on his behalf (1 Thess 5:25; Phlm 22), he does not do so with the specificity or urgency found here. The introductory "I urge" appears elsewhere in Romans only at 12:1 and 16:17. The appeal is made "through our Lord Jesus Christ and through the love of the Spirit," perhaps recalling the double intercession of Christ and the Spirit in 8:26, 34.

All of this leads to the specific request that the Roman auditors contend along with Paul in prayer on his behalf, wording that itself betrays the conflict he anticipates (by comparison with his prayer requests elsewhere; see 1 Thess 5:25; Phlm 22). First, he prays for deliverance from "the disobedient" in Judea. Given Paul's use of the language of disobedience in 10:21 and 11:30–32, he has in view those he calls "the rest" in 11:7, namely, Jews who do not recognize Jesus as the Messiah of God. The Lukan account supports Paul's remark, portraying his hostile reception in Jerusalem (e.g., Acts 21:27–28; 22:22, 30; 23:12–15). It is not necessary to take Luke's account at face value to understand the danger Paul anticipates when he speaks of the need for "deliverance," language that conveys a serious risk.[14]

His concern extends beyond bodily safety, however, as v. 31b introduces the prayer that Paul's service might be acceptable to the saints in Jerusalem. While God may have made the offering of the gentiles acceptable, it is by no means clear that fellow believers in Jerusalem will find it acceptable. The notion of a fund signaling fellowship from gentile believers could have been abhorrent to some in Jerusalem, as already noted. At the very least, it could have severed them from their own local networks of support.

Although the evidence is slender, there is reason to think that Paul's fears were realized, perhaps even exceeded. According to the account in the Acts of the Apostles, Paul was arrested in Jerusalem and transported to Rome as a prisoner (Acts 21:27–36; 26:30–32; 28:16–31). Even if Luke's narrative diverges from the facts considerably, it seems unlikely that he has created the story out of whole cloth. Perhaps more telling, Acts has nothing to say about a fund Paul took to Jerusalem for poor believers there (although see Acts 24:17). Given Luke's preoccupation with financial matters, he would scarcely have hesitated to draw attention to the collection had he known it was willingly received.

The final line of Paul's prayer (v. 32) returns him to the prospect of arrival in Rome. He anticipates arriving "with joy," a feature of early Christian texts too quickly overlooked. Already Paul has identified joy as a feature of God's

14. Paul's awareness of that risk to himself may be on evidence earlier in the letter when he writes of tribulation (5:3) and suffering (8:18), and especially as he enumerates the circumstances and agents that wish to separate "us" from God's love in Jesus Christ (8:31–39).

reign (14:17) and prayed for both joy and peace for his Roman auditors (15:13). Elsewhere he identifies it among the fruit of the spirit (Gal 5:22) and as a feature of prayer itself (Phil 1:4). Here he anticipates joy at being finally at Rome, to be "refreshed" among them through God's will (and see Phlm 20).

With v. 33 Paul brings the body of the letter to an end, invoking the "God of peace" (see also 16:20) as is appropriate for a passage in which peace among humans is in doubt. The "Amen," the last of the letter (although see below on 16:25–27) once again invites Phoebe's auditors to join in Paul's urgent prayer.

The call of "Amen" closes the body of the letter. Paul has placed the letter in an apostolic context, locating it in his own vocation to take the good news to all the gentiles. And that vocation involves the shared vocation of Jew and gentile alike. Just as all Adam's children have been ruled by Sin and Death, and God has acted in Jesus Christ to rescue all from Sin and Death, God has also given Jew and gentile occasion for shared praise (15:7–13). That news does not exist in the stratosphere, however, remote from the particulars of human life. It very much participates in matters as specific as shared relief of human need. To claim that the gospel is cosmic in its scope is not to separate it from daily necessity or from human events on either a small or large scale, but to indicate the vast extent of the gospel's implications.

16:1–16 Preparing the Letter's Way

For the first time since the prescript at 1:1, Paul introduces an individual other than Jesus or a figure from Israel's Scriptures. Most of his other letters refer either to a fellow worker (e.g., 1 Cor 1:1; 1 Thess 1:1) or to someone among the recipients (Phil 4:2), but Rom 1–15 does neither of those things. In this final chapter, however, readers encounter a bounty of individuals, from Phoebe, Prisca, and Aquila, about whom he has a good deal to say (comparatively speaking), to the unnamed members of the households of Aristobulus and Narcissus. The names appear in elements of the letter's closing familiar from ancient epistolography: a commendation (vv. 1–2; see, e.g., 1 Cor 16:15–18; Phil 2:29–30; C.-H. Kim 1972) and greetings (vv. 3–16, 21–23; see 1 Cor 16:19–20; Phil 4:21–22).

Chrysostom doubtless spoke for many readers of the letter when he compared this section with biblical genealogies in that readers are all too happy to rush past it, although it is worth noting that his comment opened a lengthy sermon devoted to the greetings (*Hom. Rom.* 31; *NPNF*[1] 11:553). Unlike the readers of Chrysostom's circles, the most recent generation of Pauline scholarship has lavished a good deal of attention on these names. Motivated by interest in the socioeconomic status of the Pauline churches, the ethnic composition of early Roman Christianity in particular, the roles of women, and the circumstances that gave rise to the letter, scholars have searched energetically for information to be gleaned from these names and Paul's comments about them.

Such reconstructions benefit readers by helping us grasp this as an actual letter to real people rather than an abstract treatise, even if all such reconstructions should be held lightly and revised regularly.

16:1 Now I commend to you Phoebe our[a] sister, who is also[b] emissary[c] of the church in Cenchreae, 2 so that her you welcome[d] in the Lord, in a way that is worthy of holy people, and assist her in whatever she needs from you in her work,[e] for she has been a benefactor[f] of many and of myself as well.[g]

3 Greet Prisca and Aquila, my fellow workers in Christ Jesus. 4 They risked their own necks on my behalf. It is not only I who give thanks for them, but all the gentile churches do as well. 5a And greet also the church at their place.[h]

5b Greet Epaenetus my beloved, who is first fruit of Asia for Christ.

6 Greet Mary, who has labored for the gospel so hard among you.

7 Greet Andronicus and Junia,[i] my kinfolk and my fellow prisoners, who are outstanding among the apostles, who also came to be in Christ before I did.

8 Greet Ampliatus, my beloved in the Lord.

9 Greet Urbanus, our fellow worker in Christ, and Stachys my beloved.

10 Greet Apelles, who is approved in Christ.

Greet those who are from the household of Aristobulus.

11 Greet Herodion my kin.

Greet those from the household of Narcissus who are in the Lord.

12 Greet Tryphaena and Tryphosa, who labor in the Lord.

Greet Persis the beloved, who has worked hard in the Lord.

13 Greet Rufus, elect in the Lord, and greet his mother, who is my mother as well.

14 Greet Asyncritus, Phlegon, Hermes, Patrobas, Hermas, and the brothers and sisters with them.

15 Greet Philologos and Julia, Nereus and his sister, and Olympas, and all the holy ones with them.

16 Greet one another with a holy kiss.

All of Christ's churches greet you.

a. "Your" (*hymōn*), which appears in 𝔓⁴⁶ A F G P, could be construed as the more difficult reading, since Paul nowhere else uses the combination "your" with the singular "brother" or "sister." Yet he employs "our" (*hēmōn*) with brother/sister elsewhere only twice (2 Cor 8:22; 1 Thess 3:2), so the basis for comparison is limited. The difference is scant, since Phoebe is sister in faith both to Paul and to the Romans (Wolter 2:457).

b. A number of early manuscripts omit the "also" (*kai*), including ℵ* A C² D F, but it is found in others, including 𝔓⁴⁶ ℵ² B C*. NA²⁸ encloses the word in brackets, indicating uncertainty. Reading "also" may draw further attention to Phoebe's leadership (as implied by Jewett 941, who takes the deletion as motivated by the desire to render Phoebe less important).

c. Translating *diakonos* as "deacon" (as in NRSVue and NIV) is not inaccurate, but it only introduces the further question of whether a deacon in this period was a "helper" (e.g., Matt 20:26) or a "leader" (e.g., Phil 1:1). "Emissary" seems a better translation, in view of evidence that a *diakonos* usually was a designated representative or go-between.

d. This unusual word order ("her you welcome") reflects most ancient manuscripts, although several reverse the order (B C D F G), and one omits the pronoun altogether (𝔓⁴⁶ᵛⁱᵈ). By placing "her" first, Paul may further underscore her importance; see the similar order in 10:9; 14:3; and cf. Eph 5:26.

e. *Pragma* is used of a range of events, occupations, and concerns (see BDAG, s.v.). "Her," which does not appear in Greek, is added on the supposition that what Phoebe needs concerns some undertaking she is to carry out, without specifying what that might be.

f. Translations of *prostatis* range from "succourer" (KJV) to "helper" (ASV) to "sponsor" (CEB) to, as here, "benefactor" (NRSVue, NIV) and reveal a good deal about the assumptions of translators regarding women's roles. The masculine noun *prostatēs*, which does not appear in the NT, clearly refers to benefaction (BDAG s.v.). While the feminine *prostatis* is more often used of the benefaction of female gods, it is also found for female mortals. Dio Cassius, for example, reports that the Egyptians regarded their queen Arsinoë IV as their *prostatis* (*Hist. rom.* 42.39). A legal document names a woman as the *prostatis* of her son following his father's death (*P.Med.Bar.* 1, line 4, discussed by Judge 1984, 21). "Benefactor" seems apt in these instances and for Phoebe also.

g. "Myself as well" reflects the addition of the intensifying *autou* (B. Longenecker 2010, 161–65). Several alternate readings smooth out the awkward expression "of many and of myself as well" by moving the self-reference forward ("of me and others," D F G) or by deleting reference to Paul ("of many others," 𝔓⁴⁶). The order above is well attested, however, by B L P Ψ 33ᵛⁱᵈ, among others.

h. An *oikos*, usually translated "house," could be any sort of residence, and "their place" leaves open what sort of residence is involved.

i. A few manuscripts read *Ioulian* (Julia) instead of *Iounian* (Junia), presumably influenced by the name Julia in v. 15 (including 𝔓⁴⁶ 6 606 1718 2685).

[16:1–2] When Paul introduces Phoebe, he provides her with the most elaborate introduction found in any NT epistle. Phoebe could be known to some of the individuals greeted in vv. 3–16, especially to Prisca and Aquila (see Acts 18:18), but that is far from certain, and the length of the introduction suggests otherwise. She requires this introduction, since she is the one charged with delivering the letter, an action that is of utmost importance to Paul.

Her name appears in Greek mythology, which likely means she was a gentile, although an enslaved Jew could have been given a Greek name (Ilan 2010, 991). In addition, she is from Cenchreae, which to date has yielded no archaeological evidence of a Jewish community in this period (Jewett 943), although

Acts 18:18 appears to presuppose the presence of Jews there. Whatever her ethnicity, Paul designates her as "our sister," which is to say that she is a fellow believer (see, e.g., 16:14, 15, 23; 1 Cor 1:1; 2 Cor 1:1; 2:13). What Paul regards as most important about himself is his relationship to Christ (Rom 1:1), and the same is to be said of Phoebe, making it unsurprising that the first thing he says about Phoebe is that she is a sister.

More specifically, Phoebe is "emissary of the church in Cenchreae." The term *diakonos* is used in a variety of ways, but what connects many usages is the notion of going between parties, as when Epictetus writes that he chooses to be God's *diakonos* and follower (*Diatr.* 4.7.20), or when Josephus identifies himself as a *diakonos* of God to the Romans (*J.W.* 3.354).[15] Along those lines, then, Phoebe is the representative or emissary of the church in Cenchreae. Apart from her role with respect to this letter, it is difficult to tease out what exactly that work entails. It seems unlikely that there is a developed office of deacon in this early period, even in Phil 1:1, but that fact does not license interpretations determined to circumscribe Phoebe's role in some predetermined way to "women's work."[16]

That Paul identifies Phoebe initially with Cenchreae rather than with his own work warrants notice. What he conveys thereby is that she represents that assembly, not Paul himself (by contrast with Timothy in 1 Thess 3:2 or Epaphroditus in Phil 2:25). Cenchreae, the eastern port city of Corinth, stands only eight miles from Paul's location as he writes this letter, however, suggesting possible connections between that assembly and the one in Corinth, where Paul writes Romans (and note the report of Acts 18:18 that associates Paul with Cenchreae).

Before going further, Paul first asks that the Romans receive Phoebe "in the Lord" and "in a way that is worthy of holy people." The verb rendered "welcome" differs from the welcome of Rom 14:1 and 15:7, but that treatment may nonetheless echo here (and see Phil 2:29). To receive Phoebe "in the Lord" is to recognize her as sister, as one for whom Christ died (14:15). Paul compounds this statement with "in a way that is worthy," a phrase that extends

---

15. These and many other examples are found in J. Collins 1990, whose rich and patient treatment of the term unsettles the pervasive notion that a deacon is a table server and that the term gradually acquires a special meaning in Christian literature. An agent or *diakonos* could take on either a serving role or a leadership role, of course, but agency between two parties is the more all-encompassing usage of the word rather than service as such.

16. One particularly egregious example appears in the Living Bible's rendering of *diakonos* as "a dear Christian woman." It is difficult to imagine a circumstance in which the seven appointed in Acts 6 would have been labeled as "dear Christian men," and in fact the Living Bible employs "deacon" for *diakonos* in Phil 1:1. My point is not to demean the role of caregiving, whether ancient or modern, but to insist that it not be assumed at the outset that women's labor on behalf of the gospel is necessarily to be defined in certain restrictive ways. As Julia Foote commented in 1879, "When Paul said, 'Help those women who labor with me in the Gospel,' he certainly meant that they did more than to pour out tea" (Andrews 1986, 209).

in both directions simultaneously: both the Romans and Phoebe belong among the holy, so the Romans should act as holy people and receive her as a holy person (and see 1:7).

Further, Paul asks that the Romans assist her in her work, but he does not specify the nature of her work. Because he anticipates a mission to Spain after his stay in Rome and hopes to be assisted by the Romans in that project (15:24, 28), Phoebe's work might be attached to that project (so Jewett 89–91). That notion is highly speculative, however, drawing on the slenderest of threads within the letter. Nonetheless, it is right to conceive of her work as connected primarily to the gospel rather than to her own business interests, except as those business interests could benefit the Pauline mission (B. Longenecker 2010, 240–44). More likely, her work in Rome directly involves the letter itself, carrying the letter, introducing and reading it, and conversing about it. For that she would require hospitality, as would most ancient travelers, but also assistance in making her way to multiple small gatherings of believers across the city of Rome.

Paul anchors this request in a final observation that Phoebe has become a *prostatis* or benefactor. He does not specify the nature of her benefaction, but it almost certainly included material support. In addition to evidence associating women with the language of benefaction (see translation note f on v. 2), the NT elsewhere assumes that women had means and used them in support of Jesus (Luke 8:1–3) and later of Christian preachers and teachers (Acts 12:12; 16:14–15, 40). Most likely Paul's comments about her benefaction to himself and others include at least her willingness to undertake travel to Rome (probably at her own expense), as well as her work there on behalf of the letter's reception.

Phoebe not only delivered the letter, but she is likely the person who initially read it aloud to small groups gathered in Rome (as has been assumed throughout this commentary). Although literacy was limited in the ancient world, some women were indeed able to read (Harris 1989, 48, 67, 96, 103, 108, 140, 173, 252–63, 271, 328; Haines-Eitzen 2011, 23–38). As a woman of at least moderate means, Phoebe may well have been able to read Paul's letter. This could be the case even if she was a freedwoman who had previously served as an enslaved reader for females in a household. At any rate, she is the sole link between Paul's writing of this letter and its reception at Rome, which makes her its most likely representative. In addition, even if she did not voice the letter in various gatherings, she would have been the one to respond to comments about it. [17]

_____

17. Head 2009, in a study of personal letters among the Oxyrhynchus papyri, found no evidence that letter carriers named within letters also functioned as letter readers, but he concedes that this silence may not be conclusive. In addition, he agrees that "the trusted letter carrier often has an

Further, Phoebe may well have had a voice in the content of the letter (see the introduction and below on vv. 21–23). Paul did not dash off this lengthy and complex letter but must have composed it over a period of time. His circle in Corinth would likely have listened at least to sections of the letter, perhaps even to full drafts, and entered into discussion of those drafts (see Starr 1987, 213–15; Gamble 1995, 83–84, 279–80, drawing on evidence from Horace, *Ars poetica* 385–90; and Pliny, *Ep.* 5.3.8–10; 5.12.1–4). As the one charged with the delivery and reading of the letter (and located in nearby Cenchreae), Phoebe would have been part of such conversations. Paul attached too much importance to the letter to hand it off without comment or direction. Her importance for Paul, for Rome, and for the origin of interpretation of this letter, begins to come into view.[18]

Phoebe's identity as a believer and her anticipated role at Rome are both reasonably clear. What this profile might suggest about her socioeconomic standing is less easy to discern. She has the means to travel and has resources that allow her to serve as benefactor to others. In addition, the fact that she appears without reference to a husband or any other male indicates a level of independence (as with Lydia in Acts 16:11–15). But benefaction in and of itself does not necessarily vault her into the realm of the elite. Economically, she likely lives comfortably above subsistence—hence, she is not as vulnerable as many in these communities—without being a member of the elite (B. Longenecker 2010, 240–44).[19]

[3–5a] Having introduced and commended Phoebe, Paul greets a large number of Roman believers. Although such greetings are a standard feature of ancient epistolography (e.g., 1 Cor 16:19–20; 1 Thess 5:26; and see Weima 2016, 182–93), several aspects of these greetings are unusual. To begin with, Paul's greetings are normally in third-person, as later in "All of Christ's churches greet you" (v. 16b; and see 16:21, 23; 1 Cor 16:19–20a; 2 Cor 13:12b; Phil 4:21b–22; Phlm 23–24). Greetings in second-person plural do appear in Paul's letters, but elsewhere such greetings are to gatherings as a whole, as below in "Greet one another with a holy kiss" (16:16a; see also 1 Cor 16:20b;

---

important role" of bringing "fuller knowledge into the communication process, which is only partly embodied in the letter." They became "personal mediators of Paul's authoritative instruction to his churches" and "the earliest interpreters of the individual letters" (297–98).

18. What is less accessible is the way a female representative of Paul might have been received, on which see Cadwallader 2015: "At least in regard to the letter most privileged in the canon, when we 'see and hear' Paul, we are seeing a Phoebeian-shaped Paul and hearing a letter *feminine/ foeminea voce*" (79).

19. Phoebe's identification with Cenchreae itself may tell against her elite status, since members of that small minority would more likely be found in a city than in a working port. Rife observes that Cenchreae was never an "autonomous municipality"; it lacked its own coinage, magistracies, and amphitheater, although it "sustained regional networks of exchange and communication" (2010, 397).

2 Cor 13:12a; Phil 4:21a; 1 Thess 5:26). Greetings to individuals but couched in second-person plural do not appear elsewhere in Paul's letters. This distinction may reflect the fact that Roman Christians do not constitute a single group but multiple gatherings (note the reference to the church in v. 5 and various greetings). Paul likely hopes that as Phoebe takes the letter from one place to another, representatives of the various groups will greet each other.

More perplexing, at least on first consideration, is the fact that Paul, who has never visited Rome, is able to identify so many individuals by name. This discrepancy has been enlisted to contend that Rom 16 does not belong to the letter, but that proposal is almost certainly wrong (on which see the introduction). Paul does know some of the people greeted, because he has met and worked with them elsewhere (minimally including Prisca, Aquila, Epaenetus, Andronicus, and Junia). Others he may know only by reputation, but he invokes their names by way of building connections with the various Roman gatherings, which of course enhances his own standing with the groups.

He begins with Prisca and Aquila, whom he does know, as evidenced not only by his remarks here but also in 1 Cor 16:19 (and see Acts 18:2, 18, 24–26, where Prisca is identified by the diminutive Priscilla; 2 Tim 4:19). Luke identifies Aquila as a Jew (Acts 18:2), and Prisca likely was a Jew as well. Both bear names associated with slavery (Lampe 2003, 181), implying that they are freedpersons. Paul places her name first (as does Acts 18:18, 26; 2 Tim 4:19), although in 1 Cor 16:19 Aquila is named first (as in Acts 18:2). Given that male names conventionally appear first in such pairings, as Andronicus does in v. 7, this reversal likely means that Prisca was the more prominent figure in Christian circles. Such deference to Prisca could convey her socioeconomic status relative to that of Aquila, if she were freeborn or wealthy, but what Paul draws attention to elsewhere in this list of greetings is relationship to the gospel, making it likely that the same consideration holds here.[20]

Paul first identifies them as "my fellow workers in Christ Jesus," an expression he elsewhere uses for the work of spreading the news of Jesus Christ (as in 1 Cor 3:9; 16:16; 2 Cor 1:24; 8:23; Phil 2:25; 4:3; 1 Thess 3:2; Phlm 1, 24). Notably, Paul makes no distinction between Prisca and Aquila in terms of their labor (as is true in Acts as well, where both are said to have instructed Apollos; 18:24–26). Luke's account also corroborates Paul's claim that they are fellow workers. According to Acts, Paul meets them in Corinth, where they have fled from Jerusalem under an edict of Claudius. Paul lives with them in Corinth, and they share in a trade. Later the two travel with him to Ephesus and are with him when he writes the letter known as 1 Corinthians (Acts 18:18, 24–26; 1 Cor 16:8, 19).

---

20. Noticing Prisca's priority goes at least as far back as Chrysostom (*Hom. Rom. 16:3*, 1.3 [PG 51.191], discussed in Mitchell 2010, 130–31).

Verse 4 continues their identification in relationship to their shared history with Paul. They "risked their own necks on my behalf." Nothing else in Acts or the letters provides specificity for this claim. Luke depicts threats to Paul and other believers both in Corinth (18:12–17) and in Ephesus (19:23–41), and scattered remarks in the letters may corroborate those threats (e.g., 1 Cor 15:32; 16:9; 2 Cor 11:26; Phil 1:12–14). Possibly Prisca and Aquila came to his aid in a way that placed them in danger; at the very least the comment serves to convey Paul's sense of their commitment to share not only in the work of the gospel but in the risks it entails; or better, the gospel and risk are intertwined.

Paul's thanksgiving goes well beyond the personal, however: "all the gentile churches" give thanks for Prisca and Aquila. This is a bold and surely hyperbolic observation, even if the couple lived in places prominent in the Pauline mission. More important than the plausibility of "all the gentile churches" is Paul's drawing attention to gentile believers and their gratitude for the leadership of these two Jews, Prisca and Aquila. In a letter deeply concerned about the relationship between Jewish and gentile believers, such gratitude is notable.

Finally, Paul greets not only the couple but the assembly of believers at their place. Uncertainty about the meeting places of earliest Christian gatherings enters at this point, with some imagining that the couple inhabits a large single residence.[21] Assuming the accuracy of Acts 18:3, however, they are skilled workers. They support themselves by their labor and, while they may have a more reliable income than others, it is unlikely that they are wealthy.[22] Probably they rented a *taberna* or workshop, where they both lived and worked. That venue would have provided space for a modest gathering.

[5b–16] The gathering hosted by Prisca and Aquila is not the only such of which Paul is aware. He adds a list of other greetings, sometimes to individuals, sometimes to groups of named individuals, sometimes to groups within households. Each begins with *aspasasthe* ("greet"). While it is impossible to know whether each separate greeting indicates a separate gathering, almost certainly Paul understands that there are multiple gatherings (as has been presupposed throughout the commentary). The size of Rome would in itself dictate the need for such.

Including Prisca and Aquila, Paul greets 26 people, of whom 17 are male and 9 are female. To some—a disproportionately large number of whom are women—he attaches more specific descriptions, while others he simply names.

21. Debate persists about the meeting places of early Christians; for a review of the proposals, together with a suggestion that some assemblies took place outside of residences, see E. Adams 2013.
22. As Lampe observes, Paul himself writes that he was in need while in Corinth (2 Cor 11:9), something that presumably would not have happened if Prisca and Aquila had been wealthy patrons (2003, 191). Lampe's discussion provides further evidence that craftsmen were associated largely with lower-class freedpersons, particularly immigrants (187–95).

Still others are gathered up anonymously in "those who are from the household of Aristobulus" or "of Narcissus."

Some of the individuals are Jewish, as signaled by the phrase "my kinfolk" for Andronicus, Junia, and Herodion. Although Paul does use familial language for fellow believers (as of Phoebe in 16:1), *syngenēs* refers to members of the same family or extended people groups (as in, e.g., 9:3; Mark 6:4; Acts 10:24). Paul does not explicitly identify Prisca and Aquila as Jews, but likely he presupposes that knowledge. The remainder of those named may well be gentile (although, as noted above, Jews in the Diaspora did bear Greek and Roman names).

Many of the names originate in the Greek east rather than in Rome and therefore likely belong to immigrants. In the case of some of them, "immigrant" is a misleading euphemism, to be sure. Epaenetus may have traveled freely to Rome (as with Prisca and Aquila), but others arrived in Rome enslaved or as the offspring of enslaved people. Hermes, for example, is a name attached to enslaved men (Lampe 2003, 173). In addition, those greeted from the household of Aristobulus and Narcissus are probably either enslaved or freedpersons, given their collective identification in terms of the head of household (Lampe 2003, 164–65). And it is quite unlikely that either Aristobulus or Narcissus was a believer, since Paul does not greet them as such.

The additional comments about others among the greeted also warrant attention. Paul identifies Epaenetus, Ampliatus, Stachys, and Persis as "beloved," a term that may convey his personal knowledge of them. Earlier in the letter he addressed the Romans collectively as "God's beloved" (1:7; and see 11:28; 12:19), but when he uses "my beloved," he does so addressing those known to him, such as Timothy (1 Cor 4:17), the Corinthians themselves (1 Cor 10:14; 15:58), and the Philippians (2:12; 4:1; and see 1 Thess 2:8). Paul calls Epaenetus the "first fruit of Asia," a phrase he uses in 1 Cor 16:15 of Stephanas's household, which could place Epaenetus in that household. Along with Prisca and Aquila, Mary and Urbanus are commended as fellow workers; Tryphaena, Tryphosa, and Persis are also labeled as workers.

Of particular interest is the pair Andronicus and Junia, on whom Paul lavishes an extensive description (v. 7). Theoretically the second name could be either Junia or Junias, because both names would take the same form in the accusative case in unaccented manuscripts. The ancient evidence is straightforward, however: there is ample evidence for Junia as a woman's name, common in the Roman world of Paul's time, and there is virtually no evidence for Junias as a man's name.[23] Early Christian writers who commented on this text

---

23. The primary evidence is conveniently available in Epp 2005, who builds on the earlier contribution of Brooten 1977. Neither is "Junia" a contracted form of the male name "Junianus" (Brooten 1977, 142–43; Epp 2005, 40–44).

consistently understood the name to be that of a woman (Epp 2005, 32–39; Belleville 2005, 232), a point with which most scholars now concur.[24]

Paul identifies Andronicus and Junia as Jews ("my kinfolk") and as his fellow captives. Where and how that captivity was shared he does not specify, but the shared captivity conveys their commitment to the gospel, as does the willingness to suffer that Paul ascribes to Prisca and Aquila. Indeed, they precede Paul in their length of commitment, having become "in Christ" before Paul.

One further comment has elicited great dispute, namely, that Andronicus and Junia are "outstanding among the apostles." As early as Chrysostom this phrase was understood to mean that they themselves *are* apostles (*Ep. Rom.* 31.2), but some scholars have recently objected that the phrase should be understood as "well known to the apostles." In the first case, the preposition *en* places Junia and Andronicus among the apostles as one of them (as in Epp 2005; Belleville 2005); in the second case, the *en* places the pair outside the apostles as someone recognized by them (as in Burer and Wallace 2001; Burer 2015). That way of putting the options is misleading, however, since there are numerous occasions when the someone might be "well known" to a group while also being a part of the group, such as "Emily Dickinson is well known to American poets." Andronicus and Junia might well be apostles who were *also* well known to the (remaining) apostles.[25]

Another factor, perhaps more compelling than either grammatical argument, is the observation that Paul does not elsewhere evaluate or otherwise commend people on the basis of their reputation with others.[26] Instead, when he identifies Andronicus and Junia as apostles who were believers before him, Paul both elevates them and ties himself to their circle at Rome (Lin 2020, 202). In short, Paul includes both Junia and Andronicus among the apostles. Unlike Luke, for whom apostleship belongs only to those males who were with Jesus during his lifetime (see Acts 1:21–22; although see Acts 14:4, 14), Paul attributes apostleship to others (as in 1 Cor 15:7), including himself as well as Andronicus and Junia.

---

24. Until the nineteenth century, most editions of the Greek NT and most English translations acknowledged the presence of "Junia" rather than "Junias." Yet late in the nineteenth century, English translations shifted to the male name "Junias," with the notable exception of Helen Barrett Montgomery's (1924). Greek editions give the impression that there is a text-critical problem, yet there is none (see the charts in Epp 2005, 62–63, 66). The commentary of Lietzmann, cited in numerous later commentaries and reference works, invoked the "context" as determinative (125). Brooten puts the matter succinctly: "Because a woman could not have been an apostle, the woman who is here called apostle could not have been a woman" (1997, 142).

25. Yii-Jan Lin makes this point and provides examples from both Greek texts and contemporary experience. As she observes, that Eldon Epp is "well known among textual critics" means both that he is a text critic and that he is well known by other text critics, but that conclusion is available only to people who know both Epp and textual criticism (Lin 2020, 197).

26. "Such reliance on human approval contradicts every indicator of Paul's stance on human judgment" (Lin 2020, 202).

Attention to Junia has focused on apostleship to the exclusion of Paul's additional comment that she and Andronicus were his fellow prisoners. This imprisonment is more than a data point in sketching the chronology of Paul's life and work. Given the character of imprisonment in the Roman world, particularly the treatment of women, the experience evoked with this word was likely horrendous (Gupta 2020, 392–95). In addition, by invoking rather than hiding the shared imprisonment of the three apostles, Paul connects apostleship directly with suffering, tacitly separating apostleship from privilege and attaching it to Christ who did not please himself (15:3).[27]

Students of the letter often attempt to identify some of the people Paul greets with individuals known elsewhere. Aristobulus, for example, might be connected with the house of the late grandson of Herod the Great (Josephus, *J.W.* 2.221; *Ant.* 20.12–13; Fitzmyer 740). Rufus is sometimes connected to the Rufus of Mark 15:21, the son of Simon of Cyrene, who carries the cross of Jesus (Byrne 454). Junia has been identified with the Joanna of Luke 8:3; 24:10, although the name is widely known (Bauckham 2002, 165–86).

Such identifications are interesting if not compelling. What the names do convey—taken together with the slender bits of information we can glean about them—is the range of Roman Christianity in this early stage of the church's life. When Paul names names, he may be doing so out of a determination not to side with one group or another.

While the most recent scholarly generation has drawn attention to the fact that women feature prominently in this list (or better, it has recovered that knowledge: see Marshall 2017; Bowens 2020, 87, 170), more is at stake here than that single question. Paul acknowledges and honors the labor of others. However much he may insist on his apostolic credentials—especially in contexts where those credentials have been challenged—he also understands that apostolic work is shared work.

Another question that lies beyond our sources is how representative this list is of Roman Christianity. Does the large number of slave and immigrant names identify Roman Christianity largely with slaves and other immigrants? Was the leadership of women prominent across Roman Christianity? How much of a template of early Roman Christianity appears in this list of names?[28] Paul may

---

27. Arminta Fox observes that here Paul's "rhetoric about apostleship is bound up with his rhetoric about imprisonment, and thus, with complex networks of others as coworkers, visitors and patrons" (2017, 38). Also, "Paul redraws the boundaries of apostleship when he pairs being imprisoned with the idea of being esteemed among the apostles" (44).

28. Some even see the greetings, addressed to the recipients in the second-person, as greetings Paul wants the addressees in Rome to extend to others beyond the believing assemblies in Rome; on that suggestion, the greetings reveal nothing about the actual audience of the letter (see the summary in Das 2007, 101–3). But that scenario raises the further question of how Paul knew, or knew

have composed this list with an eye to fairness, but that in itself sheds little light on the composition of Roman Christianity.

The greetings conclude with one final request that the letter's recipients "greet one another with a holy kiss" and an assurance that "all of Christ's assemblies greet you." This "holy kiss" is a regular feature of Paul's letters (1 Cor 16:20; 2 Cor 13:12; 1 Thess 5:26; cf. 1 Pet 5:14). As a sign of welcome or reconciliation, it is well attested (e.g., Gen 29:11; 45:14–15; Luke 7:45; Mark 14:45). These greetings serve to bring together scattered groups, not simply in Rome but beyond as well. It is often observed that Paul speaks of individual, local assemblies rather than of a general assembly of believers, but these greetings, along with the connections embodied in the collection itself, contain the seed of an enlarged understanding in which all the local churches constitute a single church.

16:17–23[25–27] Final Assurance and Greetings

To the commendation of Phoebe and the greetings Paul asks Roman believers to extend to one another, he adds a final exhortation and benediction (vv. 17–20; e.g., 1 Cor 16:13–16; Phlm 20) as the last substantive lines of the letter. These are followed by another set of greetings, this time from his companions at Corinth (vv. 21–23). The additional benediction found in vv. 25–27 probably comes from a later hand (see note g below).

17 Now I urge you, brothers and sisters, to watch out for those who, against the instruction you learned, create dissensions and traps,[a] and stay away from them. 18 For such people are not serving our Lord Christ but their own belly, and with beautiful speech and flattery they deceive the hearts of the naive. 19 For your obedience is known to all. For that reason I rejoice about you, yet I want you to be wise concerning good but blameless concerning evil. 20 And the God of peace will shortly crush Satan under your feet. The grace of our Lord Jesus[b] be with you.[c]

21 Timothy my fellow worker greets you, and Lucius and Jason and Sosipater my kinfolk greet you. 22 I, Tertius, greet you—the one writing the letter in the Lord. 23 Gaius, who is my guest[d] and that of the whole assembly, greets you. Erastus the manager of the city and Quartus our brother greet you.[e]

[25 To the one who is able to strengthen you according to my gospel and the proclamation of Jesus Christ—according to the revelation of the mystery that was kept secret for many ages 26 but that is now disclosed

of, so many other people in Rome outside Christian circles, not to mention the explicit reference to the gathering in the residence of Prisca and Aquila.

through prophetic writings, made known[f] according to the command of the eternal God for the obedience of faith for all the gentiles— 27 to the only wise God, through Jesus Christ, to whom be the glory forever. Amen!][g]

a. Most translations take the phrase "against the instruction you learned" as an adjectival phrase modifying *skandala* ("traps"), but Hassold has proposed an adverbial reading of it (2000). That option makes sense of the fact that Paul does not give *skandala* content elsewhere (9:33; 11:9; 14:13; 1 Cor 1:23; although see Gal 5:11). Like the counterfactual heavenly angel of Gal 1:8–9 who preaches contrary to what "we preached" and what "you received," these are agents who act contrary to what has been taught.

b. Numerous manuscripts read "our Lord Jesus Christ," including A C L P Ψ, but 𝔓[46] ℵ B 1881 omit "Christ," making that the more difficult and likely earlier reading.

c. Verse 20b is omitted in a few manuscripts (D*[vid] F G), where it appears instead as v. 24 (with some expansions), probably because placing the grace prior to final greetings seems disruptive.

d. By tradition, the noun *xenos* is routinely translated "host," but that translation flies in the face of the consistent use of the term for a stranger or guest, as in Matt 27:7; Eph 2:19 (Kloppenborg 2017).

e. A further benediction appears at this point in some manuscripts, as v. 24, although it takes slightly different forms. In other manuscripts it appears following v. 27. In earlier manuscripts, including 𝔓[46] 𝔓[61] ℵ A B C 81 et al., there is no additional benediction.

f. The final participle, *gnōristhentos* ("made known"), modifies "mystery," as does "kept secret" and "disclosed," but the word order is ambiguous. It could be that the mystery is made known to all the gentiles, but that seems highly unlikely, so here it is construed with "according to the command."

g. These verses appear in brackets, as they do in NA[28], to indicate serious doubt that they belong with the letter. Although they do appear at this point in 𝔓[61] ℵ B C D et al., in some manuscripts they are omitted altogether (F G 629), while in others they appear at the end of ch. 14 (L Ψ 0209[vid] 1175 et al.), or at the end of ch. 15 (𝔓[46]), or here and at the end of ch. 14 (A P 33 104), or at the end of ch. 14 and again at the end of ch. 15 (1506). Such instability as to the placement of these verses raises serious doubts about whether they belong with the letter at all, and those doubts increase given the content.

[17–20] Having concluded the long list of greetings, Paul opens his brief final appeal with the phrase "Now I urge you" (*parakalō de hymas*), recalling 12:1 and 15:30. Because these lines separate the greetings of vv. 3–16 from those of vv. 21–23, and because some of the language is unusual for Paul, numerous interpreters have proposed that vv. 17–20 are an early interpolation, perhaps crafted by someone aligned with the views espoused by the Pastoral Epistles, someone who wants to restrict the inclusive character of 16:16 to those who are "legitimate" believers (see especially the discussion in Jewett 986–88). Yet these lines appear in all extant manuscripts of Romans, and always in this place (by contrast with vv. 25–27), which makes it likely that they do belong to the letter. Further, contrary to the notion that some later writer inserted these lines by way of countering the inclusivist greetings of 16:16, Paul may be thinking of problems that would threaten any and all of the assemblies. More generally, the content of these lines, although distinctive in some respects, is not irreconcilable with the remainder of the letter.

The admonition cautions against people who generate disputes and traps for others. Paul uses the relatively rare word *dichostasia* ("dissension") only here and in Gal 5:20, where it appears in a catalog of works produced by "the flesh," that is, by-products of life lived in opposition to God. Dissension could also be understood as the antithesis of oneness in thought (12:16), or a warning connected to the divisions in ch. 14. Similarly, Paul frequently lifts up instruction (6:17; 12:7; 15:4; 1 Cor 2:13; 4:17; 12:27–29; 14:26) and learning (1 Cor 4:6; 14:31, 35; Phil 4:9, 11), even if he does not specifically refer to "the instruction you learned," although Rom 6:17 comes close.

Verse 18 engages in an ad hominem argument, in itself an indication of the seriousness of Paul's concern, even if it is less than helpful for identifying the people Paul has in mind. He claims that those who provoke dissension and entrapment are acting as if they were enslaved not to "our Lord Christ" but to "their own belly." Enslavement to Christ has figured earlier in the letter as a characterization of existence in Christ's body (12:11; 14:18; and see 1:1), which makes the charge that others live as slaves to some other master a harsh one. Notably, 6:6 characterizes the audience—and by implication all humans—as having lived as slaves of Sin.

It is easier to grasp the severity of the enslavement language than to understand what Paul means by being enslaved to "their own belly." "Belly" might be construed as a reference to the dispute of ch. 14, although in that context the problem is not gluttony as such but the prospect of a destructive use of freedom (see especially 14:15, 20). Paul uses "belly" similarly in Phil 3:19 of those "whose god is the belly," but the referent of the "they" in that context is similarly opaque. Given the way other Jewish writers associate "belly" with acts that prioritize self-aggrandizement over against faithfulness, Paul may well have the same general critique in mind (e.g., 3 Macc 7:11; Philo, *Virtues* 182; T. Mos. 7.4), although criticism associated with appearance, gluttony, and dissipation is widespread in Greco-Roman literature (Sandnes 2002, 24–93).

The second half of v. 18 further characterizes "such people" as deceiving with smooth words and flattery.[29] It is not just their own relationship with Christ (i.e., they are not acting as slaves of Christ) that is at stake but their treatment

---

29. Notably, *chrēstologia* ("beautiful speech") resembles the initial sound of *christos* in the preceding statement (perhaps explaining the unusual "our Lord Christ," which appears only in the disputed letter Col 3:24), and *chrēstologia* shares its ending with *eulogia*.

of others. As in 14:18, serving Christ involves also serving others. The notion of deception is a powerful one, recalling as it does 7:11 with its claim that "Sin deceived me and through it [the law] killed me" (and see 2 Cor 11:3; cf. also 1 Tim 2:14).

Discerning the identity of a specific group that prompts this warning is simultaneously highly desirable and highly problematic, precisely because the language Paul employs lends itself to several possibilities. His comments resemble in a general way the concerns in 1 Cor 1–4 about factions, but that does not mean he is again addressing the disputes of Rom 14. And the notion of people who wish to deceive could be connected with his characterization of the Teachers in Galatians, but that need not mean Paul anticipates the arrival of Jewish teachers in Rome or that he detects their influence (as suggested by Campbell 2009a, 495–511).

The transition from this warning to v. 19 is also puzzling. If the Romans are obedient and Paul rejoices in them, it is unclear why a warning is needed, particularly one that stands at the end of the letter. The "for" (*gar*) connecting the two verses suggests that they somehow belong together. Once again, as in the thanksgiving in 1:8, Paul makes a general statement about the standing of the Romans but does not fill it out, leaving open the possibility that he is in fact not at all convinced of their solidity.[30] The second half of v. 19 underscores that suspicion, with its urging that they be wise and innocent. Taking both halves of v. 19 together, it appears Paul may be engaging in a bit of flattery himself in order to secure their attention to his warning (Campbell 2009a, 499).

Verse 20, in substance the last line of the letter, combines promise ("The God of peace will shortly crush Satan under your feet") with blessing ("The grace of our Lord Jesus be with you"). Opening with "the God of peace" recalls 5:10, where Paul celebrates the peace God has brought about, a peace that brings to an end "our" enmity with God. In addition, God is also called "the God of peace" in 15:33 (and see also Phil 4:9; 2 Cor 13:11; 1 Thess 5:23), culminating Paul's anguished plea for prayer regarding his journey to Jerusalem. The final act of divine peacemaking is this destruction of Satan.

The sudden introduction of Satan startles, because Satan has not previously been named in this letter (although take note of 1 Cor 5:5; 7:5; 2 Cor 2:11; 11:14; 12:7; 1 Thess 2:18). On the assumption that the introductory *de* connects this verse with what precedes, implicitly Paul is associating those bad actors of vv. 17–18 with Satan. He does not identify the two (contra Jewett 994), however, and it is likely that they are evidence of Satan's work rather than that they are identified with Satan. Notably, it is Satan and not the human agents

---

30. Pelagius (152) understands the obedience of the Romans to be obedience to these false teachers, while both Origen (*Comm. Rom.* 10.35; Burns 387–88) and Chrysostom (*Hom. Rom.* 32; *NPNF*[1] 11:560) understand Paul's remark as a subtle indication that the Romans were not entirely obedient.

who are crushed, leaving open the possibility that Satan's defeat releases those being used by him.

More can be said, since the letter is replete with imagery of conflict between God and anti-God agents, especially in chs. 5–8 (Gaventa 2013b; Ryan 2020, 160–97). If Paul has not referred to Satan by name earlier, he has referred to the powers of Sin and Death, as well as a host of enemies in 8:38–39. Even the greetings recall evidence of conflict, with their references to Prisca and Aquila risking their lives for Paul and the imprisonment of Andronicus and Junia (cf. 16:4, 7 with 8:35). It is not far-fetched to identify those instances of conflict collectively as Satan's work.[31]

Paul depicts Satan's demise graphically: "The God of peace will shortly crush Satan under your feet." Some exegetes have traced this line to the influence of Gen 3:15, where God decrees hostility between the serpent and the human, saying that the human "will strike your head, and you will strike his heel." That passage becomes important in later Christian reflection, where it is read as a proto-gospel anticipating the triumph of Christ over the serpent or Satan. No verbal links connect the two passages, however, and Gen 3:15 does not feature prominently elsewhere in the NT.[32] Second Corinthians 11:3 does recall an earlier moment in the Genesis account, but there it is the serpent that deceives, not Satan. And nothing is said there of either striking or crushing the serpent.

Closer to Paul's language is Ps 110:1b (109 LXX), taken from a psalm that is highly influential in early Christian reflection (e.g., Matt 22:44; Acts 2:34–35; Eph 1:20; Heb 1:3, 13; Hay 1973):

> The LORD said to my lord, Sit at my right hand,
> until I put your enemies under your feet.

Already in 8:34 Paul has drawn on the first half of the verse ("at God's right hand"), and the second half emerges here in 16:20. Importantly, in 1 Cor 15:25 Paul employs this line for the final triumph of God: "[Christ] must rule until he puts all enemies under his feet."[33]

---

31. At several points in his discussion of Rom 5–8, Ambrosiaster writes that when Paul mentions Sin he means Satan (67–69, 167; and see Chrysostom, *Hom. Rom.* 15.37; *NPNF*[1] 11.456.) He does not, to be sure, reverse that connection when commenting on this passage.

32. Derek Brown rightly observes that Luke 10:19; Heb 2:14; and Rev 12:7 are often adduced as NT allusions to Gen 3:15, but also that the relationship is tenuous in all three cases (2010, 6).

33. There is an intriguing relationship between this line and two earlier scriptural citations in Romans. In 3:15 Paul writes that "swift are their feet for shedding blood," language that reflects the influence of Isa 59:7 LXX. And in 10:15 he draws on Isa 52:7 to elicit the joy that greets the arriving feet of messengers with good news. In both cases, "feet" is clearly metonymous for the persons as a whole; it is not simply feet that do harm or bring good news. In a way that is likely unconscious, Rom 16:20 overturns 3:15, where humans are agents of murder.

There are differences, to be sure. The verb in both Ps 110:1b and 1 Cor 15:25 is "put" or "place" (*tithēmi*), where Rom 16:20 reads "crush" (*syntribō*). But Ps 110 goes on to anticipate God's shattering of kings on the day of wrath (vv. 5–6). Further, the verb "crush" (*syntribō*) does appear in several important texts associated with the divine warrior tradition, such as Exod 15:3 ("The Lord crushes wars"), Isa 42:13 ("The Lord will crush war"), and 1 Macc 3:22 ("[God] will crush them before us; do not be afraid of them") (Ryan 2020, 238).

Genre makes a difference in this instance: this is a promise about God's future deliverance; it is not a call to human action. To say that God will do it is not to invite human beings to seek out Satan in order to destroy him or his agents; instead, it is to urge them to be on the watch for God's deliverance from those agents that threaten to separate God from God's people. In that sense it stands as something of a culmination to the end of ch. 8. God's deliverance will be complete when Satan is crushed.

With these words, Paul can usher in the final grace of the letter: "The grace of our Lord Jesus be with you." Reference to "our Lord Jesus" without the term "Christ" is unusual in Paul's letters, but it does occur (1 Cor 5:4; 1 Thess 2:19; and cf. 2 Thess 1:12). Here it serves as a bookend to the phrase "our Lord Christ" in v. 18.

[21–23] Following these final words of assurance and blessing, Paul relays a brief set of greetings from his companions in Corinth to Roman believers (as also in 1 Cor 16:19; Phlm 23–24; cf. Col 4:10–14).

First among them is Timothy, to whom Paul refers in every letter except Galatians. Here Paul calls him "my fellow worker," language he has used above of Prisca and Aquila as well as Urbanus (and see 1 Thess 3:2, where he is identified as God's fellow worker). That identifier sits well alongside the work Timothy does elsewhere. Paul names him as cosender of 2 Corinthians, Philippians, 1 Thessalonians, and Philemon. More tellingly, Timothy serves as Paul's delegate, instructing the Corinthians (1 Cor 4:17) and probing the standing of the Thessalonians (1 Thess 3:2, 6). Luke identifies Timothy as the son of a Jewish mother and Greek father and reports that Paul had him circumcised to minimize conflict with Jews (Acts 16:1–3), but the letters confirm none of those details.

Also sending greetings are Lucius and Jason and Sosipater, whom Paul identifies as fellow Jews, his "kin," like Andronicus, Junia, and Herodion in the previous greetings. Lucius and Jason are mentioned nowhere else in Paul's letters. Sosipater appears only here, although this could be the individual Luke names Sopater and includes among Paul's companions in Acts 20:4.

Verse 22 interrupts with a greeting from Tertius in first-person, explaining that he is "the one writing the letter in the Lord." Other letters imply the work of a secretary when Paul interrupts the closing with "I, Paul, write the greeting" (1 Cor 16:21; Gal 6:11; Phlm 19; cf. Col 4:18; 2 Thess 3:17). Only in Romans does the writer's name appear, attached to an awkwardly phrased claim to be "writing in the Lord." This distinctiveness has prompted the proposal that Tertius himself drafted some portions of the letter, even that he is a professional secretary who has traveled from Rome (Richards 2004, 151–52). Yet that scenario builds on parallels in the letters of Cicero, whose situation is remote from Paul; further, if Paul had direct access to someone from Rome and known to Roman believers, he would have invoked his name well before this last line of the letter. Tertius is probably a local, someone from Corinth or perhaps Cenchreae, in which case he may be an enslaved member of Phoebe's household (Cadwallader 2018, 378).[34]

Verse 23 reverts to third-person reports of greetings, from Gaius, Erastus, and Quartus. Gaius is "my guest and that of the whole assembly" (see translation note d). Paul says nothing more of Gaius, raising the possibility that the Roman audience knows him (or that some do), and that he is actually one of them, so that Paul hopes his own hospitality for Gaius will elicit Roman hospitality for Phoebe (16:1–2; as argued by Kloppenborg 2017). As with Tertius, however, if Gaius came from Rome, Paul would have referred to him and any information he brought with him earlier in the letter. The only other Gaius in the letters is in 1 Cor 1:14 (and see Acts 19:29; 20:4), a Gaius among those Paul baptized, but they need not be the same person, given the frequency of the name.

Layers of questions attach to the figure of Erastus, "the manager of the city." The name does not appear elsewhere in Paul's letters, although both Acts 19:22 and 2 Tim 4:20 place an Erastus in Paul's circle, and the name was relatively rare (Brookins 2013). An early twentieth-century recovery of an inscription in the agora of Corinth in honor of the *aedilis* "ERASTVS" prompted the identification of this figure with Paul's Erastus and the further conclusion that Erastus was a highly placed individual.[35] Serious problems attach to that conclusion because both the date and the content of the inscription are uncertain (Meggitt 1996). In addition, it is by no means clear that a city's "manager" (*oikonomos*) was a highly placed individual. Erastus may instead have been a freedman or even a slave who held a position in the local bureaucracy (B. Longenecker 2010, 236–39; Kloppenborg 2019, 189–92). Paul's identification of him through his position is odd, given that others are introduced in relationship to Paul's work, but Paul could see this connection to a local manager as somehow beneficial. Possibly Paul includes the identification because Erastus is not a believer (Friesen 2010, 249–51), but if that is the case, he likely is at least attracted to Paul's instruction sufficiently to want to make a connection to Roman believers.

34. Hultgren imagines that Tertius's greeting may be a "friendly outburst," prompted by the "roll call of names" (598).

35. Henry J. Cadbury was instrumental in drawing the inscription to the attention of biblical scholars, although he himself was cautious about identifying the textual Erastus with the inscriptional Erastus (1931).

Quartus "our brother" is otherwise unattested in Paul's letters or in Acts, and possibly he is part of Erastus's household, given his location in the list (Friesen 2010, 253). In any event, this brief reference concludes the list. The greetings come from individuals who comprise—together with Phoebe—those closest to Paul in Corinth. As Paul has developed this letter, likely over a period of time, they have listened, argued, contributed, and refined. That scenario makes it easy to understand that they would want at this point to have their names included among the greetings of people to whom they have grown attached. Although the letter was written for Rome, these people in Corinth are in effect its first audience. Even from the beginning, Paul's letter to the Romans reached well beyond its stated addressees.[36]

[25–27] This doxology appears in most standard translations of the NT, although it probably represents an early insertion into the letter.[37] Several individual elements in the doxology do cohere with the letter that precedes, including Paul's conviction that God is powerful in the lives of the audience (e.g., 14:4), the emphasis on *apocalypse* (1:18), the significance of Israel's Scriptures (1:2 and often elsewhere), the inclusion of gentiles (e.g., 1:5), and the praise of God (e.g., 1:25). Yet the inflection the doxology gives to these elements is difficult to reconcile with Pauline authorship. For example, Paul seldom speaks of the kerygma (1 Cor 1:21; 2:4; 15:14) and nowhere else of the "proclamation of Jesus Christ." Nor does he pair the nouns "gospel" and "proclamation," although he does refer to "preaching the gospel" (Gal 2:2; 1 Thess 2:9). This letter has invoked individual prophets (e.g., Rom 9:25, 27; 10:20) as well as the law and the prophets (3:21), but nowhere else does Paul adduce "prophetic writings." Nor does he speak of God elsewhere as "eternal" or "only wise."[38]

More distinctive than these individual expressions, this doxology emphasizes mystery to an extent and in a manner that does not sit well with the remainder of the letter and indeed the remainder of the Pauline canon. Attention to the structure of the doxology shows the difficulty. The opening and closing clauses praise God:

v. 25a   To the one who is able to strengthen you according to my gospel
          and [according to] the proclamation of Jesus Christ
v. 27   to the only wise God, through Jesus Christ, to whom be the glory forever

---

36. Hartwig and Theissen make this suggestion in a somewhat extended form (2004).

37. The NA[28] places these lines in brackets, indicating uncertainty as to their inclusion. Although numerous scholars agree that these lines are post-Pauline (e.g., Fitzmyer 753; Byrne 461–62; Cranfield 2:808–9; Jewett 990–1002; Wolter 2:505), others contend that the doxology does belong in the letter (e.g., Schreiner 784–5; L. Johnson 221, 223).

38. For more extensive discussion of stylistic features of the doxology, see J. Elliott 1981 and R. Collins 2002.

But "the revelation of the mystery" in vv. 25–26 interrupts, dominating the doxology and setting it apart from the remainder of the letter as well as other Pauline doxologies:

v. 25b   according to the revelation of the mystery that was *kept secret* for many ages
v. 26   but that is *now disclosed* through prophetic writings,
         made known according to the command of the eternal God for the obedience
         of faith for all the gentiles

All three of the italicized verbal forms (participles in Greek) modify the term "mystery" (Wolter 2:504–5), making it the focal point rather than the power or wisdom of God. Earlier doxological elements in this letter all focus squarely on God and God's actions (1:25; 9:5; 11:36; 15:33); by contrast, this one centers the secret-but-now-disclosed mystery, putting the emphasis in an unusual place.

In Romans "mystery" appears elsewhere only in 11:25, where it introduces Paul's conclusion about the salvation of "all Israel." It is the content of the mystery rather than its apparatus (its hiddenness and special disclosure) that is important. Even in 1 Cor 2, Paul's most extensive discussion that involves mystery, the center of attention is wisdom shared with the mature, not the ancient hiddenness of mystery itself. That interest in the disclosure of ancient mystery sounds more like Eph 3:9 or Col 1:26 and raises the possibility that this doxology was added by someone in Pauline circles later in the first century.

Both the various locations of this doxology in early manuscripts and its distinctive content prompt the judgment that it was not written by Paul. Nonetheless, the "Amen" with which it concludes Romans fittingly comments on Paul's letter.

INDEX OF SCRIPTURE
AND OTHER ANCIENT SOURCES

References in parentheses reflect LXX versification where different from English versions.

35:19	302	14:2–3 (13:2–3)	100	44:26 (43:27)	260
36:17	253	14:3 (13:3)	101	45:2 (44:3)	145, 257
Ezra		14:7 (13:7)	325	48:2 (47:3)	325
4:21	123n84	17:7 (16:7)	257	48:10 (47:11)	257
4:23	123n84	17:9 (16:9)	216	48:11 (47:12)	325
5:5	123n84	17:13 (16:13)	216	51:4 (50:6)	91, 95–96
6:8	123n84	18 title (17:1)	408	51:11 (50:13)	217
		18:2 (17:3)	371	51:18 (50:20)	325
Nehemiah		18:6 (17:7)	232	52:8 (51:10)	314
5:13	67, 67n29	18:35 (17:36)	257	55:5 (54:4)	143
5:15	364	18:41 (17:42)	232	56:9 (55:10)	252
8:6	67, 67n29	18:47 (17:48)	360n31	57:5 (56:6)	62, 171, 270, 406
8:15	314	18:35 (17:36)	371	58:10 (57:11)	147n11
9:6	68n30	18:49 (17:50)	408	60:5 (59:7)	257
9:27	143	19 (18)	298	60:8 (59:10)	360n31
		19:1–4 (18:2–5)	68n30	60:10 (59:12)	302
Esther		19:6 (18:5)	298	61:5 (60:6)	102n63
8:12b	226n129	20:6 (19:7)	257	62:12 (61:13)	79
		22:2 (21:3)	232	63:8 (62:9)	257
Job		22:5(21:6)	232	65:12–13 (64:13–14)	239n155
5:9	329	22:24 (21:25)	232	68:1 (67:2)	180
8:8	359	22:27 (21:28)	322	68:1–3 (67:2–4)	179
11:4	359	23:1 (22:1)	106	69:9 (68:10)	400
12:7–9	60n17	23:4b (22:4b)	252	69:22–23 (68:23–24)	306
26:7–13	68n30	25:22 (24:22)	112n70	69:24 (68:25)	58n13
30:20	232	28 (27)	103	69:25 (68:26)	309
34:11	79n41	29:1 (28:1)	79	69:27–28 (68:28–29)	309
36:15	223	29:11 (28:11)	102n62	69:28 (68:29)	306
37:22	79	30:4 (29:5)	30	72:1–3 (71:1–3)	48
38:16	294	31 (30)	103	72:7 (71:7)	102n62
40:4b–6	281	31:1 (30:2)	49	72:19 (71:19)	67
40:10	79	31:19 (30:20)	77	74:1 (73:1)	302
41:3	329	31:5 (30:6)	95	76:5 (75:6)	61
		32:1 (31:1)	189n69	77:9 (76:8)	302
Psalms		32:1–2a (31:1–2a)	128	78:5–6 (77:5–6)	86
	102n65, 408	32:3–4 (31:3–4)	128	78:50 (77:50)	253n170
1:1	147	32:5–7 (31:5–7)	128	78:52 (77:52)	260n176
1:2	104, 194	32:11 (31:11)	85	78:54 (77:54)	257
2:4	101	33:7 (32:7)	294	79:6 (78:6)	58n13
2:7	231	33:6–9 (32:6–9)	68n30	85:8 (84:9)	102n62
2:9	282n25	34:11 (33:12)	364	85:10 (84:11)	102n62, 141
3:4 (3:5)	232	34:14 (33:15)	102n62	86:9 (85:9)	322
4:3 (4:4)	232n138	35:2 (34:2)	182	89:3 (88:4)	24, 254
5	102	35:13 (34:13)	386	89:52 (88:53)	67
5:9b (5:10b)	101	35:24 (34:24)	49	90:10 (89:10)	163
5:11 (5:12)	85	36 (35)	102	91:4 (90:4)	182
5:11–12 (5:12–13)	103	36:1 (35:2)	364	94:11 (93:11)	61
5:12 (5:13)	182	37:1 (36:1)	308	94:14 (93:14)	301–2
7:6 (7:7)	180	37:7 (36:7)	360n31	95:7 (94:7)	260n176
7:6–9 (7:7–10)	179	37:7–8 (36:7–8)	308	95:8 (94:8)	78
7:9 (7:10)	180	40:6 (39:7)	415	96:6 (95:6)	30
7:16–18 (7:17–18)	183n60	40:8 (39:9)	104	96:7 (95:7)	79
8	68n30	40:9–10 (39:10–11)	49	96:13 (95:13)	48
8:4	60n17	41:13 (40:14)	66–67	97:10 (96:10)	347
10:18 (9:19)	103	43:3 (42:3)	377	97:12 (96:12)	30
10:7 (9:28)	101	44:9b–10a (43:10a–11a)	260	98:7–9 (97:7–9)	239n155
10:18 (9:39)	103	44:11 (43:12)	260, 302	98:1 (97:1)	257
11 (10)	102–3	44:15a (43:16a)	260	100:3 (99:3)	260n176
11–12 (10–11)	103	44:22 (43:23)	260	103:4 (102:4)	242
14 (13)	102				

Galatians (*continued*)

4:15	109
4:19	4, 198
4:21	99
4:24	231
4:25–26	418
5:1	187–88n66, 231
5:5	236
5:10	414
5:11	43, 350, 438
5:13	207n96, 346
5:13–14	372, 372n43
5:13–21	199
5:13–6:10	347
5:14	372
5:16	65
5:16–18	227
5:16–21	28
5:17	252
5:18	99
5:19	65–66
5:19–21	379
5:20	80, 80n45, 439
5:21	394
5:22	43, 346, 411, 426
5:24	65, 237
6:1	158
6:1b	347n15
6:2	121
6:4	370
6:6	417
6:8	79, 242
6:11	413n1, 442
6:14	95n58, 142
6:15	155, 166, 172, 183
6:16	322n69
6:18	67n28

Ephesians

	6
1:3	66
1:7	112n70
1:14	112n70
1:20	229, 257, 441
2:8	370
3:12	142
2:14–15	424
2:15	123n84
3:16	215
2:18	142
2:19	438
3:6	315
3:9	445
4	156
4:12	315
4:19	379
4:22	65n26, 173n45, 371
4:25	371
4:30	112n70

4:31	80n45
5:5	359
5:14	410
5:21	360
5:22–24	353n24
5:24	360
5:26	428
6:1	360n32
6:5	360n32
6:6	23n4
6:10–11	378
6:13–14	386
6:14	378

Philippians

	6
1:1	23, 31, 36n21, 188, 231, 365, 422, 429, 429n16, 442
1:3–4	39
1:3–6	36
1:3–11	34
1:4	36, 426
1:5	59
1:6	417
1:7	259
1:8	38
1:9b	284
1:11	36n21, 43
1:12	34, 14, 43, 193
1:12–14	433
1:17	80
1:17–18	37
1:20	144, 236
1:20–23	163
1:21	263
1:22	43
1:23	65, 379
1:25	411
1:28	115, 371
1:29	143n4, 254
2:2	352, 402
2:3	80
2:5–11	30
2:6–8	296
2:6–11	164, 272, 295
2:7	172
2:8	118
2:9	254, 256
2:9–11	28n16, 32
2:10	262, 328
2:10–11	324, 389
2:12	181n56, 360n32, 371, 434
2:15	84
2:16	142
2:25	25–26, 365, 415, 429, 432
2:27	344

2:27–28	269
2:29	429
2:29–30	426
3	57
3:1	43, 193, 349
3:2–11	23, 31, 44, 203, 405
3:3	38, 87, 271
3:5	303
3:7–11	51
3:8	386
3:9	47
3:10	46, 237
3:10–11	229
3:12	5, 119, 154
3:12–16	289, 289–90n33
3:13	43, 193, 237n144
3:14	119
3:15	320, 335
3:16	346
3:17	193
3:18	319, 350
3:19	439
3:20	256, 371
3:21	242n158
4:1	434
4:2	352, 402, 426
4:3	432
4:4	349
4:9	140, 402, 439–40
4:10	154
4:11	439
4:14	259
4:17	43
4:18	338
4:20	67n28
4:21–22	426
4:21a	432
4:21b–22	431
4:22	116n75

Colossians

	6, 34
1:1	428
1:2	31
1:6	199n80
1:10	199n80
1:11–17	31
1:14	112n70
1:15	25
1:26	445
2:2	444
2:9	417
2:11	87
2:12	229
2:14–15	263
3:1	257
3:8	26, 80n45, 371
3:9	173n45
3:18	353n24

Historia / History of		**XENOPHON**		*Hellenica*	
the Peloponnesian War		*Agesilaus*		6.3.14	226n129
(*continued*)		11.3	183n60	7.4.40	226n129
5.109	420	*Apologia Socratis*		*Oeconomicus*	
8.15.2	222	Apol.7	225	9.14	364
VELLEIUS PATERCULUS		*Cyropaedia*			
Historiae Romanae		5.4.51	64		
2.126.3	364				

INDEX OF SUBJECTS AND AUTHORS

John Chrysostom. *See* Chrysostom, John
Josephus, 23, 126, 341, 418, 423
Joshua, 24
joy, 395, 409–11, 425–26
Judaism/Jews
advantages of, 91ng, 93–94, 110, 123
as audience of Romans, 9–10
boastfulness of, 120
Christ, as servant of, 406–7
Christ, recognition of as Messiah by, 271, 291
criticism of, 86, 89, 121
dietary law and (*see* dietary laws)
divine judgment of, 81–84
enslavement language and, 185n62
faithfulness of, 94–95, 269
faith of, 95
gentile categories and, 87–89
gentiles, mutuality with, 422–24
gentiles as, 84–85
identification as, 84–86
innocent belief of, 41–47, 54, 58, 60, 62–63, 70–72, 99–103 (*see also* judgment, divine, as universal; Sin, power of)
vs. Israelites, 269–70
law observance by (*see* law, observance of)
misrepresentation of, 217, 221n116
priority of, 47, 75, 98, 110
rectification by God and, 121–22
sacrificial practices of, 337
salvation for, 296
as unseen, 88
as vessels of mercy, 284
word of God, entrusted with, 93
wrath of God and, 54
judges, 75–78
judgment. *See also* judgment, divine; judgment, divine, as universal
authorities and, 363
enacting on, warning against, 353–55
familial language and, 388
of hidden things, 84
shame of Christ and, 45
shared, 402
warning against, 385–86
judgment, divine. *See also* judgment
eschatological, 88
God's truth and, 96
gospel as means to, 84
law observance and, 81–84
truth and, 76
as universal (*see* judgment, divine, as universal)
wrath and, 58
judgment, divine, as universal
ethnicities and, 80–81

gentiles and, 81–84
impartiality of, 75–81
introduction to and Scripture on, 72–75
Jews and, 84–87
judicial language, 148, 150
Juel, Donald, 338n7
Julius Caesar, 366
Junia, 424n23, 434–35, 435n24, 436
"just as it is written," 99
justice, 48–49, 354

kapporet (mercy seat), 106nd, 113, 243
Karris, Robert, 381
Käsemann, Ernst, 34, 40, 51, 66, 95, 105n66, 111, 113, 149n15, 188, 188n68, 216, 221n113, 229n132, 272n11, 315, 332, 407
kata pneuma (God's own holiness), 28, 220nh, 230
kata sarka (according to flesh/physically), 28, 30, 125na, 125nc, 220nh, 230, 269, 321
Keck, Leander, 99n59, 108, 121, 218, 273, 291, 369n40, 372
Khobnya, Svetlana, 315
kin, of Paul, 268–69, 434–35
kingly language, 257. *See also* rulership
kiss, holy, 437
knowledge
corruption of, 61–62
of God, 59–60, 247
lack of (*see* ignorance)
shared, 76
of time, salvation and, 375
koinōnia (association/fellowship), 420nc. *See also* fellowship
kosher law, 394, 394n69, 396
kosmos (world), Abrahamic promise and, 132
Krisis, 4
ktisis (creation), 239–40. *See also* creation

labor, 127, 243. *See also* vocation, of Paul
Lampe, Peter, 112, 432, 433n22, 434
law, Mosaic. *See also* other law headings; Ten Commandments
Abrahamic promise and, 131–32
absence of, 108–9, 189
ambiguous use of by Paul, 374–75, 374n48
Christ and, Scripture on, 293–95
Death and, 157
of faith, 121
flesh and, 211, 223
fulfillment of, 373–74, 380
as God's gift to Israel, 104, 270–71
as holy/good, 209–10, 213
liberation and, 221
love and, 371–75

tribute tax, 367
trickery, of Israel, 291
Trinity, 146, 228
trust, 133–34, 221, 411. *See also* faith
truth, 58, 76, 95–96, 407
twins, fathers of, 276, 276n20
typos (teaching), 187

unchosen, Esau as, 276–77
uncircumcision, 82, 87, 122–24, 128–29. *See also* circumcision
undisputed texts of Paul, 6
ungodliness, 58, 58n14, 127–29, 146–47, 325
"unregenerate" Paul, 202, 202n88
upbuilding of believers, 395–96, 399

vengeance, 350, 354
vessels, 279ne, 282
  of mercy, 283–84
  of wrath, 281, 283–84
vice lists, 55, 70
victory, 261
violence, 182n58, 259
visibility, creation and, 59–60
vocation, of Paul
  as apostleship to gentiles, 9, 23, 25, 31–32, 311–12, 311n58
  Christ's work in, 416–18
  geographical markers of, 417–18
  as gift, 31, 42, 341, 414–15
  gospels and, 30, 340
  as from grace, 31, 414–15
  obligation of, 42 (*see also under* gospel: Paul's obligation to)
  self-identification of, 413–16
  summary of in prescript, 22
  travel plans for, 10–13, 39, 421–22, 430
  "where Christ has not been named," 418–19

wages, of Sin, 190
Wagner, J. Ross, 16, 266, 280–81, 284, 284nn28–29, 291, 299, 317n64, 325–26, 329, 389, 409
wakefulness/sleep imagery, 375
Wallace, Daniel, 113, 148, 179nc, 196n77, 435
warfare, 212n103. *See also* martial imagery
warrior, divine, 182n57, 185, 253, 261, 324, 408, 442
War Scroll, 378
Watson, Francis, 57, 62n20, 100, 103, 135, 194, 196, 272, 276
weakness, 245n162
  bearing others', 399
  in faith, 383–84
  of flesh, 188

of humanity, 146–47, 147n9
Spirit's role in, 245
wealth/wealthy, equality of to poor, God's favor and, 80
weapons, 178, 181–83, 185, 209, 378
weapons of light, 378
welcoming, 384–85, 406–7, 429
wickedness. *See* evil; wrongdoing
will, of creation, 242
will of God, 335nc
  about, 339
  Pharaoh and, 281, 362
  travel plans of Paul and, 39, 426
  understanding of, 85–86, 230, 316, 339, 401
Williams, Margaret, 387n63
Williams, Sam, 105n66
Wilson, Walter, 344n13, 347n15, 347n18
Winkler, John, 2
Wisdom, 101, 262
wisdom/wise, 43, 61–62
Witherington, Ben III, 62
witness, use of, 38, 38n22
Wolter, Michael, 8–9, 235, 282n26, 292n38, 320, 320ni, 344n13, 364, 445
womanist interpretation, 3–4
women
  in audience of Romans, 42
  circumcision and, 87, 92, 128n88
  divorce/adultery and, 194–96
  gospel work of, 428nf, 429, 429n16, 430, 431n18
  in greetings from Paul, 433, 436
  ordination of, 403n80
  same-sex relations between, 68–69 (*see also* same-sex relations)
wonders/signs, 417
word and work, 417
"word of faith that we preach," 295
word of God, 272, 285, 298–99
works, 79–80, 84, 127, 290, 377–79, 416–18
world, as whole of humanity, 36–37
worldly ways, 338–39
worship. *See also* glory, of God
  absence of as rejection of God, 60, 66, 111 (*see also* idolatry)
  calling on the name of Christ and, 297
  human rationality and, 335nb
  obligation of, 271
  Paul's service as, 38, 415
  sacrifice and, 337
  shared glorification of God and, 402, 402n79
worth, 142, 150
"wrapped up" in Christ, 378–79